INTERPERSONAL HELPING
Emerging Approaches
for
Social Work Practice

INTERPERSONAL HELPING

Emerging Approaches
for
Social Work Practice

JOEL FISCHER, D.S.W.

Associate Professor
School of Social Work
University of Hawaii
Honolulu, Hawaii

CHARLES C THOMAS · PUBLISHER
Springfield · *Illinois* · *U.S.A.*

Published and Distributed Throughout the World by
CHARLES C THOMAS • PUBLISHER
BANNERSTONE HOUSE
301-327 East Lawrence Avenue, Springfield, Illinois, U.S.A.

© *1973, by* CHARLES C THOMAS • PUBLISHER
ISBN 0-398-02564-9 cloth
ISBN 0-398-02565-7 paper
Library of Congress Catalog Card Number: 72-79188 √

With THOMAS BOOKS *careful attention is given to all details of manufacturing and design. It is the Publisher's desire to present books that are satisfactory as to their physical qualities and artistic possibilities and appropriate for their particular use.* THOMAS BOOKS *will be true to those laws of quality that assure a good name and good will.*

Printed in the United States of America
N-1

CONTRIBUTORS

Alexander W. Astin, Ph.D.

Sherman Barr, M.S.W.

Allen E. Bergin, Ph.D.

Irving N. Berlin, M.D.

Eli M. Bower, Ed.D.

Earl C. Brennen, D.S.W.

Scott Briar, D.S.W.

Rachel Burkholder, Ph.D.

Robert R. Carkhuff, Ph.D.

Catherine S. Chilman, Ph.D.

Emory L. Cowen, Ph.D.

Robert I. Cutts, M.D.

Allen Darbonne, Ph.D.

Joel Fischer, D.S.W.

Jacob R. Fishman, M.D.

Kalman Flomenhaft, D.S.W.

Jay Haley, M.A.

Charles Hersch, Ph.D.

Frederick H. Kanfer, Ph.D.

David M. Kaplan, Ph.D.

Leonard Krasner, Ph.D.

Donald G. Langsley, M.D.

Robert Liberman, M.D.

Perry London, Ph.D.

Michael S. March, Ph.D.

John McCormack, M.D.

Salvador Minuchin, M.D.

Gordon Paul, Ph.D.

Robert A. Porter, Ph.D.

S. J. Rachman, Ph.D.

Frank Riessman, Ph.D.

Carl R. Rogers, Ph.D.

Sue E. Sampen, Ph.D.

George Saslow, M.D.

William Schofield, Ph.D.

Howard N. Sloane, Jr., Ph.D.

Beth Sulzer, Ph.D.

Robert Sunley, M.S.W.

Paul Terrell, D.S.W.

Roland G. Tharp, Ph.D.

Charles B. Truax, Ph.D.

Edwin J. Thomas, Ph.D.

Earl Ubell

A. Dan Whitley, Ph.D.

Joseph Wolpe, M.D.

Melvin Zax, Ph.D.

Jane Zeilberger, Ph.D.

For

Ursula, Lisa *and* Nicole

PREFACE

One of the persistent challenges to individualized services might be expressed the following way: "Given the horrendous level of societal dysfunctioning, the pervasiveness of social problems such as poverty and racism, the inability of social institutions to meet the needs of people, and the concomitant extensiveness of social and psychological breakdown among families and individuals, how can we afford to offer individualized services when so much needs to be done at the institutional and societal levels?" I think the question should be rephrased: "Given the horrendous level of societal dysfunctioning, the pervasiveness of social problems, the inability of social institutions to meet the needs of people, and the extensiveness of social and psychological breakdown among families and individuals, how can we afford *not to* offer individualized services, even though one of the clear priorities for professional action exists at the institutional and societal levels?"

This book is intended as an affirmation of that belief. The reader who sees this as a plea for professional intervention *only* at the individual level has missed the point. Rather, this book, *in toto,* is an attempt to illustrate the potential for making those services as effective and efficient as possible, with the recognition that such services are only part of our job. Were our efforts to approach the ideal of the "compleat practitioner," there would be a balance of activities, including case by case helping and social action.

This book, though, deals specifically with one aspect of practice, largely involving the "direct service" model. All of the approaches in the book do not necessarily involve face-to-face activity between the client and the helper. But the intent is always to refer back to the effects of the helper's intervention on the client's well-being. Thus, the subject matter deals consistently with "interpersonal helping."

This book is intended primarily for social work practitioners and students. I think it also has relevance for members of related professions—psychologists, psychiatrists, counselors. The articles are multidisciplinary and theoretically eclectic, and reflect my own bias: no single profession, no single system of intervention has been able to deal adequately with the complex of human behaviors which we face in our everyday practice. Thus, it is the responsibility of the practitioner to be knowledgeable and competent in a variety of approaches, based on careful assessment of available alternatives on ideological, theoretical and empirical grounds. For the student and practitioner too busy to be constantly engaged in a search through the literature, this book attempts to bring together a number of approaches, which, on grounds to be explicated in the introductory chapter, appear to be significant and viable alternatives for practice.

A number of people have made the effort to put together this book most rewarding. At the top of my personal list, my wife and children have shown the ultimate in understanding, patience and support. Dean Herbert Aptekar provided me with a good deal of personal encouragement. My friends and colleagues, Doctors Harvey Gochros, Larry Lister and Fred Merritt were always ready to lend a helping hand. Louise Young, supersecretary, was a joy to work with, and served well above and beyond the call of duty. I am, of course, indebted to the authors whose works are collected here, both for their invigorating thoughts and the permission to reprint them. Finally, I would like to express my appreciation to the faculty and students of the School of Social Work, University of Hawaii and the School of Social Welfare, University of California, Berkeley, for the stimulation of their ideas, and the passion of their commitment.

J.F.

CONTENTS

PART III
THERAPEUTIC INTERVENTION _____ 307

A. General

B. The Therapeutic Relationship

C. Behavior Modification (Operant)

INTERPERSONAL HELPING

Emerging Approaches
for
Social Work Practice

INTRODUCTION

We had not walked
But for Tradition;
We walk evermore
To higher paths by
Brightening Reason's lamp.

—George Eliot

"Interpersonal helping"— the topic of this book—encompasses a wide variety of interventive practices, methods and techniques. In the broadest sense, interpersonal helping can be described as informed, purposeful intervention either directly with, or on behalf of, a given person or persons (client). The goal of such intervention is to bring about positive changes either directly in the client's functioning, or in environmental factors immediately impinging on the client's functioning. These interventions are intended to enhance aspects of the client's feelings, attitudes and/or behaviors in such a way that his personal and social functioning will be more satisfying and beneficial to him.

Although broad in scope, this definition nevertheless excludes from the rubric "interpersonal helping" a variety of potential interventions. Use of the term "purposeful" excludes any chance or unplanned change such as might occur through accidental encounters between, say, professional helpers and clients. Unintended by-products of other endeavors—e.g. the "warm" teacher who coincidentally to her teaching modifies pupil feelings and attitudes—would also be excluded. Similarly, use of the term "informed" suggests the importance of utilizing principles and procedures derived systematically from an identifiable body of knowledge, as opposed to reliance on luck, faith or intuition (although such characteristics may be powerful change factors in their own right as noted by Frank, 1961).

This implies that the intervener—or helper—is qualified to do his job, mainly on the basis of his familiarity with, and competence in, the utilization of intervention knowledge on behalf of his clients. Again, this rules out "naturally helpful" individuals, such as the kind and understanding neighbor, teacher or physician, who unwittingly apply successful interventive tactics. Obviously, these individuals can have most beneficial effects on people (see Chap. 5), but they are not a primary object of concern in this book.

In selecting the term "client," there is an attempt to convey the idea that a more or less formal process of identification—by the client, helper and/or society—has led to the determination that some aspect of dysfunctionality (Fischer, 1969) exists in the life of a given person (the client). The client himself may be voluntary or involuntary,* aware of his problem(s) or not, an apt participant in the helping process or not. But there should be a clear designation by the helper of whom he is to help. This implies that the client, himself, may not be the actual target for action, although he is to be the beneficiary of that action (Pincus and Minahan, 1970). Intervention may proceed in his environment—home or school, for example—but the helper will have identified the ways in which such intervention will affect the person(s) on whose behalf he is intervening. The term client also connotes a customer or consumer of services. Such a designation almost inherently contains a greater degree of dignity and worth than an appellation such as "patient," which suggests elements of sickness and of disease. Further, the term "patient" also implies an intervention strategy so circumscribed as to deal with individuals solely on a direct basis in a quasimedical way, while the notion of "client" implies a broader purview for intervention, encompassing social and environmental factors.

This definition of interpersonal helping also calls for an emphasis on the *functioning* of the client. This is not to disparage the value of independent changes in attitudes, feelings and so on.

---

*There are few truly "voluntary" clients, despite such an assumption in most of the literature on interpersonal helping. Aside from the obvious institutionalized and legally coerced client, most clients come to "treatment" under pressure from family, peers, employers, etc. or the unwanted pressure of their own problems. (See Miller, 1968, for a discussion of the value dilemmas involving nonvoluntary clients.)

In fact, changes in these dimensions are hard enough to come by as the research on outcome shows. Nevertheless, the point of view expressed here is that such changes as can be attributed to the helper's intervention should have results demonstrable in improved personal and social functioning in the variety of roles which constitute daily living (see Chap. 21) .*

Clearly, such a sweeping definition of interpersonal helping does not set explicit limits on the kinds of knowledge which a practitioner might utilize. Except for the suggestion here that this knowledge must deal with interventive principles and procedures, the criteria for knowledge selection (and selection of articles for this book) will be discussed in the following section. However, there does remain the matter of discussing the helper's group affiliation—profession and discipline.

Interpersonal helping provides a broad umbrella encompassing a number of the activities which traditionally have been included under such designations as psychotherapy, casework, and counseling and guidance, performed by social workers, psychologists, counselors and psychiatrists. In fact, in areas where research has been conducted, primarily views and attitudes toward clients and preferences for therapeutic techniques, little or no differences arising from professional affiliation can be detected (Strupp, 1955, 1958, 1960; McNair and Lorr, 1964; McNair, Lorr and Callahan, 1963; Eels, 1964; Henry *et al.*, 1970) . Far more importantly, there is no evidence that the profession of the helper leads to any difference in his *success* with clients (Poser, 1966; Meltzoff and Kornreich, 1970) . There may be professional differences in status and prestige, and ability to influence *colleagues,* but no differences that can be attributed to profession in the ability of helpers to help their clients.

This suggests that whatever the official designation of the process—whether, for example, it be called psychotherapy or casework—within the limits of an interpersonal influence process where the helper attempts to intervene in the psychosocial problems of clients, the various professions may be engaged in a uniform enter-

---

*This emphasis on functioning is also congruent with social work's long-standing focus on problems of social functioning.

prise (Henry *et al.,* 1970). This has been demonstrated empirically, and can be demonstrated conceptually to the extent that the approaches to intervention used by members of different professions draw systematically upon a common core of knowledge (e.g. "psychodynamic theory"). As a corollary to that notion, it might be suggested that when professionals are in fact engaged in similar activities, it would behoove them to be utilizing the best knowledge available, whether or not that knowledge has been developed by members of one's own profession.

This, of course, does not mean that differences between the various professions are lacking. Clearly, a variety of professional differences do exist, in matters of training, interests, spheres of functioning, societal mandates, areas of specialization, and so on. Overlap exists most obviously, though, in the area of clinical or therapeutic endeavors. And this suggests that when such overlap does occur, knowledge that has common relevance must be made available to all practitioners who might be able to put it to use. While social workers—to whom this book is largely directed—obviously derive a considerable portion of their knowledge from fields other than social work, the perspectives, opinions and new developments external to social work often suffer either in translation to social work terms, or through pure neglect.

In view of the above, it is the major purpose of this book to bring together in one source multidisciplinary perspectives on several areas of theory, practice and research which are pertinent to the practice of social work where interpersonal helping is concerned. The areas selected for coverage were derived from a social work perspective. Although a substantial part of the profession does engage in clinical activities, social workers are not only clinicians or therapists. As one of its unique features, social work traditionally has featured a broadly-based practice which, even in the direct service component, deals with such dimensions of practice as restoration, provision and prevention (Boehm, 1959). Thus, it would seem to be setting up a straw man to argue, for example, that casework and psychotherapy are one and the same. The caseworker, generally operating from a far broader base than the field of psychotherapy alone can provide, traditionally has supplied a wide range of services to clients. What can be argued, though, is first, the literature has not accurately reflected this broadly-based practice; second, much of the direct service literature until only recently has been preoccupied with development of rather narrow models for practice (see Fischer, 1971 re: Roberts and Nee, 1970); and third, there is a considerable amount of well-defined knowledge available that is appropriate for social work, and that could be integrated into a more flexible and comprehensive practice approach.

In essence, this orientation contains within it an appeal that social workers (and other professionals) remain open to new ideas and emerging developments in practice, and that carefully thought-out criteria be utilized to distinguish between fads, and the selection of knowledge that can be translated into constructive gains for clients. In short, the professional cannot afford premature closure around one approach, expecting to use that approach indefinitely without either awareness of new developments, or willingness to examine and utilize new developments when they are available. This book is an attempt to provide not only the tools for analysis, but a selection of knowledge from multidisciplinary sources that hopefully will update professional practice in these areas, and stimulate a broadly conceived practice resting on a careful, informed scrutiny of a number of alternatives.

A FRAME OF REFERENCE

The question obviously arises as to how knowledge selected from presumably divergent perspectives can be meaningfully integrated in a volume such as this, let alone in actual practice. In the past, many social workers have opted for a form of theoretical integration. Freudian-based ego psychology was used to "understand people," and to pull together a variety of perspectives ranging from role theory to personality development to casework practice principles. But, despite noble efforts to the contrary, this resulted in a rather unidimensional picture of man, and a clearly circumscribed practice theory. Change principles were derived from a narrow base composed of part-Freud (and his theoretical descendants) and part "practice wisdom." But since the practice wisdom itself was largely a reflection of Freudian and neo-Freudian thinking, the end-product of this ingrown and circular process was clearly lacking in the breadth necessary for a comprehensive base for practice. More importantly, use of a single "theoretical orientation," whatever its nature, as an integrating base for practice generally precludes the consideration of clearly divergent new developments in intervention technology as viable alternatives for practice.*

The frame of reference utilized in this book is atheoretical, but grounded in certain values and principles which cut across various theoretical (and professional) domains. This section of the book contains an explication of those principles.

Since social work is ultimately a profession deeply rooted in, and committed to, a number of value positions, the most appropriate way to introduce an approach to practice for social work is through a recapitulation of what might be considered the principal value premises underlying the approach. Two value propositions could be identified as furnishing direction for the contents of this book, and perhaps the social work enterprise as a whole. They can be viewed as the primary values in a hierarchy of several values.† They are: (a) respect for the dignity and worth —or more appropriately, the humanity—of every individual; and (b) a commitment endorsing man's responsibility to his fellow man. These values almost automatically render irrelevant the argument that individualized helping is a waste of time or energy with little or no palpable return. For while it is not necessary to engage all people in an individualized helping process, and it may not always be effective when we do, the primacy of these values indicates it would be even more disastrous if, when appropriate, we were not to *try*. Taken together, these two premises point toward an unabashed recognition of the inherent meaningfulness of the person-to-person approach, and the desirability of counter-

---

*See Part III, the introductory section on "Behavior Modification" for an example of such a situation.

†See *Values in Social Work: A Re-Examination*, NASW (1967), for a comprehensive discussion of major values underlying the practice of social work.

ing what might be contended are the increasing processes of de-humanization and impersonalization of modern society.

Thus, two levels of principles for examining a variety of alternatives for practice can be derived from these preeminent ethical considerations. At the broadest level, in making selections from among alternatives for practice and in integrating those selections into a practice framework, the first principle involves the extent to which utilization of an approach would be congruent with the primary values of the profession.* Secondly, in actual application, a specific procedure can be evaluated as ethically suitable if its utilization does not demean—more, enhances or maintains—the dignity and individuality of the persons involved, and can be implemented in a way consonant with the values of both client (s) and helper (s) .

As another dimension, the area of knowledge to be examined, per se, has characteristics which can be utilized both as criteria for evaluation and as principles of integration. Obviously, given the explosion of knowledge in the social and behavioral sciences in recent decades, the educator and theorist, not to mention the practitioner, needs guidelines to aid in wending his way through the constantly expanding maze of ideas. It would probably be gratuitous to note that social work has long avowed the importance of knowledge for practice which deals with both social *and* psychological characteristics of human beings, particularly as related to the practice goal of enhancing client social functioning.†
What may be less obvious, though, is that a substantial proportion of this knowledge is only minimally related to the explicit process of intervention into dysfunctional spheres of human existence. In large part, available knowledge has served mainly to bolster professional *understanding* of human behavior (no mean accomplishment in itself) , with very little to say about how maladaptive aspects of that behavior might be *changed*.

Since this topic is discussed more thoroughly in Chapter 9 and,

---

*All of these criteria are more fully explicated in Chapter 9.

†That such avowals have not always kept pace with realities of practice seems clear from the earlier example of overdependence on ego psychology as a theoretical orientation, and examples to be discussed in the following section.

particularly, Chapter 21, it need not be elaborated extensively here. But a graphic presentation might suffice at this point for facilitative purposes. Figure 1 is a representation of the two major areas of knowledge from the social and behavioral sciences which, in a gross sense, are potentially available to practitioners in the area of interpersonal helping.

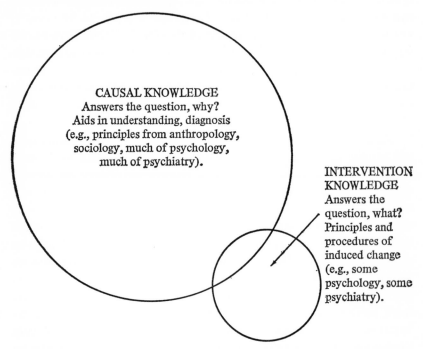

CAUSAL KNOWLEDGE
Answers the question, why?
Aids in understanding, diagnosis
(e.g., principles from anthropology,
sociology, much of psychology,
much of psychiatry).

INTERVENTION
KNOWLEDGE
Answers the
question, what?
Principles and
procedures of
induced change
(e.g., some
psychology, some
psychiatry).

Figure 1. Areas of knowledge potentially available to practitioners.

Causal knowledge, by far the bulk of the knowledge developed in the behavioral sciences, essentially serves as an aid in understanding the development of both adaptive and maladaptive behavior, and is devoted to answering the question: why did this state of affairs come about? This is, of course, valuable information for the practitioner, and crucial in assessing cases and situations. Intervention knowledge, on the other hand, prescribes principles and procedures for inducing change in (by and large) problematic situations, and seeks to answer the question: what can be done in this situation and will it be effective? Clearly, there is some overlap between these two areas of knowledge. Perhaps equally as clear is the necessity for establishing some priorities for knowledge development and selection. The position taken throughout this book is that the priority for professional practice is in the area of knowledge dealing specifically with interventive methodology.

Statements such as the above may appear to be mere truisms. By definition, a professional practice rests on a body of knowledge the purpose of which is to supply the practitioner with the capacity to influence (or control or change) "natural" events. In fact, practice theory, per se, can be described as being composed of two major elements. The first involves a systematic explication of diagnostic principles (with the goal of understanding the phenomena of concern). The second part involves a systematic explication of principles of change, and procedures for implementing those principles. Hypothetically, the diagnostic and treatment principles are to be utilized together. Unfortunately, what can be demonstrated is, first, there appears to be little or no relationship between diagnosis and treatment in major areas of traditional practice (Fischer, 1971), and second, the bulk of our current professional knowledge lies in the causal-diagnostic realm, at the expense of intervention methodology, and to the extent that some approaches even fail to prescribe any procedures for influencing client-change (see, e.g. Fischer, 1972; Roberts and Nee, 1970; Ford and Urban, 1963). This contributes to what might be termed the "etiological pitfall" (Bennis *et al.,* 1961), wherein practitioners are caught up in a process of trying to understand how the client came to be the way he is, without a concomitant ability to influence changes in those dimensions even were they to be successfully understood (see Chap. 21). Diagnostic knowledge, in and of itself, while important, is an insufficient basis for effective intervention, and is of real consequence only to the extent that it complements knowledge dealing with intervention.

Thus, an important principle both for selection of the contents of this book, and for integrating diverse approaches in practice, lies in the extent to which an approach deals with interventive practices, whether of an individual-psychological or social-environmental nature. This includes a systematic explanation of how induced change comes about, and prescription of procedures so that the change principles might be implemented by the practitioner.

The latter part of this criterion bears particularly careful scrutiny. A number of approaches ostensibly dealing with interventive practices nevertheless equivocate on the matter of delineating techniques. Since theories, or principles of theories, cannot themselves be applied with people, an absence of specific techniques which detail how to carry out change efforts means that a helping person would not actually be able to implement the approach (see e.g. Perlman, 1970; Smalley, 1970).

Specification of interventive procedures alone, while serving to narrow the field considerably, is still insufficient as a sole criterion for adequate selection from among the dozens of available approaches to intervention (see, e.g. Ford and Urban, 1963; Patterson, 1966). Thus, a crucial additional criterion for establishing the value of an approach, and applied whenever possible in the selection of articles for this book, is the extent to which there is empirical validation of successful intervention with clients when change procedures are implemented. In other words, when research establishes the efficacy of an approach, it must be considered a prime candidate for adoption for practice.

At least three implications stem from major reliance on research. In the first place, use of research findings provides clear guidelines for use in evaluation (see Chap. 6). This would tend to diminish a helter-skelter approach to knowledge selection wherein a practitioner adopts an approach because a theorist uses flowery phrases, seems impressive in his erudition, or the approach somehow "sounds good."

Second, the complexity of most theories precludes total theoretical validation. Hence, it would appear to be a near-impossibility to bring together entire theories, or comprehensive systems of change, especially on the basis of research evidence of effectiveness. Actually, research tends to be carried out on selected portions of theory, in this case, on specific change principles and procedures. So, instead of attempting to integrate several complete theories, a number of different principles and procedures, perhaps selected from different theories and used in a complementary fashion, might form the basis for practice. Thus, their utilization can be decided upon given the particular nature of the client, problem or situation. This can be accomplished on the basis of an appropriate assessment, and evidence that implementation will be efficacious (see Chap 21).

The preceding relates to the third implication of using research as an important aid in integrating diverse approaches to practice. Presumably, the studies upon which a judgment is based illustrate the conditions under which an approach is successfully utilized. This, in turn, suggests an implicit, or even explicit, client/diagnostic typology which demonstrates the types of problems and clients where a given approach can be effectively applied. Combination of effective approaches, then, can supply not only a complementary range of interventive procedures, but a range of problem-situation configurations where the procedures can be applied. The goal, of course, is the maximum in technical flexibility for the practitioner in response to the large variety of potential client problems.

In essence, what is proposed here is that the greater the degree of scientifically validated input in practice, the greater the degree of competence can be exercised by the practitioner on behalf of his clients. This does not exclude the use of intuition or "horse sense"—the art of practice. The point is not that professionals should be automatons unfeelingly implementing an intervention technology (see Part III). But the point *is* that a rigorous foundation for practice, involving the testing and evaluation of concepts and propositions, will provide a more successful base for the use of less clearly defined dimensions.

Unless posed as an alternative to the approach which has clear and considerable empirical validation, lack of research on effectiveness does not automatically render an approach without merit. In fact, a wide range of criteria exist for evaluation of such approaches on structural, substantive and ethical grounds (see Chap. 9). In some situations, and in the absence of research evidence to the contrary, such approaches may be the intervention of choice. What is looked for ultimately is some Gestalt, some careful piecing together of a complex of analytic factors. When a number of approaches can be evaluated as satisfactory on the variety of criteria suggested here, and can be seen to complement each other based on clearly defined prescriptive statements for their utilization, some degree of integration for practice can be demonstrated to have occurred.

Such integration may be facilitated through use of a framework for assessment such as the one developed by Atherton, Mitchell and Schein (1971 a and b). These authors have devised a classification scheme of client problems as related to personal roles and the structure of social systems. The problem typology is divided into three major categories: (a) Problems related to performance of legitimate and acceptable roles (e.g. impairment of role performance because of illness; or problems in role transition); (b) Problematical roles (e.g. outsider role; or stigmatized role); and (c) Problems in the structure of social systems (e.g. nonavailable roles; or excessive role expectations). Within each category, a variety of "points for intervention" are identified. Based upon these points for intervention, Atherton *et al.* have identified eleven roles—several of which are discussed in this book—for the change agent: broker, interpreter, psychosocial and sociobehavioral counselor, educator, mediator, advocate, crisis intervener, role model, catalyst, and agent of social change.

Through their attempt to systematize the assessment-intervention process, Atherton *et al.* offer an advantageous method of looking at the multiplicity of practice functions dealt with in this book. Implicit in their work, also, is the necessity for the professional helper to be equipped with an eclectic knowledge base to be able to flexibly meet the demands of the great number and variety of problems encountered in practice.

SOCIAL WORK TRADITION AND AN EXAMPLE FROM PRACTICE

There are clear potential problems of confusion and uncertainty involved both in utilizing knowledge derived from a variety of sources, and in functioning in a variety of roles. Why, therefore, should the practitioner, especially the social work practitioner, have to contend with such difficulties? Obviously, in the first place, experience points to the fact that the diversity of problems and situations encountered in practice dictates the necessity for a response in kind: diversity of knowledge and roles to more adequately deal with such situations as they arise. But beyond this is an element partly composed of professional mandate, of societal sanction, of practice experience, and of agency or institutional concerns, which, cumulatively, serves to interrelate and enhance values and knowledge and the realities of day to day practice. For want of a better term, this element might be called "tradition."

In social work, particularly, tradition operates powerfully to shape aspects of our practice. For example, one of the points of view expressed in this book is that it is a responsibility of the direct service practitioner to take on a mediating function, working to coordinate individuals with institutions. This could be seen partly as an expression of awareness and concern about the importance of interactional factors—psychological and social—influencing human behavior. But more than that, this point of view has been expressed, often implicitly, from social work's earliest days, from Richmond* to Hamilton (1952) to Reynolds (1963); identified by Wilensky and Lebeaux (1958) as social work's liaison function, and described in this book as a "broker" function (see Chap. 1, 37, 39).

Actually, like Topsy, traditional practices have a habit of "just growing up." There is, perhaps, at some point in time an "unmet need," and individual practitioners, agencies or institutions take action to attempt to fill the gap. So, as Tevya notes in "Fiddler on the Roof": "You may ask, 'How did this tradition get started?' I'll tell you. I don't know. But it's a tradition." And the traditions become developed (and even "conceptualized") and incorporated

---

*Mary Richmond stated: "I have spent twenty-five years of my life in an attempt to get social casework accepted as a valid process in social work. Now I shall spend the rest of my life in trying to demonstrate to social caseworkers that there is more to social work than social casework." Quoted in Bruno (1948), pp. 186, 187.

into practice. Thus, social workers have come to perform a mediating function, ranging in activity from helping a bedridden client deal with a hospital staff, to aiding a client in wending his way through a bureaucratic maze to secure a basic right, to the application of pressure to influence institutions to respond to the needs of individuals. And these functions are performed for an important reason: they are necessary, and very few other people are doing them in an organized or systematic way.

The interrelation of values, knowledge and tradition can be clarified by examining a prototypical form of social work, practice in a school setting. The practitioner in a school participates in a variety of activities (Vinter and Sarri, 1965): direct services aimed at remediation of individual pupils' problems and facilitation of growth and development; mediation between pupil and school personnel; consultation to teaching personnel; and a bargaining or lobbying function—advocacy on behalf of students whom the social worker has identified as clients.

A number of points can be illustrated by these activities. Whatever the form of intervention, the social worker's efforts are on behalf of the student as identified client (but not necessarily with the student as target). In fact, an important corollary to the value positions identified in the preceding section, and aptly stated in the Code of Ethics of the National Association of Social Workers, demands such a stance: "I regard as my primary obligation the welfare of the individual or group served, which includes action for improving social conditions." Another point which can be illustrated is the necessity for the practitioner to possess a wide repertoire of interventive measures—some with few obvious similarities—to adequately conduct his job. Additionally, all of the interventions in the school can be seen not only in terms of remediation or treatment, but within the context of prevention: direct intervention with the child to forestall further disruption, and consultation if not advocacy to alter the system to provide a more beneficial effect on the functioning of its constituents. And finally, it can be seen that a process of assessment is necessary as a basis for making decisions as to what form of intervention is appropriate at what point.

Again using the school system as an example, the practitioner's job at point of contact, say, with a student newly referred by a teacher, would be to begin an assessment process incorporating the following dimensions: (a) identifying (for himself) the child as his client, but not immediately accepting the child as the target for intervention; (b) assessing both personal and interpersonal circumstances based on the principle that a broad range of psychosocial variables are pertinent*; (c) making the judgment as to where intervention would be most efficacious; (d) implementing the intervention (which could involve a combination of approaches) ; and (e) evaluating the results of intervention. In sum, this process involves a continuous interaction between the practitioner's values, knowledge and a tradition of services. Together, these dimensions provide a system for decision-making which could lead to intervention at any level—in this example, from the individual child, to the family, teacher or broader school system.

It is the thesis of this book that it is dysfunctional for a profession involved in interpersonal helping to become overly dependent on one theoretical perspective. It is dysfunctional for two primary reasons: (a) exclusive reliance on one orientation frequently precludes systematic, objective examination of other orientations; and (b) no single theoretical perspective—at least to this date—has been able to successfully address the wide range of problems that practitioners encounter. And, as the above example illustrates, use of a number of discrete approaches in practice does not preclude employment of an overall perspective or orientation that serves to aid the practitioner in comprehending the array of forces which he confronts. As suggested in this book, that orientation might be integrated less at a theoretical level than at a level at which values, knowledge and tradition interre-

---

*As contrasted, say, to only psychological. This precludes immediate assignment to psychotherapeutic treatment since a form of intervention into the impinging social system might be more relevant. Immediate acceptance of the child into treatment implies that the problem rests mainly with the child as deviant, thereby hastening a labelling process (see Siporin, 1965) . Despite social work's avowal of the importance of social phenomena, practitioners often still attend more readily to psychological variables (Fischer, 1970) .

late to provide a broad framework for professional practice. The framework utilized in this book also assumes the appropriateness of an interactional model of human behavior in which individual and social phenomena interact in definable ways to produce numerous forms of dysfunctionality (see Vinter, 1967). This in turn leads to the necessity for the practitioner to be equipped with a variety of approaches to both individual and social intervention.

ORGANIZATION OF THE BOOK

In selection of areas for coverage for this book, several factors were considered, such as those dimensions of value, knowledge and tradition examined in the preceding "frame of reference" section. Among the other factors were the following criticisms of a number of major approaches to direct practice: a lack of principles and procedures of social-environmental change; overdevelopment of diagnostic knowledge at the expense of intervention methodology; lack of evidence of effectiveness in work with clients; and disregard of "the poor" as a priority population for social work attention (Fischer, 1972).

The attempt in this book is to address these concerns directly. Major portions of the book are devoted to an explication of both current issues, and potential means of dealing with the issues. Accordingly, based on the material discussed in this introductory chapter, and in view of the traditional and worthwhile arenas of social work practice in such domains as prevention, remediation and provision, the book is divided into four parts:

I. The Challenge to Interpersonal Helping
   . . . controversial issues in the field of interpersonal helping, presented from a variety of professional, scholarly and ideological perspectives, including papers delineating the tools for the analysis of both theory and research to aid the reader in evaluating new developments.

II. Preventive Intervention
   . . . major developments in preventive practice, in families, schools and at points of crisis. Both direct and indirect service perspectives are included.

III. Therapeutic Intervention

. . . papers at both a general conceptual and prescriptive practice level are included. The major current thrusts in clinical practice are covered.

IV. Intervention with the Poor

. . . services to "the poor," whose special needs generally have been neglected both theoretically and practically. The emphasis is on new developments in direct service, the advocacy and mediation functions, and service delivery.

All of the papers selected were originally published or presented in the Sixties or early Seventies. This is not to deprecate the past, but to attempt to deal more forcefully with what is new. Many of the papers provide specific, technical prescriptions for change that have a firm empirical foundation and are already available for utilization by the practitioner. Some papers contain programatic implications—e.g. the area of prevention —while others present emerging ideologies for practice—e.g. advocacy. Where possible, there was an attempt to present for each topic aspects of theory, research, practice and some of the relevant issues.

This book represents the work of scholars from many professions—social work, psychology, psychiatry, educational psychology, and counseling. Whether the subject matter involves casework, psychotherapy or counseling, it was, within this context, intended as a subcategory of interpersonal helping, and, as such, related to a potential preferred mode of intervention for the practitioner. Despite their relatively recent publication, some of the works included here have led to major repercussions in their fields, although they are not uniformly well-known in social work. But, of course, putting them together for social workers is the purpose of this book.

REFERENCES

1. Atherton, C., Mitchell, S. and Schein, E.: Locating points for intervention. *Social Casework, 52 (3)*:131-142.
2. Atherton, C.: Using points for intervention. *Social Casework, 52 (4):* 223-233.

3. Bennis, W., Benne, K. and Chin, R. (Eds.): *The Planning of Change.* New York, Holt, Rinehart & Winston, 1961.

4. Bergin, A. and Garfield, S. (Eds.): *Handbook of Psychotherapy and Behavior Change.* New York, Wiley & Sons, 1971.

5. Boehm, W.: *Objectives of the Social Work Curriculum of the Future.* New York, Council on Social Work Education, 1959.

6. Bruno, F.: *Trends in Social Work.* New York, Columbia University Press, 1948.

7. Eells, J.: Therapists' views and preferences concerning intake cases. *J Consult Psychol, 28:*382, 1964.

8. Fischer, J.: Theories of social casework: A review. *Social Work, 17 (1):* 1972.

9. Fischer, J.: Portents from the past: What ever happened to social diagnosis? *International Social Work, 13 (2):*18-29, 1970.

10. Fischer, J.: Negroes and whites and rates of mental illness: Reconsideration of a myth. *Psychiatry, 32 (4):*428-446, 1969.

11. Ford, D. and Urban, H.: *Systems of Psychotherapy.* New York, Wiley & Sons, 1963.

12. Frank, J.: *Persuasion and Healing.* Baltimore, John Hopkins Press, 1961.

13. Goldstein, A., Heller, K. and Sechrest, L.: *Psychotherapy and the Psychology of Behavior Change.* New York, Wiley & Sons, 1966.

14. Goldstein, A. and Simonson, N.: Social psychological approaches to psychotherapy research. In Bergin, A. and Garfield, S. (Eds.): *Handbook of Psychotherapy and Behavior Change.* New York, Wiley & Sons, 1971, pp. 154-196.

15. Hamilton, G.: *Theory and Practice of Social Casework.* New York, Columbia University Press, 1951.

16. Henry, W., Sims, J. and Spray, S. L.: *The Fifth Profession.* San Francisco, Jossey-Bass, 1971.

17. McNair, D. and Lorr, M.: An analysis of professed psychotherapeutic techniques. *J Consult Psychol, 28:*265-271, 1964.

18. McNair, D., Callahan, D., and Lorr, M.: Therapist 'type' and patient response to psychotherapy. *J Consult Psychol, 26:*425-429, 1962.

19. Meltzoff, J. and Kornreich, M.: *Research in Psychotherapy.* New York, Atherton, 1970.

20. Miller, H.: Values dilemmas in social casework. *Social Work, 13 (1):*27-34, 1968.

21. Patterson, C.: *Theories of Counseling and Psychotherapy.* New York, Harper & Row, 1966.

22. Perlman, H. H.: The problem-solving model in social casework. In Roberts, R. and Nee, R. (Eds.): *Theories of Social Casework.* Chicago, University of Chicago Press, 1970, pp. 129-181.

23. Pincus, A. and Minahan, A.: Toward a model for teaching a basic first-year course in methods of social work practice. In Ripple, L. (Ed.):

Innovations in Teaching Social Work Practice. New York, C.S.W.E., 1970, pp. 34-57.

24. Poser, E.: The effect of therapists' training on group therapeutic outcome. *J Consult Psychol, 30:*283-289, 1966.

25. Reynolds, B.: *An Uncharted Journey*. New York, Citadel Press, 1963.

26. Roberts, R. and Nee, R. (Eds.) : *Theories of Social Casework*. Chicago, University of Chicago Press, 1970.

27. Simon, B.: Social casework theroy: An overview. In Roberts, R. and Nee, R. (Eds.) : *Theories of Social Casework*. Chicago, University of Chicago Press, 1970, pp. 353-397.

28. Siporin, M.: Deviant behavior theory in social work. *Social Work, 10:* 59-67, 1965.

29. Smalley, R.: The functional approach to casework practice. In Roberts, R. and Nee, R. (Eds.) : *Theories of Social Casework*. Chicago, University of Chicago Press, 1970, pp. 77-129.

30. Strupp, H.: *Psychotherapists in Action*. New York, Grune & Stratton, 1960.

31. Strupp, H.: The performance of psychiatrists and psychologists in a therapeutic interview. *J Clin Psychol, 22:*219-226, 1958.

32. Strupp, H.: Psychotherapeutic technique, professional affiliation and experience level. *J Consult Psychol, 19:*97-102, 1955.

33. *Values in Social Work: A Re-Examination*. New York, National Association of Social Workers, 1967.

34. Vinter, R. (Ed.) : *Readings in Group Work Practice*. Ann Arbor, University of Michigan Press, 1967.

35. Vinter, R. and Sarri, R. Malperformance in the public school: A group work approach. *Social Work, 10 (1):*3-14, 1965.

36. Wilensky, H. and Lebeaux, C.: *Industrial Society and Social Welfare*. New York, Russell Sage Foundation, 1958.

PART I

THE CHALLENGE TO INTERPERSONAL HELPING

> He that wrestles with us strengthens
> Our nerves and sharpens our skills.
> Our antagonist is our helper.
>
> —EDMUND BURKE

THE SUGGESTION that there is "a challenge" to interpersonal helping is a vast oversimplification. There are, in fact, a multitude of challenges to practice. Not the least of these is whether or not such practice even will continue. For example, the Community Service Society, New York City's oldest private social agency, a bastion of the provision of individualized services for over 120 years, has only recently announced that the agency will no longer provide family and individual counseling except as part of a larger, overall attack on the basic problems of a block, neighborhood or community *(New York Times,* 1971).

A number of factors contribute to such basic concerns: an almost cyclical societal reawakening to the pervasiveness of social problems; impatience with the efficiency, range and limited conception of individualized services; a disgust with the inability of interpersonal helpers to clearly demonstrate their effectiveness. Yet, the thesis of this book is that, in conjunction with programs of social action and social change, services involving interpersonal helping are necessary and important. It remains, then, for the contents of this book to, first, deal openly with the myriad of issues facing the professions engaged in interpersonal helping, and second, attempt to address these issues by presenting meaningful, productive alternatives for practice. The first order of business, presenting the issues, is the task of this part of the book. The initial section of Part I presents some general perspectives on issues. The first article by Briar is an overview of major issues confronting "casework practice." It contains a plea for the continued existence of social work's individualized helping services, but proposes that these services can be made more effective by innovation, experimentation, and more judicious examination of

5

the theory and research developments in fields related to casework. Briar also calls for an expanded conception of casework
with an eye to environmentally-oriented roles such as broker, advocate, reformer, educator. The second article by London focuses
on the moral dilemmas that cut across both theory and practice in
interpersonal helping. London argues that since therapists claim
technical expertise in their ability to influence people, then they
must also assume some responsibility for the nature of that influence. So, they are ultimately moral agents since they are confronted with moral problems. Thus, values may be seen as intervening in the therapeutic situation in many ways, from concrete
instances of clash of values between helper and client, to moral
problems as the critical substantive issues in psychotherapy, to
values as determinative of the therapist's broad personality orientation, and hence (hypothetically at least) his methods of conducting treatment.

The second section of Part I deals with research. Research,
quite simply, provides a crucial base for professional decision-
making. The practitioner must use *some* criteria for making selections from among diverse claims, and the willingness and ability
to read and understand evidence accumulated in the research literature is of paramount importance. This is not to suggest either
that one study, in and of itself, is sufficient "proof" for recommending a course of action, or that, in the absence of perfectly-
designed research, no action whatsoever be taken. Rather, it is
that, since decisions about practice are in fact being made continuously, they should have as firm a grounding as possible in scientific rules of evidence. This means evaluating studies within the
context of a range of research which might provide substantiating
evidence, and making decisions on the basis of the major directions in which the evidence points at any given time. This implies
an open-ended stance toward decision-making, proceeding on the
basis of the best available current knowledge, with the understanding that such knowledge is rarely conclusive, and often subject to change when new evidence appears.

In the first, somewhat tongue-in-cheek article, Astin proscribes
those researchers and practitioners who have decided that whether

or not they are helpful to clients is an irrelevant issue. That this is also a problem in the field of casework can be seen in Roberts and Nee (1970; especially p. xiii). The second paper by Ubell is a newspaper article depicting a lay view of outcome research in casework. Discussing the study *Girls at Vocational High* (Meyer, Borgatta and Jones, 1965), and other studies of casework effectiveness, this article poses a real challenge to caseworkers: how effective are we in helping our clients? The next article by Bergin is an overview of some of the major findings in psychotherapy research. Though published originally in 1966, most of the conclusions still retain their validity (Bergin, 1971). In fact, one of Bergin's most dramatic findings—that psychotherapy can produce deterioration in clients, can be for better or for worse—has been found by Bergin to be demonstrated in over thirty studies (Bergin, 1971). Actually, though, the pitcure on outcome is not nearly as bleak as suggested by Ubell's article and Eysenck's (1966) well known pessimistic review. In fact, a recent compilation of outcome research in psychotherapy has found a number of studies illustrating positive effects from therapeutic treatment (Meltzoff and Kornreich, 1970). However, this review included such a jumble of theoretical orientations, methods and practices (ranging from behavior therapy to hypnosis to undefined counseling and therapy), that what really seems to be illustrated is that people clearly can be purposefully influenced in beneficial ways. Since interpersonal helping is composed of a variety of approaches, it still remains a major task to ferret out which of the approaches, or perhaps more specifically, which variables (e.g. personality, techniques, combinations, etc.) are responsible for the positive effects of intervention.* In the last article of this section, Paul offers an overview of approaches to outcome research, and a framework for reading and understanding such research. Paul argues that the question of whether or not "psychotherapy works" is irrelevant, if not impossible to answer. What does matter is a clear specification of pertinent variables along several dimensions: client, therapist and temporal.

    The following section deals with issues of theory and practice.

---

*Tentative answers to these questions are suggested in Part III of this book.

The basic point of this section is to pose questions which emphasize the necessity for careful informed scrutiny of both old and new models of practice. The first brief paper by Brennen offers some intriguing notions about "the casework relationship." Brennen argues that traditional models of relationship should be laid to rest, and replaced by a democratization of social work which would involve relationships based on psychological and perceptual equality between clients and workers combined with mutual honesty and openness. The following paper by Haley offers a mirror against which the practitioner might view his own practices. Haley presents twelve major factors which every practitioner can utilize as a hedge *against* success with his clients. The not-very-funny question is: how many practitioners really function much differently in practice? The final paper in this section is an elaboration of some of the ideas discussed in the Introduction of this book. This paper proposes a framework for the analysis of clinical theories for use by practitioners and students in the evaluation of this important element of the knowledge base of practice. Criteria for analysis are grouped into five categories, each with numerous subcategories: (a) structural characteristics of the theory; (b) characteristics as a theory of therapy; (c) empirical status; (d) assumptions and moral implications; and (e) applicability for social work. All of the criteria are abstracted in a single table as a guide to be utilized in analysis of a theory.

The final section of Part I deals with issues of service delivery. Whatever the source or nature of our knowledge, if the helping professions cannot make themselves accessible to the public and deliver their goods, all other issues become irrelevant. Schofield, in the first paper, points out that, in view of the pressing manpower shortage in the helping professions, it is crucial for professionals to place some delimitations on the types of problems with which we deal. He proposes a turn away from dealing with the "philosophical neuroses," and a placing of top priority on emotional and behavioral disorders which have social impact. Schofield in essence argues for professional accountability. The concluding paper by Hersch discusses a distressing problem, disengagement of the helping professions from "the poor," coupled with a disproportionally greater need of the poor for professional services. Hersch's paper serves the function of defining the problem. The next step must involve action to remedy the problem (see Part IV).

Part I of this book involves an attempt to establish a paradigm for examination of the field of interpersonal helping (or subareas of that field). The paradigm involves articulated investigation of theory, research, practice and the issues which overlap and interrelate these dimensions. Within each area selected for inclusion in this book, there was an effort, where possible, to follow that design.

REFERENCES

1. Bergin, A.: The evaluation of therapeutic outcomes. In Bergin, A. and Garfield, S. (Eds.): *Handbook of Psychotherapy and Behavior Change.* New York, Wiley, 1971, pp. 217-271.
2. Community service society changing tactics: Will drop casework. *New York Times,* January 29, 1971, p. 1.
3. Eysenck, H.: *The Effects of Psychotherapy.* New York, International Science Press, 1966.
4. Meltzoff, J. and Kornreich, M.: *Research in Psychotherapy.* New York, Atherton, 1970.
5. Meyer, H., Borgatta, E. and Jones, W.: *Girls at Vocational High.* New York, Russell Sage Foundation, 1965.

A. GENERAL ISSUES

Chapter 1

THE CURRENT CRISIS
IN SOCIAL CASEWORK

SCOTT BRIAR

I T IS SAID that social casework is in deep trouble. It is said that
caseworkers are destined for extinction. It is said—and this criticism cuts deepest of all—that casework is not responsive to the
needs of the persons it claims to serve. These criticisms, with
many variations, can be heard from persons outside the profession, from other social workers, and even, though more softly,
from some of our fellow caseworkers. In fact, just a few months
ago, Helen Perlman felt moved to ask whether casework is dead.[1]

As a teacher and practitioner whose professional career has
been centered on social casework, I am distressed by these criticisms. Unfortunately, what distresses me most is that I find myself
compelled to agree with many of these criticisms. Casework *is* in
trouble. And unless casework cures its own ills, it could very well
be destined to become, at worst, a relic of a past era or, at best, a
marginal activity in the profession. But I am not willing to stand
idly by to watch this prophecy come to pass. The initial vision
that gave rise to social casework was based on an important insight into the human condition in modern society, namely, the
realization that if social welfare programs are to be genuinely responsive to the needs of persons, they must be individualized. If
that insight is forgotten, the profession as a whole will be the
worse for it.

The recent criticisms of social casework have taken two principal forms. One questions the very existence of casework by arguing that a case-by-case approach to social problems is at best in-

---

Note: Reprinted from *Social Work Practice, 1967.* New York, Columbia University
Press, 1967, pp. 19-33. Copyright 1967, National Conference on Social Welfare, Columbus, Ohio.

efficient and at the worst hopeless and perhaps even harmful. The second declares that casework simply is not effective, a criticism that is perhaps even more fundamental than the first.

The argument against the case-by-case approach to social problems has appeared partly as an accompaniment to the rising tide of interest in social change and social reform. I want to emphasize that I see no grounds for anything but enthusiasm and optimism about this trend and the promise it portends for the profession and for social welfare. It is a welcome development, not only because social reform activities have too long been neglected, but also because there can be no doubt that many of the problems of concern to the profession will not yield to direct service alone but require intervention at other systemic levels in the social order.

In some of the burgeoning literature on the need for social reform, however, there has appeared a strand of strong and sometimes shrill criticism of social casework. Some of this criticism is well deserved, but some of it heaps on social caseworkers responsibilities they never presumed to carry, and some of its reflects a disquieting naïveté about what social change can realistically be expected to accomplish. But more important is that the growing emphasis on social change as a strategy for alleviating social problems has evoked from many caseworkers a defensiveness about their own activities. And this defensiveness threatens to block more constructive responses by caseworkers to the changes occurring in the profession.[2]

It is important at the outset to be clear about the legitimate grounds for a critique of the casework enterprise. It is fair to criticize casework—or, for that matter, group work, community organization, and social reform—for failing to accomplish what it claimed it could do; in other words, for not being effective. If caseworkers have claimed to be able to help persons with certain kinds of problems and the evidence shows that they have not done so, then caseworkers better return to the drawing board and look for other ways to accomplish their aims. It also is fair to criticize caseworkers if they lose sight of the problem, the need, the person, and the task in a preoccupation with techniques, ideologies, and theoretical concepts. In other words, if it is true, as some have argued,[3] that caseworkers, rather than devising methods tailored to the client's needs and expectations, have expected clients to adapt to the caseworker's methods, then caseworkers should pause to remind themselves that their first commitment is to the client. And, finally, it is fair to criticize casework if it cuts itself off from persons who need its services. That is, if it is true, as it appears to be, that persons who could benefit from the services of caseworkers are systematically deprived of them, then we must alter the methods of delivering and offering casework services so that they are available to such persons.

It is *not* responsible, on the other hand, to criticize social casework for failing to fulfill responsibilities it never promised to discharge—for failing, for example, to eliminate poverty, do away with delinquency, or end illegitimacy. It is possible that some caseworkers have made such rash and immodest claims, but I do not believe the field of social casework has seriously taken these responsibilities upon itself. Consequently, it is absurd to point to the continued existence of social problems as a sign of the failure of casework. Nevertheless, the misconceptions implicit in this line of argument point to the need for a clearer statement of what it is that caseworkers *are* supposed to do.

The dominant preoccupation of social casework over the past thirty-five to forty years has been devoted to the development of the therapeutic function of social casework, or what has come to be called "clinical" casework. I have no quarrel with clinical casework—most of my own practice is of this sort—except that I do not think clinical casework is nearly as effective as it ought to be. Caseworkers can no longer afford to ignore the implications of studies such as the recently published *Girls at Vocational High*.[4] The findings of that study may seem discouraging, but they cannot be written off as due to inadequacies in research design and technology. For what confronts us is not one study but a long list of studies with equally distressing results. Hunt, Kogan, and their coworkers labored long and hard at the Community Service Society in New York City to measure the outcome of casework and found an average movement of only one step on the movement scale, a result that, at the least, should have stimulated a searching reconsideration of the clinical casework approach developed in that agency and widely promulgated in the field.[5] This is not to say that casework is never effective, and it is important to be clear about that. Any caseworker can cite cases from his own experience to show that casework is effective, sometimes dramatically so. What the research indicates is simply that our batting average is too low—not that we never succeed but rather that we succeed too infrequently.

The research on the effectiveness of casework is only a small part of the story. Research on the effectiveness of psychotherapy is both more extensive and, in some respects, more rigorous than the outcome studies of casework.[6] I know that many caseworkers are quick to insist on the difference between clinical casework and psychotherapy, but it is demonstrable that the theory and techniques of treatment that inform clinical casework practice were not developed independently but carry a heavy debt to psychotherapy, and to psychoanalytic psychotherapy in particular. Thus, studies that question the efficiacy of dynamic psychotherapy also challenge the foundations of clinical casework. And the plain facts are that the effectiveness of the traditional psychotherapies, the so-called "dynamic" psychotherapies, is in grave doubt. Even defenders of the traditional psychotherapies who have surveyed this body of evidence can find only weak support in a few isolated studies and for the remainder can only question the validity of the research itself, a weak and no longer sufficent defense.[7]

Moreover, at least as far as casework is concerned, it is not simply that effectiveness is less than satisfactory, but other research has shown that the model of clinical casework dominant for many years is suitable for no more than a fraction of the clients who come to us. We now know that even in the presumably ideal conditions of the private family service agency, the conception of casework as a prolonged series of interviews between the caseworker and an individual who is seeking help with emotional or interpersonal problems appears to be applicable to at most 25 percent of the clients who seek help from such agencies.[8]

But the findings I have all too briefly summarized here should not be viewed as cause for despair. The response required is of quite another sort. The message of these findings is that caseworkers should embark on a period of active and vigorous innovation and experimentation, in a search for more effective models and methods for the conduct of clinical casework. Fortunately, some promising directions for experimentation have already appeared. Caseworkers in many places are experimenting, for example, with short-term methods of intervention. But experimentation with short-term approaches has not proceeded at a pace commensurate with their obvious relevance to the reality that a large proportion of the encounters between caseworkers and clients are of brief duration. If we are to give short-term methods the attention they deserve, we have to modify our tendency, as Lucille Austin notes, to regard them "chiefly as a matter of expedience."[9] Family treatment represents another area of active experimentation in social casework. Unfortunately, however, the family therapy movement also illustrates a characteristic weakness of innovative efforts in social work, namely, the failure to conduct systematic evaluations of effectiveness. Despite the enormous effort that has been devoted to family diagnosis and treatment over the past ten to fifteen years, the number of attempts to assess its effectiveness systematically can be counted on the fingers of one hand.[10] Thus, we continue to expand family treatment only on the basis of faith and the missionary zeal of the practitioners who have become committed to it. Faith, however, is not enough. The crucial questions to be asked of an intervention method are not "Does it sound good?" or "Is it fascinating?" but "Does it work?" and "Is it more effective than other methods?"

Appearing on the horizon are some even more fundamental innovations in treatment models and techniques. I have in mind a variety of new therapeutic strategies based on theories that depart radically from the psychoanalytic formulations that have dominated psychotherapy and casework for the past thirty to forty years. One illustration of these new departures is the attempt to apply sociobehavioral theory to social work practice. When one first hears it, the language and metaphors of this approach may seem strange or even disagreeable, but do not turn away if they do. Or, at first glance, it may seem that this theory simply puts new labels on old, familiar ideas, but that impression, too, would be invalid. The sociobehavioral approach has already had wide application and is based on theories that are backed by extensive research.[11] The results thus far are impressive, sometimes dramatically so, and perhaps the most promising aspect of sociobehavioral theory is that it suggests a strategy for the development of practice knowledge that is more systematic than those we have followed in the past. We cannot afford to ignore any perspective that is demonstrably successful or that appears to promise a more effective strategy for developing the body of knowledge we need in order to improve our effectiveness. Finally, I would mention the important innovations now being formulated in response to our increased understanding of the realities of casework with the poor.

My intent in these comments on clinical casework is to make two general points. The first is that current attempts to disparage the therapeutic function of social casework are invalid and misdirected. Clinical casework represents an essential function carried out in relation to important human problems. For that reason, the demand for caseworkers to perform this function should continue to increase, *if*—through more vigorous innovation and systematic experimentation—caseworkers can discover ways of performing this function more effectively.

My second point is that the general field of psychotherapy is in a state of exciting ferment and experimentation. Unfortunately, however, many caseworkers are effectively isolated from these developments, for it still is true that caseworkers by and large keep abreast primarily of those developments in psychotherapy that are within the psychoanalytic tradition, broadly defined. This restriction is becoming increasingly dysfunctional for clinical casework, since, as Ford and Urban recently concluded in their excellent review of developments in psychotherapy, "the innovative steam has gone out of the psychoanalytic movement. Major theoretical and technical advances in the future will probably come from other orientations."[12] In order that we can benefit from those advances in the general field of psychotherapy that may be applicable to casework practice, it is essential that we find ways of keeping informed about the many new developments in that closely related field.

I said that the disparagement of clinical casework is misplaced. The proper target of these critics, in my opinion, is the strong tendency to equate clinical casework with casework, the tendency to regard the therapeutic function as the *only* function of casework. To make this equation is to constrict the range of functions of casework and thereby to make it less flexible and less responsive to changing needs and conditions. The founders of social casework had no such narrow conception of the functions of the social caseworker. (By founders, incidentally, I have in mind persons such as Mary Richmond, Porter Lee, Edith Abbott, Shelby Harrison, and Bertha Reynolds.) The therapeutic function was part of their vision of social casework, but it was only one of several functions they thought caseworkers should perform. However, the history of social casework is in large measure a history of progressive constriction, elimination, and reduction of the functions of casework to the therapeutic or clinical function.[13] The other functions of the casework enterprise envisaged by its founders have either atrophied or have been relegated to marginal activities subsumed under the catch-all phase, "environmental manipulation." I believe this trend ought to be reversed, not simply because the founders had a broader conception of the caseworker's mission, but because changing conditions and changing conceptions of the problems facing the profession require an expanded conception of casework.

Two functions that were explicit components of the casework enterprise in its early history have since atrophied. I select these two functions only as examples; they are not the only functions that have been neglected.

One is a function that currently is being revived under the rubric of "social broker" (see chap. 37 in text).[14] The justification for this function resides in the fact that there are many persons who need services but do not know that these services are available; many others know that the services are available but do not know where to obtain them; others who know where to obtain services do not know how to get them or else face obstacles in seeking and obtaining them; and still others do not know how to gain the maximum benefits available to them. This function is vastly more important today than it was when Mary Richmond and her colleagues were preoccupied with it, because the maze of social welfare programs is far more complex and the social agencies are larger and more bureaucratic than they were in her day. Fortunately, however, we have an advantage not available to Mary Richmond, namely, a substantial body of knowledge concerning the dynamics of the welfare system and its constituent agencies. This body of knowledge could be applied—though by and large it has not been—to the performance of the social broker function, much as we have applied social and psychological knowledge in our performance of the therapeutic function.

The problem of getting what one wants and needs from the public welfare agency, the health department, the vocational rehabilitation agency, the psychiatric hospital, the public school—and on and on through the array of organizations with which persons must negotiate to get what they need—is no simple matter, as everyone knows from his own encounters with large, complex organizations. Increasingly, if a person is to gain from these agencies the benefits to which he is entitled, he requires an informed and skilled guide who knows the social welfare maze, knows the bureaucracy, and knows how to move it to get what the client needs and deserves. In our personal lives, we may be able to negotiate effectively with the organizations that directly affect us because we know how, the businessman is able to hire specialists to deal with the organizations on which he depends for services and benefits, but many of the persons we seek to serve lack the knowledge, skills, or resources to negotiate effectively with the organizations on which the satisfaction of their needs may depend.

Currently, the broker function is being revived, but only to a limited extent. As an outgrowth of the war on poverty, new careerists are being trained to perform this function. But evidence already is accumulating to indicate that subprofessionals can perform this function effectively only with professional guidance and direction and that in some instances they cannot perform it very effectively at all, partly because some of the problems encountered require the application of considerable skill and knowledge.[15] Recognition of the importance of this function also is evident in the growing interest in the creation of neighborhood information and referral centers. Thus far, however, discussion of such centers has been focused more on organizational considerations than on the roles to be performed and the knowledge and skills required for their effective performance.

Another function that was highly visible early in the history of social casework subsequently not only declined in significance but came to be regarded by some as inconsistent with the proper conduct of casework practice. Some of the early leaders in casework saw one function of the caseworker as that of a person who actively fought on the side of his client to help him meet his needs, realize his hopes and aspirations, and exercise his rights. The caseworker was to be his client's supporter, his adviser, his champion, and, if need be, his representative in his dealings with the court, the police, the social agency, and the other organizations that affected his well-being. In other words, the caseworker was to serve not only as a therapist or as a social broker, but also as an active advocate of the client's cause in relation to the various social organizations.[16] Currently, we are being told by lawyers, who at last are becoming interested in social welfare problems in sufficient numbers to make a difference, that performance of the advocacy function by social workers is essential both for the client to get what he is entitled to receive and for the social welfare system to operate as it is supposed to, especially as it becomes more institutionalized. For instance, fair and equitable procedures in an organization will remain such only if its clients are able to insist that the procedures be honored and to call the organization to task when it becomes lax. But many of the persons whom caseworkers seek to serve, especially among the poor, will not exercise their rights, press their claims and needs, or appeal actions that adversely affect them unless someone performs the role of advocate, because many of these clients are too apathetic, feel too powerless, or are too uninformed to do so. Moreover, effective performance of the advocacy function would help to insure that agencies are attentive and responsive to the needs and desires of clients.

One example will illustrate the importance of the advocacy function. The California State Department of Social Welfare provides a fair hearing procedure to be used by a welfare recipient when he believes that the welfare agency has erred or has taken improper action in his case. There are over one million welfare recipients in California. During a one-year period, from 1965 to 1966, only 1,098 recipients, or less than one tenth of one percent of all recipients, used the fair hearing procedure. There is no doubt that the proportion of recipients who have legitimate grounds for requesting a hearing is substantially greater than one tenth of one percent. For one thing, this proportion is substantially below the rate of error in the agency's favor typically found in sample case record audits. What prevents more recipients from using this procedure? Based on some research I am currently completing, I would say one reason is that only a tiny fraction of recipients know about the fair hearing or how to apply for it, in spite of the fact that they are routinely given information about this procedure.[17]

A substantial proportion of recipients who obtain fair hearings win their appeals. And the recipient's chances of winning are doubled if he brings along someone to represent him. The recipient can select anyone he wants as his representative; rarely does he bring a lawyer, but the hearings are informal and a lawyer's skills and knowledge ordinarily are not necessary to represent the client. The client's caseworker frequently is required to be present, but he is expected to represent both the client and the agency, which prevents him from serving as his client's advocate. Bear in mind that the stakes for the client may be quite high, namely, the means to feed, house, and clothe his family. I suggest that the caseworker ought to be free to represent his *client's* cause in such situations. And the agency should want to have this function performed in order to discharge its commitment to the welfare of its clients.

Finally, it should be emphasized that performance of the advocacy function to the point where the client has the experience of making his wishes felt and having them acted on can enhance, sometimes dramatically, his sense of confidence, competence, and mastery and reduce the feelings of apathy and impotence many of our clients experience in their dealings with the organizations that affect their lives.

It also is important to see both the social broker and the advocate functions in a somewhat broader context. In my view, these functions must become institutionalized if the social welfare system is to operate as it should, no matter how well planned or enlightened it is otherwise. It would be a naïve and tragic mistake to view these as residual functions that need to be performed only because the social welfare system has not yet been perfected. On the contrary, the social welfare system cannot be perfected unless these functions are performed effectively. To argue otherwise is analogous to arguing that the fact that plaintiffs and defendants still need attorneys when they go to court is symptomatic of imperfections in the court system, that if the court system were perfected, lawyers would be unnecessary. The opposite is, of course, the case. That is, the court system as a system cannot operate properly unless the functions assumed by lawyers are performed.

I have discussed three functions that originally were conceived to be integral components of the caseworker's mission: the therapeutic function, the social broker function, and the advocacy function. Subsequently, casework became preoccupied with the therapeutic function at the expense of the others. The therapeutic function flourished and underwent sophisticated theoretical development to the point where it seemed to some that this was the *only* function of casework. Recently, research has raised grave questions about the effectiveness with which caseworkers perform their therapeutic function. I have argued that our response to these questions should be vigorous innovation and systematic experimentation. I have also argued that we need to expand our conception of the casework mission to include other functions, not simply because they are part of our historic heritage but because the needs of our clients and the conditions of their lives require that we assume these responsibilities. Moreover, we should devote to these other functions the same measure of thought and skill we have long devoted to the therapeutic function, for the tasks these other functions impose on us are no less difficult or demanding than those we encounter in our therapeutic work.

I do not mean to imply that these three functions are the only ones I have in mind in calling for an expanded conception of social casework. I discussed the social broker and advocate functions as crucial examples to make the case for an expanded conception of casework. But there are other functions that caseworkers need to perform. For example, there is the vital and indispensable role that social caseworkers should be playing, as practitioners, in social policy-making. Caseworkers have virtually unique access to information indispensable to the development of sound social welfare policies and programs.

Moreover—and I cannot emphasize this point too strongly—I have in mind no fixed list of casework functions, because the central point is that these functions arise in response to the needs of the persons we seek to serve, the conditions of their lives, and our understanding of these needs and conditions. Consequently, as these needs and conditions and our knowledge of them change, our responses to them should be modified accordingly. It also follows from that, of course, that not all these functions are needed by every individual or family nor will any one caseworker necessarily perform all of them.

An expanded conception of social casework has many implications that deserve more detailed discussion than is possible here. However, two general implications are of crucial importance. First, vigorous innovation and experimentation in treatment methods and participation in the activities required in performing the advocate and social broker functions require that caseworkers have much greater professional autonomy and discretion than now prevail in many, if not most, social agencies. Ninety percent or more of all caseworkers practice in bureaucratic organizations, and the demands of such organizations have a tendency to encroach upon professional autonomy. Every attempt by the agency to routinize some condition or aspect of professional practice amounts to a restriction of professional discretion, and for that reason probably should be resisted, in most instances, by practitioners. But it will not be enough to resist bureaucratic restriction. We will need to roll back the restrictions that already constrain practice in order to gain the freedom essential to experiment, to discover new and better ways of helping the clients to whom we are primarily responsible. There are, of course, realistic limits to the amount of autonomy and discretion an organization can grant to the practitioner, but no one knows just where that limit is, and we cannot know until we have tried to reach it. It may be that when this limit is reached we will find it still too confining to engage in the kind of practice required to help some of our clients.

The second general implication is that the remedies I have proposed require a much closer relationship between practice and research than we have achieved thus far, because research is an indispensable tool in our efforts to improve the efficacy of casework. The relationships between the practitioner and the researcher continue to be problematic. There are good reasons to believe that in the long run the best solution to these problems may be to develop both sets of skills in the same person.

A brief quotation from Alfred Kahn concisely expresses a basic assumption underlying everything I have said:

> Crucial to social work is an integrative view of needs . . . The real commitment, and the unique nature of the entire social work institution . . . is not to any one method or even one concept but rather to human need. The role is dynamic—and never completed. The danger is the loss of that flexibility essential to the recognition of new horizons and the undertaking of consequent responsibilities.[18]

If we take seriously the view that the central commitment is to human need and if we keep our attention focused squarely on the needs of persons and the responsibilities these needs impose on the profession at all levels of systemic intervention, I believe the result must be an expanded and dynamic conception of the scope and multiple functions of the endeavor we call social casework.

NOTES AND REFERENCES

1. Perlman, Helen Harris: Casework is dead. *Social Casework, XLVIII:* 22-25, 1967.

2. Gronfein, Berthe: Should casework be on the defensive? *Social Casework,* *XLVII:* 650-56, 1966.

3. Cloward, Richard A. and Epstein, Irwin: Private social welfare's disengagement from the poor: The case of family adjustment agencies. In Zald, Mayer N. (Ed.): *Social Welfare Institutions.* New York, Wiley, 1965, pp. 623-44.

4. Meyer, Henry J., Borgatta, Edgar F. and Jones, Wyatt C.: *Girls at Vocational High: An experiment in Social Work Intervention.* New York, Russell Sage Foundation, 1965.

5. For a review of this research, see Briar, Scott: Family services. In Maas, Henry S. (Ed.): *Five Fields of Social Service.* New York, National Association of Social Workers, 1966, pp. 16-21.

6. The literature on research on psychotherapy is too vast to be summarized here. A recent review of major studies of traditional psychotherapy is available in Eysenck, Hans J.: *The Effects of Psychotherapy.* New York, International Science Press, 1966. An excellent source for current developments in research on psychotherapy is the chapters on psychotherapy in the *Annual Review of Psychology* published each year by Annual Reviews, Inc., Palo Alto, California.

7. See, for example, Wallerstein, Robert: The current state of psychotherapy: Theory, practice, research. *J Am Psychoanal Assoc, XIV:* 183-225, 1966.

8. Briar, *op. cit.*

9. Parad, Howard J. (Ed.): *Crisis Intervention: Selected Readings.* New York: Family Service Association of America, 1965, p. xi.

10. One of the better exceptions is Robert Macgregor *et al: Multiple Impact Therapy with Families.* New York, McGraw-Hill, 1964.

11. See, for example, Krasner, Leonard, and Ullmann, Leonard P. (Eds.): *Research in Behavior Modification.* New York, Holt, Rinehart and Winston, 1965. Also see Ullmann, Leonard P., and Krasner, Leonard (Eds.): *Case Studies in Behavior Modification.* New York, Holt, Rinehart, and Winston, 1965.

12. Ford, Donald H. and Urban, Hugh B.: Psychotherapy. In *Annual Review of Psychology, 18:333,* 1967 (Palo Alto, Calif., Annual Reviews, Inc., 1967).

13. Reynolds, Bertha: *An Uncharted Journey; Fifty Years of Growth in Social Work.* New York, Citadel Press, 1963. Bertha Reynold's autobiographical book is in part a chronicle of one person's efforts to maintain a broader conception of the casework mission in the face of her colleagues' more successful attempts to constrict it.

14. For other discussions of this concept, see Grosser, Charles F.: Community development programs serving the urban poor. *Social Work, X (No. 3):* 15-21, 1965.

15. Barr, Sherman: The indigenous worker: What he is not, what he can be.

Fourteenth Annual Program Meeting, Council on Social Work Education, 1966.

16. For other discussions of the advocacy role, see Grosser, *op cit.:* Terrell, *op. cit.;* Brennen, Earl C.: The casework relationship: Excerpts from a heretic's notebook. *New Perspectives: The Berkeley Journal of Social Welfare, I (No. 1):* 65-67, 1957; and Briar, Scott: The social worker's responsibility for the civil rights of clients. *Ibid.,* pp. 89-92.

17. Briar, Scott: Welfare from below: Recipients' views of the public welfare system. *California Law Review, LIV:* 370-85, 1966.

18. Kahn, Alfred J.: The function of social work in the modern world. *Issues in American Social Work.* New York, Columbia University Press, 1959, p. 16.

Chapter 2

THE MORALS OF PSYCHOTHERAPY

PERRY LONDON

INSOFAR as he is concerned with the diagnosis and treatment of illness, the modern psychotherapist has grown up in the tradition of medicine. But the nature of the ailments he deals with and the way he treats them set him apart from the physician and in some ways make him function much like a clergyman. He deals with sickness of the soul, as it were, which cannot be cultured in a laboratory, seen through a microscope, or cured by injection. And his methods have little of the concreteness or obvious empiricism of the physician's—he carries no needle, administers no pill, wraps no bandages. He cures by talking and listening. The infections he seeks to expose and destroy are neither bacterial nor viral— they are ideas, memories of experiences, painful and untoward emotions that debilitate the individual and prevent him from functioning effectively and happily.

Our traditional understanding of the physician is that he relieves men of their suffering regardless of their moral condition. Historically, the dedicated physician has treated the good and bad alike, ministering to their physical needs as best he could.

He has done so for reasons that are both technically and theoretically sound. In his technical work, the physician rarely needs to be concerned with the moral attributes of his patient, for they generally have no bearing on the diagnosis he will make or how he will combat an illness. In theory, the physician is committed to the task of saving and enhancing the life and physical well-being of his patients. So he treats them all, and treats them as they come—and this is perhaps the noblest tradition within medicine.

Psychotherapists have been nobly moved to adapt this tradi-

Note: Reprinted from *The Modes and Morals of Psychotherapy* by Perry London. Copyright 1964 by Holt, Rinehart & Winston, Inc. Reprinted by permission of Holt, Rinehart & Winston, Inc.

tion to their own practice. In so doing, they argue that the mental therapist is no moralist, that he has no business becoming involved in the moral, religious, economic, or political beliefs of his client, and that he has no right, in the course of his practice, to make value judgments of his client, to moralize or preach at him, or to try to dictate to him some "good" way of life. His purpose is to alleviate the suffering, the mental anguish, the anxiety, the guilt, the neurosis or psychosis of the client, not to change his way of life along moralistic or ideological lines.

This argument has a great deal in its favor. It has served the historical purpose of permitting students of mental health and illness to investigate objectively the conditions that predispose people to mental troubles and the kinds of people who suffer from such difficulties. It has allowed therapists, free of metaphysical concerns, to develop a technical armamentarium that, though limited, can often be used much as the physician uses his store of pills and skills. It has been largely responsible for the creation of a new "helping" art, one that has not only demonstrated its usefulness, but has also been able to entertain legitimate pretensions to being a scientific discipline.

It is impossible to overstate the importance of freedom from metaphysics and morals to the conduct of scientific research, especially to the objective analysis and interpretation of data. But the psychotherapist, in his actual practice, does not usually function as a researcher. He is a clinician. And much of the material with which he deals is neither understandable nor usable outside the context of a system of human values. This fact is unfortunate and embarrassing to one who would like to see himself as an impartial scientist and unprejudiced helper. It is a fact none the less, and one which, for both technical and theoretical reasons, may be painfully important to students of human behavior in general and to psychotherapists in particular. Moral considerations may dictate, in large part, how the therapist defines his client's needs, how he operates in the therapeutic situation, how he defines "treatment," and "cure," and even "reality."

Many psychotherapists are poignantly aware of this. Students of mental health find that it is difficult even to *define* such terms as "health," "illness," and "normality," without some reference to morals; and worse still, they cannot discuss the proper treatment of what they have defined without recognizing and involving their own moral commitments.

The issue is the same whether the problem is a social one like prostitution or an apparently individual one like obsessional neuroses. Neither can be called an illness on the grounds of invasion by a foreign body or of the malfunctioning of specific organs. Nor do people die directly from them. They may be abnormal in a statistical sense, but this is hardly a basis for worry. Living one hundred years or making a million dollars is also deviant in that sense. The objectionable feature of these problems concerns the violation of the public moral code, in the one case, and the experience of apparently unnecessary personal anguish—which either presupposes the virtue of comfort or abjures the discomfort of preoccupation—in the other. In both, the assumption of a moral desideratum underlies the definition.

Yet psychotherapeutic training programs in psychiatry, psychology, social work—even in the ministry—often do not deal seriously with the problem of morals. Psychotherapeutic literature is full of formal principles of procedure and somewhat vague statements of goals, but it generally says little or nothing about the possible moral implications of those procedures and goals—indeed, it often fails even to mention that there are any moral, as opposed to scientific, implications to psychotherapy, though the objectives of the latter are rationalized by the former. It is as if therapists were themselves unconscious of some of the most profound difficulties in their own work. Or perhaps the opposite is true—that they are well aware but find that, as Marie Jahoda puts it, "[it] seems so difficult that one is almost tempted to claim the privilege of ignorance." Perhaps so, but ignorance can serve no useful purpose in this matter, and may even impair the uses of the craft.

At some level of abstraction, it is probably correct to declare that every aspect of psychotherapy presupposes some implicit moral doctrine, but it is not necessary to seek this level in order to say why it is important for therapists to recognize the moral concomitants of patients' problems and the implied moral position of some of their solutions. Some problems are inevitably moral ones from the perspective of either client or therapist, and some can be viewed as strategic or technical ones and treated without reference to particular value systems. In the one case, the therapist must fulfill a moral agency in order to function at all, whereas in the other he may restrict himself to the impartial helping or contractual function with which he is usually identified. But if he does not know the difference, then his own moral commitments may influence his technical functioning so that he willy-nilly strives to mold men to his own image, or his technical acts may imply moral positions which he might himself abhor.

MORALS AS TECHNICALITIES

To be sure, there are many people and problems that clearly do not require much moralistic concern by therapist or patient. These are in fact purely technical problems and can be assessed, for the most part, on purely empirical grounds. An example might be the case of a phobia in a child. Such a condition will often succumb to fairly specific techniques without much thought to the value systems that may underlie their use. Similarly, many psychogenic physical symptoms in children and adults may be treated without seriously invading the patient's value system and without challenging his moral code or, for that matter, knowing anything about it. Some familial conflicts are resolved by fairly simple means—helping people to improve interpersonal communication, to discover that their feelings can be voiced without disastrous consequences, and so forth.

Such problems require few moral commitments from the therapist beyond the belief that children ought not have phobias, people should be free of allergies, members of families should not be in continuous conflict, and so on. It would be precious for most of us to label these as moral issues, not because they are free of moral underpinnings, but because the consensus which exists about them almost everywhere is so great that it makes them virtual universals.

The technical problem that becomes a moral problem in psychotherapy, often in a critical way, might be stated like this:

How does a psychotherapist properly deal with a client who reports that he has perpetrated a theft or been sexually delinquent? Or suppose a religiously devout patient reports that he is conflicted, guilty, and anxious about the use of birth control devices. What defines a therapeutic reply to a person who feels that his behavior, or thoughts, violate the word of God, or the Church, and that at the same time he cannot control them?

Suppose, for that matter, the converse—a patient reports particularly opprobrious behavior about which he does not experience guilt, anxiety, or conflict; suppose, in effect, he thereby violates the moral code of the therapist.

What should the therapist do? Avoid comment? Refer his comments to the ostensible code of the client without reference to his own? Should he circumvent the moral issue itself and attempt to penetrate the dynamic, or unconscious, or historical situations that may have "determined" the behavior?

A common technical objective of therapists of all schools is to help the client to be free of his unrealistic conflicts—but when conflicts revolve around moral issues, how is it possible to help without becoming directly involved in the moral issue? How is it even possible, for that matter, to decide whether a conflict is realistic without moral involvement? It is specious to argue, as some therapists do, that moral concerns are simply manifestations of "resistance" and that the underlying dynamics of the client's situation never relate to moral problems. It seems viciously irresponsible for the therapist to argue that, at such times, he must formally remove himself from the discussion by telling the client that the therapy session can be helpful for discussing "personal, emotional problems, not moral ones." The naive injunction that, regardless of what approach he *does* take, the therapist must *not* moralize at the client, has little value here—it is hard to imagine that the failure to moralize alone arranges things so that the client can then solve his own moral dilemmas.

Within the framework of technical therapeutic objectives, independent of his own scheme of values or his awareness of the relevance of the client's morality to the conflict situation, it is unclear what the therapist should do here. Most therapists, regardless of the particular psychological orthodoxy to which they adhere, would probably agree that there are a number of perfectly valid, even necessary, technical actions which may be considered in such a situation. The therapist might reflect, interpret, probe the origins of the symptom, or its intensity, or its continuities and discontinuities; he might ask the client to free-associate in general or in response to particular words or phrases. He might challenge him to explain clearly why he deprecates his own impulses, or to explore deeper underlying motives for his anxiety or his preoccupation, to describe this or think about that or understand a third thing. What unites all these technical operations in most actual cases, I believe, is first, the fact that the therapist says *something,* and second, the fact that he almost inevitably avoids expressing an opinion about the *moral issue as such.* Morality, religion, the oughts and shoulds of human behavior, are not his ostensible concern.

But these issues are surely the concern of the client; to the extent that he is in touch with reality, let alone has any care to serve his own best interests, he must necessarily be concerned with what he should and should not do. This kind of concern may be one of the things that brought him to a psychotherapist in the first place, and however independent a soul he may be, one of the main things that keeps him there is the hope that he can be helped to guide himself along lines of behavior that will make his life more meaningful and satisfying. It is largely this hope that may compel him to invest the therapist with greater importance than most other people and to view the therapist, more or less realistically, as the agent of the resolution of his conflicts. It is my contention that the force of this agency, in those conflict areas in which morality figures, propels the therapist into the practical position of moralist whether or not he wishes to assume it.

That he should not wish to assume such a role is understandable, but the studied attempt to avoid doing so sometimes leads therapists into logically untenable positions. A therapist of my acquaintance, for example, once offered her students as a cardinal rule of psychotherapy the dictum that one "does not get involved in the politics or religion of the patient." At the same time, she could not advise how to avoid doing so—once the client has made them explicit issues—except by declining to offer one's personal politics or religion as solutions to the client's problems. While this may be sound negative advice, it is of questionable use to either therapist or patient. The strategy itself requires some rationale—it seems unreasonable to propose a list of ideas, beliefs, and attitudes that are outside the scope of the therapist's function, without similarly defining relevant alternatives that are appropriate to his function. Such a task is, at best, very difficult to do, and still harder to justify. And considering only tactics, how does one explain to the patient that it is legitimate for him to talk about anything, but it would not be proper for the therapist to talk back about A, B, or C?

Another analyst of my acquaintance said to a patient, in response to queries about certain guilt-provoking behavior, "Why should I give a damn how you act?" but on another occasion, in relation to the same behavior, told him that therapy would have to terminate if the patient did not discontinue his "acting-out." In the first instance, the analyst was referring, albeit for technical reasons, to his own moral view of the patient's behavior, while in the second situation he was considering the behavior as a technical problem in the therapy. But the behavior was the same in both cases! It seems unrealistic to discuss the same behavior as a therapeutically irrelevant issue in the first instance and a therapeutically critical one in the second. Could one seriously expect the patient to honor the distinction?

The "neutralist" position is most clearly stated by a third analyst who says, "When I am working in the privacy of the analytic session, I don't care if the world is coming down around my patient's ears on the outside." He does not stipulate, incidentally, whether his attitude would be the same if the financial world of the patient were collapsing, indicating that he would no longer be paid, or if the patient were, on the outside, "acting-out" in a fashion which "interfered with the progress of the analysis."

It is obvious that, in most therapeutic situations, there are choice points at which the therapist must manifest some very real concern with the life the patient leads outside the therapy situation proper, and that some of that concern will be directed towards how the patient ought or ought not to act.

MORALS AS GENERALITIES

Consideration of the foregoing as a purely technical problem also forces a more general issue into bold relief: This concerns what the therapist wishes ultimately to accomplish: the long-range goals of his therapy. The technical problem deals with immediate goals, but this asks what he wishes to see happen to this person, not merely in therapy, but in life. In what ways does he, as therapist, want his ministrations to alter the client's life?

Ultimately, I believe, this is a moral question that is always answered by the therapist in practice, whether or not it is ever posed in words; and the answer in fact is formed in terms of some superordinate, if unvoiced, moral code of his own. Sometimes the nature of the answer is masked by the impersonal scientistic language of mental health—but it is less subtly hidden in the words of the minister who counsels against premarital intercourse because of its "unfortunate psychological consequences"; of the Catholic caseworker who opposes his client's divorce because of its "mentally disrupting effect"; of the libertarian who helps his client accept the "psychological legitimacy" of extramarital affairs. Such therapeutic goals reflect personal morals and not scientifically validated conclusions.

Perhaps the most general, and accurate, answer that sensitive and self-conscious therapists could offer to the question of their goals could be put so: "I want to reshape this person's existence so that he will emulate values which I cherish for myself, aspire to what I wish humanity to be, fulfill my need for the best of all possible worlds and human conditions."

It is a truism that the therapist is himself a human being, that he lives in society, and that wisely or unknowingly, responsibly or casually, he has made moral commitments to himself and that society. But the present argument carries this platitude to its own logical, if unheeded, conclusion—that the very nature of his interaction with the people he serves involves a moral confrontation which, at the very least, renders communication of some part of his own moral commitments an inescapable part of his therapeutic work.

No one seriously doubts the validity of this argument in the case of the pastoral counselor, for he is almost always publicly committed to a religious-moral system whose content is usually well known to his clients before they ever approach him. No one believes, for example, that a priest will "accept" crime or sexual misconduct when confessed, as something less than sinful, regardless of the immediate response he makes to the confession. And while he may be understanding of the cause of this behavior and eager and able to temper judgment of its severity, and may deeply empathize with the guilt and anguish of its perpetrator—there is still little doubt that he looks upon the action as sinful and the behaver as a sinner, independent of the determinants which contributed to the act. For the priest, despite all else, is publicly committed to the notion that every individual is ultimately responsible for paying the price of his choice—and the person who confesses knows this all along.

The notion that the psychotherapist's situation differs much from the priest's is, I believe, a convenient fiction. To any given incident revealed by his client, the psychotherapist makes some kind of response, or so he is seen. He may carefully avoid making a very emphatic positive or negative response—he may manifest a studied, neutral attitude, and he may sincerely and devoutly feel neither censure nor approval of the situation at hand. But to regard this neutrality as an amoral position, to salve his own democratic, egalitarian, or relativistic conscience, to convince himself that he "is not imposing his own value system upon his client"—merely because he does not want to impose it—is ultimately to deceive both the client and himself. For this belief implicitly denies the essence of the psychotherapeutic relationship: that its most critical points are those involving the *interactions* between participants, not the private experiences of either of them. In other words, psychotherapy is a social, interpersonal action, characterized by an exchange of individual, personal ideas and feelings. The verbal content of the exchange differs with the respective roles of client and therapist, but the relationship is, in vital respects, a reciprocal one.

The very fact of the exchange relationship dictates, I believe, the inevitability of the therapist's functioning practically as a moral agent for three reasons:

1. He influences the moral decisions of the client because the client necessarily interprets the therapist's response to his moral concerns. If the therapist approves his behavior, he may reinforce it. If the therapist disapproves, he may change it. If the therapist appears neutral, he may interpret this as either tacit approval or tacit disapproval—and in many instances, it may be either one, complicated by the therapist's fears of upsetting the client or his reluctance to "dictate" ground rules of propriety. In any case, the very fact that the therapist permits discussion of these issues largely legitimizes any attempts on the client's part to interpret the therapist's reaction to his remarks.

2. Therapists are affiliated with professional societies. These societies have generally published codes of ethical conduct that dictate ground rules of propriety to the therapist, codes that attempt to establish minimal bounds to his conduct. Breach of these codes generally results in expulsion from the professional society. Whether or not he makes the binding limits of his code explicit to his client, the ethical therapist must act on these limits at critical points in therapy—and whenever he does so, he serves an explicit moral agency.

3. Therapists have personal value systems, and it is difficult to see how they could possibly form relationships with clients even for the sole purpose of understanding them, never mind helping them, without being cognizant of their own values and making implicit comparisons between themselves and their values and those of their clients. The failure to respond in any way to those comparisons, by some process of suspension of his own beliefs, may be possible, but it may also eventually commit the therapist to suspending his interaction—for it is hard to see how he can respond to his patient without cognizance of himself, and once aware of his own values, how he can completely withhold com-

municating them and continue to interact. This communication is precisely what occurs whenever, for example, a psychotherapist makes the continuation of treatment contingent on the patient's performing or refraining from some behavior. That the value involved for the therapist is a technical rather than a moral one is beside the point. It is *his* value, not the client's, and unless he can communicate it, he cannot function therapeutically.

IMPLICATIONS

If one accepts the notion that psychotherapists are moral agents, and that this agency may be intrinsic to their functions and goals, some important issues take shape.

It becomes apparent, for one thing, that not all the matters dealt with in therapy are mental health matters, even within the broadest meaning of that term. Some of these matters refer to religion, politics, and social and economic behavior of great importance both to individuals and to society. Psychotherapists cannot claim special knowledge or competence in the discussion of such issues, but neither are they apparently free on that basis to disengage themselves from their patients' concerns.

I do not believe that this is an entirely soluble dilemma, but certainly a first step towards its solution would require that therapists become vividly aware of their own personal commitments. Students of therapy have too often been encouraged to regard their clients and themselves exclusively in terms of "dynamics," "relationships," and "perceptions." Insufficient attention has been paid to those aspects of both clients' and therapists' ideologies, philosophies, and moral codes, many of which cannot be interpreted as merely incidental aspects of people's lives.

Secondly, it is apparent that so-called moral neutrality in the psychotherapist is as much a moral position as any more blatant one. It is, from the therapist's side, a libertarian position, regardless of how the client sees it (indeed, in some respects, he may justly see it as insidious). Expressed in a variety of ways, this position is currently in vogue among psychotherapists of quite dissimilar orientations. Some of the concepts that serve to legitimize and popularize moral neutrality are "democracy," "self-realization" or "-actualization," and "existence." All these concepts are oriented towards people's freedom to do as they please. But even the most democratic general theories, in specifying assumptions and goals, limit their generosity with other terms such as "social responsibility" or "productivity." The latter kind of language seems to suggest that psychotherapists regard themselves as a genuine social force. If so, then to what extent are therapists obligated to represent themselves to the public at large, and to their clients, as a committed social agency? And according to what set of codes? For societies reflect within themselves systems of morality, and a relatively open society, such as that in America, reflects competing and contradictory codes. Is the therapist as moralist obligated, further, to participate publicly in moral arguments as they are reflected in political and economic life—or is he entitled to reserve his participation to his special area of competence?

The question becomes more immediate when it is asked in relation to the individual patient rather than to society at large. At what point, and by what means, is the therapist obligated or entitled to involve himself actively as moralist with his client? Is he entitled, perhaps obligated, to challenge the moral intent of his client when he thinks it inadequate—or immoral? Can he, in good conscience, permit in his patient any kind of behavior that serves to free him permanently of guilt, anxiety, neurosis? If so, will he not thoughtlessly be elevating the goal of personal adjustment to a supreme value—and is this not an inadequate goal for a community of men? And if so, is the therapist free of moral responsibility to that community?

Starting with an altogether technical matter, the sequence of issues that evolve seems inescapable. Either therapists can successfully influence behavior or they cannot, and they have little choice of what to claim. If they wish to say they cannot do so, or may not do so in just those areas where human concern is greatest, and are therefore not at all responsible for the behavior of their clients, one must ask what right they have to be in business. The very validity of the disclaimer destroys their most important function, so the help they can give must then be very narrowly defined.

But if, on the other hand, they affirm some technical *expertise* and wish to claim a genuine ability to influence people, then they must also assume some responsibility for the nature of that influence. In that event, they must ultimately see themselves as moral agents as they are confronted with moral problems. And the extent to which they are confronted with moral problems depends on the significance of the problems with which they deal, for morals are the ultimate values we assign to our acts.

It is not clear that psychotherapists are suited to assume this role, but it seems certain they cannot escape it. In such a strait, they may best serve themselves and those they hope to aid, by examining this agency to see what it entails.

B. RESEARCH

Chapter 3

THE FUNCTIONAL AUTONOMY OF PSYCHOTHERAPY

ALEXANDER W. ASTIN

ONCE UPON a time there was a method for treating mental problems called psychotherapy. Those who were around when it first came into vogue may remember that its principal purpose was to provide a service to troubled people who had asked for help. This function was, in fact, psychotherapy's *raison d'etre*. After people began to use this method, however, evidence of its efficacy was unimpressive and skepticism was advanced regarding whether it was really fulfilling its purpose. As had usually been the case with other treatment methods of similarly dubious value, psychotherapy should have died out. But it did not. It did not even waver. Psychotherapy had, it appeared, achieved *functional autonomy*.

The development was of especially profound significance for practitioners, who, at last freed from the petty demands of having to serve their clients, were now able to engage in hot squabbles about how psychotherapy should be done, and hotter ones about who should do it (Anderson, 1956; Ausubel, 1956; Blanton *et al.*, 1953; Brody, 1956; Kelly, 1956; Sanford, 1953). Another noteworthy by-product was the formation within the American Psychological and Psychiatric Associations of committees on relations with each other. It should be noted that these developments actually enhanced psychotherapy's emerging functional autonomy by giving it several new and expanding functions.

THE REACTIONARIES

Despite this surge of productive activity, certain reactionaries within the field attempted to lead psychotherapy back to the Dark

Note: Reprinted from *Am Psychol, 16*:75-79, 1961.

Ages. Notable among these was Eysenck (1952) who claimed that nowhere in the scientific literature was there any good evidence that psychotherapy worked. In a crushing attack on Eysenck's position, Rosensweig (1954) pointed out that neither was there any good evidence that psychotherapy *hurt* anybody. Eysenck (1955) agreed. Now that everyone agreed that the evidence was no good, psychotherapy had been vindicated.

Another reactionary position was advanced by Hoppock (1953), who believed that clients were entitled to help with the problem that they asked to be helped with. This in turn was attacked by Kaufmann and Allerhand (1953) on the grounds that it might be dangerous to try to give the client what he asks for. Hoppock (1954) replied weakly that we really know nothing one way or the other and that we must do more research.

Eysenck tried again (1954) to promote his position. This time his claim was that to squabble over who should do psychotherapy before its efficacy had been demonstrated is, in essence, to put the cart before the horse. Eysenck was answered by Raush (1954), as follows: "It is not the point to discuss the efficacy or lack of efficacy of psychotherapy here . . . psychotherapy is a method for studying the human psyche . . . whether it is a good or bad method is not at issue" (p. 588). Thus, without the bothersome business of first knowing if, how, or under what conditions psychotherapy might work, we could still engage in controversies about who should perform it and also use it to "study the psyche." Who could doubt now that psychotherapy had indeed become functionally autonomous?

ETHICS?

Ethical considerations, while not raised specifically by these reactionaries, nevertheless seemed to be involved in some of their arguments. The question of efficacy or outcome, rephrased in ethical terms, might have run as follows: since this client has asked for our help and may even be paying us for it, are we not morally and ethically *obligated* to determine if we are giving him anything for his time and money?

Fortunately, the *Ethical Standards of Psychologists.* (APA,

1953) , based on the fundamental ethical position of "contribution to the welfare of man," was being developed to insure that members of the Profession would give due consideration to any relevant ethical issue. For example, the main stated principle in the section on "Recognizing limitations of psychological techniques" warns: "The psychologist should refuse to suggest, support, or condone unwarranted assumptions . . . in the use of psychological instruments or techniques" (p. 41). An extension of this principle states that "tests [should] be made available . . . for routine use only when adequate . . . validity data are available" (p. 153). Appropriately, the Profession was questioning the "contribution to the welfare of man" of tests whose validity was still in doubt. Indeed, the only condition under which the Profession would condone the use of such tests was if they were "conspicuously marked 'experimental use only' " (p. 153).

These cautions were not similarly extended to include the "psychological technique" of psychotherapy, most likely in order to protect the therapists and clients from the possibly disturbing effects of "Experimental Use Only" signs on office doors and couches. The wary reader, who by now may detect some inconsistency or error of omission in the ethical code, will be relieved to know that any possible inconsistency was recently eliminated for good, when a revised code (APA, 1959) appeared in which the ethic having to do with "condoning unwarranted assumptions" has been dispensed with altogether.

MORE ETHICS

A serious ethical objection lodged by the practitioners against "outcome" research centered around the necessity for using controls in such investigations. Because of the limited usefulness of comparing psychotherapy with other therapies or even with therapy "wait" groups, an adequately-designed outcome study required denying treatment to a comparable group of clients. Practitioners, in their ethical concern for the welfare of their clients (see "Ethics?" above) , were opposed to the practice of refusing treatment to sick people who ask for it.

In a desperate counterargument, some reactionaries suggested that psychotherapy might conceivably be *detrimental* under certain conditions, and that ethical considerations really *demanded* that controlled outcome studies be done in order to evaluate at least these possibilities. Some even went so far as to suggest that interprofessional squabbling, legislation, quack-hunting, etc., represented more than a struggle for power and prestige, i.e. that these concerns reflected a belief that clients *could* be harmed by psychotherapy. Practitioners, on the other hand, were quick to point out (e.g. Eysenck, 1952) that nowhere in the literature was there any good evidence that psychotherapy did any harm. Scientifically minded practitioners were understandably reluctant to act on any such "belief" in the absence of valid evidence.

OUTCOME'S OUTCOME

The later history of the outcome problem can be mapped by examining the chapters on "psychotherapy" appearing in the *Annual Review of Psychology*.

In 1955 Meehl was able to find only one outcome study which "approximated" the "minimum standards" of a control group, pre- and posttherapy evaluations, and follow-up. Echoing Eysenck's reactionary arguments, Meehl made a desperate plea for better outcome studies.

The following year Harris (1956) observed: "Critical evaluations by reviewers of the literature on psychotherapy in previous years could be repeated here with undiminished relevance" (p. 143).

None of the many outcome studies reviewed the next year by Winder (1957) employed an equivalent no-therapy control group. The author also cited the need for follow-ups, concluding that "Outcome criteria could be substantially improved . . . by selecting measures which are intrinsically powerful, e.g. measures based on how the person behaves and relates to others in his life environment" (p. 328).

In the 1958 review Snyder, commenting on outcome methodology, reported: "Most of these outcome studies leave a great deal to be desired . . . in general the more rigorous the criteria the less encouraging the results" (pp. 366-367).

The following year Luborsky (1959) noted: "Fortunately there have been recently fewer of the simplistic type of outcome studies in which the end point of the study is to present percentages of patients who have improved or have not improved, broken down according to diagnostic labels" (p. 318). The reviewer does not also give his opinion on well-designed studies of outcome, perhaps because there were none. He does, however, point out that "It has yet to be demonstrated that control groups in psychotherapy research have a more than very limited usefulness" (p. 328).

That Luborsky's comments were indicative of a trend away from the outcome issue is confirmed in Rotter's 1960 review: "Research studies in psychotherapy tend to be concerned more with some aspects of the psychotherapeutic procedure and less with outcome . . . to some extent, it reflects an interest in the psychotherapy situation as a kind of personality laboratory" (p. 407). This would appear to be one more instance where psychotherapy's functional autonomy has fostered progress in the field, i.e. by being able to dismiss the question of efficacy we can now use the therapy situation as a research laboratory.

THE EXPERTS

Perhaps the most up-to-date picture of outcome's waning popularity is available in a recent monograph, *Research in Psychotherapy* (Rubinstein and Parloff, 1959), which is based on an interdisciplinary conference of twenty-seven experts in the field. In summarizing the main biases and points of view of these experts, the editors conclude: "as if by some tacit agreement the issue of outcome was skirted by the conference." An attempt was made to account for this fact by reviewing the pros and cons of doing outcome research. Accordingly, twenty-three lines were devoted to the arguments of outcome "Advocates," and 170 lines were used to review the arguments of the "Critics." Some of their major objections were:

1. We become identified with the practitioner's "simple pragmatic concerns," at the expense of basic science. Clearly, basic science must avoid the taint of pragmatics, if it is to remain pure.

(A related objection to outcome research, which was not mentioned specifically in the conference, has to do with the "scut work" necessary to conduct follow-ups in the community. No one will argue that attempting to measure our client's behavior in his natural habitat is scut work, and that attempting to measure it in the consultation room is pure science.)

2. An "unexpressed fear that patient change may not be a consequence unique to psychotherapy." (Finding out that psychotherapy does not work could create severe economic problems by putting thousands of people out of work and by requiring the dissolution of numerous committees.)

3. Everybody is already "convinced" that it works.

4. Criterion problems: any attempt to select "specific criteria [is] a premature and presumptuous value judgment." (To expect anyone to define what therapists are trying to do is admittedly unreasonable.)

It may be superfluous to point out that the sole argument of the Advocates of outcome research, i.e. that accepting a patient for treatment implies "that the patient is justified in his expectation that psychotherapy will be of benefit to him," pales when pitted against those of the Critics.

THE FUTURE

Now that the reactionaries have been crushed and psychotherapy continues to flourish, the possibilities for future progress seem limitless. If nothing else, we can be sure that the principle of functional autonomy will permit psychotherapy to survive long after it has outlived its usefulness as a personality laboratory.

REFERENCES

1. American Psychological Association: *Ethical Standards of Psychologists.* Washington, D.C., Amer Psychological Assoc, 1953.
2. American Psychological Association: Ethical standards of psychologists. *Am Psychol, 14:*279-282, 1959.
3. Anderson, W.: On the practice of psychotherapy by the nonmedically trained. *Am Psychol, 11:*197-199, 1956.
4. Ausubel, D. P.: Relationships between psychology and psychiatry: the hidden issues. *Am Psychol, 11:*99-113, 1956.

5. Blanton, R. L., Brown, L., Davis, J. E., Jr., Johnson, D. T., Kipnis, E., Kramish, A. A., Nichols, R. C., Ward, L. C., Jr., Webster, H., Weingarten, E., Cohen, L., Ellson, D. G., Kasman, S., Meyers, T. J., Schnack, G. F. and Volle, F. O.: Comments on "Relations with psychiatry." *Am Psychol, 8:*590-595, 1953.
6. Brody, E. B.: Interprofessional relations or psychologists and psychiatrists are human too, only more so. *Am Psychol, 11:*105-111, 1956.
7. Eysenck, H. J.: The effects of psychotherapy: An evaluation. *J Consult Psychol, 16:*319-324, 1952.
8. Eysenck, H. J.: Further comments on "Relations with psychiatry." *Am Psychol, 9:*157-158, 1954.
9. Eysenck, H. J. The effects of psychotherapy: A reply. *J Abnorm Soc Psychol, 50:*147-148, 1955.
10. Harris, R. E.: Clinical methods: Psychotherapy. *Ann Rev Psychol, 7:* 121-146, 1956.
11. Hoppock, R.: What is the "real" problem? *Am Psychol, 8:*124, 1953.
12. Hoppock, R.: The real problem. *Am Psychol, 9:*81-82, 1954.
13. Kaufmann, P. and Allerhand, M. E.: Comment on Hoppock's "What is the 'real' problem?" *Am Psychol, 8:*524, 1953.
14. Kelly, G. A.: Issues: Hidden or mislaid. *Am Psychol, 11:*112-113, 1956.
15. Luborsky, L.: Psychotherapy. *Annu Rev Psychol, 10:*317-344, 1959.
16. Meehl, P. E.: Psychotherapy. *Annu Rev Psychol, 6:*357-378, 1955.
17. Raush, H. L.: Comment on Eysenck's "Further comments on 'relations with psychiatry.' " *Am Psychol, 9:*588-589, 1954.
18. Rosensweig, S.: A transvaluation of psychotherapy: A reply to Hans Eysenck. *J Abnorm Soc Psychol, 49:*298-304, 1954.
19. Rotter, J. B.: Psychotherapy. *Annu Rev Psychol, 11:*381-414, 1960.
20. Rubinstein, E. A. and Parloff, M. B.: *Research in Psychotherapy.* Washington, D.C., Amer Psychological Assoc, 1959.
21. Sanford, F. H.: Relations with psychiatry. *Am Psychol, 8:*169-173, 1953.
22. Snyder, W. U.: Psychotherapy. *Annu Rev Psychol, 9:*353-374, 1958.
23. Winder, C. L.: Psychotherapy. *Annu Rev Psychol, 8:*309-330, 1957.

Chapter 4

SOCIAL CASEWORK FAILS TEST

EARL UBELL

SCIENTISTS HAVE A KIND OF COURAGE that drives them to subject their most precious ideas to objective scrutiny. Yet such courage is lacking among the people-manipulators of our time: social workers whose main goal is to help people.

People-manipulators go their do-good way, spending millions of dollars and affecting as many lives, while rarely subjecting their ideas, plans or manipulations to trial by scientific test. They are dedicated and they serve and they consider that enough.

Recently a small New York social agency, the Youth Consultation Service (YCS), an organization devoted to guiding unwed mothers, displayed the kind of scientific bravery seen only in laboratories. They laid open their deepest commitments—personal and professional—to impartial scientific scrutiny.

In a study involving four hundred city vocational high school girls, YCS permitted three scientists to test the power of social work to deter these troubled youngsters from social disaster. It was the third such study in the history of social work and for the third time it demonstrated the same result: negative. Social casework—counseling and guidance—was found to be powerless to prevent school dropout, delinquency, or other "misbehavior."

This study may revolutionize social casework, a field devoted to "helping" troubled individuals by counseling or by providing such direct service as psychotherapy, or with money or with all these techniques. If the profession remains untouched by this new investigation, it is far more intellectually corrupt than its bitterest detractors say it is.

The YCS study leaves little room for argument. It boasts an experimental design that is nearly airtight. The four hundred girls

Note: Reprinted from *New York Hearld Tribune,* Oct. 4, 1964.

involved in the study, identified first on the basis of school record as potential problems, were divided at random into two groups: one group received the social casework treatment; the other did not.

After periods of two to four years, the scientists tested the girls by psychological techniques. They also evaluated their school work, grade level, difficulties with the police, pregnancy rate, tendency to drop out of school, truancy, conduct and other factors. On not one of these measures did the casework-treated girls rank statistically higher than the untreated.

The social workers themselves, asked to rate the girls, found that the individual case approach produced hardly any change in the girls' behavior in 60 percent of the cases. However, when the girls were treated in groups, the results were better—the caseworkers detected some change in two-thirds of the girls. Nevertheless, these changes as seen by the social workers were not reflected in better social behavior outside the agency.

Such contradictions have been noted before: social workers see improvement in their clients; objective measurements show no improvement at all.

The earliest such test was carried out from 1937 to 1945 with six hundred boys, aged six to ten, judged to be potential delinquents in the Cambridge-Somerville area of Boston. Social workers mounted a total program: guidance, counseling and psychotherapy for half the boys; no treatment at all for the other half. The end result: no difference in delinquency rates.

Even in that early study, the counselors listed two-thirds of the boys as having benefited from the program. They even said that half of them showed outstanding progress. Yet the delinquency rate remained unchanged from the untreated group.

In 1962, 115 boys from Washington's slums were subjected to a social work and psychiatric program; another group remained untreated. The two groups were not distinguishable on objective measurements of behavior.

The YCS study seems to be the most elaborately planned of the three investigations.

Credits for this effort goes not only to YCS and its director,

Dr. Elizabeth P. Anderson, but to Dr. Wyatt C. Jones, associate director of research at Mobilization for Youth; Dr. Henry J. Meyer, professor of sociology and social work at the University of Michigan, and Dr. Edgar F. Borgatta, chairman of the department of sociology at the University of Wisconsin.

Furthermore, the Russell Sage Foundation put up $47,000 to pay for the research evaluations and the Grant Foundation provided $52,000 for the services provided to the girls, for a total of $99,000. The full results are to be published by the Russell Sage Foundation in April.

In commenting on the study, Dr. Jones pointed out that the findings were not entirely negative. Some slight benefit in favor of the treated group was discerned, but it was not statistically significant. That means that the effect might have occurred by chance and not as a result of treatment.

However, if the effects are slight then it is up to the community to decide if they are worth the money spent for them. How much social effort should be expended to prevent one delinquent act, one unwanted pregnancy or one school dropout? The YCS study indicates that the price may be several thousand dollars to prevent any single act, if the slight effects discerned are real and not due to chance.

"If confidence can be placed in our measures," the scientists said, "one must conclude that only powerful treatment interventions can be effective." In other words, it would take a great deal to change psychological test results.

Since no dramatic effects were found for the treatments used, the study obviously indicates the low power of guidance, counseling and psychotherapy as treatments.

Dr. Jones also pointed out that the findings suggested that the present fashion of concentrating on the psyche of troubled children may be wrong. Better results may be obtained, he said, by trying to improve the life situation of such children by giving them the competence to hold jobs, to have a decent family life and to maintain adequate health.

"However," he said, "we would have to test that scheme too."

As for YCS, the study done, they have gone back to working

with unwed mothers, in groups now, trying to help them stay out of trouble. Miss Anderson, the director, hopes to do another study of social casework some day. She is a brave woman.

Chapter 5

SOME IMPLICATIONS OF PSYCHOTHERAPY RESEARCH FOR THERAPEUTIC PRACTICE

ALLEN E. BERGIN

THE MATERIAL TO FOLLOW is a digest of research findings which have implications for practice and research in psychotherapy. It has been formulated in terms of six conclusions and implications which appear justifiable and defensible. This catalogue of conclusions is based upon a comparative handful of research reports which have been carefully selected from the present empirical chaos for their relative adequacy of conceptualization, design, and outcome. Conclusions have been drawn only in those areas where the results appear to have substance and where they have been replicated; consequently, many areas of study are excluded.

THE DETERIORATION EFFECT

CONCLUSION 1. *Psychotherapy may cause people to become better- or worse-adjusted than comparable people who do not receive such treatment.*

Recently, a curious and provocative finding occurred in the preliminary results of the Wisconsin schizophrenia project conducted by Rogers, Gendlin, and Truax (Rogers, 1961; Truax, 1963; Truax and Carkhuff, 1964). It was that the patients in psychotherapy tended to become either better or worse in adjustment than their matched control-group counterparts.

Note: Based in part on a paper presented at the Pre-Convention Institute of the Ontario Psychological Association, London, Ontario, February, 1964. Presented at a symposium: Implications of empirical research for innovations in therapeutic practice and research. American Psychological Convention, Los Angeles, September, 1964.

Reprinted from *J Abnorm Psychol, 71:*235-246, 1966.

At that time two earlier studies were analyzed (Barron and Leary, 1955; Cartwright and Vogel, 1960; Cartwright, 1956) in which similar findings had occurred; but being incidental to other results, they had not been emphasized in proportion to their true import (Bergin, 1963). Since then, four additional studies with similar findings have been discovered (Fairweather *et al.*, 1960; Mink, 1959; Powers and Witmer, 1951; Rogers and Dymond, 1954). In all seven studies, although there tends to be no difference in the average amount of change between experimentals and controls, there does tend to be a significant difference in *variability* of change. The criterion, or change, scores for treatment groups attain a much wider dispersion than do those of control groups, even though the mean change in both groups is quite similar. Typically, control *S*s improve somewhat, with the varying amounts of change clustering about the mean. On the other hand, experimental *S*s are typically dispersed all the way from marked improvement to marked deterioration. Now frequently documented, this information is alarming to say the least. Psychotherapy can and does make people worse than their control counterparts! Because of the controversial nature of this conclusion, the following material is presented as detailed substantiating evidence in its support.

Table 5-I is reproduced from Cartwright's reanalysis (1956) of the well-known Barron and Leary study (1955).
He comments on the data as follows:

> For many scales the variance results suggest that mean differences between the groups are absent because differences of two kinds, opposed in sign, are present. It seems that some therapy patients *deteriorated* to a greater extent than did the waiting-list controls, while some therapy patients *did improve* significantly more than the controls.

It should be noted that this occurred only for individual and not for group therapy.

It is a fascinating fact that Cartwright's observation has lain unattended in the literature for years, while implicit in his statement is a clear means of resolving much of the controversy over negative results in therapy outcome studies. It is even more fascinating that Cartwright himself participated in a study (Rogers

TABLE 5-I

VARIANCES OF DISCREPANCY SCORES ON MMPI SCALES FOR
INDIVIDUAL PSYCHOTHERAPY AND NONTREATMENT GROUPS

MMPI Scale	Individual Psychotherapy (N = 42)	Nontreatment group (N = 23)	F	ρ
	V*	V		
1. Lie	19.89	23.43	1.18	
2. F	215.21	22.94	9.38	.01
3. K	55.95	31.70	1.76	
4. Hs	127.46	64.16	1.99	.05
5. D	244.30	93.32	2.62	.01
6. Hy	113.21	87.80	1.29	
7. Pd	155.00	89.68	1.73	
8. Pa	111.94	68.06	1.64	
9. Pt	208.51	73.27	2.85	.01
10. Sc	272.91	74.13	3.68	.01
11. Ma	126.79	75.34	1.68	
12. Es	43.56	14.82	2.94	.01

*Variances computed from SD data reported by Barron and Leary (1955, p. 243).

and Dymond, 1954) in which a similar phenomenon occurred, but just as the data in the Barron and Leary study, it was never emphasized in proportion to its true import. The classic features in this study apparently overshadowed the passing references to a *client-deterioration phenomenon*. While the study is properly famous for other reasons, it provides supporting bits of evidence for the thesis that negative change in therapy is not an isolated or chance occurrence. A careful reading of the report indicates that of twenty-five therapy Ss, six, or 24 percent, declined in self-ideal correlation between pretherapy and follow-up testing. A quick computation of the mean change in self-ideal correlation indicates that those who increased averaged an increment of .49 in this correlations, whereas those who declined a decrement of —.40, a difference that is striking considering the fact that the mean pretherapy correlations were not different for these two subgroups. While some chance fluctuations in scores are to be expected, these changes in both directions can hardly be attributed to the effects of imperfect test reliability. While the authors do not examine these possibilities in the data, they do allude to them in passing: "It is of interest, though it does not bear directly upon the hypothesis, that there has also been a marked increase in the degree of variation of correlations [self-ideal] over this period" (Butler and Haigh, 1954, p. 63).

It may be argued, of course, that decline in self-ideal correlation can be an indication of improved adjustment, particularly when the correlation is extremely high as in the case of some paranoid subjects. However, the pretest correlations of all six subjects who declined in this study were low, ranging from .28 to —.12. The question of whether self-ideal correlations actually measure adjustment at all is still a subject of some debate, so we would not want to draw conclusions about psychotherapy in general from data based on this measure alone. In another section of the same volume, an analysis of behavior observations made of the clients independently of therapist progress ratings (p. 228) yielded results similar to those found with the self-ideal measure: "During the whole period from pretherapy to follow-up, observers saw a definite increase in the maturity of behavior of those clients whose therapy was rated as successful and a sharp decrease in the maturity of behavior of those clients rated as unsuccessful. The relationship was statistically significant."

While there are additional fragmentary evidence of deterioration phenomena in the book, these suffice to illustrate the point.

In a controlled study of counseling with high-school students, Mink (1959, p. 14) observes the same phenomenon: "Counseling affected the expression of social adjustments on the California Test of Personality. The forms of expression indicate both improvement and recession."

The excellent multifactor design executed by Fairweather *et al.* (1960) yielded similar results:

Generally, significantly different variances occurred on most instruments between treatments and diagnosis. The control group usually had the smallest variance and the three psychotherapy groups the largest (p. 24). . . . In these three interactions, one or all of the three long-term psychotic groups in psychotherapy demonstrated changes in the maladaptive scale direction [MMPI] while the controls remain relatively the same or change in the adaptive direction (p. 9).

Cartwright and Vogel (1960) discovered the same type of differential effect in a neurotic sample using different criterion measures:

> Thus, as measured by the Q score, adjustment changes, regardless of direction, were significantly greater during a therapy period than during a no-therapy period (p. 122). . . . The post-therapy tests showed those in therapy with experienced therapists to have improved significantly on both tests, whereas those in therapy with inexperienced therapists not to have improved . . . ; in fact, they bordered on a significant decrease in health on the TAT (p. 127).

Turning back several decades to the Cambridge-Somerville youth study (Powers and Witmer, 1951) which was initiated in 1937, we find the same phenomenon with a group of predelinquent boys:

> . . . when the Study Services were effectual most of the boys did function better than their C-twins. This conclusion can be accepted, however, only if its opposite is also accepted: that some of the boys who were not benefited may have been handicapped in social adjustment by the organization's efforts. If this is true, we can conclude that the apparent chance distribution of terminal adjustment ratings . . . was due to the fact that the good effects of the Study were counterbalanced by the poor (p. 455).

Elsewhere the authors indicate that in a significant proportion of cases where the counselor's efforts were judged as poor, the boys "were more socially maladjusted than their control twin" (p. 509). It is unfortunate that this excellently designed and executed study is one leaned upon most heavily by Eysenck (1960, 1965) in his bold denial of the usefulness of psychotherapy, for while the study shows no difference between experimentals and controls, it demonstrates the efficacy of treatment as well as its deteriorative effect.

Finally, we cite the recent Wisconsin project on therapy of schizophrenia which has been published thus far only in tempting bits and pieces:

> . . . high levels of therapist-offered conditions during therapy are related to patient improvement, but . . . low levels . . . are related

to patient deterioration, so that if all therapy combined is indiscrim-
inately compared to control condtions there is little average change.
Thus psychotherapy can be for better or for worse. . . . (Truax, 1963,
p. 256).

Since the length of therapy varied in these seven studies from
a few months to several years, it seems doubtful that the observed
deterioration can be accounted for by the temporary regression
that sometimes occurs during treatment. The views of most
writers would indicate that the average deterioration due to this
effect for a treatment group would be small after brief and
lengthy periods of therapy but large in between; whereas the
findings reported here suggest a consistent, rectangularly distributed, amount of regression regardless of the length of time tran-
spired prior to obtaining outcome estimates. Unfortunately, so
little controlled empirical work has been done with analytic
therapies, which are presumably the richest sources of such data,
that it is difficult to compare the findings reported here with what
might be found if research were done on them.

Fortunately, these various data indicate that psychotherapy
can make people considerably better off than control *Ss.* Therefore, contrary to the notions of some critics, psychotherapy can
produce improvement beyond that which may occur due to spontaneous remission alone. Consistently replicated, this is a direct
and unambiguous refutation of the oft-cited Eysenckian position
(Eysenck, 1960, 1965).

A general paradigm is suggested by the double-edged effect observed in the studies cited which may be schematized as shown in
Figure 5-1. Such a startling phenomenon certainly deserves a
name, and *The Deterioration Effect* is suggested here.

It is interesting to note that a phenomenon similar to the
great variability in the quality of therapeutic effects noted here
has also been observed in relation to the accuracy of diagnostic
evaluations (Garfield, 1963). Apparently, even well-known diag-
nosticians vary greatly in the accuracy of their judgments. When
all of these judgments are pooled, average predictions or discriminations often are not different from chance estimates; but some

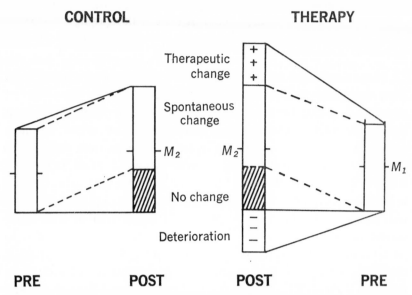

Figure 5-1. The deterioration effect. Schematic representation of pre- and post-test distributions of criterion scores in psychotherapy outcome studies.

individuals appear to far exceed chance predictions while others actually do worse than chance.

Implication No. 1. (a) We should not give up the practice of psychotherapy as some have advocated. (b) We should be more cautious and critical of our own practices, carefully eliminating any ineffective or harmful therapeutic techniques. We should find out whom we are making worse or better, and how, with all due speed. (c) We should find out if some therapists make people better and if some make them worse, or if individual therapists do both. After that, we have the ticklish business of making changes in technique, personality, or personnel as may be necessary to eliminate negative influences and accentuate positive ones.

NATURAL THERAPEUTIC CONDITIONS

CONCLUSION 2. *(a) It has been frequently replicated, and is now a well-established fact, that control Ss who do not receive psy-*

chotherapy change positively as a group with the passage of time. This is the so-called "spontaneous remission" effect (Eysenck, 1952, 1960, 1965). (b) Three studies (Frank, 1961; Gurin, Veroff and Feld, 1960; Powers and Witmer, 1951) indicate that many of these disturbed persons who receive no formal psychotherapy seek and obtain help from various professional and nonprofessional sources such as friends, clergymen, physicians, teachers, and occasionally even psychotherapists (Bergin, 1963).

All this has typically been unknown to the researchers who were depending upon these so-called controls to be a base line for comparison with their treatment cases. It seems clear that this aid has an ameliorative effect since the people improve, although it would be impossible to substantiate this fully without further study of the influences upon control Ss in their "natural" habitat. To the extent that this position is correct, it further undermines the Eysenck-type position, because it shows that control Ss often change due to the influence of therapy or therapy-like procedures. Thus, "spontaneous remission" is just another name for the effects of informal therapy.

Implication No. 2. (a) Researchers who utilize control groups should carefully ascertain that these groups are indeed controls, or, if necessary, should directly measure the effects of nonexperimental influences which they cannot control. (b) The fact that some of these previously uncontrolled influences are much like therapy, but frequently occur outside of a professional setting, implies that nonprofessional help can stimulate positive personality change. This may consist partly of individuals with "therapeutic personalities" who are sought out for counsel and catharsis by many people. It may be also that unrecognized, but powerful, therapeutic agents exist naturally in everyday life. Just as cures for various physical disorders have been discovered by studying health, so it may be possible to discover antidotes for some of the mental disorders that confront us by discovering conditions already existing in "nature" which support or promote personality integration.

INGREDIENTS OF THERAPY

CONCLUSION 3. *Therapeutic progress varies as a function of therapist characteristics such as warmth, empathy, adequacy of adjustment, and experience.*

In a recent review, Gardner (1964) cited a smattering of positive results to the effect that the more a therapist has an attitude of *liking and warmth,* the more likely he is to obtain positive change in his clients. While some of the studies enumerated are of questionable design or generalizability, they are relatively consistent when compared with many other areas of research.

A recent questionnaire study of patients' retrospective reports regarding their therapeutic experience (Strupp, Wallach, and Wogan, 1964), which was not reported by Gardner, further confirms this general finding. While the study is uncontrolled and appears to be contaminated by artifactually inflated correlations, it is of interest that it strongly emphasizes the importance of therapist warmth and genuineness in relation to patient-perceived outcome $(r = .53)$.

Additional data on this point come from the client-centered group in a series of studies with neurotics and psychotics. It should be noted that some of the therapists studied were *not* client-centered. These studies are consistent in discovering a significant relationship between operational measures of Rogers' concept of positive regard and independent indices of therapeutic progress or outcome (Truax and Carkhuff, 1964, 1965a; Barrett-Lennard, 1962). Measures of the therapist's attitudes have included ratings by both the therapist himself and the patient. Three types of analysis have resulted in similar results and in different studies with different samples of clients and therapists. It has thus become increasingly clear, within the limits of these studies, that a therapist's ability to be warm and positively inclined toward his patients is an effective therapeutic ingredient. The effects of intentional authoritarian demands or other forms of planned therapist aggression which are sometimes advocated have not been studied and thus cannot be compared with these findings.

Acknowledging the past confusion and contradiction involved in studies of *empathy,* we suggest that the recent data summarized at Chicago (Barrett-Lennard, 1962), Wisconsin (Truax, 1961a; Truax and Carkhuff, 1964), and Kentucky (Truax and Carkhuff, 1965a; Carkhuff, Kodman and Truax, 1965; Dickenson and Truax, 1965; Truax and Wargo, 1965) offer promising leads. Analyses of recorded therapist behavior and ratings by clients of their therapists during the process of treatment have yielded consistently positive relationships between empathic understanding and outcome.

The strength of these findings lies in careful design (Rogers, 1961) and in the analysis of therapist behavior *in vivo,* which is unusual in empathy research. A new empathy measure has been operationalized by Truax (1961b) and is defined as accurate ". . . sensitivity to current feelings *and* the verbal facility to communicate this understanding in a language attuned to the patient's current being" (Truax and Carkhuff, 1964). While the scale is ctill crude and might not be accepted by analysts as measuring their "kind" of empathy, its usefulness has been relatively substantial in these studies.

The third characteristic, *adequacy of adjustment,* has not been studied as thoroughly as the others, but thus far the data are relatively consistent. Those therapists who are more anxious, conflicted, defensive, or "unhealthy" are least likely to promote change in their cases.

Several studies have indicated that supervisor and client ratings of the therapists' competence are negatively related to his degree of anxiety or maladjustment (Arbuckle, 1956; Bandura, 1956; Bergin and Solomon, 1963). Other studies have yielded similar findings when the therapist's actual in-therapy behavior and the patient's response to it was evaluated and used as a criterion of competence. For example, Bandura, Lipsher, and Miller (1960) found that therapists' hostility anxiety was directly associated with avoidance responses to patients' expressions of hostility toward them. The more hostility conflict a therapist had, the more likely he was to avoid his patients' hostility and consequently the patients' self-exploration in this area diminished and his conflicts remained unresolved. A practically identical result was found by Winder, Ahmad, Bandura and Rau (1962) with regard to dependency anxiety.

In another study (Bergin and Solomon, 1963) it was found that measures of the therapists' degree of personal disturbance correlate negatively with his level of empathy as measured by ratings of tape-recorded psychotherapy interviews. Independent measures of personality strength, on the other hand, correlated positively with degree of "live" empathy. In addition, ratings of therapist anxiety level correlated negatively with independent ratings of therapeutic competence.

Additional data came from the client-centered studies already cited with regard to warmth and empathy, in their examination of therapist congruence. Congruence (Rogers, 1957; 1959) means essentially the healthiness of the therapist in his relationship with his client—his spontaneity, nondefensiveness, openness, or genuineness. Like positive regard and empathy, this variable has also been related to therapeutic progress, and further confirms the general finding of a direct connection between level of therapist adjustment and therapeutic effectiveness.

The three elements of warmth, empathy, and congruence have been found, in the Wisconsin studies, to vary directly with outcome in both negative and positive directions. That is, when these therapist characteristics were at a low level, the patients were getting worse; when they were high, the patients improved (Truax and Carkhuff, 1964) .These studies thus provide a partial answer to the question raised earlier as to how negative change occurred in the outcome studies reviewed, although they are limited in that the observed differences were not large, and there is also some question as to whether the division into high and low conditions was done before or after the fact. The other studies cited here in the same realm further clarify the point, although none of the data are precise enough to make practical selection decisions possible.

With regard to the much debated variable of therapist experience, it may be asserted that, in general more experienced therapists are more effective and successful. This is based on four studies

(Barrett-Lennard, 1962; Cartwright and Vogel, 1960; Chance, 1959; Fiedler, 1950a, 1950b, 1951), one of which suggests that highly inexperienced therapists may actually cause patient deterioration (Cartwright and Vogel, 1960).

Implication No. 3. (a) Since psychotherapists are effective partly as a function of personal adjustment, they should be selected for this quality and not solely on the basis of academic and intellectual abilities. Future practice of therapy should therefore be modified by new selection procedures which will bring healthier personalities to bear upon problems of pathology, and by closer self-scrutiny and exposure of one's work among present practitioners.

There is presently no evidence that personal therapy for a disturbed therapist can qualify him for practice and should not be depended upon until such evidence is provided. This does not, of course, prove that the experience of being treated cannot be useful to a student therapist whose functioning is within a relatively normal range. There are no studies in which treated neurotics have improved to a level of functioning which is similar to that of control normals even though they do change in level or adjustment; therefore, treatment should not be counted upon to take care of errors in selection. The behavior ratings and personality inventories used in the studies reviewed could provide a beginning in research geared specifically toward the selection problem.

(b) Given the necessary personal attributes, therapists should develop their abilities in the realm of warmth and empathic communication, particularly in the case of empathy which is known to be subject to training and experience influences. Further study should be conducted so that clear, measurable standards of performance can be required of aspirants to professional status before they are permitted to practice. As an example, the Truax Empathy Scale (Truax, 1961b) could be used as a beginning to assess one's level of functioning via analysis of recorded interviews.

(c) Inexperienced potential therapists should be very carefully introduced to practice with clients, perhaps with much more stringent care than is now commonly exercised. Since all beginners make many mistakes, it may be more useful and ethical to have them see more resilient, normal people until they reach a criterion level of interview performance, measured perhaps on dimensions such as warmth and empathy which appear to be accepted by most schools of therapy as vital though not necessarily sufficient for successful treatment.

CONCLUSION 4. *To date, the only school of interview-oriented psychotherapy which has consistently yielded positive outcomes in research studies is the client-centered approach (Rogers and Dymond, 1954; Shlien, Mosak, and Dreikurs, 1962; Truax and Carkhuff, 1964).*

The fact that other schools have not subjected their methods to systematic study of this sort is important but it should not deter us from accepting the fact that client-centered treatment has some positive value when properly conducted according to Rogers' paradigm (1957). The implications for practice seem quite clear, particularly in light of the consistently dismal reports on percentages of improvement in psychoanalytic therapy (Eysenck, 1965; Wolpe, 1964b).

It appears from these reports that the poorest results were obtained with more classical, long-term psychoanalysis, namely a lower percentage of improved cases than the 67 percent "spontaneous" remission rate. Briefer, analytically-oriented eclectic psychotherapy was more promising in that the percentage improvement equalled the spontaneous remission figure. This type of therapy was also used in some of the studies cited in this paper on the deterioration effect; therefore, despite the generally negative evidence, some analytically-oriented therapists must be having a positive effect beyond that occurring in control groups.

It should also be noted that the technique of "moderate interpretation" (Speisman, 1959), which derives from the analytic tradition, has potential therapeutic significance. Its definition is very similar to that given for "good" interpretation by various analysts (Fenichel, 1941) and it is related to productive patient self-exploration. It consists of responding to client affect just below the surface and labeling, identifying or emphasizing it. This does not involve making connections between past and present, being diagnostic or theoretical, nor telling the patient about feelings he "really has" when he is not experiencing them. It is, rather, an instance of good empathy. If one looks carefully at the definitions and operations for identifying accurate empathy and moderate or good interpretation, it is very difficult to distinguish between them. Truax and Carkhuff (1964) refer to this notion in an interesting comment:

> . . . "accurate empathy" has much in common with the "good psychoanalytic interpretation," in that it makes use of both verbal and nonverbal cues presented by the patient. It differs from some good psychoanalytic interpretations in its insistence that the therapist's empathic response focuses upon feelings and experiences of the patient from the patient's own unique viewpoint.

The importance of these observations should not be underestimated, for if they are accurate it appears that effective variables cut across schools of treatment and thus provide the basis for applying techniques on the basis of known effects rather than on doctrines promulgated by warring factions. This also indicates that titles, degrees, or years of training should not define the psychotherapist, but rather what the individual can do. Thus one might call himself "client-centered" and espouse the teachings of that school while at the same time presenting the low level of therapist empathy found to result in client deterioration. On the other hand, a psychoanalyst might be functioning at a high level according to the client-centered empathy scale.

CONCLUSION 5. *In spite of all so far stated about the possibilities for substantially improving consulting-room effectiveness, some stubborn facts still require confrontation. One is that even when the various sources of slippage and inadequacy are accounted for, interviews still do not generally produce very dramatic changes in people. Another is the now well-known fact that many types of people simply are not helped at all by this procedure.*

Studies of the relationship between client qualities and therapeutic outcome indicate consistently and clearly that positive outcome is limited or nil with many personality types. It is common for private practitioners and even clinics to either refuse to treat, or reluctantly accept for treatment, cases that do not fit their conception of psychotherapy. To a great extent this is realistic because traditional methods do not work with these cases. These "rejects" tend to be less intelligent, less anxious, less educated, less verbal and insightful, more concrete and action-oriented, more severely disturbed, more impulsive in the sociopathic sense, and often find the typical consulting room procedure rather meaningless (Barron, 1953; Cartwright, 1955; Fulkerson and Barry, 1961; Garfield and Affleck, 1961; Hollingshead and Redlich, 1958; Kirtner and Cartwright, 1958a, 1958b). This general observation has been made fairly frequently by various clinicians and is currently rather well-substantiated by the research literature.

Implication No. 5. The implication of these data, which only confirm an already widely believed idea, is that novel or modified techniques must be developed for dealing with a vast population whose problems are not amenable to standard methods. The importance of novel approaches is further emphasized by the fact that standard methods are not dramatically effective even in those cases where they are applicable, except in rare instances. The latter unusual cases would be a proper subject of study in themselves and may actually suggest innovations even though they arise in "traditional" therapy.

There are three primary sources of possible innovation that might alleviate this predicament. One is creative work in the clinical setting; another is naturally existing conditions in society; and another is that general area of research which is concerned with personality and behavior change such as studies of learning, attitude change, and personality development.

THE PROMISE OF BEHAVIOR THERAPY

CONCLUSION 6. *Studies of learning have thus far been very fruitful in generating principles and methods for promoting personality change. The work by Wolpe (1958), Lazarus (1963), Lang and Lazovik (1933), Lindsley (1963) and others has been both provocative and fruitful. The cases presented and research studies reported provide more positive evidence of the usefulness of these methods than is the case in any form of traditional interview or dynamic psychotherapy, including client-centered therapy.*

They involve clinical adaptation of learning principles, such as counterconditioning or extinction of anxiety symptoms, positive reinforcement in shaping adaptive responses and developing appropriate discriminations, aversive conditioning of maladaptive approach responses, and modeling. It is the effects of these methods which are important here. Wolpe (1964a) cites over two hundred cases of neurosis in 89 percent of which he has obtained substantial recovery. Lazarus (1963), in England, reports 408 cases with a similar improvement rate. The striking aspect of these results is that they have been achieved with difficult symptom pictures in brief periods of time. Unfortunately, these are clinical reports by individual therapists who rate their own case outcomes. Independent criteria and control subjects are completely lacking, and it is difficult to discern how comparable their cases are with those reported in other studies. Still, it is rare to find such high rates of claimed cure even in the clinical literature.

A number of well-designed studies appear to substantiate the clinical reports of Wolpe and Lazarus. Lang and Lazovik (1963) were able to significantly alter snake phobias with brief desensitization procedures. Effects of testing and training in relaxation were controlled, and no symptom substitution occurred during six-months of follow-up. Lazarus (1961) demonstrated substantial and rapid change of phobic symptoms and impotence by group desensitization methods. A comparison group being treated by traditional interpretive group therapy showed considerably less improvement, only two of seventeen cases becoming symptom-free after twenty-two sessions. These same cases were subsequently treated by group desensitization and after a mean of ten sessions each, two-thirds were symptom-free. Paul (1964) found that desensitization procedures were far more effective in eliminating speech anxieties than brief insight therapy, an attention-placebo condition, and a no-therapy control condition.

In a study of operant conditioning methods, which are different from Wolpe's techniques, King, Armitage, and Tilton (1960) found that substantial changes could be effected even in schizophrenic cases. They were able to produce clinically observable improvement in cases so treated which was greater than the changes occurring in conventional interview therapy, recreational therapy, or no therapy. Allyon and Michael (1959) effected substantial positive changes in ward behavior of psychotics by programming the reinforcements of their hospital environment according to operant principles. Lovaas, Schaeffer, and Simmons (1966) appear to have induced important changes in the social behavior of difficult cases of childhood autism by systematic use of negative reinforcement. In a review, Lindsley (1963) argues for the general promise of operant techniques. The evidence thus far pertains primarily to simple motor and verbal behaviors. Conceivably, this approach will prove to be more useful with the more primitive behaviors of psychotics and small children than with the more complex, symbolically involved adult neuroses.

A most interesting development in behavior therapy involves the systematic application of principles of imitative or observational learning. Bandura (1965c) argues persuasively from the vantage point of extensive experimental work (Bandura, 1965a, 1965b) that modeling procedures provide powerful conditions for the acquisition of new responses and the modification of old ones. Though controlled clinical applications have just begun, they already lend considerable substance to Bandura's view (Berberich and Schaeffer, 1965; Frank, 1965; Hoehn-Saric et al., 1965; Krumboltz and Thoreson, 1964; Krumboltz and Schroeder, 1965; Krumboltz, Varenhorst, and Thoreson, 1965; Nelson and Bijan, 1965; Thoreson and Krumboltz, 1965; Truax and Carkhuff, 1965b).

Several extensive reviews further substantiate the generality of conclusion six (Bandura, 1965c; Bandura and Walters, 1963; Eysenck and Rachman, 1965; Franks, 1964; Grossberg, 1964; Krasner and Ullmann, 1965; Ullmann and Krasner, 1965; Wolpe, 1964b).

In spite of the fact that the evidence is favorable, these techniques have been criticized by clinicians as removing symptoms without changing basic pathology and as being limited to very simple neuroses. Neither criticism, however, fits the evidence. Wolpe (1964a) cites data on eighty-eight cases which indicate that a high proportion of complex neuroses can be successfully treated (89%) and in a much briefer time than is typical of traditional methods (Table 5-II).

TABLE 5-II
COMPARISON OF NUMBERS OF SESSIONS IN COMPLEX AND SIMPLE NEUROSES*

	Number	Median Number of Sessions	Mean Number of Sessions
Complex Neuroses	65	29	54.8
Simple Neuroses	21	11.5	14.9
Whole group	86	23	45.4

*The total is only eighty-six because two cases that turned out to be schizophrenic are excluded.

The more telling critique of this work is Breger and McGaugh's point (1965) regarding the uncontrolled case reports, which are the basis for the high cure rates, and the rater bias in estimating outcomes encountered in many of the experimental studies. Faulty as a proportion of these reports are, the overall record still represents the best there is in the field of psychotherapy.

In addition to the fact that difficult cases show improvement in a short time, these reports indicate that significant relapses are rare. This is perhaps the most persuasive evidence that behavior therapists are right when they assert that "symptoms" are not symptoms of psychoanalytic-style pathology, but that they are learned behaviors subject to modification via relearning.

Some learning theorists have criticized Wolpe in particular, claiming that his techniques do not derive directly and logically from learning principles and thus do not have the scientific base he claims (Breger and McGaugh, 1965; Mowrer, 1963). While this may be true to some extent, it is irrelevant to the question of the techniques's effectiveness and ignores the possibility that these clinical phenomena may eventually become the basis for reformulating learning theories in terms of complex, socially significant human behavior. In this case, one would not expect principles of behavior therapy to conform rigorously to conceptions derived largely from animal research.

Implication No. 6. The implications of this work seem quite clear. Since these techniques are effective with many types of symptomatology, they should be used. With regard to some of the more complex and difficult problems, behavior therapists argue that it would be better to spend time developing more complex social learning paradigms for treatment than to expand equal energy modifying less promising traditional interview methods. It appears that special effort should be devoted to integrating these methods with others and in some cases substituting them for the other methods. It would seem important to avoid a current tendency to isolate behavior therapies from the mainstream of treatment and thus create another rigid "school" which will gradually become as impervious to new ideas as the traditional schools already are.

CONCLUSION

In conclusion, it is only regrettable that comment upon so many topics of research has had to be excluded. Suffice it to say that the results in many of those not mentioned are not as yet amenable to synthesis. A good example is the material on the patient-therapist relationship. Nearly all of this research actually pertains to therapist qualities and has nothing to do with an analysis of interactional factors. An unusual exception is the work of Barrett-Lennard which was cited briefly in the discussion of therapist qualities. The few other useful facts in this domain were also included in that section. Another promising line of investigation is that on patient-therapist similarity; but the meaning of the data is still quite ambiguous (Sussman, 1964).

In spite of the fact that much of what is called psychotherapy research is appalling in its inadequacy, to have found a handful of reliable conclusions is gratifying. The groundwork seems well laid by these studies for initial steps at productive innovation in therapeutic treatment.

REFERENCES

1. Ayllon, T. and Michael, J.: The psychiatric nurse as a behavioral engineer. *J Exp Anal Behav, 2*:323-334, 1959.
2. Arbuckle, D. S.: Client perception of counselor personality. *J Counsel Psychol, 3*:93-96, 1956.
3. Bandura, A.: Psychotherapist's anxiety level, self-insight, and psychotherapeutic competence. *J Abnorm Soc Psychol, 52*:333-337, 1956.
4. Bandura, A.: Vicarious processes: A case of no-trial learning. In Berkowitz, L. (Ed.): *Advances in Experimental Social Psychology.* New York, Academic Press, 1965 a, vol. II, pp. 3-48.
5. Bandura, A.: Behavioral modification through modeling procedures. In Krasner, L. and Ullmann, L. (Eds.): *Research in Behavior Modification.* New York, Holt, Rinehart and Winston, 1965 b, pp. 310-340.
6. Bandura, A.: Psychotherapy conceptualized as a social-learning process. Paper presented at the Kentucky Centennial Symposium on Psychotherapy, University of Kentucky, April, 1965c.
7. Bandura, A., Lipsher, D. H. and Miller, Paula E.: Psychotherapists' approach-avoidance reactions to patients' expressions of hostility. *J Consult Psychol, 24*:1-8, 1960.
8. Bandura, A. and Walters, R. H.: *Social Learning and Personality Development.* New York, Holt, Rinehart and Winston, 1963, Chap. 5.
9. Barrett-Lennard, G. T.: Dimensions of therapist response as causal factors in therapeutic change. *Psychol Monographs: General and Applied, 76 (No. 43, whole No. 562)*:1962.
10. Barron, F.: Some test correlates of response to psychotherapy. *J Consult Psychol, 17*:235-241, 1953.
11. Barron, F. and Leary, T: Changes in psychoneurotic patients with and without psychotherapy. *J Consult Psychol, 19*:239-245, 1955.
12. Berberich, J. and Schaeffer, B.: Establishment of verbal behavior through imitation. Paper read at Amer Psychol Assoc Convention, Chicago, 1965.
13. Bergin, A. E.: The effects of psychotherapy: Negative results revisited. *J Counsel Psychol, 10*:244-250, 1963.
14. Bergin, A. E. and Solomon, Sandra: Personality and performance correlates of empathic understanding in psychotherapy. *Am Psychol, 18:* 393, abstract.
15. Breger, L. and McGaugh, J. L.: Critique and reformulation of "learning-theory" approaches to psychotherapy and neurosis. *Psychol Bull, 63:* 338-358, 1965.
16. Butler, J. M. and Haigh, G.: Changes in the relation between self-concepts and ideal concepts consequent upon client-centered counseling. In Rogers, C. R. and Dymond, R. F. (Eds.): *Psychotherapy and Personality Change.* Chicago, U of Chicago Press, 1954, pp. 55-75.

17. Cartwright, D. S.: Success in psychotherapy as a function of certain actuarial variables. *J Consult Psychol, 19:*357-363, 1955.
18. Cartwright, D. S.: Note on "changes" in psychoneurotic patients with and without psychotherapy. *J Consult Psychol, 20:*403-404, 1956.
19. Cartwright, Rosalind D. and Vogel, J. L.: A comparison of changes in psychoneurotic patients during matched periods of therapy and no-therapy. *J Consult Psychol, 24:*121-127, 1960.
20. Chance, Erika: *Families in Treatment.* New York, Basic Books, 1959.
21. Dickenson, W. A. and Truax, C. B.: Group counseling with college underachievers: Comparisons with a control group and relationship to empathy, warmth, and genuineness. Unpublished manuscript, Univer. of Kentucky, 1965.
22. Eysenck, H. J.: The effects of psychotherapy: An evaluation. *J Consult Psychol, 16:*319-324, 1952.
23. Eysenck, H. J.: The effects of psychotherapy. In Eysenck, H. J. (Ed.): *Handbook of Abnormal Psychology.* New York, Basic Books, 1960, pp. 697-725.
24. Eysenck, H. J.: The effects of psychotherapy. *Int J Psychiat, 1:*97-178, 1965.
25. Eysenck, H. J. and Rachman, S.: *The Causes and Cures of Neurosis.* San Diego, Knapp, 1965.
26. Fairweather, G., Simon, R., Gebhard, M. E., Weingarten, E., Holland, J. L., Sanders, R., Stone, G. B. and Reahl, J. E.: Relative effectiveness of psychotherapeutic programs: A multicriteria comparison of four programs for three different patient groups. *Psychol Monogr, 74 (No. 5, whole No. 492):* 1960.
27. Fenichel, O.: *Problems of Psychoanalytic Techniques.* Albany, N. Y., Psychoanal. Quarterly, 1941.
28. Fiedler, F. E.: The concept of the ideal therapeutic relationship. *J Consult Psychol, 14:*239-245, 1950a.
29. Fiedler, F. E.: A comparison of therapeutic relationships in psychoanalytic, nondirective, and Adlerian therapy. *J Consult Psychol, 14:*436-445, 1950b.
30. Fiedler, F. E.: Factor analyses of psychoanalytic, nondirective, and Adlerian therapeutic relationships. *J Consult Psychol, 15:*32-38, 1951.
31. Frank, J. D.: *Persuasion and Healing.* Baltimore, Johns Hopkins Press, 1961.
32. Frank, J. D.: The role of hope in psychotherapy. Paper presented at the Univer. of Kentucky Centennial Psychotherapy Symposium, April, 1965.
33. Franks, C. (Ed): *Conditioning Techniques in Clinical Practice and Research.* New York, Springer, 1964.
34. Fulkerson, S. D. and Barry, J. R.: Methodology and research on the prognostic use of psychological tests. *Psychol Bull, 58:*177-204, 1961.

35. Gardner, G. Gail.: The psychotherapeutic relationship. *Psychol Bull, 61:* 426-437, 1964.
36. Garfield, S. L.: The clinical method in personality assessment. In J. Wepman and R. Heine (Eds.): *Concepts of Personality.* Chicago, Aldine, 1963, pp. 474-502.
37. Garfield, S. L. and Affleck, D. C.: Therapists' judgments concerning patients considered for psychotherapy. *J Consult Psychol, 25:*505-509, 1961.
38. Grossberg, J. M.: Behavior therapy: A review. *Psychol Bull, 62:*73-88, 1964.
39. Gurin, G., Veroff, J. and Feld, Sheila: *Americans View Their Mental Health.* New York, Basic Books, 1960.
40. Hoehn-Saric, R., Frank, J. D., Imber, S. D., Nash, E. H., Stone, A. R. and Battle, C. C.: Systematic preparation of patients for psychotherapy—I. Effects on therapy behavior and outcome. *J Psychiat Res, 2:*267-281, 1965.
41. Hollingshead, A. B. and Redlich, F. C.: *Social Class and Mental Illness.* New York, Wiley, 1958.
42. King, G. F., Armitage, S. G. and Tilton, J. R.: A therapeutic approach to schizophrenics of extreme pathology. *J Abnorm Soc Psychol, 61:*276-286, 1960.
43. Kirtner, W. L. and Cartwright, D. S.: Success and failure in client-centered therapy as a function of client personality variables. *J Consult Psychol, 22:*259-264, 1958a.
44. Kirtner, W. L. and Cartwright, D. S.: Success and failure in client-centered therapy as a function of initial in-therapy behavior. *J Consult Psychol, 22:*329-333, 1958b.
45. Krasner, L. and Ullmann, L. (Eds.): *Research in Behavior Modification: New Developments and Implications.* New York, Holt Rinehart and Winston, 1965.
46. Krumboltz, J. D. and Thoreson, C. E.: The effect of behavioral counseling in group and individual settings on information-seeking behavior. *J Counsel Psychol, 9:*324-333, 1964.
47. Krumboltz, J. D. and Schroeder, W. W.: The effect of reinforcement counseling and model-reinforcement counseling on information-seeking behavior of high school students. *Personnel Guid J,* 1966, in press.
48. Krumboltz, J. D., Varenhorst, Barbara and Thoreson, C. E.: Nonverbal factors in the effectiveness of models in counseling. Paper read at Amer Personnel and Guidance Assoc Convention, 1965, Minneapolis.
49. Lang, P. J. and Lazovik, A. D.: Experimental desensitization of a phobia. *J Abnorm Soc Psychol, 6:*519-525, 1963.
50. Lazarus, A. A.: Group therapy of phabic disorders by systematic desensitization. *J Abnorm Soc Psychol, 63:*504-510, 1961.

51. Lazarus, A. A.: An evaluation of behavior therapy. *Behav Res Ther, 1:* 69-79, 1963.
52. Lindsley, O. R.: Free-operant conditioning and psychotherapy. In Masserman, J. H. (Ed.): *Current Psychiatric Therapies.* New York, Grune & Stratton, 1963, vol. III, pp. 47-56.
53. Lovaas, O. I., Schaeffer, B. and Simmons, J. Q.: Building social behavior in autistic children by use of electric shock. In Palmer J. O. and Goldstein, M. J. (Eds.): *Perspectives in Psychopathology: Readings in Abnormal Psychology.* New York, Oxford Univer. Press, 1966, pp. 222-236.
54. Mink, O. G.: A comparison of effectiveness of nondirective therapy and clinical counseling in the junior high school. *School Counselor, 6:*12-14, 1959.
55. Mowrer, O. H.: Freudianism, behavior therapy, and "self-disclosure." *Behav Res Ther, 1:*1963.
56. Nelson, Karen and Bijan, Guilani: Teaching social behaviors to schizophrenic children through imitation. Paper read at Amer Psychol Assoc Convention, Chicago, 1965.
57. Paul, G. L.: Effects of insight, desensitization, and attention placebo treatment of anixety. Stanford, Calif., Stanford Univer. Press, 1966.
58. Powers, E. and Witmer, Helen: *An Experiment in the Prevention of Delinquency.* New York, Columbia Univer. Press, 1951.
59. Rogers, C. R. and Dymond, Rosalind F.: *Psychotherapy and Personality Change.* Chicago, Univer. of Chicago Press, 1954.
60. Rogers, C. R.: The necessary and sufficient conditions of therapeutic personality change. *J Consult Psychol, 21:*95-103, 1957.
61. Rogers, C. R.: A theory of therapy, personality, and interpersonal relationships, as developed in the client-centered framework. In Koch, S. (Ed.): *Psychology: A Study of a Science.* New York, McGraw-Hill, 1959 vol. III, pp. 184-256.
62. Rogers, C. R.: A theory of psychotherapy with schizophrenics and a proposal for its empirical investigation. In Dawson, J. G., and Dellis, N. P. (Eds.): *Psychotherapy with Schizophrencis.* Baton Rouge, Louisiana State Univer Press, 1961, pp. 3-19.
63. Shlien, J. M., Mosak, H. H. and Dreikurs, R.: Effect of time limits: A comparison of two psychotherapies. *J Counsel Psychol, 9:*31-34, 1962.
64. Speisman, J. C.: Depth of interpretation and verbal resistance in psychotherapy. *J Consult Psychol, 23:*93-99, 1959.
65. Strupp, H. H., Wallach, M. S. and Wogan, M.: Psychotherapy experience in retrospect: Questionnaire survey of former patients and their therapists. *Psychol Monogr, 78 (No. 11) (Whole No. 588):* 1964.
66. Sussman, Alice: Patient-therapist similarity as a factor in psychotherapy. Unpublished manuscript, Teachers College, Columbia Univer., 1964.
67. Thoreson, C. E. and Krumboltz, J. D.: Relationship of counselor rein-

forcement of selected responses to external behavior. *J Counsel Psychol,* 1966, in press.

68. Truax, C. B.: The process of group psychotherapy. *Psychol Monogr, 75 (No. 14, Whole No. 511):* 1961a.

69. Truax, C. B.: A scale for the measurement of accurate empathy. *Psychiat Inst Bull,* Wisconsin Psychiatric Institute, Univer. of Wisconsin, *1 (No. 10):* 1961b.

70. Truax, C. B.: Effective ingredients in psychotherapy. *J Counsel Psychol, 10:256-263,* 1963.

71. Truax, C. B. and Carkhuff, R. R.: For better or for worse: The process of psychotherapeutic change. In *Recent Advances in Behavioral Change.* Montreal, McGill Univer. Press, 1964.

72. Truax, C. B. and Carkhuff, R. R.: The experimental manipulation of therapeutic conditions. *J Consult Psychol, 29:*119-121, 1965a.

73. Truax, C. B. and Carkhuff, R. R.: Personality change in hospitalized mental patients during group psychotherapy as a function of the use of alternate sessions and vicarious therapy pretraining. *J Clin Psychol, 21:*225-228, 1965b.

74. Traux, C. B. and Wargo, D. G.: Human encounters that change behavior: For better or for worse. Unpublished manuscript, Univer of Kentucky, 1965.

75. Ullmann, L. and Krasner, L. (Eds.): *Case Studies in Behavior Modification.* New York, Holt, Rinehart and Winston, 1965.

76. Winder, C. L., Ahmad, Farrukh, Z., Bandura, A. and Rau, Lucy: Dependency of patients, psychotherapists' responses, and aspects of psychotherapy. *J Consult Psychol, 26:*129-134, 1962.

77. Wolpe, J.: *Psychotherapy by Reciprocal Inhibition.* Stanford, Calif., Stanford Univer Press, 1958.

78. Wolpe, J.: Behavior therapy in complex neurotic states. *Brit J Psychiat, 110:*28-34, 1964a.

79. Wolpe, J.: The comparative clinical status of conditioning therapies and psychoanalysis. In Wolpe, J., Salter, A. and Reyna, L. J. (Eds.): *The Conditioning Therapies.* New York, Holt, Rinehart and Winston, 1964, pp. 5-20. (b)

Chapter 6

STRATEGY OF OUTCOME RESEARCH
IN PSYCHOTHERAPY

GORDON L. PAUL

SHLIEN (1966) has summarized the overall impact of the past twenty-five years of psychotherapeutic research by pointing out, "Continued subscription (to psychotherapy) is based upon personal conviction, investment, and observation rather than upon general evidence" (p. 125). Eysenck's (1952) first review of the outcome literature concluded; "The figures fail to support the hypothesis that psychotherapy facilitates recovery from neurotic disorder" (p. 323). His more recent reviews (Eysenck, 1961, 1965) have led to essentially the same conclusions. In the face of such evidence, only two alternatives present themselves: (*a*) Psychotherapy does not "work;" that is, it is ineffective and should be abandoned, or (*b*) past studies have been inappropriate or inadequate evaluations of the efficacy of psychotherapy. The consensus of research workers who have considered the basic principles and methods for the evaluation of psychological treatment strongly favors the second alternative (e.g. Edwards and Cronbach, 1952; Hoch and Zubin, 1964; Rubinstein and Parloff, 1959; Strupp and Luborsky, 1962).

Parloff and Rubinstein (1959) have summarized the sociological obstacles to progress in outcome research which, combined with methodological difficulties in criterion definition, resulted in what Zubin (1964) calls a "flight into process" (p. 127). Large scale researchers came to focus on the process of therapist-client interaction. Thus, sociological difficulties were circumvented by the importance of personality theory, and criterion problems were

Note: Reprinted from *J Consult Psychol, 31:*109-118, 1967.

Psi Chi Invited Address (revised) presented at Midwestern Psychological Association, Chicago, May 1966.

eased by a focus on intratherapy measures. The assumed relationship of such studies to treatment outcome rests on the common belief that more process studies are necessary to identify all important variables before evaluations can be meaningfully made (Hoch, 1964). Similarly, "The evaluation of the effects of therapy is not a task we can handle with existing tools" (Hyman and Berger, 1965, p. 322).

A major problem with the process approach is that the importance of a variable or theory for outcome cannot be established without concurrent assessment of outcome (Greenhouse, 1964). It is precisely through outcome studies with concurrent measurement or manipulation of variables whose influence is unknown that important variables are likely to be identified. If the influence of all variables were known, the question of evaluation would be spurious from the beginning. Additionally, many statements such as that of Hyman and Berger appear to result from a confusion of what Reichenbach (1938) has called the context of discovery and the context of justification. While it may be true that psychological science may never be in a position to measure the truth of the complex experiences which take place between two or more persons (context of discovery), verifying the degree to which the goals of such an interaction are reached or not reached (context of justification) is logically no different for psychotherapy than for any other change-agency (Sanford, 1962).

Apart from emotional and sociological obstacles, the principles and methods of outcome research are basically the same as any other experimental design problem, except for the greater number and complexity of variables. As with all research in psychology, the basic purpose is to discover phenomena—behavioral events or changes—the variables which affect them, and the lawfulness of the effects. Likewise, the greatest difficulty has come from research errors, that is, discrepancies between what is concluded and what can be concluded as a consequence of the experimental operations. Unfortunately, the majority of outcome research has suffered from what Underwood (1957) terms "lethal errors"—discrepancies in which there is no way that a scientifically meaningful conclusion can be reached from the procedures used.

"These cases are best exemplified by blatant confounding of stimulus variables from different classes (environmental, task, subject) so that behavior changes measured cannot be said to be the result even of variables within a given class" (Underwood, 1957, p. 90).

VARIABLES IN PSYCHOTHERAPY RESEARCH

The major variables or domains involved in psychotherapy research, irrespective of theoretical preconceptions, are summarized in Table 6-I. Levinson (1962) and Kiesler (1966) have also considered these basic problems. Each of the variables listed in Table 6-I may be treated as independent variables through selection or manipulation, exerting main effects and interactions within domains and between domains.

TABLE 6-I

MAJOR VARIABLES (DOMAINS) INVOLVED IN PSYCHOTHERAPY
RESEARCH

1. Clients
   a. Distressing behaviors (cognitive, physiological, motoric)
   b. Relatively stable personal-social characteristics
   c. Physical-social life environment
2. Therapists
   a. Therapeutic techniques
   b. Relatively stable personal-social characteristics
   c. Physical-social treatment environment
3. Time
   a. Initial contact
   b. Pretreatment
   c. Initial treatment stage
   d. Main treatment stage
   e. Termination (pretermination stage)
   f. Posttreatment
   g. Follow-up

The essential ingredients are at least one client and one therapist who get together over some finite period of time. Clients come to treatment in order to obtain help in changing some aspect of their behavior which they, or someone else, find distressing. These distressing behaviors (1a) may vary in number and nature and may change over time. Clients may also vary on relatively stable personal-social characteristics (1b) such as age, intelligence, and expectancies. 1a and 1b thus comprise the usual experimental class of subject variables. Clients work with therapists who utilize therapeutic techniques (2a) through which they attempt to alleviate the distress of the client. Like the client's distressing behaviors, therapeutic techniques may vary in number and nature and may change over time. Therapists, just as clients, may vary on relatively stable personal-social characteristics (2b) and, in addition, on characteristics related to treatment, such as subscription to particular "schools" of therapeutic theory, experience, and type of "conditions" established. Thus, 2a and 2b comprise the usual experimental class of task variables. Although 1c and 2c comprise the usual class of environmental variables, they are listed with clients and therapists due to the greater likelihood of confounding adjacent classes. The client's physical-social life environment (1c) includes essentially all the intercurrent life experiences impinging upon him outside of the treatment situation, for example, family, drugs, and work situation. The physical-social treatment environment (2c) refers to the institutional setting in which treatment takes place. This domain may vary from private to public, fee or no fee; it may be a hospital, clinic, or private office.

The third category of Table 6-I, that of time, is usually considered a task variable. Time is separated here for expository purposes because, in addition to task variation, the events in time also mark points of research focus. As a task variable, time may vary in terms of length of treatment contact and number of sessions, that is, the time between pretreatment (3b) and posttreatment (3f). Within treatment proper (3c, d, e) time may vary within and between different stages. Likewise, time may vary between initial contact (3a) and pretreatment (3b) and between posttreatment (3f) and follow-up (3g). The second aspect of the time dimension delineates points of research focus for study or measurement of the main effects and interactions of variables, either between time periods or within time periods.

QUESTION PROBLEM

From the above list of variables and the corresponding points in time for their occurrence and measurement, it is possible to determine the necessary operations for obtaining answers to specific questions and, conversely, to see where research errors have occurred. The most obvious problem with past outcome research has been in the stage of asking questions. The initial question posed, "Does psychotherapy work?" is virtually meaningless. Psychotherapy comprehends a most diversified set of procedures ranging from suggestion, hypnosis, reassurance, and verbal conditioning to systematic sets of actions and strategies based upon more or less tight theoretical formulations. Narrowing the question to specific schools of psychotherapy, such as "Does client-centered therapy work?" or "Does behavior therapy work?" is no more meaningful than the general question, since the range of procedures remains as diversified within schools as within psychotherapy in general. Furthermore, such questions fail to take into account the characteristics of therapists (2b) which may contribute to efficacy. Even if psychotherapy were a homogeneous entity, these questions fail to specify the "what" for "does it work?" Here again, the wrong questions were asked. "Does it work for neuroses?" "Does it work for schizophrenics?" As with schools of psychotherapy, the range of individual differences within standard diagnostic categories remains so diversified as to render meaningless any questions or statements about individuals who become so labeled. The labeling process itself is notoriously unreliable, and criteria for inclusion in a particular class are vague and overlapping. Questions asked in this manner are doomed to committing lethal errors from their time of conception, allowing confounding and confusion of Domains 1 and 2 from the beginning.

The third problem with questions that have been asked in outcome research is with the term "work" itself, that is, the criteria of success or improvement. While there may be general agreement that if psychotherapy works, the client will "feel better" and "function better" (Frank, 1959), the specific goals in accomplishing this end will be as varied as the problems which are brought to treatment. Without specifying the "what" in a question of the nature, "For what does it work?" the question of success remains as confused and heterogeneous as the domains of psychotherapy and clients at large.

What is the appropriate question to be asked of outcome research? In all its complexity, the question towards which all outcome research should ultimately be directed is the following: *What* treatment, by *whom,* is most effective for *this* individual with *that* specific problem, and under *which* set of circumstances? Relating the basic question to the domains listed in Table 6-I, we find: What treatment (2a, therapeutic techniques) , by whom (2b, therapists with relatively stable personal-social characteristics) , is most effective (change in 1a, the client's distressing behaviors, from 3b, pretreatment, to 3f and g, posttreatment and follow-up) for this individual (1b, clients with relatively stable personal-social characteristics) , and under which set of circumstances (1c, the client's physical-social life environment, and 2c, the physical-social treatment environment) ? Posed in this manner, two points are obvious: (*a*) No single study of any degree of complexity will ever be capable of answering this question, and (*b*) in order for knowledge to meaningfully accumulate across separate studies and provide a solid empirical foundation for subsequent research, it will be necessary for every investigation to adequately describe, measure, or control each of the variables or domains listed in Table 6-I.

CRITERION PROBLEM

One of the most recurrent methodological difficulties in outcome research has been the criterion problem. Lack of agreement among criteria, not only between investigators, but between clients, therapists, and other sources in the same investigation was one factor which resulted in the flight into process. A major basis for the lack of relationship among criteria lies in the fact that different frames of reference may be used by persons in different roles for making overall judgments of success or improvement. Most investigators have selected criteria from some theoretical frame of reference, ignoring the heterogeneity of client populations. Criteria so selected are likely to be, at best, partially related to criteria selected from some other frame of reference. Parloff and Rubinstein's (1959) statement that an "investigator's selection of specific criteria (is) a premature and presumptuous value judgment" (p. 278) appears valid when the criteria are based upon some preconceived theoretical judgment which bears no demonstrated relationship to the client's problems, or when the criteria are deemed to be the attainment of some "ideal" which is necessarily value laden with the mores of a particular class, culture, or investigator. The normal population is heterogeneous in the extreme, allowing for broad ranges of variability in ways of living. Irrespective of any theoretical position, the real question of outcome on logical and ethical grounds is whether or not the clients have received help with the distressing behaviors which brought them to treatment in the first place (Betz, 1962; Hoppock, 1953; Rickard, 1965.) As recently stated by Jerome Frank and his colleagues (Battle, Imber, Hoehn-Saric, Stone, Nash, and Frank, 1966) :

> In the absence of adequate knowledge of the causes of psychiatric complaints, we assume that psychotherapy has removed the causes if the complaints are permanently relieved, and no new ones are substituted for them (p. 185).

While using such tailored criteria does bypass the homogeneity problem which arises from the use of varying frames of reference, it does not remove the necessity for adequately defining the dependent variables at some level of quantification with adequate reliability and validity. Although many techniques for measuring change have been used in the past, few of these methods have proved to be acceptable (Zax and Klein, 1960). Subjective reports of change by clients or therapists are notorious for their lack of reliability and validity, and specific problems negate the use of many psychological tests (Paul, 1966).

The most important and meaningful test of outcome is the change in clients' distressing behaviors outside of treatment (Luborsky and Strupp, 1962). Some guidelines for assessment may be obtained by considering the process which results in client-therapist contact; that is, the client does something, under a set of circumstances, which disturbs someone sufficiently that action results—entering treatment (Ullmann and Krasner, in press). The "something" he does has been identified as the distressing behaviors which lead him to treatment. However, since this something occurs under a set of circumstances it is unnecessary to attempt measurement of change under all circumstances. Rather, assessment should be more or less situation specific. As Zax and Klein (1960) point out, the least used but most promising criteria are, then, objective behavioral criteria external to the treatment situation. The advantages of such "work sample" assessments, which may include self-report measures, have been presented elsewhere (Paul, 1966). While multiple measures of outcome are necessary, the dependent variable in any outcome evaluation must be, to return to Table 6-I, change in the distressing behaviors which brought the client to treatment (1a), from pretreatment (3b) to posttreatment (3f), and follow-up (3g), assessed external to treatment proper by unbiased means.

APPROACHES TO OUTCOME RESEARCH

Given the basic question and criterion specifications, as with all research, the means of obtaining answers or partial answers becomes a problem of strategy. That is, what is the place of and need for different levels of outcome research? What can the varied approaches such as case studies, simplifications, and different levels of controlled experiment contribute? In view of the range and complexity of the variables involved, continuing series of well-controlled, factorially designed experiments appear to be not only the most efficient means to obtain knowledge relevant to the ultimate question (Edwards and Cronbach, 1952), but probably the only way. Both before and after factorially designed experiments there is a real value for lower levels of investigation and for studies designed to answer different questions, especially in the determination of mechanisms of change. However, these investigations must be evaluated on the basis of their possible level of product.

Since outcome studies attempt to determine cause-effect relationships, the ultimate necessity of factorial investigations is apparent upon consideration of two principles of basic research: (*a*) There is really only one principle of experimental design, and that is to "design the experiment so that the effects of the independent variables can be evaluated unambiguously" (Underwood, 1957, p. 86), and (*b*) in order to do this, "to draw a conclusion about the influence of any given variable, that variable must have been systematically manipulated alone somewhere in the design" (Underwood, 1957, p. 35). These principles again highlight the need of describing, measuring, or controlling each of the variables or domains listed in Table 6-I to prevent confounding.

The problem of necessary experimental controls for the prevention of confounding (Frank, 1959) is clear in factorial designs. Additionally, tactical decisions within a factorial study need to be made on the basis of the strength of knowledge in an area at any given time. Since the major points concerning needed controls and the practical and empirical problems of conducting factorial outcome studies have been presented elsewhere (Paul, 1966), these points will only be summarized here, with focus on strategies which appear desirable at our current level of knowledge.

An adequate definition of the client sample and the related practical problems of providing sufficient time for appraisal, adequate information prior to treatment assignment, and large enough groups constitute the first concern of the outcome study. Since change in clients' distressing behaviors (1a) is always a dependent variable, selection of the sample involves a decision on heterogeneity. In view of the likelihood that the severity of distressing behaviors will vary, even within the same class (e.g. obese women), and that resistance to change may vary across classes (e.g. obese women versus morphine addicts), the tactical choice favors selection of clients on the same class of target behaviors.

Even with selection on a homogeneous class of target behaviors, there is likely to be a wide variation in relatively stable personal-social characteristics (1b). Clients might be classified on the basis of 1b variables, and these classes might then be treated as independent variables (e.g. elderly, lower class males of average intelligence versus adolescent, middle-class females of superior intelligence). However, practical considerations suggest that the best strategy for early studies would be the selection of homogeneous samples described in enough detail for meaningful comparisons to be made across studies. With quantification of major characteristics, correlational analyses of client characteristics with outcome can provide suggestive evidence of possible influencing parameters and thus sharpen independent variables for subsequent outcome studies.

While the distressing client behaviors in Domain 1a will always be involved as independent and dependent variables, and while the relatively stable personal-social characteristics in Domain 1b may be independent variables, described or controlled, the variables in Domain 1c, the physical-social life environment of the clients, can seldom be described in detail or treated as independent variables. The task then becomes one of control, that is, to provide for the eventuality that behavioral modifications which may be observed are not due to extraexperimental life experiences. The only way of controlling for these factors appears to be to use a comparable no-treatment control group that is observed and assessed at the same time and for the same amount of time as the treatment groups. Such a group also controls for the effects of repeated testing and for so-called "spontaneous" changes over time.

Own-control designs (i.e. comparisons of 3a-3b change with 3b-3f change for the same clients) are desirable for obtaining base rates on the stability of distressing behaviors, but they do not adequately control for changes which may be related to the passage of time, season, or extraexperimental experiences. Therefore, the problem becomes one of dividing the sample into equivalent experimental and control groups. Experimentally, there are three ways of obtaining equivalent groups. The first method is to match groups, not only on target behaviors, but also on all major variables believed to be significant from Domains 1b and 1c, randomizing on other aspects. A second possibility is to equate groups by stratified sampling of major categories without matching individuals. The third method is straight random assignment. For any method, randomization of variables not matched or measured is important. In factorial studies, the present strategical choice appears to favor, at least, stratification on target behaviors and motivation. The danger of experimental procedures destroying the equivalence of the no-treatment control group in relation to other groups may be partially circumvented by strategic use of an own-control waiting period for a later treatment as the no-treatment control for current treatment groups.

Constituting the next concern are an adequate definition of the therapists and techniques of treatment and the related practical problems of providing sufficient time for assessment or training prior to treatment contact, monitoring of intratherapy procedures, and obtaining enough cooperative individuals. The usual independent variable of most interest in the outcome study is the specific therapeutic technique (2a) proposed to be effective in alleviating behavioral distress. A decision on heterogeneity is even more important with regard to therapeutic technique, since the replication of independent variables is involved. In dealing with established treatment procedures, this problem becomes even more complicated, because most experienced psychotherapists have developed their techniques to a more or less individual art. One strategic approach to this problem would be to allow complete flexibility among therapists with their preferred techniques, determine those who are reliably effective, and then return to audio or video recordings of the effective therapists to determine what they did, or conduct more elaborate process studies with these therapists as subjects. The difficulty with this approach is that it provides no information on what is ineffective treatment, nor does it allow ready comparison to other therapeutic techniques.

On the other hand, if each set of treatment techniques is relatively homogeneous within treatment groups across therapists, immediate knowledge of what constitutes effective treatment would be available. Thus, whether dealing with old or new treatment procedures, the tactical choice favors homogeniety within groups, preferably provided with a single monitor-supervisor for all therapists within individual treatments.

By using homogeneous treatment procedures, the chief problem of control is to distinguish between the effects of Domains 2a and 2b, that is, the effects of the relatively stable personal-social characteristics of the therapist versus those of the specific set of therapeutic techniques. A related problem is that of distinguishing between the specific effects of particular therapeutic techniques and the nonspecific effects which are involved in any therapeutic contact—the "placebo-effect" (Rosenthal and Frank, 1958). An adequate control for placebo effects would then be another form of treatment in which clients have equal faith, but which would not be expected to lead to behavioral change on any other grounds. By having each therapist conduct both a treatment to be evaluated and an attention-placebo treatment with several clients, equating the length and number of sessions and all other time factors, not only may nonspecific placebo effects be distinguished, but a base rate is provided for the improvement resulting from the relatively stable personal-social characteristics of the individual therapists, As with client characteristics (1b), therapist characteristics (2b) may be treated as additional independent variables (e.g. experienced versus inexperienced). However, in view of the present state of knowledge, the best strategy for early studies might limit evaluation of therapist characteristics to correlation with outcome to aid in sharpening of hypotheses for future evaluation.

In practice, the physical-social treatment environment (2c) will probably be constant for any given investigation. In this case, the major requirement is an adequate description of the facility and usual operating procedures to allow comparisons across studies. Should more than one facility be involved, however, it is important to control for possible confounding by conducting all treatments, including the attention-placebo, in all facilities. While the separate influence of the treatment setting itself appears, within normal limits, to be the least important domain, settings could be evaluated as an independent variable by having each therapist conduct each of the different treatments with several clients in two or more facilities.

With regard to the time dimension, each of the time periods listed in Table 6-I should be specified and held constant, unless time is to be treated as an independent variable. Assessments should be taken at the same points in time and the number and duration of sessions held constant across groups. If time is to be treated as an independent variable, for example, in questioning whether spacing or duration of sessions were important, it would also be necessary to systematically vary these aspects across relevant control groups.

If the investment of time and money is made for all of the above therapists and controls, it would also appear to be good strategy to evaluate two or more treatments within the same design. This could be accomplished by extending therapists across more than one treatment, in addition to the attention-placebo treatment, or by introducing different therapists into the design to conduct both a different type of treatment and the attention-placebo treatment. In either case, main effects may be evaluated for treatments and for therapists, as well as interactions. It would also seem reasonable to choose the most promising competing treatments for any particular disorder for comparative evaluation. Further, if these treatments were derived from competing theoretical formulations, an additional contribution could be made to basic science, as well as to the ethical-technological aspects.

Since factorial studies of the above type do involve a tremendous investment of time, money, and personnel, it is important to consider the place and value for lower levels of investigation and for studies designed to answer different questions both before and after factorially designed experiments. A summary of the major approaches relating to outcome research, along with a designation of the confounding possible and resulting level of knowledge obtainable for each is presented in Table 6-II. As indicated above, the factorially designed experiment with no-treatment and attention-placebo controls is the only approach which offers the establishment of antecedent-consequent relationships for specific treatments without possible confounding. With this type of design, analytic conclusions may be reached for complex variables, such as a total treatment system.

Once the effectiveness of a complex treatment is established across specified problems, populations, and therapists, a number of these alternative approaches become valuable research strategies. One of the most valuable approaches is that of "simplification" (Bordin, 1965), that is, abstracting from the originally ob-

TABLE 6-II
SUMMARY OF MAJOR APPROACHES TO OUTCOME RESEARCH

Approach	Confounding Possible	Level of Product
Case study (without measurement)	Within and between all domains	Crude hypotheses.
Case study (with measurement)	Within and between all domains	Correlational conclusions. Strengthened hypotheses.
Nonfactorial group design (without no-treatment control)*	Within and between all domains	Same as above. Hypotheses strengthened as individual studies move across domains.
Nonfactorial group design (with no-treatment control)	Within client (1a, b) Within treatment (2a, b, c)	Antecedent-consequent relationship established between classes. Determinants strengthened as individual studies move across domains.
Factorial group design (with no-treatment control and attention-placebo control)	None necessary	Antecedent-consequent relationship established for specifics within and between classes. Analytic conclusions for complex variables.
Laboratory simplification	None necessary	Antecedent-consequent relationship established for specifics within and between classes for analogues. Analytic conclusions for specific variables.

*Lower possible confounding, higher level product for "A-B-A own-control" approach (see text).

served phenomena in the clinical setting and transferring them to the laboratory, where greater precision can be obtained in experimental isolation, manipulation, and control. The term experimental analogue is often given to this approach, since in the process of simplification, one or more of the variables or domains relevant to psychotherapy is deemed to be analogous to those existent in the natural clinical setting (Maher, 1966). To the extent that the analogue shares the essential characteristics of clinical procedures and phenomena, this approach is a powerful and economical means for determining the mechanisms of operation and specific parameters of influence for complex variables identified in the factorial group design. However, any changes in procedure or hypotheses developed for other phenomena which grow from experimental analogues need to be confirmed in the clinical setting.

While both laboratory simplifications and factorial group designs in the clinical setting allow analytical conclusions to be reached, lower levels of investigation also have strategic value for the ultimate question of outcome. Nonfactorial group designs with no-treatment controls can establish antecedent-consequent relationships between treatment and outcome in the same manner as factorial designs. However, since the nonfactorial design cannot separate within-class confounding, its utility must be considered in relationship to the available knowledge concerning the effectiveness and applicability of treatment techniques. Following a factorial study, the nonfactorial design may be valuable in extending treatment evaluation across domains, that is, to different types of clients, problems, therapists, treatment settings, and variations in the time domain. The limiting factor with this usage is that, for the accumulation of knowledge to remain precise, new variation can be introduced into only one domain at a time. The second strategic use of the nonfactorial design with a no-treatment control is to provide, prior to the factorial experiment, global validation of promising treatment procedures and of new combinations of known methods. Since confounding is possible within classes of variables, from a scientific point of view, the latter usage serves only a mapping function. Practically, however, this mapping function has considerable value; only the promising therapists or treatment procedures need be included in later factorial outcome studies, and only effective treatment procedures need be continued in clinical practice. Additionally, therapists or techniques which cause clients to get worse can be immediately identified and redirected.

The three lower approaches in Table 6-II (the nonfactorial design without no-treatment controls and case studies with or without measurement) cannot provide evidence of antecedent-consequent relationships because confounding is possible between domains and classes as well as within. The individual case study without external measurement is of use only in the earliest phase of the clinical development of techniques. The case study with measurement before, during, and after treatment constitutes the first step in validation by establishing correlational conclusions and communicating procedures to others. The hypotheses of a promising treatment procedure and its parameters can be strengthened as case studies accumulate across domains and through the uncontrolled nonfactorial design; however, these approaches can at best serve an early, crude mapping function and can never validate a specific technique. One particular approach involving a nonfactorial group design without no-treatment controls does not quite fit with these statements. This is the "A-B-A own-control" design in which the client's distressing behavior is reduced, increased, and again reduced contingent upon therapeutic techniques (Ullmann and Krasner, 1965). By demonstrating these temporal relationships reliably across groups, the likelihood of between-class confounding by spontaneous fluctuation in time, or extraexperimental life experiences is quite low. The level of product for this design approaches that of the nonfactorial group design with no-treatment controls.

One other approach to outcome research which appears from time to time is the "retrospective study" in which clinical records are searched to obtain "measurement" or description on all variables, including the outcome measure itself. Although the rationale of such studies may be the same as prospective experiments, the crudeness of the data and methodological problems involved are so nearly insurmountable that these studies appear to contribute little more than confusion. With careful application of appropriate methodology and strategy, hope exists that twenty-five more years of research will no longer find psychotherapy characterized as "an undefined technique applied to unspecified problems with unpredictable outcome" (Raimy, 1950, p. 93).

REFERENCES

1. Battle, C. C., Imber, S. D., Hoehn-Saric, R., Stone, A. R., Nash, E. R. and Frank, J. D.: Target complaints as criteria of improvement. *Am J Psychother, 20:*184-192, 1966.

2. Bordin, E. S.: Simplification as a strategy for research in psychotherapy. *J Consult Psychol, 29:*493-503, 1965.

3. Betz, B.: Experience in research in psychotherapy with schizophrenic patients. In Strupp, H. H. and Luborsky, L. (Eds.): *Research in psychotherapy* Washington, D. C., American Psychological Association, 1962, vol. 2, pp. 41-60.

4. Edwards, A. L. and Cronbach, L. J.: Experimental design for research in psychotherapy. *J Clin Psychol, 8:*51-59, 1952.

5. Eysenck, H. J.: The effects of psychotherapy: An evaluation. *J Consult Psychol, 16:*319-324, 1952.

6. Eysenck, H. J.: The effects of psychotherapy. In Eysenck, H. J. (Ed.): *Handbook of Abnormal Psychology.* New York, Basic Books, 1961, pp. 697-725.

7. Eysenck, H. J.: The effects of psychotherapy. *Int J Psychiatry, 1:*99-144, 1965.

8. Frank, J. D.: Problems of controls in psychotherapy. In Rubinstein, E. A. and Parloff, M. B. (Eds.): *Research in Psychotherapy.* Washington, D. C., American Psychological Association, 1959, vol. 1, pp. 10-26.

9. Greenhouse, S. W.: Principles in the evaluation of therapies for mental disorders. In Hoch, P. H. and Zubin, J. (Eds.): *The Evaluation of Psychiatric Treatment.* New York, Grune & Stratton, 1964, pp. 94-105.

10. Hoch, P. H.: Methods of evaluating various types of psychiatric treatments: Discussion. In Hoch, P. H. and Zubin, J. (Eds.): *The Evaluation of Psychiatric Treatment.* New York, Grune and Stratton, 1964, pp. 52-57.

11. Hoch, P. H., and Zubin, J. (Eds.): *The Evaluation of Psychiatric Treatment.* New York, Grune and Stratton, 1964.

12. Hoppock, R.: What is the "real" problem? *Am Psychol, 8:*124, 1953.

13. Hyman, R., and Berger, L.: Discussion of H. J. Eysenck's: The effects of psychotherapy. *Int J Psychiatry, 1:*317-322, 1965.

14. Kiesler, D. J.: Some myths of psychotherapy research and the search for a paradigm. *Psychol Bull, 65*:110-136, 1966.
15. Levinson, D. J.: The psychotherapist's contribution to the patient's treatment career. In Strupp, H. H. and Luborsky, L. (Eds.) : *Research in Psychotherapy*. Washington, D. C., American Psychological Association, 1962, Vol. 2, pp. 13-24.
16. Luborsky, L. and Strupp, H. H.: Research problems in psychotherapy: A three year follow-up. In Strupp, H. H. and Luborsky, L. (Eds.) : *Research in Psychotherapy*. Washington, D. C., American Psychological Association, 1962, Vol. 2, pp. 308-329.
17. Maher, B. A.: *Principles of Psychopathology*. New York, McGraw-Hill, 1966.
18. Parloff, M. B. and Rubenstein, E. A.: Research problems in psychotherapy. In Rubenstein, E. A. and Parloff, M. B. (Eds.): *Research in Psychotherapy* Washington, D. C., American Psychological Association, 1959, Vol. 1, pp. 276-293.
19. Paul, G. L.: *Insight vs. Desensitization in Psychotherapy: An Experiment in Anxiety Reduction*. Stanford, Stanford University Press, 1966.
20. Raimy, V. C. (Ed.) : *Training in Clinical Psychology*. Englewood Cliffs, N. J., Prentice-Hall, 1950.
21. Reichenbach, H.: *Experience and Prediction*. Chicago, University of Chicago Press, 1938.
22. Rickard, H. C.: Tailored criteria of change in psychotherapy. *J Gen Psychol, 72*:63-68. 1965.
23. Rosenthal, D. and Frank, J. D.: Psychotherapy and the placebo effect. In Reed, C. F., Alexander, I. E. and Tomkins, S. S. (Eds.) : *Psychopathology: A Source Book*. Cambridge, Harvard University Press, 1958, pp. 463-473.
24. Rubinstein, E. A. and Parloff, M. B. (Eds.) : *Research in Psychotherapy*. Washington, D. C., American Psychological Association, 1959, Vol. 1.
25. Sanford, N.: Discussion of papers on measuring personality change. In Strupp, H. H. and Luborsky, L. (Eds.) : *Research in Psychotherapy*. Washington, D. C., American Psychological Association, 1962, pp. 155-163, Vol. 2.
26. Shlien, J. M.: Cross-theoretical criteria for the evaluation of psychotherapy. *Am J Psychother, 1*:125-134, 1966.
27. Strupp, H. H. and Luborsky, L. (Eds.) : *Research in Psychotherapy*. Washington, D. C., American Psychological Association, 1962, Vol. 2.
28. Ullmann, L. P. and Krasner, L. (Eds.) : *Case Studies in Behavior Modification*. New York, Holt, 1965.
29. Ullmann, L. P. and Krasner, L.: *Abnormal Behavior: A Psychological Approach*. Englewood Cliffs, N. J., Prentice-Hall, in press.
30. Underwood, B. J.: *Psychological Research*. New York, Appleton-Century-Crofts, 1957.

31. Zax, M. and Klein, A.: Measurement of personality and behavior changes following psychotherapy. *Psychol Bull 57*:435-448, 1960.
32. Zubin, J.: Technical issues: Discussion. In Hoch, P. H. and Zubin, J. (Eds.): *The Evaluation of Psychiatric Treatment.* New York, Grune and Stratton, 1964, pp. 122-128.

C. THEORY AND PRACTICE

Chapter 7

THE CASEWORK RELATIONSHIP: EXCERPTS FROM A HERETIC'S NOTEBOOK

EARL C. BRENNEN

T HE CASEWORKER-CLIENT relationship is what sociologists would term "sacred," and it is perhaps not merely coincidental that the definitive work on the topic bears the name of a priest (Biestek). This is not surprising, for caseworkers employ the medical model in treating those in their charge, and the aura surrounding the medicine man—whether shaman or physician—has carried over to the social agency. The sacrosanct component can be beneficial, as Jerome Frank and others have observed, but it has its disadvantages. For one thing, sacred norms are more resistant to change than are secular norms. And when such norms happen to be professional in nature the resistance is magnified. Professions change slowly, especially where client welfare conflicts with what is thought best for the profession. The American Medical Association is currently the foremost exemplar in this regard, and it is worth noting that the organization's strongest public appeal is based on the "threatened" doctor-patient relationship (never mind that doctors barely know their patients these days) .

THE PASSING OF CONVENTIONAL CASEWORK

Yet altered social conditions and advances in knowledge press for change. In social work a number of events have combined to invite changes in the nature of the casework relationship, but whether such revisions will come about gracefully hinges largely on how desperately we cling to the medical model. I say "desperately," for the pull is already in other directions. Our specific medical model, psychoanalysis, has become increasingly suspect in many quarters (some friendly) and even caseworkers themselves

Note: Reprinted from New Perspectives, 1:65-67, 1967.

are beginning to doubt its appropriateness, if not its efficacy. Recent articles in social work journals reveal that many practicing professionals are shamelessly neglectful of psychoanalytic theory, even though the Hollis text continues to offer students the venerably intact system in meticulous detail.

But again it is easy to understand why caseworkers cleave to the outmoded. The history of science is replete with instances of dedicated men continuing to work with theories already found to be invalid. Chemists, for example, persisted in using phlogiston theory as a basis for experiments although their own results repeatedly disputed the very existence of the element. Apparently scientists would rather work with an erroneous framework than no framework at all, and practitioners have doubtlessly followed suit. *In social work we are becoming disenchanted with the conventional casework model, but until a new model is developed we will continue to draw upon the old, and teach it to novices.* And since any conception of the casework relationship must be congruent with the larger body of practice theory, this too awaits the advent of a new practice model.

THE DEMOCRATIZATION OF SOCIAL WORK

What will this new model be like? In some respects it may resemble the *legal* model. The antipoverty programs and the general concern with economic rights, civil rights, and personal rights (contraceptive information, etc.) have led to an introduction of legal considerations in the dispensing of social services. Some social workers are not only paying attention to the client's point of view and to complaints of the "customers" of the welfare establishment, but they are actively taking the side of the client against the bureaucracy and the community. These practitioners work *for* rather than *on* clients. And other social workers (that is, Scott Briar) are beginning to study this virgin area.

Of course, at the onset, the legal model will apply mainly to the oppressed and stigmatized, notably poor people and Negroes. But its impact will diffuse through other segments of social work culture.

How would the legal model affect our current conception of

the casework relationship? Let us contrast the medical and legal models and venture some guesses (as students we should take advantage of the social sanction to talk "wild" at times). First, the medical model views the patient or client as sick (guilty) until proven healthy (innocent), as the prolific Dr. Szasz tells us in compelling fashion. This is a desired approach in physical matters—we all want a suspicious doctor who will examine us thoroughly. But it does not bode well in emotional and social concerns. Articles have been written on the "strangeness" between caseworker and client, and I believe (with evidence to support me) that this is in part due to caseworkers viewing so many of their clients as disturbed people who will probably not improve without intensive treatment. The casework relationship is conceived as one between a strong and knowing helper and someone with a personal defect. The legal approach would have us regard clients as normal, sensible people (much like ourselves on these two counts), until proven otherwise beyond a reasonable doubt. In a word, this model would inject a now absent element into the casework relationship: *psychological equality.*

Second, the medical model views the client as an object to be studied. We devote ourselves to *diagnostically* understanding clients (never mind that the client may not *feel* understood by us). We also have a nice legitimate word to cover this process—objectivity. Now I can almost hear someone saying, "Aw come on now, are you suggesting that we relate to them *subjectively?*" Not at all; but I would ask that we consider quite another definition of "objectivity." A fair number of social scientists and therapists hold that since the client will change only in relation to the reality he perceives, this is the only objective reality for him; all other realities are our subjective creations for the client. True, caseworkers talk much of "empathy," and maybe we achieve empathic relationships more than I think we do. It's just that I find it hard to believe when there is so much that tells us we have never understood the poor, or Negroes, or unwed mothers, or delinquents, and so on. Diagnostic understanding does not seem to pull it off. But in the legal model the client gets his "day in court," and his perception of things is often a key issue. If you feel slandered, an attorney is unlikely to claim that this is not the *real* problem. Let me suggest that the legal model would add another missing element to the casework relationship: *perceptual equality.*

Finally, the medical model holds that the patient must be completely open and honest with the doctor if he expects to be helped. But the norm is hardly reciprocal: indeed, secrecy and deception are encouraged. If the patient learns what pills he is taking he may get confused or anxious; or, if he finds out that he really hated his recently departed father he may become disabled with guilt. So we tell our clients to pour out their innermost thoughts, including what they think of us. But we tell them little in return. In fact, we would be embarrassed—and perhaps a bit ashamed—if they could read what we write about them in our case records. The legal model is quite different, and we could have fun with this comparison, especially when it comes to courtroom antics. But in general an attorney may lay out the case strategy to his client and even be candid about the probable outcome. This might seem to be far removed from what we could incorporate into casework, but other psychological helpers are already doing it. Some behavior therapists tell their patients exactly what they are doing to them (step by step) , and some family therapists come close. My guess is, then, that the legal model would supply yet another element to the casework relationship: *mutual honesty and openness.*

Is there any evidence that the addition of these elements would make for a more desirable casework relationship? Well, at least among Negroes and the poor, some spokesmen claim that indigenous nonprofessionals—who haven't learned to relate to clients as we have—get along better with those they serve than do we. Why? Among other things, these nonpros tend to: (a) take a normalizing stance toward clients; (b) enter into the client's frame of reference (as expected, for they are indigenous) ; and (c) speak their mind. In other words, the elements of *psychological equality, perceptual equality,* and *mutual honesty and openness* are present to a greater degree than in the conventional casework relationship.

Nonprofessionals own vices to match their virtues, fail as often as they succeed, and exasperate as well as refresh. But whatever else the record shows, this much seems certain at this point in time: they are democratizing social work.

Besides the legal model—and I have not exhausted its implications—there are other events which are impinging now upon the casework relationship. Short-term contacts, casework with groups, the growing tendency to focus more on change than causation . . . all will leave their mark. The prospects are exciting, and the present cadre of social work students will play its part in shaping a new practice model: one that will competently offer clients an acceptable relationship.

Chapter 8

THE ART OF BEING A FAILURE AS A THERAPIST

JAY HALEY

W HAT HAS been lacking in the field of therapy is a theory of failure. Many clinicians have merely assumed that any psychotherapist could fail if he wished. However, recent studies of the outcome of therapy indicate that spontaneous improvement of patients is far more extensive than was previously realized. There is a consistent finding that between fifty and seventy percent of patients on waiting list control groups not only do not wish treatment after the waiting list period but have really recovered from their emotional problems—despite the previous theories which did not consider this possible. Assuming that these findings hold up in further studies, a therapist who is incompetent and does no more than sit in silence and scratch himself will have at least a fifty percent success rate with his patients. How then can a therapist be a failure?

The problem is not a hopeless one. We might merely accept the fact that a therapist will succeed with half his patients and do what we can to provide a theory which will help him fail consistently with the other half. However, we could also risk being more adventurous. Trends in the field suggest the problem can be approached in a deeper way by devising procedures for keeping those patients from improving who would ordinarily spontaneously do so. Obviously merely doing nothing will not achieve this end. We must create a program with the proper ideological framework and provide systematic training over a period of years if we expect a therapist to fail consistently.

Note: Reprinted from *Am J Orthopsychiatry*, *(39)*:691-695, 1969. Copyright 1969, the American Orthopsychiatric Association, Inc. Reproduced by permission. Republished in Haley, J., *The Power Tactics of Jesus Christ and other Essays.* New York, Grossman, 1970.

An outline will be offered here of a series of steps to increase the chance of failure of any therapist. This presentation is not meant to be comprehensive, but it includes the major factors which experience in the field has shown to be essential and which can be put into practice even by therapists who are not specially talented.

1. The central pathway to failure is based upon a nucleus of ideas which, if used in combination, make success as a failure almost inevitable.

Step A: Insist that the problem which brings the patient into therapy is not important. Dismiss it as merely a "symptom" and shift the conversation elsewhere. In this way a therapist will never have to examine what is really distressing a patient.

Step B: Refuse to treat the presenting problem directly. Offer some rationale, such as the idea that symptoms have "roots," to avoid treating the problem the patient is paying his money to recover from. In this way the odds increase that the patient will not recover, and future generations of therapists can remain ignorant of the specific skills needed to get people over their problems.

Step C.: Insist that if a presenting problem is relieved, something worse will develop. This myth makes it proper not to know what to do about symptoms and will even encourage patients to cooperate by developing a fear of recovery.

Given these three steps, it seems obvious that any psychotherapist will be incapacitated whatever his natural talent. He will not take seriously the problem the patient brings, he will not try to change that, and he will fear that successful relief of the problem is disastrous.

One might think that this nucleus of ideas alone would make any therapist a failure, but the wiser heads in the field have recognized that other steps are necessary.

2. It is particularly important to confuse diagnosis and therapy. A therapist can sound expert and be scientific without ever risking a success with treatment if he uses a diagnostic language which makes it impossible for him to think of therapeutic operations. For example, one can say that a patient is passive-aggressive, or that he has deep seated dependency needs, or that he has a

weak ego, or that he is impulse ridden. No therapeutic interventions can be formulated with this kind of language. For more examples of how to phrase a diagnosis so that a therapist is incapacitated, the reader is referred to *The American Psychiatric Association Diagnostic Manual.*

3. Put the emphasis upon a single method of treatment, no matter how diverse the problems which enter the office. Patients who won't behave properly according to the method should be defined as untreatable and abandoned. Once a single method has proven consistently ineffective, it should never be given up. Those people who attempt variations must be sharply condemned as improperly trained and ignorant of the true nature of the human personality and its disorders. If necessary, a person who attempts variations can be called a latent layman.

4. Have no theory, or an ambiguous and untestable one, of what a therapist should do to bring about therapeutic change. However, make it clear that it is untherapeutic to give a patient directives for changing—he might follow them and change. Just imply that change spontaneously happens when therapists and patients behave according to the proper forms. As part of the general confusion that is necessary, it is helpful to define therapy as a procedure for finding out what is wrong with a person and how he got that way. With that emphasis, ideas about what to do to bring about change will not develop in an unpredictable manner. One should also insist that change be defined as a shift of something in the interior of a patient so that it remains outside the range of observation and so is uninvestigable. With the focus upon the "underlying disorder" (which should be sharply distinguished from the "overlying disorder"), questions about the unsavory aspects of the relationship between therapist and patient need not arise, nor is it necessary to include unimportant people, such as the patient's intimates, in the question of change.

Should student therapists who are not yet properly trained insist upon some instruction about how to cause change, and if a frown about their unresolved problems does not quiet them, it might be necessary to offer some sort of ambiguous and general idea which is untestable. One can say, for example, that the therapeutic job is to bring the unconscious into consciousness. In this way the therapy task is defined as transforming a hypothetical entity into another hypothetical entity and so there is no possibility that precision in therapeutic technique might develop. Part of this approach requires helping the patient "see" things about himself, particularly in relation to past traumas, and this involves no risk of change. The fundamental rule is to emphasize "insight" and "affect expression" to student therapists as causes of change so they can feel something is happening in the session without hazarding success. If some of the advanced students insist on more high class technical knowledge about therapy, a cloudy discussion of "working through the transference" is useful. This not only provides young therapists with an intellectual catharsis, but they can make transference interpretations and so have something to do.

5. Insist that only years of therapy will really change a patient.

This step brings us to more specific things to do about those patients who might spontaneously recover without treatment. If they can be persuaded that they have not really recovered but have merely fled into health, it is possible to help them back to ill health by holding them in long-term treatment. (One can always claim that only long term treatment can really cure a patient so that he will never ever have a problem the remainder of his life.) Fortunately the field of therapy has no theory of overdosage, and so a skillful therapist can keep a patient from improving for as long as ten years without protest from his colleagues, no matter how jealous. Those therapists who try for twenty years should be congratulated on their courage but thought of as foolhardy unless they live in New York.

6. As a further step to restrain patients who might spontaneously improve, it is important to offer dire warnings about the fragile nature of people and insist they might suffer psychotic breaks or turn to drink if they improve. When "underlying pathology" becomes the most common term in every clinic and consulting room, everyone will avoid taking action to help patients recover and patients will even restrain themselves if they begin to make it on their own. Long-term treatment can then crystallize

them into therapeutic failures. If patients seem to improve even in long-term therapy, they can be distracted by being put into group therapy.

7. As a further step to restrain patients who might spontaneously improve, the therapist should focus upon the patient's past.

8. As yet another step with that aim, the therapist should interpret what is most unsavory about the patient to arouse his guilt so that he will remain in treatment to resolve the guilt.

9. Perhaps the most important rule is to ignore the real world that patients live in and publicize the vital importance of their infancy, inner dynamics, and fantasy life. This will effectively prevent either therapists or patients from attempting to make changes in their families, friends, schools, neighborhoods, or treatment milieus. Naturally they cannot recover if their situation does not change, and so one guarantees failure while being paid to listen to interesting fantasies. Talking about dreams is a good way to pass the time, and so is experimenting with responses to different kinds of pills.

10. Avoid the poor because they will insist upon results and cannot be distracted with insightful conversations. Also avoid the schizophrenic unless he is well drugged and securely locked up in a psychiatric penitentiary. If a therapist deals with a schizophrenic at the interface of family and society, both therapist and patient risk recovery.

11. A continuing refusal to define the goals of therapy is essential. If a therapist sets goals, someone is likely to raise a question whether they have been achieved. At that point the idea of evaluating results arises in its most virulent form. If it becomes necessary to define a goal, the phrasing should be unclear, ambiguous and so esoteric that anyone who thinks about determining if the goal has been achieved will lose heart and turn to a less confused field of endeavor, like existentialism.

12. Finally, it cannot be emphasized enough that it is absolutely necessary to avoid evaluating the results of therapy. If outcome is examined, there is a natural tendency for people not fully trained to discard approaches which are not effective and to elaborate those which are. Only by keeping results a mystery and

avoiding any systematic follow-up of patients can one insure that therapeutic technique will not improve and the writings of the past will not be questioned. To be human is to err, and inevitably a few deviant individuals in the profession will attempt evaluation studies. They should be promptly condemned and their character questioned. Such people should be called superficial in their understanding of what therapy really is, oversimple in their emphasis upon symptoms rather than depth personality problems, and artificial in their approach to human life. Routinely they should be eliminated from respectable institutions and cut off from research funds. As a last resort they can be put in psychoanalytic treatment or shot.

This program of twelve steps to failure—sometimes called the daily dozen of the clinical field—is obviously not beyond the skill of the average well-trained psychotherapist. Nor would putting this program more fully into action require any major changes in the clinical ideology or practice taught in our better universities. The program would be helped if there was a positive term to describe it, and the word "dynamic" is recommended because it has a swinging sound which should appeal to the younger generation. The program could be called therapy which expresses the basic principles of *Dynamic Psychiatry, Dynamic Psychology,* and *Dynamic Social Work.* On the wall of every institute training therapists there can be a motto known as *The Five B's Which Guarantee Dynamic Failure:*

> Be Passive
> Be Inactive
> Be Reflective
> Be Silent
> Beware

Chapter 9

A FRAMEWORK FOR THE ANALYSIS AND COMPARISON OF CLINICAL THEORIES OF INDUCED CHANGE

JOEL FISCHER

IN THE PROCESS of knowledge-building for social work, one of the profession's great strengths and one of its most serious weaknesses lies in its "integrative" nature: the tendency to select from other areas knowledge appropriate for the practice of social work. The strength of this orientation is the potential flexibility such selection allows our profession; unattached as we hypothetically are to a specific professional theory, we are free to seek out and utilize from other disciplines whatever may be efficacious in work with our clients. The flaw in the process, though, lies in the paucity of available material that can serve as a reasoned guide for the study and selection of material from sources external to the profession. We therefore tend to be rather haphazard in our choices, and, as the periodic upheavals in the state of both our knowledge and our practice might well testify, frequently fail to evaluate critically what we do select, often to the detriment of our client populations.

The purpose of this paper is to propose a framework for the analysis of clinical theories of induced change—that is, theories of therapy*—in an effort to help correct what has been essentially a dysfunctional position for the profession. The framework is focused on clinical change theories for three reasons. First, a considerable portion of the curriculum in most schools of social work is structured around education in the theories and practice of in-

Note: Reprinted from *Social Service Review, 45:* 1971. Copyright 1971, University of Chicago Press.

*For definitions and a discussion of the distinction between theories of induced change and other related theories (for example, personality theories), see Fischer.[2]

tervention with individuals, families, and small groups (for example, the "methods" as opposed to the human-behavior courses), and a substantial part of our knowledge base is similarly concerned. Second, most social work practitioners are employed in agencies whose primary function is the provision of such direct services. Third, there is a dearth of readily accessible analytic material, particularly with a social work emphasis, dealing directly with clinical theories of induced change. This is not to say that several writers have not suggested criteria that are appropriate to the purposes intended here (see, for example, Hall and Lindzey,[5] Ford and Urban,[3] Thomas,[13] Briar[1]); in fact, some of the applicable material, particularly from the prototypic work of Ford and Urban,[3] has been modified for inclusion in this framework. Rather, the point is that much of this work has utilized assessment criteria that are either too gross to provide guidelines for detailed, intensive analysis of theoretical material, or that basically tend to be focused on areas of knowledge other than clinical theories.

The goals of development of this framework are twofold:

1. It can serve as a guide in the study of clinical theories by pointing out some of the significant questions that a clinical theory might address. Thus, some of the uncertainty and confusion that might confront a reader of many of the complex theories of therapy can be minimized, and some of the superfluous theoretical material bypassed.

2. Based on the way in which a theory is constructed around these dimensions, and the way it does or does not address the criteria—which is the substance of the analysis—an evaluation of the theory can take place: a judgment about the value of a given theory (or aspects of a theory) for the practice of social work.

There are two basic approaches to studying theory. The first is to step within the boundaries of the theory itself, learn what the theorist has to say, and then accept or reject it on the basis of ambiguous, poorly defined, or (as often happens) no criteria. This might be called the descriptive method since the reader, after considerable study, is generally prepared only to describe what the theory states. The second approach involves the development of a number of criteria—external to any specific theory—which a theory should or could address or around which it is constructed, and then stepping outside the boundaries of the theory to this external frame of reference and assessing the theory against those criteria. This is the analytic orientation, the frame of reference utilized here. The most important advantages this orientation offers lie in its utilization of standardized guidelines for studying diverse theories, and, although some bias is inevitably present, in its objectivity. That is, every theory is evaluated against the same criteria.

There are five basic areas in which clinical theories can be analyzed: (a) structural characteristics; (b) characteristics as a theory of therapy; (c) empirical status; (d) assumptions about the nature of man and moral implications; and, as a summary device, (e) applicability for social work.* Each of these five categories has numerous subclassifications. The extent to which the various theories address each of these criteria varies considerably. But, in this, of course, lies the analysis.

STRUCTURAL CHARACTERISTICS

In the most general sense, a theory is any more or less formalized explanatory conceptualization of the relationship of variables. The "basic building blocks" of theory construction are the concepts, generalized class names representing certain abstracted properties of the class.[7] Propositions are statements about relationships between concepts (formal) and/or observable events (empirical). All theories can be analyzed along several dimensions of their logical structure (that is, in addition to the actual content of the theory).† Of major significance for the nature of the construction of a theory is the extent to which it varies along the dimension of formality-informality. Formal theories are tightly organized, deductive systems arranged in a consistent, interdependent whole. Informal theories, on the other hand, tend to be

---

*With minor modifications, this framework is also applicable to the evaluation of selected social work approaches, such as contained in Roberts and Nee (8).

†For more extensive discussions of the structural dimensions of theories, see Hall and Lindzey,[5] chapter 1; Marx[7]; Ford and Urban,[3] section I; and Rychlak.[11]

inductive, loosely organized collections of empirical propositions. The formality or informality of a theory is generally related to the theorist's preference for nomothetic or idiographic study. The nomothetic focus of a theory refers to a concern with general statements applicable to several members of a given class, while an idiographic focus refers to the intensive study of an individual subject (see, for example, Skinner[12]) with all the potential concomitant law-making limitations this entails.

Since a major goal of theory development is the explanation of selected phenomena—in this case, the principles and procedures of therapeutic behavior change—an important analytic criterion is explanatory ability. The theory must facilitate understanding of the dimensions it seeks to explain, based on a clear and logical ordering of pertinent knowledge and clarification of the relationships between relevant variables. The theory, in other words, should prevent "the observer from being dazzled by the full-blown complexity of natural or complex events."[5:14] Many theories, though, tend to reductionistic explanations, wherein higher-level phenomena are explained at lower, more basic levels of analysis, which lead in the extreme to oversimplification. All theories are also to some extent deterministic; that is, they seek to establish causal relationships. But in the extreme—for example, Freud's psychic determinism—meaning is attributed to all behavior. That is, every form of behavior is assumed to have an antecedent condition which, somehow, can be ascertained. Finally, theories can also be more or less comprehensive, dependent upon the range of phenomena which they purport to explain. For example, Freud's theory of personality attends to a wide range of developmental phenomena, but his theory of therapy is far more circumscribed, as it deals with only limited client groups, diagnostic categories, and technical interventions.*

Theories, and particularly the concepts of which they are constructed, can be analyzed as to their level of abstraction, from concrete (molecular) to molar. The kinds, variety, and amounts

---

*Throughout this paper, the work of Freud, Rogers, and Wolpe is used for illustrative purposes. These three approaches were selected because each represents a major and distinct thrust in the clinical field.

of events to which they refer are functions of their complexity. While the more abstract theory, of course, can be more inclusive, it can also fall prey to a lack of clarity and explicitness, and thus produce confusion and conceptual muddiness. The concepts and propositions should be logically related and also clearly formulated in relation to the areas of central concern to the theory. The assumptions should be clear and germane to the context of the theory. In essence, theories must be internally consistent. A related hazard is the possibility of reification of concepts, wherein concepts are treated less as abstractions and more as actual entities in themselves (for example, "her ego is weak").

A most critical function of theory lies in its potential for generating predictions, for establishing knowledge about the nature of B, given the characteristics of A. This directly utilitarian aspect of theory is a function not only of the construction of its propositions as testable hypotheses, but of the operationalization of its concepts. The concepts used in a theory must be tied to empirical referents so that major elements of the theory are measureable and confirmable or disconfirmable. If its major concepts are not accessible to operationalization, not only is the theory untestable, and hence minimally useful in facilitating empirical investigation, but lack of identifiable referents will lead different observers to make different interpretations and observations based on the theory. Thus, the explanatory and clarifying ability of the theory will also be greatly diminished. Measurement problems, of course, are minimized if the emphasis in the theory is on utilization of concepts that are focused on observable phenomena, rather than on the use of inferential constructs, which are unobservable and difficult to operationalize.

A major function of a theory lies in its ability to stimulate related study, generate empirical research, and add to the development of a body of knowledge which, both quantitatively and qualitatively, produces a range of scholarly endeavors. Similarly, a theory must be flexible, able to stand the test of a range of empirical findings and incorporate them within its domain. This does not mean that a theory must explain everything, but an adequate theory should be adaptable to the results of empirical research focused on the area of concern to the theory. Moreover, a theory has more utilitarian value if it is somewhat congruent with other theories in the same area. Finally, a traditional principle of science has dealt with theoretical parsimony—the notion that, when two theories arrive at similar explanations, it is wiser to accept the simpler of the alternative explanations.

CHARACTERISTICS AS A THEORY OF THERAPY

The heart of the assessment of a clinical theory—and the aspect of the analysis differentiating it from other types of theories —lies in careful examination of its specific characteristics as a theory of therapy, that is, what the position of the theory is along several content dimensions. A theory of therapy, as an interrelated system intended to explain diverse phenomena of the therapeutic endeavor, can in fact be identified by an enumeration of those dimensions. Its utilitarian value can best be assessed by the manner in which it addresses those criteria. This assessment, however, consists of more than a mere description of what a theorist might say; it calls in addition for a careful, critical examination of both explicit and implicit characteristics of the theory, watching for the possibility of propositional contradictions embedded in the theory. For example, a theorist may state that, in his system, the client determines the goals, but careful reading of the theory may reveal that the theorist has already made a priori determinations of the nature of most or all psychosocial disorders and the necessary forms of treatment for those disorders. In other words, the major decisions may have been made even before meeting a given client, thus eliminating any realistic potential for setting of goals by the client.*

Given the focus on theories of therapeutic change, it is nevertheless helpful, but not always necessary, if a theory articulates with both a theory of normal development and a theory of behavior disorder. The degree of necessity for this articulation is decreased when the theorist suggests that behavior change can be

---

*The distinction, perhaps, is between paying lip service to what might be a particular value (the client determines his own goals), and the assumptions and actual content of the theory.

carried out without knowledge of antecedent conditions, that is, when the method of changing behavior is independent of the acquisition of that behavior.† Freud's theory of therapy, for example, is deeply rooted in his theories of normal and abnormal development; it is practically impossible to proceed in Freudian psychoanalysis without careful examination of developmental features. On the other hand, the behavior therapy of Joseph Wolpe[16] is only tenuously connected to developmental theory, and, in fact, the therapist may implement change procedures without knowledge of the developmental history of an individual.

A theory of induced change should indentify the client unit of concern, that is, whether, based on the theory, a therapist is equipped to deal with an individual client, a family, a group, or a combination of the three units. A critical function of a theory of therapy is a careful detailing of the behavior (broadly defined[3]) to which a therapist should attend. This means that the theory should specify not only the kinds of problems that should be included as objects of therapeutic attention, but also those that should be excluded. For example, a "symptom" might be seen only as a derivative phenomenon (Freud) or as an important focus of therapeutic effort (Wolpe). Further, a theory of therapy should define the superordinate goals of the system, so that the reader will be clear, not only about the behavior to be focused upon, but to what the behavior will be changed. Therapeutic systems also vary in their emphasis on specification of objectives. Not only is there probably an inverse relationship between the generality of such statements and their utility, but the greater the degree of specification of outcome statements, the more likely it is that specific and precise therapeutic operations will arise.[3]

Related, of course, to statements about the goals of the system are questions about who should select the goals. A theory might state that the client sets the goals, that the therapist (by way of his theory) sets the goals, or some combination of the two. Whichever way the theorist presents his case, it should be clear and congruent with both the assumptions and the remainder of the

---

†For a discussion of the potential independence of theories of change, see Fischer.[2]
The opposing point of view is presented in Ford and Urban[3]

content of the theory. Some systems also place heavy emphasis on careful assessment of the client's problems and situation, resulting in a "differential diagnosis." This process is important, not only as an individualizing procedure, but as a way of organizing the pertinent facts. However, unless there is a direct relationship between assessment and treatment, the value of any diagnostic procedure is minimal. For a system such as Wolpe's, careful assessment is particularly important since it suggests which one of several available intervention procedures should be implemented. On the other hand, Rogers[9] dispenses with diagnosis altogether, since it is philosophically and ethically objectionable to Rogers, who views objective diagnosis by an outside observer (the therapist) as practically impossible, and who espouses essentially one form of treatment for all problems anyway.

There are multiple focal points for intervention which could be emphasized by a theory of therapy. A theory might focus its treatment on phenomena occurring in the present or those occurring in the past. Similarly, a theory might place emphasis on interpersonal or intrapsychic behavior. Closely related to the above, a theory might emphasize change of observable behavior as a primary therapeutic objective, or be more concerned with the client's achieving some form of self-understanding or insight. Actually, many of these dimensions might be combined in a given system, and there is considerable blurring of the fine lines between the two extremes of each bipolar dimension. Nevertheless, for purposes of discussion, it might be assumed that such "ideal types" as a "present-interpersonal-observable behavior" constellation or a "past-intrapsychic-insight" emphasis could exist. Clearly, then, each feature or set of features would require a different perspective from client and therapist, since each set involves important implications regarding the assumptions of the theory, as well as the process of intervention itself. Summarily, the former constellation (or elements of it) not only could lead to more tangible and accessible intervention procedures (for example, focus on communication or on altering environmental contingencies), but would allow more direct measurement of outcome. The latter constellation, on the other hand, would require a process of intervention designed to tap phenomena which appear to be less accessible for manipulation (for example, emphasis on history-taking and on reordering and rethinking past experiences) , and the measurement of therapeutic success or failure would be more difficult.

The heart of a theory of therapy lies in four types of statements: (a) principles regarding extinguishing unwanted (or dysfunctional) behavior; (b) specification of procedures and techniques for extinguishing unwanted behavior; (c) principles regarding the development of new behavior; and (d) specification of procedures and techniques dealing with the production of new behavior. Two basic distinctions are involved: the first between "principles" and "procedures," the second between eliminating unwanted behavior and developing new behavior.

Principles of behavior change are propositions stating how and why problematic behavior may be altered. Statement of these principles generally is a precondition for a discussion of therapeutic techniques, which are the procedures utilized to implement the change principles. The techniques consist of a set of conditions that can be varied by the therapist;[3] a clear statement of therapeutic procedures is the crux of the therapeutic system, as it details what it is that the therapist has to do in order to produce changes in the client's behavior. As an example of the preceding material, Wolpe's principle of reciprocal inhibition is a principle by which behavior change occurs; Wolpe's procedure of systematic desensitization is a technique for implementing the principle.

Wolpe's technique of systematic desensitization might also serve to illustrate the distinction between extinguishing unwanted behavior and developing new behavior. Systematic desensitization is a procedure primarily concerned with eliminating maladaptive behavior. To induce development of new behavior, Wolpe might call on other procedures, such as behavior rehearsal.[16] This distinction is crucial; too often, theorists develop material dealing only with principles and procedures for eliminating behavior; for the adherent to such a theory who is faced with a client in need of new forms of functional behavior, only one-half of the job of therapy would be possible within the confines of such a theory. A related concern is the necessity for development of principles and procedures for transfer of change from the therapy situation to the extratherapy milieu. The ultimate goal of all theories of therapy is to produce lasting changes in the client's real-life situation. The therapist cannot always rely on automatic carry-over of in-therapy changes to the client's external situation; a whole new set of procedures may be called for. At the least, the theorist should attend to this issue and offer a discussion of how his therapy proposes to handle it.

Some theories of therapy are limited in their development of a range of procedures for changing behavior. For example, Rogers utilizes, in large part, only one type of interview procedure, of a reflective mode.[9] Other systems, for example Wolpe's,[16] have, in addition to verbal interventions, considerable technical diversity, differentially applied based on assessment of the client's problems. Some systems emphasize a systematic approach by the therapist, wherein each stage of therapy is carefully planned, objectives are determined, and specific programs are implemented and evaluated. A critical analytic criterion for social work is whether or not the theory makes provision for an environmental approach to behavior change. If, for example, the theory assumes that the source of the problem is internal and that treatment must of necessity deal with the client's reworking of his own experience, provision for "environmental manipulation," or some form of rearranging of environmental elicitors or maintainers of dysfunctional behavior, is less likely to occur. Finally, given the emphasis on delineating the functions of the therapist, a theory should also address the question of specification of in-treatment client behaviors, of what a client should do and/or talk about in therapy. Some theories also allow the therapist to explain his principles and procedures to the client, thus facilitating client understanding of the program and, presumably, facilitating client cooperation as well.

Theories of therapy vary considerably in the emphasis placed on the planned use of relationship, that is, in statements detailing how the therapist is to utilize the constellation of factors generally thought of as composing "the relationship" (for example, warmth, acceptance, genuineness, etc.). Similarly, there can be considerable variation in theorists' views of the degree of structure recommended for the relationship. This may involve such dimensions as strictness-permissiveness, directiveness-nondirectiveness, and emphasis on a planned versus an unplanned approach. Furthermore, some theorists, as does Rogers, see the major source of therapeutic change in the therapist's personality (the relationship, in itself, is viewed as "curative"), whereas others, for example, most behavior therapists, emphasize technical procedures as the basic change element in therapy. Each perspective, of course, leads to a distinctly different approach to the development of therapeutic principles and procedures.

Some theories of therapy are intended to deal only with selected client groups or diagnostic categories. Hence, their applicability to a range of both clients and problems is an important analytic criterion. Thus, if the theory placed great value on the client's psychological sophistication, verbalness, and intellectual capacity or educational attainment, large categories of clients would be viewed as inaccessible to, or unsuited for, treatment. Both Freud and Wolpe, for example, also state that their systems are intended primarily for neurotic (or nonpsychotic) clients. Related to these criteria is the degree to which the theory is culturally specific. Many theorists, based on their own life experiences, intentionally or unintentionally develop approaches so that there are particular cultural groups for whom their system is most applicable. The efficiency of the treatment process—or the length of time required for successful treatment to take place—must also be considered. It appears that, if all other things, including effectiveness, are equal, "that form of treatment is best that does it least and does it fastest."[2:20] Finally, an area that most clinical theories tend to neglect is the establishment of clear criteria for termination of treatment, including statements about when the process ends, who decides, and what the basis for the decision is.

EMPIRICAL STATUS

A most important ingredient in assessing the ultimate value of a theory of therapy lies in the degree of successful empirical verification of (a) its content and (b) its effectiveness in successfully changing clients' behavior. Success is a function not only of the degree to which the concepts and propositions are constructed so as to be testable (as discussed in the section dealing with structural characteristics of theory), but of the extent to which the theorist emphasizes the necessity for empirical testing. For many years, for example, Rogers stood by the necessity for the scientific investigation of the propositions contained in his theory. But beyond this orientation (or attitude) toward the use of scientific procedures, there should be actual attempts at conducting research, and a demonstration of success in measuring aspects of the theory. In fact, each of the content criteria specified above can be examined to assess its empirical status: the degree to which research has validated the position of a particular theorist regarding each dimension. For example, Rogers and his colleagues have been able to operationalize and reliably measure the basic ingredients of Rogers's theory—the therapist's attitudinal orientation or therapeutic conditions.[10,14] Not only is such successful measurement crucial for the transmission (or teaching) of a theory; it is even more critical in the actual implementation of the theory in practice—the model is there to be followed. Of course, successful measurement of concepts and propositions then allows the examination of the relationship to outcome of the important elements of the theory, of the idea that the theorist's procedures are in fact producing the changes intended.[3]*

The issue of outcome—or success in validating effectiveness with clients—is second to none in the evaluation of a clinical theory of induced change. Presumably, a search for the most effective means of providing help to clients is the *raison d'être* for the development of a theory of therapy, and is also an important reason for undertaking an intensive review of it. Once the theorist has made clear how outcome should be determined (that is, answered the questions—what is success and how can it be assessed?[1]) and some measurable goals have been developed, the

---

*Note the work of Rogers's (10), and Truax and Carkhuff (14), studying the relationship of the therapeutic conditions to successful outcome, and Lang's review of studies of the procedure of systematic desensitization (6).

critical job of actually validating the results of therapy remains. For the student of a theory of therapy, the task is two-fold. First, to become aware of the research that examines the effectiveness with clients of a particular approach. Second, to be able to evaluate the quality of the research as well, so as not to be confused by inadequate research methodologies or incorrect interpretations of data.*

ASSUMPTIONS ABOUT THE NATURE OF MAN AND MORAL IMPLICATIONS

All theories of therapy have embedded in them a view about the nature of man, ranging from an image of man as essentially "ugly," a seething cauldron of primordial drives, to a veiw of man as a creative, self-actualizing being. Related to this view is the degree to which the theorist is optimistic about the therapy process itself. For example, Freud thought personality very difficult to modify, and the analytic process, he suggested, was an interminable one.[4] On the other hand, on the basis of the view that all behavior is learned and therefore adaptable, behavior therapists tend to view the therapy process with optimism and consider most forms of behavior modifiable. Furthermore, theorists differ with regard to their view of man as responsible. As Ford and Urban[3] note, some theorists see "man as a pilot," able to exercise control over his own behavior. Others view "man as a robot," at the mercy of either the environment or his own drives and not responsible for the direction of his behavior.

Some theorists fail to attend to the value issues which are so critical in both the theory and the practice of methods of induced change. This neglect may be due to an oversight, or a judgment that values are not appropriate areas for discussion in theories of

---

*Actually, the most useful question to ask may not always be "does a given theory 'work'" since there are so many potential intervening and confounding variables, In fact, even the demonstrated treatment success of adherents to a particular theory does not necessarily prove the efficacy of the theory. Rather, a more valuable and certainly more precise question might be: what methods, based on what theory (the relationship to outcome must be demonstrated), with what therapists, working with what clients, with what kinds of problems, in what situations, are most successful?

therapy. Other theorists devote considerable attention to such issues. Either way, a careful reading of the theory should reveal whether or not a theorist places a primary value on man's dignity and individuality, or whether such concerns are secondary to other issues. Further, analysis should reveal whether the theorist considers it important for the therapist to attempt to avoid imposing his own values on the client and, if so, how he proposes that this can be accomplished. It is clear, at any rate, that throughout the process of theorizing about and practicing therapy—from decisions about goals to implementation of procedures—value questions do exist.

Two other important assumptions of theories of therapy deal with use of the disease model and use of the medical model, two characteristics which are generally lumped together. But there seems to be some heuristic value in separating them in the analysis of a theory. The disease model, in the first place, refers to a set of assumptions about the nature of the problem (or pathology or maladaptive behavior). Behavior would be considered disturbed (or "diseased") because of some underlying cause ("the patient is sick"); symptoms are viewed as symbolic and less worthy of attention than "the basic cause," the ferreting out of which should be the "proper" focus of the therapist's efforts. The major alternative to the disease model is the "psychological" (or behavioral) model,[15] in which both adaptive and maladaptive behaviors are seen as learned through similar processes, no underlying causes (diseases) are presumed, and the focus is on overt, objectively identifiable behaviors (the "symptoms" are the problem).

The medical model, on the other hand, deals with assumptions about the nature of treatment; like the disease model, in which dysfunctional behavior is considered as analogous to a physical illness, an adherent to the medical model might proceed in treatment as would a physician treating a physical illness. The therapist-doctor is considered the expert, who has the knowledge to "cure" the patient through the therapist's prescriptions for behavior change. Quasimedical terminology is utilized ("patient," "cure," "treatment"). Practice is conducted in the privacy of an office, within the context of the therapist-patient relationship, or in "consultation" with a small group, with the therapist in full control of treatment. Such an approach prevents the therapist from dealing with the social situation and working in the environment (that is, away from the client), since the theory is circumscribed to include only statements regarding behavior change accomplished through the application of techniques directly to the client (that is, in therapy); it is, in essence, the clinical approach.*

Theories of therapy can also be assessed by the degree to which an attempt is made to minimize client dependency. Is a by-product of the process of therapy a decrease in the competence and decision-making ability of the client, based on enforced dependency on the therapist? Or are the conditions so arranged that the client will be able to maintain some degree of independence, some sense of integrity, during the process of therapy? Related to this criterion is the importance that a theorist attributes to the client's perspective. This ranges from the client's opportunity to share in the process of goal determination to an attempt actually to "begin where the client is." Similarly, theories vary in the extent to which they maintain the client's reality orientation, ranging from an unconscious-historical-pathology focus, to a present-problem-oriented-interactional focus.

Finally, theories of therapy may be examined by considering the extent to which they permit therapist involvement. Must the therapist stay removed from the situation in a passive, neutral, "objective" posture, or does the theory make provision for an open encounter in which the therapist takes active interest in the well-being of the client? While not as clearly an ethical dimension, each theory might also be assessed by viewing its position on technical flexibility, on whether or not it emphasizes "what works." In such an approach, the therapist actively searches for procedures that will benefit the client, as opposed to placing all of his technical eggs in one basket by utilizing only one basic procedure, regardless of the problem. Theories should also make some provision for controlling for incompetent practioners, whether it be

---

*It is possible for a theory to be heavily weighted toward the medical model but not the disease model. Wolpe[16], for example, while decrying the disease model of psychopathology, quite consistently adheres to the medical model of treatment.

through training, examination, quality of past experience, or some other form of evaluative process.

APPLICABILITY FOR SOCIAL WORK

The last section of this framework deals with critieria for selecting aspects of a theory for social work. Utilization of these criteria is based on the assumption that all of the above criteria have been analyzed, that is, the selector is thoroughly knowledgeable about the theory. The first criterion has to do with whether or not the theory has relevance to the phenomena with which social work is concerned. Clearly, the profession is not interested in the adaptation of theories of physics, but is concerned with induced behavior change. If this criterion has been met, the second deals with the issue of value convergence between the theory in question and the social work profession. The profession has developed its own ethical and philosophical position, rooted in the worth and dignity of its clients; a theory of therapy whose assumptions or content contradict this position is, at best, questionable for adaptation for social work practice.

The next criterion deals with the degree of empirical validation of aspects of the theory. Of course, because of their complexity, such theories can rarely if ever be validated *in toto*. Most important, though, for a theory of therapy, is substantial empirical evidence of success in work with clients. Selection of aspects of theory must also take into account its heuristic value: the theory should serve as a tool for guiding empirical investigation, for ordering relevant knowledge, and for facilitating understanding of complex phenomena.

Adoption or use of a particular theory must mean that its principles and procedures are teachable within the social work curriculum. If, to learn a theory, the student must spend many years of preparation, or the cost of implementing training in or practice of the theory would be excessive, the theory would simply be impracticable for social work. A final dimension for assessment involves the utility of a theory, including the degree to which the crucial elements of the theory are identifiable and accessible for manipulation[13] and, of major consequence for a clinical theory, the extent to which the theory provides specific prescriptions for action. There would be little advantage in adopting a theory the major provisions of which are not available for direct action by the practitioner.

FRAMEWORK FOR ANALYSIS

As a summary device, and to aid in the utilization of this framework in the analysis of theories, all the criteria have been abstracted and included in the Appendix.

A theory—or several theories in comparison—can be rated on each criterion on a four-point scale:

1 = clear discussion of criterion; strong emphasis or high value placed by theory on criterion in question
2 = addresses criterion, but incomplete
3 = inadequately addresses criterion and/or position is highly dubious
4 = does not deal with criterion; little emphasis or value placed on criterion by theory

Thus, rating a theory "1" on any given criterion would indicate that either the theorist or the reader of the theory considers the theory to be heavily weighted on that dimension—for example, highly reductionistic (No. 5); clear specification of principles regarding extinguishing unwanted behavior (No. 35); strong emphasis on empirical testing (No. 55); or highly positive view of the nature of man (No. 60). A higher rating does not necessarily indicate that a given theory is "better" on a specific dimension than a lower rating, but differential ratings should supply information about where a particular theory stands on each dimension.

This table is not offered as a finely honed, precise scientific instrument, but as a heuristic guide to aid in the process of theory analysis. In actuality, most of the categories are not independent, and there is a clear question about the relative weighting of dimensions; some items obviously are more important than others. Nevertheless, the framework, as summarized in the table, is offered in the spirit that the use of criteria such as those proposed here will result in a more scholarly, yet, at the same time, more pragmatic approach to the assessment of relevant theories. Implicit in this view is the notion that such analysis is not a simple task, nor is it one that should be considered lightly, for the careful evaluation of available knowledge from the social and behavioral sciences has direct implications for the success or failure of work with clients.

APPENDIX
FRAMEWORK FOR ANALYSIS OF THEORIES

Item	*Theory*			
A. *Structural Characteristics*	*A*	*B*	*C*	*D*
1. Formality				
2. Informality				
3. Explanatory ability				
4. Internal consistency				
5. Reductionism				
6. Determinism				
7. Comprehensiveness				
8. Level of abstraction				
9. Clarity				
10. Explicitness				
11. Reification of concepts				
12. Capacity to generate predictions				
13. Construction of propositions as testable hypotheses ..				
14. Operationalization of concepts				
15. Focus on observables				
16. Stimulation of related study				
17. Flexibility				
18. Congruence with other theories				
19. Degree of parsimony				
B. *Characteristics as a Theory of Therapy*				
20. Articulation with theory of normal development				
21. Articulation with theory of behavior disorder				
22. Dependence on knowledge of antecedent conditions				
23. Identification of client-unit				
24. Detailing of behaviors to which therapist should attend				
25. Delineation of goals of the theory				
26. Emphasis on specification of objectives				
27. Description of who should set goals				
28. Use of differential assessment				

Theory

	A	B	C	D
29. Relationship between assessment and treatment				
30. Focus on the present				
31. Emphasis on interpersonal behavior				
32. Emphasis on intrapsychic behavior				
33. Emphasis on change of observable behavior				
34. Emphasis on self-understanding ....:......				
35. Specification of principles' regarding extinguishing unwanted behavior				
36. Specification of techniques (re: 35)				
37. Specification of principles regarding development of new behavior				
38. Specification of techniques (re: 37)				
39. Specification of principles for transfer of change				
40. Specification of techniques (re: 39)				
41. Range of procedures for changing behavior				
42. Emphasis on systematic approach by therapist				
43. Provision for environmental approach				
44. Specification of in-treatment client behaviors				
45. Facilitation of client understanding of program				
46. Planned use of relationship				
47. Degree of structure in relationship				
48. Source of change in therapist's personality				
49. Source of change in technical procedures				
50. Applicability to range of clients				
51. Applicability to range of problems				
52. Degree of cultural specificity				
53. Efficiency				
54. Specification of criteria for termination				
C. Empirical Status				
55. Emphasis on empirical testing				
56. Success in measuring aspects of theory				
57. Clarity about how outcome should be determined ...				
58. Relationship to outcome of elements of theory				
59. Success in validating effectiveness				
D. Assumptions and Moral Implications				
60. Positive view of nature of man				
61. Optimism about therapy process				
62. View of man as responsible				
63. Attention to value issues				
64. Primary value on man's dignity and individuality ..				
65. Attempt to avoid imposition of therapist's values on client				

Appendix *(continued)*

	A	B	C	D
	Theory			
66. Use of disease model				
67. Use of psychological model				
68. Use of medical model				
69. Attempt to minimize client dependency				
70. Importance of client's perspective				
71. Maintenance of reality orientation				
72. Emphasis on therapist involvement				
73. Emphasis on what works				
74. Attempt to control for incompetent practitioners				

E. *Applicability for Social Work*

	A	B	C	D
75. Relevance to phenomena of concern				
76. Value convergence				
77. Degree of empirical validation				
78. Heuristic value				
79. Teachability				
80. Utility				

REFERENCES

1. Briar, Scott: Analysis of intervention theories. Mimeographed. Berkeley, University of California, 1967.
2. Fischer, Joel: *An Eclectic Approch to Social Casework.* In press.
3. Ford, Donald, and Urban, Hugh: *Systems of Psychotherapy.* New York, Wiley, 1963.
4. Freud, Sigmund: Analysis terminable and interminable." *Collected Papers,* Vol. V. Translated by Joan Riviere. London, Hogarth, 1950.
5. Hall, Calvin and Lindzey, Gardner: *Theories of Personality.* New York, Wiley, 1957.
6. Lang, Peter: The mechanisms of desensitization and the laboratory study of human fear. In Franks, Cyril (Ed.) : *Behavior Therapy: Appraisal and Status.* New York, McGraw-Hill, 1969, pp. 160-91.
7. Marx, Melvin: The general nature of theory construction. In Marx. Melvin (Ed.): *Theories in Contemporary Psychology.* New York, Macmillan, 1963, pp. 4-16.
8. Roberts, Robert W. and Nee, Robert (Eds.) : *Theories of Social Casework.* Chicago, University of Chicago Press, 1970.
9. Rogers, Carl: A theory of therapy, personality and interpersonal relationships as developed in the client-centered framework. In Koch, S. (Ed.) : *Psychology: A Study of a Science.* New York, McGraw-Hill, 1959, Vol. II.

10. Rogers, Carl *et al.*: *The Therapeutic Relationship and Its Impact: A Study of Psychotherapy with Schizophrenics.* Madison, University of Wisconsin Press, 1967.
11. Rychlak, Joseph: *A Philosophy of Science for Personality Theory.* New York, Houghton Mifflin, 1968.
12. Skinner, B. F.: A case history in scientific method. *Am Psychol, 11*:221-33, 1956.
13. Thomas, Edwin: Selecting knowledge from behavioral science. In *Building Social Work Knowledge.* New York, National Association of Social Workers, 1964, pp. 38-48.
14. Truax, Charles and Carkhuff, Robert: *Toward Effective Counseling and Psychotherapy.* Chicago, Aldine, 1967.
15. Ullman, Leonard and Krasner, Leonard: *A Psychological Approach to Abnormal Behavior.* Englewood Cliffs, N.J., Prentice-Hall, 1969.
16. Wolpe, Joseph: *The Practice of Behavior Therapy.* New York, Pergamon, 1969.

D. SERVICE DELIVERY

Chapter 10

IN SICKNESS AND IN HEALTH

WILLIAM SCHOFIELD

MENTAL ILLNESS, UNHAPPINESS, AND PHILOSOPHICAL NEUROSIS

THERE IS A BLURRING of distinction between and confusion about the concepts of mental illness and of unhappiness. This problem is crucial to the socially effective functioning of our mental health facilities. At heart it is a definitional problem, or, perhaps, a taxonomic one. But it is a peculiarly difficult problem because of the complexity of the variables entailed in the appraisal of an individual's mental or emotional status. It is a problem because of the unsatisfactory, abstract, contradictory, and nonoperational definitions with which we presently have to work in deciding that a candidate for psychological or psychotherapeutic assistance is a bona fide patient (Schofield, 1964).

Historically, the past one hundred years has witnessed a movement away from a severely restricted and extremely crude definition of insanity to our present situation in which we struggle with unduly comprehensive and inadequately differential definitions. There is current philosophical controversy that is direct witness to the problem. On the one hand, we have the application of the concept of mental illness as a blanket rubric to cover the complete range of all behavioral, psychological, and emotional disorders. On the other hand, we have the position that mental illness is, in fact, a myth and that we violate reality when we seek to work within the framework of such a concept (Szasz, 1961). At one extreme we have the employee with a record of chronic tardiness viewed as mentally ill, and at the other extreme we have the full

Note: Reprinted from *Community Mental Health Journal,* 2:244-251, 1966. A version of this paper was given as an invited address at the annual meeting of the Wisconsin Association of Mental Health Clinics, June, 1965.

blown schizophrenic viewed as simply a nonconformer to social expectations.

Social institutions that have been created, after much effort and historical struggle, to provide the best possible treatment to those of our citizens who are psychologically ill, should be enabled to function with maximum efficiency. Mental health clinics should be able to render the most effective treatment possible in the shortest possible time to the largest number of those truly in need. We should also be concerned with the manpower problem, and with the fact that, as presently defined and accepted, the demands upon our facilities greatly exceed our personal resources.

It is my thesis that *part* of the supply-demand problem rests upon the fact that we are presently neither oriented sufficiently nor equipped in terms of reasonable standards to distinguish properly between those applicants to our services who are legitimate candidates for our therapeutic resources and those who are not. Further, a matrix of social and professional forces, broadly subsumed under the mental health movement, has encouraged the public to share in our professional confusion as to what is and what is not mental illness, and our confusion as to what is treatable, and by what means. The reality of our present social structure and the world in which we live is such that for many thousands of persons the conditions of life are far from optimal. Large numbers of our citizens suffer deprivations and stresses which would not be present in the ideal future society toward which we all strive. However, they are a hard fact of our present forms of existence and are not subject to significant alteration through the expert administration of psychiatrists, psychologists or social workers. In brief, there is a phenomenon such as unhappiness and it is not a form of mental illness.

The nature of the world and the facts of individual circumstance, one might say the fortunes of birth, deal very unkindly with many people. All of these people are in need of help and many of them need to be personally comforted. Frequently they are in need of emotional support. Sometimes they are in need of inspiration. They are always in need of a philosophy of life that enables them to live as they must, to struggle however they may toward something better, without becoming bitter, despondent, depressed, or defeated. The proper assistance of persons with whom life has dealt cruelly, and whose complaint (when they do complain—and not all of them do!) is that they are unhappy—the proper assistance for these persons is not, to my mind, appropriate to the expensive, specialized psychotherapeutic technique of the mental health clinic.

The existence of clear reality factors contributing to stress is not a sufficient basis on which to withhold the service of mental health personnel. But, the extent and nature of the reality factors must be carefully evaluated. In those instances where change or amelioration appears possible through psychological intervention, the supplicant has a right to be received and assisted. However, there are many situations and many cases in which we are not empowered legally, morally, or in terms of our techniques to change the individual's life situation. He must be assisted to learn to live, to accept his role. He must not be encouraged to think that psychotherapy will make him rich or handsome or brilliant or, in the final analysis, that it will bring him luck.

It is helpful to consider the derivation of the term happiness. It derives from the Middle English word "hap" which means chance, fortune, luck, or lot. And it has come to mean, of course, good fortune or good luck. There are many unlucky people in the world. There are many whose chances not only have been poor but have been restricted. The mental health profession cannot change the facts of an individual's life. Despite the growing public awareness of mental illness and of services to treat mental illness, it is fortunate that there are still large numbers of people who react to personal misfortune, to crushing personal defeats, to ineluctable conflicts and insuperable barriers by saying, "That's the way the ball bounces," or "It is God's will," or, "It could have been worse." It is ironical that many of our professional colleagues might be inclined to look upon such modes of acceptance as "hysterical" or unrealistic or involving the pathological use of denial.

On the other hand, growing numbers of people react to the pressing, distressing, thwarting aspects of their lives by saying,

"Why me?" and when they say, "Why me?" they imply "It is not fair . . . that my husband had a stroke . . . that my mother had cancer . . . that my daughter is illegitimately pregnant."

In our present culture, such persons frequently go to psychiatrists, psychologists, or social workers and ask an implied question, "Why did it happen to me?" These individuals may very likely be accepted for psychotherapy. Initially there may be an aura of despondency or they may appear to be depressed. But eventually, with growing clinical awareness, or earlier *with careful evaluation,* it may be determined that they are not in fact emotionally depressed. Rather, they, are suffering a philosophical neurosis. They are immersed in asking the ultimate "whys" and they are suggesting that they cannot continue to maintain a meaningful existence unless somebody proposes to answer for them those ultimate whys. The basic question, "What is the meaning of life?" is a legitimate, fundamental query that deserves the thought and perhaps the conviction of every sensitive person. But, the absence of a finished personal answer to that question is not a sign of mental illness and the mental health expert is not legally, morally, or technically best equipped to help an individual to struggle with it. It is not clear that he is *better* equipped than any other sensitive, educated person.

COMPLAINTS: JUSTIFIED AND EXPECTANT

Applicants for the services of our mental health agencies can be separated into two large groups: those with *expectant* complaints and those with *justified* complaints. The person with a justified complaint is the victim of a condition of life which is not universal, and which is causing him pain or unhappinness. He is justified in the belief that the circumstances of his life are not ideal, that he lives in a society that is concerned for his personal welfare and that there may be places and resources to which he may look for help. His complaint is justified in a broadly social sense. While the ideal society may be one which is responsible for the individual's opportunities, and for reducing the chance restrictions of the facts of birth, it is not necessarily (and I think cannot be) ultimately responsible for the individual's happiness.

In final analysis, the individual must be free to pursue his happiness and he alone is responsible for it.

This is one of the points on which we are in trouble currently. In a variety of ways we are inappropriately, uncritically, and indirectly encouraging people to relinquish responsibility for their happiness. We are encouraging them to think that there are persons or places or procedues that can somehow fix up that part of their existence, that part of their experience that has to do with being happy or unhappy. As a matter of fact, we should all be very cognizant that there is a kind of unspoken assumption which is very basic to much of what we are trying to do—and perhaps inappropriately trying to do—in our mental health endeavors, namely, that happiness is an absolute essential, or that happiness is a prime criterion of the good life. We are trying to guarantee happiness for people. We are encouraging people to view happiness as an accomplishable goal.

The individual with an expectant complaint is like the person with a justified complaint except for the crucial difference that it is in the nature of his distress and his symptoms that *he is correct in expecting* that psychotherapy, that the skills and resources of a mental health clinic, will give him relief. The nature of the distress is such that it is appropriate for the individual to anticipate that in the psychiatrist's office, in the psychologist's office, in the social worker's office, he will get meaningful help for his problem. The problem for the mental health clinic is to make this distinction between a justified complaint and an expectant complaint. Everyone that rings the bell of the clinic has some kind of complaint. There are many people coming to our centers and clinics who are misguided, whose anticipations are inappropriate, who have very real problems—in many instances problems for which social resources exist—but the mental health center is not the place and the mental health professional is not the person optimally equipped in terms of particular skills and knowledge to render the needed assistance.

The need of the clinic to accept the patient with the expectant complaint and to refer to other resources the patient with the justified complaint is a definitional problem. It entails the defini-

tion of mental illness and mental health. We must be sensitively
familiar with the literature in which many thoughtful people
have attempted to propose rather clear, formal definitions of the
criteria and characteristics of mental health, and who have tried
to deal with the problem of defining mental illness by saying—
"*this* is mental health and if these properties are not satisfied,
then the individual is mentally ill." Difficulties entailed in that
approach are well recognized (Milbank Conference, 1953;
Jahoda, 1958).

PRIORITIES FOR PATIENT ACCEPTANCE

Much of the problem is one of deciding how far we can go in
allowing the definition of mental illness to be personal rather
than social. At this stage of our development and in light of our
limited personnel resources we should place the emphasis on a
social definition. When our resources are limited, when the demand for the services of mental health personnel are clearly in
excess of the supply, we must attend to the question of priorities.
We do this in a gross sense when we try to provide immediate
assistance to emergency cases and place some cases on a waiting
list. But are there bases on which we could establish a more refined system of priorities? Are there criteria by which we might
identify the applicant who should not be accepted for psychological help?

There are some dimensions that, contrary to the great bulk of
clinical literature, should not be accepted as a basis for this determination. A potential patient should not be rejected on the
basis of his age, his education, his verbal facility, or his occupational status. There are varieties of therapeutic conversation with
real potential to help many persons who do not present the
"YAVIS" syndrome (Schofield, 1964). Our psychotherapeutic resources should not be reserved for the client who is young, attractive, verbal, intelligent, and successful.

The first consideration should be the degree to which the individual's functioning in his various *social* roles is seriously impaired. Are the symptoms of his maladjustment reflected in his
work history? Does his neurosis manifest itself in his role as par-

ent? Is he failing or frustrated as a spouse? Is he underachieving as a student? Is he ridden by guilt feelings in relation to his responsibilities to his neighbors, his church, his community? In other words, regardless of how he *experiences* his symptoms, are they of such a nature that his psychological disturbance impinges on others? It is not sufficient that the clinic applicant be dissatisfied with one or another of his social roles in order to be assigned a top priority for assistance. His complaint must be validated by external evidence that he is in fact meeting one or more of his roles in a significantly inadequate or inefficient way. When the inadequacies of his role adjustments entail actual suffering or possibly even danger to others, then he is clearly a bona fide applicant for first consideration.

A lesser priority should be given the individual who is in general meeting his role responsibilities adequately but who is aware of some frictions or some unexploited potential and whose call for help is primarily in the context of self-improvement rather than amelioration of actual deficiency or defeat. Self-actualization and the realization by the individual of his full potential is a goal to be respected and assisted. However, the clinic, with its limited personnel and resources, should not undertake this realm of mental hygiene until it has provided fully for the maximum treatment of all cases presenting actual pathology. I say this, in part, because there cannot be a *primary* locus of mental hygiene endeavor. Prophylaxis must exist "on the street," in the school, in the factory, and in the neighborhood.

This position is in opposition to an equally well-formulated, explicit position that is part of the guiding operational philosophy of many mental health centers. Good arguments can be made for saying, with all respect for the limited potency of our therapeutic techniques and with all respect for the limitations of our personnel to treat: "We will do better to concentrate on prevention; we will do better to provide an educational and a consultative role." This is a very appealing argument and not to be rejected out of hand. However, the mental health center has to be sensitive to what its charter implies if it does not specify. Few clinics or mental health centers have been chartered in a way that permits exclusion or rather definite neglect of therapeutic responsibilities in preference for prophylaxis. This is a controversial point. There are good arguments to be made on both sides. The nature of prophylaxis being what it is, the needs being so disseminated, it is doubtful that it is justifiable at this time for the limited technical, professional skills of clinic personnel to be invested primarily in prophylaxis to the negelect of treatment.

Lowest priority, and questioned acceptability for the clinic rolls, should be given the individual who suffers primarily from disenchantment, from ennui, from the impoverishment of his social relationships, from what is popularly called alienation or loss of meaning. When existence is threatened globally and catastrophically, as it has been for almost the last generation, the enduring bases of man's faith is shaken. If the orthodoxy of established religions no longer fits the spiritual needs of many modern men it does not mean that this need does not persist. Man is a spiritual animal. There must be a philosophy of life. But the pursuit and development of that philosophy is inevitably the responsibility and the great privilege of the individual. Again, in our well—intentioned desire to assist individuals we may frequently overextend the area of our justified responsibility in trying to give, literally, a philosophy of life—not recognizing that we are doing this. In searching for meaning there is help to be found in the counsel of wise men, in the documents of the ages, and in the simple sharing of the experiences of one's friends. But, it is doubtful that psychiatry or psychology have the substantive basis to offer the rationale of a way of life—in final analysis, the only or best system of ultimate values.

Members of the mental health professions should not expend their time and energies as ministers to the spiritual needs of unhappy men, to the relative neglect of their expert treatment of specific psychological and emotional problems. Some psychotherapists are indeed wise men, but there are larger numbers of wise men to be found throughout the community and the spiritually empty person must be directed to them. It is a presumptuous folly for the mental health clinic to tacitly operate as if it were the 20th century equivalent of the church, or in less institutional terms, the best home for the spiritual community.

It is obvious from the above that the appraisal of the potential client must carefully attend to the question of the extent and nature of reality factors contributing to the request for help. Furthermore, it is important to evaluate the resources and assets of the individual's life situation. The goal is to avoid the undertaking of treatment of conditions which are untreatable. The goal also is to avoid the overtreatment of conditions that can be responsive to less extended and less intensive endeavors. The goal is to adequately evaluate and respect the potentially therapeutic resources in the patient's life space. The need is to recognize that a severe neurotic *reaction* can occur in an individual with a basically strong ego. He will need skillful psychotherapeutic assistance in achieving an emotional and intellectual assimilation of the crisis in his life, but his own recuperative potential must be neglected or pushed aside. There are individuals who desperately require and who will profit from opportunities to simply ventilate their emotions. While the mental health clinic may be an appropriate place to provide such ventilation, it is certainly not the only place nor necessarily the most appropriate place.

THE IMPLICIT CONTRACT

We are in a period in the development of our mental health programs in which we can no longer afford to ignore the problem of identifying the individual who is not an appropriate candidate for psychotherapy and also of recognizing the individual who can and will profit from brief as contrasted with long term therapy. The whole area of psychotherapy until very recently has been dominated by a theoretical orientation which has caused a widely dispersed and uncritical acceptance of the notion that the only really good therapy, the only really effective therapy is intensive and long-term. It is cheering to see signs that we are beginning to have some revolution in our thinking about the modes and morals of psychotherapy (London, 1964). We are beginning to develop techniques and philosophies of therapy that make possible a flexibility in our approach to our case loads, if we are meaningfully and critically diagnostic. There is a large literature on mental health clinics, on psychotherapy, and on the research endeavors of psychologists to predict which patients will stay in therapy longest rather than which patients will achieve maximum gain by particular psychotherapy. One looks in vain for specifications for those characteristics and facts that identify the nonlegitimate client with a justified but nonexpectant complaint. It appears that our clinics may be operating in an implicit or covert contract with their clientele. This would be best expressed in a paraphrase of the familiar marriage oath: "We, X mental center, take this applicant, Y, to be our lawful wedded patient, to have and to hold, in sickness and in health, until death shall so do us part." If the patient is willing, the clinic is always willing. If the marriage occurs— and there is so far no provision of a parental supervision to evaluate the question "Is this a good and appropriate marriage"—if the marriage occurs, then divorce or separation whenever it transpires is most frequently at the initiative of the client and rarely at the initiative of the clinic. Most generally, the clinic attitude is that such divorces are bad.

The bias toward retention of patients is illustrated by a paper which deals with the importance of appraising the client's social context so as to appraise the likelihood of the patient's remaining or not remaining in treatment (Mayer and Rosenblatt, 1964). In the introduction to this paper, studies of the Family Association of America are reviewed. It is noted that 13 percent of short-term cases were closed because the client was unwilling to accept further contact, and 22 percent were the result of premature discontinuance on the part of the client. Comparable figures obtained for surveys of "short term" cases conducted in 1948 and in 1960. In commenting on these survey data, the authors write, "The dropout rate is of concern both to the mental health professions as a whole and to the various practitioners involved . . . client dropouts represent a waste of professional resources . . . Time and effort are expended upon persons who sever their ties with the helper before gains can be achieved (at least substantial ones)

. . . " What is a substantial gain, and how do we know? This is an illustration of a pervasive attitude on the part of clinics.

It is an *assumption,* not an unreasonable assumption, but an assumption. It is possible that some undetermined portion of the dropouts had benefited to a degree by their limited contact, to a degree that they feel able or willing to continue to struggle with their problems independently. It is presumptuous to assume that they are not going to be more successful than they were before they came to the clinic.

We are the victims of a variety of philosophic, theoretic and professional culture forces that lead us unwittingly into treatment where treatment is not indicated, into prolonged treatment where briefer treatment would suffice and into a relatively uniform mode of therapeutic conversation in which we are loathe to give reassurance and afraid to advise or instruct. We underestimate the therapeutic benefit from ventilation alone. We underestimated the needs of patients for simple information and for brief reassurance. We are particularly prone to overtreat the patient who is less disturbed, because he is after all a "better candidate" for psychotherapy. In so doing, we subtly encourage him to think that he is sicker than he is and to remain on the clinic rolls longer than need be.

FACTS IN SEARCH OF APPLICATION

No respectable profession allows its clients to determine unilaterally that they have a problem and that they can be helped. We in the mental health field suffer at the present time because the weight of social, cultural and historical factors has caused us to permit our clients to define their illness and that they have an illness. We must now become critical and selective especially as we must recognize the limited potency of our currently available techniques for rendering assistance and our limited resources in terms of man hours. We must recognize that propaganda effects of the mental health movement lead many persons to feel that we have a potency we do not have, while at the same time they fail to recognize resources for help in other places. In particular, we must become sensitive and responsive to the implications of the growing body of brave and pioneering research in psychotherapy. We must be more "in touch"—we must be more influenced by research findings. We are, perhaps, at a point where the primary problem is not to do research, not to collect data, not to plan studies, but to have the findings of accomplished research, the implications of things we *have discovered* effectively communicated and assimilated so that they have impact on how we operate as clinics and as individual therapists.

There are studies which have enabled us to see that "control" groups, that is to say, patients who receive periodic evaluation without any formal therapy during intervening periods, show positive changes in their status (Barron and Leary, 1955) ; studies which show that individuals who have been chronically on the rolls of outpatient clinics for months and years, do not when abruptly terminated reveal a sudden and marked exacerbation of their symptomatology (Wiener, 1959) ; and studies that show that teachers and clergy and even the greatly devalued housewife can with very conservative programs of training become effective therapeutic conversationalists (Rioch *et al.*, 1963) .

We need also to be aware of the literature that does *not* exist, the research studies that do *not* appear in our journals at the present time. As a specific example, there is an absence of data which show that if you treat symptoms and remove symptoms without affecting the presumed underlying etiology, the patient subsequently substitutes another symptom or has a recurrence of the "removed" symptom. That is a widely accepted truism in our business. "Do not treat symptoms—because you are ignoring cause, and if you simply ameliorate or remove symptoms, the patient will come back." The literature does not have good evidence that this is, in fact, so. That "truism" has been perpetrated and maintained on the basis of perhaps a half-dozen dramatic cases.

ACCOUNTABILITY

We have established the rightful and necessary place of mental health centers in the scheme of our society. For the most part we have good and improving facilities and well-trained personnel, albeit they are inadequate in numbers. We are at a point where the next significant gain will not be achieved by the establishment of new facilities or the addition of new personnel. Rather, there needs to be a conscientious attention to those questions and those kinds of data that will tell us about the efficiency with which we are carrying out our assigned task. A mental health center is in essence a psychological bank and we must now begin to become rigorous about a periodic examination of our books. We have not given this very much thought. This is in part because it is a difficult problem, but it is not insoluble. Perhaps, there is no completely satisfactory and entirely valid single index by which to measure the efficiency of a clinic's operation, but certainly there are some indices that are relevant and useful. Certainly there are indices that would permit us to know something about the variation from clinic to clinic. Why is there a relatively high rate of intake in one clinic and a relatively low rate in another clinic? Again, for example, there is an interesting paper reporting the results of a questionnaire completed by more than five hundred clinics (Kemble, 1963). The *average* clinic had 6.6 professional workers, registered 304 new cases in a calendar year, and had an interview cost index of $18.50. An individual case averaged 16.7 interviews "costing somebody $310 by the time his service was completed." Remember, when you are doing therapy in a publicly supported clinic, it is costing you because you are a taxpayer!

We must know the status of our accounts. No hospital can afford to keep a well patient in bed. No mental health center can afford to carry a person who is by any reasonable definition recovered to the level that can be reasonably anticipated. In particular, no responsible mental health facility can accept a client whose problem is not of a nature responsive to the unique facilities and resources of the clinic. We should begin to formulate a more explicit contract with our clients. Again, paraphrasing the marriage oath, we should have something of this order, "We, X mental center, take thee, applicant Y, to be our lawful wedded patient so long as it shall be proved that you are legitimately in need of the help we can render, to have and to hold you in our therapeutic environment so long as you shall be emotionally ill, and to discharge you from our rolls at the earliest moment when it may be ascertained that you have achieved maximum benefit from our ministrations."

REFERENCES

1. Barron, F. and Leary, T. L.: Changes in psychoneurotic patients with and without psychotherapy. *J Consult Psychol, 19:*239-245, 1955.
2. Milbank Memorial Fund: Definition of a case for purposes of research in social psychiatry. In *Interrelations Between the Social Environment and Psychiatric Disorders,* Annual Conference of the Milbank Memorial Fund. New York, 1953.
3. Jahoda, Marie: *Current Concepts of Positive Mental Health.* New York, Basic Books, 1958.
4. Kemble, A.: *Operational Indices for Outpatient Psychiatric Clinics.* Psychiatric Outpatient Centers of America Press, March, 1963.
5. London, P. *The Modes and Morals of Psychotherapy.* New York, Holt, Rinehart, and Winston, 1964.
6. Mayer, J. E. and Rosenblatt, A.: The client's social context: Its effect on continuance in treatment, *Soc Casewk,* 1964.
7. Rioch, Margaret J. *et al.:* National institute of mental health pilot study in training mental health counselors. *Am J Orthopsychiat, 33:*678-689, 1963.
8. Schofield, W.: *Psychotherapy: The Purpose of Friendship.* Englewood Cliffs, N. J., Prentice-Hall, 1964.
9. Szasz, T.: *The Myth of Mental Illness: Foundations of a Theory of Personal Conduct.* New York, Hoeber-Harper, 1961.
10. Wiener, D. N.: The effect of arbitary termination on return to psychotherapy. *J Clin Psychol, 15:*335-338, 1959.

Chapter 11

MENTAL HEALTH SERVICES AND THE POOR

CHARLES HERSCH

Two great and increasingly intertwined upheavals are at present underway. One of these is within the body of the orthopsychiatric professions, the other within society at large.

In independent papers by Hobbs and by Bellak, the upheaval in the professions has been granted the status of a revolution.[3,21] Both these writers agree that the first revolution in mental health was the introduction of a humane point of view toward the mentally ill, which is associated with the name of Pinel; that the second revolution was initiated by Freud through the establishment and development of psychoanalysis; and that the third and current revolution, while without its established hero, is the increasing orientation toward the community as the locus of professional concern. The essence for Hobbs is that "... *the concepts of public health have finally penetrated the field of mental health*" (p. 823).[21] For Bellak, the heart of the matter is "... *the resolve to view the individual's psychiatric problems within the frame of reference of the community and vice versa*" (p. 5).[3] (The italics are theirs.)

The second upheaval, occurring within the total society, derives from the vast stirrings of discontent among the economically, socially, and culturally deprived. Ordinarily without political power, the hitherto silent and invisible poor have begun to find new voices. Like some massive return of the repressed, the disadvantaged portion of the population is breaking through the layers of society's awareness and making its presence known. Among the manifestations are channeled demands for adequate

Note: Abridged and reprinted from *Psychiatry*, 29:236-245, 1966 by special permission of the William Alanson White Psychiatric Foundation, Inc.

147

housing, adequate schools, the right to vote, and the right to be treated with decency and respect. But other manifestations are crime and delinquency, street violence, disrupted schooling, financial dependency—in general, the staggering statistics of psychosocial breakdown and welfare economics.

The two upheavals come together in regard to the issue of quantitatively and qualitatively improved mental-health services to the poor.[46,48] At the federal level it is the point of confluence of the community mental-health program and the antipoverty program. While the relationship of these two programs is yet to be worked out, it may be said at this point that the application of the public-health perspective is particularly suited to the mental health disabilities of the poor. The interweaving of social and community problems with individual and personal problems is nowhere more evident than among the poor.[18,49] When Conant, for example, out of his evaluation of education in the slums, warns that "we are allowing social dynamite to accumulate in our large cities" (p. 10).[7] It is difficult to separate the community aspects from the individual aspects of the problem. In large measure, this interpenetration of levels provides the framework for understanding the distress of the poor and establishes the guidelines for intervention.

In providing improved services to the poor there are some special factors that have to be considered. One of these is the magnitude of the task, for the poor have a higher rate of psychiatric and social impairment than the other classes in American society. The second factor is the challenge that mental-health services, along with other services, have disengaged themselves from the problems of the poor. The third factor is the alienation of the poor, which prevents them from utilizing available services.

MAGNITUDE

In sheer numbers, the magnitude of the overall task facing the mental-health professions is awesome. The present long waiting lists show how difficult it is even to keep up with the flow of cases that are fortunate enough to have their symptoms recognized as such and referred to an appropriate resource. In the community at large, while there may be disagreement as to the extent of distress and affliction, the available evidence indicates that it is considerable. Lapouse summarizes the prevalence surveys of the fifties:

> That decade gave birth to the Midtown study in which 80 per cent of the population was said to have mild to incapacitating "pathology-denoting" symptoms, and 25 per cent was reported to have seriously impaired mental health. The Stirling County study claimed 65 per cent of the survey population as significantly psychiatrically impaired, and 37 per cent as psychiatric cases needing treatment. The Chronic Disease Commission's study of Baltimore, found that only 10 per cent of the population had sufficient symptoms to justify a psychiatric diagnosis. And the Hunterdon County study found 18 per cent with mental disorders in the survey population (p. 140) .[32]

The percentages may vary, but it is reasonably clear that there is in the community a significant degree of unattended emotional disturbance.

Regarding children only, the situation is equally serious. At a recent conference on the planning of psychiatric services for children, the following picture was drawn:

> According to a conservative 1962 estimate, there are about 60 million children under 14 years of age, making up 30 per cent of the total population. Of these, from 2,500,000 to 4,500,000 are estimated to be in need of some kind of psychiatric services because of emotional difficulties (p. 3) .

These unhappy statistics have significance not only in regard to the impaired lives that they represent. They also reveal the discrepancy between the extent of the needs for service and the extent of services available. Of the millions of children estimated to need psychiatric help, it is unlikely that more than 10 percent receive it. One example is reported by Gordon.[16] In Middlesex County, New Jersey, a local clinic conducted a mental-health survey of all of the elementary school children. Using teacher ratings based on operational definitions of adjustment, a total of 6,267 children were rated either as poorly adjusted or very poorly adjusted. This is to be compared with the fewer than six hundred cases a year that were able to be seen by the combined public and private resources of the community. Here is one instance of what is generally true: the need for mental-health manpower far exceeds the supply. Furthermore, it is not expected that this gap will decrease in the foreseeable future; the reverse is more likely. This inability to meet mental-health needs is the foundation for the increasing swell of voices calling for more imaginative programs of intervention and more strategic deployment of personnel.[20,21,38,53]

It is not surprising that these voices are never more forceful than when they speak for the need for improved services to the poor.[15,16,33,43,51] All of the background that I have just presented is by way of highlighting the problem of magnitude as it stands in regard to the impoverished. The evidence is increasing that there is an enormous piling up of mental-health disabilities and related psychosocial disorders among the poor. Harrington states it this way: "The poor are subject to more mental illness than anyone else in the society, and their disturbances tend to be more serious than those of any other class (p. 122).[18]

Here, then, are some of the things that can be documented. The population living in poverty is large in numbers. For the children, there is inherently a greater risk of disability in their encounter with the school (pp.172-87).[9,10,26,49] For the adults, there are heightened mental-health hazards in the conditions of their work (pp. 49-56).[30] They are more vulnerable to the stresses in the circumstances of their living.[31] The personal toll wrought by poverty is reflected in the high proportion of social and psychological pathology among the poor, and in the profundity of their impairment. In short, the poverty-stricken present to the mental-health professions a task of staggering dimensions.

DISENGAGEMENT

If mental-health services were organized on a completely rational basis, linking concentration of effort to high levels of need, then the disadvantaged population would have long been a focus of attention. Yet this has not been the case. If anything, the disturbing indications are that the poor, until very recently, have been systematically deterred from obtaining the services they need.

Miller has stated this as follows:

> Insufficient attention has been paid to the poor in America. Richard Cloward has written of social work's increasing disengagement from the poor. Other professions have never engaged or insufficiently engaged themselves with the plight of the poor. Each profession and social service has to confront itself with the issue of how much existing practice is aimed at dealing with the problems of the poor as they presently exist in the United States (p. 444; 11-15) .[37,48]

William Brueckner has echoed this concern, commenting on the unfortunate magnitude of the disengagement, and on its existence even among agencies located in low socioeconomic population areas.[4]

For this disengagement, the service professions have of late been richly criticized and scolded.[16,49,51] Obviously not all of the agencies or all of the groups deserve the criticism. Yet, in the overall view, the picture is somewhat disquieting. Here, from varied sources, is what one finds. Services are not geographically situated so as to be readily available to the poor. If the poor do reach the agencies, they do not find the services they expect within a context that is meaningful to them—they are not buying what the agencies are selling, and they do not return after the early encounters. The services are structured in such a way—in terms of procedures, formalized steps, waiting periods, and the like—as to fend off the poor. If they do go through the procedures, they are more readily rejected by the agencies than are those of higher socioeconomic status—there are more breaks in contact initiated by the staffs with the poor than with the classes above them. Those who are accepted for treatment are less often given the type of treatment considered most beneficial by the professionals, treatment choice being class-bound rather than bound to diganosis. Finally, if they are given the higher-status treatment, it is by less experienced or lower-status personnel.

Within this panorama of systematic deterrence, presumably not too overdrawn, the issue of psychotherapy is particularly interesting. It is a current cliché to state that individual psychotherapy is not a suitable treatment medium for the ills of the poor. It is hard to understand on what basis of experience this cliché is gaining currency. The poor are not seen by therapists in private practice, they seldom reach the stage of therapy in clinics, and they are very rarely indeed seen by the senior personnel who would be best equipped to make the therapeutic enterprise successful. Furthermore, it is just these senior personnel who would be in a position to understand and report on whatever special factors of therapeutic technique might be involved in treating the emotional disabilities of the poor.

Without such understanding, it seems premature to disqualify the poor from this form of treatment. It may turn out that the problems are insurmountable—that the inherent structure of psychotherapy is incompatible with the personal and cultural characteristics of the poor—but at this point in time, with the experience now available, there is no way of knowing whether this is the case. Perhaps modifications of technique will be required, and this would not be surprising. Here, once again, is the necessity for some well-grounded clinical research. Finally, it may be charged that, given the current manpower shortage, advocating further interest in individual psychotherapy is ill-advised. From the overall public-health perspective this may be true. Yet it may also be true that among the poor, as among the other classes, there are psychiatrically impaired people for whom individual psychotherapy is the treatment of choice, perhaps the only treatment that would be suitable to their needs. If at this point decisions are made that result in the denial of psychotherapy to the poor, then one has to ask whether this is being done on rational grounds, or whether it is another instance of the process of disengagement.

Care must be taken not to further this process in even the most progressive steps in the planning of services. The exciting new development in the mental-health field is the concept of the comprehensive community mental-health center.[2] This type of facility is aimed at providing a range of services, offering continuity of care to the individual psychiatric patient, as well as consultative and educational programs to the rest of the community.

The plan is to provide for localization and coordination of heretofore geographically and administratively scattered services. Yet should such plans develop so as to establish a centralization of functioning within the larger community, it would create an undesirable distancing from local neighborhoods that would particularly affect the adequacy of services provided to the poor. In spite of the express mandate that such centers serve the poor, without adequate safeguards there is the danger that they also will find themselves disengaged.

What is the historical background of the disengagement from the poor? The reasons are subject for speculation.

One likely factor is that the particular plight of the poor was not adequately recognized by the mental health professions until the third revolution in psychiatry brought with it a conscious orientation toward community, social class, and demographic variables. The hard evidence that poverty is a major epidemiological factor bearing on individual and family breakdown, and that there are clear associations between poverty and a number of specific psychopathological conditions, waited for the introduction of public-health viewpoints and methodologies to be brought to the fore. Prior to that point, professional thinking was dominated by what Riessman and Miller have called the psychiatric world view, which interpreted virtually all problems, whether psychological, social, political, educational, or medical, in essentially individual, psychodynamic terms.[47] The emphasis on intrapsychic factors—which Hobbs refers to as an obsession with the world inside a man's skull[21]—provided profound insights and a firm foundation for all subsequent growth, but obscured the larger context of psychopathological development and contributed to the insufficient involvement of the orthopsychiatric disciplines with the poor.

A second reason for the disengagement seems to be that the professions, wittingly or not, have joined the rest of society in a generalized rejection of the poor. The poor have a bad reputation in society and are viewed in the mass as having a number of disagreeable characteristics (pp. 205-23).[48,51] They are said to be lazy and shiftless, to have sexual lives akin to those of animals, to be disinterested in attainment or self-improvement, to be unstable and undependable, to live in dirt and be indifferent to it, and so on down the line. Agency professionals often describe the poor as unmotivated, lacking in awareness, holding unreasonable and inappropriate expectations, blaming their problems on outside forces, incapable of insight, and untreatable. They are called multiproblem, hard-core, multigeneration, action-oriented, nonverbal, impulse-ridden, concrete, and disorganized—terms in which the language of diagnosis shades into the language of abuse. While some of these characteristics may be true for some or many of the poor, making them unsuitable candidates for what the agencies have to offer, there has been a reluctance to adapt services to persons in need who would not adapt themselves to the services that were available. One is reminded here of a main theme in the summary report of the Joint Commission—that adequate care was not provided to the mentally ill because they were rejected both by the community and by the professionals.[25] A similar circumstance appears to obtain in regard to the poor: to society they are unlovely as people, and to the agencies they are unlovely as patients. While gains have been made by the mental-health professions in the past few years in overcoming this tendency to reject the poor, it must be admitted that there is still a long way to go.

ALIENATION

The disengagement on the part of the professionals is, however, only one side of the coin. The other side is the alienation of the poor, which has hindered them from making use of the services that are available to them.

Particular characteristics accompany the status of being poor in this society at the present time. Being poor in the United States in the 1960's takes one out of the mainstream of the larger community. History is more familiar with a poverty-stricken majority, where the individual at least has the consolation of being in the same boat with most of his fellows. A poor population which is in the minority, living in the context of a society of plenty, has given rise to a new situation altogether. This is "the other America"[18] or the "culture of poverty,"[8,48] made up of people who simply do not participate in the well-being of the surrounding affluent society and for many of whom aspiration has given way to defeatism and despair. It is a culture with distinguishable value patterns that differ from those of the larger society.[50] It has distinctive patterns of family life[36,44] and parent-child interaction.[29,48] It provides processes of socialization and acculturation that—for good or evil—prepare the young for participation within the culture and thus perpetuate it.[19,28]

Riessman and others have argued that there are strengths in the culture of poverty, that the characteristics which the poor show are not simply failures in the management of life but rather are functional for survival in coping with chronic conditions of disadvantage and deprivation.[45,51] One can only agree with this point of view. However, it is a point of view that should not be romanticized or sentimentalized. There are survival and adaptation, but at a cost. Although the families with multiple impairments and no money find ways to continue to live, it is not a kind of living that most people would want to share. Sufficient antidote to any sentimentalization may be found in Pavenstedt's recent portrayal of the appalling conditions under which the children of extreme deprivation live,[42] conditions reminiscent of that most famous of disadvantaged families, the Kallikaks.[14] Pavenstedt states: "The saddest, and to us the outstanding characteristic of this group with adults and children alike, was the self-devaluation" (p. 96).[42] This self-devaluation is an important feature of the estrangement of the impoverished.

The plight of the poor today is aggravated not only by their being a minority in the society, but by certain cultural and intellectual traditions as well. Democracy does not feel comfortable with the concept of a class society and does not quickly come to grips with the issues that are implied. Although social stratification is recognized, it is emphasized that this is an open society and that the boundaries between the classes are almost totally permeable. Presumably, if there is initiative and energy, one should be able to move up the ladder with relative ease. If one does not move up, but remains in deprived straits, the lack is considered to be individual and personal. Historically, Protestantism joined hands with capitalism to link ambition, productivity, and success with ethical goodness, providing as a legacy an image of free and rugged individuals conquering the undeveloped frontier. Social Darwinism, with its doctrine of survival of the fittest, added its scientific voice, decreeing that the poor are poor as a result of their own inferiority. A second and unfortunate scientific tributary appeared in the tendency of psychodynamic psychiatry and psychology to find the causes of an individual's circumstances within himself and his personal emotional history. There is an agreement with Shakespeare that the fault ". . . is not in our stars, but in ourselves, that we are underlings." The poor, then, are seen, by themselves as well as by much of the society, as having their condition caused by some curious admixture of weakness, sinfulness, and psychopathology.

This is not to say that the poor are without their share of psychiatric and emotional problems. As has been pointed out, they have them, and in great quantity. But in organizing a program of services to the poor it is important to conceptualize two domains within which problems have their origin and expression. One is internal, intrapsychic, and within the province of dynamic psychiatry. The other is external, reality-based, and related to the fields of sociology and economics. In Harrington's words:

> The drunkenness, the unstable marriages, the violence of the other America are not simple facts about individuals. They are a description of an entire group in the society who react this way because of the conditions under which they live (p. 162) .[18]

One may think, then, of two kinds of alienation, recognizing that they may work hand in hand and combine in the distress of a given person. One is alienation from the self and the other is alienation from society. Karen Horney has described alienation from the self as one of the basic and most injurious processes characterizing the psychopathological conditions.[23,24] It refers to all those ways in which a person suppresses or eliminates essential parts of himself, loses contact with what he really feels, believes, likes, or wishes, and beomes tyrannized by what he thinks he should be rather than living according to what he actually is or might be. Horney's emphasis is on the neuroses, and her intervention of choice is psychoanalysis or psychotherapy. Alienation from society is another matter; it derives from sociologic and economic origins, and it requires interventions that bring the individual into participation within the larger community. Many of these interventions need to be at the level of community action, vocational rehabilitation, and remedial education.*

The emotionally disturbed poor, large in numbers, represent the confluence of the two forms of alienation, which in combination are transmitted with peculiar regularity over the generations. Breaking into the cycle of disability in any meaningful way requires consideration of both aspects of alienation, and the development of coordinated service programs that operate simultaneously at a number of different levels. An example would be the multiservice centers that are being developed in Boston. On a smaller scale, there is the multidimensional approach reported by Massimo and Shore, in which a single practitioner offered intensive psychotherapy, remedial education, and job placement help in a combined treatment program for adolescent delinquent boys.[34]

The consequences of alienation are very somber, whether measured in terms of personal distress, social disorder, or financial cost to the community. The estrangement can be seen in the men who seek to numb their loneliness and sense of isolation through the use of alcohol. Others forfeit their responsibilities to their families and abandon them to the welfare rolls. There are the youths who cannot understand any value in continuing their education, even if it is vocationally oriented, and become school dropouts, and others who strike out at the alien society by delinquency and by often senseless acts of destruction. There is, in short, the whole range of people who cannot find a satisfying place in the society and who cannot work out an effective life within it.

---

*Similar ideas are found in Galbraith's distinction between case poverty and insular poverty, and in Cohen's distinction between emotional deprivation and economic deprivation. See refs. 12 and 8.

Out of this comes a dilemma. The people who feel apart from the society often do not trust the agencies and organizations that society has established. To put it another way, of the people who need professional services, most either cannot or will not—in any event, they do not—voluntarily take advantage of them.

The problem was underscored in an editorial in the *New York Times* late in 1964. The editorial pointed out the difficulties that the Job Corps program of the war on poverty could be expected to face in helping youngsters become suitable candidates for employment. It cited the efforts of the local draft boards to encourage draft rejects to seek job counseling and placement at their state employment offices. Of the nearly quarter of a million young men who received letters to this effect, only a small proportion appeared for interviews, and of these only one out of six was placed, even for a few days. The editorial went on:

> It is plain from these discouraging statistics that the administrators of the anti-poverty program will have to devote much of their energy to combatting the sense of alienation that makes many of those who are most disadvantaged unwilling even to avail themselves of the opportunity for help. They have become so inured to rejection that it amounts almost to a way of life.[39]

This is the challenge that faces the orthopsychiatric professions as well. The pattern of setting up services for those who feel the need for and seek out professional assistance is not workable for the disadvantaged. Rather, coming to grips with the psychiatric problems of the poor will require the development of programs that take into consideration their sense of estrangement and alienation.

CONCLUSION

It is tempting to offer here another pious and strident exhortation to the effect that we have failed the poor and that something needs to be done. The current literature, however, is sufficiently decorated with these. Yet it is true that there are many issues concerning the mental-health problems of the poor that we have not begun to master, and others that we are only beginning to face. What can be offered here, then, is a suggestion—namely, that we will be in a more strategic position in developing intervention programs for the poor if we take into consideration some of the background factors discussed above. The problem of magnitude, for example, suggests the need to build on the lesson of medical history and seek control of pathology through prevention rather than through cure; it further suggests the wisdom of extending the reach of professional personnel through the use of volunteers and specially trained subprofessionals, and through the use of such methods as mental-health consultation. Coping with the process of disengagement will require a reexamination of our models of treatment, as well as a purposive orientation to the poor based on determined decisions throughout the administrative hierarchies. The problem of alienation can be approached by developing coordinated, multilevel services that can deal with both inner and outer reality, and by bringing these services to the poor in their own neighborhoods. Underlying all this is the requirement of a spirit of innovation, in which techniques are molded to problems rather than vice versa, and in which there is a readiness to depart from tradition if what it has to offer is unsuited to the job at hand. On foundations such as these we would be in a position to build meaningful and rational mental-health programs for the poor.

REFERENCES

1. American Psychiatric Assoc.: *Planning Psychiatric Services for Children in the Community Mental Health Program.* Washington, D.C., 1964.
2. American Psychiatric Assoc.: *The Community Mental Health Center: An Analysis of Existing Models.* Washington, D.C., 1964.
3. Bellak, L.: Community psychiatry: The third psychiatric revolution. In Bellak, L. (Ed.): *Handbook of Community Psychiatry and Community Mental Health.* New York, Grune & Stratton, 1964.
4. Brueckner, W.: Current thinking on the role of the settlement. In Spiegel, A.D. (Ed.): *The Mental Health Role of Settlement and Community Centers.* Boston, Massachusetts Department of Mental Health, 1963.
5. Cambridge Planning Board: *Social Characteristics of Cambridge.* Cambridge, Mass., 1962.
6. Chilman, C., and Sussman, M. B.: Poverty in the United States in the midsixties. *J Marriage Family, 26:*391-94, 1964.

7. Conant, J. B.: *Slums and Suburbs*. New York, Signet Books, 1964.
8. Cohen, J. Social work and the culture of poverty. *Social Work, 9*:3-11, 1964.
9. Deutsch, M. P.: The disadvantaged child and the learning process. Passow, H. (Ed.) : *Education in Depressed Areas*. New York, Columbia Univ., 1963.
10. Deutsch, M.: The role of social class in language development and cognition. *Am J Orthopsychiat, 35*:78-88, 1965.
11. Dunham, H. W.: Social class and schizophrenia. *Am J Orthopsychiatry, 34*:634-42, 1964.
12. Galbraith, J. K.: *The affluent Society*. Boston, Houghton Mifflin, 1958.
13. Glueck, S.: *The Problem of Delinquency*. Boston, Houghton Mifflin, 1959.
14. Goddard, H. H.: *The Kallikak Family*. New York, Macmillan, 1912.
15. Gordon, E. W.: Help for the disadvantaged? *Am J Orthopsychiatry, 35*: 445-48, 1965.
16. Gordon, S.: Are we seeking the right patients? Child guidance intake: The sacred cow. *Am J Orthopsychiat, 35*:131-37, 1965.
17. Haggstrom, W. C.: The power of the poor. In Riessman, F., Cohen, J. and Pearl, A. (Eds.) : *Mental Health of the Poor: New Treatment Approaches for Low Income People*. New York, Free Press, 1964.
18. Harrington, M.: *The Other America*. New York, Macmillan, 1962.
19. Hess, R. D.: Educability and rehabilitation: The future of the welfare class. *J Marriage Family, 26*:422-29, 1964.
20. Heyder, D. W.: A contribution to overcoming the problem of waiting lists. *Am J Orthopsychiatry, 35*:772-78, 1965.
21. Hobbs, N.: Mental health's third revolution. *Am J Orthopsychiatry, 34*: 822-33, 1964.
22. Hollingshead, A. B., and Redlich, F. C.: *Social Class and Mental Illness*. New York, Wiley, 1958.
23. Horney, K.: *Our Inner Conflicts: A Constructive Theory of Neurosis*. New York, Norton, 1945.
24. Horney, K.: *Neurosis and Human Growth: The Struggle Toward Self-Realization*. New York, Norton, 1950.
25. Joint Commission on Mental Illness and Health: *Action for Mental Health*. New York, Basic Books, 1961.
26. Keller, S.: The social world of the urban slum child: Some early findings. *Am J Orthopsychiatry, 33*:823-31, 1963.
27. Kennedy, J. F.: *Message from the President of the United States Relative to Mental Illness and Mental Retardation*. 88th Congress, 1st. Sess. Doc. No. 58. House of Representatives, Washington, D.C., 1963.
28. Kobrin, S.: The impact of cultural factors on selected problems of adolescent development in the middle and lower class. *Am J Orthopsychiatry, 32*:387-90, 1962.

29. Kohn, M. L.: Social class and parent-child relationships: An interpretatation. *Am J Sociol, 68:*471-80, 1963.
30. Kornhauser, A.: Toward an assessment of the mental health of factory workers: A Detroit study. In Riessman, F., Cohen, J. and Pearl, A. (Eds.) : *Mental Health of the Poor: New Treatment Approaches for Low Income People.* New York, Free Press, 1964.
31. Langner, T. S., and Michael, S. T.: Life stress and mental health. *The Midtown Manhattan Study.* New York, Free Press, 1963, vol. 2.
32. Lapouse, R.: Who is sick? *Am J Orthopsychiatry, 35:*138-44, 1965.
33. Lourie, N. V.: Impact of social change on the tasks of the mental health professions. *Am J Orthopsychiatry, 35:*41-47, 1965.
34. Massimo, J. L., and Shore, M. F.: The effectiveness of a comprehensive, vocationally oriented psychotherapeutic program for adolescent delinquent boys, *Am J Orthopsychiatry, 33:*634-42, 1963.
35. McDermott, J. F., Harrison, S. I., Schnager, J. and Wilson, P.: Social class and mental illness in children: Observations of blue-collar families. *Am J Orthopsychiatry, 35:*500-8, 1965.
36. McKinley, D. G.: *Social Class and Family Life.* New York, Free Press. 1964.
37. Miller, S. M.: Poverty and inequality in America: Implications for the social services. *Child Welfare, 42:*442-45, 1963.
38. Muhlich, D. F., Hunter, W. F., Williams, R. I., Swanson, W. G., DeBellis, E. J., and Moede, J. M.: Professional deployment in the mental health disaster: The Range mental health center. *Community Mental Health J, 1:*205-7, 1965.
39. *The New York Times.* Sunday, November 15, 1964, sect. 4, p. 8 (editorial) .
40. Pasamanick, B., and Knoblock, H.: Epidemiologic studies on the complications of pregnancy and the birth process. In Caplan, G. (Ed) : *Prevention of Mental Disorders in Children.* New York, Basic Books, 1961.
41. Pasamanick, B., Knobloch, H. and Lilienfeld, A. M.: Socioeconomic status and some precursors of neuropsychiatric disorder. *Am J Orthopsychiatry, 26:*594-601, 1956.
42. Pavenstedt, E.: A comparison of the child-rearing environment of upper-lower and very low-lower class families. *Am J Orthopsychiatry, 35:*89-98, 1965.
43. Rabinowitz, C.: Human rehabilitation in the sixties. *Am J Orthopsychiatry, 33:*589-90, 1963.
44. Rainwater, L.: Marital sexuality in four cultures of poverty. *J Marriage Family, 26:*457-66, 1964.
45. Riessman, F.: Low-income culture: The strengths of the poor. *J Marriage Family, 26:*417-21, 1964.
46. Riessman, F.: *New Approaches to Mental Health Treatment for Labor*

and Low Income Groups. New York, National Institute of Labor Education, 1964.

47. Riessman F. and Miller, S. M.: Social change versus the "psychiatric world view." *Am J Orthopsychiatry, 34*:29-38, 1964.

48. Riessman, F., Cohen, J. and Pearl, A. (Eds.): *Mental Health of the Poor: New Treatment Approaches for Low Income People,* New York, Free Press, 1964.

49. Ryan, W.: *Distress in the City: A Summary Report of the Boston Mental Health Survey.* Boston, 1964.

50. Schneiderman, L.: A study of the value-orientation preferences of chronic relief recipients. *Social Work, 9*:13-18, 1964.

51. Schneiderman, L.: Social class, diagnosis and treatment. *Am J Orthopsychiatry,* 99-105, 1965.

52. Srole, L., Langner, T. S., Michael, S. T., Opler, M. K. and Rennie, T. A. C.:*Mental Health in the Metropolis: The Midtown Manhattan Study.* New York, McGraw-Hill, 1962, vol. 1.

53. Williams, R.: Trends in community psychiatry: Indirect services and the problem of balance in mental health programs. In Bellak, L. (Ed.): *Handbook of Community Psychiatry and Community Mental Health.* New York, Grune and Stratton, 1967.

54. Witmer, H. L.: Children and poverty. *Children, 11*:207-13, 1964.

55. Wortis, H. and Freedman, A.: The contribution of social environment to the development of premature children. *Am J Orthopsychiatry, 35*: 57-68, 1965.

56. Wortis, H., Heimer, C. B., Brame, M., Redlo, M. and Rue, R.: Growing up in Brooklyn: The early history of the premature child. *Am J Orthopsychiatry, 33*:535-39, 1963.

PART I:
ADDITIONAL RECOMMENDED READINGS

1. Briar, S. and Miller, H.: *Problems and Issues in Social Casework*. New York, Columbia University Press, 1971.
2. *Building Social Work Knowledge*. New York, N.A.S.W., 1964.
3. Epstein, I.: Professional role orientation and conflict strategies. *Social Work, 15(4)*:87-92, 1970.
4. Green, H.: *I Never Promised You a Rose Garden*. New York, Holt, Rinehart & Winston, 1964.
5. Halmos, P. :*The Faith of the Counselors*. New York, Shocken Books, 1966.
6. London, P.: *Behavior Control*. New York, Harper & Row, 1969.
7. Maas, H. (Ed.): *Five Fields of Social Service*. New York, N.A.S.W., 1966.
8. Maas, H. (Ed.): *Five Fields of Social Service: A Five Year Review*. New York, N.A.S.W., 1971.
9. Mayer, J. and Timms, N.: Clash in perspective between worker and client. *Social Casework, 50*:32-40, 1969.
10. Meyer, C.: Casework in a changing society. In *Social Work Practice, 1968*. New York, Columbia University Press, 1969, pp. 3-19.
11. Miller, H.: Value dilemmas in social casework. *Social Work, 13 (1)*:27-33, 1968.
12. Reynolds, B.: *An Uncharted Journey*. New York, Citadel Press, 1963.
13. Reynolds, B.: *Social Work and Social Living*. New York, Citadel Press, 1951.
14. Richmond, M.: *What Is Social Casework?* New York, Russell Sage Foundation, 1922.
15. Roberts, R. and Nee, R.: *Theories of Social Casework*. Chicago, University of Chicago Press, 1970.
16. Siporin, M.: Social treatment: A new-old helping method. *Social Work, 15 (3)*:13-25, 1970.
17. Soyer, D.: The right to fail. *Social Work, 8:*, 1963.
18. Szasz, T.: *The Manufacture of Madness: A Comparative Study of the Inquisition and the Mental Health Movement*. New York, Harper & Row, 1970.
19. Tripodi, T. P. Fellin and H. Meyer: *The Assessment of Social Research*. Itasca, Illinois, F. E. Peacock, 1969.
20. Wasserman, H.: The professional social worker in a bureaucracy. *Social Work, 16 (1)*:89-96, 1971.

PART II
PREVENTIVE INTERVENTION

> Past sorrows, let us
> moderately lament them;
> For those to come, seek
> wisely to prevent them.
>
> —John Webster

DESPITE occasional inputs into the social work literature (e.g. Rapoport, 1961; Haselcorn, 1967), the area of prevention has received disproportionately little attention from social workers when compared to such areas as clinical practice and remediation. This is despite a large outpouring of work in other fields, particularly community mental health (Cowen, Gardner and Zax, 1967), and recommendations such as those by Smith and Hobbs (1966; adopted as a position statement by the American Psychological Association) that 50 percent of our mental health resources be expended in preventive efforts, particularly work with children.

There are some tangible reasons for this foot-dragging (see Chap. 12). A philosophical and programmatic switch to a preventive emphasis requires a major redirection of time, energy and money. A preventive practice is especially difficult to undertake since its implementation calls for the identification of many procedures which are still barely accessible for manipulation. And research evidence of successful preventive efforts is still in rather short shrift.

But there are increasing grounds for the belief that such conditions are changing. This part of the book presents some of the evidence. In order to provide an element of concreteness to this still rather amorphous area, and to present specific instances where the professional helper may in fact engage in preventive interventions, the field of prevention was subdivided for purposes of this book into two (non-exhaustive) categories: (a) early childhood; and (b) crisis (Cowen, 1967). Early childhood prevention can be further subdivided into areas dealing with prevention in the school and in the family. Thus, an early childhood approach to prevention might be viewed as a combination of attempts to deal with problems at the level of the two institutions with primary societal responsibility for child-rearing, in an effort to alleviate either individual or systematic pressures before their effects become amplified. This volume, then, contains papers dealing with both subcategories—the family and the school—of an early childhood approach to prevention.

An early childhood orientation is viewed here as complementary to an orientation toward prevention involving intervention in crisis situations (whether in childhood or adult life). And, while crisis intervention could be viewed from either a preventive or a remedial framework, crisis intervention does have major preventive implications. In fact, the goal of crisis intervention is to avoid the development of further breakdown in a given situation, and to aid clients in developing coping methods which would prevent the occurrence of similar future dysfunctional situations.

The single article in the first section, by Bower, presents a general framework for viewing the prevention of emotional and mental disorders, and includes a discussion of major factors mitigating against preventive efforts. Bower not only provides a basis for a broadened perspective on issues in the field of prevention, but also discusses specific action possibilities for a wide variety of potential interventions. Bower's article serves to bring attention to the importance of a focus in practice on populations, as opposed to the narrower, clinical, case-by-case approach. Still, within the broader population perspective, there is ample room for the individualized services of interpersonal helping, since intervention efforts include dealing both with situations and with cases. Thus, a preventive orientation has, primarily, programmatic implications, which can include planning and utilization of a wide variety of services.

The following section deals with the early childhood orientation to prevention. The first paper by Cowen and Zax presents an overview of their work in the schools. They have accumulated a body of evidence suggesting that preventive intervention can be effective, and discuss a variety of strategies for allocating resources involving both professional and nonprofessional helpers. The next paper by Tharp, Cutts and Burkholder describes a program in which a community mental health center and a school collaborated in the provision of services to children. The focus of this program was on training teachers to deal more adequately with problematic situations, and is a clear delineation of some of the principles involved using a behavioral model for such a program. The last article in this section by Zeilberger, Sampen and Sloane involves a behavioral approach to intervention in the family, specifically in the area of parent-child problems. Though not an article on prevention, per se, the implications of amelioration of parent-child problems at an early stage are obvious. It might be expected, in fact, that such amelioration will have a spiraling effect, with beneficial results not only in parent-child interaction, but observable in decreased tension and difficulties in other areas of daily living for all members of the family.

The preceding two articles, and a later paper in the section on consultation, all deal with aspects of behavior modification. They were included to illustrate two areas where behavior modification may have its greatest impact in social work—intervention in the schools and in the family. Behavior modification offers the clearest available set of principles and procedures for dealing with social-environmental change in the proximate milieu, in ways that have maximum impact with minimal disruption of either school or family life. The principles are easily learned and applied by parents and teachers, and there is no necessity that the child, or identified client, be stigmatized in a deviant role. The parents and teachers are actually the major focus of intervention; they are taught new ways of interacting with their children. Further, the method of evaluation, graphically presented through charted frequencies of maladaptive-adaptive behavior, offers evidence of effectiveness. The reader unfamiliar with basic behavioral principles might profitably read the articles in Part II after reading the more general introductory section on behavior modification in Part III of this book.

The next section deals with crisis intervention, an area of theory and practice somewhat more familiar to social workers. The first paper by Darbonne presents a succinct overview of crisis theory, research and practice. Darbonne suggests that while research is still limited, it would appear that crises are periods for maximally effective intervention into dysfunctional situations, again, not only with the idea of alleviating the current condition, but of preventing its recurrence. The next paper by Flomenhaft, Kaplan and Langsley describes one of the few outcome studies using a crisis intervention model. While this study doesn't actually isolate the variable (s) that directly leads to successful outcome, the suggestion contained therein is that intervention at points of crisis demonstrably can reduce further disruption, in this instance, the necessity for psychiatric hospitalization. This paper also contains clear descriptions of the variety of procedures used by the crisis team to intervene with both individuals and families. The final paper by Porter carries the concept of crisis further by extending its use into supervision and consultation. This paper is useful as a bridge to the final section of Part II, dealing with the use of consultation as a tool in prevention.

Berlin in the first paper on consultation discusses the role of consultation as a preventive service in the schools. Berlin integrates some of the ideas of crisis and prevention, and presents six basic steps in the consultation process. The final article by Whitley and Sulzer provides a clear demonstration of how consultation using a behavioral approach helped one teacher and one child resolve their difficulties. Whitley and Sulzer argue that this approach is one clear way in which helping professionals, performing in this instance in a consultative role, can document the value of their contributions.

Several of the papers in this Part have described programs where the major thrust of professional activity has been to provide intermediaries (or "caregivers" or "mediators") such as teachers with the basic tools necessary to deal with problematic situations in the "natural environment." The importance of intervention at this level lies in the fact that a small amount of professional helpers can geometrically increase their potential for reaching clients by carrying out programs involving the training of people who have primary responsibilities for "care-giving."

REFERENCES

1. Cowen, E.: Emergent approaches to mental health problems: An overview. In Cowen, E., Gardner, E., and Zax, M. (Eds.): *Emergent Approaches to Mental Health Problems.* New York, Appleton-Century-Crofts, 1967, pp. 389-455.
2. Cowen, E., Gardner, E., and Zax, M. (Eds.): *Emergent Approaches to Mental Health Problems.* New York, Appleton-Century-Crofts, 1967.
3. Haselcorn, F.: "An Ounce of Prevention. . ." *J Educ Social Work, 3 (2):* 61-71, 1967.
4. Rapoport, L.: The concept of prevention in social work. *Social Work,* 7-15, 1967.
5. Smith, M. B. and Hobbs, N.: The community and the community mental health center. *Am Psychol, 21:*299-309, 1966.

A. GENERAL FRAMEWORK

Chapter 12

PRIMARY PREVENTION OF MENTAL AND EMOTIONAL DISORDERS: A CONCEPTUAL FRAMEWORK AND ACTION POSSIBILITIES

ELI M. BOWER

Magic and science have had a curious and interesting alliance in the history of human societies. One specific kind of science-magic which man has developed over the years is that of word power. It is illustrated by fairy or folk tales in which discovering or using an appropriate word enables the hero or heroine to gain power over a natural, supernatural or human enemy. *Ali Baba and the Forty Thieves* and *The Story of Rumpelstiltskin,* for example, utilize such magic words to move mountains and solve a complex personal problem. Folklore and myths also exemplify the solution of a problem by abstention from or disuse of an appropriate word or name. In Grimm's *The Wild Swans,* the sister's power to help her seven brothers is gained by her ability not to utter a single word. Odysseus in his adventure with the Cyclops gains power over the giant Polyphemus by telling him his name is "Noman." When Polyphemus is attacked by Odysseus he cries out, "Noman is killing me by craft and not by main force." His brother Cyclops, somewhat dismayed, answers, "Well, if no man is using force and you are alone, there's no help for a bit of sickness when heaven sends it." Odysseus continues, "With these words away they went and my heart laughed within me to think how a mere nobody had taken them all in with my machinomanations" (p. 108) .[18]

In the twentieth century our "open sesame" to the solution of problems has been the word "prevention," which has found some

Note: Abridged and reprinted from *Am J Orthopsychiatry, 32:*832-848, 1963. Copyright 1963, the American Orthopsychiatry Association, Inc. Reproduced by permission.

of its magical fruition in many of man's relationships to viruses, bacteria and protozoans. The "magic bullet" and the newer "miracle drugs" are still part of the "abracadabra" of man's relationship to microbes. Dubos observes,

> The common use of the word "miracle" in referring to the effect of a new drug reveals that men still find it easier to believe in mysterious forces than to trust to rational processes. . . . Men want miracles as much today as in the past (p. 132) .[9]

Smallpox, however, *is* prevented by a nick on the arm and polio by several shots. The magic of prevention as a word, idea or myth remains a twentieth-century Rumpelstiltskin in all branches of man's activities, except one. Little in the way of magic words, incantations or mystical emanations exists for the prevention of the emotional and behavioral disorders of man. Indeed, one would be hard-pressed to divine the kinds of conjurations and "answers oracular" a contemporary John Wellington Wells might dream up to get the job done.

Thus it appears that the lack of creativity and action in the prevention of mental and behavioral disorders originates in forces too powerful for either magic or science. We do not need a Sherlock Holmes or an Arsène Lupin to perceive that there may be more to this conceptual and research abyss in prevention than a lack of imagination and interest. Indeed, one could make a good case for the existence of explicit and implicit cultural resistances to the prevention of emotional and behavioral disorders. Perhaps a necessary first step, then, in any preventive program is to examine the antagonism realistically, and plan strategies of action that take into account the probabilities of success in light of an understanding of the opposition.[8]

COMMUNITY ANTAGONISMS TOWARD PREVENTION

A common conception of prevention often obfuscates thinking and action, namely, that little can be accomplished short of major social overhaul. Prevention of mental and emotional disorders is seen as the exclusive result of the abolition of injustice, discrimination, economic insecurity, poverty, slums and illness. To seek less is to attempt to fell a giant sequoia with a toy axe. Any effort, therefore, that is not aimed directly at major social change is viewed as an inadequate and inconsequential attack at the problem. A corollary of this notion is that prevention involves wheels within wheels. Thus, any possible action is perceived as if it were a combined luncheon check presented by an inexperienced waiter to a group of women at the end of an *a la carte* meal. The alleged magnitude of the complexities and the ungeared wheels within wheels perceived are also major deterrents to biological and social scientists who can, with little effort, find more digestible problems to define and solve. Other scientists who see some value in pursuing this kind of "elusive Scarlet Pimpernel" search in vain for something akin to Archimedes' lever with which the whole of the problem can be moved. Many believe one should concentrate on immediate needs such as the care, treatment and rehabilitation of mental patients. Such problems are real and specific. If one means to do anything in this field, "they" say, let's start with this problem. Small beginnings, however, need to be made on many fronts. Farnsworth, for example, notes, "Both the treatment of mental illness and the promotion of mental health are necessary in any well-conceived community program designed to reduce crippling emotional conflict. To throw up our hands and stop promoting mental health programs because we cannot define mental health or can portray results only inexactly is to show both lack of common sense and lack of courage."[11] There is a *need* and there is a *problem*. The need to care and treat the ill is our major concern, yet it is fairly obvious that all the king's horses and all the king's men will have little effect on the problem—how to reduce or curtail the development of the illness in the first place.

A second and related phenomenon that influences preventive efforts in the mental health field is the high, often impregnable, fortress of personal privacy—the right and privilege of each person, and family, in a free society to mind his own business and have others mind theirs. If prevention of any kind includes early effective intervention in the lives of persons in the population at large, then the intervention must take place prior to such time as the person is singled out for special help. Where it can be shown that such intervention is necessary, indeed, mandatory for the common good, as it is in automobile use, school attendance and physical hygiene and sanitation, acceptance may be given. Yet, in polio inoculations and water fluoridation, invasion of personal privacy is still a major issue in families or communities that decide to accept or reject these preventive programs.

"At present," Bellak writes,

> the governing of men and the raising of children seem to be among the very few occupations in civilized society for which no training or certified ability are required—and for fairly sound reasons. Imposition of laws on either activity could constitute a serious invasion of personal freedom (p. viii) .[1]

Laws providing sanctions for intervention by an agency or person in the private life of an individual are, therefore, clearly and with sound reason limited to situations that endanger the life or health of the person or his neighbors. In essence, one can only stop minding one's own business and become one's brother's keeper when "brother" is in pretty sad shape. Nevertheless, few persons would be prepared to sacrifice the values of a free society on any nebulous, and preventive altar.

Yet, some primary institutions are actually mobilized and authorized to help the family in a positive and potentially preventive manner. For example, the well-baby clinic and the public school are given informal and official sanction to interfere and meddle—the former, in relation to the child's health, the latter, in terms of the child's educational progress or lack of it. However, these institutions must also be alert to the dangers inherent in such sanctions. The school must find its leverage in its assigned task of educating children and carefully define and demonstrate the role of auxiliary services such as health examinations, psychological testing and mental health consultation as necessary in carrying out this assignment. The health and educational progress of children represent to most parents important and highly significant achievements; almost always, there is a strong motivation to do whatever is necessary to work with the school or well-baby clinic in enhancing their child's health or educational success.

Another major social resistance to prevention, pointed out by Ruth Eissler, lies in the realm of the reduction of criminal and antisocial behavior:

. . . modern society, with all its dazzling technological progress has not been able to protect itself from individual or mass aggression against property or life. Must we assume that this helplessness is accidental and has no psychological basis? If we take the standpoint that society needs its criminals in the same way as the mother of my delinquent patient needed his delinquency, then we understand the existence of two general tendencies. The first is the seduction of individuals into criminal acting-out. The second is the interference with or the prevention of anything which promises to prevent delinquency (p. 228).[10]

One explanation advanced for this phenomenon is related to cultural values in which success lies with virtue and failure with sin. In a free society each person has equal opportunity with his fellows to show his mettle as a conscientious, hard-working and, therefore, successful citizen. If he chooses not to be conscientious and hard-working, he has only himself to blame for the consequences. Such competition in games, school work, business and life can only be perceived as successful for all when it is unsuccessful for some. As Don Alhambra sings it in *The Gondoliers,* "In short, whoever you may be/To this conclusion you'll agree/When everyone is somebodee/Then no one's anybodee."

To a great extent, the ritual of the TV-Western, in which good wins over evil fair and square, celebrates this notion at least once or twice each evening. On the other hand, increasing clinical and research evidence supports the notion that those individuals who find positive satisfactions and relationships in family, neighborhood and school also find these satisfactions and relationships as adults; and that those who find frustration, failure and defeat in these primary institutions also tend to be defeated in adulthood. This unconscious sponsorship and enhancement of defeat and alienation in and among groups of children and adolescents is often spelled out in terms of pseudo-Darwinian theory.[17] Yet the idea of equalitarianism is in our historical bones. How have we come to place equality for all and excellence for all as one-dimensional opposites? Gardner states the question more succinctly: "How can we provide opportunities and rewards for individuals of every degree of ability so that individuals at every level will realize their full potentialities, perform at their best and harbor no resentment toward any other level? (p. 115) .[14]

WHO BELLS THE CAT?

As a specific activity, prevention still has the major problem of interesting and involving members of the professions dealing with mental illness, most of whom are involved in individual relationships with patients. Clinicians trained in treatment, rehabilitation and adjunctive therapies in a one-to-one relationship naturally find this more rewarding than they find plunging into the misty arena of prevention. The physician is responsible for the health of his patient, particularly when such health is threatened. As Fox points out:

> Curative medicine has generally had precedence over preventive medicine: people come to the doctor to be healed, and most practicing physicians still think of prevention as subsidiary to their main task— which is, to treat the sick. Though they subscribe, intellectually, to prevention, they really feel more at home when the disease has "got going" (p. 16).[12]

Often, the mental health worker, be he psychiatric technician, nurse, psychologist, social worker or psychiatrist, is deeply impressed by the mountainous obstacles to effecting positive, healthful changes in mental patients and, consequently, finds it difficult to comprehend how other less intensive types of experiences might have prevented the illness.

Yet, one is often surprised by the range, variety and quality of human experiences and human relationships that can and do produce significant changes in personality. Sanford's experience and research lead him to conclude that marked and profound changes do occur in students during the college years.

"Some students," he writes:

> undergo in the normal course of events changes of the same order as those brought about by psychotherapy. The question is, what makes these changes occur and what can be done deliberately to bring them about. . . I'm suggesting that changes of a pretty fundamental kind can be brought about by regular educational procedures or by events occurring in the normal course of events, provided we know enough about what makes changes occur (p. 8).[30]

In bringing prevention into the ken of the psychiatrist, clinical psychologist, or social worker, one may need to recognize and deal with the minimization or depreciation of change processes other than a depth peeling of defenses. Stevenson, in his study of direct instigation of behavioral changes in psychotherapy, finds that some patients often improve markedly when they have mastered a stressful situation or relationship and that by helping such patients manage a day-to-day problem, change is brought about.[31] In the early relationships of the mental health professions and the parents of retarded children, it was often assumed that being a parent of a retarded child necessitated intensive psychological help or mental health counseling. Yet, many such parents were more puzzled and distressed by a lack of information and skill in basic home management of the child, and were often best helped by simple instruction in how to help retarded children learn to feed and dress themselves.

It is possible, as Sanford suggests, that our overemphasis on individual therapy as a major community resource retards to some degree our interest in or our giving priority to prevention. The fact is, primary prevention is the concern of all the mental health professions, but the responsibility of no one group. Much preventive gold can be mined from clinicians and therapists by encouraging them to translate their clinical experiences and knowledge into programs with preventive possibilities. Such translations, however, must be within a framework of what is operationally feasible within one of the "key integrative systems" of our society. Gardner Murphy may well be right:

> The ultimate keys to the understanding of mental health will come, not through exclusive preoccupation with the pathological, but with the broader understanding of the nature of life and of growth. Perhaps the understanding of resonant health and joyful adaptation to life will help us to understand and formulate the issues regarding the prevention of mental disorder (p. 146).[24]

PREVENTION OF WHAT?

Lastly, there is the knotty problem of defining the goals of prevention. Do such goals include the development of individuals who can more easily be helped by community resources; a reduction in hospitalized schizophrenics; or making persons more amenable to psychotherapy? If our purpose is the promotion of emotional robustness, what exactly does this mean and how can this goal be translated into specific, positive and, hopefully, measurable objectives of health? Dubos notes:

> Solving problems of disease is not the same thing as creating health.
> . . . This task demands a kind of wisdom and vision which transcends specialized knowledge of remedies and treatments and which apprehends in all their complexities and subtleties the relation between living things and their total environment (p. 22).[9]

The lack of specificity as to what constitutes mental illness, plus the changing character of such illnesses, make this baseline difficult to define or use in evaluating programs. Yet, where living is equated with and therefore measured by degrees of illness rather than health, one can easily perceive the world as a giant hospital peopled by patients whose only health lies in discovering how sick they are. Nevertheless, reliable measures or indexes of health or illness of a community are the *sine qua non* of any preventive program.

A FRAMEWORK FOR PRIMARY PREVENTION

No single problem in primary prevention has a solution deserving of greater priority than the development of a platform or position from which one can begin to organize and act. One cannot exert leverage on any field of forces except from some fixed position. Without such a theoretical framework little can be done in developing hypotheses, testing them and further developing or, if need be, abandoning them.

Primary prevention of mental and emotional disorders is any specific biological, social or psychological intervention that promotes or enhances the mental and emotional robustness or reduces the incidence and prevalence of mental or emotional illnesses in the population at large. In this framework, primary preventive programs are aimed at persons not yet separated from the general population and, hopefully, at interventions specific enough to be operationally defined and measured.

Measured how—along what dimensions and by what value system? To be sure, some types of primary prevention can be specified in relation to specific diseases or impairments. In such illnesses as phenylketonuria or pellagra psychosis, an appropriate diet initiated at an appropriate time may prevent some of the serious complications of the illness. Other types of mental illness, however, may come about as the cumulative effect of a myriad of interacting social and biological causes and be relatively uninfluenced by any single intervention. Yet, if one assumes that emotional robustness is built on the interactive elements of a healthy organism with enhancing life experiences, one must consider how one could increase those social forces in a community that help the population at large to cope with normal problems, rather than to defend against them, to deal with stress effectively, and to be less vulnerable to illness, including the mental illnesses.

There is, of course, a basic assumption about human behavior and mental health in these propositions, namely, that those social, psychological and biological forces which tend to enhance the full development of the human characteristics of man are desirable and preventive of mental illness; those factors which tend to limit or block such development have greater illness-producing potential and are, therefore, undesirable. By human characteristics, the full development of which are sought, I mean the ability to love and to work productively (Freud's *Lieben und Arbeiten*). In this framework one might support those social and biological forces that tend to make man an effectively functioning organism with maximum ability to adapt to his own potential as well as to the potential of his environment. One can, therefore, hypothesize that forces which increase or enhance the degrees of freedom of man's individual and social behavior are mentally healthful, whereas those which reduce such freedom are unhealthful.

What, specifically, is meant by degrees of behavioral freedom? Behavioral freedom may be regarded as the ability of the organism to develop and maintain a resiliency and flexibility in response to a changing environment and a changing self; operationally, such freedom may be defined as the number of behavioral alternatives available in a personality under normal conditions. Such behavioral freedom is not unlike that of a sailboat that can take full advantage of changing winds and currents by changing sails and direction, but is bound by the nature of the craft and the strength and direction of the forces driving it.

In thinking of preventive action as increasing or enhancing man's behavioral degrees of freedom, one must refer to Kubie's restless pursuit of this notion in differentiating normal behavior from neurotic behavior. His contention is that socially positive behavior can be the consequence of either healthy or neurotic processes, but that there is a basic difference in organismic elasticity or homeostasis between the normal and neurotic. This elasticity manifests itself in the individual's freedom and flexibility to learn through experience, to change and to adapt to changing external circumstances.

In a defensive, neurotic pattern of behavior, inflexibility or illness would reduce the effectiveness of the organism's functioning, especially as a constructive social being. Thus, one index of the health of a community or a society could be the ways people choose to spend their time, especially their uncommitted time. Meier[23] sees the possibility of compiling an index representing the variety of life in a society—specifically, ways in which people *choose* to spend their time. He proposes that an increase in variety almost always reflects an enhancement in social integration. One could, therefore, conceive of *degrees of behavioral freedom* in terms of operational social indexes that would reflect changes in variety and patterns of life and could be used as a method of evaluating preventive programs. For example, one might examine the allocation of time of persons with personality disturbances or a mentally ill group in a hospital as compared to various other persons and communities.

A FRAMEWORK FOR PREVENTION

The zonal classifications of people and services in Figure 12-1 presents a framework and a functioning methodology for prevention. Primary prevention can be considered medical, social or psychological action within Zones I and II, which reduces the need for the services and institutions of Zones III or IV. The goals of such action, with respect to the institutions and services of Zone I and Zone II, are threefold:

1. To increase the biological robustness of human beings by strengthening those institutions and agencies directly involved in prenatal, pregnancy and early infant care.

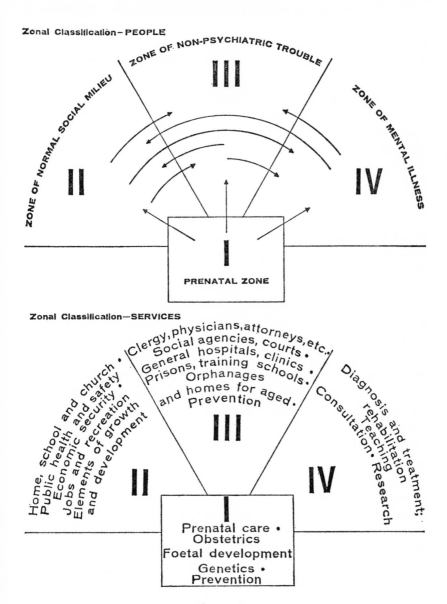

Figure 12-1.

2. To increase the flexibility of the agencies serving persons of Zones I and II, so that such agencies may encompass and affect a greater variety and number of persons in the general population. For example, the extension of school services for retarded or emotionally disturbed children may make it possible for a child usually needing Zone III or IV services to remain in Zone II. The utilization of prenatal medical or nursing advisory services for lower-class pregnant mothers may be significantly influenced by placing such services close to neighborhood shopping or laundry centers. Or the presence of a counseling center for workers may make the difference for a number of individuals in maintaining employment and family economic support.

3. To assist primary institutions in planning individual and social techniques by which stress immunity or manageability can become a natural outcome of their relationship to children and their families.

It is evident that, in this scheme of primary prevention, the preventive forces will be those affecting the operation, accessibility, adaptability and modifiability of the institutions and agencies found in Zones I and II. Particularly, one needs to determine: (a) which specific social and community forces tend to push Zone II persons into requiring Zone III or IV services; (b) how present medical, genetic and biological information can be translated into social action so as to reduce the number of Zone I infants entering Zones III or IV; and (c) how Zones I and II agencies and institutions can be reinforced, modified or developed to lessen the need for Zones III and IV services.

The institutions and agencies in Zones I and II can be denoted as the frontline defenses of a community. If such institutions and agencies cannot adequately serve individuals in their field, Zones III or IV services are required. Some of the forces moving people into Zones III or IV are the number and character of the emotionally hazardous situations and crises the individual has been required to mediate and manage, and how mediation and management were accomplished. The key, therefore, to movement from one zone to another lies in the quality of the mediation (coping or defending) of the emotionally hazardous situation or crisis.

Klein and Lindemann[20] define an emotionally hazardous situation as any sudden alteration in the field of social forces affecting an individual so that the individual's perception and expectation of self and others undergo change. In each instance an emotionally hazardous situation or crisis is a normal life occurrence that is temporarily upsetting, not always in an unpleasant sense, but one that necessitates rapid reorganization and mobilization of an individual's personality resources. Such life situations as birth of a sibling, death of a loved one, school entrance, school failure, marriage, job promotion, divorce or inheritance of a large sum of money from a dead uncle's estate are examples of emotionally hazardous situations. The hazard in these situations is that the individual may find himself unable to manage the increased stress in a healthful way. Yet, such hazards and hurdles are part of the normal process of living and are, in large part, the cutting edges that sharpen and crystallize personality development and integration.

Whether for good or bad, emotionally hazardous crises have these aspects in common: (a) They cause a rise in inner tension and uneasiness; (b) they cause some disorganization in normal functioning; and (c) they necessitate some internal change in self to manage the situation. In baseball parlance, an individual in an emotionally hazardous situation is said to "stand loose at the plate," that is, the individual is lightly balanced to be able to move quickly in any direction. During this period of relative instability, minimal forces have their greatest effects, much like the effect of a one-gram weight at one end of a delicately balanced teeter-totter. Such a gram of weight would have little effect if the forces governing the organism were relatively stable.

The implications of the emotionally vulnerable situation or crisis as a fulcrum for preventive action is clear. To the extent to which such situations can be identified and the "crisis" institution or agency prepared and strengthened to make the most of this opportunity, to that extent can it place grams of force on the side of health and personality growth. In primary prevention one is focused on the emotionally hazardous situation that occurs in the context of the operation of each of the services or agencies in

Zones I or II. Such institutions and agencies are often aware of some crises and do a great deal to help individuals deal effectively with them. Sometimes, however, the agency or service may fail to recognize relevant crises, or fail to take advantage of the health-producing potential of the situation. For example, the school may well be aware of the effect of the birth of a child on his siblings but, as an institution, it is seldom in a position to obtain and use this information systematically. Such an important and natural event in the lives of children may be sufficiently upsetting to the sibling to warrant some attention by the school. To capitalize on this emotionally hazardous situation, teachers may need to plan opportunities for the sibling to be recognized, to be helpful, to be successful—in short, to help the child, within the structure and role of the institution, to manage and mediate the crisis. In some cases, the child may need no more than an extra pat on the back from the teacher. In others, a planned conference with parents may be of some help. What is critical is the recognition by the institution of the emotionally vulnerable position of the child and a readiness to act positively upon it.

Table 12-I lists some services and institutions of Zones I and II, along with some emotionally hazardous and enhancing situations or crises that occur in relation to each institution, with some possibilities for preventive action in each case. Neither the services, hazards, nor action possibilities listed are intended to be comprehensive or exhaustive. However, this conceptualization may help provide a fulcrum for the development of pilot and experimental studies and other preventive programs that can be delineated and evaluated. For example, the first emotional hazard under "family" is that of loss of father through death, divorce or desertion. With few exceptions, the burden for breadwinning is thrust upon the mother who, in turn, finds it necessary to depend upon child-caring services for her children. In part, such services are provided by relatives, friends, nursery schools, foster homes and child-care centers. In California, child-care centers were initiated during World War II to increase the labor force, and have since continued in operation to serve one-parent families of modest incomes and some families of teachers and nurses. Such a

TABLE 12-I

Zone II Service	Normal Emotional Hazard	Possibilities for Preventive Action
Family	Loss of father through death, divorce or desertion	Reinforcement of child-care services for working mothers
	Loss of mother	Reinforcement of foster-home services
	Adolescence	Increase in staff and professionalization of high school counselors, deans, and vice-principals
	Birth of sibling	Pediatric or well-baby clinic counseling
	Death	Management of grief—religious or community agency worker
Public health	Phenylketonuria	Detection and diet
	Childhood illnesses	Vaccination, immunization
	Stress caused by children —economic, housing, etc.	Reinforcement of well-baby clinic through mental health consultation to staff
	Pregnancy	Adequate prenatal care for mothers of lower socioeconomic status
School	Birth of sibling	Recognition of event by school and appropriate intervention
	School entrance of child	Screening vulnerable children
	Intellectual retardation	Special classes and assistance
	Teacher concern and anxiety about a child's behavior	Consultation by mental health specialists
	School failure	Early identification and prevention through appropriate school program
Religion	Marriage	Counseling by clergy
Job or profession	Promotion or demotion	Opportunity to define role through services of a mental health counselor
Recreation	Appropriate and rewarding use of leisure time	Active community and city recreational programs
Housing	Lack of space—need for privacy	Working with architects and housing developers

child-care facility usually serves preschool children all day and cares for school children part of the day.

There is sufficient evidence to support the hypothesis that one-parent families are more vulnerable to stress and emotional hazards than are intact families. The child-care facility, properly staffed and oriented, would then be a potentially preventive force in developing and maintaining some type of assistance and support for the mothers and children utilizing this service. Such assistance could be provided by a psychiatric social worker or another professional person hired to work with the child-care staff or families. In theory, the child-care center as a primary institution would be reinforced as a preventive agency by enlisting trained personnel to work with parents or child-care staff on the normal problems of people who are bringing up children but who are obliged to work at the same time.

Or, let us take the emotional hazard of pregnancy and birth. One of the points made by Wortis,[34] Pasamanick,[19,27] Freedman[13] and others is that adequate prenatal and natal care is a significant and far-reaching measure in the prevention of neuropsychiatric disorders in children. In most cases, such care is available. Yet, significant numbers of mothers in lower socioeconomic neighborhoods are not normally motivated to seek medical care during pregnancy. Ordinarily they will use medical assistance only as a last resort. Many such mothers would take advantage of preventive medical services if such services were present somewhere along the paths they normally travel, or if they could be motivated to detour a few blocks for them. For example, space in empty stores near laundromats or markets could be rented for health department personnel and manned by nurses who could spend time with a mother while she was shopping or waiting for her load of wash. Such a program could be evaluated by comparing rates of premature births, birth injuries or other birth difficulties before and after the service, or with rates in neighborhoods where no such service exists.

FULCRA FOR PREVENTION

It is increasingly evident that there are three basic interrelated ingredients in primary prevention: (a) a healthful birth experience, (b) a healthful family experience, and (c) a successful school experience. Healthful birth experiences are largely the result of early medical care and advice that help prospective mothers obtain and use preventive medical care. Although the evidence is far from complete, Bowlby,[4] Brody,[5] and Ribble,[29] to name only three, have emphasized the primacy of family relationships and their effect on the mental health of children. Bowlby summarized numerous studies from various countries that illustrated the emotional impact on children of early separation from their parents. Ribble and Brody studied the pivotal relationship of mothering and personality development, and Caplan[7] pointed out how a neighborhood health center can be a preventive force in enhancing and strengthening family resources for the child. Goodrich,[16] at the Bio-Social Growth Center of the National Institute of Mental Health, studied the emotional hazard of early separation of the child from the mother in a nursery school setting. He found this crisis a potentially manageable staging area for research in primary prevention and suggested some areas of developmental influences that effect how a child or family manages a crisis. Early separation anxieties in a child often mean the possibility of greater problems later on with school entrance or bereavement.

The school has become increasingly primary to a child's personality growth. Consequently it can be the prime mover for alerting parents whose children need additional help or support within the school or, in some cases, additional services outside the school. In essence, the role of the school as a preventive force is realized to the extent to which it is able to make the educational experience a successful learning experience for all children. Two studies from widely disparate sources illustrate the intertwined threads of successful school experience and primary prevention. In a thirty-year follow-up study of children who had been referred to a municipal clinic because of problem behavior, the investigators included students from the files of the public schools who matched the patients in age, sex, IQ, race and residence. In addition, this group was selected on the basis of having no school record of behavior or discipline problems. Although the investigators were not studying the health of the control group, they were struck with the fact "that the simple criteria used to choose the control subjects—no excessive absences, no full grades repeated, no disciplinary action recorded and an IQ of 80 or better—have yielded a strikingly healthy group (p. 986) ."[26] This was particularly striking since the control group was drawn largely from disadvantaged classes and a history of broken homes was found in one-third of the cases.

The other link of evidence relating school success and primary prevention is found in Ginzberg and his associates' monumental study of the ineffective soldier of World War II. They found that, while poverty, racial discrimination and lack of industrialization could help explain higher rates of emotional instability for individuals who came from certain sections of the country, each of these factors was also related to the differentially low educational achievement of the region. The study demonstrated that, although a higher level of educational attainment was no safeguard against emotional disorders, the lower the educational level, the higher the incidence of emotional disorders. As to cause, Ginzberg noted, "A disturbed childhood is likely to be reflected in learning difficulties; children who do poorly in school are likely to develop emotional problems (p. 118) .[15]

If the school is to become an effective preventive force, it must develop ways to identify early the children who are or are becoming learning problems, so that school and community resources can help such children most effectively and economically. The potential learning difficulty may be related to intellectual, emotional or family-centered problems; even so, the problem may first manifest itself in the school, which can, if it recognizes the problem, pave the way for early help through parent conferences, counseling or psychological or remedial service.[2,3]

In job situations, the hazards seem to be just as numerous for going up the ladder as down. A person moving up in a large industrial or governmental agency may find it difficult to accept his new role or recast his loyalties with a particular group. He may have greater responsibility for men or production than he is able to manage. A staff-related mental health counselor in industry or work organization may provide some source of help for emotionally hazardous situations of this type.

Wilner and Walkley[32] and others have mapped out preliminary steps for studying the interrelationships of housing and mental health. In studying the mental health of families in relation to their housing, including such things as the extent of plumbing leaks or the number of rats, the general impression of these investigators based on preliminary short-term evaluations is that moving from poor to good housing does not, on the average, result in measurable improvement in the mental health of the family. In the matter of housing and related social economic problems, one must be continually reminded of the large body of research describing the high, positive relationship between the indicators of social class and the many kinds of human illnesses. As Wilner and Walkley point out:

> The list of pathologies so related is long, beginning with early studies on crime and delinquency. Other examples are alcoholism, broken homes, and divorce (Beverly Hills notwithstanding), syphilis, tuberculosis, and childhood communicable diseases. New entries are being made as time goes by: Reading disability has entered the lists, as has the incidence of narcotics use among teenagers, as well as the incidence of mental illness.

Housing, by and large, shows a marked negative relationship with most illnesses so that, in general, as housing deteriorates, illnesses rise. Psychoses have been found to increase with housing deterioration; neuroses, on the other hand, seem to increase with improved housing.

WHITHER PREVENTION?

Prevention is, at present, a high-status, magic word generally applicable to almost all professional endeavors in mental health. The term is applicable to newer and more effective treatment methods for schizophrenia, preventive hospitalization of suicidal patients or the use of drugs for quieting patients, or, in vague or general terms, to improved housing, better human relations, better schools, more staff, and so on. This lack of specificity in the term prevention is especially critical in a field that already has a large element of vagueness and expansiveness. If, as Freud noted, thinking is action in rehearsal, it behooves individuals interested in preventive action to get into rehearsal ideas that are primarily preventive, specific enough to be replicated in more than one locality and operational enough to be evaluated within one's lifetime. Also, it must be kept in mind that the preventive battlegrounds are the primary institutions or agencies of a society. We must determine the specific interventions or modifications these institutions can make to reduce the stress vulnerability or enhance the personality resources of the human organisms they serve.

Prevention has to do with the quality of the interactions and the degree of effectiveness of the primary institutions of a society in providing each person with increments of ego strength and personality robustness for coping with the "slings and arrows" of life. The nature of these interactions and experiences would be considered preventive to the extent to which such experiences enhance the degrees of psychological freedom of an individual to select behavioral alternatives and to act upon them. This preventive model and point of view was succinctly illustrated by an old Cornish test of insanity related by Woodward. The test situation comprised a sink, a tap of running water, a bucket and a ladle. The bucket was placed under the tap of running water and the subject asked to bail the water out of the bucket with the ladle. If the subject continued to bail without paying some attention to reducing or preventing the flow of water into the pail, he was judged to be mentally incompetent. Similarly, any society that attempts to provide more and larger buckets to contain the problems of that society, without simultaneously attempting to reduce the flow, might be equally suspect. Treatment, rehabilitation and incarceration are our necessary buckets to contain the flow. Prevention, however, deals with the tap, the sources of flow and the leverages needed to turn the faucet down or off.

REFERENCES

1. Bellak, L.: *Schizophrenia: A Review of the Syndrome.* New York, Logos Press, 1959.
2. Bower, E. M.: *Early Identification of Emotionally Handicapped Children in School.* Springfield, Thomas, 1960.
3. Bower, E. M.: Primary prevention in a school setting. In Caplan, G. (Ed.): *Prevention of Mental Disorders in Children.* New York, Basic Books, 1961, p. 353-377.
4. Bowlby, J.: *Maternal Care and Mental Health.* Geneva, Switzerland, World Health Organization, 1951.
5. Brody, S. *Patterns of Mothering.* New York, International Universities Press, 1956.
6. Bruner, J. S.: On coping and defending (mimeo).

7. Caplan, G.: A public health approach to child psychiatry. *Ment Hyg,* *35:*235-49, 1951.

8. Cumming, E. and Cumming, J.: *Closed Ranks.* Cambridge, Harvard University Press, 1957.

9. Dubos, R.: *Mirage of Health.* New York, Harper, 1959.

10. Eissler, R.: Scapegoats of society. In Eissler, K. R. (Ed.): *Searchlights on Delinquency.* New York, International Universities Press, 1955.

11. Farnsworth, D. L.: The provision of appropriate treatment: hospital and community collaboration. *Ment Hosp, 12:*18, 1961.

12. Fox, T. F.: Priorities. In *Steps in the Development of Integrated Psychiatric Services.* New York, Milbank Memorial Fund, 1960.

13. Freedman, A. *et al.:* The influence of hyperbilirubinemia on the early development of the premature. *Psychiat Res Reps, 13:*108-23, 1960.

14. Gardner, J.: *Excellence.* New York, Harper, 1961.

15. Ginzberg, E. *et al.: The Ineffective Soldier: Lessons for Management and the Nation.* New York, Columbia University Press, 1959.

16. Goodrich, D. W.: Possibilities for preventive intervention during initial personality formation. In Caplan, G. (Ed.): *Prevention of Mental Disorders in Children.* New York, Basic Books, 1961, p. 249-64.

17. Hofstadter, R.: *Social Darwinism in American Thought.* Boston, Beacon Press, 1955.

18. Homer: *The Odyssey.* W. H. D. Rouse, Trans. New York, Mentor, 1949.

19. Kawi, A. A. and Pasamanick, B.: *The Association of Factors of Pregnancy With the Development of Reading Disorders in Childhood.* Yellow Springs, Ohio, Society for Research in Child Development, 1959.

20. Klein, D. and Lindemann, E.: Preventive intervention in individual and family crisis situations. In Caplan, G. (Ed.): *Prevention of Mental Disorders in Children.* New York, Basic Books, 1961, p. 283-306.

21. Kubie, L. S.: The fundamental nature of the distinction between normality and neuroses. *Psychoanal Q, 23:*1954.

22. Kubie, L. S.: Social forces and the neurotic process. In Leighton, A. *et al* (Eds.): *Explorations in Social Psychiatry.* New York, Basic Books, 1957.

23. Meier, R. L.: Human time allocation: A basis for social accounts. *J Am Inst Planners, 25:*27-33, Nov. 1959.

24. Murphy, G.: The prevention of mental disorder: Some research suggestions. *J Hillside Hospital, 9:*1960.

25. Murphy, L. B.: Preventive implications of development in the preschool years. In Caplan, G. (Ed.): *Prevention of Mental Disorders in Children.* New York, Basic Books, 1961, p. 218-48.

26. O'Neal, P. and Robbins, L.: The relation of childhood behavior problems to adult psychiatric status. *Am J Psychiatry, 114:*1958.

27. Pasamanick, B.: The epidemiology of behavior disorders of childhood. In *Neurology and Psychiatry in Childhood*. Baltimore, Md., William & Wilkins, 1956.

28. Redlich, F. C.: The concept of health in psychiatry. In Leighton, A. et al. (Eds.): *Explorations in Social Psychiatry*. New York, Basic Books, 1957.

29. Ribble, M.: *The Rights of Infants*. New York, Columbia University Press, 1943.

30. Sanford, R. N.: The development of the healthy personality in the society of today. In *Modern Mental Health Concepts and Their Application in Public Health Education*. Berkeley, Calif., State Department of Public Health, 1959.

31. Stevenson, I.: Direct instigation of behavioral changes in psychotherapy. *Arch Gen Psychiat, 1*:99-107, 1959.

32. Wilner, D. and Walkley, R.: Housing environment and mental health. In *Epidemiology of Mental Disorder*. Washington, D.C., American Association for the Advancement of Science, p. 143-74.

33. Wilson, W.: The new freedom. In Chamberlain, Essie (Ed.): *Essays Old and New*. New York, Harcourt, Brace, 1926.

34. Wortis, H., Heimer, C. B., Braine, M., Redlo, M. and Rue, R.: Growing up in Brooklyn: An early history of the premature child. *Am J Orthopsychiatry, 33(3)*:535-39, 1963.

B. EARLY CHILDHOOD

Chapter 13

EARLY DETECTION AND PREVENTION OF EMOTIONAL DISORDER: CONCEPTUALIZATIONS AND PROGRAMMING

EMORY L. COWEN AND MELVIN ZAX

T HE OBJECTIVES of this paper are twofold and limited. The first is to articulate several primitive conceptualizations relevant to the mental health fields today. The second aim, if only by way of brief summary, is to review some of our principal research findings within the framework of our guiding philosophy.

Increasingly, mental health professionals have come to realize the insufficiency of our network of helping operations (Cowen, 1967). For example, we now recognize that our best efforts have failed to result in noteworthy progress with entire classes of disorder; schizophrenia well illustrates this point. Technology (e.g. psychotherapy) that is fundamental to our current "bag of tricks" is of limited effectiveness clinically and is certainly restricted in its scope (Schofield, 1964; Cowen and Zax, 1967). Profound biases exist in the availability of mental health services with respect to such variables as race, social class, geography, and educational level (Sanua, 1966). Unfortunately, these operate according to the rule that where help is most needed it is least available. Moreover, for vast segments of the population we have been grossly deficient in working out modes of delivery of services that are consonant with the life styles and social realities of potential recipients (Reiff, 1967; Riessman, 1967). Underlying the foregoing is the realization that the demand for helping services, let alone need, substantially exceeds available resources; present extrapola-

Note: Reprinted from Carter, J. (Ed.): *Research Contributions from Psychology to Community Mental Health.* New York, Behavioral Publications, 1968. pp. 46-59.

tions suggest that this gap is growing rather than narrowing (Albee, 1959, 1963, 1967; Nichols, 1963). The enormity of these problems dictates that careful scrutiny be given to our prior guiding assumptions and practices (Cowen, Gardner, and Zax, 1967).

Historically, "practice" in the mental health fields has focused on the goal of arrest and modification of pathology. The everyday operations of helping specialists typically begin when people experiencing emotional difficulties seek them out. Obstacles, whether economic, geographic, or psychological, are often sufficiently formidable so that the individual does not ask for help until discomfort is advanced and symptomatology well entrenched. At that time the helping specialist is seen as a knowledgeable expert who will prescribe (perhaps words rather than medicine) and cure, much as the physician does in treating flu. Professional practice has been supportive of this view. We have sought, through diagnosis, to understand the nature of psychic disorder and, through treatment, to modify it, largely within the framework of the one-to-one clinical interaction. Our stance toward mental health problems has been passive-receptive—seeking to do the best "patchwork" possible in known instances of dysfunction.

Notwithstanding dramatic increases in facilities, resources, budgets, and professional personnel in past decades, it would be difficult to argue that we have achieved proportional reduction in the number and seriousness of mental health problems. Rather, we have struggled desperately to tread water. Thus, the need for alternative conceptualizations about "cause and cure" in the mental health fields assumes paramount importance.

A critical shortcoming of society's efforts to cope with emotional perturbation resides in its historical emphasis on pathology and its cure, rather than on the origin and flow of disorder. Any comprehensive system of long-range planning in the mental health fields should accord central significance to issues of prevention. The implicit assumption of analogy between psychological and physical disorder has, doubtless, been a stultifying one. Whereas physical disorder implicates invasion by some type of pathogenic agent, psychological dysfunction more likely reflects complex, long-standing determinants and processes and varied sources of influence, including important "others" in the person's life space, and key social institutions.

Our concerns need sharper focus in these latter directions. We must learn more and do more about building for psychological resources and for health, rather than simply counterpunching against pathology. Such an orientation underscores the need for examination of influential primary institutions in modern society and establishes the centrality of questions such as: How do primay institutions influence emotional and personality development? How are these impactful systems modified; and what is the relationship between institutional change and optimal psychological development? The long-range aim of such inquiry is to create conditions to reduce the flow of disorder.

Lately, "market value" of the term prevention has gone up considerably. This should not obscure the fact that it is an expansive, elusive concept covering a variety of objectives and functions. Primary prevention implies re-doing the very fabric of society. As such, it implicates skills and know-how far beyond the combined resources of the helping professionals, let alone psychology by itself. Secondary prevention, whether defined as early in the life history of the organism or early in the course of a given episode of disorder, seeks to curtail the duration and impact of disorder through *early* detection and treatment. Tertiary prevention is aimed at entrenched, essentially irreversible pathology; its purpose is to keep impairment minimal. It is questionable that this function is properly described as prevention. Our own preferred focus when using the term is on primary prevention and on ontogenetically early secondary prevention.

Much of our particular interest in "community mental health," these days a projectivist's bonanza, is justified in terms of prospective functions rather than geography. We stand to gain little through simple transplantation of Szondi plates or intensive therapy from clinics to courthouses, schools, factories or prisons. To us, the real value of a shift from the consulting room to the community and its primary institutions lies in the opportunities for generating preventively oriented programs, for constructive modification of social systems, and for meaningful extension of the reach of our helping operations to the multitudes of heretofore unreached. Our needs for such expansion are more nearly geometric than arithmetic. That we already lack sufficient professional personnel in the mental health fields and that prospects for solutions along this dimension are, at best, dim (Albee, 1967) point up the importance of two further types of developments: (a) exploration of new ways for effective utilization of nonprofessionals, and (b) recasting a substantial portion of the role of the professional in directions elsewhere described (Cowen, 1967) as those of the "social engineer" and "mental health quarterback." This implies retrenchment on "one-to-one" clinical service activities in favor of consultative, educative, supervisory, and resource functions. To achieve these ends, there is need for change in conception and implementation of graduate training in the several helping professions.

Much of what has been said thus far is an introductory articulation, however primitive, of a conceptual credo. We now turn, at least briefly, to some of our supporting research efforts. The perceptive reader may soon detect substantial discontinuity between crystal-ball gazing and empirics. Largely, this reflects the issue of "point of address" of one's research efforts. In the armchair it is not difficult to be global and far ranging, especially if one is at all tolerant of loose ends and islands of fuzziness. The issues thus identified are broad in scope and suggest a variety of approaches, at different levels, to diverse problems—far beyond the resources and know-how of any single group of professionals. The research to be summarized is considerably narrower than the prior theoretical speculations. Our chosen "point of address" is that of early detection and early secondary prevention of emotional disorder in the school setting. This choice reflects a blend of premeditation and serendipity that defies precise itemization of ingredients. Some limited portions of our rationale, however, can be made less mystical.

One vital focus of a comprehensive, preventively oriented approach to mental health problems, historically underplayed, is the young child and his environment. In this context, the family and the school represent primary institutions of major import. In particular, the school, both because of its accessibility and inevitably heavy and enduring impact upon all members of society in their formative years, represents a unique situation for program development and research. Opportunities for curriculum modification in keeping with learning and mental health principles, concerted efforts to create school environments that favor optimal psychological development, mental health-related training for teachers and cadet teachers, early identification of emotional disturbance, and the development of interventive models designed to curtail the negative sequelae of such disturbance, each represents an area of some potential.

Much of our effort in recent years has centered around the establishment and evaluation of experimental programs for the early detection and prevention of emotional disorder in very young schoolchildren. We have focused primarily on two broad problems: (a) assessment of the effectiveness of the experimental programs, and (b) development of techniques for early identification of ineffective functioning. Implicit in the second objective is a concern about the extent to which children, so identified, are differentiable from more effectively functioning peers with respect to a series of independent performance, achievement, and behavioral measures.

Our programs for early detection and prevention have been described in detail in the literature (Cowen, Izzo, Miles, Telschow, Trost and Zax, 1963; Zax, Cowen, Izzo, and Trost, 1964; Cowen, Zax, Izzo and Trost, 1966; Zax and Cowen, 1967) and will therefore, be summarized only briefly here. Psychological evaluation of first-grade children, social work interviews with their mothers, classroom observation, and reports by teachers provided the materials for early detection of disorder. Based on an amalgam of such information, children have been divided, for research purposes, into one of two groupings. The designation Red-Tag was used for those youngsters who, on the basis of all available evidence, had already manifested disorders ranging from moderate to severe, or in whom such pathology seemed incipient. In schools we have worked in thus far that figure has run about 35 to 40 percent. All other children were called Non-Red-Tag. This has been an arbitrary, fallible, clinical impression—internal to the research staff. It is neither made part of the child's record nor known to teachers or school administrators. In subsequent research (Beach, Cowen, Zax, Laird, Trost, Izzo, 1968) we have been able to identify, in greater detail, some of the determinants of the Red-Tag judgment, particularly those deriving from the social work interview, which accounts for a goodly share of the rating variance. We have also taken steps to increase the sensitivity of the judgment by expanding it to a seven-point scale, with demonstrable reliability.

Our prevention program has gone through certain metamorphoses over the years.* Perhaps its most enduring component has been the utilization of professional staff as an educative, consultative, and resource team. School personnel, especially teachers, are provided ongoing opportunities to meet with Mental Health Clinical Services (MHCS) team members to discuss problems relating to individual children, to classroom management, and to the role of being a teacher. Initially, lunch hours and after-school times were used for such consultation. More recently, however, recognizing the centrality of this function to our program, we have acquired the services of a substitute teacher to free the classroom teacher for discussion and consultative conferences, during regular school hours. A consulting psychiatrist has also functioned centrally on the project staff as a resource person, and in individual and small group conferences with teachers and members of the MHCS staff. Other aspects of the preventive program include parent meetings, teacher meetings and, more recently, several specially designed interventive mechanisms utilizing nonprofessionals both on an "in-school" and "after school" basis.

In order to assess the effectiveness of the program a battery of objective assessment procedures was utilized, including school record data (e.g. days absent, nurses' referrals, report card grades, achievement-aptitude discrepancy scores, etc.), standard achievement tests (e.g. SRA Reading and Arithmetic), and personality

*Our appreciation is expressed to Mr. Louis D. Izzo, psychologist; Mrs. Mary Ann Trost, social worker; and Dr. Angelo Madonia, psychiatrist, who have contributed significantly to the development of this program.

and behavior measures (e.g. teacher ratings, peer ratings, and self-ratings). These indices with some modification, have been applied twice. In each instance the target group consisted of third-grade youngsters who had been exposed to the program for three years. Two control schools, demographically comparable to the experimental school, provided a frame of reference for the evaluation.

Analysis of the data has been completed for both groups. Data from the second year are basically consistent with the earlier ones; indeed, in a number of instances they appear to be even stronger and more clear-cut. Looking at the findings for both year groups, we may conclude that: (a) there is a cluster of salutary consequences of the prevention program tapping adjustive, performance, achievement and sociometric measures in children exposed to it for three years; (b) children evidencing ineffective behavior in the first school years (Red-Tag) are, by the end of the third year: performing less adequately in school, showing greater signs of maladjustment on both objective tests and behavioral ratings, obtaining lower scores on standard achievement tests, being rated more negatively sociometrically, manifesting more physical complaints in the school situation, all in comparison to their Non-Red-Tag peers (Cowen, Zax, Izzo and Trost, 1966).

We have undertaken follow-up studies of the alumni of our first prevention program, at seventh-grade level, four years after their exposure to the special program ended, in order to determine the stability or ephemerality of earlier findings. In this context, we recently reported (Zax, Cowen, Rappaport, Beach and Land, 1968) evidence indicating that the early-diagnosed "Red-Tag" child, left untreated, continued to show evidence of poorer development throughout his entire elementary school career.

Our findings, to date, point to some fairly rich potentials for a preventive approach in the schools. The high incidence of early pathology and its already serious consequences within the first three school years suggest that there is much room here for intensive exploration of secondary preventive measures. This is an area in which we have only recently become involved. The problem is this. Granted that "high-risk," Red-Tag youngsters can be identified and that, left untreated, they do very poorly in the first three school years, what if anything can be done to halt or reverse the seemingly inevitable downward spiral? Considerable effort in the past several years has been invested in the design, implementation and field-testing of several interventive programs, guided by the conceptual orientation we have described, and built on the findings of our earlier research. These programs have in common: a focus on early secondary prevention, heavy utilization of nonprofessionals, and use of the mental health professional in a consultative and resource capacity.

One of our "programs-in-action" has recruited and trained middle-aged housewives for roles as mental-health aides in the schools (Zax, Cowen, Izzo, Madonia, Merenda and Trost, 1966). Such women, though they have been incorporated in a variety of volunteer programs in the past, have tended to be used for relatively trivial jobs such as chauffeuring, distributing books, cleaning blackboards, etc., when in fact they have much to offer in interpersonal relationships and as a resource in the mental health helping enterprise. We have recruited and provided focused, time-limited training, including both didactic-discussion meetings on mental health-relevant issues and guided experience in clinical observation, for a group of six (not especially highly educated) housewives. This training sought to equip them to function as mental health aides in the school. Several models for the functioning of the housewife aide have already been explored, each of which presumes at least half-time involvement to assure continuity and relatively stable relationships with the child. One such model "stations" the housewife directly in the classroom; the second has her in the school building, combining classroom observations and "on-call" service with children. The aide is oriented toward the educational and emotional needs of the disturbed child who, in many instances, cannot receive special attention from the teacher who is charged with the progress of her entire class. Through such efforts the child with withdrawal tendencies may be encouraged to come out of his shell and the overactive child who needs attention may get this plus intelligent guidance toward useful pursuits before either type becomes rigidified in a pathological pattern.

A second program (Cowen, Zax and Laird, 1966) utilizes undergraduate education majors as companions in after-school activity programs with children referred by their teachers because of emotional difficulties—particularly acting-out problems, problems of shyness, timidity and withdrawal and those of educational underachievement. This program also involves fourth-year clinical graduate students, hopefully providing for them a meaningful experience in the community and the schools, and a taste of functioning in a consultative-resource capacity. Our pattern of operation runs roughly as follows. Each graduate student works with a group of six undergraduate volunteers. Each volunteer is assigned specifically to an individual child or a pair of children. Twice a week volunteers and graduate student leaders go to the schools. Activities with the children take place between 3:30 and 4:45 P.M. Then the entire group returns to campus for a postmortem discussion between 5 and 6 P.M. These discussions range across topics such as trying to understand the child's behavior, considering the efficacy of varying types of actions and interventions, and trying to deal with the volunteer's concerns about his own role and function (Zax and Cowen, 1967). It seems that this program may have potential not only for its effect on young children, but also by providing prospective teachers with a mental health-oriented practicum experience—a long-range step in the direction of primary prevention.

The third group of nonprofessionals that we have trained to work as mental health aides with young children in the schools consists of retired people. Here training and function, though less intensive, were guided by our experience with housewives. The results of this project (Cowen, Leibowitz, and Leibowitz, 1968) have been encouraging. Independent objective data obtained from teachers and aides indicated that referred children profited significantly from their experience. Moreover, participation in the program was a gratifying experience for the retirees as well. This latter fact may well illustrate Riessman's (1965) helper-therapy principle (i.e. the therapeutic value deriving to oneself from the process of being genuinely helpful to another human being).

While the school, as a "heavy-impact" primary institution, is necessarily a *basic* sphere of operation for preventively oriented mental health programs, it is not the only one. Nor are the specific manpower, recruitment, and training models utilized in that setting likely to be equally effective with all other groups and settings. Based on these assumptions we have also undertaken a highly exploratory program, in cooperation with a local settlement house, involving recruitment and training of indigenous Negro youth (ages 15 to 18) from Rochester's "inner-city" areas to work in a one-to-one counselor-type relationship with very young neighborhood children referred for emotional problems by agency staff. Once again advanced clinical students are actively involved in a training-resource-supervisory capacity. As in our program for retired people, and in other programs for disadvantaged urban groups (Riessman, 1967; Klein, 1967), the potential operation of the helper-therapy phenomenon may again be noted.

The foregoing examples are limited to situations in which *we* have had concrete experience. They reflect, however, a key underlying principle that should be underscored because of its potential applicability to a variety of community mental health settings.

We know that the need for professional help already far outstrips available resources. Best estimates indicate that this disparity will increase over time. Hence we must develop and exploit less saturated, mental health training situations in which considerably larger numbers of individuals are provided with appropriate background and experience. Such individuals would form a corps of field workers that would geometrically expand the range of mental health-relevant contacts with those in the community requiring help. As this model is developed and applied, there will be need for the mental health professional to exercise the vital educative, supervisory, and resource functions. Doubtless, this will entail parallel encroachment upon his traditional functions and will require modification and extension of graduate training programs and practicum experiences for helping professionals.

In closing, we offer a view, derived from our thinking and research findings, of an important direction for movement of the mental health helping professions. Fundamental marker characteristics of the professional mental health specialist several decades hence should include a clear orientation toward early detection of emotional pathology or incipient pathology, and toward preventive interventions (both primary and secondary) designed to forestall the occurrence of disorder. A substantial portion of our focus should be directed to the very young child. This is in contrast to past dominant emphases on severe symptomatology, well entrenched in older individuals, and on the one-to-one diagnostic and treatment model. The professional specialist in implementing this new, preventive orientation will inevitably act as an educator, consultant, and resource person for a new corps of nonprofessional specialists that must be created if we are to deal meaningfully with serious present-day manpower shortages. Graduate training in the helping professions must emphasize consultative and preventive orientations affecting many, as well as individual diagnosis and treatment of the few. Only by effectuating change of this general nature does it seem possible that a mental health "helping" structure capable of meeting existing, very real, social needs can come about.

REFERENCES

1. Albee, G. W.: *Mental Health Manpower Trends.* New York, Basic Books, 1959.
2. Albee, G. W.: American psychology in the sixties. *Am Psychol, 18:*90-95, 1963.
3. Albee, G. W.: The relation of conceptual models to manpower needs. In Cowen, E. L., Gardner, E. A., and Zax, M.: *Emergent Approaches to Mental Health Problems.* New York, Appleton-Century-Crofts, 1967, p. 63-73.
4. Beach, D. R., Cowen, E. L., Zax, M., Laird, J. D., Trost, M. A., Izzo, L. D.: Objectification of screening for early detection of emotional disorder. *Child Dev, 39:*1968.
5. Cowen, E. L.: Emergent approaches to mental health problems: An overview and directions for future work. In Cowen, E. L., Gardner, E. A., and Zax, M.: *Emergent Approaches to Mental Health Problems.* New York, Appleton-Century-Crofts, 1967.
6. Cowen, E. L., Gardner, E. A. and Zax, M.: *Emergent Approaches to Mental Health Problems.* New York, Appleton-Century-Crofts, 1967.
7. Cowen, E. L., Izzo, L. D., Miles, H., Telschow, E. F., Trost, M. A., and Zax, M.: A preventive mental health program in the school setting: Description and evaluation. *J Psychol, (part 2):*307-356, 1963.
8. Cowen, E. L., Leibowitz, E., and Leibowitz, G.: The utilization of re-

tired people as mental health aides in the school setting. *Am J Orthopsychiatry, 38:*1968.

9. Cowen, E. L., and Zax, M.: The mental health fields today: Issues and problems. In Cowen, E. L., Gardner, E. A., and Zax, M.: *Emergent Approaches to Mental Health Problems.* New York, Appleton-Century-Crofts, 1967.

10. Cowen, E. L., Zax, M., Izzo, L. D., and Trost, M. A.: Prevention of emotional disorders in the school setting: A further investigation. *J Consult Psychol, 30:*381-387, 1966.

11. Cowen, E. L., Zax, M., and Laird, J. D.: A college student volunteer program in the elementary school setting. *Comm Ment Health J, 2:* 319-328, 1966.

12. Klein, W. L.: The training of human service aides. In Cowen, E. L., Gardner, E. A., and Zax, M.: *Emergent Approaches to Mental Health Problems.* New York, Appleton-Century-Crofts, 1967.

13. Nichols, R. S.: The influence of economic and administrative factors on type and quality of care given to persons with psychological disease. *Working Papers in Community Mental Health, 1:*1-34, 1963.

14. Reiff, R.: Mental health manpower and institutional change. In Cowen, E. L., Gardner, E. A., and Zax, M.: *Emergent Approaches to Mental Health Problems.* New York, Appleton-Century-Crofts, 1967.

15. Riessman, F.: A neighborhood-based mental health approach. In Cowen, E. L., Gardner, E. A., and Zax, M.: *Emergent Approaches to Mental Health Problems.* New York, Appleton-Century-Crofts, 1967.

16. Sanua, V. D.: Sociocultural aspects of psychotherapy and treatment: A review of the literature. In Abt, L. E., and Bellak, L. (Eds.): *Progress in Clinical Psychology.* New York, Grune and Stratton, 1966, p. 151-190, vol. 8.

17. Schofield, W.: *Psychotherapy: The purchase of friendship.* Englewood Cliffs, N.J., Prentice-Hall, 1964.

18. Zax, M., and Cowen, E. L.: Early identification and prevention of emotional disturbance in a public school. In Cowen, E. L., Gardner, E. A., and Zax, M.: *Emergent Approaches to Mental Health Problems.* New York, Appleton-Century-Crofts, 1967.

19. Zax, M., Cowen, E. L., Izzo, L. D., Madonia, A., Merenda, J. and Trost, M. A.: A teacher-aide program for preventing emotional disturbance in young school children. *Ment Hyg, 50:*406-415, 1966.

20. Zax, M., Cowen, E. L., Izzo, L. D. and Trost, M. A.: Identifying emotional disturbance in the school setting. *Am J Orthopsychiatry, 34:* 447-454, 1964.

21. Zax, M., Cowen, E. L., Rappaport, J., Beach, D. R. and Laird, J. D.: Follow-up study of children identified early as emotionally disturbed. *J Consult Psychol, 32:*369-374, 1968.

Chapter 14

THE COMMUNITY MENTAL HEALTH CENTER AND THE SCHOOLS: A MODEL FOR COLLABORATION THROUGH DEMONSTRATION

ROLAND G. THARP, ROBERT I. CUTTS, AND RACHEL BURKHOLDER

T HE COMMUNITY MENTAL HEALTH CENTER draws upon the principles of community as well as clinical psychiatry. As we examine the potential resources for preventive mental health which exist in the community, we are convinced of the salience of the public schools. Schools are primarily concerned with the cognitive growth and development of children. But, because it is difficult to isolate cognitive from affective processes, school personnel often find themselves called upon to handle both academic and behavioral problems in the school setting.

A child must perform adequately in either the academic or social spheres (and preferably both) if he is to be regarded as a success by the important people in his life. Thus, the teacher whose job it is to train this "whole child" finds herself in a role of extreme influence and power in regard to the child, his family, and the community. This power, unfortunately, can be misused: there are ways in which the inadequacy of instruction and the teacher-child relationship can so alienate the child from his environment as to produce mental illness. School, a major force in any child's world, can become a punishing place. A feeling of inadequacy in school can, and often does, spread rapidly, becoming a pervasive and destructive life theme.

On the other hand, the power inherent in the teaching position can be used constructively. The teacher who offers the classroom as a natural setting for maximizing the academic, personal,

Note: Reprinted from *Community Ment Health J, 6:*126-135, 1970.

and social repertoire of each child allows him to learn in miniature to deal with adult society.

THE CLASSROOM AS A TREATMENT MILIEU
FOR THE DISTURBED CHILD

In addition to the prophylactic potential of the classroom, it
can be argued that there are many reasons to view the classroom
as an appropriate treatment milieu. By this point in history, it is
generally accepted that the general social resource of a community
must be marshalled for the "treatment" of disturbed individuals.
There is a clear shortage of mental health personnel; for instance,
in Tucson there is approximately one child psychiatrist for each
100,000 of population. Direct contact by highly trained professional personnel is simply not an available resource for the majority of disturbed children. Out of necessity, other treatment
possibilities have been explored; out of this exploration has come
discovery. Thus, not only is it clear that the classroom can be used
as a primary treatment modality, but in many cases it should be
used. If the interaction between the child and his school environment can be established as a significant reeducative experience,
then this six-hour block of vital learning opportunity can have
more power for good than any other conceivable therapeutic arrangement short of a totally controlled environment, such as hospitalization. Were the special education classrooms for the emotionally disturbed maximally programmed for corrective experience, then this milieu would well become the treatment of choice
for a majority of disturbed children. The classroom has so much
power over the child; enough power to teach him anything including mental, emotional, and intellectual health. Ordinarily,
however, the classroom does not have the knowledge of how to
teach emotional and personal development. Whereas the formalized education of teachers in the curriculum and content fields is
traditionally assigned to universities and colleges of education,
and in-service training is primarily the responsibility of school
districts, perhaps the specific training of school personnel in mental health skills could be a form of assistance offered by mental
health centers to school districts.

A MODEL FOR ACTION THROUGH DEMONSTRATION

However, no mental health center has unlimited resources, either. Just as direct contact between psychiatrist and every patient is impractical, so is direct contact between mental health consultant and every teacher. For instance, the treatment program at the Southern Arizona Mental Health Center must serve metropolitan Tucson and its satellite communities—perhaps 380,000 people. Although the staff numbers nearly one hundred, it cannot hope to provide continuous consultation to the multitude of teachers in Southern Arizona. Responsibilities for serving the disturbed individual, for providing education, consultation, and prophylaxis, require that a model be adopted which will geometrically expand therapeutic impact. It is to this end that a demonstration classroom for emotionally and behaviorally disturbed children has been established on the grounds of the Mental Health Center.

Thus, direct service is offered by a therapist-teacher to selected clinical cases, up to the number that architectural and staff limitations allow. Services of education for prophylaxis are achieved through the demonstration program. Through a cooperative program involving this Mental Health Center, the University of Arizona College of Education, and Tucson School District Number One, teachers of Southern Arizona are educated and trained in classroom mental health skills. A series of observations and participations in the demonstration classroom trains public school teachers for improved classroom management of their own public school pupils. Participation in the program can be at one or more phases depending on position and training. To date the demonstration school has been utilized as (a) an assignment facility for graduate students in education and psychology; (b) for specialized training of teachers and counselors employed in the public schools; and (c) for on-the-job training of special education instructors who are rotated through the classroom as part of the school's regular teaching staff.

These participants can engage in one or more phases of the instructional, research, and planning operations of the program and move in a successive progression of experiences. The four major phases consist of (a) observation, (b) data collection and processing, (c) monitoring, and (d) instructing.

Observation

The demonstration classroom is located in a small building on the grounds of the Mental Health Center. Adjoining the classroom is an observation room equipped with a one-way mirror and microphone attachments, affording an easy view of the classroom without disruption of activities. Here observers can watch a highly competent Master Teacher, on permanent assignment from Tucson School District Number One, as she shapes the behavior of her pupils. Staff members are usually on hand to discuss methods being employed in the classroom at the time. Observation sessions frequently turn into question-and-answer periods as observers relate the demonstrations to their own classroom problems.

Data Collection and Processing

Casual watching of classroom action is one thing—careful minute-by-minute observation and recording of behavior is, of course, a much more complex process demanding training, practice, and precision. The next phase in the teacher-training program, therefore, includes instruction and practice in the accurate recording of time segments of behavior. Observers are asked to chart behaviors over time and to familiarize themselves with data collected by other observers on the teacher or child in question. In this initial stage of record keeping, the teacher-trainee remains in the observation room isolated from any interaction with the children, recording but not participating in the action.

Monitoring

In the third phase of the program, the student-teacher moves out of the observation room into the classroom proper. His duties may include dispensing praise for good behavior, offering tutorial assistance, working with two or more children in a small group, supervising a class activity or managing the classroom in toto when the Master Teacher leaves the area. In these situations, the student-teacher comes face-to-face with schoolroom situations previously observed and must reach on-the-spot decisions of ways to manage the current situation.

After a few such sessions in the classroom, student-teachers become more aware of the effect of their interactions with children, not only through their own immediate perception of the situation but also through later discussion with staff and from confrontation of the cold hard data.

Instructing

Participant instructors are trainees assigned to carry designated classroom loads. Supervision is offered to them by the Master Teacher and others on the staff, but the responsibility for specified areas of instruction is carried by the teacher-trainee. This portion of the program is truly on-the-job training as the teacher must learn to juggle individualized instruction, group presentations, and the application of reinforcement principles both simultaneously and successively.

Two-hour training sessions are arranged daily for five weeks so that each day's problems can be discussed and solutions devised. In addition, all teachers and staff meet together to discuss individual cases, research findings, academic procedure, and innovative ideas.

THE CONTENT OF THE PROGRAM

Now with this elaborate program for teacher education, what is its content? Primary aims of the program are to increase the teacher's sensitivities and skills in four basic areas: (a) accuracy of observation; (b) the use of approximations; (c) the management of contingencies; and (d) the clarification of discriminations.

Accuracy of Observation

Few people are able to observe, directly and immediately, the events of their own lives. For the most part, beliefs about events are created by past experience, expectation, convention, and perceptual sets. The prime and irreducible element of scientific inquiry is the accurate observation; this element is not automatically given, but must be taught, learned, earned. Accurate observation is a more difficult achievement in social systems than in physical ones; it is probably more difficult in familiar surroundings than in a fresh environment. It is more difficult to see the actions of familar people than to accurately know the behavior of strangers. The most difficult thing to observe accurately is one's self.

For all these reasons, it is a rare teacher indeed who can accurately observe his interaction with his pupil. Yet it is surely indisputible that intelligent action cannot proceed in the absence of accurate perception of facts, and it seems that the excellent teacher is usually the accurately observing one. It is a major effort of the program to teach this skill. Perhaps it should be said that it is a major effort to teach this attitude, because the specific skills of observation always vary with the target of observation. The inclination toward accuracy, and the conviction of its necessity—this attitude can be taught, and indeed it becomes most valuable to the teacher whenever he sees the discrepancy between the unreflective perception and the accurate observation. For example: A participant teacher was asked to estimate the number of times a particular child had spoken out in class, without permission, on Tuesday as compared with Monday. She wearily reported that Tuesday had seen many more such incidents than the day previous and that she was increasingly concerned over this management problem. From the observation area, however, the observing teachers had charted on a time-unit graph the actual occurrence of the problem-behavior. It had actually declined in frequency on Tuesday. The inaccurate estimate created in her an inappropriate action pattern: she was ready to abandon her current techniques of management, even though the data suggested that they were effective.

Error factors do operate and will always in the lives of people. Techniques which will override and compensate for these factors must be developed.

The first technique is the simple one of respecting the data of accurate observations. Three basic means of achieving this attitude have been used. The first, already described, is illustrating to the participant and observing teachers the discrepancies between the two modes of perceiving. The second is to offer some basic training in the devices of observing and recording of observations. All the observer teachers do actual time-unit recording of selected behaviors of the children (and of the Master Teacher!) as they watch from the observation room. They learn methods of grouping and graphing data. They serve a brief apprenticeship, in short, as social scientists of the classroom. The "demands" of the recording sheet force the teacher into the unfamiliar behavior of looking carefully at classroom process. In addition, experience indicates that the most experienced observer will actually need to count, from time to time, particularly those behaviors of children which irritate him sufficiently that his scientific objectivity is lost. Thus, recording teaches an attitude; it is also a reliable technique upon which to draw in hard times.

The third means of achieving accuracy of observation is to have the teachers experience the usefulness of these objective data. That is to say, after they learn to discover what is happening, they can be taught to judge what should be happening. If, as in the previous example, a problem behavior is observed to decline in frequency or amplitude, it can then be decided with confidence to maintain the current "treatment-plan" for the child. If, on the other hand, the data reveal that problem behavior is not declining, or is increasing, then procedures should be reexamined, and in all likelihood changed.

The most significant experience our training-teachers have is to observe accurately, to adjust their own behavior in the light of these data, and then to observe the record of the child's improvement. This can frequently be a radical, even a "conversion" experience; the minimum achievement, however, is a worthwhile one: they come to respect facts.

The Use of Contingencies

Contingency management is a central focus of the training

program. It is not the exclusive theoretical concern: the treatment program incorporates the full range of available modalities and approaches. There is a group counseling program, one for individual psychotherapy, work-activity groups, parent-therapy groups, and the like. But behavior modification is one of these; indeed, in the classroom itself, the use of contingency management is the most salient feature to the newly assigned teacher.

Because the Center school deals with atypical pupils, motivational devices are employed which require a more structured environment than is appropriate to the typical classroom. However, no particular effort is made to train the teachers in the details of "behavioral engineering." But the effort is made to make the teacher aware of contingencies and of the effects of their own actions upon the child's behavior. For example: the participant teacher, while proctoring the independent study hour, may well be assigned to punch the reward-system coupon books of those pupils who earn this reinforcement. But this activity is perhaps less important to the participant teacher than to learn of the reinforcing value of his own presence and attention to the child. For a given child, either praise or scolding may be either rewarding or punishing; any permutation may exist, and the true functional relationship of teachers' behavior to a specific behavior of the child must be discovered. Here, the accuracy of observation aim is wedded to the use of contingencies aim. The trainees record their own reactions (smiling, scolding, retreating, ignoring, whatever) to a targeted behavior of a particular child (John argues, studies, fights, approaches, or whatever). When a teacher's action follows a particular behavior of a child, the former is contingent upon the latter. If a week's observation demonstrates that the teacher's approach nearer to the child is contingent upon the child's kicking at another pupil's desk, it is hypothesized that the teacher is inadvertently reinforcing this misbehavior. But this contingency can be "managed." The teacher can be instructed to react differently when John kicks his neighbor's desk, e.g. walk further away from him when he kicks, and then reprimand him; then this new contingency can be recorded and its functional value determined. If the frequency of kicking diminishes from the week previous, the reinforcer to John of teacher's proximity has been successfully managed. If it does not, another contingency-management technique can be attempted.

The teachers have knowledge and control of many other school-available reinforcers: eraser dusting; visits to the principal; name on the blackboard; varsity sport participation; and innumerable others. A basic technique for the rehabilitation of the neurotic or behavior-disordered child is to motivate him to attempt healthier behaviors, which then can be shaped and perfected. The teacher who understands contingency management is in the position to correct incipient problems and to encourage desirable behavior.

Approximations

It is common sense that an individual cannot be expected to produce behavior which is not in his repertoire; that is, behaviors not now possessed by a child must be taught to him. Simple though it may be, this principle is regularly violated and never more often than in the case of the problem child.

Pure research in learning principles has revealed that complex behaviors rarely occur spontaneously in their complete form. Rather than awaiting such an improbability, the wise teacher recognizes that imperfect approximations will occur, and if they are reinforced will become the secure base from which the next and improved approximation will be launched. This process—the reinforcement of successive approximations—is known as shaping.

Most problem children have very narrow ranges of responses, and these are emitted to a wide range of situation-stimuli. Thus, aggression, or withdrawal, or anxiety, or tantruming may be the only "skill" which the child may have in responding to the full range of classrooms' and teachers' complex stimuli. Because these children never emit the full-perfected criterion behavior of, say, courtesy, or homework neatness, or full silent study hour, they are never rewarded. Not only does this produce further withdrawal or counteraggression in the problem child, it also means he never learns to improve. In order to reverse these misfortunes, the child must be brought into the school's reward systems.

Many teachers are reluctant to praise or otherwise reward behavior which is patently undesirable. Yet the first approximations to improvement are frequently still in the "undesirable" range, but must be rewarded nevertheless. The child who has never studied quietly for the required fifteen minutes will never do so unless his successive approximations—three quiet minutes, five, twelve—are reinforced. Simply bringing a pencil to class may be the first approximation to completing an assignment. The first approximation to courtesy may be the absence of abusive language.

To fully achieve the habit of shaping requires much teaching of the teacher; she requires having her own approximations rewarded also.

Discrimination

A major problem for youngsters who have been removed from standard classrooms for "emotional reasons" is their inability to discriminate between many of the behaviors deemed appropriate and acceptable by their high school mentors and others termed unsuitable (intolerable). In most school settings certain actions almost always find teacher approval. For example, high academic strivings, cooperative participation in school approved functions, proper conservative dress are positively sanctioned; other behaviors such as cursing at teachers, flagrant smoking in the halls, consistent absence from class are almost never tolerated. But the consequences of many less obvious forms of behavior, unfortunately, are not as clear-cut or consistent as they might be; and frequently they are dependent on the whims of a particular staff in a particular setting at a particular time. When, for example, does a youngster's inattention become a sign of disrespect in the eyes of his teacher or his overt attempt at friendliness turn into an act of intrusion into personal affairs? When does self-assurance become cockiness; a teasing sense of humor, insolence; blowing off steam, an aggressive display of hostility? By one teacher, youthful exhuberance might be viewed with warm approval as a natural phenomenon, whereas quiet, thoughtful reflection is seen as a possible symptom of withdrawal. For a different teacher the perception might be totally reversed.

A major terminal goal of the treatment program is to reinstate students into a public school setting on a permanent full-time basis. Unfortunately many large public high schools have neither the time nor the tolerance to adjust to the eccentricities of atypical students. The usual ultimatum to a "disruptive" adolescent upon his return to a regular class is "you can remain here as long as you behave, but one false move and you're out!" What is that false move? The definition is often vague and broad. The burden of discovery is upon the student.

The teacher-therapist must, of necessity, therefore, develop acute sensitivity to a range of school behaviors, and their place on the continuum of public school tolerance. Not only must he expand his ability to discriminate between a student's behaviors which are acceptable and unacceptable to school personnel, but he also must devise means to consistently reinforce those actions sanctioned by the schools by rewarding approximations. He must continuously teach the child to discriminate between suitable and unsuitable conduct by consistently pointing out to him the appropriateness or inappropriateness of his behavior.

This process of discrimination—the feel of when a given behavior will be sanctioned or censured—can best be learned through constant exposure to an extensive repertoire of discriminative cues. A teacher-therapist, therefore, must learn to present a wide range of discriminative cues in the classroom and to follow a student's response to these cues with some form of approval or disapproval, depending on the appropriateness of the response. At first the presenting cues can be gross, easily recognized—a sharp barrage of words, an explicit set of instructions, a forceful look. Gradually the clarity of each cue lessens, until a single word, a glance, or a shrug suffices. As a student sharpens his sensitivity to a wide array of behavioral cues—from the gross to the refined—he strengthens his ability to adjust to the idiosyncratic demands of the classroom and life.

IMPLICATIONS FOR SCHOOL, COMMUNITY, AND MENTAL HEALTH CENTER

In any given year, such a demonstration classroom may offer direct treatment and education to a small number of children—perhaps eight to twenty. Certainly this is but a modest achievement; yet if these are the most difficult and alarming youngsters in a district, the contribution to the community may be substantial. Yet—and this is the thrust of the argument—the direct service contribution is paltry when compared with the indirect effects of the operation. These effects occur in all three sectors: school, community, mental health facility.

School

Teachers who have received this specialized training are more confident in the face of behavioral difficulty than most other teachers. As a consequence of this confidence, they become more willing to accept their proper responsibility to maximize the classroom potential for every child. They become more effective workers in the field of education and more effective as mental health line-workers. The impact upon numbers of children in the school reaches startling proportions: if fifteen teachers serve a time in the demonstration classroom, the ten pupils trained at the Center expand into two thousand children in the public schools who may benefit in the next year from these teachers' increased capacity to provide personal growth.

Community

All of these two thousand children will not be problem children. Alert classroom interaction will provide prophylaxis for the community which can have a profound effect on the total spectrum of community problems: delinquency and crime, psychopathology, underachievement, anomie.

Mental Health Center

Immediate benefits accrue to the institution and its staff. After all, the demonstration is not only to the schools and the community, it is to mental health professions themselves. The presence of a model classroom at the Center, and the interdisciplinary interaction which the facility provides, brings a constant input of information and challenge which a staff needs to grow and to improve. One can constantly learn how to use school resources more effectively, learn to appreciate the staggering problems involved in the organization and administration of a curriculum, and learn to understand the difficulties as well as the power which devolve upon the classroom teacher. One comes to admire the determination and dedication required of any teacher who really teaches children. The classroom is a milieu more difficult for the professional than any psychiatric ward. With adequate preparation, the classroom teacher can, for many children, make the psychiatric ward permanently unnecessary.

Chapter 15

MODIFICATION OF A CHILD'S PROBLEM BEHAVIORS IN THE HOME WITH THE MOTHER AS THERAPIST

JANE ZEILBERGER, SUE E. SAMPEN AND HOWARD N. SLOANE, JR.

T RADITIONAL FORMS of child therapy attempt to modify problem behaviors by placing the child in an artificial environment where he interacts with a highly trained specialist. Treatment is usually based upon the assumption that deviant behaviors are symptoms of some underlying emotional disturbance, and treatment is designed to modify these hypothetical underlying causes. However, a learning theory approach suggests that both desirable and undesirable behaviors of the child are maintained by their effects upon the child's natural environment (Bijou and Sloane, 1966). If this is true, the most efficient way to modify deviant behavior may be to change the reactions of the natural milieu to that behavior.

Differential social reinforcement and the use of a timeout from reinforcement have been successfully used to change children's behaviors in a nursery school setting (Harris, Wolf, and Baer, 1964; Sloane, Johnston, and Bijou, in press). In Wahler, Winkel, Peterson, and Morrison's (1965) report of the use of social reinforcement to modify children's problem behavior, the children's mothers, rather than a nursery school teacher, served as therapists. Under controlled laboratory conditions, each mother

Note: Abridged and reprinted from *J Appl Behav Anal*, *1*:47-53, 1968. Copyright 1968, the Society for the Experimental Analysis of Behavior, Inc.

This research was supported by grant MH12067-01 from the National Institutes of Health, U.S. Public Health Service and by grant 32-23-1020-6002 from the U. S. Office of Education, both to Prof. Sidney W. Bijou, and by grant NSF GY 113, 46, 32 66 156 from the National Science Foundation. The authors wish to thank Drs. Sidney Bijou and Stephanie Stolz for suggestions concerning the manuscript.

interacted with her child in specific ways on cue from the experimenter. Russo (1964) demonstrated that parents can serve as therapist in both home and clinical settings, while Hawkins, Peterson, Schweid, and Bijou (1966) used the mother as the therapist in the home.

The present study illustrates that the frequency of a child's undesirable behaviors can be controlled in the home by differential reinforcement contingencies programmed by his parents, and thus replicates the general findings of Hawkins *et al.* (1966).

METHOD

Subjects

Rorey B. was a four-year, eight-month-old boy. He was an only child and had obtained a Stanford Binet I.Q. score of 100. Because of difficulties in two other nursery schools, he was referred to the Child Behavior Preschool Laboratory at the University of Illinois.

Rorey's objectionable behaviors at the time of his enrollment were described as screaming, fighting, disobeying, and bossing. Eight months later these behaviors had reportedly declined to an acceptable level in the preschool but were still observed in his home. Therefore this experiment was conducted in the subject's home using Mrs. B. as the therapist.

Observation of Rorey at home revealed a physically well-developed and active young boy, with average or better verbal skills for his age. With his peers he screamed frequently, at times rarely talking in a normal voice at all. He continually told the other children what to do and how to play, and enforced his demands with punches, kicks, and slaps. Mr. and Mrs. B. were college educated. They were quite concerned over Rorey's behavior. Observation of the mother's interaction with the child during play situations suggested that she reinforced undesirable behavior with excessive attention, that she did not program consequences consistently, and that the contingency between aversive consequences programmed for undesirable behavior and the behavior itself was often unclear, due to the mother's frequent use of long verbal explanations. However, Mrs. B's interactions with

Rorey fell within the pattern usually considered desirable in the middle class, and could not be considered unusual.

Mrs. B. and her husband voiced willingness to cooperate with the program, and eagerness to do what they could to change Rorey's behavior. They stated that the family physician had indicated to them several times that he felt that Rorey's behavior reflected a severe emotional problem.

Procedure

Experimental sessions were held each afternoon (Monday through Friday) at the B.'s home from 3:15 to 4:15 P.M.* Rorey was free to remain in his own house or yard, or to leave. His mother increased the likelihood of Rorey's staying in his own house or yard by having an outdoor inflatable swimming pool and other toys always available. Other neighborhood mothers cooperated to insure that approximately the same children were present each day, and to insure that each child remained for the entire daily experimental period. However, there were a few sessions during the second baseline period when this was not so. The following code was used by the observers:

A: *Physical aggression:* hitting, pushing, kicking, throwing, biting, scratching. Recorded only while the subject was in his own yard or house.

Y: *Yelling.* Recorded only while the subject was in his own yard or house.

B: *Bossing:* Directing another child or adult to do or not to do something. Recorded only while the subject was in his own yard or house.

I: *Any instruction given to Rorey by his mother.* To be coded as an instruction, the statement had to include Rorey's name, and a command that he do or stop doing some specific action. Each

---

*Due to the termination of nursery school (Summer session, Child Behavior Preschool Laboratory), the neighborhood children began playing with Rorey earlier in the day and were often not present during the afternoons. Therefore, on Day 24 the experimental hour was changed for the duration of the experiment to 10:30-11:30 A.M. Observations were made on one Saturday (Day 24) because the experimenter wanted to conclude the study before many of the subject's playmates left on vacation.

different kind of instruction was assigned an arbitrary time interval the first time it occurred. Compliance with the instruction within this interval (which remained the same throughout the study) was coded as obeying by circling the symbol; if Rorey did not comply within this interval it was coded as disobedience by being left uncircled. All instructions given by Mrs. B. were recorded whether the subject was at the neighbors or at home.

The recording techniques have been described previously (Allen, Hart, Buell, Harris, and Wolf, 1964) and involved recording the occurrence or nonoccurrence of each coded behavior in successive 20-sec intervals. Interobserver reliability for each code symbol was determined by computing the percent of total intervals in a session in which two observers agreed as to the presence or absence of the code symbol under consideration. Reliability was tested during each phase of the experiment, and each time was found to be 90 percent or better on all measures described above. As the absolute frequency of aggressive behavior was rather low, reliability was recomputed with the data scored in 2-min intervals. Reliability computed this way was 100 percent. Such rescoring raises approximately five-fold the percent of intervals scored for aggressive behavior and insures that reliability is not merely due to agreement as to the rarity of aggressive incidents.

Various maternal behaviors which were part of the independent variable were also recorded. These included verbal and physical contact with the child, physical proximity, and longer verbal contacts (explanations). The reliability of these measures was not assessed.

The experimental design consisted of four different periods.

Baseline Period I. In this period the preexperimental frequency of the behaviors of interest was assessed. This phase lasted ten sessions. Mrs. B. was told to interact with Rorey as she always did during the afternoon period. Several earlier sessions in which the coding system was developed probably helped Mrs. B. and Rorey to adapt to the presence of the experimenter (S.S.) and the observer (J.Z.).

Experimental Period I. The parents were instructed to follow the program described below. The experimenter cued Mrs. B.

when necessary. When Mrs. B. followed the program correctly, the experimenter provided social approval; when Mrs. B. did not follow the instrutcions correctly, the experimenter corrected her. This phase lasted ten sessions. The instructions were:

1. Immediately after Rorey acts aggressively or disobediently, take him to the time-out (TO) room. One of the family bedrooms was modified for this use by having toys and other items of interest to a child removed.

2. As Rorey is taken to the TO room for aggressive behavior, say "you cannot stay here if you fight." As Rorey is taken to the TO room for disobedient behavior, say "you cannot stay here if you do not do what you are told." Make no other comments.

3. Place Rorey in the TO room swiftly and without conversation other than the above. Place him inside and shut and hook the door.

4. Leave Rorey in the TO room for two minutes. If he tantrums or cries, time the two minutes from the end of the last tantrum or cry.

5. When the time is up take Rorey out of the TO room and back to his regular activities without further comment on the episode, i.e. in a matter-of-fact manner.

6. Do not give Rorey explanations of the program, of what you do, of his behavior, or engage in discussions of these topics with him. If you desire to do this, have such discussions at times when the undesired behaviors have not occurred, such as later in the evening. Keep these brief and at a minimum.

7. Ignore undesirable behavior which does not merit going to the TO room. "Ignore" means you should not comment upon such behavior, nor attend to it by suddenly looking around when it occurs.

8. Ignore aggressive or disobedient behavior which you find out about in retrospect. If you are present, treat disobedient behavior to other adults the same as disobedient behavior to you.

9. Reinforce desirable cooperative play frequently (at least once every 5 min) without interrupting it. Comments, such as "my, you're all having a good time" are sufficient, although direct praise which does not interrupt the play is acceptable.

10. Always reward Rorey when he obeys.

11. Special treats, such as cold drinks, cookies, or new toys or activities, should be brought out after periods of desirable play. It is always tempting to introduce such activities at times when they will interrupt undesirable play, but in the long run this strengthens the undesired behavior.

12. Follow the program twenty-four hours a day.

Baseline Period 2. Mr. and Mrs. B. were instructed to interact with the subject exactly as they had during Baseline Period 1.

Experimental Period 2. This was a replication of Experimental Period 1.

RESULTS

The consequences provided by the parents clearly exerted strong control over the extent to which Rorey followed instructions* (see Fig. 15-1). In the first baseline period, the percent of instructions followed varied between 11 percent and 53 percent,

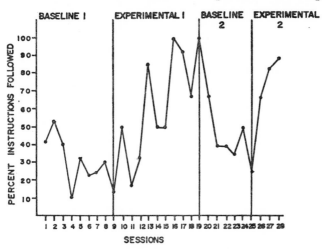

Figure 15-1. Percent of instructions followed.

---

*Percentage of instructions followed was computed by dividing the number of instructions followed by the total number of instructions given. The relative frequency of aggressive acts was computed by dividing the number of intervals in which aggressive acts occurred by the number of intervals the subject spent in his yard or house. Yelling and bossing percents were derived in the same manner as aggression.

averaging 30 percent. During the final seven sessions of the first
experimental period, Rorey followed between 50 percent and 100
percent of instructions, averaging 78 percent. Percent of instructions followed dropped to 40 percent by the second day of Baseline Period 2, and to 25 percent by the final day of this condition.
When the TO room was used again in the three days of the
second experimental period, the percent of instructions followed
rapidly rose to about 78 percent. The extreme and rapid response
of this behavior to the conditions programmed by the parents indicates its sensitivity to the consequences provided by the parents.

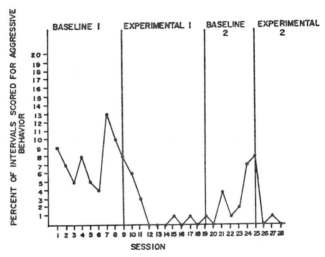

Figure 15-2. Percent of intervals scored for aggressive behavior.

Parental consequences also differentially controlled aggressive
behavior (see Fig. 15-2). In the first baseline period, aggressive behavior occurred in 5 percent to 13 percent of the scored intervals.
On the third day of the first experimental period, no aggressive
behavior was observed, and it occurred only rarely for the remainder of this phase. In the second baseline period, aggressive behavior rose to 8 percent but was quickly eliminated when the experimental conditions were reinstated, indicating the control
which parental consequences had over this behavior.

DISCUSSION

Rorey's aggressive and disobedient behaviors were clearly changed by manipulating the consequences of those behaviors. The changes in behavior were readily apparent to all who came into contact with him. Both Rorey's parents and several neighbors commented that Rorey behaved like a "different child." When aggressive behavior did occur during the experimental conditions, it was usually in self-defense. Toward the end of the first experimental period there were even several instances when the subject was hit and did not strike back.

Obedience improved even more drastically than aggression. In addition to the recorded increase in percentage of instructions followed, the latencies of the subject's responses to his mother's instructions seemed gradually to decrease as the experimental phases progressed.

There was a noticeable difference between the number of instructions given by Rorey's mother during the experimental and baseline periods, an average of six for the former and of fourteen for the latter. This may have occurred because fewer instructions were necessary during the experimental conditions; most instructions were followed the first time and all other immediately led to a TO. Another possible explanation is that it was aversive for Mrs. B. to administer a TO, and that she therefore reduced the number of instructions.

It is evident that during Baseline Period 2 the initial baseline level was not completely regained for either aggressive behavior or disobedience. Several confounding variables during Baseline Period 2 might account for this difference. Mr. B. was home for nearly all of the second baseline period, and Mrs. B. reported that Rorey was better behaved in his father's presence. In addition, Rorey and several of his friends were restricted to their own yards for several days during Baseline Period 2. On these occasions there was no one for Rorey to be aggressive toward but the experimenter, the observer, or his parents.

In comparing the two experimental periods, it is quite apparent that the drop in aggressive behavior and the rise in obedience was achieved much more quickly the second time.

The parents were very cooperative during the experimental sessions, but the program probably was not carried out as systematically at other times. Although the average number of TOs per experimental hour was 1.4, only once did the parents report giving more than two TOs during the rest of the day. Of course, the subject spent most of his time with peers during the experimental hour, increasing the opportunities for aggressive behavior during this time.

Although the experimental program did not directly apply to the subject's yelling and bossing behaviors, yelling tended to remain high or to increase during the baseline periods, and to decrease during the experimental periods. These changes were not as marked as those noted for the behaviors which were directly manipulated. Similar results were noted in a previous study (Sloane *et al.*, in press) , where experimentally induced changes in assaultive behaviors were paralleled by similar changes for verbal aggressive behavior. In the current study, the changes in yelling behavior did not appear to be due to an unplanned contingency involving yelling and the TO procedure, although a moderate decline in maternal attention after yelling was noted. Another possibility is that the decline in yelling was a function of contingencies operating on other responses.

Rorey had been in the laboratory preschool before the home behavior modification program was started. His initial objectionable behaviors in the preschool had reportedly declined to an acceptable level in school without a correlated reduction in these behaviors at home. Traditional treatment usually takes place in a "special" environment, rather than in the setting in which the problem behaviors first attract notice. Our experience has been that when the contingencies programmed for a child in two separate settings differ, discrimination learning may take place, and the child may behave differently, but appropriately, in both settings. Thus for example, we have seen children who are aggressive at home but not at school, who are obedient at school but not at home, or who are toilet trained at school but not at home. One solution appears to be to treat the problem in the environment in which it occurs.

The use of the mother as the therapist in this study had the advantage of offering treatment to the mother and her child together. As the mother learned to deal with her child more effectively, she began to make statements to the effect that her behavior might have been maintaining the objectionable behaviors of her child. As the child's behavior improved, the mother's verbalizations concerning him improved also. The change in the child's behavior may reinforce and maintain this change in the mother. Further possible advantages of modifying behavior in the environment in which it occurs (in this case the home) are that treatment may be carried out (even if not rigorously) twenty-four hours a day, that it may continue after the experimenter leaves, and that the therapeutic process is not an isolated event in the life of the mother or the child.

REFERENCES

1. Allen, K. Eileen, Hart, Betty, Buell, Joan S., Harris, Florence R. and Wolf, M. M.: Effects of social reinforcement on isolate behavior of a nursery school child. *Child Dev, 35*:511-518, 1964.
2. Bijou, S. W. and Sloane, H. N.: Therapeutic techniques with children. In Berg, I. A. and Pennington, L. A. (Eds.): *An Introduction to Clinical Psychology* 3rd ed. New York, Ronald Press, 1966.
3. Brown, P. and Elliott, R.: The control of aggression in a nursery school class. *J Exp Child Psychol, 2*:103-107.
4. Burchard, J. and Tyler, V.: The modification of delinquent behavior through operant conditioning. *Behav Res Ther, 2*:245-250, 1965.
5. Ferster, C. B. and Appel, J. B.: Punishment of S△ responding in matching-to-sample by timeout from positive reinforcement. *J Exp Anal Behav, 4*:45-56, 1961.
6. Harris, Florence R., Wolf, M. M. and Baer, D. M.: Effects of adult social reinforcement on child behavior. *Young Children, 20-1*:8-17, 1964.
7. Hawkins, R. P., Peterson, R. F., Schweid, Etta and Bijou, S. W.: Behavior therapy in the home: Amelioration of problem parent-child relations with the parent in a therapeutic role. *J Exp Child Psychol, 4*:99-107, 1966.
8. Lovaas, O. I., Freitag, G., Gold, Vivian J. and Kassorla, Irene C.: Experimental studies in childhood schizophrenia: analysis of self-destructive behavior. *J Exp Child Psychol, 2*:67-84, 1965.
9. Quay, H. C., Werry, J. S., McQueen, Marjorie and Sprague, R. L.:

Remediation of the conduct problem child in the special class setting. *Excep Child, 32:*509-515, 1966.

10. Richard, H. C. and Dinoff, M.: Shaping adaptive behavior in a therapeutic summer camp. In Ullman, L. P. and Krasner, L. (Eds.): *Case Studies in Behavior Modification.* New York, Holt, Rinehart & Winston, 1965.

11. Russo, S.: Adaptations in behavioral therapy with children. *Behav Res Ther, 2:*43-47, 1964.

12. Sloane, H. N., Johnston, Margaret K. and Bijou, S. W.: Successive modification of aggressive behavior and aggressive fantasy play by management of contingencies. *J Child Psychol Psychiatry* (in press).

13. Wahler, R. C., Winkel, G. H., Peterson, R. F. and Morrison, D. C.: Mothers as behavior therapists for their own children. *Behav Res Ther, 3:*113-134, 1965.

14. Wolf, M. M., Risley, T. R. and Mees, H. L.: Application of operant conditioning procedures to the behavior problems of an autistic child. *Behav Res Ther, 1:*305-312, 1964.

C. CRISIS

Chapter 16

CRISIS: A REVIEW OF THEORY, PRACTICE AND RESEARCH

ALLEN DARBONNE

Recently a new focus on psychological crisis suggests that crises may be periods for maximally effective intervention in emotional illnesses.

As is often the case during the stage of rapid development of a mental health concept, crisis-relevant articles appear in widely scattered journals. They demonstrate little awareness of each other, of what has been written before, and of the relationship of crisis to previously explored concepts. This article attempts a comprehensive review of crisis-relevant literature from its inception approximately twenty years ago.

Farberow *et al.* (1965) emphasized that crisis theory evolved from increasing demands made on the psychotherapeutic professions since World War II. Agencies have long waiting lists (Perlman, 1963). Among applicants who wait nine weeks or more, half do not return (Beck, 1962). This demand for treatment as well as some information from research has shifted the emphasis to shorter treatment (Cattell *et al.,* 1963) and to the group, the family and the community (Klein, 1965; Porter, 1965). These trends and their importance are delineated by the report of the Joint Commission on Mental Illness and Health (1961) and are the focus of articles in the recently established *Community Mental Health Journal* (Roen, 1965; Smith, 1965; Bodarky, 1965; and Kramer, 1965).

Querido (1965) emphasizes the effects of loss of social self, loss of family contact, and the tendency to further regression, which lead him to advise the avoidance of hospitalization when-

Note: Reprinted from *Psychotherapy: Theory, Research and Practice,* 4:49-56, 1967. Gratitude is expressed to Dr. Georgene Seward of the University of Southern California for her helpful suggestions. Literature reviewed to January, 1966.

237

ever possible. Lewis (1962) focuses on the "archaic, medically unsound, and uneconomical" features of institutionalization.

As treatment demands and dissatisfactions increased, several investigators developed early detection and intervention as a step in the direction of prevention. One of the pioneers was Lindemann (1944) who studied the bereavement reactions of families of victims who died in the Coconut Grove night club fire. His findings formed the foundation of "crisis theory." He reported that the duration of a grief reaction was dependent on the success with which a person did his "grief work." He described the stages of a normal course of grief and suggested that individuals could be helped through these stages.

In 1948, Lindemann and Caplan established a community mental health program in the Harvard area, the Wellesley Human Relations Service (Caplan, 1964), where they implemented their crisis intervention ideas. Their basic hypothesis was that, when individuals are confronted with emotional hazards, there are adaptive and maladaptive methods of attempting to cope with the problem. These methods have a sizeable effect on later adjustment and ability to cope. While the original crisis concept has had some modification and expansion over the intervening years current thinking remains along the lines suggested by Lindemann and Caplan.

DEFINITION AND CHARACTERISTICS OF CRISIS

Caplan defines crisis as a state

> provoked when a person faces an obstacle to important life goals that is, for a time, insurmountable through the utilization of customary methods of problem-solving. A period of disorganization ensues, a period of upset, during which many different abortive attempts at solution are made. Eventually some kind of adaptation is achieved which may or may not be in the best interest of that person and his fellows (1961, p. 18).

He refers to the obstacle as an "emotional hazard." His observations indicate that a crisis is usually resolved, for better or worse, in four to six weeks.

Crisis theroy is based on the concept of homeostasis (Caplan, 1964). An individual's state of balance of emotional functioning is maintained by learned coping techniques which are used to solve common problems of daily life. When a problem is greater, when it is related to significant problem areas in an individual's personality or when the previous coping techniques are unsuitable, he moves from an emotionally hazardous into a crisis situation.

Crisis refers to the person's emotional reaction to the hazardous situation, not the situation itself.

While crisis is essentially an individual matter, certain hazardous situations are thought to produce crises in a majority of instances. Among these are death of a significant other, addition of a family member, loss or change of a job, a threat to body or family integrity, entrance into a new developmental stage, change of social role, etc. Erikson (1953) has focused on the difference between "developmental" and "accidental" crises.

The crisis period has four phases (Caplan, 1964). In phase one there is an initial rise in tension which summons the homeostatic habitual problem-solving responses. Phase two includes an increase in tension, upset, and ineffectuality resulting from lack of success and a continuation of stimulus impact. In phase three the tension reaches a point where additional internal and external resources are mobilized. At this point the problem may decrease in intensity, emergengy coping techniques may be used, the problem may be defined in a new way, or certain goals may be relinquished as unattainable. The fourth phase follows if the problem is neither solved with need satisfaction nor avoided by need resignation. It is characterized by mounting tension which may cause major disorganizations and eventually an emotional break.

Morley (1964) points to several key implications arising from this theory. An individual in crisis is ripe for great change in a short period of time and he can be maximally influenced by another person during this period. A person's response to crisis is only partially determined by previous emotional struggles. Present psychological forces contribute significantly to this determination. Also, equilibrium following a crisis may be at a level of higher or lower mental health. Enduring positive change can result from adaptive crisis resolution.

Couched in these terms the concept of "crisis" sounds similar to the concept of "stress." Rapoport (1962) attempted to differentiate these two concepts. She sees stress as having pathogenic potential and crisis as growth-promoting potential. This definition of "stress" predominated at a recent conference (Richter, 1960). Caplan (1964) views crisis as time-limited whereas stress need not be. The literature of both areas indicates that these terms are at times used interchangeably, especially when stress and crisis are considered phenomenologically.

The problem of defining "crisis" was pointed up by Bloom (1963) in one of the few good experimental studies in this area. His results indicate that to expert judges crisis is defined as an episode beginning with a known precipitating event, followed by *either* no discernible reaction *or* one that was resolved in a month or so. When the precipitating event was known, judges could not reliably determine the presence of a crisis on the basis of subsequent reactions. Further refinement of the definition of the crisis concept is necessary before research on the effectiveness of crisis intervention can be undertaken.

Many workers have begun instituting these developing concepts in treatment facilities which thereby become centers for testing and generating new hypotheses. Characteristics of such facilities are described by Coleman and Zwerling (1959), Mac Leod and Middelman (1962), Cattell *et al.* (1963), Bellak, (1960), McGee (1965), Errera *et al.* (1963), Schwartz and Errera (1963), Ungerleider (1960), Clark (1963), Jacobson *et al.* (1964), Strickler (1965), Waltzer and Hankoff (1965), and Shneidman, Farberow, and Litman (1961), to cite a few. Parad (1965) has recently compiled a book of readings concerning crisis intervention which demonstrates the broad applicability of these concepts. The reported recovery rates by agencies practicing crisis therapy are very impressive.

RELATIONSHIP OF CRISIS THEORY
TO OTHER THEORETICAL SYSTEMS

Crisis theory is quite consistent with ego psychology. As Selby (1963) explains, crisis therapy is brief therapy to help the ego in its cognitive, synthesizing and integrating functions. Within the framework of prevention theory, it is considered primary prevention (Caplan, 1964). It is an action therapy which views work with significant others as very important. This factor distinguishes crisis from traditional short-term therapy (Parad, 1961). It is related to the existential approach through its emphasis on the here and now and on the growth potential forces of crisis (May *et al.*, 1958) and to the potentially constructive view of crisis found in Rank's (1945) concept of the birth trauma, and in the works of Adler, Horney, Fromm, Sullivan (Munroe, 1955) and Rogers (1961). Jahoda (1958) has discussed the importance of differentiating between positive crisis reactions and mental ill health.

Behaviorist and conditioning theorists have not focused specifically on crisis. Their general assumption that the observable behavior is the psychopathology and can be attacked directly is compatible with active crisis intervention. Shaw (1961) emphasizes that in problem resolution current success breeds future success. This is supported by experiments on an animal level that indicate infantile "stress" can be positively adaptive (Levine, 1962).

One area of psychological therapy which has not been linked with crisis theory, although the advantages of such a consideration are obvious, is that of creative problem solving. Crisis resolution is, in essence, an attempt of an individual to solve a problem which is novel to him. The problems of being "stimulus-bound" (Maier, 1933), the relevance of motivation (Birch, 1945), Frenkel-Brunswick's (1949) concept of ambiguity tolerance, and Bruner's (1956, 1964) work on concept formation and problem solving are only a few germane principles.

A review of crisis-relevant literature suggests a categorization of studies into three general aspects of crisis: situational; interpersonal and group; and individual and psychodynamic.

Situational Aspects of Crisis

Kaplan (1962) develops the theoretical difference between individual problems (chronic psychological disorder) and situational problems (acute adaptive reactions to environmental changes). Situational focus is not new. Sheffield (1937) stressed that the "individual confronted with a problem situation" is the important unit for treatment attention. Epidemiological data (Glass, 1958) indicate that the incidence of combat neurosis is related more to circumstances (social pressures and social support from the soldier's buddies) of the combat situation than to personality factors. In similar noncombat army situations (Bushard, 1958) it was concluded that it was best to leave the soldier in the situation from which he was trying to escape and to treat him there. The situational crisis of relocation through urban renewal was discussed by Brown (1965) with some proposed solutions.

Many situational investigations concern disasters. (The Disaster Research Group [1961] has inventoried 114 field studies.) Mack and Baker (1961) found that people seldom instantly adapt adequate courses of protective action after receiving a disaster warning. Moore (1958) detected several phases of social behavior in the rehabilitative process of families after tornado disasters.

Other studies include relocation from "slum housing" (Fried and Lindemann, 1961), children of parents who are hospitalized for mental illness (Irvine, 1964), hospitalized children and adolescents (Vernick, 1963), kindergarten entry (Klein and Ross, 1958), slow-learning children (Stahlecker, 1965) and the crisis of unwed motherhood (Bernstein, 1960).

Interpersonal Family and Group Aspects of Crisis

Most crisis workers emphasize working with the families of individuals in crisis. Not only is the family usually involved in the crisis situation, but it also has a great impact on the individual's technique and success in meeting the crisis.

Parad and Caplan (1960) studied fifty families in crisis and proposed the following framework: family life-style; intermediate problem-solving mechanisms; and need-response patterns. They stress the importance of cultural difference in family reactions to crisis. Koos (1946) pointed out how some families emerge from a crisis stronger, while others become weaker or dismembered. Rapoport (1962) suggests differing treatment approaches for different family types. She recommends as general therapeutic activities keeping explicit focus on the crisis and managing the affect; offering basic information; and creating a bridge to community resources.

An instrument to measure maladaptive coping in parent-child relationship patterns was devised by Hurwitz, Kaplan, and Kaiser (1962). The study represents a good beginning of experimental control and operational definitions.

Hill (1958) proposed a framework for studying families in crisis which emphasizes the family's crisis-meeting resources and ability to anticipate crisis. Ritchie (1960) describes an intensive, six- or seven-hour per day, two-day treatment of families in crisis. It is called "multiple impact therapy" and involves, at times, the family being seen simultaneously by more than one member of the treatment team. Kaffman (1963) also discusses a technique of short-term family therapy.

Rhona Rapoport (1963) has investigated the adjustment of young couples to the crises of engagement, early marriage and the first baby. Le Masters (1957) studied the reactions of couples to the birth of their first child. He views it as a crisis because it causes a shift from a two-person group to a three-person group, which frequently becomes a pair and an isolate. Controls were lacking. Dyer (1963) reports on a better designed study on the same question, but there are problems of sampling and of subjects' recall of events two years prior to interview. Cyr (1957) works during pregnancy and immediate post-partum period, preparing parents for what they can expect and helping them to understand their "conscious" attitudes and behavior. It is true that preparation for parenthood classes have been offered for years. These programs could easily be altered to include it.

Klein and Lindemann (1961) describe the advantages of discussion groups with parents of children entering school. Rosenberg and Fuller (1955) discuss a similar program with student nurses, which significantly reduced drop-out rates.

Howe (1964) indicates that a crisis can heighten or lessen the sense of community. She suggests that frequency of crises routinely imposed on individuals might serve as an index of community disorder. Certain community service agencies such as Travelers

Air have begun to take on crisis intervention functions (Chaskel, 1961).

Since crises, by their nature, are emergency situations, more crisis intervention training should be offered to personnel of community agencies which are likely to have contact with individuals during the early stages of crisis situations.

Individual and Psychodynamic Aspects of Crisis

Among the numerous extensions of crisis theory, the only major research area concerns suicidal crisis. As this field has been developed independently the reader is referred to Shneidman and Farberow (1957), and Farberow (1961 and 1965).

Much attention has been given to the relationship between current crisis and earlier experiences (Waldfogel and Gardner, 1961). During a crisis memories of old problems are linked symbolically to the present (Sarvis *et al.,* 1959; and Kalis *et al.,* 1961). Current threats to instinctual need (symbolically linked to earlier threats) are common precipitants of crisis (Parad and Caplan, 1960).

Harris *et al.* (1963) advocate focusing on the precipitating stress in brief therapy. Precipitating stress, they propose, results from the interaction of current events with the "conflict derivatives" they engender or reflect. The goal of crisis therapy is to make explicit and work through these conflict derivatives.

This view is similar to Fenichel's (1945), although his treatment approach deals less with the here and now. Gill (1954) suggests a theoretical rationale for the new adaptive balance established by working through "derivative conflicts" without working through the basic conflict.

Crisis clinic patient populations include groups of patients who are not usually represented in traditional psychiatric facilities, including usually unmotivated and lower socioeconomic and older age groups (Kalis *et al.,* 1961; Jacobson, 1964; and Strickler *et al.,* 1965).

Tyhurst (1957) warns against nonjudicious symptom removal. Alpern (1965) agrees that experience in long-term psychotherapy is necessary before a threapist can make adequate use of brief therapy. One of the major considerations here is the timing of the individual's behavior. (In times of realistic hazard, a reaction of disorganization, withdrawal, and even intense anxiety, may be an emotionally healthy reaction.)

Farberow *et al.* (1965) have stressed the importance of having treatment sources accessible (in terms of time and distance) if crisis intervention is to be made at the optimum moment. They explore the use of telephone therapy.

A study by Dewees *et al.* (1961) shows that an initial crisis interview must occur within two weeks after request for treatment. Beyond this, maladaptive coping and poor resolution, with significant resistance to intervention and insight is apt to occur. Farnsworth (1953) argues for support of adjustive attempts rather than encouraging regression in therapy.

Jacobson (1965) has outlined the following therapist's procedure: (a) formulate the dynamics in his own mind; (b) state the problem in terms the patient can assimilate in the available time; (c) help the patient see the problem in a new light and show him where his previous coping mechanisms have failed; (d) do not get involved in discussion of chronic problems. Avoid direct advice, except in rare instances, to discourage dependency; (e) begin planning discharge at first interview. Bellak and Small (1965) offer techniques and illustrations of a variety of other sorts.

Forer (1963) describes three levels: situational crises, crises of secondary narcissism, and crises of primary narcissism. He proposes that psychotherapy involves a series of successive crises, and that their resolution is the process by which rigid defenses are replaced with adaptive methods. Ruesch (1961) discusses four types of individual crises in communications terms: input crises, anticipation and recollection crises, decision-making crises, and output crises. Menninger (1954) discusses the ego under stress. Mead (1934) refers to adaptive worrying before a crisis situation as "presenting to oneself to a situation that is going to arise."

Several investigations of specific types of crises have generated valuable treatment theory. Bowlby (1960) found that young children entering a hospital proceed through three phases as a result of separation: trauma-protest, despair, and then detachment. Other studies concern children facing new life experience (Murphy, 1956) ; death anxiety in children with fatal illnesses (Morrissey, (1964) ; and the mother's crisis of premature birth (Caplan *et al.*, 1965, Kaplan and Mason, 1960). Janis (1958) found significant correlations between patients' presurgical reactions and their postsurgical adjustment.

Freeman, Kalis, and Harris (1964) developed a method of objective ratings to quantify crisis interview material. Cath (1963) considers crisis work in relation to the dynamics of middle and later years. Other studies concern adolescents (Ichikawa, 1961; Miller, 1959; Redl, 1959) and emotionally disturbed children.

To date the field of crisis intervention gives reason for optimism. Ahead lies the scientific task of converting impressions into hypotheses and clinical reports into experimental research. It might be said that the concept of psychological crisis is currently in a crisis of its own. The concept has reached a new developmental period where the old coping mechanisms of exploratory research, theorizing and clinical case reports are not in themselves contributing to the healthy growth of the concept. Whether or not the concept emerges from this crisis as vital and growing or as exhausted and regressed will depend upon the response of significant others, professional scientists interested in crisis.

REFERENCES

1. Alpern, Evelyn: Short clinical services for children in a child guidance clinic. *Am J Orthopsychiatry, 26*:314-325, 1956.
2. Beck, Dorothy F.: *Patterns in Use of Family Agency Service.* New York, Family Service Association of America, 1962.
3. Bellak, L.: A general hospital as a focus of community psychiatry. *JAMA, 174*:2214, 1960.
4. Bellak, L. and Small, L.: *Emergency Psychotherapy and Brief Psychotherapy.* New York, Grune and Stratton, 1965.
5. Bernstein, Rose: Are we still stereotyping the unmarried mother? *Social Work, 5:*(3), 1960.
6. Birch, H. G.: The role of motivational factors in insightful problem-solving. *J Com Psychol, 38*:259-278, 1945.
7. Bloom, B. C.: Definitional aspects of the crisis concept. *J Consult Psycol, 27(6)*:498-502, 1963.

8. Bodarky, C. J.: Comprehensive planning for community mental health services. *Community Mental Health J, 1*:1965.

9. Bowlby, J.: Separation anxiety. *Int J Psychoanal, XLI*:89-113, 1960.

10. Brown, H. F., Burditt, Vera B. and Lidell, C. W.: The crisis of relocation. In Parad, H. J. (Ed.): *Crisis Intervention: Selected Readings.* New York, Family Service Association of America, 1965 p. 248-260.

11. Bruner, J. S., Goodnow, J. J. and Austin, G. A.: *A Study of Thinking.* New York, Wiley, 1956.

12. Bruner, J. S.: The course of cognitive growth. *Am Psychol, 19*:1-15, 1964.

13. Bushard, B. L.: The United States Army's mental hygiene consultation service. In *Symposium on Preventive and Social Psychiatry.* Walter Reed Army Institute of Research, Washington, D.C. United States Government Printing Office, 1958.

14. Caplan, G.: *An Approach to Community Mental Health.* New York, Grune and Stratton, 1961.

15. Caplan, G.: *Principles of Preventive Psychology.* New York, Basic Books, 1964.

16. Caplan, G., Mason, E. and Kaplan, D.: Four studies of crisis in parents of prematures. *Community Mental Health J, 1*:1965.

17. Cath, S. H.: Some dynamics of the middle and later years. *Smith College Studies in Social Work, XXIII(2)*:1963.

18. Cattell, J. P., Forester, E. and McKinnon, R. A.: Limited goal therapy in a psychiatric clinic. *Am J Psychiatry, 120*:255-260, 1963.

19. Chaskel, Ruth: Assertive casework in a short-term situation. *Casework Papers, 1961.* New York, Family Service Association of America, 1961.

20. Clark, Eleanor: Round-the-clock emergency psychiatric services. *Social Work Practice, 1963. Papers from the National Conference on Social Welfare.* New York, Columbia University Press, 1963.

21. Coleman, M. D. and Zwerling, I.: The psychiatric emergency clinic: A flexible way of meeting community mental health needs. *Am J Psychiatry, 115*:11, 1959.

22. Cyr, Florence E. and Wattenburg, Shirley H.: Social work in a preventive program of maternal and child health. *Social Work, 2:* 1957.

23. Dewees, R. F., Johnson, R. F., Sarvis, M. A. and Pope, S. T.: An open service in a university psychiatric clinic. *Mental Hygiene, 47*:57, 1961.

23. Disaster Research Group. Field Studies of Disaster Behavior: An Inventory. *Disaster Study No. 14.* Washington, D.C., National Academy of Sciences—National Research Council, 1961.

25. Dyer, E. D.: Parenthood as crises: A re-study. *Marriage and Family Living, XXV(2):* 1963.

26. Erikson, E.: Growth and crisis of the healthy personality. In Kluckhohn, C. and Murray, H. (Eds.): *Personality in Nature, Society and Culture.* New York, Knopf, 1953.

27. Errera, P., Wyshak, G. and Jarecki, H.: Psychiatric care in a general hospital emergency room. *Arch Gen Psychiatry, 9*:105-112, 1963.
28. Farberow, N. L. and Shneidman, E. S.: *The Cry For Help.* New York, McGraw-Hill, 1961.
29. Farberow, N. L., Schneidman, E. S., Litman, R. E., Wold, C. I., Helig, S. M. and Kramer, Jan: Suicide prevention around the clock. *Am J Orthopsychiatry,* 1965 (In press).
30. Farnsworth, D. L.: Potential problem areas of mutual interest to the dean and the psychiatrist. *Ment Hyg, 37*:209-219, 1953.
31. Fenichel, O.: *The Psychoanalytic Theory of Neurosis.* New York, Norton, 1945.
32. Forer, B.: The therapeutic value of crises. *Psychol Rep, 13*:275-281, 1963.
33. Freeman, Edith H., Katis, Betty L. and Harris, M. R.: Assessing patient characteristics from psychotherapy interviews. *J Proj Tech Pers Assess, 28(4)*:413-424, 1964.
34. Frenkel-Brunswick, E.: Intolerance of ambiguity as an emotional and perceptual personality variable. *J Pers, 18*:108-143, 1949.
35. Fried, M. and Lindemann, E.: Socio-cultural factors in mental health and illness. *Am J Orthopsychiatry, 31*:87-101, 1961.
36. Gill, M.: Psychoanalysis and exploratory psychotherapy. *J Am Psychoanal Assoc, 2*:793, 1954.
37. Glass, A. T.: Observations upon the epidemiology of mental illness in troops during warfare. *Symposium on Preventive and Social Psychiatry.* Walter Reed Army Institute of Research, Washington, D.C. United States Government Printing Office, 1958.
38. Harris, M. R., Kalis, Betty and Freeman, Edith: Precipitating stress: An approach to brief therapy. *Am J Psychother, 17*:465-471, 1963.
39. Hill, R.: Generic features of families under stress. *Social Casework, 39:* 1958.
40. Howe, Louisa P.: The concept of the community. In Bellak, L. (Ed.): *The Handbook of Community Psychiatry.* New York, Grune and Stratton, 1964.
41. Hurwitz, J. I., Kaplan, D. M. and Kaiser, E.: Designing an instrument to assess parental coping mechanisms. *Social Casework, XLIII(10):* 1962.
42. Ichikawa, Alice: Observations of college students in acute distress. *Student Medicine, 10(2):* 1961.
43. Irvine, Elizabeth E.: Children at risk. *Case Conference, 10(10):* 1964.
44. Jacobson, G. F.: Crisis theory and treatment strategy: Some socio-cultural and psychodynamic considerations. Paper read at International Congress of Social Psychiatry. London, England, August, 1964.
45. Jacobson, G. F., Wilner, D. M., Morley, W. E., Schneider, S., Strickler, M. and Sommer, Geraldine: The scope and practice of an early-access

brief treatment psychiatric center. Paper read at American Psychiatric Association, Los Angeles, California: May, 1964.

46. Jacobson, G. F.: Some psychoanalytic considerations regarding crisis therapy. Paper presented at American Psychoanalytic Association. New York, April, 1965.

47. Jahoda, Marie: *Current Concepts in Positive Mental Health*. New York, Basic Books, 1958.

48. Janis, I.: *Psychological Stress*. New York, Wiley, 1958.

49. Joint Commission on Mental Illness and Health. *Action for Mental Health*. New York, Basic Books, 1961.

50. Kaffman, Mordecai: Short-term family therapy. *Family Process, 2(2):* 1963.

51. Kalis, Betty, Harris, M. R., Priestwood, A. R. and Freeman, Edith: Precipitating stress as a focus in psychotherapy. *Arch Gen Psychiatry, 5:*219-228, 1961.

52. Kaplan, D. M. and Mason, E. A.: Maternal reactions to premature birth viewed as an acute emotional disorder. *Am J Orthopsychiatry, 30:*539-552, 1960.

53. Kaplan, D. M.: A concept of acute situational disorder. *Social Work, 7:* 15-23, 1962.

54. Klein, D. C.: Community and mental health—An attempt at a conceptual framework. *Community Mental Health J, 1:*1965.

55. Klein, D. C. and Ross, Ann: Kindergarten entry: A study of role transition. *Orthopsychiatry and the School*. Morris Krugman (Ed.): American Orthopsychiatric Association, New York, 1958.

56. Klein, D. C. and Lindemann, E.: Preventive intervention in individual and family crisis situations.

57. Caplan, G. (Ed.) : In *Prevention of Mental Disorders in Children: Initial Explorations*. New York, Basic Books, 1961.

58. Koos, E.: *Families in Trouble*. New York, Kings Crown Press, 1946.

59. Kramer, B. M.: Links and barriers between hospital and community. *Community Mental Health J, 1:* 1965.

60. Le Masters, E. E.: Parenthood as crisis. *Marriage and Family Living, XIX(4):* 1957.

61. Levine, S.: The effects of infantile experience on adult behavior. In Bachrach, A. J. (Ed.): *Experimental Foundations of Clinical Psychology*. New York, Basic Books, 1962.

62. Lewis, F. A.: Community care of psychiatric patients versus prolonged institutionalization. *JAMA, 182:*323-326, 1962.

63. Lindemann, E.: Symptomology and management of acute grief. *Am J Psychiatry, CI:*141-148, September, 1944.

64. McGee, R. K.: The suicide prevention center as a model for community mental health program. *Community Mental Health J, 1:* 1965.

65. Mack, R. W. and Baker, G. W.: The occasion instant: The structure of

social responses to unanticipated air raid warnings. *Disaster Study, No. 15*. Washington, D. C., NAS-NRC, 1961.

66. MacLeod, J. A. and Middelman, Francine: Wednesday afternoon clinic: A supportive care program. *Arch Gen Psychiatry, 6:*56-65, 1962.

67. Maier, N. R. F.: An aspect of human reasoning. *Br J Psychol, 24:*144-155, 1933.

68. May, R. *et al.* (Eds.): *Existence: A New Dimension in Psychiatry and Psychology.* New York, Basic Books, 1958.

69. Mayo, Clara and Klein, D. C.: Group dynamics as a basic process of community psychiatry. In Bellak, L. (Ed.): *Handbook of Community Psychiatry and Community Mental Health.* New York, Grune and Stratton, 1964.

70. Mead, G. H.: *Mind, Self and Society.* Chicago, University of Chicago Press, 1934.

71. Menninger, K.: Psychological aspects of the organism under stress. *J Am Psychoanal Assoc, 2:*305, 1954.

72. Miller, Lovick C.: Short-term therapy with adolescents. *Am J Orthopsychiatry, XXIX(4):* 1959.

73. Moore, H. E.: *Tornadoes over Texas: A Study of Waco and San Angelo in Disaster,* Austin, Texas: University Press, 1958.

74. Morley, W. E.: Treatment of the patient in crisis. *Los Angeles Psychiatric Service.* Unpublished manuscript, 1964.

75. Morrissey, J. R.: Death anxiety in children with a fatal illness. *Am J Psychother, XXVII(4):* 1964.

76. Munroe, Ruth L.: *Schools of Psychoanalytic Thought.* New York, Dryden Press, 1955.

77. Murphy, Lois B. *et al.: Personality In Young Children.* New York, Basic Books, 1956.

78. Parad, H. J. and Caplan, G. A.: Framework for studying families in crisis. *Social Work, 5:*3-15, 1960.

79. Parad, H. J.: Preventive casework: Problems and implications. *The Social Welfare Forum, 1961, Papers from The National Conference on Social Welfare.* New York, Columbia University Press, 1961.

80. Parad, H. J. (Ed.): *Crisis Intervention: Selected Readings.* New York, Family Service Association of America, 1965.

81. Perlman, Helen H.: Some notes on the waiting list. *Social Casework, XLIV(4):* 1963.

82. Porter, R. A.: Crisis intervention and social work models. *Community Mental Health J, 1:*1965.

83. Querido, A.: Early diagnosis and treatment services. In *Elements of a Community Mental Health Program,* Milbank Memorial Fund, Inc., 1965.

84. Rank, O.: *Will Therapy and Truth and Reality* (Trans. by J. Taft). New York, Knopf, 1945.

85. Rapoport, Lydia: The state of crisis: Some theoretical considerations. *Social Service Review, 36:*211-217, June, 1962.

86. Rapoport, Lydia: Working with families in crisis: An exploration in preventive intervention. *Social Work, 7(3):* 1962.

87. Rapoport, Rhona V.: Normal crisis, family structure and mental health. *Family Process, 2:*68-80, 1963.

88. Redl, F.: The life space interview. Workshop, 1957. I. Strategy and Techniques of the Life Space Interview. *Am J Orthopsychiatry, XXIX(1):* 1959.

89. Richter, D.: Some current usage of the word "stress" in different fields. In Tanner, J. M. (Ed.): *Stress and Psychiatric Disorder,* Oxford, England, Blackwell Scientific Publications, 1960.

90. Rioch, D. McK.: Preface. In *Symposium on Preventive and Social Psychiatry.* Sponsored jointly by Walter Reed Army Institute of Research, Walter Reed Army Institute of Research. Walter Reed Army Medical Center and The National Research Council, April 1957. Washington, D. C. United States Government Printing Office, 1958.

91. Ritchie, Agnes: Multiple impact therapy: An experiment. *Social Work, 5(3):* 1960.

92. Roen, S. R. (Ed.) : *Community Mental Health J, 1:* 1965.

93. Rogers, C.: *On Becoming a Person: A Client's View of Psychotherapy.* Boston, Houghton Mifflin, 1961.

94. Rosenberg, Pearl P. and Fuller, Myrtrie I.: Human relations seminar: A group work experiment in nursing education. *Ment Hyg, 34:*406-432, 1955.

95. Ruesch, J.: *Therapeutic Communication.* New York, Norton, 1961.

96. Sarvis, Mary, Dewees, Sally and Johnson, Ruth: A concept of ego-oriented psychotherapy. *Psychiatry, 20:*277-287, 1959.

97. Schwartz, M. D. and Errera, P.: Psychiatric care in a general hospital emergency room. *Arch Gen Psychiatry, 9:*113-121, 1968.

98. Selby, Lola G.: Social work and crisis theory. In *Social Work Papers,* X. School of Social work, University of Southern California, Los Angeles, 11, 1963.

99. Shaw, F. J.: *Behavioristic Approaches To Counseling and Psychotherapy.* University of Alabama Press, 1961.

100. Shaw, F. J.: Counseling and psychotherapy from the standpoint of a behaviorist. In Shaw, F. J. (Ed.): *Behaviroistic Approaches to Counseling and Psychotherapy.* University of Alabama Press, 1961.

101. Sheffield, Ada E.: *Social Insight In Case Situations.* New York, Appleton-Century Company, 1937.

102. Shneidman, E. S. and Farberow, N. L. (Eds.): *Clues To Suicide.* New York, McGraw-Hill, 1957.

103. Shneidman, E. S. and Farberow, N. I. and Litman, R. E.: The suicide prevention center. In Farberow, N. L. and E. S. Shneidman (Eds.): *The Cry For Help*. New York, McGraw-Hill, 1961.

104. Smith, Elizabeth: Current issues in mental health planning. *Community Mental Health J, 1:* 1965.

105. Stahlecker, L. V.: Counseling parents of slow-learning children. *Community Mental Health J, 1:* 1965.

106. Strickler, M.: Applying crisis theory in a community clinic. *Social Casework,* May 1965.

107. Strickler, M., Bassin, Ellen G., Malbin, Virginia and Jacobsen, G. F.: The community-based walk-in center: A new resource for groups under-represented in outpatient treatment facilities. *Am J Public Health, 55:3,* 1965.

108. Tyhurst, J. S.: The pole of transition states—Including disaster in mental illness. *Symposium on Preventive and Social Psychiatry. Walter Reed Institute of Research.* Washington, D. C., United States Government Printing Office, 1957.

109. Ungerleider, J. T.: The psychiatric emergency. *Arch Gen Psychiatry, 3:* 1960.

110. Vernick, J.: The use of the life space interview on a medical ward. *Social Casework, XLIV(8):* 1963.

111. Waldfogel, S. and Gardner, G. E.: Intervention in crisis as a method of primary prevention. Caplan, G. (Ed.): *The Prevention Of Mental Disorder In Children: Initial Exploration.* New York, Basic Books, 1961.

112. Waltzer, H. and Hankoff, L. D.: One year's experience with a suicide prevention telephone service. *Community Mental Health J, 1:* 1965.

Chapter 17

AVOIDING PSYCHIATRIC HOSPITALIZATION

KALMAN FLOMENHAFT, DAVID M. KAPLAN, AND
DONALD G. LANGSLEY

HOSPITALIZATION of severely disturbed psychiatric patients has been traditional. There have been few alternatives to this, and it has generally been easier to hospitalize patients than to avoid admission. Although the custodial-care hospital has adopted a treatment orientation, the revolving door concept has resulted only in shorter but more frequent periods of hospitalization. Evaluative studies have raised a serious question about the effectiveness of mental hospital admission. It is the aim of this paper to explore some of the problems associated with psychiatric hospitalization and to describe an alternative in which the social worker may play a significant and effective role.

TREATMENT PROBLEMS IN A HOSPITAL SETTING

The label of "mental patient" does not evolve from the presence of the symptoms of psychiatric illness, but is acquired with admission to a mental hospital. The Cummings have pointed out that

clinical experience supports the impression that many people define mental illness as that condition for which a person is treated in a mental hospital . . . until they go, almost anything they do is normal.[1]

The benefits expected to accrue from hospital treatment must be balanced against the disadvantages of being labeled a mental patient. Admission to that status may diminish the individual's self-

Note: Slightly abridged and reprinted with permission of the National Association of Social Workers from *Social Work, 14: (No. 4)*:38-45, Oct. 1969.

This article is based on a study from the work of the Family Treatment Unit, which is part of an NIMH clinical demonstration and research program of Colorado Psychiatric Hospital, supported by NIMH Grant MH 16286.

253

esteem and intensify the family's picture of him as being incapable of managing his affairs. Despite the notion that society is more accepting of mental illness, the ex-mental patient is stigmatized. His application for a driver's license often must be accompanied by a medical report. Job applications for civil service and private industry may specifically ask if the applicant has had treatment in a mental hospital. A young person may be refused admission to a college or to the armed forces because of a history of psychiatric admissions.

Hospitalization disrupts the ability of the individual to perform his usual role in the family, with the result that the job of breadwinner or homemaker must be carried on by someone else. Upon discharge, there may be difficulty in reintegrating the patient into his family and community. With each successive readmission, the family further isolates the patient.

Employers usually view patients as highly undependable. A study of the work histories of 108 schizophrenic patients found that 87 percent of the sample had worked regularly prior to the first psychiatric hospitalization. There was a strong downward shift after each subsequent hospitalization, both in job level and in the percentage employed. Eight years after the first hospitalization, only 43 percent of the group were employed.[2]

Hospitalization may be used by individuals or families for destructive and manipulative purposes. Wood *et al.* studied the circumstances surrounding the mental hospital admissions of forty-eight patients and found evidence to suggest that hospitalization can, for some patients, be a way of demanding that those close to them change their behavior, just as it can be an expression by relatives that they are dissatisfied with the patient's behavior.[3] These manipulations suggest that hospitalization may be used in a power struggle. Under such circumstances, the purpose of hospitalization has more to do with controlling certain family members than with therapeutic change.

One hospitalization leads to another and yet another. Rather than utilizing community outpatient facilities to deal with current stress, the family rehospitalizes the ex-mental patient. Miller's five year follow-up study of patients discharged from California mental hospitals demonstrated that "71 percent had returned to the hospital at least once during those five years, and 24 percent had been rehospitalized an average of 4.4 times."[4]

Hospitalization does not resolve interpersonal conflicts, but postpones that resolution. It provides a temporary escape from current problems. Querido, the Dutch psychiatrist who established the Amsterdam Home Care Service, describes the process of dealing with crises by hospitalization:

> By admitting him to the hospital, his running away is met with success, a way of escape is opened to him. In many cases it is most important to keep this way closed, to frustrate the patient's attempt at running away and to teach him to keep on facing the situation with, of course, expert help. The hospital by its very nature tends to isolate itself from the rest of the community and by its very atmosphere, its history, and its organization, is apt to filter out, so to speak, a most important attribute of the patient, that is his social and personal aspects, what we may call his relational life.[5]

Finally, hospitalization is far more expensive than outpatient treatment, and the total cost of any single hospitalization will depend not only on the cost per day, but also the length of hospitalization. A six-month stay at a $10-a-day custody-oriented state mental hospital is more expensive than a twenty-five-day admission to an acute treatment-oriented hospital at $50 per day. There are no comparative figures for the cost of outpatient crisis services other than the estimates in a report from the Family Treatment Unit of Colorado Psychiatric Hospital, but it is clear that the cost of brief outpatient treatment would be less than that for inpatient treatment.[6]

DEVELOPMENT OF EMERGENCY SERVICES

The historical roots of emergency psychiatric treatment are to be found in the military experiences of World War II and the Korean War. Under extreme combat conditions, soldiers who developed acute psychiatric illnesses were treated close to the front lines with rest, medication, and nonspecific support. Most were returned to duty rapidly and only a small percentage were permanently removed from the combat area. Recent newspaper accounts of the Vietnam war report that only 1 percent of the psychiatric casualties require permanent transfer from combat duty.

Civilian emergency psychiatric services originated in Europe following World War II. For example, the lack of psychiatric hospital bed space compelled Amsterdam psychiatrists to develop techniques for treating psychiatric patients at home. In England, to relieve the strain on mental hospitals, serving one District Mental Health Service, the Worthing experiement found that providing emergency psychiatric services reduced the number of admissions by 59 percent.[7] Similarly, in Boston in 1957, the Community Extension Service of the Massachusetts Mental Health Center found that 52 percent of the patients awaiting admission to the center could be treated by outpatient facilities.[8] These projects have all demonstrated that many psychiatric patients who would otherwise have been hospitalized can be treated outside the hospital.

FAMILY-ORIENTED TREATMENT

The treatment methods just described focused primarily on the identified patient and for the most part were concerned with his internal problems. The patient's family was viewed as a necessary ally in problem management, but not as having made a significant contribution to the problem itself. Within the past ten years, however, there has been increasing interest in the family's contribution to the decompensation of the member labeled "patient." The illness is

> often as much a reflection of dis-equilibrium within the family as it is of individual malfunction . . . without seeing the family and observing the dynamics of family interaction and the meaning of the patient's illness to the entire family, one cannot obtain a comprehensive picture of the illness.[9]

Although most studies of reaction to stress have focused on personality factors, there is considerable reason to believe that stress outcome is not determined by prestress personality alone. Current object relationships can tip the balance in favor of healthy or unhealthy stress resolution. Susceptible individuals may be bolstered by the support of significant persons and healthy personalities may be hindered in mastering the stress by current conflictual relationships. Family members who decompensate in the face of stress are rarely responding exclusively to internal factors. More typically, precipitating factors consist of family problems.

Stress may arise from a variety of sources such as marital problems, parent-child conflicts, difficulties with the extended family, normal developmental processes, or crises associated with change within a family (e.g marriage, family separations, or retirement). Stress may also stem from problems originating outside the family such as unemployment or relocation. But no mater where the stress arises, the family as a whole is involved in attempts to master the problem.

Too frequently the family has been ignored as an ally in crisis resolution. When stress cannot be adaptively mastered within the family, the decompensation of a susceptible member may ensue. This decompensation may be seized on by the family as a way of dealing with the stress itself (scapegoating). Unfortunately, the request for hospitalization too often represents an avoidance of family problems rather than a resolution. Scapegoating permits other members of the family to avoid their part in the difficulty. By labeling one member as "crazy and in need of hospitalization," they can consider his behavior to be incomprehensible and uncontrollable. The family is frightened by his behavior and seeks to remove him until he has been "brought back to his senses" by hospitalization.

FAMILY CRISIS THERAPY

Since 1964, the Family Treatment Unit (FTU) of Colorado Psychiatric Hospital has been using crisis-oriented therapy with families who have requested mental hospitalization for one of their members, after the psychiatric admission service has agreed the patient should be hospitalized. The clinical team is composed of a psychiatrist, social worker, and nurse. Once a patient has been selected for crisis therapy, the team takes immediate responsibility for the case, responding to the family's distress and the patient's symptoms with an air of calm professional assurance that the problem can be resolved. The family is told that the patient's problem is manageable on an outpatient basis with professional help and that the unit has successfully aided other families in similar situations. Present and past family problems are carefully reviewed with emphasis being placed on health as well as pathology and on the level of prestress equilibrium of the family. When appropriate, members of the extended family, friends, and significant others in the community (such as an employer, caseworker, or priest) are called in from the beginning.

To forestall the exclusion process, the identified patient's psychotic behavior is interpreted as a regressive form of communication and the family is assured that he is not really "crazy." The team emphasizes adaptive social functioning as proof of his family membership. Previously the family had generally exempted the patient from his usual role demands because he had been labeled "sick." If the patient is employed, he is told clearly that a return to work is expected. When the patient is a housewife, she is expected (and helped) to cook, clean, and take care of her family. The patient is encouraged to give up his sick role and to use more adaptive modes of communication. Symptoms of a regressive illness are discouraged.

The FTU team emphasizes that, with help, the patient can manage, and as the patient's behavior becomes more comprehensible, the family regains confidence. The team's aim is to restore the confidence of the patient and family sufficiently so that they can manage their own problems, cope more adaptively with expected future problems, and proceed with less need in the future to exclude a member.

TECHNIQUES OF FAMILY CRISIS THERAPY

The general techniques of family crisis therapy may be summarized as follows:

1. *Family-oriented interviews.* All members of the patient's immediate family and significant others (relatives, friends, clergymen, employers, physicians, caseworkers) are interviewed immediately in order to understand and resolve current family prob-

lems. Although the family is the final pathway through which all interactional problems are channeled, the source of stress may be the immediate family itself, the extended family, a community institution (such as a school or employer), or a social or health agency. Temporarily, the family may not be able to cope with the pressures from the outside systems. The clinical team may serve as a spokesman for the family or as an intermediary with these external systems in an effort to relieve pressure on the family or to assist them in resolving the issues. For example, in one case involving a fourteen-year-old school-phobic boy who was about to face juvenile court action for truancy, the team worked with the court to effect a delay until the parents could be helped to get the boy back into school.

2. *Twenty-four-hour availability.* The team is available twenty-four hours a day, seven days a week. This promise of immediate and constant help is one of the most important nonspecific factors in crisis treatment.

3. *Home visits.* By seeing the family in its own environment within twenty-four hours after the initial contact, the team conveys its involvement and obtains a more complete understanding of the situation. Home visits can also be used to motivate the depressed housewife to function more efficiently. The team member may review on the spot details of important home activities. He may mobilize other family members to help the identified patient to function more adaptively.

4. *Drugs.* In many situations the psychiatrist will prescribe drugs to lessen anxiety and control psychopathological symptoms. Although medication is usually for the identified patient, it may be given to the family members when required. Specific tranquilizers or energizers are chosen for their value in helping the patient or other family members carry on his expected activities. Adequate rest and chemical means of reducing tension permit the patient and family to use problem-solving capacities that are not available in a state of extreme tension.

5. *Use of a holding bed in the emergency room.* Occasionally, when the patient and family are so distraught with each other that a brief respite is necessary, it is advisable to hold a patient in

the general hospital emergency room overnight. Patient and family are temporarily separated without the stigma of a psychiatric hospitalization. Some situations are so confusing that an overnight stay in the emergency room allows the family treatment team an opportunity to sort it out.

6. *Postcrisis contacts.* When the patient has recompensated and resumed his previous level of functioning, chronic or long-term problems may then be evaluated. It is possible to refer the patient or family to a community resource for help with long-standing difficulties. The referral may be for supportive treatment by a public health nurse, for job training and counseling through vocational rehabilitation, to the welfare department for financial assistance, or for treatment in a community mental health clinic. The team has learned to make the referral a live and vital process in which a continuing interest in the patient is demonstrated. It makes itself available for consultation in regard to the family and for emergencies that may occur in the treatment process. Both referred and nonreferred families are advised that they can contact the FTU in times of subsequent crises.

TREATMENT RESULTS

During the first year of operation of the FTU (1964-65), thirty-six pilot cases were treated by family crisis therapy. For a more controlled comparison of the results of out-patient family crisis therapy with hospital treatment, during the years 1965 to 68 a sample of 150 cases was randomly selected for treatment by an FTU clinical team from a group of patients living in the metropolitan Denver area and sick enough to require immediate hospitalization. The comparison group consisted of 150 cases from the same population who were routinely treated as inpatients at Colorado Psychiatric Hospital. Baseline data were collected and follow-up studies conducted six and eighteen months after termination of treatment and annually thereafter. The average hospital stay of patients in the control group was 26.1 days; the family crisis treatment cases were seen for an average of $2\frac{1}{2}$ weeks. Outpatient treatment consisted of an average of approximately five office visits, one home visit, and three telephone contacts. Of the first thirty-six cases (the pilot series) three patients were admitted to the hospital during treatment. Of the 150 experimental cases, hospitalization was avoided in all cases. Termination of therapy took place when the patient was over the acute crisis and had resumed his precrisis level of functioning.

The avoidance of hospitalization with all 150 experimental patients and in thirty-three of thirty-six pilot cases is in itself a significant accomplishment. However, in order to test the relative effectiveness of the two kinds of treatment, it is also necessary to compare the outpatients with a hospitalized sample. All patients (experimentals and controls) were given baseline measures of recent social adaptation, and much information was gathered about the patients and their families. Sufficient data have been accumulated to analyze the baseline and six-month measures for half the experimentals and half the controls. These data demonstrate that six months after treatment experimentals were doing as well as controls on two measures of functioning, and that the experimentals returned to prestress functioning much more rapidly than did controls. Approximately the same number of experimentals were subsequently hospitalized as the number of controls who were rehospitalized during the first six months following discharge from baseline treatment (14 and 16 respectively). The duration of hospitalization for control cases, however, was approximately three times as long as that for experimental cases.

DISCUSSION

A history of previous psychiatric hospitalization is a key factor in determining the potential success of outpatient crisis therapy. With each mental hospital admission, the family's image of the patient and the patient's own self-image are further altered. All are convinced that the identified patient cannot be treated outside a hospital. In contrast, most patients with no previous hospitalizations easily accept outpatient therapy, since the patient and his family have not been conditioned to any specific style of treatment.

Repeated admissions to a general hospital are often equivalent to mental hospital admission. Such cases are frequently women in the involutional period with a history of polysurgery and repeated general hospital admissions for psychophysiological disorders. Although they have no history of mental hospital treatment, they eventually are admitted to a psychiatric inpatient service. The hospital comes to have significance as an avenue for dealing with problems.

Among patients who do require hospitalization, even after family crisis therapy, the course of the decompensation is often insidious rather than acute. The symptoms are long-standing. These patients have had a low level of role functioning within the family for a considerable period of time before seeking admission to a mental hospital. The families of such patients have learned to function without that member and, in effect, had long ago excluded him.

When the family's disequilibrium is not of recent origin, interpersonal conflicts are not really a crisis but merely a continuation of a chronic problem. The original sources of the conflict have often been long forgotten by the protagonists. Considerable bitterness is usually apparent. An impasse develops within the family and they are deadlocked. They resist attempts to compromise and continue to follow a pathological pattern. Confrontations are useless.

The FTU has slowly learned from such cases. Although early attempts were made to alter long-term patterns, these were met with a lack of cooperation on the part of the family. They missed appointments, refused to take medication, and sabotaged any attempts to reinvolve the patient in family life. The clinical team has painfully learned that there is no point in becoming involved in a power struggle with such families. If they are determined to have the patient hospitalized, they will eventually succeed in this.

IMPLICATIONS FOR SOCIAL WORKERS

Patients treated by the FTU are seen in almost any setting—welfare department, family service agency, mental health clinic. Previously such patients were largely treated by confinement to a state mental hospital. However, the development of community-based comprehensive mental health centers (including emergency and crisis services) means that many patients can be seen and treated locally. These centers are often staffed by social workers as well as members of other mental health professions.

In such a setting there is frequently less medical backup than is found in large psychiatric hospitals. Consequently, social workers have had to learn to deal on their own with a variety of disturbed patients. Experience and skill in family crisis therapy give the clinical social worker confidence that he can manage a variety of seriously ill patients and families. He learned to use the psychiatrist as an appropriate medical resource, especially in regard to the use of medication, although he will himself become familiar with the most-often-used drugs and their expectable effects. The social worker on the FTU team has learned to work relatively independently, which has encouraged other social workers at the center to follow suit. The social worker used to doing crisis therapy will not immediately refer patients for hospitalization, but will attempt to deal with disturbed behavior on an outpatient basis.

The essential ingredients of the FTU approach are in accord with traditional social work services. Casework has always emphasized the role of the family, current interaction, role functioning, and home visits. The specific components of this approach are well-known to social workers in a variety of settings varying from psychiatric clinics to public welfare agencies.

SUMMARY

This is a preliminary report on the use of outpatient family treatment with individuals who have been deemed in need of psychiatric hospitalization. Tentative findings at six months' follow-up suggest that the results achieved by out- and inpatient treatment are equivalent, but the former appears to be more economical and less stigmatizing.

REFERENCES

1. Cumming, Elaine and Cumming, John: *Closed Ranks*. Cambridge, Mass., Harvard University Press, 1957, pp. 101-102.

2. Cole, N.J., Brewer, D.J. and Branch, C.H.: Socio-economic adjustment of a sample of schizophrenic patients. Paper presented at the 119th Annual Meeting of the American Psychiatric Association, St. Louis, Mo., May 8, 1963.
3. Wood, E.C., Rauskin, J.M. and Morse, Emanuel: Interpersonal aspects of psychiatric hospitalization: I. The admission. *Arch Gen Psychiatry, 3 (No. 6):* 632-641, Dec. 1960.
4. Miller, Dorothy H.: Worlds that fail. *Transaction, 4 (No. 2):* 38, Dec. 1966.
5. Querido, Arie: Early diagnosis and treatment services. *Elements of a Community Mental Health Program.* New York, Milbank Memorial Fund, 1956, p. 163.
6. Langsley, D.G., Pittman, F.S., Machotka, Pavel and Flomenhaft, Kalman: Family crisis therapy—results and implications. *Family Process, 7 (No. 2):*148-158, Sept. 1968.
7. Carse, Joshua *et al.:* A district mental health service: The Worthing experiment. Lancet, 2 *(No. 1):*39-41, Jan., 1958.
8. Greenblatt, Milton *et al.: The Prevention of Hospitalization: Treatment Without Admission for Psychiatric Patients.* New York, Grune & Stratton, 1963.
9. Becker, Alvin and Weiner, Leonard: Psychiatric home treatment service: Community aspects. *Psychiatric Opinion, 3 (No. 1):* 8, Winter, 1966.

Chapter 18

CRISIS INTERVENTION AND SOCIAL WORK MODELS

ROBERT A. PORTER

THE INCREASING USE of crisis intervention in social agency practice can be combined effectively with concepts of mental health consultation to form strategic preventive programs in community mental health. This paper will discuss crisis theory in relation to a mental health consultation project with visiting teachers and the adaptability of the supervisory model in social work to the consultation task.

CONCEPT OF CRISIS

The individual, in the course of his life span, experiences a number of developmental and accidental crises, which we have come to know in clinical practice as the precipitating stresses leading to emotional disorder or mental illness. The developmental crises relate to such episodes as the child's first leaving home to attend school, biological changes at puberty, the establishment of an independent existence away from the parental home, marriage, childbearing, old age, and death. The accidental crises include such matters as separation and divorce, abandonment, pregnancy out of wedlock, unemployment, etc.—problems characteristically presented to social agencies. In these critical moments, the manner in which the individual copes with, or is helped to cope with, the stress may have far reaching consequences for his future mental health as well as that of other persons who may be caught in the problem network with him. At these times, when he is struggling to find some resolution and when his coping system is still open and fluid, he may achieve mastery of the problem without future restriction to his person-

Note: Reprinted from *Community Mental Health J*, 2:13-21, 1966.

ality; he may compromise with the situation and find some sort of adjustment; or he may use regressive devices which will be detrimental to his future mental health. Under the emotional impact of the crisis, the individual, still in the throes of problem solving, and not yet settled (or perhaps only tentatively settled) on a coping system, is more receptive to help and more subject to influence than he is once a coping system has evolved and become crystallized. Professional intervention at this point, by aiding the individual to adopt reality-based adjustive or adaptive devices, will usually yield maximum results for minimum efforts. If one succeeds in helping the individual to choose an effective coping system, it is fair to say that he has accomplished a bit of preventive psychiatry in that he has helped the individual to avert psychopathological sequelae which would result from maladaptive or maladjustive patterns.

Now it is usually assumed in clinical practice that the defensive or coping pattern, which the individual uses when confronted with significant stress, is determined by predisposing factors in the individual personality. Epidemiological research done in recent years by community psychiatrists, however, calls this assumption into question. These studies have concluded that the vulnerability of the individual to neurotic resolution in a crisis situation is more significantly related to factors in the social system in which the crisis occurs than to predisposing factors in the personality. For instance, Caplan (1964) cited a study done in the late 50's by a group of military psychiatrists, oriented in community psychiatry, which bears on this point.

> These psychiatrists have emphasized the significance for the onset and continuation of mental disorder in a soldier of the emotional milieu of the military unit of which he is a member. Glass (1959) has shown that epidemiological data indicate that the incidence of "combat neurosis" is related to the circumstances of the combat siuation rather than to previously existing personality factors in the individual exposed to stress. These situational circumstances relate to the intensity and duration of the battle, but more significantly to the degree of support given the individual by buddies, group cohesiveness, and leaders. Moreover, he showed that the defensive patterns adopted by individuals in the face of stress are molded by the social pressures of the group [p. 14]

A related study done in England by Brown (1959) concluded that the prognosis for the discharged psychiatric patient is more significantly related to factors in the social environment to which the patient returns than to the clinical diagnosis. Such studies as these stimulate a great deal of reflection regarding possibilities for preventive concepts in mental health in agency programming and administration, leadership role, group process, social action, and community organization. Our society is equipped with a great many health, welfare, social, religious, legal, and other institutions which have direct and immediate contact with individuals in crisis situations. Mental health consultation with the caretakers who operate these institutional programs can be an effective means of preventive psychiatry.

Case Illustrations

Two case illustrations of crisis intervention, selected from a group consultation project with visiting teachers, will be presented. These cases, along with similar ones not here discussed, will be used as the basis for inferring some generalizations about the characteristics of cases which best lend themselves to crisis intervention.

A Case of "School Phobia." A visiting teacher brought in a case of a ten-year-old, fourth grade girl, an only child, who had refused to attend school for two successive weeks at the point of referral. She was a somewhat retiring, timid little girl with tentative speech. She had good intelligence and had performed quite well academically. She was presenting the initial symptoms of the so-called "school phobia."

It was significant that the father accompanied the child to the interview. The mother worked and was unable to attend. An examination of the child's relationships with the significant persons in her life revealed nothing to account for her symptoms. Exploration of the father's current adjustment, however, immediately yielded clinically significant material. He had had a heart attack in recent months, had become preoccupied with fears of another such attack, and had developed considerable anxiety about death. He had been a mechanic for many years, but had given up his job in favor of doing farm work on the small acreage where he lived so that he might be close to home in the event of another heart attack. His wife, of course, was not at home during the day. As the father revealed his fears and anxieties about himself, the child indicated that she was fully aware of them.

She acknowledged and could talk about her fear that her father might die while she was away at school. The father had effectively communicated to the child his need for her to remain at home as a symbol of security and protection for himself in the event of the feared catastrophe, yet he was consciously quite amazed to learn of the burden which his anxiety about himself had imposed on the child. He was encouraged to seek medical assessment of his heart condition so that he might gain a realistic perspective of the limitations it imposed. The following week the visiting teacher reported that the father had returned to his earlier job as auto mechanic and that the child had returned to school. A follow-up investigation a year later revealed that the child had had no further recurrence of the school phobia.

While one might attribute the dramatic results in this case to a good bit of luck, a closer analysis of the circumstances of the case offers a more satisfying explanation. Most importantly, the case was detected early and referred promptly by the visiting teacher. One can only conclude, judging from the change in both father and child, that the maladjustive coping system which both had been using had not yet become firmly crystallized. Focusing the anxiety for both father and child and discussing, mostly by implication, the negative consequences for both of the maladjustive patterns they were using to cope with this anxiety was apparently all that was needed to motivate them to use a healthier pattern. No treatment was used, certainly not in the usual psychotherapeutic sense, and neither father nor child was pushed into a patient role. Neither the father's depression and self-destructive impulses nor the child's generally inhibited demeanor went unobserved clinically. However, the father did not present himself as a candidate for psychotherapy, and one did not want to demoralize him by suggesting it, unless his subsequent behavior, as observed by the visiting teacher, should indicate that this step should be taken. Resolution of the difficulty was achieved at the social problem level, namely, by the child's return to school and by the father's resumption of his occupational role. The visiting teacher, in view of her particular knowledge and skills, was not encouraged to delve deeper into it.

It is tempting to speculate what might have happened had this child been placed on a six months' waiting list at some child guidance clinic. Probably the maladjustive pattern in both father and child would have become so sufficiently set or so fixed that it would yield only to extensive psychotherapeutic intervention. Meantime, the secondary complications of both a psychic and social nature would have made the therapeutic task a more complex and belabored one. The eventual interdisciplinary diagnostic study, six months removed from the onset of the problem, would probably find the isolation and identification of the precipitating stress more difficult. Of course, if the case had been admitted to outpatient treatment at a later date, both father and child may well have had their other problems attended to. Preventive psychiatry, however, is aimed primarily at the prevention of mental illness and incapacitating emotional disorder, and cannot aspire, at this stage of our knowledge, if ever, to making maximally healthy persons out of all human beings.

A Case of Rebellion. The second case concerns a fourteen-year-old Negro girl who was referred for recent school failure, truancy, and sexually acting-out behavior. At home the girl had become passively rebellious and difficult to deal with. The school became alarmed when the girl was discovered nude in an apartment near the school with a group of teen-agers. The girl was referred last November and had been presenting difficulty since the beginning of the school term. Previously her academic achievement was good and she had gotten along quite well at home and at school. She appeared for the interview with her grandmother who had raised her from infancy. The child was born out-of-wedlock and her natural mother had moved to the midwest soon after her birth. The grandmother was a lower middle class woman with strong middle class moral values. She was a little rigid but quite material, adequate, mature, and giving. No headway was made in understanding the girl's behavior until she was questioned about her natural mother. This proved to be a highly sensitive area; she dissolved into tears when it was suggested that she missed her mother very much. She then revealed that her natural mother had visited her three months previously, for the first time in five years, and on departing had promised to send the girl bus fare so that she might visit the mother in the midwest. Meanwhile, the girl's older brother, who had also been raised by the grandmother, did visit the natural mother and returned to report that the mother continued to be as promiscuous as the grandmother had known her to be in earlier years. The grandmother, feeling the mother would be a bad influence, thereupon refused to let the girl visit her mother. It was from this point that the girl's difficult behavior began to develop. In the interview it became apparent that the girl had idealized her absent mother and refused to believe the negative reports about her. She was quite depressed in the interview, did little talking, and cried most of the time. The grandmother had made no connection between the earlier conflict situation and the girl's current behavior difficulties. She accepted the connection which was made for her, was able to identify with the girl's sense of loss and anger, and accepted the suggestion that she let the girl visit the mother. I felt safe in making this suggestion for two reasons: (a) a continuation of the girl's current behavior pattern could only lead to a worsening of the situation and to a fulfillment of the grandmother's fears; and (b) the rather adequate nurturance of this child by her grandmother throughout her earlier life made it unlikely that she would be susceptible to negative influence from the mother. The grandmother was given considerable support in this regard. The visiting teacher subsequently reported that the child had returned to school; and six months later, there has been no further evidence of truancy or of promiscuous behavior. She is achieving academically at her earlier level. I later had occasion to see the grandmother a second time, and learned that she had promised to let the girl visit her mother at the end of the school year and that they had talked out many of their feelings about their earlier conflict.

Again, it is interesting to consider what might have happened to the girl had her problem behavior continued for another six months. If the grandmother had been more adequate to the child's needs at this strategic moment in her life, would the maladjustive behavior have developed at all? Was the girl's choice of behavioral response determined primarily by predisposing factors in her personality, or was it a socially prescribed pattern adopted from her peers who were involved in the same behavior? It should be emphasized that the intervening activities on my part were primarily directed toward the grandmother rather than the girl.

Some Generalizations

A few generalizations regarding the characteristics of those cases which most readily lend themselves to this kind of preventive intervention can be made:

1. The onset of the psychosocial problem is usually clear-cut, often even dramatic.

2. The level of adjustment prior to the crisis situation, although it may have been neurotic, is stable in the homeostatic sense.

3. Judging from the fact that the focal anxieties are easily elicited, and that the change in behavior subsequent to intervention may be as dramatic as the change in behavior following the crisis situation, one must conclude that the emergency-coping pattern used by the individual is not yet fixed. Or, put in terms of the theory of neurosis, we might say that the adjustment reaction is largely situational and has not yet been firmly internalized. This might be contrasted with the chronically neurotic or char-

acter disordered personality where the repressive forces are so strongly entrenched that anxiety is firmly bound by a variety of defenses, especially denial, displacement, etc.

4. The nascent state of the adjustment reaction, characterized by high anxiety levels, and the exigencies of the crisis situation, usually characterized by considerable social pressures, engenders a dependency in the client which makes him most susceptible to influence. Once the crisis has passed and the maladjustive behavior pattern is fixed, motivation for help may be proportionately reduced.

5. The crisis situation does not seem to be a one person phenomenon. The crisis is usually generated out of an intimate, interpersonal complex. In case work, of course, we look closely at the social role relationships, which are always reciprocal, and for interruptions in complementary nurturance. Breakdown in the one part always has repercussions for the reciprocal partner or partners.

6. The parties involved in the crisis situation obviously have a knowledge of the social problem or behavioral difficulty for which they seek help. Investigation will reveal that they also have a conscious knowledge of the precipitating conflict or stress, but that they usually do not make a connection between the two.

7. Treatment of the crisis situation typically involves the identification and focusing of the anxiety, the relating of this to the precipitating stress or conflict, the ventilation and communication among the parties of the dormant feelings about the conflict or stress situation, and the interjection by the therapist of his corrective reality-based observations and judgments which permit the client to find a more adaptive method of problem solution.

Investigation of the crisis situation or problem behavior generally does not need to exceed the bounds of the current life situation. Examination of current social role relationships and environmental influence will usually yield the genetic data which will account for the crisis situation and the emergency behavior. Exploration of early life experiences, while perhaps enlightening, yields little or no data of relevance to the treatment task. Character structure can usually be adequately discerned in the current context. Anxiety is identified as it fulminates when sensitive areas are touched. This task is made easy by the fact that the anxiety is as yet poorly defended against. It is not usually met vigorously with denial or other defensive maneuvers. As the parties ventilate the impounded affect surrounding the conflict or stress situation, with encouragement from the therapist, anxiety levels are lowered and corrective adjustments tend to be made. The interjection by the therapist of his reality-based observations and judgments aid in this process. The impounded affect is almost entirely contained at preconscious levels. The social pressure implicit in the visiting teacher's follow-up contacts, along with the support he offers, constitutes an important contribution to the client's sustained efforts at problem solution.

8. Preventive intervention may focus more treatment actively on collaterals in the social system network of the primary client than on the client himself. This would, of course, be consistent with the research findings of the community psychiatrists, quoted above, to the effect that susceptibility of the individual to neurotic resolution or other maladaptive response to crisis appears to be more significantly related to inadequate nurturance in the social milieu than to predisposing factors in the personality. In the case of the school phobic girl, it would certainly appear that the father's return to work, for all the shifting in his psychic economy which that act represented, was the crucial factor which released the child from the burden of anxiety which kept her from attending school. And in the second case of the acting-out teen-ager, it would seem that the relaxation of the rigidity in the grandmother was the principal factor which permitted the child to resume her earlier pattern of stable adjustment. We might look at the matter another way by asking, in reference to the first case, whether the little girl would ever have developed the school phobia had the father not become so anxious about his own health; or, in the second case, whether we would ever have come to know the teen-age girl if her grandmother had been more understanding of the child's needs when she was confronted with the brutal facts about her natural mother.

9. Early detection and referral are crucial to the success of

this type of preventive intervention. The location of the mental health consultant in an institutional program such as the public school system permits maximum exploitation of opportunities for preventive treatment.

10. This kind of preventive intervention requires a considerable amount of activity on the part of the consultant. The professional passivity of analytically-oriented psychotherapy will not work in these kinds of situations. The initial or exploratory phase of the interview, where one is attempting to identify the anxiety and establish its cause, may move more in the traditionally passive approach. However, once this information is established, effective intervention requires a fairly active playback by the consultant of his assessment in a fashion appropriate to the vernacular and level of understanding of the client.

The cases on which these generalizations are based are fairly simple ones, if any behavior can be said to be simple, in the sense that the psychodynamic formulation is fairly easily established, and the client is easily susceptible to remedial or reparative influence. However, it is probable that more complex cases, if approached with the same spirit of preventive intervention, will yield to attempts at classification and the development of modifications of this approach appropriate to the differing levels of complexity of the cases studied.

CONSULTEE-CENTERED CASE CONSULTATION

So far the discussion has been directed toward client-centered case consultations in crisis intervention. The topic now will shift to a type of mental health consultation which focuses on the alleviation in the consultee of countertransference phenomena which obstruct his efficient and objective treatment of the client. This kind of consultation can be readily adapted from the supervisory model in social work. The client is not seen by the consultant, and the process focuses entirely around the case material presented by the consultee. A brief outline of the supervisory model in social work will be described as this relates to the emerging body of consultation theory in community psychiatry and will be followed by an illustration of this type of consultation in my visiting teacher group using Caplan's (1964) concept of the theme interference, reduction type of consultee-centered, case consultation.

The Supervision Model

Social work supervision is somewhat different from its counterpart in psychiatry. The learner in any of the mental health disciplines will inevitably find that certain unresolved problems in his own personality will at times interfere with the efficiency of his efforts to help his client or patient. Psychiatry typically handles this problem by encouraging the resident to seek some type of psychotheraputic experience as a part of his training program. Psychiatric supervision, therefore, remains primarily patient centered. That is, the supervisor addresses his efforts primarily to helping the resident understand the complexities of diagnosis and treatment with reference to his patient. Social work, on the other hand, cannot generally rely on a formal therapeutic experience as a safety valve or control over the patient needs of the social work student, and has had to build into its supervisory process a device for dealing with countertransference in the learner. Although this is not a psychotherapeutic device, psychic change in the learner is achieved. Supervision in social work is largely learner centered, rather than client centered, and we establish an educational diagnosis of each student which prescribes the nature of much of our supervisory task. The educational diagnosis is largely an assessment of the student's capacities and learning blocks. For instance, interruption of the learning process in the student may be indicated by undue resistance to the supervisor as the student struggles to shift his loyalties from past mentors with a different theoretical frame of reference to present ones, or by regressive behavior as he demonstrates that his intellectual grasp of theoretical considerations is quite in advance of his development of skills to implement his knowledge.

Not infrequently, however, the learning task may be interfered with by the intrusion of a countertransference phenomenon, evoked by the life situation or problem of the client, so that the student becomes unable to perceive his client realistically or to offer him effective help. For instance, a student in a child protective agency may be assigned a case in which he must explore evidence of alleged parental neglect in a mother who apparently failed to make adequate provision for supervision of her children in her absence while working. Following his interview of the mother, the student reports to his supervisor an array of evidence to demonstrate that the mother is indeed quite neglectful and concludes that the child should be taken from her. He is somewhat emotional in his presentation, perhaps even moralistic or punitive in his attitude toward the mother. While he may report some evidence of the mother's adequacy, he assesses it lightly, and shows little understanding of the mother's anxieties and little or no disposition to help her. The clue to the student's countertransference problem lies in his overidentification with the victimized child, with his stereotyped perception of the mother, and with his distorted or skewed data collection. Or the student in a family service agency, working with the depressed wife of a man who is threatening divorce, may feel that he must save the marriage at all costs and adopts the same hostile attitudes toward the husband as his client.

The wise supervisor will not direct the student's attention to unresolved problems in himself as this would not only increase his anxiety and invite resistance, but also convert the supervisory hour into a therapeutic session with the student. Instead, he will keep the discussion on the client's problem situation and emphasize evidence in the case which will serve to counteract the student's distorted or stereotyped perception of the client. In the first illustration above, he might invite a discussion of the mother's anxieties and needs, or point to evidence of the mother's adequacy. The supervisor's essential aim is to loosen the student's neurotic perception and to hold out the prospect of a reality-based resolution. In a sense, this is the essential goal of the psychotherapeutic encounter, though it is unlike it in that the therapeutic message is mediated indirectly through a discussion of the client's rather than the student's, problem. The validity of this technique is demonstrated only as the student is freed to help his client, or by his demonstration in subsequent but similar cases that he is able to perceive his client more objectively. Note particularly, in this supervisory model, that it is not necessary for the supervisor to explore the life history material in the student that would explain or account for the countertransference phenomenon; in fact, such a procedure is definitely contraindicated. Even if the student voluntarily injects anamnestic material into the discussion, it is tacitly acknowledged but not encouraged, and the supervisor brings the focus back to the task, namely, that of understanding and helping the client. Allowing the student to lapse into a patient role not only diverts his energies, but threatens his sense of adequacy. And in any case, the supervisor would find himself frustrated in following through with any interpretation of the student's behavior because he has no contract with the student that would allow him to deal with the student's resistance.

Model Adapted to Consultation

The social worker with a good command of this model can adapt his knowledge and skills readily to the requirements of consultee centered mental health consultation. Both models are learner centered and proceed on the basis of a diagnosis of psychic processes operating in the student or consultee. Both are highly structured and aim at resolving obstructions impeding learning or effective job performance. Either process aims at psychic change without the use of direct psychotherapeutic measures or the investigation of life history material. In both, corrective reality-based messages aimed at the emotional obstruction in the learner are mediated by a displacement of the discussion onto the client group.

Case Illustration

The desire here is to approach a discussion of this type of consultee-centered mental health consultation by offering an illustration from a visiting teacher group, and then to use this as the basis for developing a presentation of the theoretical and technical considerations involved.

This past year two Negro men were in the visiting teacher group for the first time. During the course of the year they both presented several cases of truant children where the overt problem did not extend beyond that of truancy. That is, there was no evidence of delinquency or of other marked conflict in the home. These children simply had no motivation for attending school, and their truancy was met either with indifference or actual encouragement on the part of their parents. These children were typically from economically deprived homes where the parents were either illiterate or virtually so, and where there was no identification with middle class values regarding education. The attitude of the Negro visiting teachers toward these families was one of condemnation. They overtly spoke of the parents as "no-count," "bums," and "no good." They complained of the lack of ambition in these parents and were pessimistic regarding the child's future, feeling that, if something wasn't done, the child would turn out to be a replica of the "no good" parent. To save the child from this fate, these two visiting teachers typically suggested that the child be removed from the home and put in a foster home where the effects of a middle class orientation might save him.

Recently one of the teachers presented a case of this nature involving two siblings, a 14-year-old boy, and his 15-year-old sister. They began truanting last September shortly after school began and following the death of their mother from cancer. They were out-of-wedlock children and the grandmother was the only remaining adult in the home. She made idle promises to the visiting teacher to get the children off to school, but this never came about. It became apparent that she was not only indifferent to the truancy issue, but wanted the girl to remain at home to help with the domestic chores. In response to my questions, the visiting teacher indicated that there were no other significant problems presented by the children or the home situation. The grandmother was described as a "nice lady." In February the visiting teacher brought the fifteen-year-old girl before the juvenile court, and that confrontation with the law was apparently sufficient to induce her to attend school, which she has done with regularity since that time. The visiting teacher expressed open hostility toward the girl and voiced his earlier resolve that he would see to it that she stayed in school. More recently the teacher brought the fourteen-year-old brother into court with the recommendation that he be placed in detention, and this was accomplished. The boy's detention posed, for the visiting teacher, the problem of a disposition for the child following his release. He pessimistically predicted that the boy would not attend school and expressed reservations as to whether the influence of the court would continue to hold in the fall when the girl would normally resume school. He was strongly thinking of recommending to the court that both children be placed in foster homes.

Now the theme interference in this case, relating to the visiting

teacher's condemning attitude toward the parent, his pessimistic outlook for the children's future in the present home situation, and his
rescue fantasy that would have led him to separate these children from
their natural home, was the focal point around which I built my consultation message. I emphasized that the girl had responded quite well
to court intervention, that the boy had not yet been given an opportunity to demonstrate how he would respond to the detention experience; otherwise, the consultation pointed to strengths in the family,
which were mostly elicited from the teacher, and to the fact that the
absence of other significant psychosocial pathology in the situation
bespoke the relative adequacy of the home environment. I expressed
my feeling that the case was moving along well. As the discussion
closed the visiting teacher decided he had done a good job and abandoned plans to separate the children from the home.

In the discussion no reference was made to the visiting teacher's
emotional involvement in the case, and obviously no efforts were made
to investigate the life history sources of the interfering theme. The
defensive projection and displacement of the countertransference anxiety onto the client group was not undone, and the relaxation of the
interfering theme was achieved with the consultation message mediated entirely through a discussion of the client situation. The consultant asks questions of the consultee about the client situation only
to elucidate the countertransference theme in the consultee, and not to
clarify the diagnosis of the client. The consultation message is focused
entirely on the countertransference problem in the consultee.

The Consultation Model

Caplan (1964) stated that the cornerstone of this consultation
method is the maintenance of the unconscious nature of the defensive displacement in the consultee which allows the consultant
to discuss the theme upsetting the consultee by discussing the
client. This means, of course, that the consultant must work
against the development of insight in the consultee, which would
lead him to connect the client's difficulties and his personal emotional problems. The displacement in the consultee protects him
from facing his own psychological problems, and if he becomes
aware of the personal link between himself and the client, the
displacement is weakened or undone. The consultee will then feel
exposed, anxiety develops, and his attention and energies are di-
verted from understanding and helping the client to understand-

ing and helping himself. It then becomes impossible for the consultee to work out his own problems in terms of the client.

This kind of development must be avoided. Otherwise, the consultation session is likely to degenerate into a psychotherapeutic one and, as with the supervisory model, psychotherapy is not the function of the mental health consultant. His function is that of enhancing the effectiveness of the consultee's work performance by bringing to bear his expert knowledge of behavior on the consultee's understanding of the psychological aspects of his cases. Moreover, if it becomes known generally among the staff of the consultee institution that sessions with the consultant typically result in exposure of the personal problems of the consultee, then there is likely to develop such fear, resistance, and hostility in the consultees toward the consultant that he is likely to find himself without a function in the institution at all. The mental health consultant is an expert with superior knowledge in his specialty and his role is best sustained by a respectful regard for the consultee as a peer with whom he is collaborating to get the job done.

The interfering or countertransference theme in the consultee is typically manifested by the usual clinically significant reactions of anxiety, shame, guilt, anger, condemnation, and oversolicitude. His observations of the client are usually colored by preconceptions, oversimplifications, stereotyping, significant omissions, and other perceptual distortions. Typically, he feels helpless with regard to the client and fears a bad outcome for him. For instance, the delinquent client is seen as headed for prison, the retarded child will be exploited, or, in the case of the visiting teacher, the lower class child of illiterate parents will turn out to be an unambitious ne'er-do-well like his parents. This pessimistic preconception of the client is not challenged, for this would force the consultee to reclassify the client and then the countertransference theme could not be dealt with. Reassurance that the client does not fit the consultee's preconceived pattern imposed on him might relieve his anxiety about the particular client and therewith free him to be more objective in helping the client, but then the consultee would have to find another displacement object on which to work out his problems. The consultant leaves the displacement intact and then organizes a message which will invalidate the expectation of a bad outcome. The message is designed to influence the consultee to realize that, in at least one case, reality does not confirm his fantasies of doom. In the visiting teacher case, for instance, the consultation message, which did not question the teacher's preconception of the client group, pointed to evidence in the case which demonstrated that his pessimistic prognosis for the children was not necessarily so. Caplan (1964) pointed out that since the disordered expectation is couched in terms of global inevitability, even one instance which refutes the expected outcome will have a significant effect in invalidating the preconception emanating from the countertransference anxiety.

Crisis intervention is used extensively in social work practice, for it lends itself admirably to the social work task. Mental health consultation, both client centered and consultee centered, is readily adaptable from social work models and provides a valuable addition to the working equipment of the mental health specialist.

REFERENCES

1. Brown, G. W.: Experiences of discharged chronic schizophrenic patients in various types of living groups. *Milbank Mem Fund, 37*:105-131, 1959.
2. Caplan, G.: *Principles of Preventive Psychiatry.* New York, Basic Books 1964.

D. CONSULTATION

Chapter 19

PREVENTIVE ASPECTS OF MENTAL HEALTH CONSULTATION TO SCHOOLS

IRVING N. BERLIN

T HE VAST number of emotionally disturbed children, adolescents, and adults is dramatically illustrated by swelling numbers of nonlearners in schools, unabating delinquency, violence, and pregnancies among adolescents, and increased divorce rates and decreased job and interpersonal satisfactions among adults. All these have made society increasingly conscious of psychologic problems and the need for treatment.

Studies have indicated that there will never be sufficient mental health professionals to give treatment to the children who need it, not to mention the disturbed adult population. Prevention must concern us as one attack on this overwhelming problem.

In the schools we are concerned primarily with secondary prevention.[1] The prenatal and early infancy and childhood problems antedate school—that is, problems that may stem from mothers' depression, from parental conflicts that affect the infant and small child, from mother-infant and mother-toddler alienation, resulting from mothers' personality problems or inexperience in the mothering process, or problems caused by the unhappy child's reaction to his environment, to neurophysiologic dysfunction, or to sociocultural deprivation, which increases the child's turmoil and thereby increases family troubles in a vicious circle. All these have already had their effects by the time the child enters kindergarten or first grade. There are, however, a few areas of primary prevention in which educators do play a vital role, especially in cases of crisis in a child's life, in which an educator's sensitivity to the child and his response may be of crucial importance.

Secondary prevention centers around the early identification

Note: Reprinted from *Ment Hyg, 51:*34-40, 1967.

of emotional disturbance due to interpersonal, neurophysiologic, or sociocultural factors and early intervention by the educator, through the mental health consultation process. In many instances this process includes involving the parents; in a few instances referral must be made to community resources. However, preventive work centers essentially around learning to recognize and to use the potentially healing or therapeutic aspects of the educative process. Prevention also depends on the alertness of educators to "normal" maturational and school crisis that may affect the vulnerable child adversely if they are not recognized, understood, and reacted to helpfully.

Our concern here is with some general aspects of prevention in schools, the role of mental health consultation as a means of facilitating and enhancing prevention, and a specific technique or method of mental health consultation found effective by some mental health specialists and educators.

The School's Role in Prevention

Most teachers are capable of early recognition of behavioral disturbances due to emotional factors, or of a child's inability to learn because of maturational lag, sociocultural deprivation, or manifestations of brain dysfunction. Bower[2] and others have compared the reliability of teachers' concerns and evaluations of a child's functioning in school with later diagnostic studies by mental health professionals and have found teachers' observations very trustworthy. Thus, the early recognition of a child's problems in school is possible.

The central problems are subsequent assessment of the disturbance by educators and others in terms of the child's sociocultural background, neuromuscular maturation, emotional instability, and possible organic retardation. Once a tentative diagnosis is made, the experienced educator can begin to make some prognoses and attempt to verify them by observations in the classroom. He may then be better able to decide whether a youngster needs further, prompt evaluation. Inherent in the process of early identification of problems is contact with the parents to obtain their observations on the child and his development and to assess any evident troubles in and between parents that may be affecting the child.

It needs to be stressed and restressed that, even when evaluation and treatment are undertaken by outside agencies, the school still has the challenging problem of determining how educative methods and classroom experiences can be used to take maximal advantage of the early recognition of disturbance and to enhance the therapeutic process. Since treatment is a slow process, it requires all the additional help possible in the everyday life of the child. Mental health consultation is often helpful in developing collaboration between the educator and the psychotherapist. The consultant is also able to help educators recognize that learning expectations are often supportive to the sick child's ego.

Maturational Crises of the School-age Child

Leaving the protection of home and mother at age five or six represents a crisis for some children. How the school deals with the child and parents and with the child's fear of school and desire to stay home can affect the prevention of future disability.

Restriction of gross motor activity, learning to attend and to begin to learn may precipitate a crisis, especially for slowly maturing boys who are not yet able to contain large muscle activity in favor of the pleasures to be obtained from increased fine motor coordination. The recognition of these problems, and of the crises that may result from pushing a child and not providing frequent outlets for large muscle movement and suitable rewards for sitting still, using small muscles, and acquiring fine motor coordination, is important to the learning future of the child.

The use of imaginative stimulation of all the senses and of special educational techniques to help the socioculturally deprived child achieve learning readiness is among the educator's most important preventive activities. The third grade—in which learning commences with real seriousness and most children are maturationally ready to learn—may find many children still unable to read, poorly motivated to learn, and unable to sit still, yet wanting to learn and to experience the fun of learning and the excitement of acquiring knowledge so evident in their classmates. The educator's failure to recognize increased hyperactivity, truculence, and opposition to learning as evidence of possible acute conflict about the desire to learn and the inability to find the means of learning may aggravate this crisis and alienate the child from the learning process and its potential satisfactions.

Similarly, it is often difficult for educators to keep in mind the fact that, for most youngsters, any sudden spurt in growth means that energy is being mobilized for the growing process and that there may be less energy available for learning. Thus, the correlation of growth spurts with falling-off in grades points to a need for increased understanding of the youngster rather than pressure for performance, but without permitting a serious drop in performance. Usually, vigorous engagement in learning returns in a few weeks.

In early adolescence, the development of secondary sexual characteristics, growth spurts, and flowering of social activities—especially for girls—often result in reduced energy for learning.

The shift from elementary school to the middle school or junior high school, in which the child has many teachers instead of one, may present crises for particular children who emotionally need the support, the firm expectations, and the rewards of a single parental figure. These children may begin to do badly in the larger and more impersonal junior high school, and may need to form a tie with a central person to facilitate their adaptation.

If the situation is correctly assessed and dealt with, each of these potential crises offers the educator opportunities to help a youngster mobilize his integrative capabilities and learn to cope more effectively with the external world.

Preventive Implications of Students' Life Crises

Many children, in the course of their school experience, undergo serious crises in their family situations that may require alert aid from the teacher to prevent serious impairment of the child's mental health. For example, death or divorce of parents, death of siblings or other family members, unemployment of the father, instability in the parents' financial or emotional support, serious illness of, or accident to, the student or another member of the family, with its potentially ominous import—all may have a marked impact on the child.

Perhaps the best single indicator of a serious crisis in a child's life is an abrupt change in behavior, such as a sudden loss of interest in learning, withdrawal from social interaction, explosive behavior (i.e. "blowing up" or crying), or silence and isolation on the part of a hyperactive child. Such changes should be a signal for inquiry. In these instances, the continued interest and support of teachers and others may be a vital factor in the child's ability to deal with the home crises. All experienced teachers can cite examples of how their support and, sometimes, intervention have been important to a child's emotional survival during a crisis in which the child felt alone and helpless. Here, also, the mental health consultant may be helpful in finding the best ways for a teacher to approach a difficult and nonrelating child.

The Therapeutic Effect of Learning

In order to be an effective adult in our technical society, the child must master ever more difficult and complex subject matter and acquire a variety of increasingly more refined skills. Mastery of academic materials depends on the satisfaction, pleasures, and rewards of the learning process. These often have not been acquired in the preschool years if the child has lived with deprived, troubled, not very effective, and not very nurturant or supportive parents. The school's efforts to help a child learn, through a variety of sensory experiences and pleasurable early learning experiences, may begin to help him to develop habits and successes in learning that can be critical to his future living as an effective adult.

Thus, inherent in the learning process itself are preventive and therapeutic implications that the mental health consultant may be able to help the teacher make more explicit for particular children.

The Role of Mental Health Consultation in Schools

The mental health consultant in a school is usually a social worker, clinical psychologist, or psychiatrist employed by the administration. This consultant may be helpful in the school in a variety of ways, depending upon the needs of the school, its personnel, and the skill and experience of the consultant himself.[3,4]

First, he may be of factual help. He may provide information about growth and development, the impact of certain sociocultural experiences, diagnostic implications of a particular type of behavior of child or parents, or the community resources available for diagnosis or treatment of particular children.

Second, he may be of interpretive help. His knowledge of interpersonal dynamics and the developmental process may permit him to piece together the data gathered by the teacher, administrator, school nurse, and others and to give some picture of the origins of, and reasons for, the child's difficulties. He may be able to draw implications from the child's present behavior and past experiences for corrective classroom experiences. He may be able to delineate what the child may need from an adult that the teacher can give as part of his job as educator.

Third, the consultant may be of help in clarifying the integrative part that learning may play in the child's life and in the reduction of the child's troubles. He may be able to help teachers recognize that emotional disturbance, and even severe mental illness, may be benefited by the teacher's firm expectation that a child can learn and, through learning, feel more effective and intact. He may also be able to trace the nonintegrative experiences of the distractible, hostile, hyperactive child, so that the teacher can begin to recognize the kind of attitudes, the personal investment, stimulation, concerned firmness, persistence, and rewards required to help a particular child begin to learn. He may also be able to help the educator become alert and sensitized to certain aspects of a child's behavior that indicate—often through negative and challenging behavior—the child's increased readiness for certain expectations, for increased tolerance of closeness, or for more firmness, required by the child to take the next step in learning and personality integration.

Fourth, the consultant may be in a position to help the educator preserve his own mental health in the face of the many pressing mental health problems of his students and the students' parents. He may be able to aid the educator with his own self-expectations, which are often inconsistent with the harsh realities. Thus, he may assist the teacher who feels a failure if his youngsters are not up to grade or if he is unable to generate in his students responsive pleasure and excitement in learning. By enabling the teacher to recognize the obstacles to learning and the therapeutic function of learning for certain children, the consultant may encourage him to find satisfaction in the bite-size increments of learning that occur as children begin to work through the initial turmoil of the learning process. He may help the teacher recognize, with more and more genuine pleasure and satisfaction, the learning and consequent changes that occur as the teacher provides the appropriate milieu for change. He may also be in a position to interpret the pressures of the community and administration for heroic action so that the teacher sees the realities of his day-to-day job in terms of accumulation of tiny increments of learning and behavior change.

Hopefully, the consultant can also aid the teacher, under the trying conditions of very difficult classrooms, to recognize his human feelings of despair, anger, and even hate, as well as a sort of general guilt at not being able to love all the children and work miracles for them. When she or he understands these as common human feelings, the teacher often feels less frustrated and is able to work more effectively bit by bit and day by day. A not-so-incidental result of this is that the teacher provides an example to his students of what they need to do, showing that achievement comes not with wishing, but with hard and unremitting work. As the teacher evaluates the reality of his situation more objectively and scales down his self-expectations, he begins to try to clarify where each student is and what he needs to learn. He also then begins to expect realistic increments of learning from each student. And, as his students do learn more under these conditions, he feels better about himself and his job.

Inherent in all this is a serious problem. Mental health consultation is designed to help educators deal more effectively with disturbed children in their schools rather than get rid of them. The reality of the situation is this: there is nowhere to refer all the problems and no way to wash one's hands of them since there are so many problem children. Educators must understand the function of consultation—to help teachers learn to work with more children more effectively so that only the most seriously disturbed youngsters will require referral.

A Method of Mental Health Consultation

There are four or five steps in the process of mental health consultation—often not consecutive steps, but all important to successful consultation.[5] Perhaps the most important guideline is that the process is designed to promote collaboration between educator and mental health specialist, with the goal of helping the former to do a better job with students who have mental health problems.

The first step is the consultant's efforts to become acquainted with the organization, structure, and problems of schools in general, the usual burdens of the teacher, and the special problems of the particular school. The consultant must become sufficiently immersed in the school setting so that he can understand the teacher's comments in the context of the special milieu in which the teacher works.

The second step centers around the consultant's efforts to facilitate the educator's acceptance of the mental health consultant as a potentially helpful person rather than one who is concerned with analyzing the educator and uncovering character problems and unconscious motivations. In short, the consultant's concern is the educator's work problems, and not his personal ones. The educator should experience the mental health consultant as a fellow human being whose task is to engage him as a collaborator, *not,* in any way, as a patient or client.

This phase of the work may take some time. The working-through is focused on the consultant's trying to indicate, in a variety of ways, that he can understand the teacher's feelings about the particular students he teaches in his particular setting. The consultant's projection of empathy with, and acceptance of, the teacher's feelings as both human and understandable should lead to collaboration in the service of the student.

The third stage of consultation is concerned with relieving

the anxieties, self-recriminations, and feelings of failure that result from attempting to teach difficult and disturbed children. The
reduction of teacher anxiety is a prerequisite to being able to
explore methods of working with the child. Unless the educator's
self-blame, tension, and feeling that he should be able to handle
such problems without help are dealt with, he is not able to listen
to and consider alternative courses of action. Teacher anxiety is
best reduced by the consultant's discussing similar problems that
he or others have been confronted with, which clearly demonstrates his understanding of similar feelings and moments of
impasse.

(The teacher who has to deal with hostile, aggressive, hyperactive children knows that I understand her problems when I describe some harrowing experiences of my own in a playroom with
a child who had similar problems; but I have had to contend with
only one youngster for one hour once or twice a week, rather than
with thirty-six children daily for six or seven hours. Since I, too,
have experienced the kind of wounds that come from being
rendered "temporarily" ineffectual by a child, teachers seem to
know, from my comments, that I understand their feelings.)

The fourth step is an effort to increase the teacher's distance
from the problem and his objectivity by using all the data provided to draw a picture of the etiology of a particular child's
problems, showing how experience with the important adults in
the child's life have affected him and resulted in his present behavior. This not only helps the teacher feel less responsible for
the child's problems and for his immediate cure, but also indicates
the conditions in which the child's problems developed and where
it may be necessary to take hold, or what adult behavior is required to alter the child's view of the adult and of himself. In
instances of sociocultural deprivation, it may also help the teacher
to understand that, as a teacher, he has an important function in
the community. Not only does he help children become more
effective persons, but also, by participating in community activities, he may enhance his access to parents in the service of their
children.

The fifth step is considering alternative methods of dealing with the child's behavior that, in the consultant's experience, or that of other educators, have been effective. Often the consultant's understanding of the origin of the child's problems can be restated to the educator so that, from this, certain attitudes, attentions, and expectations seem to evolve for mutual consideration. Alternative possibilities congruent with the teacher's experience and ideas need to be explored. The consultant who makes a recommendation or gives a prescription instead of fostering a consideration of alternatives usually learns that the teacher has already tried what he proposes and found that it didn't work; or, if the teacher tacitly accepts a recommendation to which he has not contributed, he is apt to report back the next time that it hasn't worked. Thus, the consultant needs not only to help the educator consider alternatives, but also to suggest that these be *tentatively* tried and reported on the next time for mutual reconsideration.

The sixth step is the follow-up of consultation, in which sustained interest, concern, and supportive help provide a recurrent opportunity for the teacher to learn to deal with his problems more effectively.

Inherent in all of these phases of consultation is the probability that much of the effect of the process results from the identification of the educator with the consultant, his attitudes, and his methods of interaction. The consultant's attitudes, which are based on respect for the teacher as a potentially effective collaborator who can learn to use teaching and learning as a means of helping disturbed students, are often adopted by the teacher. Very clearly, teachers often act toward their difficult students as consultants have acted toward them.

In my own work, I have felt it important that the administrator be present as the key person in the school who not only needs to agree that the ideas to be tried are consonant with his own philosophy, but also to mediate between teacher and consultant. In addition, the administrator can learn from observing the consultation process what aspects of it he can use to make his own work more effective.

Each successful consultation not only reduces the child's present learning and behavior disturbance, but also prevents future learning disability and personality disorder. The youngster's increased learning ability and effectiveness in school may change his view of himself and his functioning in the world. The teacher is frequently able to apply what he has learned in consultation about one child to other children in the classroom. The consultation process thus helps the teacher to feel ever more effective and successful as a teacher and furthers the goal of prevention through both pupil and teacher.

REFERENCES

1. Eisenberg, L., and Gruenberg, E. M.: *Am J Orthopsychiatry, 31:*355, 1961.
2. Bower, E. M.: Early identification of emotionally handicapped children in school. Springfield, Thomas, 1960.
3. Berlin, I. N.: *Mental Hyg, 40:*215, April, 1956.
4. Berlin, I. N.: *J Am Acad Child Psychiatry, 1:*671, October, 1962.
5. Berlin, I. N.: *Mental Hyg, 48:*257, April, 1964.

Chapter 20

REDUCING DISRUPTIVE BEHAVIOR
THROUGH CONSULTATION

A. DAN WHITLEY AND BETH SULZER

Teachers are continually confronted with many complex maladaptive child behaviors that disrupt the educational process. When unable to resolve these problems, the teacher often refers the child to a pupil personnel worker such as the school psychologist, social worker, or counselor. Communication between the personnel worker and the teacher is often referred to as a consultation process (Dinkmeyer, 1968a, 1968b; McClain and Boley, 1968).

The idea of elementary school counselors performing in a counseling role has received a great deal of support in the literature (Dinkmeyer, 1963; Faust, 1967; Kaczkowski, 1967; Mayer and Munger, 1967; *Report of the ACES-ASCA Committee on the Elementary School Counselor, 1966*). Kennedy (1968) and Zimmer (1967) endorsed this role for elementary school counselors with a different approach that advocated the consultant's use of operant conditioning procedures. This study is an extension of this position since it illustrates the use of operant procedures by a classroom teacher with the consulting assistance of a counselor.

The purpose of this study was to determine if instructing the teacher to pay attention to the child when he was behaving properly would improve his general classroom behavior. Others have shown similar procedures to be effective (Allen, Hart, Buell, Harris and Wolf, 1964; Becker, Madsen, Arnold and Thomas, 1967; Hall, Lund and Jackson, 1968; Hart, Reynolds, Baer, Brawley and Harris, 1968; Madison, Becker and Thomas, 1968;

Note: Reprinted from *Personnel Guidance J, 48*:836-841, 1970.

The authors wish to thank Mona Marcec, a fourth grade teacher who made this study possible, and William Bach, Carl Wallin, Pamela Hentze, and Andrew Wheeler for their assistance in reliability measures.

Thomas, Becker and Armstrong, 1968; Walker and Buckley, 1968; Zimmerman and Zimmerman. 1962).

METHOD

The student was a nine-year, ten-month-old fourth grader, whose cumulative folder indicated that he was of average intelligence. At the end of the third grade he had achieved a low fourth grade level on the Metropolitan Achievement Battery. His health records reported no physical abnormalities except for hyperactivity, a characteristic confirmed by his teacher and mother. His teacher expressed concern about his "talking-out" and "out-of-seat" behavior.

PROCEDURE

The parents, teacher, and counselor jointly decided to change the student's behaviors in the classroom setting rather than referring him for individual counseling sessions. First, behavioral definitions of out-of-seat and talking-out were agreed upon by the teacher and counselor. Then a record of the frequency of the student's typical disruptive behaviors was obtained. A series of consultations between teacher and counselor was held at the end of this period. Instruction and role-playing were used to help the teacher learn to pay attention to the child only at appropriate times.

Observing the Student's Behaviors

The child was observed on Mondays, Wednesdays, and Fridays from 8:50 A.M. until 10:00 A.M. during reading class. Typically, the class worked on Science Research Associates "Reading Laboratory Series" and "Pilot Library Series."

A recording system similar to those used in other studies (Bijou, Peterson, and Ault, 1968; Hall, Lund and Jackson, 1968; Walker and Buckley, 1968) was developed, containing the list of inappropriate behaviors. Madsen, Becker, and Thomas' (1968) definition was used for the list: ". . . the occurrence of one or more behaviors listed under Inappropriate Behavior . . . during any observation interval." Observers were undergraduate and graduate volunteer students and an assistant building principal. They watched the student's behavior for ten seconds, and then used symbols to record what they saw within a five-second interval. Observation-recording was continuous for five minutes, followed by a two-minute interlude. These students were provided with identical, synchronized, Bel-Air stopwatches, clip boards, and recording sheets.

Observers were trained to identify out-of-seat and talking-out behaviors by referring to a mutually accepted set of definitions. Demonstrations of behavioral responses were role-played by the counselor, and the observers' subsequently recorded responses were checked. Once reliability agreement stabilized at 80 percent or above, recording was done in the classroom. Training required from thirty to forty-five minutes. Two observers, sitting in different physical locations in the classroom, independently recorded the child's behavior. Reliability was determined by dividing the number of agreements by the number of agreements plus disagreements (Bijou, Peterson and Ault, 1968). The average of seven reliability checks was 87 percent.

Observing the Teacher's Behaviors

The teacher's behavior was also observed and recorded. Teacher attention was defined as being near the child, looking at him, giving directions to him, praising him, and several others that were listed and clearly defined for the observers. Whether the teacher's attention followed the desirable or disruptive behaviors of the student was recorded. The percentage of agreement between two independent observers of teacher behavior averaged 84 percent on seven different occasions.

Experimental Conditions

The phases of the program consisted of looking at both the child's and teacher's behaviors at these times: (a) during normal classroom routine (Baseline 1); (b) when the teacher attended to desirable behaviors (Contingent Teacher Attending 1); (c) when the teacher returned to normal classroom routine (Baseline 2);

(d) when the teacher again attended to desirable behavior (Contingent Teacher Attending 2) ; and (e) follow-up.

Normal Classroom Routine (Baseline 1)

The child's normal classroom behavior was measured by recording the frequency of time blocks in which he either talked out or was out of his seat without permission before counselor instructions to the teacher were instituted.

Teacher Attending to Desirable Behavior
(Contingent Teacher Attending 1)

The teacher was instructed to attend to the child only when he was not talking out or was not out of his seat. When he took his seat in the morning, the teacher was to approach and compliment him on his behavior. When appropriate, she was encouraged to commend him to the class as "setting a good example." If he raised his hand, the teacher was to call on him for a response as soon as possible. If an academic response possessed degrees of correctness, she was to voice approval of the correct aspects and try to ignore the inaccurate portions. Since he seemed to prefer being out of his seat, provisions were made for him to do this as a consequence of not talking out. For example, when the teacher responded to his raised hand and he asked permission to pass out the reading material, she might have responded, "Certainly, since you raised your hand and did not talk out, you may pass out the books." In general, she was instructed in giving praise systematically, nodding, smiling, and being near the child whenever he raised his hand, sat in his seat, and responded positively to the classroom environment.

When inappropriate behaviors were observed, the teacher was to move away from the child's desk, look the other way when possible, ignore his calls when a hand was not raised, and generally not attend to behaviors that interfered with the desired learning environment.

Throughout the study, twenty-minute consultation meetings between the counselor and teacher were held in the afternoon of each day that an observation took place. The counselor brought current graphs of the teacher's and child's behaviors to the meeting (see Fig. 20-1) .

Return to normal classroom routine (Baseline 2)

After eighteen sessions of observation, a probe was instituted to determine whether the behavioral alterations effected in the consultation-treatment period were related to the attending behavior of the teacher. This procedure was originally planned for five days but was discontinued after three days due to teacher concern. During the probe period, the teacher paid attention to the student when he was out of his seat or when he was talking, a condition paralleling the normal classroom situation at the initiation of the study.

Teacher Attending to Desirable Behavior: Two (Contingent Teacher Attending 2)

After reversal procedures were established, the previous conditions were reinstated. The teacher again used her attention to increase the child's desirable classroom behavior. Seven sessions were involved in this period of the experiment.

Follow-up

A two-month follow-up was conducted after the study was concluded. Observers recorded both the child's and the teacher's behavior one day a week for eight weeks. Ten randomly chosen one-minute observations were gathered each session. The conditions established during the last phase were maintained.

RESULTS

Percentage of observation intervals in which talking-out and out-of-seat behaviors occurred as a function of conditions is shown in Fig. 20-1. Major alterations in the desired direction occurred when the teacher was praising and attending to the student. Conversely, inappropriate behavior was high when the teacher was paying attention after disruptive behaviors.

The upper portion of Fig. 20-1 indicates the frequency of teacher responses following both desirable and disruptive student

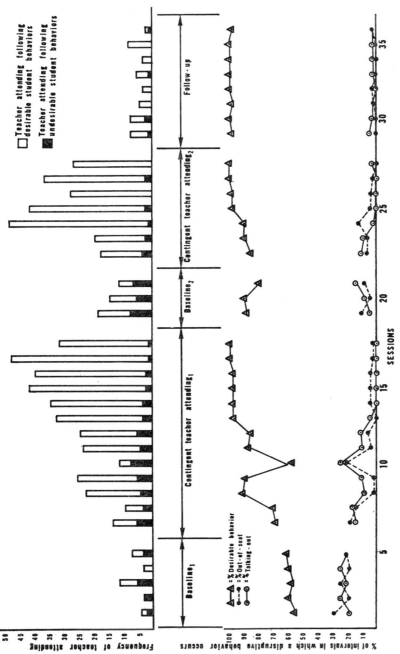

Figure 20-1. Occurrences of various pupil behavior in relation to teacher attending.

behaviors. Inspection of the figure shows that as the teacher attended to desirable student behaviors, the percentage of disruptive student behaviors decreased and the percentage of desired student behaviors increased. During session 10, when the teacher inadvertently gave a disproportionate amount of attention to the child following disruptive behaviors, the disruptive behaviors showed an increase. During the return to normal classroom conditions, when the teacher substantially reduced her frequency of attending to desirable behaviors, there was a reduction in percentage of desirable student behaviors.

Follow-up over the two-month period after the termination of the study indicated that the student continued to raise his hand and remain in his seat (even though the teacher paid less attention to him).

DISCUSSION

Kennedy (1968) and Zimmer (1967) have argued for a behavioral approach since such an approach has established data-gathering procedures that are useful to the consultant. Subsequently, this study is an applied response to their suggestions and is based on their rationale. It is only logical to seek more effective consulting procedures and to do more applied research on the consulting role of the counselor, since it is so widely recommended as a legitimate professional responsibility.

This study demonstrates that a counselor can effectively function as a consultant to the classroom teacher. By recommending specific procedures in a consultation process, the counselor assisted in the resolution of a difficult problem. The teacher learned that the form and timing of her attention had a substantial effect on her student's behavior. More specifically, the teacher acquired a general procedure appropriate for dealing with other classroom problems. Knowledge of such procedures can serve her in the future in (a) dealing with a problem early in its inception, and (b) preventing similar problems from occurring in her classroom.

Such counselor techniques as the use of systematic observation and recording systems in the actual classroom environment can provide objective data. The subsequent analysis of data should result in specific recommendations to the teacher, thereby enhancing classroom management techniques. Counselors are constantly saying, "I cannot demonstrate to my administrator my professional contributions." The techniques used in this study suggest that such contributions can indeed be documented.

REFERENCES

1. Allen, K. E., Hart, B. H., Buell, J. S., Harris, F. R. and Wolf, M. M.: Effects of social reinforcement on isolate behavior of a nursery school child. *Child Dev, 35:*511-518.
2. Becker, W. C., Madsen, C. H., Jr., Arnold, C. R. and Thomas, D. R.: The contingent use of teacher attention and praise in reducing classroom behavior problems. *J Special Educ, 1:*287-307, 1967.
3. Bijou, S. W., Peterson, R. F. and Ault, H.: A method to integrate descriptive and experimental field studies at the level of data and empirical concepts. *J Appl Behav Anal, 1:*175-191, 1968.
4. Dinkmeyer, D. C.: The consultant in elementary school guidance. In Peters, H. Riccio, A. and Quaranta, J. (Eds.): *Guidance in the Elementary School.* New York, Macmillan, 1963.
5. Dinkmeyer, D. C.: The counselor as consultant: rationale and procedures. *Elementary School Guidance and Counseling, 2:*187-194, 1968a.
6. Dinkmeyer, D. C. (Ed.): *Guidance and Counseling in the Elementary School.* New York, Holt, Rinehart & Winston, 1968b.
7. Faust, V.: The counselor as a consultant to teachers. *Elementary School Guidance and Counseling, 1:*112-117, 1967.
8. Hall, R. V., Lund, D. and Jackson, D.: Effects of teacher attention on study behavior. *J Appl Behav Anal, 1:*1-12, 1968.
9. Hart, B. M., Reynolds, N. J., Baer, D. M., Brawley, E. R. and Harris F. R.: Effects of contingent and non-contingent social reinforcement in the cooperative play of a preschool child. *J Appl Behav Anal, 1:*73-76, 1968.
10. Kaczkowski, H.: The elementary school counselor as consultant. *Elementary School Guidance and Counseling, 1:*103-111, 1967.
11. Kennedy, D. A.: Use of learning theory in guidance consultation. *Elementary School Guidance and Counseling, 3:*49-56, 1968.
12. Madsen, C. H., Jr., Becker, W. C. and Thomas, D.R.: Rules, praise, and ignoring: Elements of elementary classroom control. *J Appl Behav Anal, 1:*139-150, 1968.
13. Mayer, G. R. and Munger, P. F.: A plea for letting the elementary school counselor counsel. *Counselor Education and Supervision, 6:*341-346, 1967.

14. McClain, A. D and Boley, J. J.: Counseling and consulting interrelationships. *Elementary School Guidance and Counseling, 3:*32-39, 1968.
15. *Report of the ACES-ASCA Joint Committee on the Elementary School Counselor.* Washington, D.C., American Personnel and Guidance Association, 1966.
16. Thomas, D. R. Becker, W. C. and Armstrong, M.: Production and elimination of disruptive classroom behavior by systematically varying teacher's behavior. *J Appl Behav Anal, 1:*35-45, 1968.
17. Walker, H. M. and Buckley, N. K.: The use of positive reinforcement in conditioning attending behavior. *J Appl Behav Anal, 1:*245-250, 1968.
18. Zimmer, J. M.: Learning principles strategy: an approach for guidance in the elementary school. *Elementary School Guidance and Counseling, 2:*43-50, 1967.
19. Zimmerman, E. H. and Zimmerman, J.: The alteration of behavior in a special classroom situation. *J Exp Anal Behav, 5:*59-60, 1962.

PART II.
ADDITIONAL RECOMMENDED READINGS

1. Bindman, A. and Spiegel, A. (Eds.): *Perspectives in Community Mental Health*. Chicago, Aldine, 1969.
2. Bolman, W. and Westman, J.: Prevention of mental disorder: An overview of current programs. *Am J Psychiatry, 123(9):*1058-1068, 1967.
3. Caplan, G.: *The Theory and Practice of Mental Health Consultation*. New York, Basic Books, 1970.
4. Caplan, G.: *Principles of Preventive Psychiatry*. New York, Basic Books, 1964.
5. Carter, J. (Ed.): *Research Contributions from Psychology to Community Mental Health*. New York, Behavioral Publications, 1968.
6. Cowen, E., Gardner, E. and Zax, M. (Eds.): *Emergent Approaches to Mental Health Problems*. New York, Appleton-Century-Crofts, 1967.
7. Golan, N.: When is a client in crisis? *Social Casework, 50:* 1969.
8. Golann, S. and Eisdorfer, C. (Eds.): *Handbook of Community and Social Psychology*. New York, Appleton-Century-Croft, 1972.
9. Holland, C.: An interview guide for behavioral counseling with parents. *Behav Ther, 1:*70-79, 1970.
10. Karp, H. N. and Karlas, J.: Combining crisis therapy and mental health consultation. *Arch Gen Psychiatry, 14:*536-542, 1966.
11. Kellam, S. and Schiff, S.: The Woodlawn Mental Health Center: A community mental health center model, *Social Service Review, 40(3):* 255-263, 1966.
12. Parad, H. (Ed.): *Crisis Intervention: Selected Readings*. New York, F.S.A.A., 1965.
13. Peck, H., Kaplan, S. and Roman, M.: Prevention, treatment and social action: A strategy of intervention in a disadvantaged area. *Am J Orthopsychiatry:* 57-68, Jan. 1966.
14. Rapoport, L.: Crisis-oriented short-term casework. *Social Service Review, 41(1):*31-43, 1967.
15. Wadsworth, H.G.: Initiating a preventive-corrective approach in an elementary school system. *Social Work, 15(3):*60-66, 1970.
16. Wagner, M.: Parent therapists: An operant conditioning method. *Ment Hyg:*452-455, July, 1968.

PART III

THERAPEUTIC INTERVENTION

> Cans't thou not minister
> to a mind diseased?
>
> —William Shakespeare

THE NEGATIVE answers to the question posed (above) by Shakespeare (e.g. Eysenck, 1966) have become so entrenched in clinical lore that the clinician, bombarded by doubts from all sides, really has only one step available to him: a careful search through the literature to see if, in fact, there *are* any courses which he might chart to insure a practice based on some predictable record of success. As discussed in relation to the section on research in Part I, there have indeed been a number of positive findings in the literature, coupled with the development of new approaches to practice. One point though, made in the Introduction, must be clear: use of research findings as a guide to practice is not infallible. Individual studies must be put into the perspective of both the theory (or approach) which generated them, and other studies which support or contradict them. Decision-making is a never-ending process since, at any time, new findings might invalidate old. But because the practitioner must make judgments since he is continuously rendering services, those judgments should be tempered by the best the research can offer at any given point in time. Closure around one area of theory and practice should be avoided.

The first paper in the "General" section sets the tone for Part III. The paper presents a framework for an eclectic practice, based on the two positions that: (a) professionals must do all in their power to find procedures that are effective, and (b) no single approach has been found uniformly successful. The paper also presents several areas where research findings point to potentially useful modes of practice. The next paper is a brief description of a study involving short-term versus open-ended casework. (Reid and Shyne, 1969). Placing the Reid and Shyne study in the context of other research conducted on this topic, the paper points to the generally greater or equal effectiveness, and clearly greater efficiency, of short-term time-limited treatment over extended open-ended treatment. This has major implications for practice. If the same or even better results can be achieved using short-term treatment, what justification can there be (in comparable situations) for the use of long-term treatment? In other words, with effectiveness held constant, that form of treatment is best that does it least and does it fastest (Fischer, 1970). The third paper in this introductory section is by Kanfer and Saslow and deals with issues involving diagnosis and assessment. Kanfer and Saslow illustrate many of the difficulties associated with traditional modes of diagnostic classification, and propose an alternative based on a functional analysis of individual behavior. They discuss the methods of data collection for such an analysis, and develop a framework to guide in the collection of information. The final paper in this section, by Carkhuff, poses some disturbing questions. Carkhuff argues that there are no training programs in the helping professions that have established their efficacy in terms of demonstrated translation to client benefits. Carkhuff presents some evidence that lay counselors may be systematically trained to offer beneficial therapeutic conditions to clients. He also presents a model for practice involving a core of facilitative conditions, around which a variety of potential helping methods may be grouped.

Carkhuff's work serves as a bridge to the following section, since his model of core facilitative conditions deals directly with the next topic—the Therapeutic Relationship. In her overview of the various systems of social casework, Simon (1970) notes that most of them utilize "the relationship" as the keystone of the casework process. Unfortunately, with one exception, traditional conceptions of the therapeutic relationship, while of considerable interest, have been of minimal practical value since most theorists were unable to provide systematic ways for practitioners to implement their ideas about relationship. The major exception to this dilemma is discussed in this section. Here, a substantial body of research, with a sound conceptual foundation and associated methods for training, points to the efficacy of certain operational-ized variables of the therapeutic relationship: warmth, empathy and genuineness.

The first paper of this section is a presentation by Carl Rogers of the nature of these characteristics. Evolving out of his own theory of therapy, Rogers describes the core conditions of the therapeutic relationship—warmth, empathy and genuineness—which he hypothesizes are crucial for the achievement of positive change in clients. Truax and Carkhuff in the following paper present some of the evidence which their research program has produced on these and other variables. Not only do high levels of these therapeutic conditions lead to positive client change, but low levels possessed by the helper are related to client *deteriora-tion*. The final paper in this section, by Carkhuff and Truax, describes the successful implementation of a program in which students were trained to develop higher levels of therapeutic con-ditions. Without such evidence of trainability, the work described in this section would be questionable in terms of its application in educational, and consequently, practice situations. *With* this evi-dence, and increasing evidence that such training is specifically adaptable to social work education (Fischer, 1972), the implica-tions of this work are far-reaching. Actually, since social work in general has been exposed to little of this material, the papers presented here describe basic elements of the approach. There has been some expansion of this work, particularly by Carkhuff (1971), to include additional variables such as "confrontation" and "immediacy." But the dimensions of warmth, empathy and genuineness remain the foundation upon which the remainder of the model is constructed.

In fact, a distinct pattern has emerged. Since most "tradition-al" schools of therapeutic endeavor report approximately the same levels of success, and no schools* have demonstrated their super-iority in helping clients, these results might be explainable in terms of relationship variables which cut across all schools of

---

*Even Roger's client-centered therapists in general appear no more successful than the "average" therapist, unless they are functioning at high levels on these rela-tionship variables.

thought and tend to level out results. This further suggests the distracting but potent idea that the "theory" to which one ascribes is, in practice, minimally relevant since effectiveness seems to be attributable to other factors. In fact, the positive but undifferentiated effects of "psychotherapy" found in several studies by Meltzoff and Kornreich (1970) and discussed in Part I of this book, might now, at least partially, be explainable on the basis of the integrating principles of the therapeutic relationship, indeed the "keystone" of successful practice.

The final two sections of Part III deal with Behavior Modification. This area has, at best, received a lukewarm reception from social workers.† Part of the reason perhaps involves a problematical circularity: little knowledge about behavior modification was being directed specifically at social workers, social workers were thus little exposed to behavioral principles, therefore, social workers were doing little to develop and disseminate knowledge about behavior modification.* The articles in this section are intended as beginning efforts to dispel this theoretical/professional lag.

The first section deals with the operant approach to behavior modification.‡ In the first paper, Krasner presents an overview of

---

†As evidence of this, the first paper dealing solely with behavior modification to appear in a social work journal (Thomas, 1968), appeared many years after several journals had been established dealing only with the topic of behavior modification, after publication of several books on the topic, and after the psychological journals had been replete with references to behavior modification for a period of several years.

*This is despite efforts at the two major centers of social work education where behavior modification was being developed for social work practice, the School of Social Work, University of Hawaii (Nagoshi, 1969) and the School of Social Work, University of Michigan (Thomas, 1967).

‡Generally, the terms "behavior modification" and "behavior therapy" are used synonymously (despite Krasner's notion to the contrary expressed in Chap. 28). Actually, because of major differences between the operant and respondent approaches, there may be some heuristic advantages in the future in distinguishing between the two by considering the operant perspective as behavior modification and the respondent approach as behavior therapy. To distinguish briefly between the two perspectives, and in a gross sense, the operant approach deals with *voluntary*, purposeful behavior (e.g. walking, playing, studying), with application in practice to date focused predominantly on altering the controlling *consequences* of such behavior (see Chapters 15 and 20). The respondent approach deals with

some basic terms, history, the behavioral model of abnormal behavior, and several program examples using operant methods. The second paper by Thomas is perhaps the clearest extant presentation of basic operant concepts and principles, and some techniques for implementing them. The third paper by Liberman elaborates on the use of behavioral approaches to family and couple therapy. Actually, social workers are familiar with a different form of family therapy, one that emphasizes changes in communication patterns as a major therapeutic goal (e.g. Scherz, 1970). However, given the fact that none of these communication-oriented approaches (e.g. Ackerman, 1966; Satir, 1964, etc.), have demonstrated their success in empirical research, it seems time to consider an alternative model. The model presented here, based on behavioral principles with common relevance at a variety of levels of human interaction, at least offers a new and clearly differentiated approach to treatment, and one that possesses major built-in advantages involving guidelines for evaluation.

The three papers on operant behavior modification, taken as a whole, describe not only basic assumptions and principles of the operant approach, but discuss a variety of areas for implementation, ranging from work with individuals and families as voluntary clients, to programs designed to facilitate the recovery of institutionalized clients. Along with the case studies presented in Chapters 15 and 20 demonstrating both effective implementation of principles and the operant single case study research design (see also Stuart, 1971), the reader should be able to piece together major elements of the approach.*

The final section of Part III deals with the respondent approach to behavior therapy. In its most significant aspect of theory and practice, this approach is largely a product of the work

---

involuntary, automatic behavior elicited by an antecedent stimulus (e.g. emotional behavior such as anxiety), and the focus in practice (illustrated in Chapter 31) is on altering the *response* to a particular stimulus or set of stimuli. For a more thorough discussion of basic practical and theoretical distinctions between the two perspectives, see Fischer and Gochros (1973).

*For a comprehensive discussion of the operant approach written specifically for social workers and involving guidelines for assessing where (and where not) behavior modification intervention would be appropriate, see Fischer and Gochros (1973).

of Joseph Wolpe (1969). Despite the existence of other respond-ent-related procedures, Wolpe's technique of systematic desensiti-zation, the subject of both papers in this section, has received the bulk of attention from behavioral theorists, researchers, and prac-titioners. Wolpe, in the first paper, discusses the principle of reciprocal inhibition out of which the technique of systematic de-sensitization was developed, the way the therapist actually imple-ments the technique on a step-by-step basis, and presents some case illustrations. The following paper by Rachman gives an overview of the large amount of research that has been conducted on the technique. Clearly, systematic desensitization deserves primary consideration as the treatment of choice when the problem in-volves client anxieties or fears in response to identifiable stimuli; this includes the bulk of those problem/situations traditionally classified as "neurotic."

The emphasis on behavioral approaches in this book was placed as it was for one major reason: research evidence indicates that in a number of situations, implementation of behavioral tech-niques provides most efficacious results (Franks, 1968; Bergin and Garfield, 1971). These results are often dramatic, so much so that many professionals have succumbed to the temptation to hail behavior modification as a new "panacea" (the fourth psychiatric revolution?). This does not seem to be the case. But, in an inte-grated, comprehensive approach, behavior modification tech-niques clearly have their place, as long as the research continues to indicate that their use will produce desirable benefits for clients. This is not to deny special problems or ethical con-siderations that may arise through the use of behavior modi-fication procedures (see e.g. London, 1970). In fact, it would be wise to deal openly and clearly with these issues, as in the pre-sentation by Morrow and Gochros (1970), rather than to deny their existence. But the grounds for this evaluation must be clear. Behavior modification is an *intervention* technology, not a system designed to explain the *development* of behavior. Thus, the ques-tion is, does the application of behavior modification procedures produce beneficial changes in clients (irregardless of how the problematic behaviors came about in the first place). Secondly, behavior modification is not a philosophy, although, like every other intervention system, it should be evaluated on philosophical grounds (see Chap. 9). In fact, the inherently difficult nature of values questions means they cannot be dispensed with simply by disclaiming their presence.

Part III of this book covers the two major current thrusts in clinical practice—the core therapeutic conditions and behavior modification—and places them within the context of an eclectic framework. Though disparate on the surface, these approaches in actual practice appear complementary. There is both experimental and case study evidence (Vitalo, 1970; Mickelson and Stevic, 1970; Bergin, 1969) that their joint use leads to more effective helping.

REFERENCES

1. Ackerman, N.: *Treating the Troubled Family.* New York, Basic Books, 1966.
2. Bergin, A.: A technique for improving desensitization via warmth empathy and emotional re-experiencing of the hierarchy event. In Rubin, R. and Franks, C. (Eds.): *Advances in Behavior Therapy, 1968.* New York, Association Press, 1969, pp. 117-130.
3. Bergin, A. and Garfield, S. (Eds.): *Handbook of Psychotherapy and Behavior Change.* New York, John Wiley, 1971.
4. Carkhuff, R.: The development and generalization of a systematic resource training model. *J Res Dev Educ, 4:*3-16, 1971.
5. Eysenck, H.: *The Effects of Psychotherapy.* New York, International Science Press, 1966.
6. Fischer, J.: Training for effective social work practice. I. The therapeutic conditions. (in press), 1972.
7. Fischer, J.: Eclecticism: A model for social casework. Paper presented at Continuing Education Colloquium, School of Social Work, University of Hawaii, February, 1970.
8. Fischer, J. and Gochros, H.: *Changing Behavior: The Application of Behavior Modification To Social Work Practice.* Free Press, 1973.
9. Franks, C. (Ed.): *Behavior Therapy: Appraisal and Status.* New York, McGraw-Hill, 1969.
10. London, P.: Moral issues in behavior modification. In Bradfield, R. (Ed.): *Behavior Modification: The Human Effort.* San Rafael, California, Dimensions, 1970, pp. 185-197.
11. Mickelson, D. and Stevic, R.: The differential effects of facilitative behavioral counselors. *J Counsel Psychol, 17:* 1970.

12. Morrow, W. and Gochros, H.: Misconceptions regarding behavior modification. *Social Service Review, 44:*293-307, 1970.
13. Nagoshi, J. (Ed.): *Progress in Behavior Modification.* Honolulu, Social Welfare Development and Research Center, 1969.
14. Reid, W. and Shyne, A.: *Brief and Extended Casework.* New York, Columbia University Press, 1969.
15. Satir, V.: *Conjoint Family Therapy.* Palo Alto, Science and Behavior Books, 1964.
16. Scherz, F.: Theory and practice of family therapy. In Roberts, R. and Nee, R. (Eds.): *Theories of Social Casework.* Chicago, University of Chicago Press, 1970, pp. 219-265.
17. Simon, B.: Social casework theory: An overview. In Roberts, R. and Nee, R. (Eds.): *Theories of Social Casework.* Chicago, University of Chicago Press, 1970, pp. 353-397.
18. Stuart, R.: Research in social work: Social casework and social group work. In Morris, R. *et al.* (Eds.): *Encylopedia of Social Work,* 16th Issue. New York, National Association of Social Workers, Vol. II 1971, pp. 1106-1122.
19. Thomas, E.: Selected socio-behavioral techniques and principles: An approach to interpersonal helping. *Social Work, 13:*12-25, 1968.
20. Thomas, E. (Ed.): *The Socio-Behavioral Approach and Application to Social Work.* New York, Council on Social Work Education, 1967.
21. Vitalo, R.: Effects of facilitative interpersonal functioning in a conditioning paradigm. *J Counseling Psychol, 17(2):*141-144, 1970.
22. Wolpe, J.: *The Practice of Behavior Therapy.* New York, Pergamon Press, 1969.

A. GENERAL

Chapter 21

AN ECLECTIC APPROACH TO
THERAPEUTIC CASEWORK*

JOEL FISCHER

ALL CASEWORK should, of course, be therapeutic. But of all the criticisms that are currently being raised against casework (e.g. Briar, 1968), perhaps the most serious is that casework is indeed *not* therapeutic, i.e., that caseworkers are not effective in helping their clients. Many caseworkers tend to shrug off this criticism as unjust, or to cite inadequate methodologies in the outcome research as an explanation of the generally negative findings, or to just plain ignore it. But the unfortunate fact is that casework, specifically clinical or psychotherapeutic casework, *has* failed to unequivocally demonstrate its effectiveness in research designed to look exactly at that question (Fischer, 1971). It is the thesis of this paper, then, that after fifty years of effort, failure to demonstrate effectiveness is tantamount to a demonstration of ineffectiveness, and sufficient evidence that changes are desperately needed.

But this paper is not intended to be a catalog of casework's failings, real or imagined, nor is it to be an attack on casework. It is instead a *defense* of casework—or, more properly, of helping on a case by case or individualized basis—through the development of an approach to practice that is feasible, practical and will hopefully meet the most basic criterion for the justification of the casework enterprise—effectiveness in work with our clients.

Some important qualifications before proceeding further: therapeutic casework is used here as a synonym for clinical, direct or psychotherapeutic casework, which to date has been based predominantly on a particular, rather narrow, model for practice (al-

---

*An earlier version of this paper was presented at a Continuing Education Colloquium, University of Hawaii, School of Social Work, February, 1970.

though there is scattered evidence that this is changing). It is primarily this model—derived essentially from an ego-psychological, psychoanalytic base—that has been indicted by research findings, and to which this paper is addressed. But casework is not a unitary phenomenon, and attention to one aspect is not intended to imply downgrading of other aspects. Thus, the large and equally significant branch of casework—indirect or environmentally-oriented casework (as represented by such functions as broker, reformer, advocate, and so on)—is not under consideration here.

THE PLACE OF THEORY

There are two broad classes of theory possibly germane to casework practice. The first is causal theory (e.g. theories of personality development), and the second is intervention or change theory (e.g. theories of therapy).* Both types of theory, of course, are intended to explain certain phenomena. The former explains how and why individuals develop as they do, the latter explains how and why individuals can be changed. Unfortunately, casework has for years attempted to use causal theory—the sum total of which, in casework practice, is the "diagnostic formulation"—as a substitute for intervention theory. But causal theory may be only tentatively related, if at all, to notions about intervention, accounting perhaps for some of the current confusion and upheaval in the field regarding the problem of therapeutic efficacy.

Stemming from this also has been a preoccupation with searching for, and working with, "causes" in most problem-situations. This generally assumes that there *are* specifiable causes for each problem. However, the notion of specific causality is part and parcel of the so-called "disease model" of psychopathology in which psychological and social problems are treated basically as analogous to physical diseases. This leads logically to the necessity for discovering the etiology of each "illness," with treatment focused on ferreting out and dealing with this underlying cause.

But, in the first place, we have very little validated data as to

*The author is indebted to Dr. Scott Briar for making clear the distinction between these two classes of theory, a distinction which is basic to the assumptions underlying this paper.

just what *are* the "causes" of some of the problems with which we deal. At best, there seem to be numerous salient factors (multi-causality) (Rapoport, 1967). In fact, the extensive histories that for so long have seemed to be such an intimate part of casework practice—the better to see the "causes" of the problems of our clients—may be meaningless. Research by Renaud and Estess (1961) found that it was impossible to distinguish the histories of a group of "normals" from the histories of a group of "abnormals." Put two other ways, the assumption that there is a linear relationship between early disruption and later pathology may be incorrect (Orlansky, 1948; Caldwell, 1964), and/or we can find something in *everybody's* history which, interpreted in light of later events, seems to be pathogenic. However, even were we to be correct in such a diagnosis, there is little or no evidence to show that this accuracy has a positive effect on the outcome of treatment since the current level of our knowledge simply precludes us from taking direct interventive action on such "causal" variables.

Secondly, our preoccupation with causal theory led to a situation in which we are far more sophisticated in our diagnostic than our change knowledge, a condition which seems to be an anomaly in a profession whose prior commitment is, presumably, to the development of effective measures of intervention. This is not to say that understanding our clients, through the process of sensitive assessment, is not important. But it is important mainly to the extent that this understanding articulates with specific notions regarding how to bring about changes, i.e. when the "diagnosis" is stated in terms which are amenable directly to interventive measures. Finally, and perhaps most importantly, numerous examples in the literature testify to our ability to help a wide variety of people without knowing the etiology of their problems*; factors influencing the genesis of problems simply may not be involved at all in successful intervention into the course of those problems.

This is not, however, an argument for the removal of diagnostic theory from the curricula of schools of social work. It is instead an argument for the necessity of a shift in priorities from

---

*Pasamanick *et al.*, 1968; Truax and Carkhuff, 1967; Franks, 1969; etc.

emphasis on use of systems that are basically devoted to helping us develop an elaborate diagnostic methodology, to more appropriate utilization and development of theories of change. In other words, the inexorable need to know "causes" just shouldn't be so inexorable. In fact, for much of our work, it may not be necessary to be concerned with causal theory at all.

This leaves theories of intervention or induced change (induced, because change alone is worthless. To be valuable, the change must be guided and predictable. Ford and Urban, 1963). There seems to be little question that a systematic theory of intervention has several advantages. It tells us who is treatable, what and how to treat, and why treatment works (or doesn't work). Moreover, a theory of induced change should allow predictions (e.g. of outcome), and predictive knowledge is our ultimate aim in developing knowledge about effective change principles.

But, while as Kurt Lewin pointed out, there may not be anything as practical as a good theory, there also may be nothing as unfortunate as a *bad* theory. The attempt to fit all change efforts into the mold of a single theory seems nonsensical, although most practitioners do exactly that. In the first place, people may just be too complicated for practitioners to use only one approach to resolve all problems. Perhaps even more significantly, there is no empirical evidence that one theory of intervention produces consistently superior results across the total range of either people or problems. So, while it *is* important to know conceptually what we are doing so we can do it better and to the advantage of more people, the current state of our knowledge leaves us with the possibility that we may need more than one theoretical approach to intervention. Indeed, there are so many principles that may influence the modification of behavior (e.g. insight, cognitive dissonance, reciprocal inhibition, "faith," extinction, various forms of conditioning, social modeling, situational manipulation, and so on) that it seems "the best strategy at this point would be to consider the hypothesis that different kinds of responses may be governed by different principles and may require different procedures for their modification" (Ford and Urban, 1967, p. 345). In other words, a unitary theoretical perspective seems unlikely at this time. Perhaps it is undesirable as well, for the dangers are great that use of a single theoretical orientation would lead practitioners to attempt to force a number of significantly different people and problems into an incompatible mold, with disastrous results.

What this all points to, then, is the necessity to begin development of an approach to practice which can make use of the best knowledge available from a number of diverse orientations, or, specifically, the development of an *eclectic* approach to casework practice. Such an approach would consist of a variety of interventive measures, derived from different systems of induced change, and applied with people and problems where the evidence indicates that such application has a substantial chance to produce successful outcome.

Unfortunately, though, the notion of "eclecticism" seems objectionable both to many caseworkers (and this is rather strange for an allegedly "integrative profession"), and to members of related disciplines. As an example of the distaste aroused by the concept of eclecticism, Joseph Wolpe, one of the major developers of modern behavior therapy, has disdainfully accused the intellectual position of eclecticism as "inevitably barren," because the eclectic "has no consistent rules to guide either his thoughts or his actions" (Wolpe, 1969, p. XII).* Eclecticism, in short, has an aura of the unscientific, of having no systematic basis to guide its implementation.

But, such ideas seem rooted in a basic misconception about the nature and potentialities of a systematic approach to eclecticism. In fact, as Wolberg states:

> Eclecticism does not presuppose a disordered conglomeration of disparate devices thrown together into an expedient potpourri. Rather it involves the selection and studied amalgamation of aspects from varied sources that are compatible with and reinforce one another. In this way a fusion of concordant doctrines is implemented which

---

*This, in itself, is an unusual statement coming from a person who has stated unequivocally that he (and behavior therapists) ". . . will always do *what the evidence indicates* . . . [we] will in appropriate circumstances willingly employ other methods that have empirically been shown to be effective" (Wolpe, 1968, p. IX.)

buttresses up weaknesses in the individual system. The synthesis, har-
monious as it may seem for the moment, is subject to constant reorganization as new ideas and methods make themselves available.
(1966, p. 177).

Eclecticism most basically refers to a commitment to being
guided in our practice by what is most effective for our clients, a
commitment which takes precedence over devotion to any theory.
If our primary allegiance becomes attached to a particular theoretical orientation, rather than to the basic value of our responsibility to effectively help the people we serve, the entire enterprise
would be in danger of drowning in a sea of misguided irrelevance.
For casework is casework independent of the theories we use;
adherence to one particular theory is neither a necessary or sufficient condition for the existence of casework. Thus, as professionals who claim to be capable of helping our clients, we must take
the responsibility of ensuring that we are in fact capable of helping, and of competently utilizing the vast amount of knowledge
generated by disciplines engaged in endeavors related to ours.
This means, in short, that we look wherever we can for methods
that "work."

In order to properly assess what works, with whom, and how
effectively it can be used, the necessity for empirically grounding
our practice becomes readily apparent. This requires some allegiance to what has been called the "scientific method" of rational
and orderly procedures of observation and testing as the most
productive avenue of inquiry, both in the development and evaluation of "indigenous" knowledge, and as a governing principle in
the selection of knowledge from other sources.

And there *are* principles governing this selection of knowledge, based on the ability to critically evaluate systems of induced
change on the basis of meaningful criteria (Fischer, 1972). This
does not mean that all systems must be integrated into a mushy
and unwieldy supertheory. Rather, it suggests that diverse systems
of intervention should be reviewed in the event that they do, in
fact, have elements worthy of adaptation for an eclectic practice.
Careful application of the following criteria—perhaps the most
essential of several possibilities—is at the core of responsible use of

eclecticism: (a) first and foremost, a value base which appraises the appropriateness, and compatability with social work values and philosophy, of the material under consideration; (b) relevance to the phenomena of our concern (induced change in individuals) ; (c) practicability-utility—we can identify and manipulate that which is selected to the benefit of our clients (Thomas, 1964) , based on clear delineation of procedures for implementing change principles; (c) teachability—the principles and procedures are sufficiently developed to be transmissible in the casework curriculum; and, of special importance for this approach, (e) empirical evidence, obtained from controlled research utilizing significant outcome criteria, of effectiveness with clients. This is to say that while many forms of knowledge may be germane to casework practice, the most desirable knowledge, in a profession committed to inducing positive change in its clients, is that knowledge that will tell us what is effective in accomplishing our aims, and with whom.

A major portion of the remainder of this paper, then, consists of illustrations of the application of this approach in the selection of already-available knowledge. A variety of principles and procedures, derived from extant systems of intervention and/or the results of empirical study will be reviewed for potential inclusion in a single framework, focused on the competent and successful practice of therapeutic casework.

GOALS AND OBJECTIVES

In order to achieve some sense of direction for the enterprise, it would seem appropriate to establish a superordinate criterion as a guideline for the derivation of individualized goals for each client. Taking into account the traditional and worthwhile emphasis of social work on the area of client "social functioning," it appears as though a "social adjustment" criterion would best reflect that concern, and would be both realistic and attainable in treatment.

The concept of "social adjustment" is one that is repugnant to many social workers, conjuring up, as it does, images of a client-group of conforming robots, or of a profession devoted only to maintaining the status quo. But, hopefully, this would not be the case. Social adjustment (which has many popular variants such as "adaptation" and "coping") merely refers to the ability to deal with the serious conflicts and problems of life, and is recognition of the fact that people don't exist *"in vacuo."* Furthermore, there is no evidence that practitioners really know how to accomplish such objectives as helping people "self-actualize," "become more mature" or "enhance their creativity." These rather elaborate, nebulous and somewhat mystical goals may be asking too much of the available knowledge in casework. And a recent study, utilizing a nationwide sample of caseworkers and psychotherapists, discovered that practitioners, implicitly or explicitly, use a social adjustment criterion anyhow (Goldman and Mendelsohn, 1969). Finally, and perhaps most importantly, a large percentage of our *clients* define their problems in terms of social adjustment. (Gurin *et al.,* 1960; Mayer and Timms, 1969) .

The behavioral manifestation of social adjustment is social functioning. Social functioning essentially refers to the sum of an individual's activities in interaction with other individuals and/or situations in his environment (Boehm, 1959) , as delineated through the enactment of roles. And role performance is essentially made up of a series of behaviors an individual is expected to perform by virtue of his membership in particular social groups (Boehm, 1959) . If problems in social adjustment—or social functioning—arise, then, they are most likely to be problems in the performance of certain behaviors. Thus, if our practice is to be oriented by the goals which most directly affect our clients, the most reasonable arena for casework activity would seem to involve behavioral goals, or goals which involve essentially a complex of observable and measurable tasks and activities.* Actually, most problems aren't problems until they are observable anyhow, or, more appropriately, are not *labelled* as problems until they involve an observable failure to adequately handle social responsibilities.

---

*The assumptions here are that most clinical systems, implicitly or explicitly, are concerned with bringing about behavioral changes in their clients, and that there are several different potentially successful approaches to the production of such changes.

In actual practice, general goals must be translated into *specific* behavioral objectives for each client, arrived at through skillful assessment of clients' problems, a process which includes specification of the overtly identifiable aspects of the behavior defined as problematic, and identification of the conditions in the immediate environment affecting the problematic behavior. Such general and vague goals as "enhance self-esteem," or "increase ego strength" can be replaced by delineating which specific *behaviors* will accomplish the desired ends, how the client will be behaving when the aims are achieved, and the conditions under which the behaviors can be expected to occur (Bandura, 1969). This kind of specification permits the development of distinct outcome measures for evaluative purposes. It would also seem to be an absolute necessity for treatment itself as it allows more exact specification of the therapeutic procedures necessary to accomplish the individualized objectives. Finally, it also appears that specificity of goals—not to be confused with the selection of *inconsequential* goals—also leads to more *effective* treatment.*

STRUCTURING TREATMENT

If the principle is accepted that the goal of clinical casework is to help our clients achieve planned changes in their behavior, it would appear that a most crucial element to introduce into the casework situation is the use of structure. Structure, as used here, is more of a perspective than a particular set of techniques. Structure is an approach to treatment, that, in keeping with an eclectic perspective, may draw upon a wide variety of verbal, technical or experimental measures designed to influence the behavior of our clients. More specifically, structure may be defined as placing emphasis on "the therapist's use of external controls and manipulations that will lead to self-control and direction where needed. . . Structure in therapy means observing the relationship between given antecedent and resultant elements, interfering in pathology to realign variables so as to produce a different outcome or effect;

---

*Phillips and Wiener, 1966; note also the number of positive findings for time-limited treatment implying some specificity of goals, and behavior therapy's apparent success with goal-setting (to be discussed below).

using environmental manipulations (encompassing persons outside of therapy) to bring about desired effects; introducing and assuring as much certainty and dependability and control in heretofore uncontrolled and uncertain situations as possible; and above all, making these changes in ways consonant with the integrity and values of the individual" (Phillips and Wiener, 1966, p. 25).

The most crucial aspect of structure is *planning*. Planning involves: (a) assessment of the client and the relevant environmental factors; (b) selection of the variables accessible to behavior change; (c) delineation of intermediate and long-range goals; (d) development of a plan for the modification of behavior including the provision of specific means for change; (e) proceeding with the implementation of the plan in an orderly sequence; and (f) continued evaluation of progress. This sequential approach, wherein progress is carefully observed, also suggests that if a particular program does not appear to be having the desired effect it should be replaced by an alternative plan. This, in turn, demands great flexibility on the part of the caseworker, plus (obviously) the knowledge and capacity to implement alternative plans.

Utilizing a structured approach, the caseworker would function as an active teacher and a role model, encouraging the client to participate in treatment by defining mutual expectations and responsibilities. The caseworker would provide a sequence of steps—encompassing both intermediate and long-range objectives —designed to bring about the desired changes in behavior. And together, caseworker and client implement the plan, as the client, with the caseworker's assistance, learns to attend to, and attempt, however tentatively, behaviors that previously were unattainable or avoided.

In addition to the general framework mandated by a structured perspective, there are several concrete ways in which structure might be utilized. For example, a number of researchers, using variants of the same approach, have demonstrated that continuance can be increased, and positive outcome enhanced, when the practitioner devotes the first one or two interviews to structuring the role of the client, specifically, clarifying what it is he and the agency can offer, what the client can expect treatment to be like, and how the client is expected to behave in treatment (Hoehn-Saric *et al.*, 1965; Truax and Carkhuff, 1967; Perlman, 1968). Similarly, structuring might be used in the provision of procedures to enhance the transfer of positive change from the therapeutic situation to real life—e.g. leading the client through the behaviors he would be expected to participate in outside of treatment, or carrying out aspects of treatment outside the office in situations in which the client eventually will have to respond (Goldstein *et al.*, 1966). Lastly, structuring treatment by the use of time limits which shorten the process (10 to 12 sessions), fairly consistently has been found to be as effective—or even more effective—than open-ended treatment of longer duration, with improvement lasting just as long as that produced by long-term services (e.g. Reid and Shyne, 1969; Shlien *et al.*, 1962; Muench, 1965; Goldstein *et al.*, 1966).

Finally, a structured approach to therapeutic casework is considered here because of its apparent demonstrably successful results with clients. The use of a structured approach, when compared with more open-ended treatment in a number of controlled studies, has produced consistently superior results involving both efficiency and effectiveness (Phillips and Wiener, 1966; Muench, 1965; Shlien *et al.*, 1962, etc.).*

SYSTEMATIC DESENSITIZATION

The field of "behavior therapy" has blossomed forth with so many potentially important clinical innovations that it would be impossible to sort them all out for explication here. They are, though, for the most part founded on some basic postulates: (a) maladaptive and adaptive behaviors are learned through the same basic principles and can be modified through application of those principles; (b) deemphasis on "history"; (c) emphasis on those responses which are objectively identifiable; (d) focus on dis-

---

*The utilization of any approach is potentially problematic. For a discussion of some of the problems and delimitations involved in adapting each of the approaches discussed here, see Fischer (1970).

covering the conditions eliciting and/or maintaining the maladaptive behavior; (e) the goal is not to alter inner states, but to
alter the behavior; and (f) once the behavior is altered, the
problem is removed (i.e. the maladaptive behavior *is* the problem).

Behavior therapy is increasingly being applied—with considerable success—to a wide range of problems (Franks, 1969). Organized around some fundamental principles of learning (see Bandura, 1969), a large number of imaginative change procedures,
with varying applicability, have been developed. One of these
procedures—systematic desensitization—has received probably the
most rigorous and widespread research evaluation of any extant
psychotherapeutic procedure. Because of this evaluation, the resulting validation of its effectiveness when used appropriately, and
its particular relevance for clinical practice in the open (e.g.
office) setting, it has been selected for inclusion here.

Systematic desensitization (along with several other related
techniques) was developed by Joseph Wolpe (1969). In brief, it
is assumed that the core of neurotic behavior lies in anxiety.
Wolpe's principle of *reciprocal inhibition* holds that certain behaviors (relaxation in this case) are antagonistic to anxiety, and
that when performed simultaneously, inhibit anxiety. Initial interviews using systematic desensitization, after the assessment has
established this as the treatment of choice, revolve around an attempt to organize clients' problems into common themes consisting of the stimuli which produce anxiety responses. Each theme is
ordered into a heirarchy from lesser to greater anxiety situations.
The client is trained in relaxation procedures, and, while relaxing,
imagines these progressively greater anxiety-producing situations
to which he is "systematically desensitized."

This is apparently an extremely effective technique for dealing with phobias, anxiety neuroses and other specific or specifiable
problem areas involving fear or anxiety, as reported in several
well-controlled studies (Wolpe, 1969; Paul, 1966, 1969). The results do in fact appear to be due to the technique of systematic
desensitization and not suggestion, or nonspecific effects of the
therapist-client relationship (Lang, 1969). Further, these proce-

dures can be carried out with minimal psychological sophistication on the part of the client, and, hence, would seem to have rather widespread applicability. The "diagnosis" and the plan are shared with the client; he is involved with a specific program to carry out. Systematic desensitization, moreover, is not extremely difficult for the practitioner to learn (see, e.g. Paul, 1966). Compared with traditional, psychoanalytically-oriented treatment, systematic desensitization is more "efficient," more clearly defined, and does not produce adverse reactions in treatment. And systematic desensitization is compatible with much of what has been discussed in this paper.

THE HELPING RELATIONSHIP: CORE FACILITATIVE CONDITIONS

A possible legitimate concern with much of what has been discussed so far is the apparent exclusion of provisions for making the helping relationship warm, nurturing and capable of producing positive changes. There does seem to be some consensus that "relationship" is a critical variable in casework and psychotherapy. However, it is not really clear as to how or why "the relationship" is helpful. Numerous attempts to conceptualize the therapeutic relationship—from Freud to the present day—have been unable to satisfy an important criterion: operationalization of the variable(s) involved in "relationship." It might be argued that once relationship qualities are identified and measured, their importance to outcome might be more clearly evaluated.

This seems to be the case. A recent publication by Truax and Carkhuff (1967) has reviewed the efforts of a group of counselor-researchers to operationalize and measure the effects of three qualities of relationship: (a) *Accurate empathy:* the helper's ability to perceive and communicate, accurately and with sensitivity, the feelings of the client and the meaning of those feelings; (b) *Non-possessive warmth:* acceptance, liking, commitment, unconditional regard; and (c) *Genuineness:* openness, spontaneity, congruence, the opposite of "phoniness." These dimensions together have been termed "core facilitative conditions"; "core" in that they are shared by all interactive human processes independent of theoretical orientation; and "facilitative" in that they free the client to attain higher and more personally rewarding levels of intrapersonal and interpersonal functioning (Carkhuff and Berenson, 1967).

These researchers have carried out an impressive array of evaluative studies. The research program was conducted with diverse client groups, in and out of institutions and cutting across several diagnostic categories. Both individual and group methods of counseling and therapy were used. Participating therapists included professionals and nonprofessionals, experienced and non-experienced therapists, and differing professional and theoretical orientations. A wide range of both subjective and objective outcome criteria was utilized. The overall results: a clear demonstration of the positive and significant effects of the therapist's provision of high levels of the core conditions on the outcome of counseling and psychotherapy.

Thus, for essentially the first time, there is an objective, empirically validated reason (over and beyond the moral reasons) for training caseworkers in qualities of relationship. Significantly, these conditions *can* be learned. But, because the research indicates that their existence at high levels is relatively infrequent even among experienced counselors and therapists (Truax and Carkhuff, 1967; Carkhuff and Berenson, 1967), traditional rather unstructured methods of relationship training must be modified in favor of a far more systematic approach involving both didactic and experiential learning, wherein each of the three dimensions are, in turn, the focus of training. While it is of course possible to possess high levels of the three conditions prior to training (as they do appear, basically, to be qualities of personality), it is not absolutely necessary. Several studies of lay personnel and graduate students in counseling have shown significant upward changes on the three dimensions after relatively brief training (Truax and Carkhuff, 1967).

Thus, the implications again seem clear: caseworkers, especially in this approach, but probably regardless of orientation, should be trained to provide high levels of these three dimensions. A convergence of empirical evidence with ethical standards makes this conclusion almost unavoidable.

Provision of the three conditions is not all that is important, however. Many of the studies cited by Truax and Carkhuff reveal that even with the same levels of conditions, some therapists achieve more effective results than others (i.e.—the total variance of the outcome is not explained by the "core dimensions"). Thus, the relationship, as defined by these three dimensions, "may be viewed as a *prerequisite* for therapeutic influence rather than an end in itself. It may be regarded as the matrix within which planful interventions occur" (Strupp and Bergin, 1969). Hence, the rest of this approach.

CONCLUSIONS

An eclectic approach to the practice of casework cannot be taught in a vacuum, but, in a complete casework program, should be taught in accord with both empirically derived and theoretical material of diverse backgrounds, in order to produce a practitioner knowledgable in several areas relating to assessment of, and provision of services to, clients. Consequently, an intrinsic and essential characteristic of this approach is the assessment of every client and his problems with great skill and sensitivity in order to employ those procedures which—based on empirical evidence—seem most appropriate. Thus, utilization of this perspective requires the development of a set of specific techniques that can be differentially applied under specifiable conditions to specific problems, behaviors or cases (Strupp and Bergin, 1969). As emphasized earlier, specific plans and goals must be made for each client, so that there should be indications early in the process as to whether or not a particular plan is succeeding. If one plan is not successful, another can be substituted, since, of utmost importance, the caseworker is not hampered by practicing within the limits of a single theory. Several alternatives—depending on the knowledge, skill and the imagination of the caseworker—may be available.

Now it may seem as though this approach is a retreat to an overly technical, method-centered approach, recently under fire from so many of the critics of casework. But if the techniques work, if our clients are helped, that's an *advance,* not a retreat. Nor should it be assumed that this is a plea for clinical casework to operate independently of, or in opposition to, environmentally-oriented casework and programs of social change. Therapeutic casework is only one arm of social work intervention, selectively applied at a particular problem-level. And it is not necessary to believe that, with a program of individualized services, all problems are the result of personality inadequacies. Rather, a simple more fundamental assertion is made: regardless of cause, certain problems can be *resolved* through individualized services.

Since this is an attempt to proceed from "what is known" about interventive practices, it might appear as though eclecticism could be a rather stagnant approach, with the implication that we should wait for others to develop validated procedures while we remain content with only what is already known. But the various components brought together into an eclectic approach to casework practice would, at any given time, likely be far from exhaustive as are the elements selected for discussion in this paper. For we must live with the awareness that as new research is performed, some currently acceptable conclusions may be negated. Thus, basic to appropriate utilization of an eclectic approach are certain principles: (a) What works is what is important. It *is*, after all, the client, who is our primary concern. (b) Research interest must be built in from the outset. This means awareness of what others are finding through their research, plus the ability to conduct our own research, especially of an experimental-evaluative nature. Hopefully, this attitude can be engendered through awareness that the components of this approach are *not* the "last word," and that it is the caseworker's responsibility to continually search for new and better ways to help his clients. Thus, each segment of this model was, and should be, chosen, in part, because of its emphasis on, or susceptibility to, research evaluation.

There may be a problem, however, in attempting to fit together within a single framework a number of obviously divergent procedures. But, the evaluation of compatibility, as well as the testing of differential applicability, are problems for further research. At this time, there seems to be no *inherent* reasons why these—and other—elements cannot be combined into a uniform productive whole. In fact, at least one case report has already been published which utilized two of the elements discussed here—

systematic desensitization and the core conditions—suggesting there was considerable clinical advantage and enhanced outcome due to their combined use in treatment (Bergin, 1969) .

What is central to this approach is first, its orientation to the client's welfare above all else; second, its orientation to the use of empirically validated procedures, and third, the use of eclecticism as the most viable framework for combining the first two dimensions. Yet, there is clearly no attempt at explication of a unifying, all-encompassing theory of change which could embrace the bulk of what could conceivably be included as components of an eclectic approach. While the importance of such a broadly-based theory would lie in the potential of increased knowledge of differential application of intervention procedures, acceptance of such a theory would hinge on empirical verification of its propositions, a prospect which seems rather remote at this stage in the development of our theoretical and research wisdom.

In the meantime, people are suffering, and it appears as though, in many cases, we do have considerable knowledge of ways to help them.

REFERENCES

1. Bandura, A.: *Principles of Behavior Modification.* New York, Holt, Rinehart & Winston, 1969.
2. Berenson, B. and Carkhuff, R. (Eds.): *Sources of Gain in Counseling and Psychotherapy.* New York, Holt, Rinehart & Winston, 1967.
3. Bergin, A.: A technique for improving desensitization via warmth, empathy and emotional re-experiencing of the hiearchy event. In Rubin, R. and Franks, C. (Eds.): *Advances in Behavior Therapy, 1968.* New York, Association Press, 1969, pp. 117-130.
4. Boehm, W.: *The Social Casework Method in Social Work Education.* New York, C.S.W.E., 1959.
5. Briar, S.: The casework predicament. *Social Work,* I. 5-11, Jan. 1968.
6. Caldwell, B.: The effects of infant care. In M. Hoffman, and Hoffman, L.: *Review of Child Development Research.* New York, Russell Sage Foundation, 1964, vol. I, pp. 9-87.
7. Carkhuff, R. and Berenson, B.: *Beyond Counseling and Therapy.* New York, Holt, Rinehart and Winston, 1967.
8. Fischer, J. :"A framework for the analysis and comparison of clinical theories of induced change. *Social Service Review* (in press), 1972.

9. Fischer, J.: Eclecticism: A model for social casework. Paper presented at Continuing Education Colloquium, School of Social Work, University of Hawaii, February, 1970.

10. Fischer, J.: To help or not to help: The state of outcome research in social casework. Paper presented at Tripler General Hospital, Honolulu, Hawaii, February 23, 1971.

11. Ford, D. and Urban, H.: *Systems of Psychotherapy*. New York, John Wiley and Sons, 1963.

12. Ford, D. and Urban, H.: Psychotherapy. In Fransworth, P. *et al.* (Eds.): *Annual Review of Psychology*. Palo Alto, California, Annual Reviews, Inc., 1967, pp. 333-372.

13. Franks, C. (Ed.): *Behavior Therapy: Appraisal and Status*. New York, McGraw-Hill, 1969.

14. Goldman, R. and Mendelsohn, G.: Psychotherapeutic change and social adjustment. *J Abnorm Psychol, 74*:164-172, 1969.

15. Gurin, G. *et al.*: *Americans View Their Mental Health*. New York, Basic Books, 1960.

16. Hobbs, N.: Sources of gain in psychotherapy. *Am Psychol, 17*:18-34, 1962.

17. Hoehn-Saric, R. *et al.*: Systematic preparation of patients for psychotherapy. I. Effects on therapy behavior and outcome. *J Psychiat Res, Z*:267-281, Dec. 1963.

18. Lang, P.: The mechanisms of desensitization and the laboratory study of human fear. In Franks, C. (Ed.): *Behavior Therapy: Appraisal and Status*. New York, McGraw-Hill, 1969, pp. 160-191.

19. Mayer, J. and Timms, N.: Clash in perspective between worker and client. *Social Casework, 50*:32-40, Jan., 1969.

20. Muench, G.: An investigation of time-limited psychotherapy. *J Counsel Psychol, 12*:294-299.

21. Orlansky, H.: Infant care and personality. *Psychol Bull, 46*:1-48, 1949.

22. Pasamanick, B. *et al.*: *Schizophrenics in the Community: An Experimental Study in the Prevention of Hospitalization*. New York, Appleton-Century-Crofts, 1967.

23. Paul, G.: *Insight vs. Desensitization in Psychotherapy*. Stanford, Calif., Stanford University Press, 1966.

24. Paul, G.: Outcome of systematic desensitization. In Franks, C. (Ed.): *Behavior Therapy: Appraisal and Status*. New York, McGraw-Hill, 1969, pp. 105-159.

25. Perlman, H.: *Persona*. Chicago, University of Chicago Press, 1968.

26. Phillips, E.L. and Wiener, D.: *Short-term Psychotherapy and Structured Behavior Change*. New York, McGraw-Hill, 1966.

27. Rapoport, L.: Crisis-oriented short-term casework. *Social Service Review, 41*:31-43, 1967.

28. Reid, W. and Shyne, A.: *Brief and Extended Casework.* New York, Columbia University Press, 1968.
29. Renaud, H. and Estess, F.: Life history interviews with 100 normal American males: "Pathogenicity" of childhood. *Am J Orthopsychiatry, 31:*786-802, 1961.
30. Rubin, R. and Franks, C. (Eds.): *Advances in Behavior Therapy, 1968.* New York, Association Press, 1969.
31. Shlien, J. *et al.:* Effects of time limits: A comparison of two psychotherapies. *J Counsel Psychol, 9:*31-34, 1962.
32. Strupp, H. and Bergin, A.: Some empirical and conceptual bases for coordinated research in psychotherapy. *Int J Psychiatry, 7 (whole No. 37):* February, 1969.
33. Thomas, E.: Selecting knowing from behavioral science. In Bartlett, H. *et al.* (Eds.): *Building Social Work Knowledge.* New York, N.A.S.W., 1964, pp. 38-48.
34. Thomas, E.: The socio-behavioral approach: Illustrations and analysis. In Thomas, E. (Ed.): *The Socio-Behavioral Approach and Applications to Social Work.* New York, C.S.W.E., 1967, pp. 1-15.
35. Truax, C. and Carkhuff, R.: *Toward Effective Counseling and Psychotherapy.* Chicago, Aldine Publishing Co., 1967.
36. Wolberg, L.: *Psychotherapy and the Behavioral Sciences.* New York, Grune & Stratton, 1966.
37. Wolpe, J.: *The Practice of Behavior Therapy.* New York, Pergamon Press, 1969.
38. Wolpe, J.: Presidential Address, Second Annual Meeting of the Association for the Advancement of Behavior Therapy. In Rubin, R. and Franks, C. (Eds.): *Advances in Behavior Therapy, 1968.* New York, Association Press, 1969.

Chapter 22

SHORT-TERM VS. EXTENDED CASEWORK*

W<small>HICH IS MORE EFFECTIVE</small> under given circumstances, brief or
extended casework? Evidence from an increasing number of researchers and practitioners suggests that preplanned brief service
may be the better, yet many caseworkers and their agencies continue to prefer long-term treatment. However, if brief casework
is indeed more effective, this is a finding of the highest importance for the social welfare field, where the shortage of professional workers and the means to train them becomes ever more
acute as the number of clients and their needs increase.

This project (Grant No. 185) investigated the relative merits
of preplanned brief service vs. open-ended service. Other goals
were to study these treatment processes in relation to client
change and develop guidelines for planning services. One hundred and twenty lower middle-class families who voluntarily
sought help with chronic marital or parent-child problems which
had recently become worse were assigned randomly to differing
service patterns involving long and short-term help.

All caseworkers on the project had master's degrees and three
or more years of casework experience. Four well-qualified caseworkers, with no service responsibility obtained research data by
home interview at completion of intake, termination of casework,
and six months later. Outcome was assessed from the point of
view of the client, caseworker, and these independent research

Note: This *Brief* is based on *Brief and Extended Casework, N.Y.* Columbia University Press, 1969, by William J. Reid and Ann W. Shyne (Project Director). The book grew out of Grant No. 185, funded by the Cooperative Research Grants Branch of this Division, under Title II, Section 1110, of the
Social Security Act. The reesarch was carried out by caseworkers and researchers at the Community Service Society, 105 East 22nd Street, New
York, N.Y. 10010.

*Prepared by the Research Utilization Branch, Office of Research and Demonstra-
tions, Social and Rehabilitation Service, Department of Health, Education, and
Welfare, Washington, D.C. 20201.

interviewers. Sixteen key ratings of family's overall problem situation and functioning were used to test differences in outcome. The clients were young (21 to 50) and well-motivated. Almost all were high school graduates, and one-third had either attended or graduated from college.

SUPPORTING FINDINGS

- The problems of 84 percent of families receiving short-term services were improved at closing, compared to only 64 percent of those given extended help. Further, 17 percent of the "extended-help" families showed some deterioration, compared to only 2 percent of briefly helped families.

- Of thirty-two comparisons between long- and short-term services, ten were significantly different and nine of these favored brief casework.

- Brief therapy gave greater gains in "perception of self" for both husband and wife than long therapy, even though psychotherapists usually believe lengthy service is necessary to induce such change.

- Short-term casework was just as good as long-term in relation to parental and child-related problems, and consistently improved marital functioning.

- Each caseworker did somewhat better with his short-term clients, even though 85 percent of them initially preferred the long term approach. Brief treatment placed the caseworker under more pressure but was more beneficial for the client.

- A third of those receiving brief service disliked its brevity, feeling a need for at least a few more interviews. This was especially true of wives.

- At followup after six months, short-term cases retained their gains just as well as families given long-term help.

THREE GENERALIZATIONS FROM LITERATURE REVIEW

- Planned, short-term treatment yields results at least as good as, and possibly better than, open-ended treatment of longer duration.

● Improvement associated with short-term treatment lasts just as long as that produced by long-term services.

● Short-term treatment can be used successfully under most conditions if its objectives are appropriately limited.

IMPLICATIONS FOR ACTION

● The findings from this study and related research offer substantial evidence for wider use of brief, more economical, and better structured casework.

● Such casework is indicated for intact families who come voluntarily for help with chronic marital and child-related problems which have worsened.

● The proportion of cases meeting these criteria is "substantial for most agencies," ranging up to 50 percent of total caseload. This seems to warrant the introduction or gradual expansion of brief casework in most agencies, with testing along the way.

● A "treatment contract" specifying the amount and duration of service should be offered at the end of the first interview, and the caseworker conducting this interview should carry the case to completion.

● To convince the client that it is a contract to be taken seriously, the caseworker may say: "The best way to help you is for us to have a series of eight interviews—no more. What do you want to work on during these interviews?" Acceptance signifies a definite contract. From ten to fifteen interviews may be specified if desired, although eight were used on this project.

● The caseworker herself must believe in the validity of this approach and keep it within prescribed limits.

● Seminars and other means may be needed to reorient staff toward short-term service, lest they feel uneasy about letting clients go after brief periods.

ADVANTAGES OF BRIEF CASEWORK NOTED BY AUTHORS

● The most compelling advantage is cost-effectiveness. In this study, extended casework was three times as costly as short-term. with no better results to show for it.

● The money saved can be spent elsewhere in the agency's program, or used to help three times as many families of the sort served on this project. The waiting list can be made shorter and more predictable, with less delay for clients. And a higher portion of clients can be expected to complete a short "planned course of treatment."

● Since there is no basic distinction between intake and service, the same caseworker can handle both and so avoid many of the problems inherent in compartmentalized service.

● With service of a fixed and limited duration, feedback is more rapid and complete from client to caseworker. Practitioner, client, and agency can correct mistakes promptly and build upon successes.

● Field tests of different types of short-term service can be completed quickly, and the results from a sequence of such experiments can be fed into programs to improve service.

● The success of brief service may stimulate efforts to alleviate some of the more troublesome weaknesses of extended casework.

AUTHORS' ASSESSMENTS OF MAJOR RESULTS

● A more active approach by the caseworker early in treatment may yield special advantages for both short- and long-term treatment. Specifically, the first interview after intake should begin to stimulate specific changes through advice, logical discussion, and confrontation.

● Formulating more specific and limited goals, and focusing on them, may have contributed to the greater success of short-term treatment.

● Advance planning of treatment objectives and even the content of specific interviews (more easily done when treatment is short) may have enhanced success.

● The time limits of short-term help may have mobilized the caseworker's energies and caused a more active, efficient, and focused approach.

● Similarly, the brevity of the service period, and readiness for change, may have called forth an extra effort from the client, producing better outcome.

● Conversely, longer term treatment may have caused frustration in these "ready" clients and stirred up many dormant problems better left alone. Or, the client's interpersonal difficulties may in time have caused a negative reaction toward the caseworker.

● The data offer *no* basis for arguing that long-term service is really the more effective of the two patterns, or that the effectiveness of the two approaches somehow got reversed in the measurement process.

Chapter 23

BEHAVIORAL ANALYSIS
An Alternative to Diagnostic Classification

FREDERICK H. KANFER AND GEORGE SASLOW

DURING THE PAST DECADE attacks on conventional psychiatric diagnosis have been so widespread that many clinicians now use diagnostic labels sparingly and apologetically. The continued adherence to the nosological terms of the traditional classificatory scheme suggests some utility of the present categorization of behavior disorders, despite its apparently low reliability,[1,21] its limited prognostic value,[7,26] and its multiple feebly related assumptive supports. In a recent study of this problem, the symptom patterns of carefully diagnosed paranoid schizophrenics were compared. Katz et al,[12] found considerable divergence among patients with the same diagnosis and concluded that "diagnostic systems which are more circumscribed in their intent, for example, based on manifest behavior alone, rather than systems which attempt to comprehend etiology, symptom patterns and prognosis, may be more directly applicable to current problems in psychiatric research" (p. 202).

We propose here to examine some sources of dissatisfaction with the present approach to diagnosis, to describe a framework for a behavioral analysis of individual patients which implies both suggestions for treatment and outcome criteria for the single case, and to indicate the conditions for collecting the data for such an analysis.

I. PROBLEMS IN CURRENT DIAGNOSTIC SYSTEMS

Numerous criticisms deal with the internal consistency, the explicitness, the precision, and the reliability of psychiatric classi-

Note: Reprinted from Arch Gen Psychiatry, 12:529-538, 1965. Copyright 1965, American Medical Association.

fications. It seems to us that the more important fault lies in our lack of sufficient knowledge to categorize behavior along those pertinent dimensions which permit prediction of responses to social stresses, life crises, or psychiatric treatment. This limitation obviates anything but a crude and tentative approximation to a taxonomy of effective individual behaviors.

Zigler and Phillips,[28] in discussing the requirement for an adequate system of classification, suggest that an etiologically-oriented closed system of diagnosis is premature. Intsead, they believe that an empirical attack is needed, using "symptoms broadly defined as meaningful and discernible behaviors, as the basis of the classificatory system" (p. 616). But symptoms as a class of responses are defined after all only by their nuisance value to the patient's social environment or to himself as a social being. They are also notoriously unreliable in predicting the patient's particular etiological history or his response to treatment. An alternate approach lies in an attempt to identify classes of dependent variables in human behavior which would allow inferences about the particular controlling factors, the social stimuli, the physiological stimuli, and the reinforcing stimuli, of which they are a function. In the present early stage of the art of psychological prognostication, it appears most reasonable to develop a program of analysis which is closely related to subsequent treatment. A classification scheme which implies a program for behavioral change is one which has not only utility but the potential for experimental validation.

The task of assessment and prognosis can therefore be reduced to efforts which answer the following three questions: (a) which specific behavior patterns require change in their frequency of occurrence, their intensity, their duration or in the conditions under which they occur, (b) what are the best practical means which can produce the desired changes in this individual (manipulation of the environment, of the behavior, or the self-attitudes of the patient), and (c) what factors are currently maintaining it and what are the conditions under which this behavior was acquired. The investigation of the history of the problematic behavior is mainly of academic interest, except as it contributes information about the probable efficacy of a specific treatment method.

Expectations of Current Diagnostic Systems

In traditional medicine, a diagnostic statement about a patient has often been viewed as an essential prerequisite to treatment because a diagnosis suggests that the physician has some knowledge of the origin and future course of the illness. Further, in medicine diagnosis frequently brings together the accumulated knowledge about the pathological process which leads to the manifestation of the symptoms, and the experiences which others have had in the past in treating patients with such a disease process. Modern medicine recognizes that any particular disease need not have a single cause or even a small number of antecedent conditions. Nevertheless, the diagnostic label attempts to define at least the necessary conditions which are most relevant in considering a treatment program. Some diagnostic classification system is also invaluable as a basis for many social decisions involving entire populations. For example, planning for treatment facilities, research efforts and educational programs take into account the distribution frequencies of specified syndromes in the general population.

Ledley and Lusted[14] give an excellent conception of the traditional model in medicine by their analysis of the reasoning underlying it. The authors differentiate between a disease complex and a symptom complex. While the former describes known pathological processes and their correlated signs, the latter represents particular signs present in a particular patient. The bridge between disease and symptom complexes is provided by available medical knowledge and the final diagnosis is tantamount to labeling the disease complex. However, the current gaps in medical knowledge necessitate the use of probability statements when relating disease to symptoms, admitting that there is some possibility for error in the diagnosis. Once the diagnosis is established, decisions about treatment still depend on many other factors including social, moral, and economic conditions. Ledley and Lusted[14] thus separate the clinical diagnosis into a two-step pro-

344 *Interpersonal Helping*

cess. A statistical procedure is suggested to facilitate the primary or diagnostic labeling process. However, the choice of treatment depends not only on the diagnosis proper. Treatment decisions are also influenced by the moral, ethical, social, and economic conditions of the individual patient, his family and the society in which he lives. The proper assignment of the weight to be given to each of these values must in the last analysis be left to the physician's judgment (Ledley and Lusted[14]).

The Ledley and Lusted model presumes available methods for the observation of relevant behavior (the symptom complex), and some scientific knowledge relating it to known antecedents or correlates (the disease process). Contemporary theories of behavior pathology do not yet provide adequate guidelines for the observer to suggest what is to be observed. In fact, Szasz[25] has expressed the view that the medical model may be totally inadequate because psychiatry should be concerned with problems of living and not with diseases of the brain or other biological organs. Szasz[25] argues that "mental illness is a myth, whose function it is to disguise and thus render more potable the bitter pill of moral conflict in human relations" (p. 118).

The attack against use of the medical model in psychiatry comes from many quarters. Scheflen[23] describes a model of somatic psychiatry which is very similar to the traditional medical model of disease. A pathological process results in onset of an illness; the symptoms are correlated with a pathological state and represent our evidence of "mental disease." Treatment consists of removal of the pathogen, and the state of health is restored. Scheflen suggests that this traditional medical model is used in psychiatry not on the basis of its adequacy but because of its emotional appeal.

The limitations of the somatic model have been discussed even in some areas of medicine for which the model seems most appropriate. For example, in the nomenclature for diagnosis of disease of the heart and blood vessels, the criteria committee of the New York Heart Association[17] suggests the use of multiple criteria for cardiovascular diseases, including a statement of the patient's functional capacity. The committee suggests that the functional capacity be "... estimated by appraising the patient's ability to perform physical activity" (p. 80), and decided largely by inference from his history. Further,[17] "... (it) should not be influenced by the character of the structural lesion or by an opinion as to treatment or prognosis" (p. 81). This approach makes it clear that a comprehensive assessment of a patient, regardless of the physical disease which he suffers, must also take into account his social effectiveness and the particular ways in which physiological, anatomical, and psychological factors interact to produce a particular behavior pattern in an individual patient.

Multiple Diagnosis. A widely-used practical solution and circumvention of the difficulty inherent in the application of the medical model to psychiatric diagnosis is offered by Noyes and Kolb.[18] They suggest that the clinician construct a diagnostic formulation consisting of three parts: (a) a *genetic* diagnosis incorporating the constitutional, somatic, and historical-traumatic factors representing the primary sources or determinants of the mental illness; (b) a *dynamic* diagnosis which describes the mechanisms and techniques unconsciously used by the individual to manage anxiety, enhance self-esteem, i.e. that traces the psychopathological processes; and (c) a *clinical* diagnosis which conveys useful connotations concerning the reaction syndrome, the probable course of the disorder, and the methods of treatment which will most probably prove beneficial. Noyes' and Kolb's multiple criteria[18] can be arranged along three simpler dimensions of diagnosis which may have some practical value to the clinician: (a) etiological, (b) behavioral, and (c) predictive. The kind of information which is conveyed by each type of diagnostic label is somewhat different and specifically adapted to the purpose for which the diagnosis is used. The triple-label approach attempts to counter the criticism aimed at use of any single classificatory system. Confusion in a single system is due in part to the fact that a diagnostic formulation intended to describe current behavior, for example, may be found useless in an attempt to predict the response to specific treatment, or to postdict the patient's personal history and development, or to permit collection of frequency data on hospital populations.

Classification by Etiology. The Kraepelinian system and portions of the 1952 APA classification emphasize etiological factors. They share the assumption that common etiological factors lead to similar symptoms and respond to similar treatment. This dimension of diagnosis is considerably more fruitful when dealing with behavior disorders which are mainly under control of some biological condition. When a patient is known to suffer from excessive intake of alcohol his hallucinatory behavior, lack of motor coordination, poor judgment, and other behavioral evidence of disorganization can often be related directly to some antecedent condition such as the toxic effect of alcohol on the central nervous system, liver, etc. For these cases, classification by etiology also has some implications for prognosis and treatment. Acute hallucinations and other disorganized behavior due to alcohol usually clear up when the alcohol level in the blood stream falls. Similar examples can be drawn from any class of behavior disorders in which a change in behavior is associated primarily or exclusively with a single, *particular* antecedent factor. Under these conditions this factor can be called a pathogen and the situation closely approximates the condition described by the traditional medical model.

Utilization of this dimension as a basis for psychiatric diagnosis, however, has many problems apart from the rarity with which a specified condition can be shown to have a direct "causal" relationship to a pathogen. Among the current areas of ignorance in the fields of psychology and psychiatry, the etiology of most common disturbances probably takes first place. No specific family environment, no dramatic traumatic experience, or known constitutional abnormality has yet been found which results in the same pattern of disordered behavior. While current research efforts have aimed at investigating family patterns of schizophrenic patients, and several studies suggest a relationship between the mother's behavior and a schizophrenic process in the child,[10] it is not at all clear why the presence of these same factors in other families fails to yield a similar incidence of schizophrenia. Further, patients may exhibit behavior diagnosed as schizophrenic when there is no evidence of the postulated mother-child relationship.

In a recent paper Meehl[10] postulates schizophrenia as a neuro-
logical disease, with learned content and a dispositional basis.
With this array of interactive etiological factors, it is clear that the
etiological dimension for classification would at best result in an
extremely cumbersome system, at worst in a useless one.

Classification by Symptoms. A clinical diagnosis often is a summarizing statement about the way in which a person behaves. On
the assumption that a variety of behaviors are correlated and consistent in any given individual, it becomes more economical to
assign the individual to a class of persons than to list and categorize all of his behaviors. The utility of such a system rests heavily on the availability of empirical evidence concerning correlations among various behaviors (response-response relationships),
and the further assumption that the frequency of occurrence of
such behaviors is relatively independent of specific stimulus conditions and of specific reinforcement. There are two major limitations to such a system. The first is that diagnosis by symptoms, as
we have indicated in an earlier section, is often misleading because it implies common etiological factors. Freedman[7] gives an
excellent illustration of the differences both in probable antece-
cedent factors and subsequent treatment response among three
cases diagnosed as schizophrenics. Freedman's patients were diagnosed by at least two psychiatrists, and one would expect that the
traditional approach should result in whatever treatment of
schizophrenia is practiced in the locale where the patients are
seen. The first patient eventually gave increasing evidence of an
endocrinopathy, and when this was recognized and treated, the
psychotic symptoms went into remission. The second case had a
definite history of seizures and appropriate anticonvulsant medication was effective in relieving his symptoms. In the third case,
treatment directed at an uncovering analysis of the patient's adaptive techniques resulted in considerable improvement in the patient's behavior and subsequent relief from psychotic episodes.
Freedman[7] suggests that schizophrenia is not a disease entity in
the sense that it has a unique etiology, pathogenesis, etc., but that
it represents the evocation of a final common pathway in the same
sense as do headache, epilepsy, sore throat, or indeed any other

symptom complex. It is further suggested that the term "schizo-phrenia has outlived its usefulness and should be discarded" (p. 5). Opler[19,20] has further shown the importance of cultural factors in the divergence of symptoms observed in patients collectively labeled as schizophrenic.

Descriptive classification is not always this deceptive, however. Assessment of intellectual performance sometimes results in a di-agnostic statement which has predictive value for the patient's be-havior in school or on a job. To date, there seem to be very few general statements about individual characteristics which have as much predictive utility as the IQ.

A second limitation is that the current approach to diagnosis by symptoms tends to center on a group of behaviors which is often irrelevant with regard to the patient's total life pattern. These behaviors may be of interest only because they are popu-larly associated with deviancy and disorder. For example, occas-ional mild delusions interfere little or not at all with the social or occupational effectiveness of many ambulatory patients. Neverthe-less, admission of their occurrence is often sufficient for a diag-nosis of psychosis. Refinement of such an approach beyond cur-rent usage appears possible, as shown for example by Lorr *et al.*[15] but this does not remove the above limitations.

Utilization of a symptom-descriptive approach frequently focuses attention on by-products of larger behavior patterns, and results in attempted treatment of behaviors (symptoms) which may be simple consequences of other important aspects of the pa-tient's life. Emphasis on the patient's subjective complaint, moods and feelings tend to encourage use of a syndrome-oriented classifi-cation. It also results frequently in efforts to change the feelings, anxiety, and moods (or at least the patient's report about them), rather than to investigate the life conditions, interpersonal reac-tions, and environmental factors which produce and maintain these habitual response patterns.

Classification by Prognosis. To date, the least effort has been devoted to construction of a classification system which assigns patients to the same category on the basis of their similar response to specific treatments. The proper question raised for such a classification system consists of the manner in which a patient will react to treatments, regardless of his current behavior, or his past history. The numerous studies attempting to establish prognostic signs from projective personality tests or somatic tests represent efforts to categorize the patients on this dimension.

Windle[26] has called attention to the low degree of predictability afforded by personality (projective) test scores, and has pointed out the difficulties encountered in evaluating research in this area due to the inadequate description of the population sampled and of the improvement criteria. In a later review Fulkerson and Barry[8] came to the similar conclusion that psychological test performance is a poor predictor of outcome in mental illness. They suggest that demographic variables such as severity, duration, acuteness of onset, degree of precipitating stress, etc., appear to have stronger relationships to outcome than test data. The lack of reliable relationships between diagnostic categories, test data, demographic variables, or other measures taken on the patient on the one hand, and duration of illness, response to specific treatment, or degree of recovery, on the other hand, precludes the construction of a simple empiric framework for a diagnostic-prognostic classification system based only on an array of symptoms.

None of the currently used dimensions for diagnosis is directly related to methods of modification of a patient's behavior, attitudes, response patterns, and interpersonal actions. Since the etiological model clearly stresses causative factors, it is much more compatible with a personality theory which strongly emphasizes genetic-developmental factors. The classification by symptoms facilitates social-administrative decisions about patients by providing some basis for judging the degree of deviation from social and ethical norms. Such a classification is compatible with a personality theory founded on the normal curve hypothesis and concerned with characterization by comparison with a fictitious average. The prognostic-predictive approach appears to have the most direct practical applicability. If continued research were to support certain early findings, it would be indeed comforting to be able to predict outcome of mental illness from a patient's premorbid social competence score,[28] or from the patient's score on an ego-strength scale,[4] or from many of the other signs and single variables which have been shown to have some predictive powers. It is unfortunate that these powers are frequently dissipated in cross-validation. As Fulkerson and Barry have indicated,[8] single predictors have not yet shown much success.

II. A FUNCTIONAL (BEHAVIORAL-ANALYTIC) APPROACH

The growing literature on behavior modification procedures derived from learning theory[3,6,11,13,27] suggests that an effective diagnostic procedure would be one in which the eventual therapeutic methods can be directly related to the information obtained from a continuing assessment of the patient's current behaviors and their controlling stimuli. Ferster[6] has said ". . . a functional analysis of behavior has the advantage that it specifies the causes of behavior in the form of explicit environmental events which can be objectively identified and which are potentially manipulable" (p. 3). Such a diagnostic undertaking makes the assumption that a description of the problematic behavior, its controlling factors, and the means by which it can be changed are the most appropriate "explanations." It further makes the assumption that a diagnostic evaluation is never complete. It implies that additional information about the circumstances of the patient's life pattern, relationships among his behaviors, and controlling stimuli in his social milieu and his private experience is obtained continuously until it proves sufficient to effect a noticeable change in the patient's behavior, thus resolving "the problem." In a functional approach it is necessary to continue evaluation of the patient's life pattern and its controlling factors, concurrent with attempted manipulation of these variables by reinforcement, direct intervention, or other means until the resultant change in the patient's behavior permits restoration of more efficient life experiences.

The present approach shares with some psychological theories the assumption that psychotherapy is *not* an effort aimed at removal of intrapsychic conflicts, nor at a change in the personality structure by therapeutic interactions of intense nonverbal nature (e.g. transference, self-actualization, etc.). We adopt the assumption instead that the job of psychological treatment involves the utilization of a variety of methods to devise a program which controls the patient's environment, his behavior, and the consequences of his behavior in such a way that the presenting problem is resolved. We hypothesize that the essential ingredients of a psychotherapeutic endeavor usually involve two separate stages: (a) a change in the perceptual discriminations of a patient, i.e. in his approach to perceiving, classifying, and organizing sensory events, including perception of himself, and (b) changes in the response patterns which he has established in relation to social objects and to himself over the years.[11] In addition, the clinician's task may involve direct intervention in the patient's environmental circumstances, modification of the behavior of other people significant in his life, and control of reinforcing stimuli which are available either through self-administration, or by contingency upon the behavior of others. These latter procedures complement the verbal interactions of traditional psychotherapy. They require that the clinician, at the invitation of the patient or his family, participate more fully in planning the total life pattern of the patient outside the clinician's office.

It is necessary to indicate what the theoretical view here presented does *not* espouse in order to understand the differences from other procedures. It does *not* rest upon the assumption that (a) insight is a *sine qua non* of psychotherapy, (b) changes in thoughts or ideas inevitably lead to ultimate changes in actions, (c) verbal therapeutic sessions serve as replications of and equivalents for actual life situations, and (d) a symptom can be removed only by uprooting its cause or origin. In the absence of these assumptions it becomes unnecessary to conceptualize behavior disorder in etiological terms, in psychodynamic terms, or in terms of a specifiable disease process. While psychotherapy by verbal means may be sufficient in some instances, the combination of behavior modification in life situations as well as in verbal interactions serves to extend the armamentarium of the therapist.

Therefore verbal psychotherapy is seen as an *adjunct* in the implementation of therapeutic behavior changes in the patient's total life, pattern, not as an end in itself, nor as the sole vehicle for increasing psychological effectiveness.

In embracing this view of behavior modification, there is a further commitment to a constant interplay between assessment and therapeutic strategies. An initial diagnostic formulation seeks to ascertain the major variables which can be directly controlled or modified during treatment. During successive treatment stages additional information is collected about the patient's behavior repertoire, his reinforcement history, the pertinent controlling stimuli in his social and physical environment, and the sociological limitations within which both patient and therapist have to operate. Therefore, the initial formulation will constantly be enlarged or changed, resulting either in confirmation of the previous therapeutic strategy or in its change.

A Guide to a Functional Analysis of Individual Behavior

In order to help the clinician in the collection and organization of information for a behavioral analysis, we have constructed an outline which aims to provide a working model of the patient's behavior at a relatively low level of abstraction. A series of questions are so organized as to yield immediate implications for treatment. This outline has been found useful in clinical practice and in teaching. Following is a brief summary of the categories in the outline.*

1. Analysis of a Problem Situation:† The patient's major complaints are

---

*A limited supply of the full outline is available and copies can be obtained upon request from us.

†For each patient a detailed analysis is required. For example, a list of behavioral excesses may include specific aggressive acts, hallucinatory behaviors, crying, submission to others in social situations, etc. It is recognized that some behaviors can be viewed as excesses or deficits depending on the vantage point from which the imbalance is observed. For instance, excessive withdrawal and deficient social responsiveness, or excessive social autonomy (nonconformity) and deficient self-inhibitory behavior may be complementary. The particular view taken is of consequence because of its impact on a treatment plan. Regarding certain behavior as excessively aggressive, to be reduced by constraints, clearly differs from regarding the same behavior as a deficit in self-control, subject to increase by training and treatment.

categorized into classes of behavioral excesses and deficits. For each excess or deficit the dimensions of frequency, intensity, duration, appropriateness of form, and stimulus conditions are described. In content, the response classes represent the major targets of the therapeutic intervention. As an additional indispensable feature, the behavioral assets of the patient are listed for utilization in a therapy program.

2. Clarification of the Problem Situation: Here we consider the people and circumstances which tend to maintain the problem behaviors, and the consequences of these behaviors to the patient and to others in his environment. Attention is given also to the consequences of changes in these behaviors which may result from psychiatric intervention.

3. Motivational Analysis: Since reinforcing stimuli are idiosyncratic and depend for this effect on a number of unique parameters for each person, a hierarchy of particular persons, events, and objects which serve as reinforcers is established for each patient. Included in this hierarchy are those reinforcing events which facilitate approach behaviors as well as those which, because of their aversiveness, prompt avoidance responses. This information has as its purpose to lay plans for utilization of various reinforcers in prescription of a specific behavior therapy program for the patient, and to permit utilization of appropriate reinforcing behaviors by the therapist and significant others in the patient's social environment.

4. Developmental analysis: Questions are asked about the patient's biological equipment, his sociocultural experiences, and his characteristic behavioral development. They are phrased in such a way as (a) to evoke descriptions of his habitual behavior at various chronological stages of his life, (b) to relate specific new stimulus conditions to noticeable changes from his habitual behavior, and (c) to relate such altered behavior and other residuals of biological and sociocultural events to the present problem.

5. Analysis of self-control: This section examines both the methods and the degree of self-control exercised by the patient in his daily life. Persons, events, or institutions which have successfully reinforced self-controlling behaviors are considered. The deficits or excesses of self-control are evaluated in relation to their importance as therapeutic targets and to their utilization in a therapeutic program.

6. Analysis of social relationships: Examination of the patient's social network is carried out to evaluate the significance of people in the patient's environment who have some influence over the problematic behaviors, or who in turn are influenced by the patient for his own satisfactions. These interpersonal relationships are reviewed in order to plan the potential participation of significant others in a treatment

program, based on the principles of behavior modification. The review also helps the therapist to consider the range of actual social relationships in which the patient needs to function.

7. Analysis of the social-cultural-physical environment: In this section we add to the preceding analysis of the patient's behavior as an individual, consideration of the norms in his natural environment. Agreements and discrepancies between the patient's idiosyncratic life patterns and the norms in his environment are defined so that the importance of these factors can be decided in formulating treatment goals which allow as explicitly for the patient's needs as for the pressures of his social environment.

The preceding outline has as its purpose to achieve definition of a patient's problem in a manner which suggests specific treatment operations, or that none are feasible, and specific behaviors as targets for modification. Therefore, the formulation is *action oriented.* It can be used as a guide for the initial collection of information, as a device for organizing available data, or as a design for treatment.

The formulation of a treatment plan follows from this type of analysis because knowledge of the reinforcing conditions suggests the motivational controls at the disposal of the clinician for the modification of the patient's behavior. The analysis of specific problem behaviors also provides a series of goals for psychotherapy or other treatment, and for the evaluation of treatment progress. Knowledge of the patient's biological, social, and cultural conditions should help to determine what resources can be used, and what limitations must be considered in a treatment plan.

The various categories attempt to call attention to important variables affecting the patient's *current* behavior. Therefore, they aim to elicit descriptions of low-level abstraction. Answers to these specific questions are best phrased by describing classes of events reported by the patient, observed by others, or by critical incidents described by an informant. The analysis does not exclude description of the patient's habitual verbal-symbolic behaviors. However, in using verbal behaviors as the basis for this analysis, one should be cautious not to "explain" verbal processes in terms of postulated internal mechanisms without adequate supportive evidence, nor should inference be made about nonobserved processes or events without corroborative evidence. The analysis includes many items which are not known or not applicable for a given patient. Lack of information on some items does not necessarily indicate incompleteness of the analysis. These lacks must be noted nevertheless because they often contribute to the better understanding of what the patient needs to learn to become an autonomous person. Just as important is an inventory of his existing socially effective behavioral repertoire which can be put in the service of any treatment procedure.

This analysis is consistent with our earlier formulations of the principles of comprehensive medicine[9,22] which emphasized the joint operation of biological, social, and psychological factors in psychiatric disorders. The language and orientation of the proposed approach are rooted in contemporary learning theory. The conceptual framework is consonant with the view that the course of psychiatric disorders can be modified by systematic application of scientific principles from the fields of psychology and medicine to the patient's habitual mode of living.

This approach is not a substitute for assignment of the patient to traditional diagnostic categories. Such labeling may be desirable for statistical, administrative, or research purposes. But the current analysis is intended to replace other diagnostic formulations purporting to serve as a basis for making decisions about specific therapeutic interventions.

III. METHODS OF DATA COLLECTION FOR A FUNCTIONAL ANALYSIS

Traditional diagnostic approaches have utilized as the main sources of information the patient's verbal report, his nonverbal behavior during an interview, and his performance on psychological tests. These observations are sufficient if one regards behavior problems only as a property of the patient's particular pattern of associations or his personality structure. A mental disorder would be expected to reveal itself by stylistic characteristics in the patient's behavior repertoire. However, if one views behavior disorders as sets of response patterns which are learned under particular conditions and maintained by definable environmental and internal stimuli, an assessment of the patient's behavior output is insufficient unless it also describes the conditions under which it occurs. This view requires an expansion of the clinician's sources of observations to include the stimulation fields in which the patient lives, and the variations of patient behavior as a function of exposure to these various stimulational variables. Therefore, the resourceful clinician need not limit himself to test findings, interview observations in the clinician's office, or referral histories alone in the formulation of the specific case. Nor need he regard himself as hopelessly handicapped when the patient has little observational or communicative skill in verbally reconstructing his life experiences for the clinician. Regardless of the patient's communicative skills the data must consist of a description of the patient's behavior *in relationship* to varying environmental conditions.

A behavioral analysis excludes no data relating to a patient's past or present experiences as irrelevant. However, the relative merit of any information (as e.g. growing up in a broken home or having had homosexual experiences) lies in its relation to the independent variables which can be identified as controlling the current problematic behavior. The observation that a patient has hallucinated on occasions may be important only if it has bearing on his present problems. If looked upon in isolation, a report about hallucinations may be misleading, resulting in emphasis on classification rather than treatment.

In the *psychiatric interview* a behavioral-analytic approach opposes acceptance of the content of the verbal self-report as equivalent to actual events or experiences. However, verbal reports provide information concerning the patient's verbal construction of his environment and of his person, his recall of past experiences, and his fantasies about them. While these self-descriptions do not represent data about events which actually occur internally, they do represent current behaviors of the patient and indicate the verbal chains and repertoires which the patients has built up. Therefore, the verbal behavior may be useful for description of a patient's thinking processes. To make the most of such an approach, variations on traditional interview procedures may be obtained by such techniques as role playing, discussion, and interpretation of current life events, or controlled free association. Since there is little experimental evidence of specific relationships between the patient's verbal statements and his nonverbal behavioral acts, the verbal report alone remains insufficient for a complete analysis and for prediction of his daily behavior. Further, it is well known that a person responds to environmental conditions and to internal cues which he cannot describe adequately. Therefore, any verbal report may miss or mask the most important aspects of a behavioral analysis, i.e. the description of the relationship between antecedent conditions and subsequent behavior.

In addition to the use of the clinician's own person as a controlled stimulus object in interview situations, *observations of interaction with significant others* can be used for the analysis of variations in frequency of various behaviors as a function of the person with whom the patient interacts. For example, use of prescribed standard roles for nurses and attendants, utilization of members of the patient's family or his friends, may be made to obtain data relevant to the patient's habitual interpersonal response pattern. Such observations are especially useful if in a later interview the patient is asked to describe and discuss the observed sessions. Confrontations with tape recordings for comparisons between the patient's report and the actual session as witnessed by the observer may provide information about the patient's perception of himself and others as well as his habitual behavior toward peers, authority figures, and other significant people in his life.

Except in working with children or family units, insufficient use has been made of material obtained from *other informants* in interviews about the patient. These reports can aid the observer to recognize behavioral domains in which the patient's report deviates from or agrees with the descriptions provided by others. Such information is also useful for contrasting the patient's reports about his presumptive effects on another person with the stated effects by that person. If a patient's interpersonal problems extend to areas in which social contracts are not clearly defined, contributions by informants other than the patient are essential.

It must be noted that verbal reports by other informants may be no more congruent with actual events than the patient's own reports and need to be equally related to the informant's own credibility. If such crucial figures as parents, spouses, employers can be so interviewed, they also provide the clinician with some information about those people with whom the patient must interact repeatedly and with whom interpersonal problems may have developed.

Some observations of the patient's daily *work behavior* represents an excellent source of information, if it can be made available. Observation of the patient by the clinician or his staff may be preferable to descriptions by peers or supervisors. Work observations are especially important for patients whose complaints include difficulties in their daily work activity or who describe work situations as contributing factors to their problem. While freer use of this technique may be hampered by cultural attitudes toward psychiatric treatment in the marginally adjusted, such observations may be freely accessible in hospital situations or in sheltered work situations. With use of behavior rating scales or other simple measurement devices, brief samples of patient behaviors in work situations can be obtained by minimally trained observers.

The patient himself may be asked to provide samples of his own behavior by using tape recorders for the recording of segments of interactions in his family, at work, or in other situations during his everyday life. A television monitoring system for the patient's behavior is an excellent technique from a theoretical viewpoint but it is extremely cumbersome and expensive. Use of recordings for diagnostic and therapeutic purposes has been reported by some investigators.[2,5,24] Playback of the recordings and a recording of the patient's reactions to the playback can be used further in interviews to clarify the patient's behavior toward others and his reaction to himself as a social stimulus.

Psychological tests represent problems to be solved under specified interactional conditions. Between the highly standardized intelligence tests and the unstructured and ambiguous projective tests lies a dimension of structure along which more and more responsibility for providing appropriate responses falls on the patient. By comparison with interview procedures, most psychological tests provide a relatively greater standardization of stimulus conditions. But, in addition to the specific answers given on intelligence tests or on projective tests these tests also provide a behavioral sample of the patient's reaction to a problem situation in a relatively stressful interpersonal setting. Therefore, psychological tests can provide not only quantitative scores but they can also be treated as a miniature life experience, yielding information about the patient's interpersonal behavior and variations in his behavior as a function of the nature of the stimulus conditions.

In this section we have mentioned only some of the numerous life situations which can be evaluated in order to provide information about the patient. Criteria for their use lies in economy, accessibility to the clinician, and relevance to the patient's problem. While it is more convenient to gather data from a patient in an office, it may be necessary for the clinician to have first-hand information about the actual conditions under which the patient lives and works. Such familiarity may be obtained either by utilization of informants or by the clinician's entry into the home, the job situation, or the social environment in which the patient lives. Under all these conditions the clinician is effective only if it is possible for him to maintain a nonparticipating, objective, and observational role with no untoward consequences for the patient or the treatment relationship.

The methods of data collecting for a functional analysis described here differ from traditional psychiatric approaches only in that they require inclusion of the physical and social stimulus field in which the patient actually operates. Only a full appraisal of the patient's living and working conditions and his way of life allow a description of the actual problems which the patient faces and the specification of steps to be taken for altering the problematic situation.

SUMMARY

Current psychiatric classification falls short of providing a satisfactory basis for the understanding and treatment of maladaptive behavior. Diagnostic schemas now in use are based on etiology, symptom description, or prognosis. While each of these approaches has a limited utility, no unified schema is available which permits prediction of response to treatment or future course of the disorder from the assignment of the patient to a specific category.

This paper suggests a behavior-analytic approach which is based on contemporary learning theory, as an alternative to assignment of the patient to a conventional diagnostic category. It includes the summary of an outline which can serve as a guide for the collection of information and formulation of the problem, including the biological, social, and behavioral conditions which are determining the patient's behavior. The outline aims toward integration of information about a patient for formulation of an action plan which would modify the patient's problematic behavior. Emphasis is given to the particular variables affecting the *individual* patient rather than determination of the similarity of the patient's history or his symptoms to known pathological groups.

The last section of the paper deals with methods useful for collection of information necessary to complete such a behavior analysis.

This paper was written in conjunction with Research grant MH 06921-03 from the National Institutes of Mental Health, United States Public Health Service.

REFERENCES

1. Ash, P.: Reliability of psychiatric diagnosis. *J Abnorm Soc Psychol, 44:* 272-277, 1949.
2. Bach, G.: In Alexander, S.: Fight promoter for battle of sexes. *Life, 54:* 102-108, May 17, 1963.
3. Bandura, A.: Psychotherapy as learning process. *Psychol Bull, 58:*143-159, 1961.

4. Barron, F.: Ego-strength scale which predicts response to psychotherapy. *J Consult Psychol, 17*:235-241, 1953.
5. Cameron, D. E. *et al.:* Automation of psychotherapy. *Compr Psychiatry, 5*:1-14, 1964.
6. Ferster, C. B.: Classification of behavioral pathology. In Ullman, L. P. and Krasner, L. (Eds.): *Behavior Modification Research.* New York, Holt, Rinehart & Winston, 1965.
7. Freedman, D. A.: Various etiologies of schizophrenic syndrome. *Dis Nerv Syst, 19*:1-6, 1958.
8. Fulkerson, S. E. and Barry, J. R.: Methodology and research on prognostic use of psychological tests. *Psychol Bull, 58*:177-204, 1961.
9. Guze, S. B., Matarazzo, J. D. and Saslow, G.: Formulation of principles of comprehensive medicine with special reference to learning theory. *J Clin Psychol, 9*:127-136, 1953.
10. Jackson, D. D. A.: *Etiology of Schizophrenia.* New York, Basic Books, 1960.
11. Kanfer, F. H.: Comments on learning in psychotherapy. *Psychol Rep, 9:* 681-699, 1961.
12. Katz, M. M., Cole, J. O. and Lowery, H. A.: Nonspecificity of diagnosis of paranoid schizophrenia. *Arch Gen Psychiat, 11*:197-202, 1964.
13. Krasner, L.: Therapist as social reinforcement machine. in Strupp, H. and Luborsky, L. (Eds.): *Research in Psychotherapy,* Washington, D.C., American Psychological Association, 1962.
14. Ledley, R. S., and Lusted, L. B.: Reasoning foundations of medical diagnosis. *Science, 130*:9-21, 1959.
15. Lorr, M., Klett, C. J. and McNair, D. M.: *Syndromes of Psychosis.* New York, Macmillan, 1963.
16. Meehl, P. E.: Schizotaxia, schizotypy, schizophrenia. *Am Psychol, 17*:827-838, 1962.
17. New York Heart Association: *Nomenclature and Criteria for Diagnosis of Diseases of the Heart and Blood Vessels.* New York, New York Heart Association, 1953.
18. Noyes, A. P. and Kolb, L. C.: *Modern Clinical Psychiatry.* Philadelphia, Saunders, 1963.
19. Opler, M. K.: Schizophrenia and culture. *Sci Am, 197*:103-112, 1957.
20. Opler, M. K.: Need for new diagnostic categories in psychiatry. *J Natl Med Assoc, 55*:133-137, 1963.
21. Rotter, J. B.: Social learning and clinical psychology. New York, Prentice Hall, 1954.
22. Saslow, G.: On concept of comprehensive medicine. *Bull Menninger Clin, 16*:57-65, 1952.
23. Scheflen, A. E.: Analysis of thought model which persists in psychiatry. *Psychosom Med, 20*:235-241, 1958.

24. Slack, C. W.: Experimenter-subject psychotherapy—A new method of introducing intensive office treatment for unreachable cases. *Ment Hyg, 44*:238-256, 1960.

25. Szasz, T. S.: Myth of mental illness. *Am Psychol, 15*:113-118, 1960.

26. Windle, C.: Psychological tests in psychopathological prognosis. *Psychol Bull, 49*:451-482, 1952.

27. Wolpe, J.: *Psychotherapy in Reciprocal Inhibition.* Stanford, Calif., Stanford University Press, 1958.

28. Zigler, E. and Phillips, L.: Psychiatric diagnosis: Critique. *J Abnorm Soc Psychol, 63*:607-618, 1961.

Chapter 24

TRAINING IN THE COUNSELING AND THERAPEUTIC PRACTICES: REQUIEM OR REVEILLE?

ROBERT R. CARKHUFF

It is clear that traditional counseling and clinical training programs of all kinds have simply not established their efficacy in terms of client benefits. Indeed, the dominant programs are universally resistant to the notion of assessing the outcomes of their programs. They settle too early for process variables (such as grades) which research in counseling and psychotherapy has long since laid to rest. The few carefully controlled studies present a distressing composite picture. The trained clinician's ability to judge the personality characteristics of others bears an inverse relationship to the actual measured characteristics (Taft, 1955). With increasing training and expressions of confidence in clinical judgment, we find decreasing validities (Kelly and Fiske, 1950) and reliabilities (Arnhoff, 1954) in these judgments. Further, persons with the same amount of graduate training (physical scientists), irrelevant to the understanding and judgment of behavior, judge personality characteristics with a high degree of accuracy (Taft, 1955) and are better predictors of behavior with increasing information and personal encounters (Weiss, 1963). To be sure, we might even question the relationship to client benefits of these inquiries into the effects of training. However, one study stands out in this regard as the most enlightened and systematic effort to relate training process variables to client outcome variables. Bergin and Soloman (1963) found the level of empathic understanding of final year, postinternship graduate students [a level which was remarkably low compared to the baserate findings of Berenson, Carkhuff, and Myrus (1965) ; Martin,

Note: Reprinted from *J Consult Psychol*, *13*:360-367, 1966.

Carkhuff, and Berenson, (1965); and Pierce (1965) suggesting, perhaps, the deteriorative consequences of traditional graduate training] in a long-standing program of some repute to be positively correlated with therapeutic competence. Their study is another in a long and growing list of studies relating the dimensions such as empathy to a variety of outcome criteria. However, Bergin and Soloman found their ratings of *empathy to be slightly negatively correlated with both (a) the students' grade point average —and most important—(b) with the students' practicum grade averages,* with the judgments of the clinical faculty once again being brought into doubt.

Rather than ultimate concern with client outcome variables, an analysis of the training literature, in general, in all of the helping professions suggests an interesting analogue of personality and process. Medical educators (Lester, Gussen, Yamamoto and West, 1962; Romano, 1961, Schwartz and Abel, 1955; Ward, 1962; Wolberg, 1954) in the great majority focus primarily upon the more pedagogic dimension of "shaping" behavior in training and treatment to develop "rational understanding." Social workers (Austin, 1963; Bloom and Chere, 1958; Boehm, 1961; Towle, 1961; Wessel, 1961) by and large emphasize the therapeutic dimensions involved in a nurturant supervisor-supervisee relationship calculated to cultivate the experiential base leading to the kind of self-understanding which might free the student to become his most facilitative self. Clinical and counseling psychology and education, especially in its counseling emphasis, run the gamut from the direct control in training beginning with Korner and Brown (1952) and presently implied by Krasner (1962) to the views of Rogers (1957) which emphasizes the experiential base. Fluctuating in between these extremes are the views promulgated by Arbuckle (1963) and Patterson (1964) and others. One cannot help but conjecture that the attitudes and orientations found in the literature reflect the dominant and assertive disposition of the medical profession, the passive and submissive disposition of social work and the intensified role conflicts of applied psychology. Even further, the possible dominance of the emphasized dimensions by the attitudinal dispositions of the profession involved brings into clear focus the question of the critical and artificially exclusionary nature of any one of these dimensions. Indeed, both the didactic and the experiential dimensions, as well as other dimensions such as the oft-neglected role model provided by those designated as "more knowing," may constitute significant sources of learning in all effective interpersonal learning processes.

Consistent with the emphasis upon the direct shaping of behavior, a number of impersonal programmed training approaches have been implemented with the main finding being that trainees change their response patterns in the direction of their recorded supervisors (Fosmire and Palmer, 1964; Palmer, Fosmire, Breger, Straughan, and Patterson, 1963) but that they do not demonstrate gains in conditions related to therapeutic outcome (Baldwin and Lee, 1964). These findings question the possibility of programming conditions such as empathy, warmth and congruence in the contextual absence of such conditions (Berlin and Wyckoff, 1964, Ward, 1962). In this regard, Magoon's (1964) suggestion for the use of audiovisual films in brief and vicarious occupational counseling may be extended to supervisory films which make supervisory sessions unnecessary: supervisory films may be matched to trainee types who provide counseling films matched to counselee types. *No one has to see anyone!*

While a number of programs have advocated the direct experiential involvement of the trainees in supervision and client treatment (Adams, 1958: Arbuckle, 1963; Fleming and Hamburg, 1958; Flint and Rioch, 1963; Lott, 1957; Patterson, 1964; University of Minnesota counselor education staff, 1960; Workman, 1961), none have researched the process or outcome of their programs. More specifically integrative programs (Adams, Ham, Mawardi, Scali and Weisman, 1964; Fleming, 1953; Fleming and Benedek, 1964; Truax, Carkhuff and Douds, 1964) have focused upon essentially three principle sources of learning which operate consistently and concurrently in training or for that matter counseling or psychotherapy: (a) the didactic or direct shaping of behavior, (b) the experiential base of learning, and (c) the role model for effective counseling which the trainer establishes. Research evidence related to both therapy process and outcome variables for integrated programs, systematically implemented and researched, is promising (Berenson, Carkhuff and Myrus, 1965; Carkhuff and Truax, 1965a, 1965c) ; trainee-products offer high levels of empathy, positive regard, genuineness and concreteness and elicit client process involvement and movement demonstrating constructive gain or change. A number of less systematically implemented and research NDEA guidance institutes (Demos, 1964; Demos and Zuwaylif, 1963; Hansen and Barker, 1964; Jones, 1963; Munger and Johnson, 1960; Webb and Harris, 1963) have established essentially the same findings, an increased tendency for trainees to make more understanding and less evaluative responses, with the problem of possible short-term effects (Enelow, Adler and Manning, 1964; Munger, Myers and Brown, 1963) and the lack of demonstration of substantial changes in actual counselor behavior (Meadow and Tillem, 1963) perhaps reflecting the short-term nature of training.

It is interesting to note that one area where researchers have vigorously and rigorously sought to assess the translation of their training efforts in terms of client benefits is the area of lay counselor training, many of the programs of which have been built in large part around a central core of facilitative conditions of empathy, positive regard and congruence (Carkhuff and Truax, 1965b; Truax and Carkhuff, 1964) and all of which have striven primarily to enable the trainees to become their most facilitative selves. Here the evidence is extensive that the lay trainees demonstrate counseling outcomes at least as constructive as their training supervisors or professional practitioners in general (Appleby, 1963; Carkhuff and Truax, 1965, 1965a; Harvey, 1964; Mendel and Rapport, 1963; Rioch, Elkes, Flint, Udansky, Newman and Silber, 1963; Tudor, 1952) .

A RESEARCH OVERVIEW

The conjectured dimensions and process finding (where one process measure correlates with another but neither has an established relationship with the client's improvement in functioning) are, to be sure, interesting. However, we must conclude the following: *There are no well designed, controlled and implemented studies assessing the efficacy of training programs.* There are few systematic attempts to provide appropriate training control groups and pre- and post-training measures. With few notable exceptions, there are no systematic specifications of the antecedent training conditions of the behavioral change which we have implicitly asked for from our trainees in therapeutic training. With the exception of the highly positive body of literature on lay therapist training, there have been no systematic assesments of the translation of training to client or patient improvement or deterioration in functioning. An example may be warranted here. In assessing, for example, a program providing training in a dimension such as empathy we might attempt to accomplish the following: (a) to make some kind of naturalistic assessment of the level of empathy currently offered and the outcome currently achieved in therapeutic processes in a particular setting; (b) to assess in some way the level of empathy offered by both the trainees and their controls both prior to and subsequent to the training; (c) to introduce control groups including those which meet together for a similar amount of time with an instructor for obtuse purposes other than therapeutic training per se; (d) to specify the more didactic methods by which empathy will be taught; (e) to assess in some way the level of empathy provided the trainees in the context of the training; and lastly, and perhaps most important, (f) to asses the patient encounters and conduct follow-up studies in order to determine whether or not the training program has indeed led to better results than those established in the initial naturalistic studies. To be sure, process and outcome measures continue to provide great difficulty but strides of progress have been made in the last decade (Truax and Carkhuff, 1964). With the possible exception of the lay training programs, no consistent and extensive body of training literature has established its ultimate efficacy in terms of client and patient benefits.

Thus, there is substantial support for a solid core of the helping processes, a body of primary facilitative interpersonal dimensions which account for much of the variability in a variety of the outcome criteria which we may employ to assess our "helping."

While, for example, the weights of these dimensions may vary with therapist, client and contextual variables, preliminary evidence suggests that in the general case we may be able to account for between one-third to one-half of the variability in our change indices at this point in time (Truax, 1961; Truax and Carkhuff, 1964).

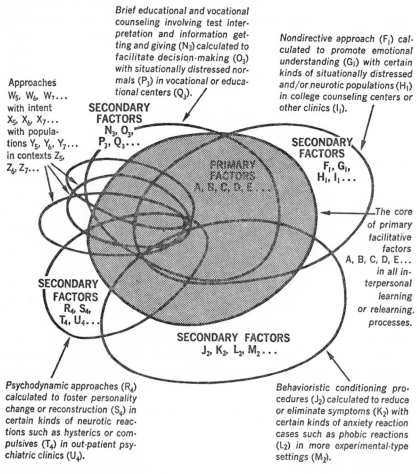

Brief educational and vocational counseling involving test interpretation and information getting and giving (N_3) calculated to facilitate decision-making (O_3) with situationally distressed normals (P_3) in vocational or educational centers (Q_3).

Nondirective approach (F_1) calculated to promote emotional understanding (G_1) with certain kinds of situationally distressed and/or neurotic populations (H_1) in college counseling centers or other clinics (I_1).

Approaches W_5, W_6, W_7... with intent X_5, X_6, X_7... with populations Y_5, Y_6, Y_7... in contexts Z_5, Z_6, Z_7...

SECONDARY FACTORS N_3, O_3, P_3, Q_3...

SECONDARY FACTORS F_1, G_1, H_1, I_1...

PRIMARY FACTORS A, B, C, D, E...

The core of primary facilitative factors A, B, C, D, E... in all interpersonal learning or relearning processes.

SECONDARY FACTORS R_4, S_4, T_4, U_4...

SECONDARY FACTORS J_2, K_2, L_2, M_2...

Psychodynamic approaches (R_4) calculated to foster personality change or reconstruction (S_4) in certain kinds of neurotic reactions such as hysterics or compulsives (T_4) in out-patient psychiatric clinics (U_4).

Behavioristic conditioning procedures (J_2) calculated to reduce or eliminate symptoms (K_2) with certain kinds of anxiety reaction cases such as phobic reactions (L_2) in more experimental-type settings (M_2).

Figure 24-1. The interpersonal core of primary facilitative factors and some possible examples of secondary forces.

Some qualifications are in order. If we are talking of dimensions common to all effective interpersonal processes, we may not be talking so much about the "techniques" of making empathic responses like the reflective technique, etc., which in the past may have bogged us down in our thinking and doing, as we are about a way of life," a way of living effectively in facilitating others and ourselves. In addition, secondary dimensions may, for some therapists, clients and situations, singularly or in their various interactions, operate to facilitate or even retard the effects of the primary conditions. Figure 24-1 demonstrates several notable possibilities concerning "preferred" modes of treatment. Given particular interaction patterns of therapist, client and contextual variables, brief educational or vocational counseling, nondirective therapy, behavioristic conditioning, psychoanalytic therapy or any one of the many other available approaches may with all their full implications concerning goals, techniques, etc., constitute preferred modes of treatment. Further elucidation may be warranted here: for example, a knowledge of psychodynamic developmental phenomena may increase the accountable variability 10 percent for a psychoanalytically-oriented therapist working with a case involving an adjustment reaction to adolescence or, on the other hand, contribute nothing or actually depress the predictability for a hospitalized psychotic patient.

Clinical psychology, psychiatic and social work training centers throughout the country, in their focus upon psychodynamic thinking, have built their programs around what may be a negligible, albeit at times an important, contribution to the treatment process, when compared to the contribution of the central core of facilitative conditions. Some counseling psychology programs have mistakenly followed suit. Others have variously concentrated upon personality, interest and aptitude testing and interpretation, "theories" of vocational choice and educational and vocational information getting and giving, all of which are, perhaps, significant in and of themselves but for each of which is no support for the likelihood of accounting for a major part of the variation in the change indices. Most programs have neglected or disregarded any systematic attention to the core of facilitative interpersonal conditions.

The intent is not to negate the potential significance of the various training orientations but rather to put them in proper perspective in building around a common interpersonal core. Due attention must be given those other aspects of the helping processes according to their efficacy in a given interaction of therapist, client and contextual variables. A dramatic and current case in point deserves some comprehensive attention, i.e. the therapist employing the conditioning principle of reciprocal inhibition with a phobic patient (Wolpe, Salter and Renya 1964) where the statistics cited for symptomatic improvement or recovery are truly strong, although not unqualified. "Behavior" therapy may well be the preferred mode of treatment here with these particular goals—*in the context of high levels of facilitative conditions.* In this regard, Murray (1963) has challenged the need of many behavior therapists to conduct an impersonal therapy and has found support for his challenge in the warm, personal and empathic relationships of the therapists in the conditioning therapy and theory of many leading behaviorists. In addition, the behavior therapists, if pushed to their logical extensions, must hold some hope for the symptom reduction in patients to lead to improvement in other areas of functioning, including especially the potential ability to engage in constructive love relationships (with appropriate discrimination learning of course). It might be facilitative to offer the patient such an experience in any therapy.

It is clear, however, that the success rate, at least as assessed by the goals established, which Wolpe and others have achieved in counterconditioning certain kinds of anxiety reactions cannot be accounted for by interpersonal factors alone. Wolpe (1958) himself, while attributing nearly all "fundamental psychotherapeutic effects" of all treatment approaches to the reciprocal inhibition of neurotic anxiety responses, i.e. the complete or partial suppression of the anxiety responses as a consequence of the simultaneous evocation by nonspecific "relationship" factors of other responses physiologically antagonistic to anxiety, concedes the following:

> If the favourable results of the present series are, to the extent of 60 percent, regarded as due to the nonspecific reciprocal inhibition that would occur in any kind of interview situation, the additional 30 percent of good results appear to be attributable to the special conditioning process and may even in particular cases account for a greater amount of the variability than the facilitative conditions, but together these two aspects of learning may constitute independent sources of variability and in given instances account for a significantly greater success rate.

We are continually reminded that learning theory in no way dictates that the therapist be an impersonal programmed reinforcement machine, but rather if carried to its logical conclusion must indeed indicate a very personal process. We are continually reminded that the magnitude of certain response patterns and reinforcement effects may well be contingent upon certain personal relationship factors.

To be sure, it becomes incumbent upon all training programs to incorporate more than a passing educational exposure to approaches constituting possible preferred modes of treatment. Further, we have good reason to believe that the very evolution of different treatment cults is born of continuing experiences involving particular interaction patterns of therapist, client and situational variables.

Nevertheless, the overwhelming preponderance of systematic evidence available today indicates that the primary conditions of effective treatment are conditions which minimally trained nonprofessional persons can provide. The conditions are not the monopoly of doctoral training and there is strong reason to believe that they are often not achieved in doctoral training. In some cases graduate training may even retard or contribute to the deterioration of the trainee's ability to offer these conditions. At the very minimum, the extensive psychoanalytic training program of Rioch *et al.* (1963), which can be severely questioned on many counts, has established that one doesn't need a doctorate degree of any kind to operate at the level of experienced doctoral trained clinicians when seen from the viewpoint of continuing traditional albeit questionable modes of practice.

It would then appear that helping persons can be trained in less than the four or usually more years it takes for doctoral training. The growing social urgency can be met most effectively and efficiently in shorter term programs for practitioners, perhaps a one or two year "mental health counselor" program designed to produce "therapeutic agents." It is clear that these minimally trained persons can provide the levels of conditions commensurate to those of their trainers. It also appears, however, that training and supervision are essential (with some issues involved here concerning who provides the training). The primary role of the doctoral person as we see it would be to attempt to explicate the effective dimensions in the therapeutic or facilitative processes, to implement these constructs in training and to assess the efficacy of the training, especially in its client and patient outcome. To do so, with all due consideration to our early developmental levels reflected in our limitations in both research as well as practice, necessitates the possession of some research skills and tools, and not simply reading or consumption skills.

CONCLUSIONS

Resistance is to be anticipated. The effect of recommendations is always in large part contingent upon the readiness of the profession. However, if we were to do properly controlled research on the practice of law and found that, all other things being equal, defendants who were defended by minimally-trained nonprofessional "friends" were more likely or even as likely to obtain acquittal than those who had professional counsel, we would be horrified and would call for extensive reform in professional legal practice. The studies reviewed here demand that we in the applied psychological sciences do likewise. How many such studies must we mount before we will take action?

We appeal for the same change in many of the practicing members of our profession which we must ask for in our trainees or for that matter our clients: a chance to become their most open and flexible, facilitative selves. We appeal to the unbiased experiences of our colleagues to find in themselves the dimensions of those relationships which have been most rewarding and fulfilling for both parties and in which they have been most efficacious. Or, if they cannot find these experiences in themselves, perhaps they can open up and attempt to understand the encounters of their colleagues whose clients improve in functioning as a consequent of "real" helping relationships. Perhaps we can further operationalize these dimensions and implement investigations of them. Perhaps we can build our programs around those dimensions for which we find extensive support. Bordin's (1962) editorial suggests the critical need for the study of that form of intervention which can best enhance the psychological growth of the individual client. We might add a concern for that form of intervention which might best enhance the growth of the trainee, for if change cannot occur for the individual trainee in the direction of effective and facilitative functioning in four or five years and several thousand hours of graduate study, then how can we expect to effect change in from one to fifty or even one hundred sessions of counseling or psychotherapy with clients? To put the question another way: If we believe constructive change or gain can occur in ten or twenty sessions, then how much more can we achieve in years of graduate study? We might also add a concern for that form of intervention which might be to enhance the growth of practitioners whose clients and own personal experiences are not left improved for the counseling or therapeutic encounter, and, in some frighteningly large number of cases as indicated by extensive research now available to us, are retarded in their development.

Our plea is not for a more delimited and dichotomous sphere of operation in practice and research as the Clark report (Clark *et al.*, 1965) recommends, but rather for an expanded role. The intent is neither to downgrade the doctorate nor to attempt to attain a perhaps unattainable Frommian society. Rather, the intent is to upgrade the position to one involving effective training and practices. We would attempt to establish shorter-term programs which facilitate the development of the interpersonal skills which allow those individuals, who are not likely to make profound contributions at other levels, to make the optimum contribution to a client's welfare. The preponderance of evidence of the foregoing review suggests that the outcomes of "low level" lay therapist training programs, and possibly some NDEA institute programs, constructed primarily around a core of "cross-cult" dimensions of effective interpersonal functioning have been most impressive, whereas more traditional, highly cognitive programs are of highly questionable and certainly unestablished efficacy.

If lay persons can accomplish in the therapeutic encounter results comparable to those of professionals, then what is it that those of us with doctorates have to offer if not some skill in explicating, operationalizing and implementing in training, practice, research and consultation the dimensions of effective interpersonal learning and relearning processes? For example, I envisualize the doctoral person in a service setting continually assessing ongoing forms of training and treatment and introducing and assessing experimental forms of training and treatment based upon extensive documentation. I see him serving to train, as well as to consult on preferred modes of treatment with, say perhaps, ten mental health counselors who can then pass the benefits on to one hundred patients instead of carrying his present ten-patient caseload (which may be a high estimate from what we know about doctoral persons in most service settings). In addition, I see the doctoral practitioner overseeing continuous and comprehensive community care. In brief, I see the doctoral person knowing *all* that is knowable concerning truly therapeutic processes—and continually striving for more understanding and effectiveness.

Surely "the rights and interests of society are paramount" (Clark *et al.*, 1965). We must strive to broaden our training efforts so that new understanding can be translated into benefits for clients and patients by trained therapeutic agents such as mental health counselors of more limited educational backgrounds. The need for doctoral-status, "pure" practitioners would appear to be *superfluous,* except insofar as the doctoral training equips the practitioners to make enlightened and systematic inquiry into that which they are attempting to accomplish and to provide the appropriate training and consultation in the hope of improving the efficacy of the therapeutic or facilitative processes involving those for whom we serve.

REFERENCES

1. Adams, W. R.: The psychiatrist in an ambulatory clerkship for comprehensive medical care in a new curriculum. *J. Med Educ, 33:*211-220.
2. Adams, W. R., Ham, T. H., Mawardi, Betty H., Scali, H. A. and Weisman, R. A.: A naturalistic study of teaching in a clinical clerkship. *J Med Educ, 39:*164-174.
3. Appleby, L.: Evaluation of treatment methods for chronic schizophrenia. *Arch Gen Psychiatry, 8:*8-21.
4. Arbuckle, D. S.: The learning of counseling: process not product. *J Counsel Psychol, 10:*163-168., 1963.
5. Arnhoff, F. N.: Some factors influencing the unreliability of clinical judgments. *J Clin Psychol, 10:*272-275, 1954.
6. Austin, Lucille N.: The changing role of the supervisor. In Parad, H. and Miller R. (Eds.): *Ego-oriented Casework: Problems and perspectives.* New York, Family Service Assoc of America, 1963, pp. 273-291.
7. Baldwin, T. and Lee, Joan: Evaluation of programmed instruction in human relations. *Am Psychol, 20:*489 (Abstract).
8. Berenson, B. G., Carkhuff, R. R. and Myrus, Pamela: An investigation of the level of interpersonal functioning of college students. Submitted. *J Counsel Psychol,* 1965.
9. Bergin, A. and Soloman, Sandra: Personality and performance correlates of empathic understanding in psychotherapy. Paper read at Amer Psychol Assoc, Philadelphia, Sept. 1963.
10. Berlin, J. I. and Wyckoff, L. B.: Human relations training through dyadic programmed instruction. Paper presented, Amer Personnel Guid. Assoc., 1964.
11. Bloom, L. and Chére, H.: A problem of relationship in supervision. *Soc Casework, 37:*402-406, 1958.
12. Boehm, W.: Social work: Science and art. *Social Serv Rev, 35:*144-151, 1961.
13. Bordin, E. S.: Narrowness or breadth? *J Counsel Psychol, 10:*2, 1962.
14. Carkhuff, R. R. and Truax, C. B.: Lay mental health counseling: the effects of lay group counseling. *J Consult Psychol,* in press, 1965 a.
15. Carkhuff, R. R. and Truax, C. B.: Toward explication of facilitation and retardation in interpersonal learning processes. *Personnel Guid J* in press, 1965 b.
16. Carkhuff, R. R. and Truax, C. B.: Training in counseling and psycho-

therapy: an evaluation of an integrated didactic and experiential approach. *J Consult Psychol, 29:*333-336, 1965c.

17. Clark, K. E. *et al.:* Committee on the scientific and professional aims of psychology. Report to Board of Directors and Council of Representatives of APA. *Am Psychol, 20:*95-100, 1965.

18. Demos, G. D.: The application of certain principles of client-centered therapy to short-term vocational counseling. *J Counsel Psychol, 11:* 280-284, 1964.

19. Demos, G. D. and Zuwaylif, F. H.: Counselor movement as a result of an intensive six-week training program in counseling. *Personnel Guid J, 42:*125-128, 1963.

20. Enelow, A. J., Adler, L. M. and Manning, P. R.: A supervised psychotherapy course for practicing physicians. *J Med Educ, 39:*140-146, 1964.

21. Fleming, Joan: The role of supervision in psychiatric training. *Bull Menninger Clin, 17:*157-169, 1953.

22. Fleming, Joan and Benedek, Therese: Supervision: a method of teaching psychoanalysis. *Psychoanal Q, 33:*71-86, 1964.

23. Fleming, Joan and Hamburg, D. A.: An analysis of methods for teaching psychotherapy with a description of a new approach. *Arch Neurol Psychiat, 79:*179-200, 1958.

24. Flint, A. A. and Rioch, Margaret J.: An experiment in teaching family dynamics. *Am J Psychiat, 118:*940-944, 1963.

25. Fosmire, F. R. and Palmer, B. E.: A comparison of a method of programmed instruction and of personal supervision in psychotherapy. Paper presented National Society for Programmed Instruction, Trinity Univer., San Antonio, Texas, April 1964.

26. Hansen, J. C. and Barker, E. N.: Experiencing and the supervisory relationship. *J Counsel Psychol, 11:*107-111, 1964.

27. Harvey, L. V.: The use of non-professional auxiliary counselors in staffing a counseling service. *J Counsel Psychol, 11:*348-357, 1964.

28. Jones, V.: Attitude changes in an N.D.E.A. Institute. *Personnel Guid J, 42:*387-389, 1963.

29. Kelly, E. L. and Fiske, D. W.: The prediction of success in the VA training program in clinical psychology. *Am Psychol, 5:*395-406, 1950.

30. Korner, I. N.: and Brown, W. H.: The mechanical third ear. *J Consult Psychol, 16:*81-84, 1956.

31. Krasner, L.: The therapist as a social reinforcement machine. In Strupp, H. H. and Luborsky, L. (Eds.): *Research in psychotherapy,* Washington, D.C., American Psychol. Assoc., 1962, vol. II.

32. Lester, B. K., Gussen, J., Yamamoto, J. and West, L. J.: Teaching psychotherapy in a longitudinal curriculum. *J Med Educ, 37:*28-32, 1962.

33. Lott, G. M.: Multiple psychotherapy: The efficient use of psychiatric treatment and training time. *Psychiat Q, 2:*1-19, 1957.

34. Magoon, T.: Innovations in counseling. *J Counsel Psychol, 11:*342-347, 1964.

35. Martin, J. C., Carkhuff, R. R. and Berenson, B. G.: Process variables in counseling and psychotherapy: A study of counseling and friendship. *J Consult Psychol,* 1965.

36. Meadow, L. and Tillem, K.: Evaluating the effectiveness of a workshop rehabilitation program. *Personnel Guid J, 42:*541-545, 1963.

37. Mendel, W. M. and Rapport, S.: Outpatient treatment for chronic schizophrenic patients: Therapeutic consequences of an existential view. *Arch Gen Psychiat, 8:*190-196, 1963.

38. Munger, P. F. and Johnson, C. A.: Changes in attitudes associated with an N.D.E.A. counseling and guidance institute. *Personnel Guid J, 38:*751-753, 1960.

39. Munger, P. F., Myers, R. A. and Brown, D. F.: Guidance institutes and the persistence of attitudes. *Personnel Guid J, 41:*415-419, 1963.

40. Murray, E. J.: Learning theory and psychotherapy: Biotropic versus sociotropic approaches. *J Counsel Psychol, 10:*250-255, 1963.

41. Palmer, B., Fosmire, F. R., Breger, L., Straughan, J. H and Patterson, G. R.: First report of a program of research in psychotherapy training. Mimeographed report, Univ. of Oregon Psychological Clinic, 1963.

42. Patterson, C. H.: Supervising students in the counseling practicum. *J Counsel Psychol, 11:*47-53, 1964.

43. Pierce, R.: An investigation of the relationship between grade point average and the level of interpersonal functioning. Unpublished doctoral dissertation, Univer. of Massachusetts, 1965.

44. Rioch, Margaret J., Elkes, C., Flint, A. A., Udansky, B. S., Newman, R. G. and Silber, E.: N.I.M.H. pilot study in training mental health counselors. *Am J Orthopsychiat, 33:*678-689, 1963.

45. Rogers, C. R.: Training individuals to engage in the therapeutic process. In Strother, C. R. (Ed.): *Psychology and Mental Health.* Washington, D.C. Amer. Psychol, Assoc., 1957.

46. Romano, J.: Teaching of psychiatry to medical students. *Lancet.* 93-95, July, 1961.

47. Taft, R.: The ability to judge people. *Psychol Bull, 52:*1-23, 1955.

48. Towle, Charlotte: Role of the supervisor in the union of cause and function in social work. *Soc Serv Rev, 35:*144-151, 1961.

49. Truax, C. B.: The process of group psychotherapy. *Psychol Monogr, 75 (No. 14,* Whole No. *511):* 1961.

50. Truax, C. B. and Carkhuff, R. R.: Significant developments in psychotherapy research. In Abt, L. E. and Reiss, B. F. (Eds.): *Progress in Clinical Psychology.* New York, Grune & Stratton, 1964, vol. VI.

51. Truax, C. B., Carkhuff, R. R. and Douds, J.: Toward an integration of

the didactic and experiential approaches to training in counseling and psychotherapy. *J Counsel Psychol, 11*:240-247, 1964.

52. Tudor, Gwenn: A socio-psychiatric nursing approach to intervention in problem of mutual withdrawal on a mental hospital ward. *Psychiat, 15*:193-217, 1952.

53. Univer. of Minnesota counselor education staff. Supervised field practice in student personnel work. *Personnel Guid J, 39*:308-309, 1960.

54. Ward, C. H.: Electronic preceptoring in teaching beginning psychotherapy. *J Med Educ, 37*:1128-1129, 1962.

55. Webb, A. J. and Harris, J. T.: A semantic differential study of counselors in an N.D.E.A. institute. *Personnel Guid J, 42*:260-263, 1963.

56. Weiss, J. H.: The effect of professional training and amount and accuracy of information on behavioral prediction. *J Consult Psychol, 27*: 257-262, 1963.

57. Workman, S. L.: Teaching the interpretive process to medical students. *Am J Psychiatry, 117*:897-902, 1961.

58. Wessel, Rosa: Social work education and practice. *Soc Serv Rev, 35*:151-160, 1961.

59. Wolberg, L. R.: *The Technique of Psychotherapy.* New York, Grune and Stratton, 1954.

60. Wolpe, J.: *Psychotherapy by Reciprocal Inhibition.* London, Oxford Univer., 1958.

61. Wolpe, J., Salter, A. and Renya, L. J.: *The Conditioning Therapies: The Challenge in Psychotherapy.* New York, Holt, Rinehart & Winston, 1964.

B. THE THERAPEUTIC RELATIONSHIP

Chapter 25

THE INTERPERSONAL RELATIONSHIP

CARL R. ROGERS

I would like to share with you in this paper a conclusion, a conviction, which has grown out of years of experience in dealing with individuals, a conclusion which finds some confirmation in a steadily growing body of empirical evidence. It is simply that in a wide variety of professional work involving relationships with people—whether as a psychotherapist, teacher, religious worker, guidance counselor, social worker, clinical psychologist—it is the *quality* of the interpersonal encounter with the client which is the most significant element in determining effectiveness.

In recent years I have thought a great deal about this issue. I have tried to observe counselors and therapists whose orientations are very different from mine, in order to understand the basis of their effectiveness as well as my own. I have listened to recorded interviews from many different sources. Gradually I have developed some theoretical formulations,[4,5] some hypotheses as to the basis of effectiveness in relationships. As I have asked myself how individuals sharply different in personality, orientation and procedure can all be effective in a helping relationship, can each be successful in facilitating constructive change or development, I have concluded that it is because they bring to the helping relationship certain attitudinal ingredients. It is these that I hypothesize as making for effectiveness, whether we are speaking of a guidance counselor, a clinical psychologist, or a psychiatrist.

What are these attitudinal or experiential elements in the counselor which make a relationship a growth-promoting climate? I would like to describe them as carefully and accurately as I can, though I am well aware that words rarely capture or communicate the qualities of a personal encounter.

Note: Originally, The interpersonal relationship: The core of guidance. Abridged and reprinted from *Harvard Educational Rev, 32*:416-429, 1962. Copyright 1962, by President and Fellows of Harvard University.

CONGRUENCE

In the first place, I hypothesize that personal growth is facilitated when the counselor is what he *is*, when in the relationship with his client he is genuine and without "front" or facade, openly being the feelings and attitudes which at that moment are flowing in him. We have used the term "congruence" to try to describe this condition. By this we mean that the feelings the counselor is experiencing are available to him, available to his awareness, that he is able to live these feelings, be them in the relationship, and able to communicate them if appropriate. It means that he comes into a direct personal encounter with his client, meeting him on a person-to-person basis. It means that he is *being* himself, not denying himself. No one fully achieves this condition, yet the more the therapist is able to listen acceptantly to what is going on within himself, and the more he is able to *be* the complexity of his feelings without fear, the higher the degree of his congruence.

I think that we readily sense this quality in our everyday life. We could each of us name persons whom we know who always seem to be operating from behind a front, who are playing a role, who tend to say things they do not feel. They are exhibiting incongruence. We do not reveal ourselves too deeply to such people. On the other hand each of us knows individuals whom we somehow trust, because we sense that they are being what they *are*, that we are dealing with the person himself, and not with a polite or professional facade. This is the quality of which we are speaking, and it is hypothesized that the more genuine and congruent the therapist in the relationship, the more probability there is that change in personality in the client will occur.

I have received much clinical confirmation for this hypothesis in recent years in our work with randomly selected hospitalized schizophrenic patients. The individual therapists in our research program who seem to be most successful in dealing with these unmotivated, poorly educated, resistant, chronically hospitalized individuals, are those who are first of all real, who react in a genuine, human way as persons, and who exhibit their genuineness in the relationship.

But is it always helpful to be genuine? What about negative

feelings? What about the times when the counselor's real feeling toward his client is one of annoyance, or boredom, or dislike? My tentative answer is that even with such feelings as these, which we all have from time to time, it is preferable for the counselor to be real than to put up a facade of interest and concern and liking which he does not feel.

But it is not a simple thing to achieve such reality. I am not saying that it is helpful to blurt out impulsively every passing feeling and accusation under the comfortable impression that one is being genuine. Being real involves the difficult task of being acquainted with the flow of experiencing going on within oneself, a flow marked especially by complexity and continuous change. So if I sense that I am feeling bored by my contacts with this student, and this feeling persists, I think I owe it to him and to our relationship to share this feeling with him. But here again I will want to be constantly in touch with what is going on in me. If I am, I will recognize that it is *my* feeling of being bored which I am expressing, and not some supposed fact about him as a boring person. If I voice it as my *own* reaction, it has the potentiality of leading to a deeper relationship. But this feeling exists in the context of a complex and changing flow, and this needs to be communicated too. I would like to share with him my distress at feeling bored, and the discomfort I feel in expressing this aspect of me. As I share these attitudes I find that my feeling of boredom arises from my sense of remoteness from him, and that I would like to be more in touch with him. And even as I try to express these feelings, they change. I am certainly not bored as I try to communicate myself to him in this way, and I am far from bored as I wait with eagerness and perhaps a bit of apprehension for his response. I also feel a new sensitivity to him, now that I have shared this feeling which has been a barrier between us. So I am very much more able to hear the surprise or perhaps the hurt in his voice as he now finds *himself* speaking more genuinely because I have dared to be real with him. I have let myself be a person—real, imperfect—in my relationship with him.

I have tried to describe this first element at some length because I regard it as highly important, perhaps the most crucial of the conditions I will describe, and because it is neither easy to grasp nor to achieve. Gendlin[2] has done an excellent job of explaining the significance of the concept of experiencing and its relationship to counseling and therapy, and his presentation may supplement what I have tried to say.

I hope it is clear that I am talking about a realness in the counselor which is deep and true, not superficial. I have sometimes thought that the word transparency helps to describe this element of personal congruence. If everything going on in me which is relevant to the relationship can be seen by my client, if he can see "clear through me," and if I am *willing* for this realness to show through in the relationship, then I can be almost certain that this will be a meaningful encounter in which we both learn and develop.

I have sometimes wondered if this is the only quality which matters in a counseling relationship. The evidence seems to show that other qualities also make a profound difference and are perhaps easier to achieve. So I am going to describe these others. But I would stress that if, in a given moment of relationship, they are not genuinely a part of the experience of the counselor, then it is, I believe, better to be genuinely what one is, than to pretend to be feeling these other qualities.

EMPATHY

The second essential condition in the relationship, as I see it, is that the counselor is experiencing an accurate empathic understanding of his client's private world, and is able to communicate some of the significant fragments of that understanding. To sense the client's inner world of private personal meanings as if it were your own, but without ever losing the "as if" quality, this is empathy, and this seems essential to a growth-promoting relationship. To sense his confusion or his timidity or his anger or his feeling of being treated unfairly as if it were your own, yet without your own uncertainty or fear or anger or suspicion getting bound up in it, this is the condition I am endeavoring to describe. When the client's world is clear to the counselor and he can move about in it freely, then he can both communicate his understanding of what is vaguely known to the client, and he can also voice meanings in the client's experience of which the client is scarcely aware. It is this kind of highly sensitive empathy which seems important in making it possible for a person to get close to himself and to learn, to change and develop.

I suspect that each of us has discovered that this kind of understanding is extremely rare. We neither receive it nor offer it with any great frequency. Instead we offer another type of understanding which is very different, such as "I understand what is wrong with you" or "I understand what makes you act that way." These are the types of understanding which we usually offer and receive —an evaluative understanding from the outside. It is not surprising that we shy away from true understanding. If I am truly open to the way life is experienced by another person—if I can take his world into mine—then I run the risk of seeing life in his way, of being changed myself, and we all resist change. So we tend to view this other person's world only in our terms, not in his. We analyze and evaluate it. We do not understand it. But when someone understands how it feels and seems to be me, without wanting to analyze me or judge me, then I can blossom and grow in that climate. I am sure I am not alone in that feeling. I believe that when the counselor can grasp the moment-to-moment experiencing occurring in the inner world of the client, as the client sees it and feels it, without losing the separateness of his own identity in this empathic process, then change is likely to occur.

Though the accuracy of such understanding is highly important, the communication of intent to understand is also helpful. Even in dealing with the confused or inarticulate or bizarre individual, if he perceives that I am *trying* to understand his meanings, this is helpful. It communicates the value I place on him as an individual. It gets across the fact that I perceive his feelings and meanings as being *worth* understanding.

None of us steadily achieves such a complete empathy as I have been trying to describe, any more than we achieve complete congruence, but there is no doubt that individuals can develop along this line. Suitable training experiences have been utilized in the training of counselors, and also in the "sensitivity training" of industrial management personnel. Such experiences enable the person to listen more sensitively, to receive more of the subtle meanings the other person is expressing in words, gesture, and posture, to resonate more deeply and freely within himself to the significance of those expressions.*

POSITIVE REGARD

Now the third condition. I hypothesize that growth and change are more likely to occur the more that the counselor is experiencing a warm, positive, acceptant attitude toward what *is* in the client. It means that he prizes his client, as a person, with somewhat the same quality of feeling that a parent feels for his child, prizing him as a person regardless of his particular behavior at the moment. It means that he cares for his client in a non-possessive way, as a person with potentialities. It involves an open willingness for the client to be whatever feelings are real in him at the moment—hostility or tenderness, rebellion or submissiveness, assurance or self-depreciation. It means a kind of love for the client as he is, providing we understand the word love as equivalent to the theologian's term "agape," and not in its usual romantic and possessive meanings. What I am describing is a feeling which is not paternalistic, nor sentimental, nor superficially social and agreeable. It respects the other person as a separate individual, and does not possess him. It is a kind of liking which has strength, and which is not demanding. We have termed it positive regard.

There is one aspect of this attitude of which I am somewhat less sure. I advance tentatively the hypothesis that the relationship will be more effective the more the positive regard is unconditional. By this I mean that the counselor prizes the client in a total, rather than a conditional way. He does not accept certain feelings in the client and disapprove others. He feels an *unconditional* positive regard for this person. This is an outgoing, positive feel-

---

*I hope the above account of an empathic attitude will make it abundantly clear that I am not advocating a wooden technique of pseudounderstanding in which the counselor "reflects back what the client has just said." I have been more than a little horrified at the interpretation of my approach which has sometimes crept into the teaching and training of counselors.

ing without reservations and without evaluations. It means *not* making judgments. I believe that when this nonevaluative prizing is present in the encounter between the counselor and his client, constructive change and development in the client is more likely to occur.

THE CLIENT'S PERCEPTION

Thus far all my hypotheses regarding the possibility of constructive growth have rested upon the experiencing of these elements by the counselor. There is, however, one condition which must exist in the client. Unless the attitudes I have been describing have been to some degree communicated to the client, and perceived by him, they do not exist in his perceptual world and thus cannot be effective. Consequently it is necessary to add one more condition to the equation which I have been building up regarding personal growth through counseling. It is that when the client perceives, to a minimal degree, the genuineness of the counselor and the acceptance and empathy which the counselor experiences for him, then development in personality and change in behavior are predicted.

This has implications for me as a counselor. I need to be sensitive not only to what is going on in me, and sensitive to the flow of feelings in my client. I must also be sensitive to the way he is receiving my communications. I have learned, especially in working with more disturbed persons, that empathy can be perceived as lack of involvement; that an unconditional regard on my part can be perceived as indifference; that warmth can be perceived as a threatening closeness, that real feelings of mine can be perceived as false. I would like to behave in ways, and communicate in ways which have clarity for this specific person, so that what I am experiencing in relationship to him would be perceived unambiguously by him. Like the other conditions I have proposed the principle is easy to grasp; the achievement of it is difficult and complex.

THE ESSENTIAL HYPOTHESIS

Let me restate very briefly the essentially simple but somewhat radical hypothesis I have set forth. I have said that constructive personality growth and change comes about only when the client perceives and experiences a certain psychological climate in the relationship. The conditions which constitute this climate do not consist of knowledge, intellectual training, orientation in some school of thought, or techniques. They are feelings or attitudes which must be experienced by the counselor and perceived by the client if they are to be effective. Those I have singled out as being essential are: a realness, genuineness, or congruence in the therapist; a sensitive, emphathic understanding of the client's feelings and personal meanings; a warm, acceptant prizing of the client; and an unconditionality in this positive regard.

SOME LIMITATIONS

I would like to stress that these are hypotheses. But they are beginning hypotheses, not the final word.

I regard it as entirely possible that there are other conditions which I have not described, which are also essential. Recently I had occasion to listen to some recorded interviews by a young counselor of elementary school children. She was very warm and positive in her attitude toward her clients, yet she was definitely ineffective. She seemed to be responding warmly only to the superficial aspects of each child and so the contacts were chatty, social and friendly, but it was clear she was not reaching the real person of the child. Yet in a number of ways she rated reasonably high on each of the conditions I have described. So perhaps there are still elements missing which I have not captured in my formulation.

I am also aware of the possibility that different kinds of helping relationships may be effective with different kinds of people. Some of our therapists working with schizophrenics are effective when they appear to be highly conditional, when they do *not* accept some of the bizarre behavior of the psychotic. This can be interpreted in two ways. Perhaps a conditional set is more helpful with these individuals. Or perhaps—and this seems to me to fit the facts better—these psychotic individuals perceive a conditional attitude as meaning that the therapist *really* cares, where an unconditional attitude may be interpreted as apathetic noncaring. In any event, I do want to make it clear that what I have given are beginning formulations which surely will be modified and corrected from further learnings.

THE PHILOSOPHY WHICH IS IMPLICIT

It is evident that the kind of attitudes I have described are not likely to be experienced by a counselor unless he holds a philosophy regarding people in which such attitudes are congenial. The attitudes pictured make no sense except in a context of great respect for the person and his potentialities. Unless the primary element in the counselor's value system is the worth of the individual, he is not apt to find himself experiencing a real caring, or a desire to understand, and perhaps he will not respect himself enough to be real. Certainly the professional person who holds the view that individuals are essentially objects to be manipulated for the welfare of the state, or the good of the educational institution, or "for their own good," or to satisfy his own need for power and control, would not experience the attitudinal elements I have described as constituting growth-promoting relationships. So these conditions are congenial and natural in certain philosophical contexts but not in others.

CONCLUSION

Let me conclude with a series of statements which for me follow logically one upon the other.

The purpose of most of the helping professions is to enhance the personal development, the psychological growth toward a socialized maturity, of its clients.

The effectiveness of any member of the profession is most adequately measured in terms of the degree to which, in his work with his clients, he achieves this goal.

Our knowledge of the elements which bring about constructive change in personal growth is in its infant stages.

Such factual knowledge as we currently possess indicates that a primary change-producing influence is the degree to which the client experiences certain qualities in his relationship with his counselor.

In a variety of clients—normal, maladjusted, and psychotic— with many different counselors and therapists, and studying the relationship from the vantage point of the client, the therapist, or the uninvolved observer, certain qualities in the relationship are quite uniformly found to be associated with personal growth and change.

These elements are not constituted of technical knowledge or ideological sophistication. They are personal human qualities— something the counselor *experiences,* not something he *knows.* Constructive personal growth is associated with the counselor's realness, with his genuine and unconditional liking for his client, with his sensitive understanding of his client's private world, and with his ability to communicate these qualities in himself to his client.

These findings have some far-reaching implications for the theory and practice of guidance counseling and psychotherapy, and for the training of workers in these fields.

REFERENCES

1. Barrett-Lennard, G. T.: Dimensions of therapist response as causal factors in therapeutic change. *Psychol Monogr* (In press).
2. Gendlin, E. T.: Experiencing: A variable in the process of therapeutic change. *Am J Psychother, 15:*233-245, 1961.
3. Halkides, G.: An experimental study of four conditions necessary for therapeutic change. Unpublished doctoral dissertation, University of Chicago, 1958.
4. Rogers, C. R.: The necessary and sufficient conditions of therapeutic personality change. *J Cons Psychol, 21:*1957, 95-103.
5. Rogers, C. R.: A theory of therapy, personality, and interpersonal relationships as developed in the client-centered framework. In Koch, S. (Ed.): *Psychology: A Study of a Science.* New York, McGraw-Hill, 1959, pp. 184-256. vol. III.
6. Wisconsin Psychiatric Institute: Research reports (unpublished).
   a. Spotts, J. E.: The perception of positive regard by relatively successful and relatively unsuccessful clients.
   b. Truax, C. B.: Comparison between high conditions therapy, low conditions therapy, and control conditions in the outcome measure of change in anxiety levels.
   c. Truax, C. B.: Constructive personality change in schizophrenic patients

receiving high-conditions therapy, low-conditions therapy, and no-therapy.

d. Truax, C. B.: Effects of therapists and effects of patients upon the amount of accurate empathy occurring in the psychotherapeutic interaction.

e. Truax, C. B.: Effects of therapists and effects of patients upon the level of problem expression and experiencing occurring in the therapeutic interaction.

f. Truax, C. B.: The relationship between the patient's perception of the level of therapeutic conditions offered in psychotherapy and constructive personality change.

g. Truax, C. B., Liccione, J. and Rosenberg, M.: Psychological test evaluations of personality change in high conditions therapy, low conditions therapy, and control patients.

h. van der Veen, F.: The effects of the therapist and the patient on each other's therapeutic behavior early in therapy: A study of the beginning interviews of three patients with each of five therapists.

i. Truax, C. B.: Perceived therapist conditions and degree of disturbance: A comparison of conditions perceived by hospitalized schizophrenic patients and counseling center clients.

j. Wargo, D. G.: The Barron Ego Strength and LH4 Scales as predictors and indicators of change in psychotherapy.

Chapter 26

THE OLD AND THE NEW:
THEORY AND RESEARCH IN
COUNSELING AND PSYCHOTHERAPY

CHARLES B. TRUAX AND ROBERT R. CARKHUFF

T HE MORE we learn from our research, the more acutely aware we become of the limitations and inadequacies of our current theoretical formulations. Individual schools of counseling and psychotherapy cannot account for the multitude of variables which in all probability ultimately will constitute the process of psychotherapeutic personality change. However, these varied approaches have proved themselves to be of research value in the past. Any attempted formulations in the future should, therefore, leave themselves open to their potential contributions to research in the therapeutic process. Indeed, common elements, stemming from, yet cutting across these various theoretical approaches, have already demonstrated significant heuristic meaning.

The central question for counseling and psychotherapy is: What are the essential elements in the psychotherapeutic process that lead to constructive behavioral change in the client? It seems certain that not all that the therapist or counselor does in the relationship is beneficial for the client. What, then, are the common elements for effective counseling and psychotherapy?

NEW MEANING FOR OLD VARIABLES

In spite of the multitude of theories and techniques reflecting the disciplines and dispositions of their promulgators, there have

Note: Abridged and reprinted from *Personnel and Guidance, 42:* 1964, the American Personnel and Guidance Association.

This article is based on an address given at the American Personnel and Guidance Association Convention, Boston, Massachusetts, April, 1963.

The authors wish to acknowledge the able assistance in data analysis of Edward P. Williams.

been some recurring themes in the many formulations designed to describe effective psychotherapy. Psychoanalytic theorists such as Alexander,[1] Ferenczi,[7] Halpern and Lesser,[10] and Schafer[20]; client-centered theorists such as Dymond,[6] Jourard,[12] Rogers,[16,17] and Snyder,[22] as well as eclectic theorists such as Fox and Goldin,[8] Raush and Bordin,[15] Strunk,[23] and Strupp,[24] have emphasized the importance of the therapist's ability sensitively and accurately to understand the client. They have all emphasized that the therapist accurately and empathically know the client's "being" and respond in such a manner as to communicate this deep understanding. Also, they have all uniformly stressed the importance of non-possessive warmth and acceptance of the client by the therapist and have emphasized that the therapist be integrated, mature or genuine within the counseling or therapeutic relationship. These three elements of the psychotherapeutic relationship are aspects of the therapist's behavior that cut across the parochial theories of psychotherapy and appear to be common elements in a wide variety of psychoanalytic, client-centered, and eclectic approaches to psychotherapy and counseling. Rogers[17-19] presented an organized theoretical statement to this effect.

Another aspect of the psychotherapeutic or counseling process commonly pointed to by these writers has been the exploration by the client of his feelings, his values, his perceptions of others, his relationships, his fears, his turmoil, and his life choices. Most have pointed to the client's exploration of self as one of the central happenings in the client's engagement in the process of psychotherapy. Truax[28] has for heuristic reasons specified "intrapersonal exploration" as a sufficient antecedent condition for the consequence of constructive personality change and has presented research evidence from several sources bearing on this hypothesis.

In a revision of Rogers's formulations, Truax[32] has added a fourth therapist-focused element common to a wide variety of therapists: the degree of therapist intensity and intimacy in the therapeutic encounter. The revised statement is, then:

> The greater the degree of the therapist's accurate empathic understanding of the client, the greater the degree to which the therapist shows unconditional or nonpossessive warmth towards the client, the greater the degree of genuineness or integration of the therapist with-

in the relationship, and the more intense and intimate the therapist in the relationship, the greater will be the degree of the client's intra-personal exploration and the greater will be the consequent extent of positive behavorial change.

While Rogers' hypothesized "necessary and sufficient conditions of therapeutic personality change" have in the past given both impetus and directionality to the exploration of the process of psychotherapy, many of us engaged in research have become acutely aware of the heuristic limitations of such a formulation. Current statements of the theoretical model are obviously incomplete.

Other therapist characteristics, such as personal and personality variables, as well as influences upon the therapist's role-concept and the specialized techniques employed by the therapist, must be taken into consideration. Most striking, there is no consideration of patient characteristics, such as the patient's degree of disturbance, or situational variables, such as the atmosphere in which therapy takes place and the "set" which is created for the patient.[13] It should be clearly anticipated that as current research develops, the model will be expanded to include these other therapist, patient, and situational variables so as to incorporate substantive findings of elements common to effective counseling and psychotherapy.[5]

Recent research growing out of a program of psychotherapy and research with schizophrenics initiated by Carl R. Rogers and a program of research into group psychotherapy initiated by Charles B. Truax,* with normals, delinquents, outpatients, and hospitalized patients at the Wisconsin Psychiatric Institute bears directly on the current theoretic formulation. For the most part the Wisconsin studies are based upon a group of thirty-two hospitalized schizophrenic patients, half of whom have received psychotherapy and half of whom have served as matched control sub-

*These findings are part of an ongoing research program supported in part by NIMH Grant No. M 3496 to Drs. Rogers, Truax, and Eugene T. Gendlin; and in part by a grant from the Vocational Rehabilitation Administration. No. RD-906-PM to Drs. Truax and Carkhuff. This research was carried out with patients at Mendota State Hospital with the generous support of Dr. Walter J. Urben, Superintendent, and his staff.

jects. The findings obtained were based upon numerous studies, most of them using randomly selected samples taken either from early and late in therapy or from throughout the whole course of psychotherapy. These samples were coded and randomly presented to groups of highly trained, naive lay raters who made use of specifically designed scales to evaluate the elements of accurate therapist empathy, therapist unconditional warmth, therapist genuineness, and therapist intensity and intimacy of interpersonal contact, as well as the patient's degree of intrapersonal exploration.

The findings from thirty studies to date are surprisingly uniform: each of the therapist "conditions" is significantly related to both the amount of patient intrapersonal or self-exploration, and, most importantly, each of the therapist conditions was significantly related to the degree of client improvement as measured by a wide variety of standard psychological tests including both the Rorschach and the Minnesota Multiphasic Personality Inventory, as well as such concrete and objective behavioral indices as length of hospital stay.

Of importance for the theoretical model, the crucial link between the patient's degree of intrapersonal exploration and the expected consequent constructive personality change was also confirmed by the research. That is, patients who explored "self" to a greater degree throughout the course of psychotherapy also showed the greatest constructive personality change, while patients who showed relatively little self-exploration throughout psychotherapy showed very little constructive personality change.

In comparing patients who received high levels of therapeutic conditions with patients who received low levels of therapeutic conditions and matched control patients, very disquieting findings emerged. Patients who received low conditions throughout psychotherapy tended to show clear negative change in personality functioning. This seems to say, that with schizophrenics at least, low conditions lead to a deterioration in personality functioning. This latter finding has a special significance since if comparisons had been made only between the combined therapy group and the control group, no differences in outcomes would have appeared.

That is, while high conditions lead to positive change, low conditions lead to negative change so that the overall net result of "good" and "bad" therapy combined is comparable to that seen in matched control groups.

One finding of particular significance was that the relationship between therapist conditions and case outcome were the same for schizophrenics as for counseling cases: the very same "conditions" had their therapeutic effect through the intermediary process of depth of intrapersonal or self-exploration. However, recent research has shown that unconditional warmth has an additional therapeutic value beyond that involved in facilitating client self-exploration.

Many theorists such as Alexander and French[2] and Strupp, have already conceptualized "warmth" in terms of a role of facilitating a "corrective" emotional experience. It would seem that they were right!

NEW VARIABLES

Our research interests have led us to explore variables beyond those tied directly to past theoretic models.

Two "environmental" factors that have recently been theoretically posited as facilitating the psychotherapeutic process should now be added to our tentative model. These are (a) vicarious therapy pretraining for psychotherapy, and (b) the use of alternate sessions where the therapist is himself absent from the therapy sessions.

Wolf,[35] Wolf and Schwartz[36] and Truax[30] have suggested especially for group psychotherapy that sessions in which the therapist is absent, if alternated with regular group meetings, would prove therapeutic and thus almost double the number of therapy hours that a given therapist could offer. In a very recent research effort[29] growing out of a program of group psychotherapy and research, it was found that both hospitalized mental patients and juvenile delinquents showed the same general depth of intrapersonal exploration or therapeutic process during the "alternate" sessions as they did during regular therapy sessions. In fact, with the juvenile delinquents there was a tendency for the deepest level of therapeutic process to occur in the "alternate" sessions when the therapist was absent!

Vicarious Therapy Pretaining (VTP), first proposed by Truax,[29] can be easily used in either group or individual psychotherapy. It simply involves presentation to prospective clients of a thirty-minute tape recording of excerpts of "good" client therapy behavior. The tape itself illustrates in a very concrete manner how clients often explore themselves and their feelings. It provides both cognitive and experiential structuring of "how to be a good client."

In short, it allows for a vicarious experiencing of deep psychotherapy prior to the initiation of the psychotherapeutic or counseling relationship.

While this VTP tape seems clinically to substantially facilitate individual psychotherapy, our empirical findings are yet to be analyzed. Recent research completed using VTP in group psychotherapy with both mental hospital and juvenile delinquent clients[31] provides both clinical and research confirmation of its facilitating effect. When early psychotherapy sessions from groups receiving VTP are compared with sessions from non-VTP groups, patients from VTP groups show the higher levels of intrapersonal exploration or the deeper level of therapeutic process.

THE REDISCOVERY OF FORGOTTEN VARIABLES

While it is too early for us to know with any degree of certitude the final meaning of any of the present findings, in listening to hundreds and hundreds of samples of the kind of psychotherapeutic relationship studied in the overall research program and from the personal therapeutic encounters themselves, a number of other learnings have emerged.

One of the perhaps most useful learnings is that the cases high in conditions, high in patient intrapersonal exploration, and high in case outcome seem heavily loaded with specificity or concreteness of interaction. The concreteness of the therapeutic interaction, an element influenced directly by the therapist, seems clinically quite crucial.

Concreteness or specificity of the therapist response seems to

serve three important functions: first, by ensuring that the therapist response does not become abstract and intellectual and, thus,
more emotionally removed from the patient's feelings and experiences; secondly, by forcing the therapist to be more precisely accurate in his understanding of the client (thus even small mis-
understandings become quite clear when the feelings and experiences are stated in specific terms and corrections can be immediately made) ; and thirdly, the client is directly influenced to attend
with specificity to problem areas and emotional conflicts.

Although this characteristic of psychotherapy has not been
specifically discussed as a variable in theories of psychotherapy,
or in research in general, the crucial importance of concreteness
for psychotherapy is implied in the discussions of client-centered,
analytic, and eclectic theory. Freud's[9] initial position stressed two
points, both of which remain basic to psychoanalytic theory: (a)
the recovery of repressed memories, and (b) the handling of repressed affects. Relief from repressions is stated as essential to
therapy. From Freud's discussion, it is quite clear that even when
these memories and affects are fantasy productions they are specific
and concrete and not abstract. In Rogers's discussion of empathic
understanding, too, there is reference to specific experiencings of
the patient rather than to abstract experiencings.[16] Eclectic theorists, too, regard abstract interactions as nontherapeutic. Indeed,
therapists and counselors from almost all "schools" regard a patient's discussion of abstractions as defensive rather than exploratory.

While explicit treatment of concreteness as a variable underlying a significant portion of the therapeutic process is new to research in psychotherapy, it is perhaps quite at home in counseling
and guidance.

Concreteness appears to be an emphatically integral part of
the counseling process. Indeed, concreteness has been incorporated
into counseling's very evolution. When the Veterans Administration first made use of psychologists who were concentrated on
helping the patient take his place in the world of work and community life, the counselor's main function was to focus upon the
specific and concrete realities of the patient's life during their

therapeutic encounter. While some lack of clarity in defining the distinctive aspects of counseling as both process and profession remains,[3,11,21,25] a constant thread running through most definitions involves highly specific considerations of the plans and decisions that individuals, whether healthy or sick, normal or abnormal, must make to play more productive roles in their social environments.[26,33,34] The concreteness of the discussions of role problems, such as educational, vocational, and marriage[4,14] rather than the usually more vague aspects of intrapersonal problems, suggest that the clinicians can learn a great deal about the importance of concreteness from the counselor.

The crucial importance of concreteness as an element common to successful psychotherapy emerged from a recent study that was designed to look at a number of elements common to a wide variety of psychotherapies. Comparative evaluations were made of the roles of empathic understanding, accurate empathy, genuineness of the therapist, unconditional positive regard, leadership, responsivity, concreteness, or specificity of expression, and several other variables.

In the analyses of sixteen different variables, concreteness or specificity of expression was the variable most highly related to the criteria measures of therapeutic process. Concreteness yielded correlations ranging from 0.47 to 0.63 with the various criterion measures. Only one condition, the genuineness of the clients, a condition influenced indirectly by the therapist, approached correlations in this range. Further, all of the therapist variables that related positively to the criteria were also found to be positively and significantly related to the concreteness variable. Concreteness, thus, might appear to underlie effective therapy.

Concreteness or specificity, since it is less tied to one's emotional make-up and "life style," would seem to be more easily under the control of the therapist or counselor than would be his communication of the other therapist conditions or elements of psychotherapy. That is, while it is difficult for the therapist to maintain control over his degree of accurate empathy, his unconditional warmth for his client, his own integration and self-congruence or even his intensity and intimacy in the interpersonal relationship, the degree of concreteness versus abstraction of his communication seems easily varied by him. Also, concreteness appears to transcend the theoretical and emotional commitments to "schools" of therapy. Thus, as future learnings add more to our knowledge of the role of concreteness, learnings could be applied easily by psychoanalytic therapists, behavior therapists, counselors, client-centered therapists, or eclectic therapists without the usual barriers presented by commitments to theories and "schools."

Again, the intention here is not to emphasize the element of concreteness to the exclusion of others. Rather, it appears that concreteness operates most effectively in the context of high levels of the other posited therapeutic ingredients, as the correlations with other effective therapist variables attest. As we search and research to account for the therapeutic process which we assume to be a lawful, predictable and directive process, we come to account more and more for the variation in our criteria measures of outcome. Sometimes we find new dimensions; at other times we rediscover old ones, as we have with concreteness.

Some old elements, such as the therapist's positive warmth, take on a new meaning; some new "environmental" factors are newly tried, while some forgotten elements are rediscovered. We must ask ourselves why concreteness is a forgotten element in current theoretical and research formulations dealing with the process of psychotherapy. We must ask ourselves if it was simply too pedestrian, too familiar? Or, have the traditional variables of the past intimidated us? Have the tribal customs of counseling and psychotherapy restricted us from stepping forward to claim new dimensions or from claiming new meanings for old dimensions? Certainly counseling in all fields is most familiar with such concepts as concrete explorations. Has it been blinded by its ties to the past in such a manner as to sterilize its theoretical and research efforts?

Finally, we must ask ourselves what practical significance these new learnings about the process of effective psychotherapy or counseling might have for us as educators, as scientists, and as professionals. While we may each draw our own meanings from these findings depending upon our own setting, the implications themselves are large.

Perhaps the greatest meaning of these findings lies in their implication of the breadth of theory and practice necessary to explain and produce constructive personality change. They together point to old and to newly conceived factors, to therapist and patient variables, and to relationship and environmental factors. They forced us to admit the inadequacy of our current theories and to hold in deep distrust the value of "schools" of psychotherapy or counseling built solely around such oversimplified theories.

REFERENCES

1. Alexander, F.: *Fundamentals of Psychoanalysis.* New York, Norton, 1948.
2. Alexander, F. and French, T.: *Psychoanalytic Therapy.* New York, Ronald Press, 1946.
3. Berdie, R. F.: Counseling. *Annual Review of Psychology.* Palo Alto, Calif., Annual Reviews, Inc., 1959.
4. Brigante, T. R., Haefner, D. P. and Woodson, W. B.: Clinical and counseling psychologists' perceptions of their specialties. *J Counsel Psychol,* in press.
5. Carkhuff, R. R.: On the necessary conditions of therapeutic personality change. *Discussion Papers, Wisconsin Psychiatric Institute,* 1963, No. 47.
6. Dymond, Rosalind: A scale for the measurement of empathic ability. *J Consult Psychol, 13:*127-233, 1949.
7. Ferenczi, S.: The principle of relaxation and neocatharsis. *Int J Psychoanal, 11:*428-443, 1930.
8. Fox, R. E. and Goldin, P. C.: The empathic process in psychotherapy: A survey of theory and research. Unpublished manuscript, 1963.
9. Freud, S.: Analysis terminable and interminable. *Collected Papers.* New York, Hogarth Press, 1950, vol. 5.
10. Halpern, H. and Lesser, Leona: Empathy in infants, adults, and psychotherapists. *Psychoanal Rev, 47:*32-42, 1960.
11. Hobbs, N. and Seeman, J.: Counseling. *Ann Rev Psychol.* Palo Alto, Calif., Annual Reviews, Inc., 1955.
12. Jourard, S.: I-thou relationship versus manipulation in counseling and psychotherapy. *J Ind Psychol, 15:*174-179, 1959.
13. Krasner, L.: The therapist as a social reinforcement machine. In Strupp, H. H. and Lubrosky, L. (Eds.): *Research in Psychotherapy.* Washington, D.C., American Psychological Association, 1962, vol. II.
14. Perry, W. G.: The findings of the commission in counseling and guidance. *Ann NY Acad Sci, 63:*396-407, 1955.

15. Raush, H. L. and Bordin, E. S.: Warmth in personality development and in psychotherapy. *Psychiat, 20 (No. 4):*351-363, 1957.
16. Rogers, C. R.: *Client-centered Therapy.* Cambridge, Mass., Riverside Press, 1951.
17. Rogers, C. R.: The necessary and sufficient conditions of therapeutic personality change. *J Consult Psychol, 21:*95-103, 1957.
18. Rogers, C. R.: A theory of therapy, personality, and interpersonal relationships as developed in the client-centered framework. In Koch, S. (Ed.): *Psychology: A Study of a Science. Formulations of the Person and the Social Context.* New York, McGraw-Hill, 1959, vol. III, pp. 184-256.
19. Rogers, C. R.: The interpersonal relationship: the core of guidance. *Harv Rev, 32:*416-429, 1962.
21. Schafer, R.: Generative empathy in the treatment situation. *Psychoanal Q, 28:*342-373, 1959.
21. Shoben, E. J., Jr.: Counseling. *Annual Review of Psychology.* Palo Alto, Calif., Annual Reviews, Inc., 1956.
22. Snyder, W. V.: *The Psychotherapy Relationship.* New York, Macmillan, 1961.
23. Strunk, O., Jr.: Empathy: A review of theory and research. *Psychol Newsletter, 9:*47-57, 1957.
24. Strupp, H. H.: Nature of psychotherapist's contribution to the treatment process. *Arch Gen Psychiat, 3:*219-231, 1960.
25. Tiedeman, D. V. and Mastroianni, W. J.: Scuttle the division of counseling psychology? Nonsense! Unpublished manuscript, 1961.
26. Tiedeman, D. V., Wrenn, C. G. and Tyler, Leona: The current status of counseling psychology. Mimeographed report of Special Committee, Division of Counseling Psychology, American Psychological Association, 1961.
27. Truax, C. B.: The process of group psychotherapy. *Psychol. Monogr., 75 (No. 14, Whole No. 511),* 1961.
28. Truax, C. B.: Therapeutic conditions. *Discussion papers, Wisconsin Psychiatric Institute,* 1961, No. 13 a.
29. Truax, C. B.: The therapeutic process in group psychotherapy: A research investigation. Mimeographed paper, Wisconsin Psychiatric Institute, 1961 b.
30. Truax, C. B.: Depth of intrapersonal exploration or therapeutic process in group alternate sessions and during regular sessions. Mimeographed paper, Wisconsin Psychiatric Institute, 1962.
31. Truax, C. B.: Depth of intrapersonal exploration or therapeutic process in group psychotherapy with and without vicarious therapy pretraining. Mimeographed paper, Wisconsin Psychiatric Institute, 1963.
32. Truax, C. B.: Effective ingredients in psychotherapy: An approach to

unraveling the patient-therapist interaction. *J Counsel Psychol, 10:* 256-263, 1963.

33. Tyler, Leona E.: Counseling. *Ann Review of Psychology.* Palo Alto, Calif., Annual Reviews, Inc., 1958.

34. Vance, F. L. and Volsky, T. C.: Counseling and psychotherapy: Split Personality or siamese twins? *Am Psychol, 17:*565-570, 1962.

35. Wolf, A.: Group psychotherapy with adults: The alternate meeting. Paper read at APGA Conference, New York, January 27, 1961.

36. Wolf, A. and Schwartz, E. K.: *Psychoanalysis in Groups.* New York, Grune & Stratton, 1962.

Chapter 27

TRAINING IN COUNSELING AND PSYCHOTHERAPY: AN EVALUATION OF AN INTEGRATED DIDACTIC AND EXPERIENTIAL APPROACH

ROBERT R. CARKHUFF AND CHARLES B. TRUAX

A RECENT ATTEMPT (Truax, Carkhuff and Douds, 1964) was made to implement a view of training in counseling and psychotherapy that would integrate the didactic-intellectual approach which emphasizes the shaping of therapist behavior with the experiential approach which focuses upon therapist development and growth. Briefly, the approach set forth involves the supervisor's didactically teaching the trainee the former's accumulated research and clinical learnings concerning effective therapeutic dimensions in the context of a relationship which provides the trainee with experiences which the research and clinical learnings suggest are essential for constructive change or positive therapeutic outcome. For example, the teacher-supervisor might teach about high levels of empathic understanding while himself attempting to provide high levels of this dimension in his relationships to the trainees. Supervision is itself viewed as a therapeutic process: a learning or relearning process which takes place in the context of a particular kind of interpersonal relationship which is free of threat and facilitative of trainee self-exploration.

This integrated approach has grown out of programs of re-

Note: Reprinted from *J Consult Psychol*, 29:333-336, 1965.

The authors wish to acknowledge the critical technical contributions of Edward P. Williams to the training program and data analyses and the cooperative efforts of John Corcella, Robert DeBurger, and Logan Gragg.

Robert Carkhuff's work was supported by Public Health postdoctoral research fellowship number 7 FMH-19,912-02, and the program was supported by Research and Development Grant No. 906-PM to the authors from the Vocational Rehabilitation Administration.

search into the processes of individual and group counseling and psychotherapy which appear to have identified at least four critical process variables in effective therapeutic processes. The dimensions include (a) therapist accurate empathic understanding, (b) therapist warmth or positive regard; (c) therapist genuineness or self-congruence; and (d) patient depth of self-exploration. There is extensive evidence to indicate that the three therapist-offered conditions predictably relate to the patient process variable of intrapersonal exploration, and all four dimensions have been shown to relate significantly to a variety of positive patient personality and behavioral change indexes (Barrett-Lennard, 1962; Bergin and Solomon, 1963; Braaten, 1961; Halkides, 1958; Rogers, 1962; Tomlinson and Hart, 1962; Truax, 1961; Truax and Carkhuff, 1964a, 1964b; Wagstaff, Rice, and Butler, 1960) .

A central part of the training program involves the application of research scales which have been predictive of positive patient outcome in researching these dimensions. With the help of the scales which had successfully measured or estimated the levels of the therapeutic conditions in previous research, the trainees are didactically taught the therapeutic conditions involved. The beginning counselors are then exposed to tape-recorded samples of counseling or psychotherapy rated at various levels of therapist-offered conditions and client-process involvement. The trainees get practice at discriminating levels of therapist and client conditions. Further, the trainees receive empathy training in which the trainee listens to patient statements and then is asked to formulate his response in terms of the feeling and content of the communication. The trainees then role-play, and finally their initial clinical interviews with hospitalized patients are recorded and then rated so as to give them immediate and concrete informational feedback on how well they are learning to put into operation the concepts involved.

Two separate, but essentially identical, training programs have been successfully implemented. The first program involved twelve advanced graduate students, ranging in age from the 20's to the 30's, in a regular university graduate course in "Individual Psychotherapy." The second and simultaneously run program involved five volunteer but otherwise unselected lay hospital personnel, ranging in age from the 30's to the 50's. These five volunteers consisted of three aides, a volunteer worker, and an industrial therapist. Only the industrial therapist had a college education. The programs lasted one semester of sixteen weeks. The classes met twice a week for two hours on each occasion. In addition, the trainees spent approximately two additional hours per week listening on their own to recorded therapy.

METHODOLOGY

During the last week of the semester of training, each trainee had a single clinical interview with each of three hospitalized patients. From the three tapes of each trainee, six four-minute excerpts were randomly selected, two excerpts from each tape. For purposes of comparison, excerpts of therapy interviews were similarly selected from the recordings of sessions in which eleven patients from a similar patient population were seen by experienced therapists in the Schizophrenic Project of the Wisconsin Psychiatric Institute. In addition, random excerpts were obtained from the publicly dispersed tapes of therapy interviews of four prominent therapists. The combined experienced therapists included the following: Albert Ellis, William Fey, Eugene T. Gendlen, Rollo May, Allyn Roberts, Carl R. Rogers, Jack Teplinsky, Charles B. Truax, Julius Seeman, Al Wellner, and Carl Whitaker. The experienced therapists ranged in age from the thirty's to the sixty's.

Following the pattern of rating upon which much of the extensive body of research in support of the four dimensions has been built, undergraduate students who were not psychology majors and who were naive concerning therapeutic practices were trained on the particular individual scales involved to a degree of intrarater reliability of not less than .50 in order to insure that the ratings were not random. While .50 was the cut-off level, in most cases the rate-re-rate reliabilities hovered in the 70's and 80's. In the rater training, the prospective raters were exposed to therapy excerpts selected because of a high dgree of rating agreement by a variety of raters, including experienced therapists, at the various levels of the scales involved in order to insure a spread in the therapy process levels which the prospective raters were to rate. In the Wisconsin Schizophrenic Project and the Kentucky Group Therapy Project and in the analyses of data from other resources such as Chicago and Stanford, the therapy process ratings of undergraduate students trained on these particular individual scales successfully predicted therapeutic outcome (Rogers, 1962; Truax and Carkhuff, 1964a, 1964b). Four raters were trained to rate the therapist accurate empathy scale; four different raters rated patient depth of self-exploration; two other raters rated therapist positive regard; and two still different raters rated therapist congruence.

The therapist accurate empathy (AE) scale is a nine-point scale attempting to specify stages along a continuum. At the lowest stage, for example," . . . the therapist seems completely unaware of even the most conspicuous of the client's feelings. . . ." At the highest stage, Stage 9, the therapist ". . . unerringly responds to the client's full range of feelings in their exact intensity . . . ." The product moment correlations between the four raters employed on the AE training data ranged in the .40's and .50's with one correlation falling to .24*

The scale measuring therapist unconditional positive regard (UPR) is a five-point scale running from the lowest point where ". . .the therapist is actively offering advice or giving clear negative regard. . . ." to the highest point where ". . . the therapist communicates unconditional positive regard without restriction. . . ." The product-moment correlation between the two raters employed was .48*

Therapist self-congruence (TSC) is estimated by a seven-point scale where Stage 1 is indicated by a ". . . striking evidence of contradiction between the therapist's experiencing and his current verbalization. . . ." and Stage 7 is noted when ". . . the therapist is freely and deeply himself in the relationship. . . ." The correlation between the two raters employed was .62.*

Client depth of self-exploration (DX) is measured by a nine-point scale running from the lowest stages where ". . . the patient actively evades personally relevant material. . . ." to the highest stages where ". . . the patient is deeply exploring and being himself. . . ." The product-moment correlations between the four raters employed on the DX training data ranged in the .50's and .60's with only one correlation falling below .47.*

RESULTS

The results appear in Tables 27-I and 27-II. It can be readily seen that, with the notable exception of the critical DX variable, where the lay therapists' mean scores were approximately equal to those of the students and the experienced therapists, the groups

---

*All intercorrelations for the ratings on all scales were significant beyond the .01 level.

TABLE 27-I

MEAN SCALE VALUES OF THERAPY PROCESS VARIABLES FOR GROUPS
OF TRAINEES AND EXPERIENCED THERAPISTS

Scale	Number of Points	Lay* (n = 5)	SD	Students* (n = 12)	SD	Experienced (n = 15)	SD
	(9)	4.58	.30	5.14	.69	5.22	.84
AE	(9)	4.58	.30	5.14	.69	5.22	.84
UPR	(5)	2.82	.62	3.05	.32	3.16	.40
TSC	(7)	4.86	.35	5.23	.48	5.51	.45
DX	(9)	4.66	.30	4.56	.60	4.86	.56

*Personnel involved in training program.

TABLE 27-II

t-TESTS FOR SIGNIFICANT DIFFERENCES OF THERAPY PROCESS
VARIABLES FOR GROUPS OF TRAINEES AND EXPERIENCED
THERAPISTS

Scale	Students Versus Lay	Students Versus Experienced	Lay Versus Experienced
AE	1.750	.267	1.641
UPR	1.045	.786	1.417
TSC	.487	1.556	2.955*
DX	.357	1.304	.741

*Significant at the .01 level.

consistently performed in the following rank order: (a) the experienced therapists; (b) the graduate students; and (c) the lay personnel. While a hierarchy of performance was established, the experienced therapists did not effect significantly better process levels than the graduate students on any dimensions, and the latter were not significantly higher than the lay group on any indexes. The only significant difference was found in the comparison of the experienced and the lay groups on the therapist self-congruence dimension.

DISCUSSION

The results suggest that in a relatively short training period, i.e. approximately one hundred hours, both graduate students and lay hospital personnel can be brought to function at levels of therapy nearly commensurate with those of experienced therapists.

It is notable that on the empathy dimension all of the groups functioned near Stage 5, which is characterized by the ". . . therapist accurately respond[ing] to all of the client's more readily discernible feelings. . . ." All groups hovered around Stage 3 of the unconditional positive regard scale where ". . . the therapist indicates a positive caring for the patient or client but it is a semi-possessive caring. . . ." On the therapist self-congruence scale all groups functioned near Level 5 where ". . . there are no negative cues suggesting any discrepancy between what he says and what he feels, and there are some positive cues indicating genuine response to the patient. . . ." The patients of all the groups of therapists are engaged in the therapeutic process of self-exploration at Levels 4 and 5 where ". . . personally relevant material is discussed . . ." and frequently, ". . . either with feeling indicating emotional proximity, or with spontaneity. . . ." To sum: it may be said that the trainees, both students and lay personnel, engaged almost as well as the more experienced therapists in what would commonly be characterized as *effective psychotherapy.*

For purposes of comparison, there is Bergin and Solomon's (1963) analysis of six different supervisory groups of postinternship fourth-year graduate students from a more didactically and psychoanalytically oriented clinical training program of a school of some repute in the field on an expanded version of the empathy scale. By inserting a stage between Levels 2 and 3 of the present scale, the authors obtained the following average ratings, with many of the ratings between Levels 2 and 3 and all of those above Stage 3 tending to be inflated if compared to assessments employing the nine-point empathy scale: Group A, 2.14; Group B, 3.84; Group C, 3.20; Group D, 2.02; Group E, 1.91; Group F, 2.08. It should be noted here that Bergin and Solomon also found empathy to be positively related to outcome. While we have only empathy ratings for comparison, it can easily be seen that the highest of these levels of functioning on empathic understanding is nowhere near those produced by the integrated program described here.

That the experienced therapists are significantly higher than the lay personnel, as well as relatively higher than the graduate students, on the self-congruence dimension, suggests that with experience the therapists come to be more freely, easily, and deeply themselves in the therapeutic encounter. In this regard, one handicap with which the lay personnel may have been operating is the lack of any real theoretical orientation to indicate to them where they were going in their encounters. The very notion that counseling and therapy may take place devoid of any theoretical knowledge is currently being assessed in a lay group counseling treatment study. While the present program did not emphasize outside readings, the graduate students tended to glean from other sources some direction for themselves and their activities.

It is perhaps noteworthy that the lay personnel, consistently the lowest on all scales assessing the level of therapist-offered conditions, engage their patients in a depth of intrapersonal exploration commensurate with that of the experienced therapists and the students. The suggestion is that other dimensions come into play in effecting patient self-exploration which, in turn, is so highly correlated with patient outcome criteria. Perhaps the oft-noted social class variables are relevant here in the sense that lower socioeducational class therapists are in some way more facilitative in engaging their patient counterparts in the therapeutic process.

REFERENCES

1. Barrett-Lennard, G. 'T.: Dimensions of therapist response as causal factors in therapeutic change. *Psychol Monogr, 76 (43, Whole No. 562):* 1962.
2. Bergin, A. E. and Solomon, Sandra: Personality and performance correlates of empathic understanding in psychotherapy. *Am Psychol, 18:393,* 1963.
3. Braaten, L. J.: The movement of non-self to self in client-centered psychotherapy. *J Counsel Psychol, 8:*20-24, 1961.
4. Halkides, Galatia: An investigation of therapeutic success as a function of four variables. Unpublished doctoral dissertation, University of Chicago, 1958.
5. Rogers, C. R.: The interpersonal relationship: The core of guidance. *Harvard Educ Rev, 32:*416-429, 1962.
6. Tomlinson, T. M. and Hart, J. T. Jr.: A validation study of the process scale. *J Consult Psychol, 26:*74-78, 1962.

7. Truax, C. B.: The process of group psychotherapy. *Psychol Monogr, 75 (14, Whole No. 511):* 1961.
8. Truax, C. B. and Carkhuff, R. R.: For better or for worse: The process of psychotherapeutic personality change. Chapter in Wigdor, Blossom T. (Ed.): *Recent Advances in Behavior Change.* Montreal, Canada, McGill Univer. Press, 1964 a.
9. Truax, C. B. and Carkhuff, R. R.: Significant developments in psychotherapy research. Chapter in Abt, L. and Riess, B. F. (Eds.): *Progress in Clinical Psychology.* New York, Grune & Stratton, vol. VI, 1964 b.
10. Truax, C. B., Carkhuff, R. R. and Douds, J.: Toward an integration of the didactic and experiential approaches to training in counseling and psychotherapy. *J Counsel Psychol, 11:*240-247, 1964.
11. Wagstaff, A. K., Rice, L. N. and Butler, J. M.: Factors in client verbal participation in therapy. *Counseling Center Discussion Papers, University of Chicago, 6(9):*1-14, 1960.

C. BEHAVIOR MODIFICATION (OPERANT)

Chapter 28

THE BEHAVIOR MODIFICATION APPROACH IN THE HELPING PROFESSIONS

LEONARD KRASNER

I N DEALING WITH PROCESSES of changing human behavior, four concepts must be discussed and differentiated: behavior influence, behavior modification, evocative psychotherapy and behavior therapy.

One person may program the environment, including his own behavior, to affect a second person's behavior. Because other people are a major source of acquired reinforcers, this is probably the largest general category of behavior in which socialized humans engage. When such behavior is effective, it is called *behavior influence*.

Behavior influence, then, is a term which includes situations in which one human being exerts control over another human being. Formal school education would fall in this category as would psychological studies involving opinion change, techniques of learning, and sensory deprivation. The focus in these situations is upon the process of change itself and does not evaluate the social desirability of the behavior being changed.

Behavior modification, on the other hand, primarily involves the changing of behaviors which have been labeled *socially* deviant. In effect behavior modification involves changing the actions of individuals who have been brought within a social labeling system.

There are people such as teachers, parents, and therapists who attempt to change people for the long-term benefit of the person being influenced. The term *behavior modification* may be applied

Note: Reprinted from Nagoshi, J. (Ed.): *Progress in Behavior Modification.* Honolulu, Social Welfare Development and Research Center, 1969, pp. 1-15.

to this process. Behavior modification involves a wide range of psychological influence. The term may be applied to many different techniques used with a broad spectrum of educational and behavioral problems by people of varying professional and non-professional affiliation. For example, a recent volume (Krasner and Ullmann, 1965) on research in behavior modification dealt with shaping, modeling, verbal conditioning, computer simulation, and hypnosis among other techniques. The people influenced by these procedures ranged from retardates to college students, from schizophrenics to normal children. In similar fashion, a book on clinical applications of behavior modification (Ullmann and Krasner, 1965) reported the efforts not only of psychologists, psychiatrists, social workers, but also of classroom teachers, parents, nurses, peers, people working in correctional institutions, retardate centers, community agencies, hospitals of all sorts, and, literally, in all institutions involved in changing behavior labeled as deviant.

Within the realm of behavior modification there are two conceptually different approaches. Treatment deducible from a sociopsychological or behavioral or social learning model that aims to alter a person's principles can be called *behavior therapy*. Treatment deducible from a medical or psychoanalytic model that aims to alter a person's behavior *indirectly* by first altering intrapsychic organizations can be called *evocative psychotherapy*. That is, the aim is to evoke something inside the individual to bring about change. In these techniques, the therapist does *not deliberately* apply response contingent reinforcement in the manner of behavior therapists.

Both evocative psychotherapy and behavior therapy are forms of behavior modification which in turn is one type of behavior influence.

It follows from these two models that the treatment procedures subsumed under each will have very different objectives and techniques. Behavior therapy, as contrasted with evocative psychotherapy, usually involves *direct* treatment of the problem behaviors, the *deliberate* use of social influence, reliance upon *laboratory* findings from basic human and animal experiments, a focus on *training* relevant people in the social environment, the most important element, emphasis on and manipulation of present environmental events, and a very active therapist. The research efforts which derive from these two models and approaches are consequently very different in design, purpose, and in the relationship between the laboratory and "real life." These points will be expanded upon.

Within behavior therapy it is becoming increasingly difficult to differentiate the various techniques into discrete categories. At one point, it was relatively simple to describe behavior therapy research in terms of operant conditioning, systematic desensitization, modeling, and extinction. Early reviews of the techniques and research involved used some variation of these. Bandura (1961) organized his review of behavior therapy around the topics of extinction, discrimination learning, reward, punishment, and social imitation. Grossberg (1964) organized his review around the topics of aversion, negative practice, positive conditioning, reinforcement withdrawal, and desensitization. Kalish (1965) reduced the techniques to extinction and conditioning.

Behavior therapy, then, is not operant conditioning per se, as some operant investigators might prefer to believe, nor is it desensitization as others would agree. All of these are part of a more generic approach.

This new approach which we are labeling behavior therapy, a branch of behavior modification, has now extended into virtually every area into which the helping professions are involved. Traditional psychotherapy of the one-to-one relationship was one of the first to be influenced as we will see when we describe the early contributions of Eysenck and Wolpe. This has developed into the current investigation and application now referred to as systematic desensitization or reciprocal inhibition.

The early work of Lindsley and Skinner has developed into the current operant programs, some using token economies in mental hospitals.

The early operant work of Bijou and Ellis with retardates and of Ferster with autistic children has been extended into institutions for retardates and for severely emotionally disturbed children.

Within the past four or five years the behavioral approach has burst out in all directions from the hospital and office to the schoolroom, guidance and counseling office, physical rehabilitation wards.

Thomas (Chapter 29), has spelled out the implications of what he called the sociobehavior approach for social case work. I think the impact of this argument is that problem and task of the social case worker is essentially the same as that of any mental health professional, namely to modify human behavior. The social worker's opportunities to do this are perhaps greater than other mental health professionals to the extent that they come in contact with the family and to the extent that they are able to influence the home environment. Unfortunately, social workers have a large extent hitched their stars to the wrong horse to the extent that they let their work be guided by psychodynamic formulations of personality.

HISTORY OF BEHAVIOR MODIFICATION

I feel that in setting the framework, it is necessary to give a little of the historical background to the field. History is not a dead, boring retelling of the past but rather history is current, essentially the current generation's interpretation of the past. This is particularly relevant for our interest here because what is now happening is a change from one theoretical model of deviant behavior, the medical model, to that of a behavioral model of deviant behavior. To those of us receiving professional training in the 1940's and 1950's and early 1960's, the disease model was presented to us as a given fact as if it were always true. Yet as we look back we find surprising things. Models of abnormality continually change. The current widely accepted but beleaguered model had its origin in a particular time and place. A good starting place would be the era of the end of moral treatment.

Moral treatment is the generic label for the procedures of Pinel, Tuke, Rush and the heads of a few hospitals influenced by them in the early 1800's. It represented the first effort to provide systematic and responsible care for large numbers of deviant people. The use of the term "moral" was equivalent to our present words such as emotional, psychological or even behavioral.

Moral treatment strove to create a complete therapeutic environment—social, psychological and physical. Although emphasis was placed on the relationships between physician and patient, moral treatment embraced a much larger psychological approach than individual psychotherapy. Indeed, "perhaps the greatest asset of moral treatment was the attention it gave to the value of physical setting and social influences of hospital life as curative agents." (Bockoven, 1963, p. 25).

The humanitarian treatment based on a psychological model and the expectation of improvement (Goldstein, 1962) were major reasons for the effectiveness of moral treatment. The reports that are available for this period (See Bockoven, 1963 and Dain, 1964) indicate a higher discharge rate than for previous and most subsequent periods of time.

From 1850 onward there was a strong shift away from this behavioral model to a medicine model. Aside from the building of larger, centralized state hospitals resulting from the campaign of Dorothea Dix there was an increased number of immigrants among patients, particularly in New England. The psychiatrists had difficulty in communicating with these individuals because of difference in language, social class and background. It was much easier to view such alien people as being sick, which would explain their deviant behavior, instead of having problems in living which would imply, as it did to the moral therapists, that they were basically no different from their therapists. Further, the success of *physical medicine* in overcoming many of the major diseases afflicting humanity, which had made enormous strides in the late 19th century, led to its adoption as a model for psychiatric treatment and research. Finally, there was decline in expenditures for treatment of the abnormal in large hospitals. Such hospitals, skimping on even the basic amenities of life, were relatively inexpensive. The ordinary citizen felt relieved of his responsibilities to these people and found it easy to be indifferent to them when they were out of sight. Increased size and reduced expenditure led to overcrowding and consequently to even further decreased effectiveness (Ullmann, 1967). Space which had been devoted to manual therapy and recreation was increasingly used to house patients.

Patients with behavior problems were viewed as being afflicted in the same manner as patients with organic diseases and this is the stumbling block. The patients were cast in the same role as other medically ill people, a role which required a passive, submissive, quiet, untroublesome waiting for the discovery of a cure. Remissions were looked upon with disbelief, if not downright disfavor. If no treatment were known, none could be given, and none was given.

Thus we can almost pinpoint the origin of our current version of the medical model of abnormal behavior.

By disease or medical model is meant that the individual's behavior is considered peculiar, abnormal, or diseased because of some *underlying* cause usually physical in nature. The analogy is made to physical medicine in which germs, viruses, lesions, and other insults foreign to the normal working of the organism lead to the production of symptoms. This approach in physical medicine represented a major break-through during the 19th century. It permitted effective specific treatment of physical ailments where previously the history of medicine had been almost completely the story of "placebo" (Shapiro, 1960).

The medical model has effects upon the general views with which the labeler and therapist approach the patient. First, there is an *underlying cause* and consequently maladaptive behaviors cannot be treated directly because they are products of these causes. Second, any change in behavior is not really important unless the "real" trouble has been dealt with and eliminated. Third, the well-springs or causes of behavior may be hidden from sight. Thus the distinction between the patient's overt behavior, and what the clinician experts, or *knows to be there,* is often blurred. Falure to find the expected cause merely confirms the *severity* of the problem.

Szasz (1961) has written extensively from both a historical and semantic-philosophical viewpoint on the concepts involved in the medical model. Szasz holds many of the same views we have expressed here about the medical model within the context of what he labels "the myth of mental illness." The myth lies not in the existence of the deviant or disturbed behaviors but rather in the label of mental illness.

The more direct origin of current behavior therapy has other philosophical and experimental roots. In fact, there is a current controversy as to the origins of either the term or the useage of "behavior therapy." Wolpe most recently has pointed out that Lindsley and Skinner used the term "behavior therapy" to describe their program of operant conditioning at Metropolitan State Hospital in 1953 to 54. Although that program was clearly not that of the later classically-oriented Wolpe porgram, it certainly was in the same framework.

Two books represent the application of laboratory research to develop new methods of behavior modification. The first of these was B. F. Skinner's (1953) *Science and Human Behavior,* which provided emphasis and intellectual tools for the measurement and manipulation of individual and hence more relevant, social behavior.

A second crucial book was Wolpe's (1958) *Psychotherapy by Reciprocal Inhibition,* the first half of which included a summary of the laboratory work leading to the therapeutic techniques detailed in the latter half. Eysenck's anthology (1960) of writing on behavior therapy and the establishment of the journal, *Behavior Research and Therapy,* in 1963 brought together much of the material which had been widely scattered throughout the literature.

Recent investigators have reflected and supplemented the major factor in the marked increase in the use of behavior therapy, namely the direct use of research results (Krasner and Ullmann, 1965). During the period of the 1950's, there were an increasing number of researchers and practitioners who turned their attention to studies of the change of behavior, particularly clinically relevant human activities. A number of anthologies (Bachrach, 1962; Berg and Bass, 1961; Biderman and Zimmer, 1961; Krasner and Ullmann, 1965; Ullmann and Krasner, 1965) brought together a fair sampling of this material which includes studies of attitude change, group behavior, verbal behavior in interview situations, classical conditioning, sensory deprivation, drugs, hypnosis, and physiological correlates of social stimuli.

CONCEPTUALIZATION OF ABNORMAL BEHAVIOR

A definition of abnormal behavior which could serve as the framework into which the operant conditioning approach can be fit should be presented. This approach must be clearly differentiated from the procedures which derive from the medical model. If you view the locus of psychopathology as some basic malfunctioning within the organism, then evocative psychotherapy which attempts to extirpate the pathology makes sense. If however the locus of malfunctioning is external then behavior therapy is the treatment of choice.

Ullmann and Krasner (1969) present a conceptualization of abnormal behavior which is compatible with and necessary for operant conditioning procedures.

Behavior which is called abnormal must be studied as the interaction of three variables: the behavior itself, its social context, and an observer who is in a position of power. No specific behavior is abnormal in itself. Rather, an individual may do something (e.g. verbalize hallucinations, hit a person, collect rolls of toilet paper, refuse to eat, stutter, stare into space, or dress sloppily) under a set of circumstances (e.g. during a school class, while working at this desk, during a church service) which upsets, annoys, angers, or strongly disturbs somebody (e.g. employer, teacher, parent, or the individual himself) sufficiently that some action results (e.g. a policeman is called, seeing a psychiatrist is recommended, committment proceedings are started) so that the society's professional labelers (e.g. physicians, psychiatrists, psychologists, judges, social workers) come into contact with the individual and determine which of the current sets of labels (e.g. schizophrenic reaction, sociopathic personality, anxiety reaction) is most appropriate. Finally, there follow attempts to change the emission of the offending behavior (e.g. institutionalization, psychotherapy, medication). The label applied is the result of the training of the labeler and reflects the society which he represents.

The labeling itself leads others to react to the individual in terms of the stereotypes of that label (e.g. "Be careful; he's a dangenous schizophernic"; "Poor girl, she's hysterical").

It is important to emphasize that behavior therapy should be approached within a framework which conceptualizes the behavior to be changed as *deviant,* not as psychopathology. The implications of the latter view (the medical model) is that behavior cannot change unless underlying causes are extirpated, since other undesirable behavior will replace them (symptom substitution). The implication of the view expressed above (social labeling) is that deviant behavior is a learned social phenomenon, hence changed behavior will represent "real" changes in the individual because every change will have social consequences changing the individual's environment specifically in eliciting new responses from others.

PROGRAM EXAMPLES

Token Economy Programs:

Token economy programs are the most recent illustration and culmination of the operant conditioning approach. They are a good example of the point made throughout this chapter that the operant techniques cannot be separated from a more general social influence approach. The critique and evaluation of these studies will differ if they are considered solely as operant conditioning or if they are put in a social influence context.

At the simplest level a token economy program involves the setting up of a contingent reinforcement program. This involves three aspects: First the designation by the institutional staff of certain specific patient *behaviors* as good or desirable, hence reinforceable. Second, there is a *medium of exchange,* an object that "stands for" something else, the tokens. These may be plastic rectangles shaped like credit cards, small metallic coins, poker chips, marks on a piece of paper, or even green stamps. Third, there is a way for utilizing the tokens, the *back-up* reinforcers themselves. These are the good things in life, the desirable things for a given individual, and may range from food to being allowed to sit peacefully in a chair. The "economy" part of the term appropriately relates to the "supply and demand" aspects of the programs which determine changing token values.

The goals of a token program are to develop behaviors which will lead to social reinforcement from others, to enhance the skills necessary for the individual to take a responsible social role in the institution and eventually, to live successfully outside the hospital. Basically, the individual learns that he can control his own environment in such a way that he will elicit positive reinforcement from others.

One of the first uses of *tokens* to replace primary reinforcers was that by Staats (1965) to help train reading discrimination in children. The responses of the children in his study were reinforced with marbles, which were exchangeable for various back-up reinforcers. Staats reported that there were scheduling effects which depended upon the way in which tokens and back-up reinforcers were related in addition to the schedules involving the manner in which tokens were made contingent upon the behavior of the individual.

However, the simple analogue from animal operant conditioning studies is not appropriate since it is human beings who deliver the reinforcement and hence bring into the situation complex social influence variables. I will present a brief description of several token programs.

Ayllon and his colleagues (Ayllon, 1963; Ayllon and Houghton, 1962, 1964; Ayllon and Michael, 1959) reported a series of applications of operant principles to a mental hospital setting. These represented dramatic illustrations of the ABA design and opened the way for introduction of the more encompassing token economy program.

Ayllon and Azrin (1965) report the results of the first application of a token economy to a psychiatric hospital ward. The behaviors selected for reinforcement included such things as serving meals, cleaning floors, sorting laundry, washing dishes, and self-grooming. Reinforcement consisted of the opportunity to engage in activities that had a high level of occurrence when freely allowed. The reinforcers selected were part of the naturalistic environmental context.

Ayllon and Azrin made no *a priori* decisions about what might be an effective reinforcer for schizophrenic patients. Instead their approach involved the observation of patients' behavior to discover what patients *actually* did. They applied the general principle expressed by Premak (1959) that any behavior with a high frequency of occurrence can be used as a reinforcer. Thus, the reinforcers included such things as having a room available for rent; selecting people with whom to dine; passes; a chance to speak to the ward physician, chaplain, or psychologist; opportunity to view T.V.; candy; cigarettes; and other amenities of life. Tokens serve as *acquired* reinforcers that bridge the delay between behavior and an ultimate reinforcement. The investigators placed particular emphasis on the objective definition and quantification of the responses and reinforcers and upon programming and recording procedures.

Ayllon and Azrin report a series of six experiments in each of which they demonstrated that target behavior *systematically* changed as a function of the token reinforcement. One experiment is typical of the procedures developed by these investigators. The response they were interested in consisted of off-ward work assignments. A patient would select from a list of available jobs for which he received tokens which he preferred. After ten days he was told that he could continue working on his job but there would be *no* tokens for the work. Of the eight patients involved, seven immediately selected another job which had previously been nonpreferred. The eighth patient switched a few days later. In the third phase of the experiment, the contingencies were reversed and the perferred jobs led to tokens. All eight patients immediately switched back to their previously preferred, original jobs.

The results of the six experiments demonstrated that the reinforcement procedure was effective in maintaining desired performance. In each experiment the performance fell to a near zero level when the established response-reinforcement relation was discontinued. On the other hand reintroduction of the reinforcement procedure restored performance almost immediately and maintained it at a high level.

The Ayllon and Azrin token economy functioned on a ward in a midwestern state hospital with a population of longterm female patients. Another token economy program (Atthowe and Krasner, 1968) was set up in a Veteran's Administration Hospital in California with male patients averaging fifty-eight years of age and a median length of hospitalization of twenty-four years. Most of these patients had been labeled chronic schizophrenics and the remaining had an organic label. As a group, their behavior was apathetic and indifferent, manifested by inactivity, dependency and social isolation. The procedures used were similar to those developed by Ayllon and Azrin. However, one of the major differences was in the amount of total control exerted by the experimenters. The Atthowe and Krasner program was designed to be an *open* ward on which patients could come and go, *if*, of course, they had the right number of tokens for the gate keeper. The token economy had to compete with the extra-ward economy which used dollars and cents as their tokens. Many kinds of economic problems had to be faced. To cope with those problems, special procedures had to be developed such as a banking system to foster savings, a monthly discount rate to cut down hoarding and yellow tokens to prevent stealing.

Prior to the introduction of tokens, most patients refused to go to any of the activities available to them and showed little interest in their environment. The patients sat or slept on the ward during the day. In effect, their behavior represented the end point of years of shaping of compliant and apathetic institutional behavior. The investigating team decided that there were better things in life for these people to do than to sit and waste away their lives. Among the valued things were enacting the role of responsible people who are adept at self-grooming, keeping their living facilities clean, dressing neatly, holding a job, and interacting with other people. Responsibility also involved their being responsive to normal social reinforcement. Thus each time tokens were given it was accompanied by social reinforcement such as "good," "I'm pleased," "fine job," and an explicit statement as to the contingencies involved, e.g. "You received three tokens because you got a good rating from your job supervisor."

This token economy program was a significant success as measured by changes in specified behavior, observer's ratings, and reactions of hospital staff. The changes in behaviors, such as attendance at group activity, were a function of the number of tokens (value) given for the activity. Group attendance increased as more tokens were given for them, and then decreased as the "pay off" returned to its previous value.

The greatest change was in the appearance and atmosphere of the ward and in the staff expectations of what the patients were capable of. The token program had an enormous effect on the attitudes of staff throughout the hospital. The staff found that they could have a therapeutic effect on patient behavior by the kinds of acts they performed. Staff morale increased and it became a matter of prestige to work on the token ward. Finally, in the hospital where the Atthowe and Krasner program was underway, two additional wards adopted similar token economies as a way of life because of its apparent usefulness in changing patient behavior.

Winkler (1968) reports the results of a token economy program which has many of the same features as that of the earlier programs with some additional novel features. Winkler's program was established in a closed female ward with patients averaging forty-nine years and twelve years hospitalization in Gladesville Hospital, New South Wales, Australia. The patients' behavior was characterized by an excessive amount of violence and screaming as well as apathy and general lack of response to the ward environment. Winkler gave particular emphasis to economic factors. For example, prices and wages were initially arranged so that the patients' average daily income tended to exceed their average daily expenditure. This basic economic fact of life, that income must equal or exceed outgo is a probable necessity for a viable economy. However, the economic aspects of token economy may be in dispute just as a Keyesian approach in our broader society may differ from a more standard conservative approach.

Winkler reported a significant improvement in staff morale as indicated by a drop in absenteeism. Absenteeism in the four months after the program began was 24 percent below the absenteeism for the four months before the program, while in a comparable ward, absenteeism over the same periods dropped only 3 percent. This emphasizes, as is clear in every study, that staff morale as mediated by the training program is a necessary ingredient in an operant program. It usually occurs when the staff gets feedback as to the effectiveness of its procedures.

Without exception, Winkler reports every type of behavior that was reinforced improved. In addition, behaviors not specifically in the program such as violence and loud noise decreased. Winkler also carried out a number of studies designed to determine whether the patients' behavior were really under the control of the tokens. In one experiment tokens for shoe cleaning were stopped for three weeks and then reintroduced. There was an immediate decrease of this behavior with a discontinuation of tokens and an immediate increase in their reintroduction. Similar results occurred with other behaviors.

THE BEHAVIOR THERAPIST AS TRAINER

One of the most important of recent developments is the continued movement in the direction of the behavior therapist as trainer. This follows from the kind of model which we have been describing. This has developed on a line from the earlier operant conditioning role. There are several models for the training, perhaps the most clearly worked out by Tharp and Wetzel (1969). In their report of the behavior research project undertaken in Tuscon, Arizona, they describe the relationship among four environmental figures: the consultant, the trainer, the mediator and the trainee. The traditional relationship in psychotherapy has been between the therapist and the patient and includes all of the behaviors involved in these two social roles. The next step by daring therapists involved adding a key person to the therapeutic situation, a person directly involved with the patient such as a parent or a spouse. But this was still done with a disease model framework. The rationale was that the disease or pathology had to be cured in the spouse or parent before the patient could cure his own disease. After all, diseases are catching and so may their cure be. A variation of this theme is to view the family itself as the unit of illness, hence that which is to be treated, or a variation of this which views the patient as a pathogenic agent with reciprocal pathogenisis in the family. That is, as one member of the family gets better another may get worse. It is very difficult to break out of the disease analogy.

The first variation offered by the behavior therapist began to work with the parent as a mediator or intervening trainer, not as a sick patient. The behavior therapist trained the parent in techniques of modifying the behavior of the child. A number of things were necessary in order to move to the next stage. First and most important it was necessary to have a set of principles which can be taught to the parent and which the parent can follow in his dealings with the child. The most important characteristic of these principles must be that they work. The evidence at this point seems to be that the behavior therapy or operant conditioning principles do indeed work. But there are more changes implied than simply transmitting a set of principles. As an old style practicing therapist I know that in the past, if a parent told me of difficulties with a child and asked me for specific advice as to what to do, I would reply to the parent that if she really loved the child or accepted the child then all would be well. Or if she could solve her own problems, and who indeed has no problems, then all would be well. Needless to say this reinforces any feelings of guilt on the part of the parents by implying the children's difficulties are the parent's fault. On the other hand, training the parent as a behavior modifier puts the parent in a more objective educational role vis a vis the child. This in itself affects the behavior of the parents. Now there is something specific they can do and see the consequences of what they do.

The key word in the new model is that of training. Implicitly and explicitly we are moving in the direction of the model of the therapist traning an intermediary to modify the behavior of the individual whose behavior had gotten him into the social labeling process. Tharp and Wetzel (1969) referred to the consultant, mediator and target.

CASE REPORTS

Another series of operant studies are essentially case reports, although they may involve some own-control procedures. They are of significance for the fact that they suggest areas of investigation for which more carefully controlled research studies may be applied. Such a study is that of Burgess (1968) on the application of contingency management to depressive behaviors. Depression may well be the last type of behavior to come within the behavior therapy paradigm. It has only been briefly referred to in the behavior therapy literature (Ferster, 1966; Lazarus, 1968). Burgess followed the implication of Ferster's view of depression resulting as a consequence of decreased reinforcement by arguing that a broad class of active, task-oriented responses can be labeled a performing behavior class. Retarded motor response rate, sad face and body appearances, and mournful verbalizations can be labeled a depressive behavior class. "As the frequency of performing behaviors begins to diminish, the very absence of reinforcement becomes the occasion for reinforcement. Concurrent with the extinction of performing behaviors may be the conditioned acquisition of depressive behaviors." It would follow from this analysis that the treatment procedures should involve the reversal of all contingencies. Reinforcement should be made contingent upon performing behaviors and depressive behaviors not being responded to should extinguish.

Following this paradigm, Burgess reports on the treatment of six clients seen in a university counseling center. The treatment methods ran as follows: If the history of the individual indicated the loss of a specific reinforcer which was available, efforts to reinstate it were made. If reinforcement losses were more generalized or nonspecific, the client was required from the first to emit a few performing behaviors which required minimal effort for completion. The client's attention was brought to the importance of successful completion rather than to the nature or value of the task. Gradually task requirements were increased so that behaviors accelerated in frequency, duration, quality, and successively approximated former behaviors from the client's repertoire. If available, a mate was taught to augment treatment by providing reinforcement specified according to prescribed contingencies. Clients were seen daily for the first week to maximize therapist reinforcing power and then seen with decreasing frequency as natural reinforcers began to become effective. Therapist attention and approval were used as reinforcers during the interviews as the clients reported either orally or in writing about their activities. No attention was paid to depressive behaviors after the first interview. "It should be noted that techniques changed as a function of individual reinforcement histories, contingencies, and environmental components." Burgess concluded that ". . . contingency management, which promotes reinforcement for the completion of performing behaviors and extinction of depressive behaviors seems to be effective for the treatment of depression when reinstatement of a reinforcer cannot be accomplished. All clients were able to perform in their life situation with at least passable facility within three weeks of treatment inauguration. Case reports, however, are not adequate to establish the efficacy of any treatment method. The need for controlled research is obvious."

A variation of the case report is represented by those studies which are more systematically own-control designed. They also derive from the earlier operant investigations. They combine a research approach with clinical applications (a "real life" genuine problem). They use a baseline period which measures the target behavior before any attempt at modification as a comparison point from which to measure the effectiveness of the procedure. They stress quantification and measurement of behavior often with the individual involved trained to quantify his own behavior. The ABA, off-on-off design is usually used. Social influence procedures are usually used in such a way as to maximize the likelihood of the operant procedures working. There is usually a follow-up over a period of some time. There is some attempt to determine if there has been changes in other behaviors which may be related to the target behaviors. They may move directly into the home as the locus for setting the conditions for change. As a prototype of these studies and as one of the most interesting and ingenious of them, the report by Stuart (1968) is cited.

The design was an own-control one with a baseline period, a treatment period, and then a follow-up report. The general framework was that of treatment of marital problems. Stuart presents certain assumptions about the character of marital interaction upon which his treatment procedure rests. These assumptions are important because they lay the basis for the extension of the operant approach into the ordinary everyday activities of individuals seeking help in an outpatient setting. Stuart assumes that, ". . . the exact pattern of interaction which takes place between a husband and his wife at any point in time is the most rewarding of all of the currently available alternatives. While the specifics may vary for each couple, most married adults expect to enjoy reciprocal relations with their partners. In order to modify an unsuccessful marital interaction, it is essential to develop the power of each partner to mediate rewards for the other." Based upon this formulation, the "operant interpersonal approach" (a term which Stuart uses in a manner similar to that of King, Armitage and Tilton, 1966) seeks to construct a situation in which the frequency and intensity of mutual positive reinforcement is increased. The treatment procedure then follows from this assumption in a logical manner.

The first step is to train the couple in the logic of the approach. The next step is to ask each of the two partners to list the three behaviors which each would like to accelerate in the other. Even this phase comprises elements of training, that of training people in the ways of observing and conceptualizing just what is a behavioral sequence. The third step is to train each individual in transferring the observed data onto a graph on which each person is to keep a record of the other's positive behavior. Step four consists of working out a series of exchanges of desired behaviors. "The typical couple complain of a lack of communication which is a euphemism for a failure to reinforce each other." At this point Stuart introduced a token system into the home situation. Stuart reports on the use of such a system with four couples who had sought treatment in a last effort to avoid divorce. One behavior which was much desired by each of the wives was that of having the husband converse with them more fully. The wives were instructed to purchase a timer and to give the husband a token after each hour in which the husband talked for a sufficient time with the wife to meet her criterion. However, an important part of the procedure was that the wife must feed back to the husband within the first thirty minutes of each hour cues as to his performance if it is unsatisfactory. If she fails to do this he must be given a token at the end of the hour even if he did not perform adequately. With the four couples, tokens were redeemable at the husband's request "from a menu stressing physical affection." A different "menu" was constructed for each couple which took into account the baseline level of sexual activity, the desired level of activity, and the number of hours available for nonsexual (conversational) interchange. On this basis, husbands were charged three tokens for kissing, "lightly petting" with their wives, five tokens for "heavy petting," and fifteen tokens for intercourse. The results indicated that, as compared with baseline measures, the "rates of conversation and sex increased sharply after the start of treatment and continued through twenty-four and forty-eight week followups." The participants were asked to fill out inventories about their own satisfaction and their perception of their spouse's satisfaction in marriage. These reports also increased dramatically as the behaviors changed. The actual sessions which were held with the therapist (by each individual couple) numbered only seven, during the first, fourth, the sixth, eighth and tenth weeks of the treatment program.

This study emphasizes most of the major points about the operant approach. In effect, the individual is trained so that he is able to provide new stimuli to the key people in his life so as to elicit different behavior from them. "Each spouse was directed in specific modifications of his own behavior in an effort to modify the behavioral environment in which his partner's behavior occurred." Actually the therapist did not introduce anything really new in terms of behavior. Stuart points out that he merely suggested behaviors which had doubtless been requested, cajoled and demanded by each party many times in the past. In that sense they were of no different an order than the many items of behavior which pay off for a hospitalized patient in a token economy (in the one instance conversing more, in the other self-grooming). But in this instance the therapist clarified and spelled out the contingencies involved. He introduced the clear expectation of change in the partners and, most important of all, he removed the situation from that of a coercive context. In the home situation when a request is put in the form of a demand, which is what had been occurring in these families, then adherence to the request involves the reinforcing of "demands," something usually held to be undesirable by most people. Nor should the importance of the game-like qualities which the therapist gave to the treatment be ignored. In fact, the game was termed "prostitution" because "all games must have names and prostitution appealed to the fantasies of all concerned."

SUMMARY

At this point I'd like to summarize the major points that have been made.

1. A model of man which argues for viewing human behavior as primarily learned, and unusual behaviors learned and modified as all behaviors. We are dealing with a social labeling process, not intrinsically abnormal behaviors.

2. It follows that if we are not dealing with sick behavior then the province of dealing with these problems does not belong to any one healing profession, be it psychiatry, psychology, or social work.

3. There is now a clear set of behavioral principles which can be applied to change human behavior and most importantly can be taught to human beings.

4. This extends enormously the range of potential help to human beings in their everyday problems. This means that increasingly the locus of help to others will move from the office, clinic and hospital to the home, school, the community and the planning boards of future society.

5. There are important implications for the professional role of the modifier, consultant, programmer, therapist.

6. If environmental contact does determine behavior, as behavior therapists say, then this opens the door to social and ec-

onomic educational planning in addition to rehabilitation or undoing the past mistakes.

REFERENCES

1. Atthowe, J. and Krasner, L.: A preliminary report on the application of contingent reinforcement procedures (Token Economy) on a 'chronic' psychiatric ward. *J Abnorm Psychol, 73:*37-43, 1968.
2. Ayllon, T.: Intensive treatment of psychotic behavior by stimulus satiation and food reinforcement. *Behav Res Ther, 1:*53-61, 1963.
3. Ayllon, T. and Haughton, E.: Control of the behavior of schizophrenic patients by food. *J Exp Anal Behav, 5:*343-352, 1962.
4. Ayllon, T. and Michael, J.: The psychiatric nurse as a behavioral engineer. *J Exp Anal Behav, 2:*323-334, 1959.
5. Ayllon, T. and Azrin, N.: The measurement and reinforcement of behavior of psychotics. *J Exp Anal Behav, 8:*343-352, 1965.
6. Bachrach, A. (Ed.): *Experimental Foundations of Clinical Psychology.* New York, Basic Books, 1962.
7. Bandura, A.: Psychotherapy as a learning process. *Psychol Bull, 58:*143-159, 1961.
8. Berg, I. and Bass, B. (Eds.): *Conformity and Deviation.* New York, Harper, 1961.
9. Biderman, A. and Zimmer, H. (Eds.): *The Manipulation of Human Behavior.* New York, Wiley, 1961.
10. Bockoven, J.: *Moral Treatment in American Psychiatry.* New York, Springer, 1963.
11. Burgess, E.: The modification of depressive behaviors. In Rubin, R. and Franks, C. (Eds.): *Advances in Behavior Therapy, 1968.* New York, Academic Press, 1969, pp. 193-200.
12. Dain, N.: *Concepts of Insanity in the United States, 1789-1865.* New Brunswick, New Jersey, Rutgers University Press, 1964.
13. Eysenck, H. (Ed.): *Behavior Therapy and the Neuroses.* New York, Pergamon, 1960.
14. Ferster, C.: Animal behavior and mental illness. *Psychol Rec, 16:*345-356, 1966.
15. Goldstein, A.: *Therapist-Patient Expectancies in Psychotherapy.* New York, Pergamon, 1962.
16. Grossberg, J.: Behavior Therapy: A Review. *Psychol Bull, 62:*73-88, 1964.
17. Kalish, H.: Behavior therapy. In Wolman, B. (Ed.): *Handbook of Clinical Psychology.* New York, McGraw-Hill, 1965.
18. King, G., Armitage, S. and Tilton, J.: A therapeutic approach to schizophrenics of extreme pathology: An operant-interpersonal method. *J Abn Soc Psychol, 61:*276-286, 1960.

19. Krasner, L. and Ullman, L. (Eds.): *Research in Behavior Modification.* New York, Holt, Rinehart and Winston, 1965.
20. Lazarus, A.: Learning theory and the treatment of depression. *Behav Res Ther, 6:*83-89, 1968.
21. Premack, D.: Toward empirical behavior laws. I: Positive reinforcement. *Psychol Rev, 66:*219-233, 1959.
22. Shapiro, A.: A contribution to a history of the placebo effect. *Behav Sci, 5:*109-135, 1960.
23. Skinner, B. F.: *Science and Human Behavior.* New York, MacMillan, 1953.
24. Staats, A.: A case in and a strategy for the extension of learning principles to problems of human behavior. In Krasner, L. and Ullman L. (Eds.): *Research in Behavior Modification.* New York, Holt, Rinehart and Winston, 1965, pp. 27-55.
25. Stuart, R.: Token reinforcement in marital treatment. In Rubin, R. and Franks, C. (Eds.): *Advances in Behavior Therapy, 1968.* New York, Academic Press, 1969, pp. 221-230.
26. Szasz, T.: *The Myth of Mental Illness: Foundations of a Theory of Personal Conduct.* New York, Hoeber-Harper, 1961.
27. Tharp, R. and Wetzel, J.: *Behavior Modification in the Natural Environment.* New York, Academic Press, 1969.
28. Ullman, L.: *Institution and Outcome: A Comparative Study of Psychiatric Hospitals.* New York, Pergamon, 1967.
29. Ullman, L. and Krasner, L. (Eds.): *Case Studies in Behavior Modification.* New York, Holt, Rinehart and Winston, 1965.
30. Ullman, L. and Krasner, L.: *A Psychological Approach to Abnormal Behavior.* Englewood Cliffs, Prentice-Hall, 1969.
31. Winkler, R.: Management of chronic psychiatric patients by a token reinforcement system. Paper presented at the Annual Meeting of the Australian Psychological Society, Brisbane, Australia, August, 1968.
32. Wolpe, J.: *Psychotherapy by Reciprocal Inhibition.* Stanford, California, Stanford University Press, 1958.

Chapter 29

BEHAVIOR MODIFICATION: SELECTED OPERANT TECHNIQUES AND PRINCIPLES

EDWIN J. THOMAS

THE FIELD of casework confronts at least two perplexing problems. The first is the relatively rudimentary state of the conceptualization of its techniques. Despite the articulate efforts of such scholars as Hollis, there still have been too few efforts to identify, codify, and conceptualize casework techniques.[1] Many new ones —and some old ones, too—have not yet been adequately explicated. In addition, important knowledge about behavioral maintenance and change that may have utility for casework exists in related behavioral science disciplines and helping professions and certain areas of social work practice.

The second problem concerns whether the techniques are actually effective. The results of evaluative studies of casework and other traditional forms of interpersonal helping have been consistently disappointing.[2] Despite occasional methodological shortcomings, enough careful studies have been done to sustain the conclusion that, in general, it has not yet been demonstrated that casework and related forms of conventional helping are effective. This is not to say that research has proved such treatment to be ineffective—that judgment has not been corroborated and probably never will be. As for the comparative effectiveness of the various conventional casework techniques themselves, even less is known. In fact, some of the inquiries done in related fields show that techniques such as insight therapy produce very modest results as compared with selected sociobehavioral techniques.[3]

The infusion of selected sociobehavioral techniques into social

Note: Originally: Selected socio-behavioral techniques and principles: An approach to interpersonal helping. Slightly abridged and reprinted with permission of the National Association of Social Workers, from *Social Work,* *13 (No. 1)*:12-25, Jan. 1968.

work practice may help. Many of these may directly augment the existing battery of conventional techniques in casework. Despite their newness in the therapeutic marketplace, sociobehavioral techniques have already been utilized with uncommon success in a variety of settings.[4] Although virtually no evaluative studies have yet been conducted on them in social work, the techniques evaluated in related fields have generally involved behavioral problems similar to those regularly dealt with in casework. Some sociobehavioral techniques may be readily adapted to the professional activities of caseworkers, as will be noted in the later discussion, and perhaps eventually we will find some use for all of them.

Furthermore, because some of the therapeutic activities in which caseworkers currently engage have sociobehavioral features, this review of selected techniques may serve to help crystallize and distinguish these sociobehavioral features of practice. As will be noted later, when applied to the techniques of behavioral maintenance or modification in casework, the sociobehavioral approach suggests fruitful, alternative ways to analyze selected, existing casework techniques.

ELEMENTS OF THE APPROACH

The sociobehavioral approach is a recent development. With the exception of a few pioneering efforts, many of the innovations in "behavioral practice" have occurred in the last twenty years, and most within the last ten years. The body of knowledge (which has an even longer history than this) that forms the basis of sociobehavioral theory derives mainly from research on learning and behavioral modification in the field of psychology, although behaviorally oriented research in such areas as personality, social psychology, and sociology has been relevant too. Practice, at present, consists largely of procedures and techniques from several emerging schools of behavioral therapy—the Pavlovian, the operant, the "personalistic," and that of the specialized technique (e.g. Wolpe's systematic desensitization). Increasingly, however, the practice is becoming more eclectic.

Despite important differences, all the behavioral approaches to therapeutic problems are based on several common assumptions. Only a few can be mentioned here.

First, most proponents agree about features of the nature of human behavior. Without denying differences in native endowment and the behavioral effects of organic and chemical factors, *behavioral approaches emphasize the learned aspects of behavior.* Learned behavior, including problem and deviant behavior, has natural, empirical antecedents, according to its advocates, and the behavior may be modified through application of the findings derived from research on learning and behavioral modification. In this sense, problem behavior is regarded as being no different from normal behavior, despite differences in response repertoires and in labels for the behavior.

By this time the reader has undoubtedly observed from the repeated use of the term "behavior" that behavior is viewed generically. The observable responses of human activity are behavior. All activity is pertinent—"thoughts," "affect," as well as the more obvious motor action—provided only that it is denotable through the senses of the observer. Real internal workings of mind occur, of course, and some of these have been studied scientifically by means of chemical and electrical indicators as well as through overt response. Although dubious hypothetical inner psychic states are not postulated, this view of behavior is much less narrow than is sometimes alleged. A good rule of thumb is that anything is fair game for behavioral analysis—"ego state," "defense," "habit," or whatever it happens to be called—if the behavior that controls the use of the verbal labels can be pointed to and known to an observer's senses.

Second, various assumptions are made about treatment. If a central assumption does indeed exist, it probably would be that *treatment consists of achieving behavioral maintenance or modification.* Modification, in turn, may be specified as the acquisition, strengthening, weakening, or elimination of behavior. In this context, treatment consists of the activities of the helper and others that serve to bring about desired modification or stabilization of the client's behavior. The roles of the helper as a modifier and stabilizer of behavior revolve mainly around producing direct behavioral change in the client, around instruction of the client on how he may alter the variables that control his behavior, or around behavioral "programming" of others so that they in turn may modify or maintain the client's behavior.

Third, behavioral approaches are based on the conviction that knowledge used in practice should have empirical corroboration. Every major school of behavioral therapy rests upon what would be considered a strong research edifice, at least in comparison with the conventional methods. Every major type of behavioral technique—for example, the operant group to be discussed later—has scores, if not hundreds, of laboratory studies behind it and now numerous applied research studies buttress the principles being used. (The reader may not realize that the principles of classical, Pavlovian conditioning rest upon over six thousand laboratory studies conducted with humans and animals.) Although the basic and applied research on which behavioral approaches are based varies in volume and quality, it is generally much superior to research connected with conventional techniques of interpersonal helping.

In this brief introduction some of the common assumptions in behavioral approaches have been stated, but there are some important uncommon ones as well. Also, many other general characteristics of the knowledge and practice of sociobehavioral theory exist, to say nothing of the specific researches and practices themselves. For lack of space, the reader is necessarily referred elsewhere.[5]

THE TECHNIQUES

In contrast to most familiar techniques, sociobehavioral techniques derive from knowledge about the modification and maintenance of behavior, they are specific behaviorally in their operations and consequences, and in their use they bear an explicit relationship to behavior designated as problem behavior, to the controlling conditions for such behavior, and to the treatment objectives. The basis for the assertions will be more apparent to the reader as the paper develops.

Although full agreement does not yet exist on what specific

techniques constitute a set that can be identified as sociobehavioral, there is already concurrence on the essential features of, and even the labels for, many of the techniques. Still, no satisfactory taxonomy has been developed to date.[6] As a matter of fact, this paper grew out of the author's efforts to find a way to order and systematize sociobehavioral techniques. Apparently, the most sensible way to do this is around two major axes. The first is the *class* of behavior dealt with (to be explained shortly) and the second is the specific concrete *operations* of the helper that will produce known consequences. The objectives of sociobehavioral intervention correspond directly to the known behavioral consequences produced by using these techniques. These objectives (and consequences) are the *acquisition, strengthening, maintenance, weakening, or elimination* of behavior.[7]

The discussion of selected operant techniques will illustrate these observations. Seventeen sociobehavioral techniques have been isolated and ordered through this framework by the author, but because of space limitations only five will be covered in this article.

SELECTED OPERANT TECHNIQUES AND PRINCIPLES

Operant behavior is one of at least two fundamental classes of behavior, the other class being respondent behavior (Chapters 31 and 32).[8] Operant behavior involves "voluntary" actions of the skeletal-muscular system. Here the striated muscles under the individual's "control" are implicated in the conditioning process. Walking, talking, writing, and many features of thinking are examples.

The main premise relating to the emergence and alteration of such behavior is that operant behavior is governed by its consequences.[9] The first recognition of operant behavior came from Thorndike, after he observed that cats who had some experience with a puzzle box could subsequently solve puzzles with greater ease. From this initial observation he formulated the Law of Effect, which stated essentially that behavior was influenced by the effects of such behavior in the environment.[10] Essentially, the operant techniques are names for specific "operations," or activities, that are known to produce identifiably different consequences for operant behavior.

Six operant techniques have been identified: positive reinforcement, extinction, differential reinforcement, response-shaping, punishment, and negative reinforcement. The first five are elaborated on in this article.

POSITIVE REINFORCEMENT

Let us begin with a case that derives from a demonstration project in which probation officers were trained to use various techniques of behavior modification.

Claire is a bright, reasonably attractive sixteen-year-old who was referred to the project for truancy, poor grades, and incorrigibility at home. The referral came from the local high school where it was stated that Claire was about to be expelled for being delinquent. The project staff persuaded the school to hold up expulsion for several days, during which time they instituted a new regimen with Claire's mother, the only parent in the home. At the time the staff intervened, Claire had been staying home from school and was threatening to run away. All money, the use of the telephone, and dating privileges had been withdrawn despite the fact that all these were potentially very powerful reinforcers for Claire and her mother had not provided any definite way for Claire to earn them back.

The intervention plan, agreed to by the mother, Claire, and a staff member, consisted of the following. Telephone privileges and weekend dates were made contingent on attending school all day. If Claire attended all classes for a given day, the school attendance officer would dispense a note to Claire at the end of each day. Upon presenting the note to the mother, Claire would then earn telephone privileges that day (both receiving and calling out). If four out of five notes were obtained during the week, one weekend date was earned; two weekend dates were earned if five out of five notes were sent home. The use of the phone on the weekend was not included in the plan. Although the mother had always been inconsistent and ineffective in her relations with Claire, she was surprised to discover that Claire accepted the plan. Despite many family difficulties, Claire attended school regularly from the first day of intervention. The plan was altered after a month so that Claire would have to receive only two notes a week. If classes were attended on Monday, Tuesday, and Wednesday, one note was required to certify to this; and this note earned the privilege of one weekend night out. A second note, on Friday, certified to the full attendance on Thursday and Friday, which earned a second night out on the weekend. Telephone privileges were removed entirely from contingency. Notes were stopped entirely about seven weeks later.

Claire's school attendance improved immediately. Whereas during the period prior to intervention Claire had missed thirty days of school out of the first forty-six days, she was only absent illegally twice during the three months that the project was involved. What is more impressive, however, was that she was never absent illegally again following termination of the project, and this involved a period of the entire second semester of school. The project staff was thus successful in preventing Claire from being expelled from school and probably from running away from home, and accomplished this with very small investment of staff time.[11]

This case illustrates various points. (a) Before the staff intervened, the indigenous and powerful reinforcers in the situation—money, telephone use, and dating—had been withdrawn, and Claire had no way of earning them back. Other behavioral controls had obviously not been effective either. (b) The treatment regimen consisted essentially of restoring these reinforcers, making their availability contingent on attending school. (c) There was a schedule of reinforcement—every desired set of responses was reinforced. Telephone privileges were provided each day and depended on whether Claire attended school that day. The number of weekend dates also depended on how many days she attended school. Later the schedule was altered so that, for example, telephone use was taken off "contingency." (d) There were no other apparent elements in the contingency system. No punishment was provided for not going to school, only the absence of available indigenous reinforcers.

As for the concept of reinforcement itself, it should be observed that there are related concepts in social work practice. Notions such as "reassurance" and "support" often pertain to phenomena for which the concept of reinforcement would be appropriate. However, these practice concepts do not *specify* the behavior of the worker that produces given consequences and may not be considered synonymous with reinforcement. The fact that the reinforcement of client behavior occurs widely in social work under different names should not be confused with the fact that, in general, reinforcement is not often utilized as a technique in casework in the deliberate, conscious manner described here.

Positive reinforcement may be defined as the use of stimuli following a response in such a way that the future rate of responding is increased. Any stimulus that is used following a response and serves to increase the rate of responding may therefore be called a positive reinforcer.

Some reinforcers—called primary—function innately to increase the rate of responding. Food, sex, and water are examples, provided that the organism is in a state of deprivation ("need"). Shock, cold and rest are additional primary reinforcers. Other reinforcers, commonly called *secondary* (or learned) reinforcers, have acquired their capacity to increase the rate of responding because of a learning history in which they have been paired together in time with various conditions of primary reinforcement. Money, approval, domination, submissiveness, and affection are generally, but not always, examples of such secondary reinforcers. These also illustrate a third type, namely, the *generalized secondary reinforcer*, which is the reinforcer that has been learned on the basis of its relationship to primary reinforcers and whose effectiveness, in general, is presumed to be relatively independent of states of deprivation involving such primary reinforcers.

Both primary and generalized secondary reinforcers have been used frequently in intervention based on principles of behavior modification. Thus, institutionalized psychotic patients who had had a history of not feeding themselves were enabled to eat regularly and on time merely by making the availability of food contingent on eating behavior.[12] Verbal behavior in interviews has been shown to be clearly affected through the use of such generalized secondary reinforcers as a smile, a nod, or "mmm-hmm."[13] Through the use of diverse reinforcers that may be exchanged for "tokens" (e.g. poker chips or other substitutes for money), institutionalized mental patients have been enabled effectively to perform a variety of on- and off-ward jobs.[14]

Positive reinforcement is widely applicable to problems that involve strengthening and maintaining behavior. However, it may also be used to weaken behavior, depending on the nature of the schedule of reinforcement used.[15] In general, it is believed that reinforcement is not effective for acquiring new behavior. Rather, reinforcement has been found to affect the *rate* of behavior, once behavior has been acquired or has occurred. And, properly speaking, it may not be used to eliminate behavior.[16]

Positive reinforcement is considered to be of primary use in strengthening behavior. Following are listed some of the conditions that relate to its effectiveness when used toward this end:

1. The response to be reinforced must first be emitted, otherwise reinforcement is impossible.

2. Reinforcement must not be delayed; in general, the more immediate the reinforcement, the better. (It has been found that in general reinforcement is most effective when given at .5 of a second after the response.)

3. Reinforcement of every desired response emitted is most effective for establishing behavior.[17]

4. Not reinforcing every desired response during response establishment, while less effective in achieving immediate high rates of responding, is generally more effective in producing responses that endure after reinforcement is terminated.

5. The stimuli suitable to reinforce one individual's behavior may not be the most appropriate for another. In general, each individual has his own profile of reinforcers.[18] Recent research suggests that one important clue to what the reinforcing conditions are in the profile is simply the rank order of activities in which a person engages in his free time.[19]

EXTINCTION

Extinction has two features. Its operation consists of withholding the reinforcer when a response, previously reinforced by that reinforcer, is emitted. The consequence of this operation, if completely and steadfastly maintained, is to reduce the rate of responding to the original level.

It is important not to confuse extinction with punishment. The extinction procedure merely involves the *withholding* of the reinforcing stimuli that previously sustained the rate of respond-

ing. No "aversive" stimuli are presented and no positive reinforcers removed.

In social work practice, one may find some partial analogs to
the extinction process in such activities as the withholding of support, reassurance, or "limit-setting." But not all behavior so
labeled is necessarily an extinction procedure. The concept of
extinction itself and the principles relating to it are not part of
social work's present conceptual framework.

The following case example involves a relatively common
problem in institutional contexts and some others as well. It refers
to approach behaviors, such as having persons come to see the
workers, in which there is no therapeutic gain associated with
contact.

> Consider the case of Lucille, a patient in the mental hospital who
> had been making frequent visits to the nurses' office for a period of
> two years. During the pretreatment study it was found that she en-
> tered the nurses' office an average of sixteen times a day. The nurses
> had resigned themselves to this activity on the grounds that such efforts
> as pushing her back bodily onto the ward had failed in the past and
> because the patient had been classified as mentally defective and
> therefore "too dumb" to understand.
>
> In order to extinguish the problem behavior in question, the nur-
> ses were informed simply that during the program the patient must not
> be given any reinforcement (attention) for entering the nurses' office.
> It was found that as soon as the extinction schedule was introduced,
> there was a gradual and continuing diminution of entries to the
> nurses' office. The average frequency was down to two entries per
> day by the seventh week of extinction, at which time the program was
> terminated.[20]

The diminution of behavior during extinction will occur
gradually or rapidly, depending on the maintenance schedule. Besides its downhill slope, the extinction curve typically has two
other features worth noting. One is that immediately after the
withholding of reinforcement in the extinction procedure, there
is often a temporary increase in the rate of responding. What appears to be a clinical instance of this will be seen in the case
example below. The other feature of the curve is that *as the behavior diminishes* to a low level there occurs quite regularly a
small but temporary increase in responding, called a spontaneous

recovery. If reinforcement continues to be withheld, this small apparent recovery of the response will again diminish.

Extinction is probably one of the most important means of reducing or eliminating operant responses and has wide applicability in social work. Undesirable motor habits, verbal behavior such as "psychotic talk," voluntary crying, and many forms of misbehavior and difficulties associated with child management may all be handled effectively through extinction.

Anyone attempting to make use of extinction in practice should anticipate the characteristics associated with the extinction curve mentioned earlier. Furthermore, there may be minor emotional reactions of a relatively temporary sort associated with the introduction of an extinction procedure.

The principal difficulty associated with the use of extinction derives from the fact that most of the operant responses called problem behavior have typically been sustained over long periods of time by intermittent reinforcement. As such, these responses are highly resistant to extinction. Thus the extinction process must be carefully controlled and monitored. Given a response history of intermittent reinforcement, it is especially important that extinction be abrupt and complete in order to differentiate it from intermittent reinforcement. The results of research in this area are absolutely clear: The worker should cease reinforcement completely. If he has little control over the reinforcement community, the chances of utilizing extinction successfully are greatly reduced.

DIFFERENTIAL REINFORCEMENT

Differential reinforcement consists of a particular amalgamation of positive reinforcement and extinction. Positive reinforcement is used to strengthen prosocial behavior while the extinction technique is used to reduce or eliminate problem behavior.

There are numerous examples of the use of differential reinforcement in behavior modification. Rational speech has been reinforced while an extinction procedure has been adopted for a patient's psychotic talk; overactive behavior has been extinguished for mentally retarded children in a playroom while also reinforcing more sedentary activities; operant crying in a nursery school has been extinguished while the use of words, as incompatible responses to crying, were simultaneously reinforced; operant vomiting has been extinguished while at the same time reinforcing alternative prosocial behaviors. Indeed, most of the examples labeled reinforcement in the literature on behavior modification are really differential reinforcement.

The use of differential reinforcement to alter the verbal behavior of a ten-year-old girl is illustrated in the following example.

> Mary was a member of a treatment group for delinquent girls and among her problems was that she talked so rapidly she could not be understood. The behavior was apparently maintained by the attention that this obtained from others. Thus they would say, "Mary, what did you say?" and "Slow down." The behavior antagonized adults as well as children and the latter often became so irritated that they attacked her physically as well as verbally.
>
> In order to have Mary speak more slowly and understandably, the following plan was instituted. The other children in the treatment group were encouraged to ignore rapid talking and not to respond to it. Furthermore, the children were encouraged to pay attention to Mary when she spoke slowly and to compliment her for this, and the social worker acted similarly.
>
> It is interesting that during the course of the first meeting following the implementation of the plan, Mary began to speak faster and faster (apparently revealing here the slight increase in responding, following the introduction of extinction, of which we spoke before), but she soon reduced the speed of her talking at the end of the meeting. During the second meeting she occasionally speeded up but usually talked slowly. Several girls commented that they liked Mary better. During the third meeting Mary speeded up only once and then, during the same episode, reduced her speed again. In subsequent meetings, her tempo was slowed so that persons could easily follow her.
>
> Of more than incidental interest is that in the course of the five-week period Mary was no longer the object of criticism or physical abuse by the girls. Furthermore, her complaining disappeared and she seemed to be better liked, at least by two of the girls in the group.[21]

Because differential reinforcement consists of positive reinforcement for some behaviors as well as the extinction of others, the comments made earlier about some of the practical considerations involving the use of positive reinforcement as well as extinction are likewise applicable to differential reinforcement.

RESPONSE-SHAPING

Schwitzgebel and Kolb have experimented with an unusual means to reach recalcitrant adolescent delinquents. Although there are many features of their change effort, only the efforts pertaining to response-shaping are referred to here:

> Young teen-age delinquent boys were both the clients in the project as well as the subjects of the research. At the outset, these hard-to-reach delinquents were met in neighborhood contexts, largely on street corners, and simply asked if they would like to take a job talking into a tape recorder. Each prospective subject was told that he could talk about anything he wanted to and could quit whenever he wished. He was warned, however, that some of the other employees had changed their opinions about many things, but that this was not really a condition of the job.
>
> Periodic bonuses were given, both in the form of primary and secondary reinforcers, in addition to paying the subjects for coming for the interviews. If a subject came for an interview he was paid and, depending on the other behaviors he engaged in, given additional bonuses. If the subject did not come for the interview, the researcher would seek the boy out a few days later and try to get him to come, somewhat on his own terms. If a boy came late, he would be welcomed and nothing would be said about his tardiness. Whenever a boy came he would be welcomed, but if he came at a time that was an improvement over his prior tardiness or earliness, he would be given a special bonus. Most of the boys eventually ended up coming precisely on time, over the course of several sessions.
>
> Furthermore, the boys began to talk about themselves in considerable detail, established strong positive relationships to the professional helpers functioning as researchers, and engaged in a number of pro-social tasks such as preparing for a driver's license test, building simple electronic equipment, or answering correspondence.[22]

As part of the general response-shaping procedure, the following points merit elaboration. First, the investigators began with high probability behaviors. In effect, they were "beginning where the client is." Specifically, the boys were met in their own neighborhoods, they were placed in the role of subjects and employees rather than of clients or delinquents, and they were asked to en-

gage in an activity that for most of them was relatively easy, namely, talking about themselves or their favorite subjects. Second,
there was a step-by-step successive approximation of desired
terminal behaviors. Attendance behavior was emphasized at the
outset, then various subjects that the boys talked about received
bonuses, and, still later, the prosocial tasks in which the boys
engaged were not only used to break the monotony but also to
train work-related behaviors. Third, differential reinforcement
was utilized throughout the procedure. First there was reinforcement for coming, then additional bonuses were given for coming
on time; later, bonuses were given for talking about particular
subjects and engaging in certain activities.

Although many gradual step-by-step procedures are used in
social work practice, there is no concept in social work that is
really synonymous with response-shaping. Two principles are
involved in the achievement of response-shaping: differential reinforcement of selected responses and the use of differential reinforcement in a step-by-step procedure that involves the gradual
shifting of the criterion of differential reinforcement for successive
approximations of the desired terminal behavior.

Response-shaping presents a general solution to the apparent
dilemma posed by reinforcement theory and by the practitioner's
frequent need to reinforce desired behavior that has a low probability. Often the worker may wish to develop response strength
of behaviors not presently in the client's repertoire—behaviors
that are new, complex, or not easily accessible. For example, a
social worker may wish to reinforce sensible talk in a psychotic
who has been mute for many years. A prime requirement of reinforcement, however, is that the response to be reinforced must
first be emitted. How then can one reinforce a response that is
most unlikely to appear freely? Shaping offers a solution to this
dilemma, for it involves the selective use of reinforcement to ap-
proximate successively the desired behavior.

The behavioral phenomenon on which response-shaping
builds is called *response induction.* In effect, this phenomenon involves the tendency of the strength of a reinforced response to increase the strength of more closely related responses than more

distantly related responses. Thus, if one is attempting to reinforce audible speech for a person who speaks very softly, the reinforcement of higher levels of volume will tend to increase the probability of emitting responses having higher volume more than responses having lower volume. By means of response induction, the differential reinforcement of only closer and closer approximations of desired terminal behavior progressively strengthens these approximations while it simultaneously weakens more remote responses.

Sidman has suggested some rules relevant to shaping. These are as follows:

1. Behavior must be reinforced immediately; a delay of even a few seconds may result in the inadvertent reinforcement of undesired behavior.

2. The shaper must not give too many reinforcements for approximations of the desired response. Excessive reinforcement at one of the intermediate levels may result in no further movement toward the final objective.

3. The shaper must not give too few reinforcements of approximations of the desired response. Each response level must be securely established before proceeding to the following one, and this can only be done through an adequate reinforcement period. Sidman believes that inadequate reinforcement is a primary reason for failures of shaping.

4. There must be careful specification of the response to be reinforced at each successive level.[23]

PUNISHMENT

Punishment expresses still another relationship between the rate of responding and consequences in the environment. Tyler and Brown have reported an intriguing demonstration of the use of mild punishment to control the misbehavior of delinquent boys committed by the courts to a training school.

One of the problems met by the staff was the misbehavior of the boys while playing pool during free time. Misbehavior in this situation consisted of such behaviors as breaking the rules of the game, throwing pool cues, and scuffling. The punishing regimen consisted simply of the matter-of-fact removal of the offending boy, immediately following his offense, to a small time-out room for a period of fifteen minutes. It was found that this simple operation served to suppress the level of infractions without untoward side effects.

The condition of mild punishment was compared with a condition of no punshment in which conventional verbal controls were attempted. "Now cut that out," "I'm warning you," and "Don't let that happen again" were among the verbal controls. It was found that punishment was much more effective than these verbal controls, although the effect of punishment, following the removal of time-out regulations, was temporary.

The mild punishment was easy to administer and worked despite its mildness in a situation in which it was alleged that much more harsh punishment was relatively common. Furthermore, the punishment worked when in competition with peer group influences, which often are stronger when placed in competition with staff influences.[24]

Punishment is used at various times in social work practice but usually the punishing behavior is cloaked with euphemistic labels. Thus one speaks of the worker's "expression of disapproval," of "withdrawing privileges," of the "use of authority," and of "limit-setting behavior." The writer will use here a more exact conception of punishment consistent with the usage of Azrin and Holz.[25] These researchers emphasize punishment as being a consequence of responding that reduces the future rate of that response. There are two operations following an operant response that may have this effect. One is the presentation of a stimulus that is usually "aversive," and the other is the removal of a positive reinforcing condition, such as is illustrated in time out from reinforcement. The reduction of the rate of responding, if it is the essential consequence of these operations, may be temporary, as was illustrated in the case demonstration, or it may be a continuing partial reduction or even complete suppression.

There are many misconceptions about punishment in this society. Likely ones can be illustrated through imaginary criticisms of the demonstration just described. It might be contended, for instance, that the use of punishment of even this mild sort was downright unethical on grounds that it was aversive. It is not the aversiveness alone that is important, for life is rarely devoid of naturally or socially induced adversity. What is important are the effects of aversiveness. Not only were there no side effects in the demonstration described, the research literature indicates that only under highly restricted conditions are there likely to be any of the dire effects sometimes alleged to accompany punishment.[26] (A related issue is the general question of ethics, which is touched on briefly below.)

Another possible criticism is that punishment has an ephemeral, short-lived effect. This is really an instance of the general criticism that punishment is ineffective and therefore of no use. This has been amply demonstrated to be false in recent inquiries. Furthermore, the mild punishment used in this study at least had the virtue of controlling misbehavior in a situation in which many conventional verbal controls had been singularly ineffective.

Still another criticism of punishment is that other behavior-reducing procedures are more effective. The research evidence on this matter is not at all unequivocal, although there is some evidence in one comparison of five behavior-reducing procedures that punishment was the most effective by all comparison criteria.[27] It remains to be seen whether there are alternative procedures that are as effective as punishment in reducing behavior.

Punishment is clearly a technique to be used for the reduction of behavior, either to weaken it or in some cases to eliminate it. Recent research suggests that in order to increase the efficacy of the punishing operations at least the following should be kept in mind:

1. The punishment should be neither so mild as to be inconsequential nor so strong as to be immobilizing or devastating.

2. The punishment should be tied immediately to the response that one wishes to reduce and should be administered matter-of-factly after the response.

3. Punishment of every response to be reduced should generally be used for obtaining immediate suppressive effects under the conditions during which the punishment is applied.

4. Alternative prosocial responses incompatible with the punished response should be allowed and reinforced.[28]

Among the side effects that have to be seriously weighed when considering the possible uses of punishment is that by using it a professional helper may come to be avoided. Azrin and Holz have observed that perhaps the most serious and well-documented side effect of punishment is the possibility that the punishing agent may lose control of the person punished.[29] This possibility has of course been well-recognized in social work practice. Another side effect is the possibility of aggression directed against the punishing agent.

The general matter of the ethical use of punishment is a most valid concern. There are at least four factors that must be weighed when appraising the ethical suitability of using punishment. One is the aversiveness (and social costs in general) to the client and others of *not* reducing the problem behavior; another is the availability of alternative behavior-reducing techniques that would do the job with less cost to clients; a third is the probable effectiveness of punishment in achieving suppression, and it should be effectively reducing or otherwise its use is irresponsible; and a fourth is the side effects for the client and helper that would result from the use of punishment.

COMPLEX TECHNIQUES

Techniques are designated as complex because more than one operant technique may be involved or, more commonly, features of both operant and respondent techniques are entailed. Also, these are almost always used in order to accomplish at least two behavioral objectives. Behavioral rehearsal, for example, is often used to reduce problems responses as well as to increase alternative pro-social responding.

The complex techniques are *negative practice*,[30] *satiation*,[31] *stimulus-shaping ("fading")*,[32] *verbal instructions*,[33] *behavioral rehearsal* (one aspect of role-playing),[34] *rule-making*,[35] *model presentation*,[36] and *position-structuring*.[37] There will no doubt be others to add to the list as theoretical and practical work continues.[38]

SOME MISTAKEN CONCEPTIONS

The sociobehavioral approach is only one of several alternatives with potential utility in practice. But as a new viewpoint, it is subject to many of the same ethical issues customarily raised with the introduction of any powerful technique or theory. Ethical issues were raised when psychoanalytic theory first was introduced, and now some critics of sociobehavioral theory contend that it is unethical (e.g. that it is "Machiavellian" or "manipulative"). One can only reply that the knowledge of the sociobehavioral approach, like all knowledge, is instrumental, and as such may be used for good or ill. Knowledge is itself ethically neutral and values become engaged only when knowledge is used. The ethical issue is generally not applicable if this new knowledge is used within the context of existing professional ethics.

Another label sometimes applied to this approach is that the sociobehavioral approach is "mechanistic." Knowledge is not "mechanistic," unless perhaps it is knowledge *about* physical mechanisms or psychodynamic mechanisms. Again, this allegation applies to its use. The method of change suggested by the sociobehavioral approach requires for its implementation a well-trained, ethical, intelligent, and sensitive helper. The qualities in practitioners valued in current social work practice will not become outmoded by this new orientation since similar skills are needed for both approaches.

The third question often raised about a new treatment strategy is the extent to which it has been clinically tested and verified. We will find that a great deal of this knowledge has been applied in diverse contexts, many of these being similar to social work endeavors; but social workers have just begun to absorb this knowledge. As indicated before, there is already an impressive body of evaluative literature on the subject garnered from these related fields.[39]

CONCLUSION

Social work should give serious attention to the selective and careful use of these techniques. Because they promise to make social work practice more effective, they cannot be ignored. Admittedly they cannot be adopted *en masse* and uncritically. They must be tried out and the results appraised. In this way, sociobehavioral techniques will get the least of what they deserve—a fair trial in the court of professional opinion.

NOTES AND REFERENCES

1. Hollis, Florence: *Casework: A Psychosocial Therapy.* New York, Random House, 1964.

2. For psychotherapy *see,* for example, Eysenck, Hans J.: The effects of psychotherapy: An evaluation. *J Consult Psychol, 16 (No. 5):*319-323, October, 1952; for a more recent and detailed review *see* Eysenck and Rachman, Stanley: *The Causes and Cures of Neurosis.* San Diego, Knapp, 1965, pp. 242-267; and for reviews of evaluative studies in family services *see* Briar, Scott: Family Services. In Maas, Henry S. (Ed.): *Five Fields of Social Service: Reviews of Research.* New York, National Association of Social Workers, 1966, pp. 16-21. An important evaluative study in social work having a control group design is Meyer, Henry J., Borgatta, Edgar F. and Jones, Wyatt C.: *Girls at Vocational High: An Experiment in Social Work Intervention.* New York, Russell Sage Foundation, 1965.

3. *See,* for example, Paul, Gordon L.: *Insight vs. Desensitization: An Experiment in Anxiety Reduction.* Stanford, Stanford University Press, 1966; Lang, Peter J. and Lazovik, A. David: Experimental desensitization of a phobia. *J Abnorm Soc Psychol, 66(No. 6):*519-525, June, 1963; and Lazarus, Arnold A.: Group therapy of phobic disorders by systematic desensitization. *J Abnorm Soc Psychol, 63 (No. 3):*504-510, Nov. 1961.

4. For relevant reviews, *see* Eysenck and Rachman, *op. cit.;* Wolpe, Joseph and Lazarus, Arnold A.: *Behavior Therapy Techniques: A Guide to the Treatment of Neuroses.* Oxford, Eng., Pergamon Press, 1966, pp. 154-165; Grossberg, John M.: Behavior therapy: A review. *Psychol Bull, 62(No. 2):*73-89, August, 1969; and Feldman, M. P.: Aversion therapy for sexual deviations: A critical review. *Psychol Bull, 65(No. 2):*65-80, February, 1966.

5. For a general statement concerning the nature of the sociobehavioral approach, Thomas, Edwin J.: The sociobehavioral approach: Illustrations and analysis. In Thomas (Ed.): *The Socio-behavioral Approach and Applications to Social Work.* New York, Council on Social Work Education, in press. For two relevant statements applicable to interpersonal helping, *see* Stuart, Richard B.: Applications of behavior theory to social casework in *ibid.;* and Rose, Sheldon D.: A behavioral approach to group treatment of children, in *ibid.*

6. For some contemporary examples of classification of techniques for behavioral therapy, *see* Grossberg, *op. cit.;* Eysenck and Rachman, *op. cit.;* and Staats, Arthur W. and Staats, Carolyn K.: *Complex Human Behavior: A Systematic Extension of Learning Principles.* New York, Holt, Rinehart & Winston, 1964, pp. 465-512.

7. The relevance of these observations to remedial action should be apparent, but the question sometimes arises concerning whether the problems of prevention can be handled in this way. The writer believes that they can, provided one acknowledges that intervention in the present, directed toward such matters as preventing the occurrence of a future problem, must necessarily involve some behaviorally active features in the present; these present interventions would appear to be nothing other than behavioral acquisition, strengthening, maintenance, weakening, or elimination.

8. Although there are other classes of behavior, such as the instinctual, the differences between operant and respondent behavior are well established and the principles for these two realms of behavior are different. For a good discussion of these matters, *see* Verhave, Thom: An introduction to the experimental analysis of behavior. In Verhave (Ed.): *The Experimental Analysis of Behavior: Selected Readings.* New York, Appleton-Century-Crofts, 1966, pp. 1-47. It is essential to acknowledge that despite the importance of the differences between the operant and respondent realms of behavior, there would appear to be at least some interrelationships. For more details *see* Kimmel, H. D.: Instrumental conditioning of autonomically mediated beavior, *Psychol Bull, 67* (No. 5):337-346, May, 1967: and Rescorla, Robert A. and Solomon, Richard L.: Two-process learning theory: Relationships between Pavlovian conditioning and instrumental learning. *Psychol Rev, 74* (No. 3):151-183, May, 1967.

9. For a succinct summary of the principles of operant conditioning, *see* Verhave, *op. cit.* More detailed reviews on specialized subjects in operant behavior are to be found in Werner K. Honig (ed.): *Operant Behavior: Areas of Research and Application.* New York, Appleton-Century-Crofts, 1966. Among the basic secondary sources here are Keller, Fred S. and Schoenfeld, William N.: *Principles of Psychology: A Systematic Text in the Science of Behavior.* New York, Appleton-Century-Crofts, 1950; Skinner, B. F.: *Science and Human Behavior.* New York, Macmillan, 1953; Honig, *op. cit.;* and Staats and Staats, *op. cit.* For more elementary statements *see,* for example, Keller, Fred S.: *Learning: Reinforcement Theory.* New York, Random House, 1954, and the beginning lectures for social workers on this subject by Thomas, Edwin J. in Goodman, Thomas and Esther (Eds.): *Socio-behavioral Theory and Interpersonal Helping in Social Work: Lectures and Institute Proceedings.* Ann Arbor, Campus Publishers, 1965.

10. Thorndike, E. L.: *Fundamentals of Learning.* New York, Teachers College, Columbia University, 1932.

11. Thorne, Gaylord L., Tharp, Roland G. and Wetzel, Ralph J.: Behav-

ioral modification techniques: New tools for probation officers. *Federal Probation, 31 (No. 2)*:21-27, June, 1967.

12. Ayllon, T. and Haughton, E.: Control of the behavior of schizophrenics by food. In Staats, Arthur W. (Ed.): *Human Learning: Studies Extending Conditioning Principles to Complex Behavior.* New York, Holt, Rinehart & Winston, 1962, pp. 458-465.

13. For a review of these studies, *see* Krasner, Leonard: Studies of the conditioning of verbal behavior. *Psychol Bull, 55 (No. 3)*:121-148, May, 1958.

14. A basic research report on tokens is to be found in Ayllon, Teodoro and Azrin, Nathan H.: The measurement and reinforcement of behavior of psychotics. *J Exp Anal Behav, 8 (No. 6)*:357-385, Nov., 1965.

15. An introduction to schedules may be found in texts such as Staats and Staats, *op. cit.*, pp. 61-70; more detailed treatment is found in Ferster, C. B. and Skinner, B. F.: *Schedules of Reinforcement.* New York, Appleton-Century-Crofts, 1957.

16. In this context we shall speak of extinction as a means to eliminate behavior. Although extinction involves one type of reinforcement schedule—namely, the special case of no reinforcement—it is related to positive reinforcement only in this way.

17. *See,* for example, Ferster and Skinner, *op. cit.*

18. For a fascinating report, *see* the description of the study by O. R. Lindsley, B. F. Skinner, and H. C. Solomon, September 1955-November 1956, referred to in Sidman, Murray: Operant techniques. In Bachrach, Arthur J. (Ed.): *Experimental Foundations of Clinical Psychology.* New York, Basic Books, 1962, pp. 202-203.

19. The writer is referring here to research on reinforcing activities and the so-called Premack Principle. *See* Premack, David: Reinforcement theory. In Levine, David (Ed.): *Nebraska Symposium on Motivation.* Lincoln, University of Nebraska Press, 1965, pp. 123-180.

20. Ayllon, Teodoro and Michael, Jack: The psychiatric nurse as a behavioral engineer. *J Exp Anal Behav, 2* (No. 4):323-334, Oct. 1959.

21. A case from the Hartwig Project, Neighborhood Service Organization, Detroit, Mich. The author is indebted to Sheldon Rose, research director, for permission to cite this case.

22. Schwitzgebel, R. R. and Kolb, D. A.: Inducing behavior change in adolescent delinquents. *Behaviour research and therapy, 1 (No. 4)*:297-304, March, 1964.

23. Sidman, *op. cit.*, pp. 173-174.

24. Tyler, Vernon O. and Brown, G. Duane: The use of swift, brief isolation as a group control device for institutionalized delinquents. *Behaviour Research and Therapy, 5 (No. 1)*:1-11, Feb., 1967.

25. Azrin, N. H. and Holz, W. C.: Punishment. In Honig, *op. cit.*, p. 381.

26. *Ibid.* For details, *see* especially pp. 438-441.
27. Holz, W. C. and Azrin, N. H.: A comparison of several procedures for eliminating behavior. *J Exp Anal Behav, 6 (No. 3)*:399-406, July 1963.
28. Among recent reviews of interest are Azrin and Holz, *op. cit.;* Solomon, Richard L.: Punishment. *Am Psychol, 19 (No. 4)*:239-254, April, 1964. Church, R. M.: The varied effects of punishment on behavior. *Psychol Rev, 70 (No. 5)*:369-402, Sept. 1963 and Kushner, Malcolm and Sandler, Jack: Aversion therapy and the concept of punishment. *Behav Res Ther, 4 (No. 3)*:179-187, Aug. 1966.
29. Azrin and Holz, *op. cit.,* pp. 439-440.
30. For example, *see* Lehner, G. F. J.: Negative practice as a therapeutic technique. In Eysenck, (Ed.): *Behaviour Therapy and the Neuroses,* pp. 194-206.
31. For a practice example *see* Ayllon, Teodoro: Intensive treatment of psychotic behavior by stimulus satiation and food reinforcement. In Ullmann, Leonard P. and Krasner, Leonard (Eds.): *Case Studies in Behavior Modification.* New York, Holt, Rinehart & Winston, 1965, pp. 77-84; for a comparative research study on the effectiveness of satiation and other behavior-reductive procedures *see* Holz and Azrin, *op. cit.*
32. A recent experimental study is reported by Sidman, Murray and Stoddard Lawrence T.: The effectiveness of fading in programming a simultaneous form discrimination for retarded children. *J Exp Anal Behav, 10 (No. 1)*:3-17, Jan. 1967.
33. An example of the explication of selected features of verbal instructions in Adams, J. Stacy and Romney, A. Kimball: A functional analysis of authority. *Psychol Rev, 66 (No. 4)*:234-251; *see also* Staats and Staats, *op. cit.,* pp. 185-199 and 321-324. For a sociobehavioral procedure that draws heavily on verbal instructions *see* Stuart, Richard B.: Behavioral control of overeating. *Behav Res Ther,* in press.
34. For selected examples and procedures *see* Corsini, Raymond, with the assistance of Cardone, Samuel: *Roleplaying in Psychotherapy: A Manual.* Chicago, Aldine, 1966.
35. For a procedure and rationale useful for parents *see* Smith, Judith M. and Smith, Donald E. P.: *Child Management: A Program for Parents.* Ann Arbor, Ann Arbor Publishers, 1966; for theoretical factors relating to prescriptive phenomena *see* Thomas, Edwin J. and Biddle, Bruce J.: Basic concepts for classifying the phenomena of role. In Biddle and Thomas (Eds.): *Role Theory: Concepts and Research.* New York, John Wiley & Sons, 1966, pp. 26-28. The technique of rule-making, to the writer's knowledge, has not been identified as a technique in prior writing. This technique along with position structuring, likewise a "new technique," will be explicated, with the other

techniques, in a book on sociobehavioral theory currently in preparation by the author.

36. A recent statement addressed to an explication of aspects of imitation is in Bandura, Albert: Vicarious processes: A case of no-trial learning. In Berkowitz, Leonard (Ed.): *Advances in Experimental Social Psychology*. New York, Academic Press, 1966, Vol. 2, pp. 3-48.

37. For an example of position change for the "dingup" *see* Crain, William: The chronic 'mess-up' and his changing character. *Federal Probation, 28 (No. 2)*:50-56, June, 1964; for a discussion of role factors that one would have to consider in changing a deviant position *see,* for example, Thomas, Edwin J.: Role problems of offenders and correctional workers. *Crime and Delinquency, 12 (No. 4)*:354-365, Oct., 1966; for a discussion of role modification and adjustment *see* Maas, Henry S.: *Building Social Work Theory with Social Science Tools: The Concept of Role.* Special Report No. 41. Los Angeles, Welfare Planning Council, Los Angeles Region, 1954.

38. For example, stimulus change, physical force, and deprivation are among other possible candidates.

39. This section was taken, with some modification, from a portion of a lecture by the author, prepared in writing with the assistance of Esther Goodman, in Thomas Edwin J. and Goodman, Esther (Eds.): *Socio-behavioral Theory and Interpersonal Helping in Social Work —Lectures and Institute Proceedings.* Ann Arbor, Campus Publishers, 1965, pp. 8-9.

Chapter 30

BEHAVIORAL APPROACHES TO FAMILY AND COUPLE THERAPY

ROBERT LIBERMAN

T HE CURRENT splurge of couple and family therapies is not simply an accident or passing fad. These increasingly used modes of treatment for psychiatric problems are anchored in a sound foundation and are not likely to blow away. The foundation of these newer therapies lies in the opportunity they offer to induce significant behavioral change in the participants by a major re-structuring of their interpersonal environments.

Couple and family therapy can be particularly potent means of behavior modification because the interpersonal milieu that undergoes change is that of the day-to-day, face-to-face encounter an individual experiences with the most important people in his life—his spouse or members of his immediate family. When these therapies are successful it is because the therapist is able to guide the members of the couple or family into changing their modes of dealing with each other. In behavioral or learning terms, we can translate "ways of dealing with each other" into consequences of behavior or *contingencies of reinforcement.* Instead of rewarding maladaptive behavior with attention and concern, the family members learn to give each other recognition and approval for desired behavior.

Since the family is a system of interlocking, reciprocal be-haviors (including affective behavior), family therapy proceeds best when each of the members learns how to change his or her responsiveness to the others. Family therapy should be a learning experience for all the members involved. For simplification, how-

Note: Abridged and reprinted from *Am J Orthopsychiatry,* 40:106-118, 1970. Copy-right 1970, the American Orthopsychiatric Association. Reproduced by per-mission.

ever, this paper will analyze family pathology and therapy from the point of view of the family responding to a single member.

Typically, families that come for treatment have coped with the maladaptive or deviant behavior of one member by responding to it over the years with anger, nagging, babying, conciliation, irritation, or sympathy. These responses, however punishing they might seem on the surface, have the effect of reinforcing the deviance, that is, increasing the frequency or intensity of the deviant behavior in the future. Reinforcement occurs because the attention offered is viewed and felt by the deviant member as positive concern and interest. In many families with a deviant member, there is little social interaction and the individuals tend to lead lives relatively isolated from each other. Because of this overall lack of interaction, when interaction does occur in response to a member's "abnormal" behavior, such behavior is powerfully reinforced.[14]

Verbal and nonverbal means of giving attention and recognition can be termed *social reinforcement* (as contrasted with food or sex, which are termed *primary reinforcement*). Social reinforcement represents the most important source of motivation for human behavior.[6,19] Often massive amounts of such "concern" or social reinforcement are communicated to the deviant member, focused and contingent upon the member's maladaptive behavior. The deviant member gets the message: "So long as you continue to produce this undesirable behavior (symptoms), we will be interested and concerned in you." Learning the lesson of such messages leads to the development and maintenance of symptomatic or deviant behavior and to characterological patterns of activity and identity. Sometimes, the message of concern and interest is within the awareness of the "sick" member. Individuals with a conscious awareness of these contingencies are frequently termed "manipulative" by mental health professionals since they are adept at generating social reinforcement for their maladaptive behavior. But learning can occur without an individual's awareness or insight, in which case we view the maladaptive behavior as being unconsciously motivated.

Massive amounts of contingent social reinforcement are not

necessary to maintain deviant behavior. Especially after the behavior has developed, occasional or *intermittent reinforcement* will promote very durable continuation of the behavior. Laboratory studies have shown that intermittent reinforcement produces behavior that is most resistant to extinction.[6]

Many family therapists[7,8,21] have demonstrated that the interest and concern family members show in the deviance of one member can be in the service of their own psychological economy. Maintaining a "sick" person in the family can be gratifying (reinforcing) to others, albeit at some cost in comfort and equanimity. Patterson[15] describes how this reciprocal reinforcement can maintain deviant behavior by using the example of a child who demands an ice cream cone while shopping with his mother in a supermarket. The reinforcer for this "demand behavior" is compliance by the mother, but if she ignores the demand, the effect is to increase the rate or loudness of the demand. Loud demands or shrieks by a child in a supermarket are aversive to the mother; that is, her noncompliance is punished. When the mother finally buys the ice cream cone, the aversive tantrum ends. The reinforcer for the child's tantrum is the ice cream cone. The reinforcing contingency for the mother was the termination of the "scene" in the supermarket. In this reciprocal fashion, the tantrum behavior is maintained. I shall return to this important aspect of family psychopathology—the mutually reinforcing or symbiotic nature of deviance—in the case studies below. Indeed, the balance between the aversive and gratifying consequences of maladaptive behavior in a member on the other family members is the crucial determinant of motivation for and response to treatment.

Changing the contingencies by which the patient gets acknowledgment and concern from other members of his family is the basic principle of learning that underlies the potency of family or couple therapy. Social reinforcement is made contingent on desired, adaptive behavior instead of maladaptive and symptomatic behavior. It is the task of the therapist in collaboration with the family or couple to (a) specify the maladaptive behavior, (b) choose reasonable goals which are alternative, adaptive behaviors,

(c) direct and guide the family to change the contingencies of their social reinforcement patterns from maladaptive to adaptive target behaviors.

Another principle of learning involved in the process of successful family therapy is modeling, also called imitation or identification. The model, sometimes the therapist but also other members of the family, exhibits desired, adaptive behavior which then is imitated by the patient. Imitation or identification occurs when the model is an esteemed person (therapist, admired family member) and when the model receives positive reinforcement (approval) for his behavior from others.[3] The amount of observational learning will be governed by the degree to which a family member pays attention to the modeling cues, has the capacity to process and rehearse the cues, and possesses the necessary components in his behavioral experience which can be combined to reproduce the more complex, currently modeled behavior.

Imitative learning enables an individual to short-circuit the tedious and lengthy process of trial-and-error (or reward) learning while incorporating complex chains of behavior into his repertoire. Much of the behaviors which reflect the enduring part of our culture are to a large extent transmitted by repeated observation of behavior displayed by social models, particularly familial models. If performed frequently enough and rewarded in turn with approval by others, the imitated behavior will become incorporated into the patient's behavioral repertoire. The principles of imitative learning have been exploited with clinical success by researchers working with autistic children,[12] phobic youngsters,[4] and mute, chronic psychotics.[18] How modeling can be used in family therapy will be discussed below.

I will limit the scope of the discussion to couples and families; however, the same principles of learning apply to group therapy[11,17] and with some modification to individual psychotherapy.[9] Although learning theory has been associated in clinical psychiatry with its systematic and explicit application in the new behavior therapies, it should be emphasized that learning theory offers a generic and unitary explanation of the processes mediating change in all psychotherapies, including psychoanalytic ones.[1,13]

TECHNIQUE

I would like to outline the main features of an application of behavior theory to family therapy. The three major areas of technical concern for the therapist are: (a) *creating and maintaining a positive therapeutic alliance;* (b) *making a behavioral analysis of the problem(s); and* (c) *implementing the behavioral principles of reinforcement and modeling in the context of ongoing interpersonal interactions.*

Without the positive therapeutic alliance between the therapist and those he is helping, there can be little or no successful intervention. The working alliance is the lever which stimulates change. In learning terms, the positive relationship between therapist and patient(s) permits the therapist to serve as a social reinforcer and model; in other words, to build up adaptive behaviors and allow maladaptive behaviors to extinguish. The therapist is an effective reinforcer and model for the patients to the extent that the patients value him and hold him in high regard and warm esteem.

Clinicians have described the ingredients that go into this positive therapist-patient relationship in many different ways. Terminology varies with the "school" of psychotherapy to which the clinician adheres. Psychoanalysts have contributed notions such as "positive transference" and an alliance between the therapist and the patient's "observing ego." Reality therapists call for a trusting involvement with the patient. Some clinicians have termed it a "supportive relationship" implying sympathy, respect, and concern on the part of the therapist. Recent research has labeled the critical aspects of the therapist-client relationship: nonpossessive warmth, accurate empathy, and genuine concern.[20] Truax and his colleagues[20] have been able to successfully operationalize these concepts and to teach them to selected individuals. They have further shown that therapists high on these attributes are more successful in psychotherapy than those who are not. Whatever the labels, a necessary if not sufficient condition for therapeutic change in patients is a doctor-patient relationship that is infused with mutual respect, warmth, trust, and affection.

In my experience, these qualities of the therapeutic alliance can be developed through a period of initial evaluation of the patient or family. The early therapist-family contacts, proceeding during the first few interviews, offer an opportunity to the therapist to show unconditional warmth, acceptance, and concern for the clients and their problems.

Also during the first few sessions, while the therapeutic relationship is being established, the therapist must do his "diagnostic." In a learning approach to family therapy, the diagnostic consists of a *behavioral* or *functional analysis* of the problems. In making his behavioral analysis, the therapist, in collaboration with the family, asks two major questions:

1. What behavior is maladaptive or problematic—what behavior in the designated patient should be increased or decreased? Each person, in turn, is asked, (a) what changes would you like to see in others in the family, and (b) how would you like to be different from the way you are now? Answering these questions forces the therapist to choose carefully *specific behavioral goals.*

2. What environmental and interpersonal contingencies currently support the problematic behavior—that is, what is maintaining undesirable behavior or reducing the likelihood of more adaptive responses? This is called a "functional analysis of behavior," and also can include an analysis of the development of symptomatic or maladaptive behavior, the "conditioning history" of the patient. The mutual patterns of social reinforcement in the family deserve special scrutiny in this analysis since their deciphering and clarification become central to an understanding of the case and to the formulation of therapeutic strategy.

It should be noted that the behavioral analysis of the problem doesn't end after the initial sessions, but by necessity continues throughout the course of therapy. As the problem behaviors change during treatment, so must the analysis of what maintains these behaviors. New sources of reinforcement for the patient and family members must be assessed. In this sense, the behavioral approach to family therapy is dynamic.

The third aspect of behavioral technique is the actual choice and implementation of therapeutic strategy and tactics. Which interpersonal transactions between the therapist and family members and among the family members can serve to alter the problem behavior in a more adaptive direction? The therapist acts as an educator, using his value as a social reinforcer to instruct the family or couple in changing their ways of dealing with each other.

A helpful way to conceptualize these tactics is to view them as "behavioral change experiments" where the therapist and family together reprogram the contingencies of reinforcement operating in the family system. The behavioral change experiments consist of family members responding to each other in various ways, with the responses contingent on more desired reciprocal ways of relating. Ballentine[2] views the behavioral change experiments, starting with small but well-defined successes, as leading to (a) a shift toward more optimistic and hopeful expectations; (b) an emphasis on doing things differently while giving the responsibility for change to each family member; (c) "encouragement of an observational outlook which forces family members to look closely at themselves and their relationships with one another, rather than looking "inside" themselves with incessant why's and wherefores"; and (d) "the generation of empirical data which can be instrumental to further change, since they often expose sequences of family action and reaction in particularly graphic and unambiguous fashion."

The therapist also uses his importance as a model to illustrate desired modes of responding differentially to behavior that at times is maladaptive and at other times approaches more desirable form. The operant conditioning principle of "shaping" is used, whereby gradual approximations to the desired end behavior are reinforced with approval and spontaneous and genuine interest by the therapist. Through his instructions and example, the therapist teaches shaping to the members of the couple or family. Role playing or behavioral rehearsal are among the useful tactics employed in generating improved patterns of interaction among the family members.

The therapist using a behavioral model does not act like a teaching machine, devoid of emotional expression. Just as therapists using other theroetical schemas, he is most effective in his role as an educator when he expresses himself with affect in a comfortable, human style developed during his clinical training and in his life as a whole. Since intermittent reinforcement produces more durable behavior, the therapist may employ trial terminations, tapering off the frequency of sessions prior to termination and "bootser" sessions.[1] A more systematic and detailed outline of the behavior modification approach is presented in Table 30-I. The specification and implications of the items in this outline can be found in the manual by Reese.[16]

TABLE 30-I
A BEHAVIORAL MODEL FOR LEARNING

1. Specify the final performance (therapeutic goals):
   • Identify the behavior.
   • Determine how it is to be measured.
2. Determine the current baseline rate of the desired behavior.
3. Structure a favorable situation for eliciting the desired behavior by providing cues for the appropriate behavior and removing cues for incompatible, inappropriate behavior.
4. Establish motivation by locating reinforcers, depriving the individual of reinforcers (if necessary), and withholding reinforcers for inappropriate behavior.
5. Enable the individual to become comfortable in the therapeutic setting and to become familiar with the reinforcers.
6. Shape the desired behavior:
   • Reinforce successive approximations of the therapeutic goals.
   • Raise the criterion for reinforcement gradually.
   • Present reinforcement immediately, contingent upon the behavior.
7. Fade out the specific cues in the therapeutic setting to promote generalization of acquired behavior.
8. Reinforce intermittently to facilitate durability of the gains.
9. Keep continuous, objective records.

Note: Adapted from E.P. Reese.[16]

DISCUSSION

There is too much confusion in the rationales and techniques underlying current practices in family therapy. Although attempts to convey the method of family therapy always suffer when done through the written word, I do not share the belief that "the vital communications in all forms of psychotherapy are intuitive, felt, unspoken, and unconscious."[7] Although this article is not meant as a "how to do it" treatise for family therapists, I do intend it as a preliminary attempt to apply a few of the basic principles of imitative learning and operant conditioning to couple and family therapy.

Although the rationalized conceptualization of family therapy practiced by psychoanalytically oriented therapists differs from the learning and behavioral approach described here, closer examination of the actual techniques used reveals marked similarity. For example Framo,[7] in explaining the theory behind his family therapy, writes:

> The overriding goal of the intensive middle phases consists in understanding and working through, often through transference to each other and to the therapists, the introjects of the parents so that the parents can see and experience how those difficulties manifested in the present family system have emerged from their unconscious attempts to perpetrate or master old conflicts arising from their families of origin. . . The essence of the true work of family therapy is in the tracing of the vicissitudes of early object-relationships, and . . . the exceedingly intricate transformations which occur as a function of the intrapsychic and transactional blending of the old and new family systems of the parents. . . .

Despite the use of psychoanalytic constructs, Framo describes the actual process of family therapy in ways that are very compatible within a learning framework. He writes:

> Those techniques which prompt family interaction are the most productive in the long run. . . . It is especially useful to concentrate on here-and-now feelings; this method usually penetrated much deeper then dealing with feelings described in retrospect. . . . As we gained experience in working with families we became less hesitant about taking more forceful, active positions in order to help the family become unshackled from their rigid patterns.

Framo goes on to give illustrations of his work with families in which differential reinforcement for behavior considered more desirable and appropriate is given by the therapists. In dealing with angry and aggressive mothers, "we learned to avoid noticing what they did (e.g. emotional in-fighting) and pay attention to what they missed in life." Trying to activate passive fathers, "the therapists make every conscious effort to build him up during the sessions. . . . A number of techniques have been tried: forcing more interaction between the husband and wife; assigning tasks; having a female therapist give encouragement in a flattering way; occasional individual sessions with the father." Zuk[23] describes his technique of family therapy in ways that fit into a reinforcement framework. He views the cornerstone of the technique the exploration and attempt "to shift the balance of pathogenic relating among family members so that new forms of relating become possible." Zuk further delineates the therapist's tactics as a "go-between" in which he uses his leverage to "constantly structure and direct the treatment situation."

It should be emphasized that the behavioral approach does not simplistically reduce the family system and family interaction to individualistic or dyadic mechanisms of reinforcement. The richness and complexity of family interaction is appreciated by the family therapist working within a behavioral framework. For instance, Ballentine[2] states: ". . . behavior within a system cannot be so easily modified by focusing on the behavioral contingencies existing within any two-person subsystem, since one person's behavior in relation to a second's is often determined by behaviors of others within the system . . . the behavioral contingencies within a family system are manifold and constitute a matrix of multiple behavioral contingencies."

A behavioral and learning approach to family therapy differs from a more psychoanalytic one. The therapist defines his role as an educator in collaboration with the family; therefore, the assigning of "sickness" labels to members, with its potential for moral blame, does not occur as it does under the medical model embodied in the psychoanalytic concept of underlying conflict or disease. There is no need for family members to acknowledge publicly their "weaknesses" or irrationality since insight per se is not considered vital.

The behavioral approach, with its more systematic and specific guidelines, makes it less likely that a therapist will adventitiously reinforce or model contradictory behavior patterns. The behavioral approach, consistently applied, is potentially more effective and faster. When patients do not respond to behavioral techniques, the therapist can use his more empirical attitude to ask why and perhaps to try another technique. The orientation is more experimental and "the patient is always right," with the burden on the therapist to devise effective interventions. In the psychoanalytic approach, the tendency has been for the therapist to decide that their failures are caused by patients who were inappropriate for the technique rather than viewing the technique as needing modification for the particular patient.

The work of behaviorally oriented family therapists is not restricted to the here-and-now of the therapy sessions. As the cases described reveal, much of the effort involves collaboration and involvement with adjunctive agencies such as schools, rehabilitation services, medication, and work settings. Family therapists are moving toward this total systems approach.

The advantages of behavioral approaches to family therapy sketched in this paper remain to be proven by systematic research. Such research is now proceeding.[5,10,15,22] Much work will go into demonstrating that family processes are "essentially behavioral sequences which can be sorted out, specified and measured with a fair degree of accuracy and precision."[2] Hopefully, further clinical and research progress made by behaviorally oriented therapists will challenge all family therapists, regardless of theoretical leanings, to specify more clearly their interventions, their goals, and their empirical results. If these challenges are accepted seriously, the field of family therapy will likely improve and gain stature as a scientifically grounded modality.

REFERENCES

1. Alexander, F.: The dynamics of psychotherapy in the light of learning theory. *Int J Psychiat, 1*:189-207, 1965.
2. Ballentine, R.: The family therapist as a behavioral systems engineer . . . and a responsible one. Paper read at Georgetown Univ. Symp. on Fam. Psychother. Washington, 1968.
3. Bandura, A. and Walters, R.: *Social Learning and Personality Development.* New York, Holt, Rinehart and Winston, 1963.
4. Bandura, A., Grusec, J. and Menlove, F.: Vicarious extinction of avoidance behavior. *Personality Soc Psychol, 5*:16-23.
5. Dunham, R.: Ex post facto reconstruction of conditioning schedules in family interaction. In *Family Structure, Dynamics and Therapy.* Irving M. Cohen (Ed.): Psychiatric Research No. 20, Amer. Psychiat.

Assoc., Washington, pp. 107-114.

6. Ferster, C.: Essentials of a science of behavior. In Nurnberger, J. I., Ferster, C. B. and Brady, J. P. (Eds.): *An Introduction to the Science of Human Behavior.* Appleton-Century-Crofts, New York, 1963.

7. Framo, J.: Rationale and techniques of intensive family therapy. In Boszormenyi-Nagy, I. and Framo, J. L. (Eds.): *Intensive Family Therapy.* New York, Hoeber Medical Division, 1965.

8. Handel, G. (Ed.): *The Psychosocial Interior of the Family.* Chicago, Aldine, 1967.

9. Krasner, L.: The therapist as a social reinforcement machine. In Strupp, H. and Luborsky, L. (Eds.): Washington, Amer. Psychol. Assoc., 1962.

10. Lewinsohn, P., Weinstein, M. and Shaw, D.: Depression: A clinical research approach. In *Proceedings, 1968 Conference.* San Francisco, Assoc Advan. Behav. Ther., 1969.

11. Liberman, R.: A behavioral approach to group dynamics. *Behav Ther.* In press.

12. Lovaas, O. *et al.*: Acquisition of imitative speech by schizophrenic children. *Science, 151:*705-707, 1966.

13. Marmor, J.: Theories of learning and psychotherapeutic process. *Br J Psychiat, 112:*363-366, 1966.

14. Patterson, G. *et al.*: Reprogramming the social environment. *Child Psychol Psychiatry, 8:*181-195, 1967.

15. Patterson, G. and Reid, J.: Reciprocity and coercion: Two facets of social systems. Paper read at 9th Ann. Inst. for Res. in Clin. Psychol. Univ. of Kansas.

16. Reese, E.: The analysis of human operant behavior. Dubuque, Iowa, Brown, 1966.

17. Shapiro, D., and Birk, L.: Group therapy in experimental perspectives. Internat. *J Group Psychother, 17:*211-224, 1967.

18. Sherman, J.: Use of reinforcement and imitation to reinstate verbal behavior in mute psychotics. *J Abnorm Psychol, 70:*155-164, 1965.

19. Skinner, B.: Science and human behavior. New York, Macmillan, 1953.

20. Truax, C. and Carkhuff, R.: *Toward Effective Counseling and Psychotherapy: Training and Practice.* Chicago, Aldine, 1967.

21. Vogel, E. and Bell, N.: The emotionally disturbed child as the family scapegoat. In Bell, N. W. and Vogel, E. F. (Eds.): *A Modern Introduction to the Family.* New York, Free Press, 1960.

22. Zeilberger, J., Sampens, S. and Sloane, H.: Modification of a child's problem behaviors in the home with the mother as therapist. *J Appl Behav Anal, 1:*47-53, 1968.

23. Zuk, G.: Family therapy. *Arch Gen Psychiatry, 16:*71-79, 1967.

D. BEHAVIOR MODIFICATION (RESPONDENT)

Chapter 31

THE SYSTEMATIC DESENSITIZATION
TREATMENT OF NEUROSES

JOSEPH WOLPE

SOME YEARS AGO, studies on the induction and elimination of experimental neuroses in animals[23] showed that these conditions were persistent habits of unadaptive behavior acquired by learning (conditioning); and that their therapy was a matter of unlearning. The central constituent of the neurotic behavior was anxiety, and the most effective way of procuring unlearning was repeatedly to feed the animal while it was responding with a weak degree of anxiety to a "weak" conditioned stimulus. The effect of this was to diminish progressively the strength of the anxiety response to the particular stimulus so that it eventually declined to zero. Increasingly "strong" stimulus situations were successively dealt with in the same way; and finally, the animal showed no anxiety to any of the situations to which anxiety had been conditioned. The basis of the gradual elimination of the anxiety response habit appeared to be an example, at a more complex level, of the phenomenon of *reciprocal inhibition* described originally by Sherrington.[17] Each time the animal fed, the anxiety response was to some extent inhibited; and each occasion of inhibition weakened somewhat the strength of the anxiety habit. The experiments suggested the general proposition that *if a response inhibitory to anxiety can be made to occur in the presence of anxiety-evoking stimuli so that it is accompanied by a complete or partial suppression of the anxiety response, the bond between these stimuli and the anxiety response will be weakened.*

I have argued elsewhere[24,27,28] that human neuroses are quite parallel to experimental neuroses. On this premise and during the

Note: Reprinted from *J Nerv Ment Dis,* *132:*189-203, 1961. Copyright 1961, the Williams and Wilkins Co. Reproduced by permission.

past twelve years, the writer has applied the reciprocal inhibition principle to the treatment of a large number of clinical cases of neurosis, employing a variety of other responses to inhibit anxiety or other neurotic responses. In a recent book[27] an analysis has been given of the results in 210 patients, of whom 89 percent either recovered or were much improved, apparently lastingly, after a mean of about thirty interviews.

In the case of neurotic responses conditioned to situations involving direct interpersonal relations, the essence of reciprocal inhibition therapy has been to instigate in the situations concerned new patterns of behavior of an anxiety-inhibiting kind whose repeated exercise gradually weakens the anxiety response habit.[16, 19,20,25,27,28] Neurotic responses conditioned to stimuli other than those arising from direct interpersonal relations do not lend themselves, as a rule, to behavioral treatment in the life situation of the patient; and consulting-room applications of the reciprocal inhibition principle have been necessary. The most straightforward examples of neurotic responses requiring such measures have been the phobias. Relatively "simple" though they are, they have hitherto constituted a difficult therapeutic problem. For example, Curran and Partridge[2] state, "Phobic symptoms are notoriously resistant to treatment and their complete removal is rarely achieved." A very different picture is in prospect with the use of conditioning methods,[1,4,10-12,14,15] which are no less effective when used for much more subtle neurotic constellations. Examples will be found below.

In the office treatment of neuroses by reciprocal inhibition, any response inhibitory of anxiety may in theory be used. The almost forgotten earliest example of therapy of this kind[7] involved inhibiting the anxiety of phobic children by feeding (just as in the animal experiments mentioned above). Conditioned motor responses have occasionally served the same end (p. 173);[27] and Meyer[14] and Freeman and Kendrick[4] have made use of ordinary "pleasant" emotions of daily life (see also p. 198).[27] But the behavioral response that has had the widest application is deep muscle relaxation, whose anxiety-inhibiting effects were first pointed out by Jacobson.[5,6] It has been the basic of the technique known as *systematic desensitization* which, because of its convenience, has been most widely adopted.[1,9,11,12]

Though several descriptions of the technique of systematic desensitization have been published,[26,27] it is now clear that more details are needed to enable practitioners to apply it without assistance. It is the aim of this paper to present a more adequate account, and also for the first time to give a separate statistical analysis of results obtained with this treatment.

THE TECHNIQUE OF SYSTEMATIC DESENSITIZATION

It is necessary to emphasize that the desensitization technique is carried out *only after a careful assessment of the therapeutic requirements of the patient*. A detailed history is taken of every symptom and of every aspect of life in which the patient experiences undue difficulty. A systematic account is then obtained of his life history with special attention to intrafamilial relationships. His attitudes to people in educational institutions and to learning and play are investigated. A history of his work life is taken, noting both his experiences with people and those related to work itself. He is questioned about his sexual experiences from first awareness of sexual feelings up to the present. Careful scrutiny is made of his current major personal relationships. Finally, he is asked to describe all kinds of "nervousness" that may have afflicted him at any time and to narrate any distressing experiences he can remember.

The problems posed by the case are now carefully considered; and if there are neurotic reactions in connection with direct interpersonal relations, appropriate new behavior based on the reciprocal inhibition principle is instigated in the patient's life situation.[19,20,25,27,28] Most commonly, it is assertive behavior that is instigated. When systematic desensitization is also indicated, it is conducted as soon as possible, and may be in parallel with measures aimed at other sources of neurotic anxiety.

Systematic desensitization is used not only for the treatment of classical phobias involving anxiety responses to nonpersonal stimulus constellations (like enclosed spaces or harmless animals), but also for numerous less obvious and often complex sources of neurotic disturbance. These may involve ideas, bodily sensations, or extrinsic situations. Examples of each are to be found in Table 31-I. The most common extrinsic sources of anxiety relate to people in contexts that make irrelevant the use of direct action, such as assertion, on the part of the patient. As examples, one patient reacts with anxiety to the mere presence of particular persons, another to definable categories of people, a third to being the center of attention, a fourth to people in groups, a fifth to inferred criticism or rejection, and so forth. In all instances, *anxiety has been conditioned to situations in which, objectively, there is no danger.*

In brief, the desensitization method consists of presenting to the imagination of the deeply relaxed patient the feeblest item in a list of anxiety-evoking stimuli—repeatedly, until no more anxiety is evoked. The next item of the list is then presented, and so on, until eventually, even the strongest of the anxiety-evoking stimuli fails to evoke any stir of anxiety in the patient. It has consistently been found that at every stage a stimulus that evokes no anxiety when imagined in a state of relaxation will also evoke no anxiety when encountered in reality.

The method involves three separate sets of operations: (a) training in deep muscle relaxation; (b) the construction of anxiety hierarchies; and (c) counterposing relaxation and anxiety-evoking stimuli from the hierarchies.

TRAINING IN RELAXATION

The method of relaxation taught is essentially that of Jacobson[5] but the training takes up only about half of each of about six interviews—far less time than Jacobson devotes. The patient is also asked to practice at home for a half-hour each day.

The first lesson begins with the therapist telling the patient that he is to learn relaxation because of its beneficial emotional effects. He is then directed to grip the arm of his chair with one hand to see whether he can distinguish any qualitative difference between the sensations produced in his forearm and those in his hand. Usually he can, and he is asked to take note of the forearm sensation as being characteristic of muscle tension. He is also enjoined to remember the location of the flexors and extensors of the forearm. Next, the therapist grips the patient's wrist and asks him to pull, making him aware of the tension in his biceps; and then, instructing him to push in the opposite direction, draws his attention to the extensor muscles of the arm.

The therapist now again grips the patient's wrist and makes him tense the biceps and then relax it as much as possible, letting go gradually as the patient's hand comes down. The patient is then told to "keep trying to go further and further in the negative direction" and to "try to go beyond what seems to you to be the furthest point." He may report sensations like tingling and numbness which often accompany relaxation. When it appears that the patient has understood how to go about relaxing he is made to relax simultaneously all the muscles of both arms and forearms.

At the second lesson in relaxation, the patient is told that from the emotional point of view the most important muscles in the body are situated in and around the head, and that we shall therefore go on to these next. The muscles of the face are the first to be dealt with, beginning with the forehead. This location lends itself to demonstrating to the patient the step-like manner in which tension is decreased; and I do this by contracting the eyebrow-raising and the frowning groups of muscles in my own forehead very intensely simultaneously, and then relaxing by degrees. The patient is then made aware of his own forehead muscles and given about ten minutes to relax them as far as possible. Patients frequently report spontaneously the occurrence of unusual sensations in their foreheads, such as numbness, tingling, or "a feeling of thickness, as though my skin were made of leather". These sensations are characteristic of the attainment of a degree of relaxation beyond the normal level of muscle tone. At this session attention is drawn also to the muscles in the region of the nose (by asking the patient to wrinkle his nose) and to the muscles around the mouth (by making him purse his lips and then smile). After a few minutes he is asked to bite on his teeth, thus tensing his masseters and temporales. The position of the lips is an important indicator of successful relaxation of the muscles of mastication. When these are relaxed the lips are parted by a few millimeters. The masseters cannot be relaxed if the mouth is kept resolutely closed.

At the third lesson, attention is drawn to the muscles of the tongue, which may be felt contracting in the floor of the mouth when the patient presses the tip of his tongue firmly against the back of his bottom incisor teeth. Thereafter, with active jaw-opening, infra-hyoid tensions are pointed out. All these muscles are then relaxed. At the same session, the tensions produced in the eye muscles and those of the neck are noted and time given for their relaxation.

The fourth lesson deals with the muscles of the shoulder girdle, the fifth with those of the back, thorax and abdomen, and the sixth with those of the thighs and legs. A procedure that many patients find helpful is to coordinate relaxation of various other muscles with the automatic relaxation of the respiratory muscles that takes place with normal exhalation.

CONSTRUCTION OF ANXIETY HIERARCHIES

This is the most difficult and taxing procedure in the desensitization technique. Investigation of any case of anxiety neurosis reveals that the stimuli to anxiety fall into definable groups or *themes*. The themes may be obvious ones, like fear of heights, or less apparent ones, like fear of rejection.

Hierarachy construction usually begins at about the same time as relaxation training, but alterations or additions can be made at any time. It is important to note that the gathering of data and its subsequent organizing are done in an ordinary conversational way and *not under relaxation*, since the patient's *ordinary* responses to stimuli are under scrutiny.

The raw data from which the hierarchies are constructed have three main sources: (a) the patient's history; (b) responses to the Willoughby Questionnaire,[22] and (c) special probings about situations in which the patient feels anxiety though there is no objective threat. Abundant material is often obtained by setting the patient the homework task of listing all situations that he finds disturbing, fearful, embarrassing, or in any way distressing.

When all identified sources of neurotic disturbance have been listed, the therapist classifies them into groups if there is more than one theme. The items of each thematic group are then re-written to make separate lists and the patient is asked to rank the items of each list, placing the item he imagines would be most disturbing at the top and the least disturbing at the bottom of the list.

In many instances, the construction of a hierarchy is a very straightforward matter. This is true of most cases of such fears, as of heights (where the greater the height the greater the fear), or enclosed spaces, or, to take a somewhat more complex instance, fears aroused by the sight of illness in others. In such instances as the last, exemplified in Case 1 below, although the items have only a general thematic linkage and do not belong to a stimulus continuum (as do, for example, the items of a height hierarchy), all that has to be done is to obtain a list of situations embodying illnesses in others and then to ask the patient to rank the items according to the amount of anxiety each one arouses.

In other cases, hierarchy construction is more difficult because the sources of anxiety are not immediately revealed by the patient's listing of what he avoids. For example, it may become clear that he reacts to social occasions with anxiety, and that different kinds of social occasions (e.g. weddings, parties, and musical evenings) are associated with decreasing degrees of anxiety. There may then be a temptation to arrange a hierarchy based on these types of social occasions, with weddings at the top of the list and musical evenings at the bottom. Usually, little effective therapy would follow an attempt at desensitization based on such a hierarchy, and more careful probing would almost certainly reveal some facet of social occasions that is the real source of anxiety. Frequently, fear and avoidance of social occasions turns out to be based on fear of criticism or of rejection; or the fear may be a function of the mere physical presence of people, varying with the number of them to whom the patient is exposed. The writer once had a patient whose fear of social situations was really a conditioned anxiety response to the smell of food in public places. A good example of the importance of correct identification of relevant sources of anxiety is to be found in a previously reported case (p. 152) [27] where a man's impotence was found to be due to anxiety related not to aspects of the sexual situation as such, but to the idea of trauma, which in certain contexts, especially defloration, enters into the sexual act.

It is not necessary for the patient actually to have experienced each situation that is to be included in a hierarchy. The question before him is of the order that, "If you were today confronted by such and such a situation, *would you expect* to be anxious?" To answer this question he must *imagine* the situation concerned, and it is usually not much more difficult to imagine a merely possible event than one that has at some time occurred. The temporal setting of an imagined stimulus configuration scarcely affects the responses to it. A man with a phobia for dogs has about as much anxiety to the idea of meeting a bulldog on the way home this evening as to recalling an encounter with this breed of of dog a year previously.

A small minority of patients do not experience anxiety when they imagine situations that in reality are disturbing. In some of these, anxiety is evoked when they *describe* (verbalize) the scene they have been asked to imagine. As in other patients, the various scenes can then be ranked according to the degree of anxiety they evoke.

To a therapist inexperienced in the construction of anxiety hierarchies, the most common difficulty to be encountered is to find that even the weakest item in a hierarchy produces more anxiety than can be counteracted by the patient's relaxation. In many cases, it is obvious where weaker items may be sought. For example, in a patient who had an anxiety hierarchy on the theme of loneliness, the weakest item in the original hierarchy—being at home accompanied only by her daughter—was found to evoke more anxiety than was manageable. To obtain a weaker starting point all that was needed was to add items in which she had two or more companions. But it is not always so easy, and the therapist may be hard put to find manipulatable dimensions. For example, following an accident three years previously, a patient had developed serious anxiety reactions to the sight of approaching automobiles. At first it seemed that anxiety was just noticeable when an automobile was two blocks away, gradually increasing until a distance of half a block and then much more steeply increasing as the distance grew less. This, of course, promised plain sailing, but at the first desensitization session even at two blocks the imaginary car aroused anxiety much too great to be mastered: and it was revealed that the patient experienced anxiety at the very prospect of even the shortest journey by car, since the whole range of possibilities was already present the moment a journey became imminent. To obtain manageable levels of anxiety, an imaginary enclosed field two blocks square was postulated. The patient's car was "placed" in one corner of the field and the early items of the hierarchy involved a trusted person driving his car up to a stated point towards the patient's car, and of bringing this point ever closer as the patient progressed. Another case in whom weak anxiety stimuli were not easily found was a patient with a death phobia, whose items ranged in descending order from human corpses through such scenes as funeral processions to dead dogs. But even the last produced marked anxiety, when they were imagined even at distances of two or three hundred yards. A solution was found in retreating along a temporal instead of a spatial dimension, beginning with the (historically inaccurate) sentence, "William the Conqueror was killed at the Battle of Hastings in 1066."

DESENSITIZATION PROCEDURE

When the hierarchies have been constructed and relaxation training has proceeded to a degree judged sufficient, desensitization can then begin. First "weak" and later progressively "strong" anxiety-arousing stimulus situations will be presented to the imagination of the deeply relaxed patient, as described below.

When relaxation is poor, it may be enhanced by the use of meprobamate, chlorpromazine, or codeine given an hour before the interview. Which drug to use is decided by trial. When pervasive ("free-floating") anxiety impedes relaxation, the use of carbon

dioxide-oxygen mixture by La Verne's[8] single inhalation technique has been found to be of the greatest value[27] (p. 166) and
with some patients this method comes to be used before every
desensitization session. In a few patients who cannot relax but
who are not anxious either, attempts at desensitization sometimes
succeed, presumably because interview-induced emotional responses inhibit the anxiety aroused by the imagined stimuli.[27]

It is the usual practice for sessions to be conducted under hypnosis with the patient sitting on a comfortable armchair. He may
or may not have been hypnotized in an exploratory way on one
or more occasions during earlier interviews. With patients who
cannot be hypnotized, and in those who for any reason object to
it, hypnosis is omitted and instructions are given merely to close
the eyes and relax according to instructions. (There is a general
impression that these patients make slower progress.)

The patient having been hypnotized, the therapist proceeds to
bring about as deep as possible a state of calm by verbal suggges-
tions to the patient to give individual attention to relaxing each
group of muscles in the way he has learned.

The presentation of scenes at the first session is to some extent
exploratory. The first scene presented is always a neutral one—to
which a patient is not expected to have any anxiety reaction whatsoever. This is followed by a small number of presentations of the
mildest items from one or two of the patient's hierachies. To illustrate this, we shall make use of a verbatim account of the first
session of Case 2, whose hierarchies are given below. After hypno-
tizing and relaxing the patient, the therapist went on as follows.

> You will now imagine a number of scenes very clearly and calmly.
> The scenes may not at all disturb your state of relaxation. If by any
> chance, however, you feel disturbed, you will be able to indicate this
> to me by raising your left index finger an inch or so. *(Pause of about
> 10 seconds.)* First, I want you to imagine that you are standing at a
> busy street corner. You notice the traffic passing—cars, trucks, bicycles,
> and people. You see them all very clearly and you notice the sounds
> that accompany them. *(Pause of about 15 seconds.)* Now, stop imagin-
> ing that scene and again turn your attention to your muscles. *(Pause
> of about 20 seconds.)* Now, imagine that it is a work day. It is 11 A.M.
> and you are lying in bed with an attack of influenza and a tempera-

ture of 103°. *(Pause of about 10 seconds.)* Stop imagining the scene and again relax. *(Pause of 15 seconds.)* Now, imagine exactly the same situation again. *(Pause of 10 seconds.)* Stop imagining the scene and relax. *(Pause of about 20 seconds.)* Now, I want you to imagine that you are at the post office and you have just sent off a manuscript to a journal. *(Pause of 15 seconds.)* Stop imagining the scene and only relax. *(Pause of about five seconds.)* In a few moments, I will be counting up to five and you will wake up feeling very calm and refreshed. *(Pause of about five seconds.)* One, two, three, four, five. *(The patient opened his eyes looking somewhat dazed.)*

On being brought out of the trance, the patient is asked how he feels and how he felt during the trance, since it is important to know if a calm basal emotional state was achieved by the relaxation. He is then asked to indicate whether the scenes were clear or not. (It is essential for visualizing to be at least moderately clear.) Finally, the therapist inquires whether or not any of the scenes produced any disturbance in the patient, and if they did, how much. It is not common for a patient to report a reaction to the neutral control scene. It is worth remarking that even though the patient has a signal at his disposal with which to indicate disturbance, the fact that he has not done so during a scene by no means proves that it has not disturbed him at all, for it is a rare patient who makes use of the signal if only mildly disturbed. But the provision of a signal must never be omitted, for the patient will use it if he has a strong emotional reaction, which may not be otherwise manifest. *Exposure, and prolonged exposure in particular, to a very disturbing scene can greatly increase sensitivity.* With less marked disturbance there may be perseveration of anxiety, which makes continuance of the session futile.

At subsequent sessions, the same basic procedure is followed. If at the previous session there was a scene whose repeated presentations evoked anxiety that diminished but was not entirely extinguished, that scene is usually the first to be presented. If at the previous session the final scenes from a hierarchy ceased to arouse any anxiety, the scene next higher is now presented, except in a few patients who, despite having had no anxiety at all to a final scene at a previous session, again show a small measure of anxiety to this scene at a subsequent session. It must again be presented several times until all anxiety is eliminated before going on to the next scene.

In order to gauge progress, the following procedure is adopted after two to four presentations of a particular scene. The therapist says, "If you had even the slightest disturbance to the last presentation of this scene, raise your left finger now. If you had no disturbance, do nothing." If the finger is not raised, the therapist goes on to the next higher scene in the hierarchy. If the finger is raised, the therapist says, "If the amount of anxiety has been decreasing from one presentation to the next, do nothing. If it has not been decreasing, raise your finger again." If the finger is now not raised, this is an indication for further presentations of the scene, since further decrements in anxiety evocation may be confidently expected; but if it is raised, it is clear that the scene is producing more anxiety than the patient's relaxation can overcome, and it is therefore necessary to devise and interpose a scene midway in "strength" between this scene and the last one successfully mastered.

There is great variation in how many themes, how many scenes from each, and how many presentations are given at a session. Generally, up to four hierarchies are drawn upon in an individual session, and not many patients have more than four. Three or four presentations of a scene are usual, but ten or more may be needed. The total number of scenes presented is limited mainly by availability of time and by the endurance of the patient. On the whole, both of these quantities increase as therapy goes on, and eventually almost the whole interview may be devoted to desensitization, so that whereas at an early stage eight or ten presentations are the total given at a session, at an advanced stage the number may rise to thirty or even fifty.

The *duration* of a scene is usually of the order of five seconds, but it may be varied according to several circumstances. It is quickly terminated if the patient signals anxiety by spontaneously raising his finger or if he shows any sharp reaction. Whenever the therapist has a special reason to suspect that a scene may evoke a strong reaction he presents it with cautious brevity—for one or two seconds. By and large, early presentations of scenes are briefer, later ones longer. A certain number of patients require fifteen or more seconds to arrive at a clear image of a scene.

The *interval* between scenes is usually between ten and twenty seconds, but if the patient has been more than slightly disturbed by the preceding scene, it may be extended to a minute or more, and during that time the patient may be given repeated suggestions to be calm.

The *number* of desensitizing sessions required varies according to the number and the intensity of the anxiety areas, and the degree of generalization (involvement of related stimuli) in the case of each area. One patient may recover in as few as a half-dozen sessions; another may require a hundred or more. The patient with a death phobia, mentioned above, on whom a temporal dimension had to be used, also had two other phobias and required a total of about a hundred sessions. To remove the death phobia alone, a total of about two thousand scene presentations were needed.

The *spacing* of sessions does not seem to be of great importance. Two or three sessions a week are characteristic, but the meetings may be separated by many weeks or take place daily. Occasional patients, visiting from afar, have had two sessions in a single day. Whether sessions are massed or widely dispersed, there is almost always a close relation between the extent to which desensitization has been accomplished and the degree of diminution of anxiety responses to real stimuli. Except when therapy is nearly finished, and only a few loose ends of neurotic reactions are left (that may be overcome through emotions arising spontaneously in the ordinary course of living[27]) very little change occurs, as a rule, between sessions. This was strikingly demonstrated by Case 1 (below) in whom the marked improvement of a severe claustrophobia achieved by a first series of sessions remained almost stationary during a three and one-half year interval, after which further sessions overcame the phobia apparently completely.

EXAMPLES OF HIERARCHIES FROM ACTUAL CASES

Single or multiple anxiety hierarchies occur with about equal frequency. Each of the following two cases had multiple hierarchies. (*The most disturbing item, as always, is at the top of each list with the others ranked below it.*)

Case I

Mrs. A. was a fifty-year-old housewife, whose main complaint was of very disabling fears on the general theme of claustrophobia. The fears had begun about twenty-five years previously, following a terrifying experience with general anesthesia, and had subsequently spread in a series of steps, each associated with a particular experience, to a wide range of situations. The patient also had other phobias, the most important of which, concerning illness and death, had its origin during childhood. In forty-six desensitization sessions between March and July, 1956, all phobias were overcome except the most severe of the claustrophobic possibilities indicated in the first three items of the hierarchy given below, and with item 4 still incompletely conquered therapy was terminated when the writer went overseas for a year. The patient returned to treatment in October, 1959, having maintained her recovery in all areas, but having made very little additional progress. During the next two months, sixteen additional sessions were devoted to desensitizing to numerous scenes relevant to the "top" of the claustrophobia hierarchy. She was eventually able to accept, in the session, being confined for two hours in an imagined room four feet square, and reported complete freedom from fear in tunnels and only slight anxiety in "extreme" elevator situations.

Hierarchies

A. *Claustrophobic Series*
   1. Being stuck in an elevator. (The longer the time, the more disturbing.)
   2. Being locked in a room. (The smaller the room and the longer the time, the more disturbing.)
   3. Passing through a tunnel in a railway train. (The longer the tunnel, the more disturbing.)
   4. Traveling in an elevator alone. (The greater the distance, the more disturbing.)
   5. Traveling in an elevator with an operator. (The longer the distance, the more disturbing.)

6. On a journey by train. (The longer the journey, the more disturbing.)
7. Stuck in a dress with a stuck zipper.
8. Having a tight ring on her finger.
9. Visiting and unable to leave at will (for example, if engaged in a card game).
10. Being told of somebody in jail.
11. Having polish on her fingernails and no access to remover.
12. Reading of miners trapped underground.

B. *Death Series*
1. Being at a burial.
2. Being at a house of mourning.
3. The word *death*.
4. Seeing a funeral procession. (The nearer, the more disturbing.)
5. The sight of a dead animal, *e.g.* cat.
6. Driving past a cemetery. (The nearer, the more disturbing.)

C. *Illness Series*
1. Hearing that an acquaintance has cancer.
2. The word *cancer*.
3. Witnessing a convulsive seizure.
4. Discussions of operations. (The more prolonged the discussion, the more disturbing.)
5. Seeing a person receive an injection.
6. Seeing someone faint.
7. The word *operation*.
8. Considerable bleeding from another person.
9. A friend points to a stranger, saying "This man has tuberculosis."
10. The sight of a blood-stained bandage.
11. The smell of ether.
12. The sight of a friend sick in bed. (The more sick looking, the more disturbing.))
13. The smell of methylated spirits.
14. Driving past a hospital.

Case 2

Dr. B. was a forty-one-year-old gynecological resident who had felt anxious and insecure for as long as he could remember. Five years earlier, when anxieties were intensified by divorce proceedings, he had consulted a follower of Harry Stack Sullivan, who had tided him over the immediate situation but left him with attitudes of "acceptance" which had resulted in his becoming more anxious than before. After a few weeks' assertive training, he felt considerably better, but was left with the anxious sensitivities ranked in the hierarchies below. After six desensitization sessions he was completely free from anxiety responses to any actual situations similar to those contained in the hierarchies.

Hierarchies

A. *Guilt Series*
1. "Jackson (Dean of the Medical School) wants to see you."
2. Thinks "I only did ten minutes work today."
3. Thinks "I only did an hour's work today."
4. Thinks "I only did six hours' work today."
5. Sitting at the movies.
6. Reading an enjoyable novel.
7. Going on a casual stroll.
8. Staying in bed during the day (even though ill).

B. *Devaluation Series*
1. A woman doesn't respond to his advances.
2. An acquaintance says, "I saw you in Jefferson Street with a woman." (This kind of activity had locally acquired a disreputable flavor.)
3. Having a piece of writing rejected.
4. Awareness that his skill at a particular surgical operation left something to be desired. (Anxiety in terms of "Will I ever be able to do it?")
5. Overhearing adverse remarks about a lecture he delivered that he knows was not good.
6. Overhearing, "Dr. B. fancies himself as a surgeon."
7. Hearing anyone praised, e.g., "Dr. K. is a fine surgeon."
8. Having submitted a piece of writing for publication.

RESULTS

Table 31-I presents basic details of thirty-nine cases treated by desensitization. These patients, comprising about one-third of the total number so treated up to December, 1959, were randomly selected (by a casual visitor) from the alphabetical files of all patients treated. They are considered to be a representative sample of the total treated patient population. Rather than to summarize results from nearly 150 cases, it was felt desirable to present some details about a more limited series.

Many of the patients had other neurotic response habits as well, that were treated by methods appropriate to them. Interspersed among the thirty-nine cases reported were six others

TABLE 31-I
BASIC CASE DATA

Patient, Sex, Age	No. of Sessions	Hierarchy Theme	Outcome	Comments
1. F, 50	62	a) Claustrophobia	++++	See case data above.
		b) Illness and hospitals	++++	
		c) Death and its trappings	++++	
		d) Storms	+++	
		e) Quarrels	++++	
2. M, 40	6	a) Guilt	++++	See case data above.
		b) Devaluation	++++	
3. F, 24	17	a) Examinations	++++	
		b) Being scrutinized	++++	
		c) Devaluation	++++	
		d) Discord between others	++++	
4. M, 24	5	a) Snakelike shapes	++++	
5. M, 21	24	a) Being watched	++++	
		b) Suffering of others	++++	
		c) "Jealousy" reaction	++++	
		d) Disapproval	++++	
6. M, 28	5	Crowds	+++	
7. F, 21	5	Criticism	++++	
8. F, 52	21	a) Being center of attention	0	No disturbance during scenes. Was in fact not imagining self in situation.
		b) Superstitions	0	
9. F, 25	9	Suffering and death of others	+++	
10. M, 22	17	Tissue damage in others	++++	
11. M, 37	13	Actual or implied criticism	++++	
12. F, 31	15	Being watched working	+++	

TABLE 31-1—*Continued*

Patient, Sex, Age	No. of Sessions	Hierarchy Theme	Outcome	Comments
13. F, 40	16	a) "Suffering" and eeriness	++++	This case has been reported in detail.[26]
		b) Being devalued	++++	
		c) Failing to come up to expectations	++++	
14. M, 36	10	a) Bright light	++++	
		b) Palpitations	++++	
15. M, 43	9	Wounds and corpses	+++	No anxiety while being watched at work.
16. M, 27	51	a) Being watched, especially at work	+++	Anxious at times while watched playing
		b) Being criticized	++++	cards.
17. M, 33	8	Being watched at golf	+++	
18. M, 13	8	Talking before audience (stutterer)	0	No imagined scene was ever disturbing
19. M, 40	7	Authority figures	++++	
20. M, 23	4	Claustrophobia	++++	
21. F, 23	6	a) Agoraphobia	0	Later successfully treated by conditioned
		b) Fear of falling	0	motor response method.[27]
22. M, 46	19	a) Being in limelight	+++	
		b) blood and death	++++	
23. F, 40	20	Social embarrassment	++++	
24. F, 28	9	Agoraphobia	0	
25. F, 48	7	Rejection	+++	
26. M, 28	13	a) Disapproval	+++	
		b) Rejection	++++	
27. M, 11	6	Authority figures	++++	
28. M, 26	217	a) Claustrophobia	++++	Finally overcome completely by use of Mal-
		b) Criticism (numerous aspects)	+++	leson's method.[13]
		c) Trappings of death	+++	

TABLE 31-I—Continued

Patient, Sex, Age	No. of Sessions	Hierarchy Theme	Outcome	Comments
29. F, 20	5	Agoraphobia	++++	
30. M, 68	23	a) Agoraphobia	++++	
		b) Masturbation	++++	
31. F, 36	5	Being in limelight	++++	
32. M, 26	17	a) Illness and death	+++	
		b) Own symptoms	+++	
33. F, 44	9	a) Being watched	++++	
		b) Elevators	++++	
34. F, 47	17	Intromission into vagina	+++	After 15th session gradual *in vivo* operation with objects became possible, and subsequently coitus with husband.
35. M, 37	5	a) Disapproval	++++	
		b) Rejection	++++	
36. F, 32	25	Sexual stimuli	++++	
37. M, 36	21	a) Agoraphobia	++++	
		b) Disapproval	++++	
		c) Being watched	++++	
28. M, 18	6	a) Disapproval	+++	Instrumental in overcoming impotence
		b) Sexual stimuli	++++	
39. F, 48	20	a) Rejection	++++	Stutter markedly improved as anxiety diminished, partly as result of desensitization, and partly due to assertive behavior in relevant situations.
		b) Crudeness of others	++++	

eligible for desensitization who had between two and six sessions, but who are excluded from the series because they terminated treatment for various reasons (even though usually showing some evidence of progress). It is felt proper to exclude these, as in evaluating the therapeutic efficacy of an antibiotic it would be proper to omit cases that had received only one or two doses. Also excluded are two cases that turned out to be schizophrenic. Psychotic patients do not respond to this treatment and of course receive it only if misdiagnosed as neurotic. On the other hand, every presenting neurotic case is accepted for treatment.

Outcome of treatment is judged on the basis of several sources of information. In addition to the patient's report of his reactions to stimuli from the hierarchies during sessions, there frequently is observable evidence of diminished anxious responding, inasmuch as many patients display, when disturbed, characteristic muscle tensions (such as grimaces or finger movements). The greatest importance is attached to the patient's report of changed responses, in real life, to previously fearful situations. I have not regularly checked these reports by direct observation, but in several cases in whom I have made such checks the patient's account of his improved reaction has invariably been confirmed. In general, there is reason to accept the credibility of patients who report *gradual* improvement. A patient who wished to use an allegation of recovery in order to get out of an unsuccessful course of treatment, would be likely to report recovery rather suddenly, rather than to continue in treatment to substantiate a claim of gradual recovery.

Degree of change is rated on a 5-point scale ranging from 4-plus to zero. A 4-plus rating indicates complete, or almost complete, freedom from phobic reactions to all situations on the theme of the phobia; 3-plus means an improvement of response such that the phobia is judged by the patient to retain not more than 20 percent of its original strength, 2-plus means 30 to 70 percent, and 1-plus indicates that more than 70 percent of the original strength of the phobia is judged retained. A zero rating indicates that there is no discernible change. (It will be noted that only 4-plus, 3-plus and zero ratings have been applicable to the patients in this series.)

TABLE 31-II
SUMMARY OF DATA OF TABLE I

Patients	39	
Number of patients responding to desensitization treatment	35	
Number of hierarchies	68	
Hierarchies overcome	45	} 91%
Hierarchies markedly improved	17	
Hierarchies unimproved	6	9%
Total number of desensitization sessions	762	
Mean session expenditure per heirarchy	11.2	
Mean session expenditure per successfully treated hierarchy	12.3	
Median number of sessions per patient	10.0	

Table 31-II summarizes the data given in Table 31-I. There were sixty-eight phobias and neurotic anxiety response habits related to more complex situations among the thirty-nine patients, of whom nineteen had multiple hierarchies. The treatment was judged effective in thirty-five of the patients. Forty-five of the phobic and other anxiety habits were apparently eliminated (4-plus rating) and seventeen more were markedly ameliorated (3-plus rating). (It is entirely possible that most of the latter would have reached a 4-plus level if additional sessions could have been given; in cases 16 and 29, progress had become very slow when sessions were discontinued, but this was not so in the other cases.)

Among the failures, cases 8 and 18 were unable to imagine themselves within situations; case 22 could not confine her imagining to the stated scene and therefore had excessive anxiety, but was later treated with complete success by means of another conditioning method (p. 174);[27] case 25 had interpersonal anxiety reactions that led to erratic responses and, having experienced no benefit, sought therapy elsewhere.

The thirty-nine patients had a total of 762 desensitization sessions, including in each case the first exploratory session although in many instances scenes from the hierarchies were not presented at that session. The mean number of sessions per hierarchy was 11.2; the median number of sessions given to patients 10.0. It should be noted that a desensitization session usually takes up only part of a three-quarter hour interview period, and in cases that also have neurotic problems requiring direct action in the life situation there may be many interviews in which a session is not included.

At times varying between six months and four years after the end of treatment, follow-up reports were obtained from twenty of the thirty-five patients who responded to desensitization. There was no reported instance of relapse or the appearance of new phobias or other neurotic symptoms. I have never observed resurgence of neurotic anxiety when desensitization has been complete or virtually so.

DISCUSSION

The general idea of overcoming phobias or other neurotic habits by means of systematic "gradual approaches" is not new. It has long been known that increasing measures of exposure to a feared object may lead to a gradual disappearance of the fear. This knowledge has sometimes,[21] but unfortunately not very often, contributed to the armamentarium of psychiatrists in dealing with phobias. What is new in the present contribution is (a) the provision of a theoretical explanation for the success of such gradual approaches and (b) the description of a method in which the therapist has complete control of the degree of approach that the patient makes to the feared object at any particular time. The situations, being imaginary, are constructed and varied at will in the consulting room.

The excellent results obtained by this method of treatment are naturally viewed with skepticism by those who in the psychoanalytic tradition regard phobias and other neurotic anxiety response habits as merely the superficial manifestations of deeper unconscious conflicts. Some attempt to clarify the issue must be made. In the majority of cases a phobia is found to have begun at a particular time and in relation to a particular traumatic event. Before that time, presumably the patient already had his assumed unconscious conflicts, but did not feel any need for treatment. At the very least, then, it must surely be admitted that if through desensitization the patient is restored to the state in which he was before the traumatic event, something important has been gained from the point of view of his suffering. The reply could, of course, be made that unless the unconscious conflicts are brought to light and resolved the patient will relapse or develop other symptoms; but in keeping with follow-up studies on the results of nonanalytic psychotherapy in neurotic cases in general my experience has been that relapse or the appearance of new reactions is rare, unless a major group of stimuli in a desensitized area has been neglected.

At the same time, it is indisputable that only a minority of individuals exposed to a given traumatic event develop a phobia; some predisposing condition or conditions must determine which individuals do. The psychoanalysts are undoubtedly right in insisting on this point. But we are not therefore compelled to accept their version of the nature of the predisposing conditions, especially as the factual foundations of that version are far from satisfactory.[30] Objective behavior theory can also point to factors that may predispose an individual to particularly severe conditioning of anxiety. First, some people are apparently endowed with much more active autonomic nervous systems than others.[18] Second, previous experience with similar stimulus constellations may have induced low degrees of anxiety conditioning which would sensitize a person to the traumatic experience. Third, there may be circumstances in the moment of trauma that may bring about an unusually high degree of focusing upon certain stimulus constellations. The second of these suggested factors is probably the most important, for patients do frequently tell of minor sensitivity having pre-existed the precipitating event. In the course of desensitization, these original sensitivities also come to be removed, along with whatever has been more recently conditioned.

Critics of the conditioned response approach to therapy of the neuroses frequently assert that when the desensitization method leads to recovery, it is not the method as such that is responsible, but the "transference" established between patient and therapist. If these critics were right—if desensitization were incidental to rather than causal of recovery—it would be expected that improvement would affect all areas more or less uniformly, and not be confined to those to which desensitization had been applied. The facts are directly contrary to this expectation, for practically invariably it is found that *unless different hierarchies have unmistakable common features desensitization to one hierarchy does not in the least diminish the reactivity to another (untreated) hierarchy.* For example, a recent patient had both a widespread agoraphobic constellation, and a fear of airplanes, extending to the sight and sound of them. Having constructed hierarchies to both series, the writer proceeded to desensitize the patient to the agoraphobia, but ignored the airplane phobia until the agoraphobia had been almost completely overcome. At this stage, reassessment of the airplane phobia revealed not the slightest evidence of diminution. This is in accord with observations made in connection with experimental neuroses, in which eliminating anxiety conditioned to visual stimuli does not affect the anxiety-evoking potential of auditory stimuli that were conditioned at the same time as the visual stimuli.[23,27]

From the point of view of the scientific investigator the desensitization method has a number of advantages that are unusual in the field of psychotherapy: (a) the aim of therapy can be clearly stated in every case; (b) sources of neurotic anxiety can be defined and delimited; (c) change of reaction to a scene is determined during sessions (and accordingly could be measured by psychophysiological means); (d) there is no objection to conducting therapy before an unconcealed audience (for this has been done without apparent effect on the course of therapy); and (e) therapists can be interchanged if desired.

SUMMARY

The desensitization method of therapy is a particular application of the reciprocal inhibition principle to the elimination of neurotic habits. The experimental background and some theoretical implications of this principle are discussed.

A detailed account is given of the technique of desensitization and an analysis of its effects when applied to sixty-eight phobias and allied neurotic anxiety response habits in thirty-nine patients. In a mean of 11.2 sessions, forty-five of the neurotic habits were overcome and seventeen more very markedly improved. Six month to four year follow-up reports from twenty of the thirty-five successfully treated patients did not reveal an instance of relapse or the emergence of new symptoms.

REFERENCES

1. Bond, I. K. and Hutchison, H. C.: Application of reciprocal inhibition therapy to exhibitionism. *Can Med Assoc J, 83:*23-25, 1960.
2. Curran, D. and Partridge, M.: *Psychological Medicine.* Edinburgh, Livingstone, 1955.
3. Eysenck, H. J.: *Behavior Therapy and the Neuroses.* New York, Pergamon Press, 1960.
4. Freeman, H. L. and Kendrick, D. C.: A case of cat phobia. *Brit Med J, 2:*497-502, 1960.
5. Jacobson, E.: *Progressive Relaxation.* Chicago, Univ. of Chicago Press, 1938.
6. Jacobson, E.: Variation of blood pressure with skeletal muscle tension and relaxation. *Ann Intern Med, 13:*1619-1625, 1940.
7. Jones, M. C.: The elimination of children's fears. *J Exp Psychol, 7:*382-390, 1924.
8. LaVerne, A. A.: Rapid coma technique of carbon dioxide inhalation therapy. *Dis Nerv Syst, 14:*141-144, 1953.
9. Lazarus, A. A.: The elimination of children's phobias by deconditioning. *Med Proc, 5:*261, 1959.
10. Lazarus, A. A.: New group techniques in the treatment of phobic conditions. Ph.D. dissertation. Univ. of the Witwatersrand, 1959.
11. Lazarus, A. A. and Rachman, S.: The use of systematic desensitization in psychotherapy. *S Afr Med J, 31:*934-937, 1957.
12. Lazovik, A. D. and Lang, P. J.: A laboratory demonstration of systematic desensitization psychotherapy. *J Psychol Stud, 11:*238, 1960.
13. Malleson, N.: Panic and phobia. *Lancet, 1:*225-227, 1959.
14. Meyer, V.: The treatment of two phobic patients on the basis of learning principles. *J Abnorm Soc Psychol, 55:*261-266, 1957.
15. Rachman, S.: The treatment of anxiety and phobic reactions by systematic desensitization psychotherapy. *J Abnorm Soc Psychol, 58:*259-263, 1959.

16. Salter, A.: *Conditioned Reflex Therapy.* New York, Creative Age Press, 1950.

17. Sherrington, C. S.: *Integrative Action of the Nervous System.* New Haven, Yale Univ. Press, 1906.

18. Shirley, M.: *The First Two Years.* Minneapolis, Univ. of Minnesota Press, 1933.

19. Stevenson, I.: Direct instigation of behavioral changes in psychotherapy. *AMA Arch Gen Psychiatry, 1:*99-107, 1959.

20. Stevenson, I. and Wolpe, J.: Recovery from sexual deviations through overcoming nonsexual neurotic responses. *Am J Psychiatry, 116:*737-742, 1960.

21. Terhune, W. S.: The phobic syndrome. *Arch Neurol Psychiat, 62:*162-172, 1949.

22. Willoughby, R. R.: Some properties of the Thurstone Personality Schedule and a suggested revision. *J Soc Psychol, 3:*401-424, 1932.

23. Wolpe, J.: Experimental neuroses as learned behavior. *Br J Psychol, 43:* 243-268, 1952.

24. Wolpe, J.: Learning versus lesions as the basis of neurotic behavior. *Am J Psychiatry, 112:*923-927, 1956.

25. Wolpe, J.: Objective psychotherapy of the neuroses. *S Afr Med J, 26:* 825-829, 1952.

26. Wolpe, J.: Psychotherapy based on the principles of reciprocal inhibition. In Burton, A. (Ed.): *Case Studies in Counseling and Psychotherapy.* Englewood Cliffs, N. J., Prentice-Hall, 1959, pp. 353-381.

27. Wolpe, J.: *Psychotherapy by Reciprocal Inhibition.* Stanford, Stanford Univ. Press, 1958.

28. Wolpe, J.: Reciprocal inhibition as the main basis of psychotherapeutic effects. *Arch Neurol Psychiatry, 72:*205-226, 1954.

29. Wolpe, J.: Recoveries from neuroses without psychoanalysis: Their prognosis and its implications. *Am J Psychiatry,* in press.

30. Wolpe, J. and Rachman, S.: Psychoanalytic "evidence": A critique based on Freud's case of Little Hans. *J Nerv Ment Dis, 131:*135-148, 1960.

Chapter 32

SYSTEMATIC DESENSITIZATION

S. J. RACHMAN

SYSTEMATIC desensitization is the most widely used method of behavior therapy. It was derived from and is closely connected with experimental psychology. Moreover, its operations and effects can be explicitly described and properly examined. The purpose of the present paper is to consider the experimental and clinical justification for this procedure.

The clinical effectiveness of desensitization has been discussed by Wolpe (1958, 1961), Eysenck and Rachman (1965), and Rachman (1965b). The success rates reported with behavior therapy (in which desensitization usually features very prominently) are usually in the region of 75 percent. The three most recent clinical reports have all yielded a similar outcome (Hain, Butcher and Stevenson, 1966; Marks and Gelder, 1966; Meyer and Crisp, 1966). It would appear that Rachman's (1965a) conclusion regarding behavior therapy in general, can be applied with equal merit to desensitization—"It is a promising technique which is virtually certain to be effective in a large number of phobic and anxiety states but the treatment of severe, chronic patients needs to be improved." In the present paper, however, we shall be considering primarily the experimental use of systematic desensitization.

Some of the most important experimental work on this subject has been carried out by Lang and Lazovik. In 1963, they reported on the results of an experiment carried out on nonpsychiatric subjects who suffered from an excessive fear of snakes. This pioneer experiment was carefully and elaborately prepared and the experimental design and execution were of a high quality. The stringent controls which they applied enhanced the signifi-

Note: Abridged and reprinted from *Psychol Bull, 67*:93-103, 1967.

cance of their findings. The aims of the experiment were described by Lang and Lazovik (1963) as follows:

1. To evaluate the changes in snake phobic behavior that occur over time, particularly the effect of repeated exposure to the phobic object.

2. Compare these changes with those that follow systematic desensitization therapy.

3. Determine the changes in behavior that are a direct function of the desensitization process.

Lang and Lazovik chose to study snake phobia because of its fairly common occurrence (Geer, 1965) and also because of the assumed symbolic sexual significance attributed to snakes (e.g. Brill, 1949; Hendrick, 1948). Twenty-four college student volunteers were finally selected by a combination of interview, questionnaire, and direct exposure to a nonpoisonous snake. Only those subjects who rated their fears as intense and whose behavior in the presence of the snake confirmed the subjective report were used in the experiment. The subjects were divided into two matched groups, an experimental group ($n = 13$) and a control group ($n = 11$). The experimental treatment comprised two essential parts: training, and desensitization proper. The training procedure consisted of five sessions of forty-five minutes duration, during which an anxiety hierarchy consisting of twenty situations involving snakes was constructed. The subjects were then trained in deep relaxation and taught how to visualize the feared scenes vividly while under hypnosis.

Following this training period, the experimental subjects were given eleven sessions of systematic desensitization, during which they were hypnotized and instructed to relax deeply. The anxiety items from the hierarchy were then presented, starting with the least frightening scenes and working up the scale to the most frightening scenes. As the experimental design demanded that each treated subject receive only eleven treatment sessions, some of the subjects were not desensitized to all of the items in the hierarchy. In order to assess the effectiveness of reality training, half of the experimental subjects were exposed to the snake before treatment on a number of occasions. The control subjects did not participate in desensitization but were evaluated at the same time as their opposite numbers in the experimental series, and their behavior in the presence of the snake was ascertained at the beginning and the end of the experiment. All of the available subjects were seen and evaluated six months after the completion of therapy.

The authors summarized their results in the following way:

> The results of the present experiment demonstrate that the experimental analogue of desensitization therapy effectively reduces phobic behavior. Both subjective rating of fear and overt avoidance behavior were modified, and gains [compared to the control group] were maintained or increased at the six-months follow up. The results of objective measures were in turn supported by extensive interview material. Close questioning could not persuade any of the experimental subjects that a desire to please the experimenter had been a significant factor in their change. Furthermore, in none of these interviews was there any evidence that other symptoms appeared to replace the phobic behavior.
>
> The fact that no significant change was associated with the pretherapy training argues that hypnosis and general muscle relaxation were not in themselves vehicles of change. Similarly, the basic suggestibility of the subjects must be excluded . . . . Clearly, the responsibility for the reduction in phobic behavior must be assigned to the desensitization process itself [p. 524].

Lang and Lazovik also found a very close connection between the degree of improvement and the amount of progress made in the desensitization of hierarchy items within the eleven sessions provided by the experiment. They also made three general points on the basis of their results. First, as has been argued on previous occasions (see Eysenck and Rachman, 1965), it is not necessary to "explore with the subject, the factors contributing to the learning of a phobia or its unconscious meaning in order to eliminate the fear behavior." Second, they were not able to find any evidence to support the presumed claim that symptom substitution will arise if the symptoms are treated directly. Third, they pointed out that in reducing phobic behavior, it is not necessary to alter the basic attitudes, values, or personality of the subject.

Lang, Lazovik, and Reynolds (1965) recently reported further developments with this experimental procedure. They completed a study which included the experimental treatment of twenty-three subjects by systematic desensitization, eleven untreated controls, and ten subjects who participated in "pseudotherapy." This last group of subjects is a particularly important addition since they received the same preliminary training as the desensitization group and participated in the same number of interview sessions. The major difference was that the pseudotherapy group was relaxed in the interview sessions but not desensitized—instead the therapist carefully avoided presenting any anxiety-provoking stimuli. These subjects were under the impression that they were being given a form of dynamic or interpretative therapy. The essential difference in the treated and pseudotherapy groups lay then in the use of systematic desensitization. Consequently, any difference in the treatment outcome had to be attributed to the use of this behavior therapy technique. The results were clear-cut and indicated that the subjects treated by systematic desensitization showed significant reductions in phobic behavior. The untreated subjects and the subjects who participated in pseudotherapy showed no improvement whatever. Among the subsidiary observations made by Lang *et al.*, the following are of particular interest. (a) None of the successfully treated subjects showed signs of developing substitute symptoms. (b) Again, it was found to be unnecessary to delve into the presumed basic causes of their fear of snakes. (c) Simply being in a therapeutic relationship with the therapist was not sufficient to effect significant changes in the phobia (see also Paul, 1966). (d) Successful behavior therapy was completely independent of the subject's basic suggestibility (as assessed on the Stanford scale). (e) The systematic desensitization of the specific fear generalized positively to other fears and an all-around improvement was observed.

Substantially confirmatory results were also reported in an experiment by Paul (1966). He investigated the effectiveness of desensitization in reducing interpersonal performance anxiety (actually, fear of public speaking). Five groups of carefully matched students were randomly allotted to the following groups: (a) systematic desensitization ($n = 15$), (b) insight therapy ($n = 15$), (c) attention placebo ($n = 15$), (d) no treatment control

$(n = 29)$, and (e) no contact $(n = 22)$. Each of the seventy-four students comprising the first four groups was assessed before and after the completion of the experiment on three different types of scales. These measures included a number of self-report questionnaires, physiological measures (pulse rate and palmar sweating), and a rating of their behavior in a real-life stress situation (which involved speaking in public). Five experienced therapists participated in the experiment after having received brief but intensive training in the desensitization technique. One of the interesting sidelights to emerge from this experiment was the apparent success with which these predominantly interpretative or nondirective therapists acquired the ability to use desensitization treatment. Each therapist was allotted patients from the three treatment groups (i.e. desensitization, insight, attention placebo). On the completion of a comparatively short period of treatment (5 hours over 6 weeks), all subjects, including the nontreatment controls, were retested. Subjects who had received desensitization treatment showed a significantly better response to treatment than any of the other subjects. This superiority was evident on all three types of measurement—subjective report, physiological arousal, and reaction to stress. The superiority of the desensitized group was maintained at the six-week follow-up period. Like the experiments conducted by Lang and Lazovik (1963), the work of Paul (1966) indicates that it is possible to bring about significant reductions in fear, even long standing fears, by the use of systematic desensitization. It also indicates that fears can be eliminated without any exploration in depth. It should be pointed out, however, that this study by Paul is best regarded as an investigation of the effectiveness of desensitization in its own right, and not as a demonstration of the superiority of this technique over other forms of therapy, particularly interpretative or insight treatment. Such a brief period of treatment cannot be regarded as a fair test of "insight therapy" which, by general agreement, is a procedure requiring a great deal of time to execute. Paul anticipated this objection by referring to reports of the success of brief psychotherapy and counseling and by pointing out that most patients suffering from anxiety currently receive *brief* therapy. These

arguments are of practical importance and well-taken. Nevertheless, it seems to be unfair to long-term therapies such as psychoanalysis to refer to the procedure as "insight" treatment; "brief
psychotherapy" is perhaps a more accurate description of Paul's
procedure. Furthermore, Paul's use of the term "follow-up" to
denote the reassessment carried out six weeks after the completion
of the experiment can be misleading. This is not in the ordinary
sense a follow-up, but should be regarded more correctly as a posttreatment assessment. Only one of the ten assessment procedures
was readministered *twice* after treatment had been completed.
The stability of changes induced by desensitization therapy was
better tested by other studies such as those carried out by Lang
and Lazovik (1963). Nevertheless, the corroborative value of
Paul's study is impressive.

In a recent development of this study, Paul and Shannon
(1966) demonstrated that systematic desensitization "can be
efficiently combined with group discussion and administered in
groups without loss of effectiveness in the treatment of interpersonal performance anxiety." Ten chronically anxious students
were treated in two groups of five each: nine weekly sessions were
given. Significant improvements were obtained at the completion
of group treatment; the ten subjects were shown to be considerably less anxious than the ten untreated control subjects with
whom they were compared. A comparison between the group-
treatment results with the individual-desensitization-treatment
results obtained in Paul's (1966) earlier study indicated that "the
changes obtained for the group treatment equalled or excelled
those obtained for individual treatments on every scale."

A very tightly controlled investigation of the effect of desensitization was recently carried out by Davison (1965). He had two
main aims in designing his study. First, he wanted to examine the
overall effect of desensitization treatment when compared with
a no-treatment group. Second, he was interested in teasing out the
effective elements of desensitization treatment. He used twenty-
eight nonpsychiatric female subjects, all of whom complained of,
and demonstrated, excessive fear of snakes. The subjects were
divided into four matched groups on the basis of their behavior

in the presence of real snakes. The four groups were treated in the following manner: Group 1 received desensitization under relaxation, in the usual manner. Group 2 received relaxation training, but during the treatment sessions these subjects were given irrelevant images to consider while under deep relaxation. Group 3 was given desensitization without either receiving training in relaxation or being relaxed in the actual treatment sessions. Group 4 received no active treatment but was merely assessed prior to and after the completion of the experiment. The subjects in Groups 2 and 3 were "yoked" to the systematic desensitization subjects, thereby ensuring that all of the girls who received treatment of any kind received the same number and durations of exposure to imaginary stimuli. The same therapist acted for all the subjects. At the completion of treatment, the retest avoidance exposures showed that the "desensitization under relaxation" group showed greater improvements than the other three groups, which did not differ. It was also observed that the subjects who were asked to imagine the anxiety-evoking stimuli without first being relaxed signalled anxiety far more often during treatment sessions than the other subjects. The importance of this study, apart from providing another demonstration of the effectiveness of desensitization in eliminating or reducing fears, is that it helps to isolate the mechanisms which produce the reductions in fear. Davison has demonstrated in this experiment that it is neither relaxation alone nor desensitization alone which produces the improvements. Rather, it is a combination of desensitization *and* relaxation which reduces fear. Apart from its practical importance, this experimental result goes partway towards confirming Wolpe's theoretical account of his treatment procedure. One would predict on the basis of his ideas of reciprocal inhibition that neither desensitization nor relaxation would in themselves be adequate procedures for eliminating fear.

A very similar result was also reported by Rachman (1965b). In this study, four small groups of spider phobic, nonpsychiatric subjects were allocated to the following experimental groups: desensitization with relaxation, desensitization without relaxation, relaxation only, no-treatment controls. The purpose of the experiment was "further to explore the effective mechanism contained in the treatment called 'systematic desensitization' based on relaxation":

> What are the necessary parts of the treatment procedure? Three specific questions are framed: is the treatment more effective than no-treatment? Is the treatment more effective than relaxation alone? Is the treatment more effective than desensitization without relaxation? (p. 256).

The effects of treatment were assessed by subjective reports, avoidance tests, and fear estimates. Marked reductions in fear were obtained only in the desensitization-with-relaxation group, and it was concluded that the combined effects of relaxation and desensitization were greater than their separate effects. Commenting on the results, Rachman (1965b) said that

> neither relaxation nor desensitization is effective in its own right. The catalytic effect of the two procedures is greater than their separate actions. It means also that the learning process involved is probably conditioned inhibition rather than extinction. This is not meant to imply that extinction is never responsible for the reduction of fear. In the present context however, inhibition is a more effective process [p. 250].

Like Davison, Paul, and Lang and Lazovik, Rachman could adduce no evidence of symptom substitution. Moreover, the improvements in phobic behavior observed at the end of treatment were found to be reassuringly stable over a 3-month follow-up period.

Cooke (1966) compared the relative effectiveness of two types of desensitization treatments—imaginal desensitizing versus real-life desensitizing. He employed three groups of nonpsychiatric subjects with excessive fears of rats. Each group consisted of four subjects, and their fear reactions were ascertained by avoidance tests in the usual manner (see Lang and Lazowik, 1963; Paul, 1966). The first group was relaxed and then exposed in a graded and gradual manner to real rats, while the second group was relaxed and desensitized to similar items in imagination only. The third group consisted of a no-treatment control. Cooke found no overall difference between the two types of treatment, both of which produced significant decreases in fear (compared to the control group). He showed, however, that highly anxious subjects showed more fear reduction when treated in the Wolpeian fashion with imaginal stimuli. This difference in the response to treatment of slightly and highly anxious subjects is of some interest because of the clinical reports which have suggested that anxious patients do not respond to behavior therapy as well as less anxious patients (see Lazarus, 1963; Marks and Gelder, 1966, Wolpe, Salter and Reyna, 1965). In a sense, Cooke's results run counter to these clinical findings which all tend to show that anxious subjects respond more slowly to behavior therapy. Clearly this is a point which needs further investigation. Some other findings to emerge from Cooke's study and which are of interest include the fact that no symptom substitution was observed nor were any increases in anxiety noted after treatment. Cooke also remarked on the consistency and reliability of the avoidance test scores and the subjective fear estimates.

A slightly atypical experiment was carried out by Lazarus in 1961 and also affords some evidence in support of the effectiveness of systematic desensitization. This study was unusual in that the treatment was carried out in groups rather than in individual treatment sessions and because of the heterogeneity of the sample used. The group desensitization technique had never been used before so that Lazarus' study to a large extent was exploratory rather than confirmatory. The results were nevertheless favorable to the desensitization approach and have now received a measure of support from the experiment recently reported by Paul and Shannon (1966). Altogether, Lazarus treated seventeen control subjects and eighteen experimental subjects. The samples consisted of four types of patients. These were eleven acrophobics, fifteen claustrophobics, five cases of impotence, and four mixed disorders. The experimental subjects were treated in four separate groups, varying in size from two to five subjects, and the control subjects were treated in groups of no less than three subjects at a time. The experimental subjects were trained in relaxation and were given desensitization training and, eventually, desensitization treatment. The first control group was given group interpretative therapy, and the second control group (consisting of eight patients) received interpretative therapy and relaxation. Although the subjects treated by Lazarus were not drawn from a psychiatric population, they were nevertheless severely limited in their social relationships and general psychological adjustment because of their complaints. Before commencing treatment, each subject was interviewed and given psychometric tests and, where possible, was observed in a real-life fear situation. The assessment of the treatment effect was carried out by the interview method and also by a further excursion into the relevant feared situation. The results showed that a high degree of success was obtained with the group desensitization method, whereas those patients who received interpretative treatment did not show any recoveries. Of the eight patients treated by group interpretative therapy and relaxation, only two recovered. Follow-up studies were conducted on all the patients who had shown any sign of recovery. The follow-ups were carried out by means of a questionnaire, and any patient who revealed even a slight phobic recurrence was considered to have relapsed. Although Lazarus paid attention to the question of possible symptom substitution, no evidence of this phenomenon was encountered. Lazarus summarized his results this way:

> Group desensitization was applied to 18 patients of whom 13 initially recovered and three subsequently relapsed. Group interpretation was applied to nine patients. There were no recoveries in this group. Group interpretation plus relaxation was applied to eight patients of whom two recovered and one subsequently relapsed. The 15 patients who had not benefitted from the interpretative procedures were then treated by group desensitizaiton. There were 10 recoveries of whom two subsequently relapsed [p. 508].

Of the eighteen subjects who were treated by group desensitization, thirteen recovered in a mean of 20.4 sessions. The fifteen patients who were not symptom-free after undergoing interpretative group therapy and who were treated by desensitization showed a 66 percent recovery rate after a mean of only 10.1 sessions. Lazarus suggested that the fact that these patients recovered in a shorter time than did the original experimental subjects indicates that they may have received some form of nonspecific benefit from either the relaxation training or from the relaxation training in association with the interpretative therapy. Unfortunately, Lazarus's results cannot be accepted without reserve because the experimental design contained some weaknesses. The possibility that rater contamination and experimenter bias distorted the results cannot be ruled out because both the treatment and assessments were carried out by Lazarus himself.

In an experiment on a small group of asthmatic patients who acted as their own controls, Moore (1965) obtained a greater degree of improvement with desensitization treatment than that recorded when the patients received either relaxation or relaxation and suggestion. An interesting aspect of the treatment outcome in this study was that when the subjects were merely relaxed, their subjective reports suggested some improvements in their condition, whereas the physiological measurements (respiratory flow) reflected little change. The results obtained revealed significant improvements after systematic desensitization, apparently attributable to the *desensitization* procedure. In the case of this procedure, subjective reports and physiological tests improved together. For this reason, and because of the intrinsic clinical interest of this study, replications and extensions of this experiment would be extremely useful.

The present state of the experimental evidence on desensitization permits the following conclusions: (a) Desensitization therapy effectively reduces phobic behavior. (b) The elimination of phobic behavior is analogous to the elimination of other responses from the subject's repertoire. (c) Although it is often useful clinically, the *experimental* studies show that it is not essential to ascertain the origin of a phobia in order to eliminate it and neither is it necessary to change the subject's basic attitudes or to modify his personality. (d) The elimination of a phobia is not followed by symptom substitution. (e) The response to treatment is not related to suggestibility. (f) Relaxation alone or hypnosis alone does not reduce the phobia. (g) Relaxation and hypnosis accompanied by pseudotherapeutic interviews do not reduce the phobia. (h) The establishment of a therapeutic relationship with the patient does not in itself reduce the phobia—at best it produces marginal improvements. (i) Desensitization administered in the absence of relaxation appears to be less effective than systematic desensitization treatment. (j) Interpretative therapy combined with relaxation does not reduce phobic behavior. (k) A limited number of observations raise the possibility that reductions in fears which are produced by desensitization occur almost immediately; in a large minority of instances, a proportion of the fear-reduction accomplished in experimental treatment sessions reappears within twenty-four hours.

Although some of these conclusions are still tentative (the last two in particular), as a body they constitute a very important advance in our ability to reduce phobias. It is clear nevertheless that there is a great deal which still needs to be investigated and understood. Perhaps the most immediate need is for further experimental studies which attempt to apply these findings to psychiatric patients. While it is true that the clinical reports which have been published to date are, with some exceptions, consistent with the experimental evidence discussed in this paper, there remains a need for careful experimental investigation. of the clinical application of desensitization. The recent study reported by Marks and Gelder (1966) is an example of the type of application which is required. The bulk of the work which has been reported so far has of course been carried out on phobic subjects. There is therefore a need for further investigation of both psychiatric and nonpsychiatric subjects who suffer from complaints other than excessive fears or phobias. Clearly, it is necessary to find other psychiatric and nonpsychiatric analogies on which to carry out similar experiments to those already described. One such example is the study carried out by Moore (1965) on asthmatic patients. From an experimental point of view, the full range of applicability of desensitization treatment remains to be explored. One of the specific problems which will have to be reexamined in clinical experiments is the role of anxiety in facilitating or impeding the progress of desensitization treatment. The clinical reports tend on the whole to indicate that the presence of high anxiety impedes or entirely prevents the progress of desensitization treatment

(Eysenck and Rachman, 1965). On the other hand, the experiment reported by Cooke (1966) suggests that, in certain instances at least, the presence of high anxiety might be associated with a speedy response to desensitization. Closely allied to this problem is the question of the role of depression in desensitization treatment. Several clinical reports (e.g. Hain, Butcher and Stevenson, 1966; Meyer and Crisp, 1966) have pointed out that the presence of depression in psychiatric patients tends to interfere, often quite seriously, with desensitization treatment. The comparative effectiveness of different therapists is another matter which needs to be examined. In the main, the results available from the experiments in which this variable has featured tend to suggest that intertherapist differences are of minor significance—at least where nonpsychiatric phobic subjects are concerned. However, it may well be that in the management of severely disturbed patients the ability (or personality?) of the therapist may be of some significance. It must be pointed out, however, that there have been some surprising indications from the experiments on nonpsychiatric subjects suggesting that it is possible to bring about the reduction or elimination of excessive fears with comparatively little training in the desensitization procedure. Needless to say, the management of psychiatric patients would by its very nature require more prolonged training and experience. In their retrospective analysis of the effects of behavior therapy in general, Marks and Gelder (1964) adduced some evidence to indicate that clinical experience was an important factor in determining the outcome of such treatment.

Another methodological innovation which merits clinical investigation is the administration of group desensitization. The experiments of Lazarus (1961), of Paul and Shannon (1966), and the author's personal experience of group treatment suggest that it may prove to be as effective as individual treatment.

Finally, two theoretical advances are worth noting. When behavior therapy was first introduced, numerous objections were raised, particularly in psychoanalytic circles, and two of the most serious and widely expressed criticisms were these: first, it was argued that the tendency of behavior therapists to treat manifest neurotic behavior would, if successful, lead to symptom substitution; that is, the patient would develop new and possibly even worse symptoms if the so-called defensive reactions were removed by the behavior therapist. This phenomenon of symptom substitution has proved to be of minimum importance and occurs very rarely. In none of the experiments described above was symptom substitution observed, even though it was in almost all cases carefully sought. In the clinical reports the occurrence of symptom substitution is also rare (see Eysenck and Rachman, 1965; Rachman, 1965).

A second objection which was raised was that it is impossible to bring about the reduction or elimination of neurotic symptoms and behavior unless one first eliminated the presumed basic causes of the illness. It was said that behavior therapy could not succeed because it was directing its attention to the wrong idea. This objection, too, has now been firmly eliminated. In the experimental investigations and in the clinical reports there is overwhelming evidence that substantial improvements in neurotic behavior can be obtained by systematic desensitization (and other methods of behavior therapy) even when little or no attention is paid to the possible or presumed underlying causes of the illness.

REFERENCES

1. Agras, W. S.: An investigation of the decrement of anxiety responses during systematic desensitization therapy. *Behav Res Ther,* 2:267-270, 1965.
2. Brill, A. A.: *Basic Principles of Psychoanalysis.* New York, Doubleday, 1949.
3. Cooke, G.: The efficacy of two desensitization procedures: An analogue study. *Behav Res Ther,* 4:17-24, 1966.
4. Davison, G.: The influence of systematic desensitization, relaxation, and graded exposure to imaginal stimuli in the modification of phobic behavior. Unpublished doctoral dissertation, Stanford University, 1965.
5. Eysenck, H. J. (Ed.): *Behaviour Therapy and the Neuroses.* Pergamon Press, Oxford, 1960.
6. Eysenck, H. J. (Ed.): *Experiments in Behaviour Therapy.* Pergamon Press, Oxford, 1964.
7. Eysenck, H. J. and Rachman, S.: *The Causes and Cures of Neurosis.* London, Routledge and Kegan Paul, 1965.

8. Friedman, D.: A new technique for the systematic desensitization of phobic symptoms. *Behav Res Ther, 4:*139-140 1966a.

9. Friedman, D.: Treatment of a case of dog phobia in a deaf mute by behaviour therapy. *Behav Res Ther, 4:*141-142, 1966b.

10. Gale, D. S., Sturmfels, G. and Gale, E. N.: A comparison of reciprocal inhibition and experimental extinction in the therapeutic process. *Behav Res Ther, 4,* in press.

11. Geer, J. H.: The development of a scale to measure fear. *Behav Res Ther, 3:*45-53.

12. Hain, J., Butcher, R. and Stevenson, I.: Systematic desensitization therapy: An analysis of results in twenty-seven patients. *Br J Psychiatry, 112:*295-308, 1966.

13. Hendrick, I.: *Facts and Theories of Psychoanalysis,* 2nd ed. New York, Knopf, 1948.

14. Jacobson, E.: *Progressive Relaxation.* Chicago, Chicago University Press, 1938.

15. Lang, P. J. and Lazovik, A. D.: The experimental desensitization of a phobia. *J Abnorm Soc Psychol, 66:*519-525, 1963.

16. Lang, P., Lazovik, A. D. and Reynolds, D. J.: Desensitization, suggestibility and pseudotherapy. *J Abnorm Soc Psychol, 70:*395-402, 1965.

17. Lazarus, A. A.: Group therapy of phobic disorders by systematic desensitization. *J Abnorm Soc Psychol, 63:*504-510, 1961.

18. Lazarus, A. A.: The results of behaviour therapy in 126 cases of severe neurosis. *Behav Res Ther, 1:*69-79, 1963.

19. Lazarus, A. A.: Crucial procedural factors in desensitization therapy. *Behav Res Ther, 2:*59-64.

20. Lomont, J. F.: Reciprocal inhibition or extinction? *Behav Res Ther, 3:* 209-220, 1965.

21. Lomont, J. F. and Edwards, J. E.: The role of relaxation in systematic desensitization. *Behav Res Ther,* in press, 1967.

22. Marks, I. and Gelder, M.: A controlled retrospective study of behaviour therapy in phobic patients. *Br J Psychiatry, 111:*561-573, 1965.

23. Marks, I. and Gelder, M.: Severe agoraphobia. A controlled prospective trial of behaviour therapy. *Br J Psychiatry, 112:*309-320, 1966.

24. Meyer, V. and Crisp, A. H.: Some problems of behaviour therapy. *Br J Psychiatry, 112:*367-382, 1966.

25. Moore, N.: Behaviour therapy in bronchial asthma: A controlled study. *J Psychosom Res, 9:*257-274, 1965.

26. Paul G. L.: *Insight versus Desensitization in Psychotherapy.* Stanford, Stanford University Press, 1966.

27. Paul, G. L. and Shannon, D. T.: Treatment of anxiety through systematic desensitization in therapy groups. *J Abnorm Psychol, 71:*124-135, 1966.

28. Rachman, S.: The current status of behaviour therapy. *Arch Gen Psychiatry, 13*:418-423, 1965a.
29. Rachman, S.: Studies in desensitization: I. The separate effects of relaxation and desensitization. *Behav Res Ther, 3*:245-252, 1965b.
30. Rachman, S.: Studies in desensitization: III. The speed of generalization. *Behav Res Ther, 4*:7-16, 1966.
31. Ramsay, R., Barends, J., Breuker, J. and Kruseman, A.: Massed versus spaced desensitization of fear. *Behav Res Ther, 4*:205-208, 1966.
32. Wolpe, J.: *Psychotherapy by Reciprocal Inhibition.* Stanford, Stanford University Press, 1958.
33. Wolpe, J.: The systematic desensitization treatment of neuroses. *J Nerv Ment Dis, 132*:189-203, 1964.
34. Wolpe, J., Salter, A. and Reyna, J.: *The Conditioning Therapies: The Challenge in Psychotherapy.* New York, Holt, Rinehart and Winston, 1964.

PART III:
ADDITIONAL RECOMMENDED READINGS

1. Bandura, A.: *Principles of Behavior Modification*. New York, Holt, Rinehart and Winston, 1969.
2. Bergin, A. and Garfield, S. (Eds.): *Handbook of Psychotherapy and Behavior Change*. New York, Wiley, 1971.
3. Carkhuff, R. and Berenson, B.: *Beyond Counseling and Therapy*. New York, Holt, Rinehart and Winston, 1967.
4. Carkhuff, R.: *Helping and Human Relations*. New York, Holt, Rinehart and Winston, 1969, 2 vol.
5. Fischer, J. and Gochros, H.: *Changing Behavior: The Application of Behavior Modification to Social Work Practice*. Free Press, 1973.
6. Ford, D. and Urban, H.: *Systems of Psychotherapy*. New York, Wiley, 1963.
7. Franks, C. (Ed.): *Behavior Therapy: Appraisal and Status*. New York, McGraw-Hill, 1969.
8. Goldstein, A., Heller, K. and Sechrest, L.: *Psychotherapy and the Psychology of Behavior Change*. New York, Wiley, 1966.
9. Group for the Advancement of Psychiatry: *Treatment of Families in Conflict*. New York, Science House, 1970.
10. Hobbs, N.: Sources of gain in psychotherapy. *Am Psychol, 17*:18-34, 1962.
11. Meltzoff, J. and Kornreich, M.: *Research in Psychotherapy*. New York, Atherton, 1970.
12. Morrow, W. and Gochros, H.: Misconceptions regarding behavior modification. *Soc Serv Rev, 44*:293-307, Sept. 1970.
13. Nagoshi, J. (Ed.): *Progress in Behavior Modification*. Honolulu, Social Welfare Development and Research Center, 1969.
14. Tharp, R. and Otis, G.: Toward a theory for therapeutic intervention in families. *J Consult Psychol, 30*:426-434, 1966.
15. Tharp, R. and Wetzel, J.: *Behavior Modification in the Natural Environment*. New York, Academic Press, 1969.
16. Truax, C. and Carkhuff, R.: *Toward Effective Counseling and Psychotherapy*. Chicago, Aldine, 1967.
17. Ullman, L. and Krasner, L.: *A Psychological Approach to Abnormal Behavior*. Englewood Cliffs, Prentice-Hall, 1969.
18. Wilson, G. T. and Hannon, A.: Behavior therapy and the therapist-patient relationship. *J Consult Clin Psychol, 32*:103-109, 1968.

19. Wolpe, J.: *The Practice of Behavior Therapy*. New York, Pergamon, 1969.
20. Yates, A.: *Behavior Therapy*. New York, Wiley, 1970.

PART IV

INTERVENTION WITH THE POOR

O God! that bread should
be so dear,
And flesh and blood
so cheap!

—Thomas Hood

THE VERY fact that there must be a focus on "the poor" is potentially dysfunctional. While the usual intent of such a focus is benevolent, without clearer specification of the population of concern, there is a danger of overgeneralizing, oversimplifying, and losing the very element which interpersonal helping is supposed to provide: individualization. It is clear, e.g., that the mere act of labelling a client as being from the lower social class is sufficient to ascribe to him all manner of pernicious characteristics (Fischer and Miller, 1972). Thus, the intent here is not to stereotype all low income people but to deal with a particular segment of the poor —where the situation involves a complex of individual and group hopelessness and apathy; environmental circumstances which limit development and growth potential; where powerlessness, real and imagined, is typical; and where, when our moral priorities are clarified, the bulk of our professional endeavors would likely be concentrated.

The articles in this part of the book are intended to supplement that which earlier parts of this book have covered. This means that there is no substantial evidence that many of the practices described in Parts II and III are not applicable to the poor. But it also suggests that special environmental conditions, and social-psychological ramifications of those conditions, require additional considerations to supplement more generalized practices. Actually, much of the "traditional" literature is predicated on the assumption that the "typical" client is highly motivated, psychologically sophisticated, verbal, and prepared to engage in a long-term psychotherapeutic experience in which the therapist more or less passively induces the client to explore his own motives and life-patterns with a goal of self-understanding. That a large percentage of our clients do not fit these categories is undeniable. Most clients—up to 80 percent—drop out of treatment before five interviews (Beck, 1962; Pfouts *et al.*, 1963; Overall and Aronson, 1964). Many clients want, and can benefit from, advice (Reid and Shapiro, 1969; Mayer and Timms, 1969). Many clients have expectations of treatment totally incongruent with those of the professional (Briar, 1966; Mayer and Timms, 1969). And all of these conditions are related, at least partially, to social class differences between clients and helpers. The task of Part IV of this book, then, is to present approaches which deal directly with some of these dilemmas of practice with lower income people.

The first set of articles deals with direct remedial-facilitative work with the poor. Riessman in the first article presents an overview of approaches to treatment which are designed, or were modified, particularly for direct practice with the poor. Riessman develops a model contrasting middle-class psychotherapy with low income expectations, and describes intervention procedures which would best seem to articulate with the characteristics ascribed to that particular segment of the poor. The next paper by Chilman proceeds on the basis of implications for practice suggested by research conducted with poor families. She contrasts patterns of child-rearing and family life of middle class society and "the very poor," and reviews the practice of several social workers who have done a considerable amount of work with lower-income people. On these bases, Chilman develops specific proposals for implementation in practice. Both of these papers contain a similar core, organized around the importance for professional helping of such concepts as action, directness, giving, coordinating and interceding, and a concrete, practical approach to helping (Weimandy, 1964). This assumes, of course, appropriate, sensitive and ethical use of such concepts (Miller, 1969). The third paper in this section, by Minuchin, suggests an ecological approach to practice, utilizing supportive forces in the environment. Minuchin illustrates how coordinated intervention with the total family and interlocking systems of support, can be of potentially greater benefit than either environmental intervention or family therapy alone.

The following section is composed of several papers which differ significantly from much of what has been presented in this book. They are concerned with the social worker as he functions to enhance the articulation of persons with institutions, based on the principle that direct service, alone, is insufficient to overcome the effects of an oppressive environment. They deal, in substance, with advocacy and mediating roles. Although, as discussed in the Introduction, these are (at least implicitly) traditional social work functions, their characteristics have until recently only been vaguely defined in the literature. They involve, primarily, a major ideological commitment, and as such, still have a weakly developed technical or procedural base. But, with the foundation of practice viewed here as rooted in a system of values, such commitment is a rather good place to begin.

The first paper by an N.A.S.W. Ad Hoc Committee on Advocacy gives a general overview of the concept of advocacy. The paper deals forthrightly with some of the problematic issues involved in an advocacy stance, and also identifies some of the basic content areas in which the advocate would need technical competence. This paper proposes that, stemming from the N.A.S.W. code of ethics, the professional social worker is ethically bound to take an advocacy role in situations where environmental action is necessary, if the social worker is to fulfill his professional responsibilities. The following paper by Terrell contains an impassioned plea for disengagement from commitments to organizations and traditional consensus-oriented values, and partisan engagement in a commitment to the poor. Terrell discusses two major types of advocacy. The first is broker advocacy wherein the advocate functions on behalf of a client to remedy difficulties stemming from the actions of public bodies. The second type is group advocacy, aimed at developing neighborhood and action groups to represent the interests of the disadvantaged. This advocate also serves as spokesman for these groups at a variety of institutional levels. The following paper by Sunley specifies fourteen forms of intervention in which a practitioner might engage in an advocacy program within the context of an agency. By integrating an advocacy component into a family agency program, Sunley expands the conceptual and ideological base of functioning for the family agency along the same lines as those recently taken by the New York Community Service Society (New York Times, 1971). The final paper in this section is drawn from the experience of Mobilization for Youth, the large-scale juvenile delinquency and social action program in New York. In this paper, Barr describes a broker-mediation role for the social agency, in which the agency disseminates information to the poor and assists in developing clients' ability to use it. This function would be congruent with the conclusion from Mobilization for Youth's program of psychological counseling for the poor that the single most important dimension of the program was the provision of concrete services (Jones and Weissman, 1969). This point of view is echoed also in the papers in the first section of Part IV of this book. Together with direct services, advocacy and broker functions comprise a continuum of practice which, based on the social worker's assessment of the problem and the situation, ranges from intervention directly with individuals to intervention into impinging, dysfunctional social systems.

The final section of the book deals with the problem of service delivery, especially delivery of services to the poor. It seems unquestionable that the entire gamut of methods of service delivery has long been inadequate, essentially due to a neglect of those most in need (Rein, 1964). That there are alternative courses of action, based on development of new strategies for innovation in service delivery, is also evident. For example, a recent paper by Morris (1970) suggests a number of building blocks for strategies of innovation in delivering services: (a) developing a sense of strategy; (b) diversifying strategies; (c) updating conventional approaches through increased allocations for research and development; (d) taking an adversary stance against agencies when necessary; (e) using the courts and the law; (f) publicly visible accounting of programs; (g) abandoning the preoccupation with service duplication in favor of some modest competition; and (h) actively forging new coalitions and alliances. Such strategies must include the necessity for protection by the profession of the individual worker who challenges the priorities of his agency.

Given the necessity for such strategies in attempting to modify a variety of inequities in the service delivery system, it remains for the papers in this section to describe some alternatives for action. The first paper by Fishman and McCormack discusses the development of a community mental health program in the ghetto. They suggest that action-oriented programs based on community involvement and unhampered by "psychiatric labels," and linking meaningful work, compensation, education and social competency, have great potential for application in the ghetto. The goal of such a development: a program "without walls." The final paper in this book presents a comprehensive review of one of the newer methods for improving the delivery of services—the multipurpose neighborhood service center. In his paper, March analyzes the developments leading to use of the neighborhood center concept, discusses the difficulties associated with traditional, disjointed methods of delivery of services, and presents some alternative models of neighborhood service center organization. The basic goal of all the approaches involves increasing the accessibility and coordination of services. The ultimate purpose of such coordination, March suggests, is not coordination for its own sake. Rather, it is to help solve the social and human resource problems of our communities, and to improve methods for preventing and treating a wide range of disorders resulting in diminished capacity for functioning among individuals and families. And, after all, is that not really what interpersonal helping is all about?

REFERENCES

1. Beck, D.: *Patterns in Use of Family Agency Service.* New York, Family Service Association of America, 1962.
2. Briar, S.: Family Services. In Maas, H. (Ed.) : *Five Fields of Social Service.* New York, National Association of Social Workers, 1966.
3. Community service society changing tactics: Will drop casework. *New York Times,* January 29, 1971, p. 1.
4. Fischer, J. and Miller, H.: The effect of client characteristics on caseworkers' clinical judgments. (in press) , 1972.

5. Jones, H. and Weissman, H.: Psychological help for the poor. In Weissman, H. (Ed.): *Individual and Group Services*. New York, Association Press, 1969.

6. Mayer, J. and Timms, N.: Clash in perspective between worker and client. *Social Casework, 50:*32-40, 1969.

7. Morris, R.: Strategies for innovation in service delivery. In Richan, W. (Ed.): *Human Services and Social Work Responsibility*. New York, National Association of Social Workers, 1970, pp. 281-293.

8. Overall, B. and Aronson, A.: Expectations of psychotherapy in patients of lower socioeconomic class. *Am J Orthopsychiatry, 33 (3):*421-430, 1963.

9. Pfouts, J., Wallach, M. and Jenkins, J.: An outcome study of referrals to a psychiatric clinic. *Social Work, 8 (3):*79-87, 1963.

10. Reid, W. and Shapiro, B.: Client reactions to advice. *Social Serv Rev, 43:*165-173, 1969.

11. Rein, M.: The social service crisis. *Trans-action,* 3-6; 31-32, 1964.

12. Weimandy, J.: Casework with tenants in a public housing project. *J Marriage Family,* 452-455, Nov. 1964.

A. DIRECT SERVICES

Chapter 33

NEW APPROACHES TO MENTAL HEALTH TREATMENT FOR LOW-INCOME PEOPLE

FRANK RIESSMAN

T HE NEW COMMUNITY-BASED mental health plans, arising from the late President Kennedy's Mental Health-Retardation Centers Act, promise a tremendous breakthrough in the treatment of blue-collar and low-income people.[1] Under the law, federal matching grants will be made available to the states for the construction of community mental health centers. The major challenge now is what to put into these buildings; in other words, what adaptations and modfications of traditional treatment are needed in order to put life into the new structures?

Miller and Swanson state the need succinctly:

... the increasing number of blue-collar workers who are seeking help for their personal problems has made it obvious that traditional goals and methods must be modified. In clinics which serve patients in both social classes, a disproportionate number of blue-collar workers drop out of therapy very early because of dissatisfaction with the therapeutic procedure. It is important that psychotherapists learn more about the characteristics of manual laborers and about conditions under which these people mature. ...

Our results indicate the desirability of exploring a variety of new psychotherapeutic techniques, particularly those in which words and concepts are subordinated to nonverbal and even motoric activities.[2]

Numerous studies confirm these observations. They indicate that community mental health organizations have, by and large, failed to provide effective services to working people and low-in-

Note: Reprinted from *Social Work Practice, 1965*. New York, Columbia University Press, 1966, pp. 174-187. Copyright 1966, National Conference on Social Welfare, Columbus, Ohio. Portions of the present article appeared in a monograph published by the National Institute of Labor Education Mental Health Project in 1964, and will appear in the *Int J Soc Psychiatry* (London, England).

come groups. Low-income individuals suffering from mental illness have either wound up in city- or state-supported mental institutions where, in President Kennedy's words, they have been "out of sight and often forgotten," or they have remained in the community without help until their behavioral deviations were such as to bring them to the "emergency attention" of corrective agencies.

A primary reason for the failure of community mental health programs to reach these large sections of the population has been their reluctance to modify the traditional forms of psychotherapy, which have constituted their principal treatment tool. The present-day institutional features of psychotherapy are primarily congenial to middle-class life styles. Thus middle-class patients are preferred by most treatment agents;[3] they are considered to be more treatable; psychotherapy is more frequently recommended as the treatment of choice;[4] and diagnoses are more hopeful (with symptomatology held constant).[5] Conversely, treatment as presently organized is not congenial to low-income clients, is not congruent with their traditions and expectations, and is poorly understood by them. In essence, these clients are alienated from treatment.

We suggest that this situation calls for a twofold strategy: modification of the traditional treatment approaches to accommodate the low-income client, and education and preparation of the low-income client for the necessary aspects of treatment not suited to his expectations.

With the aim of encouraging further experimentation, we have surveyed a wide spectrum of treatment techniques appropriate to low-income clients in different types of settings rather than presenting one or two in detail and with fully developed rationale. This has been done, to some extent, in other papers by the author.[6]

NEW APPROACHES TO INTAKE AND DIAGNOSIS

There is increasing evidence that most of the clinician's diagnostic tools, whether in the cognitive sphere (intelligence tests) or in the emotional sphere, are class-linked and class-biased.

Haase[7] found that Rorschach records were interpreted quite differently depending upon the designated social class origin of the patient. The protocols of individuals reported as "lower-class" were diagnosed as more maladjusted with poorer prognosis than were their middle-class counterparts whose essentially similar records were used as controls. It is also interesting to note that the lower-class records were more frequently categorized in terms of psychosis and character disorder while the virtually identical records of middle-class clients were diagnosed as neurotic and normal.

Haase does not object to a class differential analysis per se, but rather to the fact that the analysis unwittingly but consistently concludes that the lower class is more maladjusted. Considering the lack of opportunity and difficult life conditions of the worker, a lower-class record which is identical with that of a middle-class person might be presumed to indicate greater health and better prognosis.

Apart from biases in interpretation, traditional diagnostic techniques which rely heavily on testing and interview procedures are not well-suited to the low-income style, which is far more oriented to physical forms of expression. For this reason we strongly urge the use of role playing and situational tests as diagnostic tools and the employment of more game-like devices in general.

The following are some general recommendations regarding intake and diagnosis:

1. Telescope the initial interview and intake (shorten; cut red tape).[8] Use group intake procedures. Start the therapeutic process at once. Permit fuller catharsis while gathering case history; be very open and flexible.

2. Utilize pictorial interview and diagnostic techniques.[9] Consider hypnosis, role-playing, and dreams as diagnostic devices. Use home interviews where possible; have problem-centered discussions.

3. Do not diagnose with middle-class standards and categories; do not presume inner conflict, acting-out, lack of values, lack of guilt, or lack of verbal facility.

4. Attempt to determine the style of the individual—work style, cognitive style, interpersonal style; learn to understand his individual language; note the idiom. Note the client's humor, leisure pattern, interests, friendship pattern, extent of family relationships, identification models, defense mechanisms, role functioning.

5. Clarify the processes and goals of therapy; determine the life possibilities and specific direction of the particular patient.

DEVELOPMENT OF RAPPORT

During the first series of interviews, every effort should be made to overcome the role distance and impersonality which contribute to the low-income client's alienation from the treatment agent. As steps in this direction, we suggest less stress on obtaining and recording objective information about the client's problem, background, and situation, and less emphasis on defining the agency's role, functions, and mode of operation.

Instead of these emphases, the therapist might want to:

1. Encourage the client to talk about his problems and feelings subjectively, to express himself without regard to dates, places, details and the like. Much useful information might be obtained in this way, but this would not be the emphasis or the goal.

2. Talk about himself where relevant and possible: "I had a problem like that once." "I come from a neighborhod (family) like yours." "I have trouble making both ends meet." "A friend of mine has a situation a lot like yours."

3. Record at the *end* of the meeting whatever minimum specific information is needed. The therapist or caseworker could indicate that this recording of information was as unpleasant to him as to the client. He could share the low-income client's alienation toward impersonal bureaucratic procedure by saying that "we have to do this—let's get it over with as easily as we can" (so that we can go back to really coming to grips with your problems).

4. Provide whatever advice, service, or anticipation of improvement can be given at this stage.

In other words, "stage one," beginning with the initial interview and proceeding through the first four or five meetings, could be cathartic, supportive, informal, and should provide immediate service and appropriate advice. The assumption here is that low-income clients can accept directive authority when it is combined with informal friendliness.

In addition to these modifications, another very different initial approach might be explored. Role playing[10] can be introduced at the very beginning, not on a group basis at first, but simply on a one-to-one basis where the therapist and the client act-out relevant situations (parent-child problems, marital difficulties, vocational guidance, problems of an interpersonal nature, and so forth). Role playing of this kind is especially useful with young males, who are not receptive to "just talk," and in family counseling, and furnishes an excellent transition to group sessions. Role-playing sessions can be used diagnostically, while at the same time providing catharsis, support, problem objectification, problem-sharing, and group solution.

ROLE-PLAYING TECHNIQUES

Role-playing techniques have long been popular in educational programs with blue-collar workers in labor unions and industry. Experience at Mobilization for Youth and various community organizations further indicates an exceptionally positive response to role-playing by low-income people. While more systematic research is needed to validate these observations, there are a number of reasons why this technique may be of special value in therapeutic work with lower socioeconomic groups:

1. It is a technique that appears congenial with the low-income person's style: physical (action-oriented, doing vs. talking); down to earth, concrete, problem-directed; externally oriented rather than introspective; group-centered.[11]

2. It allows the practitioner (social worker, psychiatrist, educator) to reduce in an honest fashion the role distance between himself and the disadvantaged individual. It also permits the practitioner to learn more about the culture of the low-income

person from the "inside" (through playing the latter's role in role reversal, for example).

3. It changes the setting and tone of what often appears to the low-income person as an office-ridden, institutional, bureaucratic, impersonal foreign world.

4. It appears to be an excellent technique for developing verbalization and verbal power in the educationally deprived person, and seems to be especially useful for the development of leadership skills:

> In role-playing sessions we have had occasion to observe that the verbal performance of deprived children is markedly improved in the discussion period following the session. When talking about some *action* they have *seen,* deprived children are apparently able to verbalize much more fully. Typically, they *do not verbalize well in response to words alone.* They express themselves more readily when reacting to things they can see and do. Words as stimuli are not sufficient for them as a rule. Ask a juvenile delinquent who comes from a disadvantaged background what he doesn't like about school or the teacher and you will get an abbreviated, inarticulate reply. But have a group of these youngsters act out a school scene in which someone plays the teacher, and you will discover a stream of verbal consciousness that is almost impossible to shut off.[12]

Some cautions are in order, however. As Young and Rosenberg pointed out some years ago, role playing with low-income groups should assiduously avoid the theatrical aspects often connected with psychodrama.[13] Role playing seems to be more easily accepted by disadvantaged people when there are no stage or lighting effects, and when it is conducted very simply and directly. In work with homemakers and school aides from low-income groups, for example, it was found that they were able and willing to participate in role playing almost immediately, with practically no warm-up or even preparatory discussions to explain the technique.

Indeed, it sometimes appears that the more preparation and disscussion prior to role playing, the more resistant and fearful low-income people become. In view of this, it is best to introduce role playing directly through a discussion centered on a specific problem, such as how to persuade a member of the family to come to the clinic. It can then easily be suggested that the group "do the problem" so that it can be dealt with more effectively.

It should also be pointed out that while low-income people readily accept the basic technique, including role reversal, they are far less accepting of such features as "doubles," "soliloquies," and the like. More advanced technology of this nature seems to arouse feelings of inadequacy ("I'm not an actor"), and although it is possible to utilize them, these techniques require considerably more preparation than is needed with middle-class audiences.

Finally, it is important, as Levit and Jennings warn,[14] to guard against the overuse of role playing and to keep in mind that it should be employed intermittently for well-defined purposes—as a stimulus for discussion, for example.

THE USE OF NONPROFESSIONALS

The use of indigenous personnel drawn from low-income communities can perhaps be a decisive factor in helping treatment agencies reorganize their approaches to low-income people. Neighborhood people functioning as nonprofessionals appear to be highly successful in developing rapport with low-income clients, including the most deprived and disadvantaged individuals in the community.[15] Their success seems to stem from the fact that they are similar to the clients in terms of background, style, language, ethnicity, and interests.

For this reason, and also because they serve as excellent role models, we recommend that a great many more nonprofessionals be employed in hospitals and social agencies in various capacities. One such capacity which we feel has an important potential but has thus far been little utilized is as an auxiliary in group treatment. Under the guidance of the professional therapist or group leader, the nonprofessional aide can participate in the group therapy sessions and perform the valuable function of maintaining continuity of contact with the participants by visiting each of them daily between sessions. Moreover, the integration of the aide's home visiting and extrasessions experiences with the patient could be integrated into the group sessions, thus enriching and enhancing their therapeutic value.

THE "HELPER" THERAPY PRINCIPLES

What appears to be one of the most effective treatment mechanisms—the use of people in trouble to help other people in trouble—may have special significance in a therapeutic model for the poor. While it may be uncertain whether the people who *receive* help are always benefited, it seems clearer that those who *give* the help profit from their their role. This appears to be the case in a wide variety of group "therapies," including Synanon (for drug addicts), Recovery Incorporated (for psychologically disturbed people), Alcoholics Anonymous, and the Chicago YMCA detached workers program for delinquents.[16]

Cressey formulates this principle as one of his five social psychological principles for the rehabilitation of criminals:

> The most effective mechanism for exerting group pressure on members will be found in groups so organized that criminals are induced to join with noncriminals for the purpose of changing other criminals. A group in which criminal A joins with some noncriminals to change criminal B is probably most effective in changing criminal A not B. . . .[17]

Community programs that utilize indigenous nonprofessionals as homemakers, community organizers, youth workers, and the like record similar experiences. Some of these people have had fairly serious problems in the recent past. Some were former delinquents. It has been observed, however, that in the course of their helping role their own problems diminish greatly and they appear to grow remarkably.[18]

We suspect that while the helper principle probably has universal therapeutic application, it may be especially useful in group treatment programs with low-income people for two reasons:

1. It may circumvent the special interclass role-distance difficulties that arise from the middle-class-oriented therapy (and therapist) being at odds with the low-income clients' expectations and style. The alienation that many low-income clients feel toward professional treatment agents and the concomitant rapport difficulties may be greatly reduced by utilizing the low-income person himself as the helper-therapist.

2. It may be a principle which is especially attuned to the cooperative trends in lower socioeconomic groups and cultures. In this sense it may be beneficial to both the helper (the model) and the helped.

The helper therapy principle has wide implications for various types of group work (detached workers and youth groups, group discussions with job trainees, groups at halfway houses, tenant groups), and for group therapy as well. Since the idea basically is to structure and restructure the groups so that different group members play the helper role at different times, the principle can be utilized in a great variety of therapeutic programs which make use of some form of group process to effect change in the individual.

NEW FAMILY APPROACHES

Rachel Levine, working at the Henry Street Mental Hygiene Clinic, has developed an unusual and apparently effective type of treatment in the home which she calls the technique of "demonstration." In essence, the approach consists of the treatment agent bringing simple games, cards, and clay to the multiproblem home, and engaging as many members of the family as possible in these activities. When family conflicts arise around the games, they are discussed and worked out by the social worker right on the spot. Aside from the fact that this approach is much more involving than most office discussions, "it also eliminates the distortions which are common when conflict situations are reported after the fact and discussed in the office."[19] (Levine also uses role playing in the home treatment approach.)

Spiegel's approach emphasizes "the importance of the extended family and the community to the functioning of the individual." He states:

> Although therapy concentrates mainly on the mother, father and child, we attempt to see and make ourselves known to a wide assortment of relatives. This means that we become assimilated, to a certain extent, to the lineal chains of influence which bear upon the pathologic deviations in the family members. In addition, members of the therapeutic team became known, not simply as individuals, but

also as members of a readily identifiable organization. This approximation of individuals and organizations reduces the fear of the strange, unknown group and, simultaneously, raises its prestige.[20]

Speigel has developed some striking modifications in the traditional setting of psychotherapy: "The therapists have at times attended family celebrations, have accompanied the father to his place of work, and have conducted therapeutic interviews in this setting, as well as in trucks, bars, and other unusual places."[21]

SOCIOTHERAPY AND INVOLVEMENT

Frequently it is found that the psychological difficulties of an individual appear to diminish in importance when the individual becomes involved in some activity or social movement, which may vary from a religious organization to a hobby, to a labor union, to a block committee. Wittenberg found, for example, that participation in a neighborhood block committee led to marked personality development and growth in a woman on welfare, who despite some leadership potential had considerable personal difficulty.[22] Wittenberg's approach combined casework, group work, and community organization principles in a program directed toward "personality adjustment through social action," or what might be termed "sociotherapy." Here "the organization is the tool, while personality growth is the goal. . . . Essentially, this is using whatever available healthy ego structure there is and building from there by using environmental pressures as a catalytic agent."[23]

Many low-income clients, because they are members of the Negro and Spanish-speaking minority groups, have great interest, sometimes manifest, sometimes latent, in the present-day movements and community organizations that represent their aspirations. Treatment agents accustomed to more clinical models tend to underemphasize the therapeutic possibilities of these types of involvement.

While certainly opposing any mechanical pressuring of all Negro clients to become interested in the Negro movement, we would argue that therapists should be alert to such possibilities whenever the client shows even slight interest in this direction. There are two reasons for advocating this:

1. Use is made of a possible source of strength in the client and his traditions that is independent of the therapist. Continued dependence and the tendency to deepen attention upon pathology, so characteristic of much treatment, are thus avoided.

2. A spread effect, a self-generator of positive change, is put into motion, and it may lead the client to feel a growing sense of power and conviction which transfers to various areas of his life, his family, his friends, and the community, and this indirectly produces broad behavioral modifications and feedback effects.

We are reminded in this connection of the success claimed by the Black Muslim movement in curtailing the use of drugs and alcohol among some of the members who previously had been active addicts and alcoholics. If their contentions are accurate, one must acknowledge that the effect of social ideology is quite impressive, regardless of one's particular convictions about the Muslim movement.

Marshall[24] points up the issue by noting that the social worker who just tries to change the drug addict "without offering him a faith in addition"—without embodying this change in a "central ideology" that might involve the addict—has a much harder task than does the Muslim movement. It is striking that there appears to have been "a sharp decline in the incidence of crime among the Negro population of Montgomery, Alabama, during the year of the boycott [1955]."[25]

In countering the sociotherapeutic approach, it is sometimes contended that although a particular symptom may disappear, it is merely displaced and is expressed in different form in the very nature of the new involvement. In support of this thesis, irrational, distorted, and inappropriate aspects of the client's behavior in the new activity are sought and cited. There is little doubt that this pattern operates on some occasions and perhaps partially in all such cases, but as an overall criticism it appears far too oversimplified. It overlooks at least two important possibilities. One is that the new behavior may have emerged from, or taken root in, nonpathological aspects of the patient's personality (the "conflict-free portion of the ego") .[26] The other possibility—and perhaps one more appealing to the traditional clinician——is the likelihood that the new behavior pattern may be a well-sublimated expression of the patient's character. In either case, there is much room for therapeutic guidance to insure against negative symptom displacement.

Unquestionably, there are some dangers in this involvement approach, but perhaps it is time to err in new directions.

In the past decade, two trends have emerged in the field of psychiatry: a physiological trend highlighted by the appearance of a variety of new drugs; and an environmental-social trend reflected in community psychiatry, social psychiatry, milieu therapy, and so forth. It is striking that these two developments appear to be most in harmony with treatment expectations and desires of low-income patients. It is possible, too, that physiological and environmental psychiatry are also most relevant, not only to the expectations of blue-collar people, but to their actual problems as well.

It may be that intrapsychic, psychodynamic treatment is more suited to middle-class expectations and problems, while social and physiological therapies are more appropriate for low-income problems. This is probably an oversimplification, however. What is more likely is that the emphasis in treatment should perhaps be class-related but that each stratum could probably benefit from treatment at the various levels: intrapsychic and interpersonal, environmental, and physiological. Thus, low-income treatment programs might utilize social and physiological orientations as their starting point (and, in general, use them more extensively), but would nevertheless be concerned with internal psychological forces, and might perhaps give these factors greater attention as the therapy progressed. On the other hand, therapy attuned to middle-class clients might begin with the psychological level and move outward toward the environment and inward toward the physiological.

In a sense, the emphasis on environmental and physiological causes, in part powered by the needs of low-income clientele, may contribute to the further development of a universal psychiatry.

Much of what has been said here may have wider implications than our low-income focus might seem to imply.

TABLE 33-I

SUMMARY MODEL

Middle-Class Psychotherapy vs. Low-Income Expectations

The following is a model for contrasting the middle-class character of psychotherapy with the expectations of low-income individuals. The contrast is intentionally presented in the form of extremes or ideal types in order to clarify the differences.

	Middle-Class Model	*Low-Income Beliefs, Expectations, and Preferences*
Goals	Self-actualization, growth, understanding	Specific behavior change: vocational, marital, health
Cause of problem	Internal, self, emotional, psychological, past (childhood, family)	External (environmental), physiological, caused in present or recent past
Setting	Office	Home visit
Agent	Psychiatrist-psychologist (non-medical in outlook and appearance); segmented role relationship of professional to professional, where the "service" motivation of the psychiatrist is accepted	Doctor and clergy: more rounded informal, person-centered relationship; motivation of the psychologist or caseworker often not understood, or looked upon suspiciously
"Defense" mechanisms stressed	Rationalization; isolation-intellectualization and loss of affect; self-blame and introjection; compensation and reaction formation	Externalization-projection; scapegoating; "acting-out"; somatization; withdrawal; primitive denial
Cognitive style	Intellectual, introspective, highly verbal, quick, clever, deductive, temporal	Physical, motoric, visual, spatial, slow, careful, inductive, action-centered, verbal around the concrete stimulus
Therapeutic processes employed	Do-it-yourself, change-yourself responsibility	Formal and informal direction
	Individual therapy (or individualized groups)	Group therapy, role-playing, peer-centered
	Introspective, "think"-centered, word-focused	Work, action (talk deprecated)
	Unstructured, permissive	Structure and organization
	Stress on the past	Focused on present
	Self-focused	More emphasis on family and group

TABLE 33-I (Continued)

Middle-Class Model	Low-Income Beliefs, Expectations, and Preferences
Physically inactive, lying down, free association	Moving, gesturing, acting, role-playing, face-to-face
Stress on resistance and transference	Problem-focused
Symbolic, often circuitous interpretations and explanations	Simple, concrete, demonstrable explanations
Intensive transference and countertransference	Less intense relationships; informal friendliness, respect, sympathetic, nonpatronizing understanding

NOTES AND REFERENCES

1. "Low-income" is used as an all-inclusive term to refer to blue-collar workers and "disadvantaged," "deprived," and "underprivileged" lower socioeconomic groups.
2. Miller, Daniel R. and Swanson, Guy E.: *Inner Conflict and Defense.* New York, Henry Holt, 1960, pp. 397-98.
3. Hollingshead, August B. and Redlich, Fredrick S.: *Social Class anl Mental Illness.* New York, John Wiley & Sons, 1958.
4. Brill, Norman Q. and Storrow, Hugh: Social class and psychiatric treatment. *Arch Gen Psychiatry, III:*340-44, 1963.
5. Haase, William: Rorschach diagnosis, socioeconomic class, and examiner bias. Unpublished dissertation, New York University, 1956.
6. *See* Riessman, Frank: Role-playing and the poor; The "helper" therapy principle; and The revolution in social work: The new nonprofessional.
7. Haase: *op. cit.*
8. *See* Levine, Rachel A.: A short story on the long waiting list. *Social Work, VIII (No. 1):*20-22, 1963, for suggestions as to how to shorten intake procedures.
9. Cartoon-like tests, such as the Rosenzweig frustration test, and simple picture selection instruments, such as the Szondi, may be especially valuable.
10. Role-playing is the flexible acting-out (doing) of various types of problems in a permissive group atmosphere, such as a caseworker interviewing a withdrawn client or a person being interviewed by a housing project manager in a low-income housing project. As few as two people can role-play, such as therapist and client; but most role-playing is usually done in groups where two people act-out a situa-

tion and the group discusses it. Since it is free of tensions of an actual problem situation, role-playing stimulates the trying out of alternatives and solutions in lifelike situations without the consequences which in reality might be punishing. Role-playing thus increases the participant's role flexibility in an atmosphere where he can safely take a chance with different kinds of behavior.

11. While the style of the poor probably includes a strong emphasis on informality, humor, and warmth, the disadvantaged also like a content that is structured, definite, and specific. It is often assumed that role-playing is highly unstructured, open and free. In part this is true, particularly in the early phase of setting the problem and mood. But in the middle and later phases (especially the role-training stage), where the effort is made to teach very specific behaviors, role-playing can be highly structured, reviewing in minute detail the various operations to be learned (such as how to run a meeting, organize a conference, talk to a housing manager). Educationally disadvantaged people appear to prefer a *mood* or feeling tone that is informal and easy, but a *content* that is more structured and task-centered. Role playing may suit both needs.

12. Riessman, Frank: *The Culturally Deprived Child.* New York, Harper & Brothers, 1963, p. 77.

13. Young, Bruce F. and Rosenberg, Morris: Role-playing as a participation technique. *J Social Issues, V:*42-45, 1949.

14. Levit, Gertrude and Jennings, Helen: Learning through role-playing. In *How to Use Role-Playing.* Chicago, Adult Education Association, 1960, p. 10.

15. Riessman, Frank: The revolution in social work: The new nonprofessional. 1963; mimeographed.

16. We are not suggesting that there is good research evidence that these programs are effective; but various reports, many of them admittedly impressionistic, point more to improvement in the givers of help than in the receivers. Careful research to evaluate these programs is needed.

17. Volkman, Rita and Cressey, Donald R.: Differential association and the rehabilitation of drug addicts. *Am J Sociol, LXIX:*139, 1963.

18. See Goldberg, Gertrude: The use of untrained neighborhood workers in a homemaker program. Unpublished Mobilization for Youth report, 1963.

19. Levine, Rachel A.: Treatment in the home. *Social Work, IX (No. 1):* 22, 1964.

20. Spiegel, John P.: Some cultural aspects of transference and countertransference. In Masserman, Jules H. M.D. (Ed.): *Individual and Familial Dynamics.* New York, Grune & Stratton, 1959, p. 180.

21. *Ibid.*, p. 161.
22. Wittenberg, Rudolph M.: Personality adjustment through social action. *Am J Orthopsychiatry, XVIII*:207-21, 1948.
23. *Ibid.*, pp. 208, 220.
24. Kenneth Marshall, speech on Negro culture, Mobilization for Youth training program, 1962.
25. Kahn, T.: *Unfinished Revolution.* New York, Igal Rodenko Printer, 1960, quoted by Fishman, Jacob R. and Solomon, Frederic: Youth and Social action: I. Perspectives on the student sit-in movement. *Am J Orthopsychiatry, XXX*:876, 1963.
26. See Cumming, John and Cumming, Elaine: *Ego and Milieu.* New York, Atherton Press, 1962, pp. 13-14, for an illuminating application of Heinz Hartmann's concept of a "conflict-free portion" of the ego.

Chapter 34

SOCIAL WORK PRACTICE WITH VERY POOR FAMILIES

Some Implications Suggested By The Available Research

CATHERINE S. CHILMAN

Some suggestions for social work practice are presented here for consideration by staff members of social agencies who are concerned with helping chronically poor parents and their children escape from the multiple burdens of extreme poverty. These suggestions grow out of a recent overview and analysis of the child-rearing and family life patterns that are more characteristic of the very poor than of other socioeconomic groups. These findings are compared with child-rearing and family life patterns associated with ratings of positive adjustment in five fields: mental health, educational achievement, social acceptability, conscience formation, and marital satisfaction and stability. A condensed summary of these research findings appeared in an earlier issue of Welfare in Review.[1] The major focus of this article is on some of the possible implications of these findings for social work practice.

FAMILY LIFE PATTERNS OF THE POOR

When findings from studies of the child-rearing and family patterns more characteristic of the very poor are compared to research findings from the five "success" fields listed above, it becomes clear in light of present knowledge that the very poor, more than other socioeconomic groups, tend to conduct their family lives in ways that are nonconducive to favorable outcomes in the five crucial areas noted above.

Note: Reprinted from *Welfare in Review,* 4:13-21, 1966.

Poverty environments are seen as being the most important causative factors in the development of poverty subcultures to which these child-rearing and family life patterns are related. But subcultural responses to poverty conditions also play a part in trapping many of the poor in a network of economic, social, educational, occupational, and related disabilities.

Some of the outstanding features of these subcultural life styles as they relate to child-rearing and family life patterns are presented in the following table, together with comparative statements as to child-rearing and family life patterns revealed by research to be associated with positive mental health, educational achievement, adequate socialization, and family stability. This table greatly condenses research findings related to two major areas: (a) child-rearing patterns more characteristic of the very poor and (b) child-rearing patterns associated with five crucial areas in child growth and development. For detailed references to related research, see Welfare in Review, January 1965.

There are limitations to the research findings presented above as well as their implications for action programs. Some of the outstanding limitations are summarized as follows: gaps in research based knowledge still exist; these findings apply to some, but not necessarily all, chronically poor families; "success" conducive child-rearing patterns are closely associated with middle-class norms and question arises as to whether the middle-class way is a "better" way than that of the lower-lower social class. In this regard, it might be conceded that in our technically advanced society the middle-class way brings far greater social and economic rewards than do poverty group patterns. Since most of the poor, like the rest of our citizens, seem to want these rewards, it appears to be defensible for members of the service professions to work with the poor to help them change their life styles so that they have a better chance of joining the "haves" in our generally affluent society. Working with parents and children to break entrenched poverty patterns is quite different from imposing a middle-class value system on a captive client group.

For those who agree that the child-rearing and family life styles of some of the very poor tend to be seriously handicapping,

TABLE 34-I

CHILD-REARING AND FAMILY LIFE PATTERNS MORE CHARACTER-
ISTIC OF THE VERY POOR COMPARED WITH SOME OUTSTANDING
COMPARABLE PATTERNS REVEALED BY RESEARCH TO BE ASSOCIATED
WITH SUCCESSFUL ADAPTATION TO MODERN SOCIETY

Child-rearing and Family Life Patterns Reported to Be More Characteristic of the Very Poor	*Child-rearing and Family Life Patterns Reported to Be Conducive to Successful Adaptation to Our Predominantly Middle-class Society*
1. Inconsistent, harsh, physical punishment.	1. Mild, firm, consistent discipline.
2. Fatalistic, subjective attitudes, magical thinking.	2. Rational, evidence-oriented, objective attitudes.
3. Orientation toward the present.	3. Future orientation, goal commitment.
4. Authoritarian, rigid family structure—strict definitions of male and female roles.	4. Democratic, equalitarian, flexible family behavior patterns.
5. "Keep out of trouble," alienated, distrustful approach to society outside of family, constricted experiences.	5. Self-confident, positive, trustful approach to new experiences, wealth of experiences.
6. Limited verbal communication, relative absence of subtlety and abstract concepts, a physical action style.	6. Extensive verbal communication, values placed on complexity, abstractions.
7. Human behavior seen as unpredictable and judged in terms of its immediate impact.	7. Human behavior seen as having many causes and being developmental in nature.
8. Low self-esteem, little belief in one's own coping capicity, passive attitude.	8. High self-esteem, belief in one's own coping capacity, active attitude.
9. Distrust of opposite sex, ignorance of physiology of reproductive system.	9. Acceptance of opposite sex, positive sex expression within marriage by both husband and wife valued as part of total marital relationship, understanding of physiology of reproductive system.
10. Tendency not to clearly differentiate one child from another.	10. Each child seen as a separate individual and valued for his uniqueness.
11. Lack of consistent parental warmth and support, abrupt and early granting of independence.	11. Consistent parental warmth and support, with gradual training for independence.
12. Rates of marital conflict higher, higher rates of family breakdown.	12. Harmonious marriage, both husband and wife present.
13. Low levels of educational-occupational achievement by parents.	13. Educational and occupational success of parents.

that these patterns are at least partially related to subcultural styles, and that intervention strategies might well be designed to modify these patterns, the question becomes: how can subcultural patterns be changed? Some relevant suggestions are sketched here with the thought that specialists in the profession of social work might use them as at least a stimulant to their own thinking as they search for ways to work with the poor to help them find a way out of poverty and its multitudinous miseries.

SPECIFIC SUGGESTIONS FOR SOCIAL WORK PRACTICE

Changing Poverty Patterns:
Within the Family or in Other Settings?

Major attention today is being focused on changing the children of the poor—especially the very young children. This focus is based, to a considerable degree, on research evidence that the preschool years are crucial ones, especially in terms of intellectual, physical, and emotional development. Thus, preschool and other programs directed toward intervention for infants and very young children[2,3] tend to be highly favored. Important as the early years of life may well be, it would seem important, insofar as possible, to work with whole families in an effort to change, when indicated, the child-rearing and family life capacities and subcultures of disadvantaged parents and their children.

It seems premature to place children in facilities away from home or to put major emphasis on preschool and related programs unless there is little or no possibility of strengthening the family unit or modifying, when indicated, inappropriate child-rearing and family life patterns. For the concept of the family as a basic social unit of society is not to be tossed aside lightly. While some social scientists and practitioners are questioning the "sacred nature" of the nuclear family and its viability in a highly technical, predominantly urban society, others point to the importance of the sense of identity and significance that a child develops in the small family group to which he clearly and lastingly belongs.

However, it is possible to cling too rigidly to the concept of the importance of the child's own family. For too long, there has been a strict adherence by some professionals to the belief that an infant or child must be in the permanent, continuing care of his own mother or of a carefully selected parent substitute. Bowlby's earlier work[4] impressed this basic policy on many professionals in the child-care field. A later reconsideration of his previously firm convictions has failed to gain general understanding and acceptance in some quarters.[5] Some specialists, however, have extended this reconsideration to broader fields. Impressed by child-care models from the Soviet Union, Israel, and Sweden, they now raise question as to whether we might not, in this country, provide more care for infants and children outside their own homes. However, there is conflicting evidence for and against such programs, especially as they relate to all-day or total care of infants.[6]

Small, experimental projects patterned on the foreign models are being launched in this country and their effects are being evaluated. A cautious approach of this sort is certainly wise. As more projects are studied, guides should develop which will help determine: what kinds of infants and children from what kinds of families will profit most from (a) care within their own home; (b) partly within their own home and partly within other settings; (c) completely outside of their own home.

Related to the last alternative, we have the evidence presented by Leontine Young[7] in her recent study of two groups of children: (a) severely mistreated and (b) seriously neglected. She pleads that careful, realistic studies should be made of the family situations of these children and, when indicated, youngsters should be removed from homes in which extreme cruelty or extreme neglect exists and in which parents are unable to change their behavior. Severely neglecting parents, as she describes them, have characteristics that are similar, in an extreme form, to the characteristics found to be associated with the subcultures of poverty. In Dr. Young's experience, severely neglecting parents who have the benefit of adequate casework help are often relieved to give up their children to child-care agencies since these parents lack the multifaceted resources to act responsibly toward their young.

Although it is quite possible that some children of the very poor have very little chance for adequate development unless they are removed from their parents for full-time or most-of-the-time custody in a more growth-conducive setting, it seems that there is a danger in putting too much emphasis on saving children without sufficient regard for the total family unit.

The importance of the family unit as a crucial, dynamic, interacting force in all aspects of human behavior has been pointed out by theorists, researchers, and practitioners.[8] Recently, the extended kinship network has been rediscovered[9] as a still-potent force in American society, particularly for lower-class families. The full potentials of this kinship system are worthy of careful exploration before the child is plucked from a dynamic interaction network. This comment is made in reference to the welfare of the child as well as of his own family. Attention must be given not only to the rejection and insecurity that a child may feel when removed from his siblings and parents but also to the insecurity and rejection his own relatives may feel, if they are judged to be inadequate in their familial roles.

Enrichment for Parents

It seems inappropriate and premature to assume that parents are incapable of further growth and change. Among the intervention strategies that might be tried more extensively for very poor parents is that of parent education—as it is broadly defined. A group approach to working with very poor parents may be highly effective—at least it has been judged to be with some parents. This approach seems promising, partly because cultural change appears to be brought about, to some extent, through acceptance and identification with an individual who serves as an "ego ideal." This is particularly true if this person is the leader of a group, and more particularly if he or she is liked and admired by group members. As new patterns emerge through group activities, it is important that they be rewarded. It is also important that group members recognize these patterns as providing a better coping mechanism for reality situations than previous patterns. As the group leader serves as an ego ideal, and as patterns are gradually absorbed by the group, they may also be gradually reinforced through group action.

Group programs are not visualized as the only way of helping the very poor, but they are suggested as a potentially important way. To be more specific, it has been found by some practitioners that clubs for AFDC* mothers can have a strong appeal and seem to achieve good results.[10] The loneliness and social isolation of these mothers have been well-documented. Emphasis on group activities at the present time is placed on participation of mothers, since it appears to be extremely difficult to reach fathers. However, encouraging both parents to become group members remains an important task.[10,11]

In planning group activities for adults, it would seem important to bear in mind that many of the very poor are likely to have high levels of anxiety associated with past frustration and failure. Probably group programs should therefore focus on providing the poor an opportunity for attaining, in the shortest possible time, a maximum degree of success with a minimum degree of frustration. Since the life styles of the chronically poor are apt to be largely pragmatic and oriented toward doing rather than talking, these programs might well be centered on immediate, concrete reality problems, such as difficulties in clothing and feeding the family, procuring health services, and the like.

Since many of the very poor tend not to be goal- or time-oriented—at least not in the middle-class way—programs might generally be planned around immediate objectives. Planning probably should be flexible in terms of the scheduling of activities. For example, some leaders who work successfully with the very poor say that they keep a kind of open house which is available to mothers and fathers as they feel ready to use it. A more definite structuring of time may be planned at a later point, after new ways of life take on more meaning to group members.

It appears that very poor parents often need a great deal of nurturing themselves.[7] Most of them have been so deprived in

---

*Aid to Families with Dependent Children.

their growing-up experiences that they are limited in their ability to meet the demands of parenthood. The well-worn concept that in order to be a good parent one must have been well-parented himself has application here. A supporting, nonfrustrating experience in a small group may make up for some of the earlier deprivations of group members.

A reaching-out approach is indicated if one expects to involve many of the very poor in agency programs. Their tendency to distrust all that is middle-class, their sense of being rejected, their fear of the unfamiliar, tend to keep them from making use of the services planned in their behalf. The person-to-person style that is warmly accepting and encouraging has generally far more meaning than a more rational approach to the effect that such and such a program will be helpful in certain ways. Fear of broader experiences and larger worlds also suggest that programs be established in the neighborhoods of the very poor.[10]

A good deal has been done in reference to providing "higher horizons" for children and youth. It is suggested that more thought be given to the same concept in relation to parents. A constricted, fearful life-style—more often than not their heritage —is frequently communicated to the children.

Enlarging the horizons of lower-lower class adults would entail offering them broader experiences planned specifically along the lines of what they themselves most value and what will benefit them most as individuals. There has been a tendency—on those rare occasions when programs are planned for adults—to think in terms of providing experiences that are interpretive of programs that have been devised for their children. Appropriate adult experiences might include a shopping expedition to department stores, a trip to a supermarket outside the immediate neighborhood, a picnic in a nearby park, an excursion to an adult movie, and the like. As parents find that they can move into the larger community and that the larger community has rewards for them as well as for their children, they would seem to be more likely to integrate this broader participation into the life of the family. As participation acquires such meaning, parents may be more apt to enlarge their children's lives spontaneously, without being specifically indoctrinated to do so. And spontaneous parenting is more likely to have a deep and lasting effect on both parents and children.

Guidance in Self-Control for Parents

Accepting, supportive approaches to many of the very poor have been stressed. This does not mean, however, that a totally permissive style is indicated. It is impressive that research evidence has strongly suggested that firm, mild, consistent discipline is closely associated with many areas of success in life functioning. Characteristics more typical of the subcultures of the very poor seem to imply not only a depressed life style but, by middle-class standards, a very immature one. Such characteristics as magical thinking, subjective judgment, impulse gratification, use of force rather than reason, alienation from authority figures, lack of goal commitment, distrust of heterosexual relationships, projection of problems on to others, and other similar characteristics might be termed immature, at least in middle-class value terms. Emotional growth toward maturity rests not only on meeting and accepting the needs of individuals but also on guidance toward impulse control. Those who work with very poor adults probably should provide kindly, firm, consistent guidance of self-control and more effective reality coping for many of them.

This comment about guidance is derived from clues from a variety of sources. These sources indicate that a direct, assertive, specific approach appears to be more effective with disadvantaged adults than the more subtle, abstract, insight-oriented method often used with middle-class clients.[7,12]

Structured Learning

Role-playing and learning-by-doing projects also seem to be useful.[13,14] Considerable experimentation is going on at present along these lines. For example, instead of relying on internal personality changes developed from verbalized insights and a therapeutic relationship, the external environment is specifically structured and individuals are taught to play certain roles in this environment. By acting differently in a structured situation, it appears that some people, at least, begin to feel and think differently. Specific instruction as to appropriate behavior may facilitate this.

Somewhat along this line, recent experiments in the field of family therapy may be adapted to highly disadvantaged families. Specific help in family communication, family problem solving, and role-playing within the family has shown promise in a variety of settings.[15,16,17]

Some Applications of Learning Theory

To some extent, learning theory and its associated findings have been applied to changing the behavior of the very poor. There are a number of ways in which this theory and findings might be further applied. In general (but not always), rewarded behavior is more apt to persist than behavior that is punished. The type of reward makes a difference. In attempting to change child-rearing practices of the very poor, for instance, it seems as if further attention might be paid to the planned use of concrete, behavior-related, valued rewards. For example, a low-income mother who manages to get her children to school clean and on time for a month, might be given a certificate of recognition, plus a monetary reward. The latter might be rationalized as recognition that clean, well-fed, rested children cost the mother money as well as effort. Parenthood, in general, tends to be expensive, and its rewards are often abstract and long in coming. Middle-class parents, with a wide range of other rewards in status, range of activities, and income, do not need rewards for good parenting in the same way that lower-lower class parents do—especially the woman who lacks a husband and faces the job of parenting alone.

Family Life Education

Continuing problems of broken families among the very poor suggest a number of relevant strategies. One of these is experimentation in providing family life education and counseling programs for low-income boys and girls. Realistic programs of this sort, adapted to the situations and subcultures of the very poor, seem called for since lower-lower class cultural characteristics frequently include attitudes of hostility and distrust between the sexes, problems in communication, lack of knowledge about reproduction and male and female anatomy, and a conviction that men and women belong to two different worlds. The usual family life education and counseling approach, however, is quite middle-class.[18] Assumptions are generally made as to values, attitudes, and resources that are closely associated with the middle-class situation, style, and vocabulary. In order for such programs to have meaning for very poor adolescents, new methods and materials need to be developed. At least one settlement house has experimented with a couples' club for very poor, newly married, young people. The program includes organized sports for the boys, homemaking classes for the girls, a nursery for babies, and a gradual introduction of social activities and discussion groups for young husbands and wives together.

A coeducational recreation, guidance, and work program for younger boys and girls might be developed. One objective could well be guidance toward the deferment of impulsive early marriages. It was found in one high school program that when individual counseling was included for parents and their youngsters, along with a family life education program for students, there was more success in reducing high-school age marriages than when family life education was the only approach. One of the reasons for this higher rate of success was probably that a number of young people drift into early marriage at least partly because of difficulties in their home situation.

Family planning centers are developing in a number of localities as the communities are ready to accept them. A variety of methods in planning is offered, in keeping with the religious values of the clinic patients. There is growing recognition that free clinics of this kind must be made available to the very poor. A number of studies indicate that a sense of helplessness in coping with what they consider to be fate tends to be characteristic of the relationships between the sexes in lower-lower class groups. Ability to limit family size could be an important ingredient in reducing such fatalistic negative attitudes and promoting marital stability.[19] New developments in contraceptive techniques offer hope for more ready and effective use of family planning devices for all socioeconomic groups.[20] This may be especially true of lower-lower class members who have tended to shun more complex methods in the past.[19,20]

Adaptation of Casework Practice

Much of what has been said in the earlier pages applies to casework practice with the very poor. Applicable points will have been obvious to the casework practitioner. More specific suggestions follow. The writer is particularly indebted here to the work of such highly experienced specialists in this field as Janet Weinandy,[12] Leontine Young,[7] and Berta Fantl.[21]

All of these specialists note that a direct, specific, assertive approach is generally called for in working with the very poor. According to Fantl, for instance, "Clear, forthright, and correct statements are ego-supportive. Mere passive listening on the part of the worker may be felt as hostility and may increase anxiety or 'acting-out' behavior. However, if the worker intervenes insensitively, the client is likely to withdraw."[21]

Dr. Leontine Young, in her recent book describing her study of neglected and abused children and their parents, offers comments along the same lines. In conceptualizing good casework practice, she writes in part about the application of standards:

> The logical question, of course, is how can they be imposed unless or until the parents want such help or can respond to such an imposed structure. There is one need in many of these parents that makes such a motivation possible: the need and longing to be dependent upon someone who is able to see them as they are and still be concerned for them. Their need for dependence is so great that it can become a focal point for whatever strengths they do have. Like children they respond to strength which substitutes the reality judgment of maturity for the distorted perspectives of their immaturity, that shares the too heavy responsibilities, that makes the everyday rules within which they can find some direction.
>
> The caseworker who insists upon treating a neglecting parent as an adult finds that he has no relationship with that parent. No amount

of financial assistance or continuing contacts is likely to alter the hostility and indifference that grows up between them . . . They wanted borrowed strength, not freedom of choice—a freedom they lacked the strength to use.

With neglecting parents the use of protective authority is usually a relief. It lifts the weight of responsibility from them, protects them against their own confusion as well as from the consequences that would ensue from the unchecked expression of their destructive impulses. It is often their first encounter with consistent strength. Punishment they have been familiar with a long time, but strength has too often been unknown. Even when they grow angry at the limits imposed by authority, they show obliquely, like children, that they are glad it is there.[7]

Weinandy, Young, and Fantl are unanimous in their agreement that casework with the very poor requires a mutual focus of workers and client on the immediate, concrete situation. The subcultural patterns frequently found in this group, plus the severity of presenting specific problems, generally require such an approach. A tendency of the "hard-core, multiple-problem poor" to "swing" helplessly from crisis to crisis demands not only a focus on the immediate situation but also a firm competency on the part of the caseworker in joining with the client to resolve the present crisis and to take steps to prevent the next one. Again, to quote Fantl, "By successfully helping clients around immediate crisis situations, the following may be accomplished: (1) some relief is experienced in his ability to control his behavior, and (2) there is a growing feeling of confidence in the worker because he understood the client's feeling of extreme anger, fear of losing control or isolation from others without becoming frightened, 'hopeless,' and discouraged about the client or deserting him as others have done in the past."

Weinandy points out that this kind of crisis and desperation sharing can bring with it exhaustion and despair to the social work staff.[12] Professionals engaged in such work need replenishment of their own emotional reserves through frequent, mutually supporting staff meetings, opportunities for consultation, and backing from agency administrators.

The same three writers also emphasize the importance of

working with the entire neighborhood: key neighborhood leaders and communicators and the network of relevant business establishments, churches, schools, protective services, and health and welfare agencies.

Adequate Income Support

It has been proposed by a number of social scientists and social workers that resources should be found to provide a minimum income floor to all persons in the country. While the variety of strategies proposed is too large a subject to discuss here, it is relevant to note that the kinds of intervention suggested in the foregoing pages are hardly likely to have much effect if parents do not have sufficient money to provide themselves and their children with the basic essentials of life. An experiment might be conducted in which a group of very poor families is supplied with enough money to live above the so-called poverty line. It might be found that a steady, adequate income is sufficient for many of the recipients to give them a base for changing life styles of hopelessness, impulsiveness, fatalism, alienation, and apathy, to life styles more conducive to positive mental health, educational achievement, social acceptability, "moral" character, and family stability. Not only might such a steady income accomplish these results; it might be the most economical approach to the problem.

A variety of modifications of the above general proposal might be tried, such as adequate income, plus specialized services of various kinds; adequate income, through earnings from a public works program; slightly inadequate income with "salary raises" for certain desired behaviors such as adequate child care and housekeeping.

CONCLUSION

The foregoing has been a presentation of some of the services and programs that may be effective in implementing changes in the cultural patterns of the very poor. This has not been an all-inclusive presentation by any means. Other programs, such as community action, neighborhood counseling centers, legal aid, employment training and placement, day-care centers, homemaker services, literacy education, public housing services, improved protective services, use of indigenous personnel, camping programs, and tutorial projects are among those that come to mind.

All of the suggestions made here are made in an experimental spirit. All are viewed as being subject to tentative application and careful evaluation. None are thought to be prescriptions for the prevention and treatment of poverty. Poverty, as a function of a number of socioeconomic systems, has many causes and many modifiers. Poor people, as members of these systems, are individuals whose endowments and behaviors are infinite in variety and complexity. Therefore, a multiplicity of approaches, both to the systems and to the children and adults who interact with them, is called for. Social workers make up but one of the professional groups that may be able to help some of the poor cross the deep valley that currently separates many of them from the rest of society.

REFERENCES

1. Chilman, Catherine S.: Child-rearing and family relationship patterns of the very poor. *Welfare in Review,* January 1965.
2. An invitation to help project head start. Washington, D.C. Community Action program, Office of Economic Opportunity, 1965.
3. Bandler, Louise: A comparison of the child-rearing environment of upper lower-class and very low-class families. Boston, South End Family Program, Boston University, 1965. (Mimeo)
4. Bowlby, John: Maternal care and mental health. *Monogr, (No. 2):* 1952.
5. Prugh, Dange G., Harlow, Robert G., Andry, R. G. Mead, Margaret, Wootton, Barbara, Lebovici, S. and Ainsworth, Mary D.: Deprivation of maternal care—A reassessment of its effects. *World Health Organization Public Health Paper No. 14.* New York, International Documents Service, Columbia University Press.
6. Nimkoff, M. F.: *Comparative Family Systems.* New York, Houghton Mifflin, 1965, pp. 357-369.
7. Young, Leontine: *Wednesday's Children.* New York, McGraw-Hill, 1964.
8. Ackerman, Nathan: *The Psycho-dynamics of Family Life.* New York, Basic Books, 1958.
9. Sussman, M. B.: The isolated nuclear family: Fact or fiction. In Sussman, M. B. (Ed.): *Sourcebook in Marriage and the Family.* New York, Houghton Mifflin, 1963.

10. Chilman, Catherine and Kraft, Ivor: Helping low-income families through parent education groups. *CHILDREN,* July-August 1963.
11. Hill, Esther: Helping low-income families. *CHILDREN,* July-August, 1963.
12. Weinandy, Janet: Case work with tenants in a public housing project. *J Marriage Family, 26 (No. 4):* 1964.
13. Alpert, Richard: Recent studies of the adolescent's search for significance. *Recent Research on Creative Approaches to Environmental Stress.* Iowa City, Iowa, State University of Iowa, 1963.
14. Riessman, Frank: New approaches to mental health treatment for labor and low income groups. Mental Health Report No. 2, New York, National Institute for Labor Education, 250 West 57th Street, 1964.
15. Kluckhohn, Richard: Creative approaches to family conflicts. *Recent Research on Creative Approaches to Environmental Stress.* Iowa City, Iowa, State University of Iowa, 1963.
16. Leslie, Gerald R.: The field of marriage counseling. In Christensen, Harold T. (Ed.): *Handbook of Marriage and the Family.* Chicago, Rand McNally, 1964.
17. Levine, Rachel A.: Treatment in the home: An experiment with mental health of the poor. In Riessman, Frank, Cohen, Jerome and Perl, Arthur (Eds.): *Mental Health of the Poor.* New York, The Free Press of Glencoe, 1964, pp. 329-335.
18. Kerckhoff, Richard K.: Family life education in America. In Christensen, Harold T. (Ed.): *Handbook of Marriage and the Family.* Chicago, Rand McNally, 1964.
19. Lieberman, E. James: Preventive psychiatry and family planning. *J Marriage Family, 26 (No. 4):*471-477, Nov. 1964.
20. Rainwater, Lee: *Family Design.* Chicago, Aldine, 1965.
21. Fantl, Berta: Intergrating social and psychological theories in social work practice. *Smith College Studies in Social Work, XXXIV (No. 3):* June 1964.

Chapter 35

THE PLIGHT OF THE POVERTY-STRICKEN FAMILY IN THE UNITED STATES

SALVADOR MINUCHIN

T HE TITLE of this paper is not merely a title; it is also a diagnosis. The "poverty-stricken family" has become a target for intervention by mental health professionals, and because we are presumably change-agents, our target logically must be something that needs change-producing help. The poverty-stricken family (a term that covers about 20 million people whose strengths and problems are bewilderingly diverse) is conceptualized as an entity that must be sick. The poverty-stricken family is seen as a locus of pathology.

This paper deals with the misuse of this kind of undifferentiated diagnosis, with the impossibilities of the task that faces mental health interveners who enter this broad social arena with an inadequate psychological armamentarium, and with the way social agencies have inadvertently rendered ineffective, and sometimes harmful, their own services for the poor. Our interventions with the poor have been the product of genuine concern. Unfortunately, we have been hampered by ignorance of the field, by a set of ill-defined assumptions about the "poor," and by a predominantly middle-class set of values. The institutions that affect poverty-stricken families have been organized according to a philosophy of delivery of services that sees the recipient, or client, as a sick patient. Our diagnostic systems have been organized to determine normality or pathology in a middle-class framework that does not correspond to the life styles of the poor family. Variations from the modes and mores of the mainstream society,

Note: Reprinted from Child Welfare, *49*:124-130, 1970.
This paper was presented at the CWLA Eastern Regional Conference at Baltimore in 1969.

such as the intact nuclear family, are seen as abnormal and injurious.

In general, our concepts of problems and services have been related to those of dynamic psychiatry, which has conceptualized pathology as existing within the individual and has paid little or no attention to the ways in which the systems surrounding the individual maintain or program his responses. The same tendency has been carried over into our work with families. Because we do not take into account the family's ecological systems, family problems and pathology are seen as arising from within the family. Therefore, our interventions are designed to impinge upon the family.

THE ECOLOGICAL APPROACH

Though the mental health field has always recognized that the child can be understood only as an organism within its environment, particularly the family, the field has been less accepting of the general concept of the importance of the ecosystem, that is, the framework of systems surrounding and interacting with the individual, including the family, school, job, and so on. But lately, mental health theories have been enriched by the "ecological systems approach." The family is conceptualized as a group of people involved in constant mutual impingement. If one member of the family changes, this change affects the rest of the system. If we remove one member of the family by sending him to a residential institution for juvenile delinquents, for instance, we affect not only him, but his siblings and parents. The family system itself is seen as an entity in constant interaction with larger systems, such as the neighborhood, a racial group, and society in general.

With this view, pathology is no longer seen as a predominantly internal phenomenon. It can also be seen in, and as a product of, transactions between the individual and other systems and between the family and other systems. We do not lack conceptual knowledge of the importance of the life circumstances of our clients. But our armamentarium of interventions has failed to change in response to our broadening conceptualizations.

A major problem blocking the development of new interventions is our lack of knowledge about normal development and normal reactions to different contexts. Researchers have tended to concentrate on the observation of people we have labeled schizophrenic, phobic, delinquent, antisocial, or poor, and observations are tinged with suspicion that every part of their life styles represents part of the pathological syndrome. More knowledge of normal people's interactions with contexts would allow us to differentiate the parts of a syndrome that actually are pathological, and the parts that are a reaction to contexts and can change if the context changes. Knowledge of normality would provide the field-ground structure we badly need. This is especially true in the study of the poverty-stricken family. In research at the Wiltwyck School for Boys, for instance, my coworkers and I found definite consequences traceable to our index patients' socialization in disorganized families. We reported our data in a book we entitled *Families of the Slums.*[1] The material for this book was gathered specifically from unstable, disorganized, low socioeconomic families, mostly in clinical surroundings. But we gave the book a title that implied it encompassed the whole heterogeneous group living in the slums, in all contexts. When we finished that book and began to study similar families in their natural social surroundings, we were impressed by how much we had not seen. Certain aspects of disorganized families, such as the extended family structure, which we had labeled pathological, could be seen in the larger context as significant systems of support. But social agencies, accepting the model of the nuclear family as correct, willingly or not penalized other structural types.

In general, our interventions have not been ameliorative. Welfare, as Moynihan points out,[2] was originally designed to tide people over until better times. The existence of "third-generation welfare" families shows that some families crystallize in the welfare position. I need not elaborate this problem; what I am interested in elaborating is the non-change-producing aspects of interventions that were designed to help and change the family. Perhaps the best way to do this is to present a composite poverty-stricken family, with familiar characteristics and problems, and discuss the effects of interventions on it.

THE COMPOSITE FAMILY

This family consists of a mother and her six illegitimate children, the oldest of whom is twelve. The mother was born in the South, the youngest of seven children. When she was sixteen, she came North to live with her married sister. A year after her arrival, her first child was born. The sisters rented a crumbling brownstone and pooled money and work. The older sister lived on the top floor with her two children, and the younger sister and her children lived below. The women made out fairly well until the need to take care of her children made the younger go on relief. At this point she became homebound, caring for her children and her sister's, while the sister worked as a maid.

After several years of trying, the older sister was admitted to a low-income housing project. She and her children moved, and at that time the younger sister bore her sixth child. She began to drink, and became promiscuous. The older sister visited the family as often as possible, doing the laundry, and so forth, but the main responsibility for the children fell on the oldest daughter, twelve. The mother became more and more depressed; the children's situation deteriorated. The oldest girl was responsible, but subdued. She was doing well enough in school, but the teachers were worried about her tendency to withdraw. The oldest boy, eleven, was a truant; he stole and otherwise acted out. The younger children showed no symptoms of pathology yet.

At the urging of the caseworker, the mother consented to have the children placed. After court procedures, the children were put in a shelter. From there, the oldest daughter went to a foster home, the oldest son was placed in a residential institution for delinquent youths, and the nine- and eight-year-olds were placed in different foster homes. The eight-year-old lived in three different foster homes during this period. The five-year-old spent some months in the shelter because of hyperactive behavior that suggested minimal brain dysfunction. He was finally placed in an institution. The baby remained with his mother, whose caseworker continued to work with her.

It is difficult to calculate the cost to the children of this separation from their mother and each other. But the financial cost is staggering.[3]

The mother was eager to get her children back. Finally, the caseworker helped her petition the department of welfare and the children in foster care were returned to her. The family was referred for treatment to a child guidance clinic, since childrearing problems remained. When a clinic social worker visited the home, he found all the children dressed up, waiting to greet him. The mother put the children through rehearsed routines to show that they minded her and that she could take care of them. She said to him: "I love my kids and I want them. But if that judge takes them away again—well, I'm thirty-four now. That gives me about ten years. If they take these away from me, I'll have ten more."

NATURE OF THE INTERVENTIONS

The social interventions for this family were designed in good faith to assist them and, theoretically, to help them change. But the effect of the interventions was to fragment the family and increase their difficulties. Let us look at these interventions before we consider how to organize services according to a conceptual framework that sees the family as a whole system and takes into account the effect interventions with individual members have upon the family. First, the mother received welfare checks for years. These helped feed, shelter, and clothe the children, but this was only maintenance. Payments were made to the mother; in effect, the state was paying her to babysit. No attempt was made to help the family change or to change their circumstances. The main concern was the well-being of the children, and as long as the sisters lived together, the children received satisfactory care. The mother was given no employment counseling, and if she had been, her sense of ineffectiveness would have made the counseling futile. In any case, someone had to look after the children, and even if she had been able to hold a job, the lack of adequate day care facilities would have made it impossible for her and her sister to keep their children together. Birth control information was not made available to her. The caseworker did not mention it, and the mother never sought it. She did not know where to go to get family planning advice, and had only a vague idea of the function of social agencies; furthermore, she felt that no man would accept her use of a birth control device. The department of welfare intervened only when the mother's deterioration threatened her children. That intervention took the form of breaking up the family for two years.

The older sister's departure to the housing project is also illustrative. She was a widow with two children, a good candidate for low-income housing. Her application was approved, though it took a year because of an overload of applications. But the younger sister, mother of more than two illegitimate children, was never considered as a possible candidate. If she had been, her oldest son's record of truancy and stealing would have labeled her family ineligible. Thus, a system of interdependence and support between the two families was shattered, and nothing was supplied to take its place.

SYSTEMS OF SUPPORT

We know from studies of the low socioeconomic population that many systems of support exist within the neighborhood, including churches, social groups, and "social networks." We also know that the various forms of the extended family can be important systems of support. But this knowledge is not carried over into interventive techniques. Cases such as that of our composite family are not uncommon. It never occurred to the social worker to try to help repair the loss of support represented by the break-up of the joint family; the only intervention was to break up the family still more.

What would be more helpful to a family like our composite? For such a family an ecologically oriented intervener would first study the ecology of the family, to pick out the supportive systems and the harmful components, particularly those that tended to keep the family dependent. He would determine the relevant kinds of intervention, deciding whether to concentrate on the nuclear family or younger sister and her children, subunits of this group, the extended family, the neighborhood, the school, or a variety of targets. He would decide who should intervene—a social worker, a teacher, a counselor, or a community worker. He would then plan goals for family change and plot interventions directed toward those goals, based on the realization that the true family unit was the joint family. The smallest effective target of intervention would be the younger sister and her children, but the operant nuclear target would be the two sisters and their children.

The therapist would also consider three other sisters who were living in the immediate area. He would take into account two fathers of the younger sister's children, still in the area, not stable members of the family unit, but in contact with their children. Also part of the family's ecosystem would be the children's teachers and the school guidance counselor, the department of welfare caseworker, the minister of the neighborhood storefront church, the personnel of the medical clinic the children attended, two staff members of the child guidance clinic with whom the children had formed relationships, and other unmapped contacts.

Interventions to help the composite family could take various forms. Some would require the expertise of a mental health practitioner and some would require the work of an educator. The help of the area committee woman might be needed. The mental health intervener would have to coordinate these steps carefully, so that the interventions would not add to the chaotic impingement of life upon this family.

A COURSE OF TREATMENT

Here is a hypothetical course of treatment:

The clinician would conduct family therapy sessions in the clinic and the home. From the family's interactions, he might conclude that the family fell in the category designated as the disorganized family.[4,5] As such, they would have a particular style of communicating. They would tend to focus on the end-product of behavior, rather than on content. They would be oriented toward externalization and projection, and be unskilled in readings of interpersonal causality. They would be untrained in self-observation, and therefore unavailable for traditional therapeutic techniques. Family conflicts would be expressed in a global way, rendering them unavailable for problem-solving. The children, reared in an environment of impermanence and unpredictability, would have difficulty defining themselves in relation to the world. Such rules as were set would be largely the responsibility of the parental child. The mother would alternately defer to her and try to wrest some of her power back. All of the children, handicapped by the random and erratic rules, would look to adult responses for cues as to behavior, instead of depending on internalized rules.[6]

At the same time, there would be good features in the family that could be utilized. Immediately obvious would be the warmth and love within the family, and the mother's determination to keep her children. The availability of the older sister for support could be utilized. A neighbor who made a pet of the youngest boy could be enlisted as a babysitter so the mother could go to a "slimnastics" class she has been wanting to take at the YWCA.

A community worker could join clinic sessions designed to help the mother establish rules for the children and to offer guidance instead of the excessive control she had adopted after the children's return. The medical clinic would aid the youngest boy, seven, whose hyperactivity might cause great problems in school. Dexadrine might be prescribed, and the school counselor and teacher would consult with the combined medical and mental health team. Through a community worker, the mother might become a member of a neighborhood social club.[7] If the group had a speaker to discuss job training programs, she might enroll in a training course for sewing machine operators. At this point, if in the judgment of the clinicians the family had attained a certain degree of change and autonomy, they might enter a period of discontinuous treatment. The community worker would keep in close touch with the family, and the clinic would always be available in any crisis, but the family would be seen in the clinic only once every six weeks or so. This type of service relates to that of a family medical practitioner, who establishes a base of health and then remains available for crises.

The emphasis throughout would be not on exploring pathology, but on finding, enhancing, and rewarding competence. People change not only through the lifting of inhibitions, as in traditional psychoanalytic theory, but through the development of competences. The family would be hooked into therapy rapidly because they would perceive the therapist as responsive to their needs. The impact of the interventions would be multiplied by the use of natural systems of support within the family and community. The therapist would have to be supersensitive to the danger that his interventions would further rob the mother of her executive power and increase her dependency on social agencies, but this danger could be avoided. The intervention with this family would not be short term. But the redoubled nature of the interventions and the possibility of discontinuous clinical interventions would make the work effective and thrifty.

DEALING WITH THE TOTAL FAMILY

Family services oriented toward the total family within its ecosystem are becoming more and more the treatment of choice for a wide range of mental health and social problem families, not just members of the low socioeconomic groups. But the response of social agencies in general is still to break up the family. The records of improvement in foster care and residential treatment are not encouraging, and the costs of these approaches are discouraging, but there still has not been an organized, overall conceptualization of the delivery of services to families in this country. The family is studied and respected as a viable socialization unit when it is working; when trouble arises, the response is to split it.

This is part of the American philosophy of individualism; we are oriented toward the individual child and his rights. But this does seem to have been carried to extremes. In most countries, the function performed here by the ADC is fulfilled by family allowances, but in the United States, support goes through the mother to the child. This is an antifamilial force even without the concomitant problems of "man-in-the-house" rules.

Only recently are we beginning to develop a concept of services to the child in his ecological systems—the family, the school, the neighborhood, and so on. Within this new concept, what are the changes we should sponsor in ourselves and push for on larger levels?[8] At the level of intervention with specific family units, we must change our goals. Instead of discovering and inadvertently maintaining pathology, we must discover and enhance competence. We must change the locality of our change-producing interventions, moving into the home and community in order to study and develop goals for change in the particular family in its day-by-day life and interactions with its surrounding systems. In doing so, we will discover the natural systems of support that exist in the community and be able to work with them to enhance their supportive function.

In moving away from clinic-centered interventions into the actual life of a family, we find many new ways to help and to change the family. Auerswald[9] found that some multiproblem families were in contact with seven or more agencies, all impinging upon one part of the family's life. A family might be dealing with the school counselor and truant officer, the court's parole officer and probation officer, the social workers of a residential school for delinquents, and the caseworker of the department of welfare. It is helpful to bring all the interveners and the family together to discuss overall goals and plans.

Looking at people as they interact with their environment and social institutions, we cease to consider the intervener the only major variable in the development of change. We will become more concerned with allowing natural systems of support to function more effectively. Studying the feedback processes between the family and its surroundings, we will change the delivery of our services. To make the total family the focus of integrated services, we have to reconceptualize, and realize that we are delivering services to people with rights, people who are responding to an ecosystem of which we are part.

We are beginning to understand the importance of ecological systems and the way they affect health and mental health. Slowly, we are beginning to incorporate this understanding in the development of services. In the measure in which this concept is taken into account in our planning and execution of interventions, those interventions will become truly change-producing and helpful.

NOTES AND REFERENCES

1. Minuchin, Salvador, Montalvo, Braulio *et al.:* New York, Basic Books, 1967.
2. Moynihan, Daniel Patrick and Barton, Paul: *The Negro Family: The Case for National Action.* Washington, D.C., U.S. Department of Labor, 1965.
3. The Children's Aid Society of Pennsylvania estimates the average yearly cost of keeping a child in residential treatment is $7975. For keeping an older child in foster care, the acerage cost is $2304. Thus, the cost of keeping three children in foster care and two children in institutional care for two years would exceed $40,000.
4. Pavenstedt, Eleanor: A comparison of the childrearing environment of upper-lower and very low-lower class families. *Am J Orthopsychiatry, XXXV (No. 1):* 89 ff, 1965.
5. Minuchin, *op. cit.*
6. For a more thorough discussion, see Minuchin, *op. cit.*
7. Richard Taber: A systems approach to the delivery of mental health services to children in a low socioeconomic black community: Work with two natural groups. Presented to the American Orthopsychiatric Association, March 1969. Mimeo.
8. See Auerswald, E. H.: Cognitive development and psychopathology in the urban environment. In Graubard, P. S. (Ed.): *Children Against Schools.* Chicago, Follet Educational Corporation, 1969; Hoffman, Lynn and Long, Lawrence: A Systems Dilemma, mimeo; Speck, Ross V.: Psychotherapy and the social network of a schizophrenic family. *Family Process, VI:* 1967; and Taber, *op. cit.*
9. Auerswald, E. H.: Interdisciplinary versus ecological approach. *Family Process, VII (No. 2):* 1968.

B. ADVOCACY-MEDIATION

Chapter 36

THE SOCIAL WORKER AS ADVOCATE: CHAMPION OF SOCIAL VICTIMS

THE AD HOC COMMITTEE ON ADVOCACY

T HE NEW interest in advocacy among social workers can be traced directly to the growing social and political ferment in our cities in the past decade. Social workers connected with Mobilization For Youth[1] (which took its form in the context of this ferment) first brought the advocacy role to the attention of the profession.[2] But the notion that the social worker needs to become the champion of social victims who cannot defend themselves was voiced long ago by others, and has recently been revived.[3]

Present events are forcing the issue with new urgency. Externally the urban crisis and the social revolution of which it is the most jarring aspect are placing new demands on social work; internally, the profession is re-examining itself with an intensity that has few precedents. The profession's faith in its own essential viability is being severely tested. It is especially timely that social work turn its attention to the role of advocate at this time, both because of its clear relevance to the urban crisis and because it has been an integral part of the philosophy and practice of the profession since its earliest days.

Note: Reprinted with permission of the National Association of Social Workers from *Social Work, 14* (No. 2) : 16-22, April, 1969.
The Ad Hoc Committee on Advocacy was established by the NASW Task Force on the Urban Crisis and Public Welfare Problems, which itself had been established by the Board of Directors early in 1968 to coordinate and redirect NASW's program to make it more responsive to current national crises. Members of the advocacy committee were Willard C. Richan (chairman), William Denham, Charlotte Dunmore, Norma Levine, Howard McClary, Eva Schindler-Rainman, Sue Spencer, Jacob Zukerman, Alfred Stamm (staff), Sam Negrin (liaison with Division of Practice and Knowledge).

WHAT IS ADVOCACY?

The dictionary defines advocate in two ways. On one hand, he is "one that pleads the cause of another."[4] This is the meaning given to the legal advocate—the lawyer—who zealously guards the interests of his client over all others. Another definition describes the advocate as "one who argues for, defends, maintains, or recommends a cause or a proposal."[5] This definition incorporates the political meaning ascribed to the word in which the interests of a class of people are represented; implicitly, the issues are universalistic rather than particularistic.

Both meanings of advocacy have been espoused in the social work literature. Briar describes the historical concept of the caseworker-advocate who is

> . . . his client's supporter, his adviser, his champion, and, if need be, his representative in his dealings with the court, the police, the social agency, and other organizations that [affect] his well-being.[6]

For Briar, the social worker's commitment to the civil rights of *his own client* "takes precedence over all other commitments."[7] This is, in essence, the orientation of the lawyer-advocate.

Brager takes another view. He posits the "advocate-reformer" who

> . . . identifies with the plight of the disadvantaged. He sees as his primary responsibility the tough-minded and partisan representation of their interests, and this supersedes his fealty to others. This role inevitably requires that the practitioner function as a political tactician.[8]

Brager does not rule out of his definition the direct-service practitioner who takes on the individual grievances of his client, but his emphasis is on the advocacy of the interests of an aggrieved *class* of people through policy change. The two conceptions do overlap at many points, as for instance when the worker must engage in action to change basic policies and institutions in order to deal effectively with his client's grievances.

SOCIAL WORK'S COMMITMENT TO ADVOCACY

Advocacy has been an important thread running throughout social work's history. Some individuals have been elevated to heroic status because they have fulfilled this role—Dorothea Dix and Jane Addams come most readily to mind. However, it would be safe to say that most social workers have honored advocacy more in rhetoric than in practice, and for this there are at least two reasons.

To begin with, professional education and practice have tended to legitimate a consensus orientation and oppose an adversary one, and this has been perpetuated in the literature. A combative stance, often an essential ingredient in the kind of partisan alignment implied by the concept of advocacy, is not a natural one for many social workers. As a result, most social workers lack both the orientation and the technical skills necessary to engage in effective advocacy. Finally, the employee status of social workers has often restricted their ability to act as advocates.[9]

At the same time that the current upheaval in society adds a note of urgency to the issue of social work's commitment to advocacy, it also adds complications to the task of fulfilling that commitment because of the emotion surrounding many of the issues. For example, some members of the profession feel strongly that fighting racism and deepening the social conscience are the only means to combat these social evils; others—equally adamant —feel that social workers are not equipped to solve these ills, which are a problem of the whole society. There is still another group of social workers who tend to avoid involvement with controversial issues at any cost. What is needed is a consistent approach on the basis of which each social worker can feel confident in fulfilling his professional commitment, an approach that can be responsive to the current crisis but must also outlive it.

OBLIGATIONS OF THE INDIVIDUAL SOCIAL WORKER

The obligation of social workers to become advocates flows directly from the social worker's Code of Ethics.[10] Therefore, why should it be difficult for a profession that is "based on humanitarian, democratic ideals" and "dedicated to service for the welfare of mankind" to act on behalf of those whose human rights are in jeopardy. According to Wickenden:

In the relationship of individuals to the society in which they live, dignity, freedom and security rest upon a maximum range of objectively defined rights and entitlements.[11]

As a profession that "requires of its practitioners . . . belief in the dignity and worth of human beings"[12] social work must commit itself to defending the rights of those who are treated unjustly, for, as Briar asserts:

> The sense of individual dignity and of capacity to be self-determining . . . can exist only if the person sees himself and is regarded as a rights bearing citizen with legitimate, enforceable claims on, as well as obligations to, society.[13]

Each member of the professional association, in subscribing to the Code of Ethics, declares, "I regard as my primary obligation the welfare of the individual or group served, which includes action to improve social conditions." It is implicit, but clear, in this prescript that the obligation to the client takes primacy over the obligation to the employer when the two interests compete with one another.

The code singles out for special attention the obligation to "the individual or group served." The meaning seems clearest with respect to the caseworker or group worker who is delivering services to identified individuals and groups. It would appear to be entirely consistent with this interpretation to extend the obligation to the line supervisor or the social agency administrator who then is bound to act as an advocate on behalf of clients under his jurisdiction. A collateral obligation would be the responsibility of the supervisor or administrator to create the climate in which direct-service workers can discharge their advocacy obligations. As one moves to consider other social work roles, such as the consultant, the community planner, and the social work educator, the principle becomes more difficult to apply. But how can an obligation be imposed on one segment of the profession and not on another?

The inherent obligation is with respect to the work role and to those persons on whose lives the practitioner impinges by dint of his work role. It is in this role that the individual social worker is most clearly accountable for behaving in accordance with professional social work norms. Through this role he is implicated in the lives of certain groups of people; thus his actions affect their lives directly, for good or ill. Similarly, his work role gives him authority and influence over the lives of his clients; thus he has special ethical obligations regarding them. Finally, there are expected behaviors inherent in the work role on the basis of which it is possible to judge professional performance.

At this point it is important to remind ourselves of the distinction between the obligation of the social worker to be an advocate within and outside of his work role, both of which constitute an obligation of equal weight. However, the obligation to be an advocate outside the work role is general, not specific, and does not have the same force as the obligation to the client. In a sense, this obligation is gratuitous, or, as some might say, "above and beyond the call of duty." An additional problem is that there are no external criteria for judging whether a person is fulfilling this broad responsibility adequately. To use an extreme example: voting might be considered a way of carrying out the role of the advocate-reformer, yet would one say that failure to vote was failure to fulfill a professional obligation? To lump together the two obligations, i.e. to be an advocate in one's work role and outside of it, might appear to reinforce the latter. In reality, it only weakens the former.

Yet the profession as a whole has consistently treated the broad social responsibilities of social workers as important to fulfillment of their responsibilities. Schools of social work make an effort to provide their students with both the orientation and skills to become involved in social issues well outside their future assigned responsibilities. The difference between the two obligations is a moral, not a formal, one. In other words, enforcement of the obligation to be an advocate outside the work role would have to be self-enforcement.

COMPETING CLAIMS

Until now, most discussions of the advocacy role in social work have limited their consideration of competing claims to those of the employing agency[14] or society as a whole.[15] These have overlooked the possibility that in promoting his clients' interest the social worker may be injuring other aggrieved persons with an equally just claim. Suppose, for instance, that a child welfare worker has as a client a child who is in need of care that can only be provided by a treatment institution with limited intake. Does he then become a complete partisan in order to gain admission of his client at the expense of other children in need? What of the public assistance worker seeking emergency clothing allowances for his clients when the demand is greater than the supply? Quite clearly, in either case the worker should be seeking to increase the total availability of the scarce resource. But while working toward this end, he faces the dilemma of competing individual claims. In such a situation, professional norms would appear to dictate that the relative urgency of the respective claims be weighed.

A second dilemma involves conflict between the two types of advocacy—on behalf of client or class. Such conflicts are quite possible in an era of confrontation politics. To what extent does one risk injury to his client's interests in the short run on behalf of institutional changes in the long run? It seems clear that there can be no hard and fast rules governing such situations. One cannot arbitrarily write off any action that may temporarily cause his clients hardship if he believes the ultimate benefits of his action will outweigh any initial harm. Both ethical commitment and judgment appear to be involved here. (Is it, perhaps, unnecessary to add that institutional change does not always involve confrontation?)

A third dilemma is the choice between direct intercession by the worker and mobilization of clients in their own behalf. This is less an ethical than a technical matter. One can err in two directions: it is possible to emasculate clients by being overly protective or to abdicate one's responsibility and leave them to fend for themselves against powerful adversaries.

TECHNICAL COMPETENCE

Questions of competence can compound these dilemmas, for good intentions are not enough for the fulfillment of the advocacy role. Workers must not only be competent, they must also be sophisticated in understanding the appropriate machinery for redressing grievances and skilled in using it. If social workers are required by the profession to carry the obligation to be advocates, they must be equipped to fulfill the role.

While any responsible profession constantly strives to improve its technology, the dissatisfaction of social workers with their skills at advocacy seems to go beyond this. For a variety of reasons, most social workers seem wholly deficient in this area. On the direct practice level, the traditional techniques of environmental manipulation have tended to become peripheral to the practice of social workers, as they have become more sophisticated in the dynamics of inter- and intrapersonal functioning. Second, knowledge of the law, which is vitally tied up with client entitlements, has had less emphasis in the social work curriculum in recent years. Even though increased attention has been given to the client in deprived circumstances—the one who is most likely to need an advocate—this emphasis in the curriculum must be further strengthened.

Regardless of the type of advocacy in which the practitioner engages, knowledge of service delivery systems, institutional dynamics, and institutional change strategies are crucial. Although great advances in this technology have taken place in certain sectors of practice and education, they must be disseminated to the field.

Among the basic content areas that need development and expansion both in school curricula and in continuing education of social workers are the following:

1. Sensitization to the need for and appropriateness of advocacy.

2. Techniques of environmental manipulation and allied practice components.

3. Knowledge of the law, particularly as it bears on individual rights and entitlements.

4. Knowledge of service delivery systems and other institutions that impinge on people's lives and from which they must obtain resources.

5. Knowledge and skill in effecting institutional change.

6. Knowledge and skill in reaching and using the influence and power systems in a community.

The relative emphasis on these different components would vary, depending on the specific work role, although all are necessary in some degree for all social workers.

PROFESSIONAL AUTONOMY AND THE ROLE OF NASW

But lack of technical skills is not the greatest deterrent to advocacy by social workers; actually, it is their status as employees of organizations—organizations that are frequently the object of clients' grievances. Unless social workers can be protected against retaliation by their agencies or by other special interest groups in the community, few of them will venture into the advocacy role, ethical prescripts notwithstanding. It would seem to be a *sine qua non* of a profession that it must create the conditions in which its members can act professionally. For the profession to make demands on the individual and then not back them up with tangible support would betray a lack of serious intent.

This does not mean that all risks for the worker can or should be eliminated. A worker's job may be protected—but there is no insurance that he will advance within his organization as far or as fast as he would have if he had not been an advocate. Rather, the object is to increase the social worker's willingness to take risks to his self-interest in behalf of his professional commitment.

This brings us to the role and obligation of the professional association—NASW—and once again back to the context of social unrest, social change, and militancy in which this discussion is taking place. In view of the need for the profession to act quickly and decisively to focus on advocacy as being germane to the effective practice of social work, a program is needed—one that should be undertaken by NASW as soon as possible.[16] This program would do the following:

1. Urge social workers to exercise actively and diligently, in the conduct of their practice, their professional responsibility to give first priority to the rights and needs of their clients.

2. Assist social workers—by providing information and other resources—in their effort to exercise this responsibility.

3. Protect social workers against the reprisals, some of them inevitable, that they will incur in the course of acting as advocates for the rights of their clients.[17]

Certain assumptions are implicit in these three program objectives, namely:

• That the social worker has an obligation under the Code of Ethics to be an advocate.

• That this obligation requires more than mere "urging."

• That under certain circumstances, as discussed later, the obligation is enforceable under the Code of Ethics.

• That the *moral* obligation to be an advocate is not limited to one's own clients, although this cannot be enforced in the same way.

• That encouragement of advocacy and provision of certain kinds of assistance to advocates need not be limited to members of the professional association.

To return to the relationship of NASW to the social work advocate who gets into trouble with his agency because of his attempts to fulfill a professional obligation: *NASW has an obligation to the worker that takes priority over its obligation to the agency.* In effect, the worker is acting in behalf of the professional community. While the conditions of such responsibility of NASW must be spelled out precisely (to avoid misleading members or jeopardizing the interests of the profession), there can be no question about the member's prior claim on NASW support. Without this principle, the association's claim on the member is meaningless.

The Committee on Advocacy considered two extensions of NASW's obligation. One was in relation to the social work employee who is not a member of NASW. Should the same aids and protections be offered to nonmembers of NASW as to members? It was recognized that a majority of social work positions are held by nonmembers and that they are concentrated particularly in public agencies, which are often the object of client grievances. Furthermore, many indigenous workers in poverty and other neighborhood programs are especially likely to be performing an advocacy function. Obviously, the profession cannot impose a professional obligation on such persons, yet it is consistent with professional concerns that such efforts be supported even when NASW members are not involved. As is spelled out later, the committee recommends that certain types of help be provided, but states that NASW is not in a position to offer the same range of support to nonmembers as to members.

The other extension of NASW's obligation is the possible assumption by NASW of the role of advocate when a client has no alternative channel for his grievances. The committee agreed that NASW could not become, in effect, a service agency, offering an advocacy service to all who request it, although it was felt that the association should work toward the development of such alternative channels. The association should be encouraged to engage in selected advocacy actions when the outcome has potential implications for policy formulation and implementation in general. An example of this would be participation in litigation against a state welfare agency for alleged violation of clients' constitutional rights; in this instance NASW would be using the courts to help bring about social policy change instead of interceding in behalf of the specific plaintiffs in the case.

Broadly stated, then, the proposed program for NASW calls for concentrated and aggressive activities coordinated at local, regional, and national levels, to achieve the needed involvement by individual social workers, backstopped by members in policy-making and administrative positions and community leaders, through education, demonstration and consultation in program planning; adaptation of NASW complaint machinery to facilitate the adjudication of complaints against agencies with stringent sanctions when indicated; and assistance to individuals who may experience retaliatory action by agencies or communities, ranging from intervention with employers to aid in obtaining legal counsel or finding suitable new employment.

NOTES AND REFERENCES

1. Mobilization For Youth, Inc., started as an action-research program in juvenile delinquency control on New York City's Lower East Side.
2. *See* Brager, George A.: Advocacy and political behavior. *Social Work,*

13 (No. 2):5-15, April, 1968; and Grosser, Charles F.: Community development programs serving the urban poor. *Social Work, 10 (No. 3)*:18-19, July, 1965.

3. *See,* for example, Cohen, Nathan E. (Ed.): *Social Work and Social Problems.* New York, National Association of Social Workers, 1964, p. 374.

4. *Webster's Third New International Dictionary.* Springfield, Mass., Merriam, 1961, p. 32.

5. *Ibid.*

6. Briar, Scott: The current crisis in social casework. *Social Work Practice, 1967.* New York, Columbia University Press, 1967, p. 28. *See also* Briar: The casework predicament. *Social Work, 13 (No. 1)*:5-11, Jan. 1968.

7. Briar, Scott: The social worker's responsibility for the civil rights of clients. *New Perspectives, 1 (No. 1):* p. 90, Spring, 1967.

8. *Op. cit.,* p. 6.

9. It is not the intent to blame the agencies entirely for lack of advocacy in the discharge of a worker's daily duties. It is recognized that progressive agencies have already inculcated advocacy in their workers, often in the face of adverse community reactions and resistance by staff.

10. This code was adopted by the Delegate Assembly of the National Association of Social Workers, October 13, 1960, and amended April 11, 1967.

11. Wickenden, Elizabeth: The indigent and welfare administration. In *The Extension of Legal Services to the Poor.* Washington, D.C., U.S. Department of Health, Education, and Welfare, 1964.

12. "Code of Ethics."

13. Briar: The social worker's responsibility for the civil rights of clients.

14. *See* Brager, George A.: *op. cit.*

15. *See* Briar, Scott: The current crisis in social casework, p. 91.

16. As the first step in implementing the program, the Commission on Ethics reviewed these findings of the Ad Hoc Committee on Advocacy and recommended that they be widely disseminated. The commission interprets the Code of Ethics as giving full support to advocacy as a professional obligation.

17. This is the wording of the charge given to the Ad Hoc Committee on Advocacy by the NASW urban crisis task force.

Chapter 37

THE SOCIAL WORKER AS RADICAL: ROLES OF ADVOCACY

PAUL TERRELL

INTRODUCTION

THE RADICAL in social work is hard pressed to define for himself a professional role commensurate with his politics. Although much of his vocabulary has in recent years been incorporated into the social welfare rhetoric, activity in the schools and in the field still reflects a generation of practice enmired in the essentially restrictive Freudian approach. So long as ameliorism and strategies of individual adjustment remain the social worker's primary tools, he will continue to practice a stigmatized pursuit, one resented by the poor, subsidized by paternalistic philanthropists, dismissed by academicians, and ignored by decision-makers. If social work is not to become further superfluous to humanistic endeavors, professional roles addressing themselves to meaningful social change must be developed. The ideology and action requisite to such a radicalization of social work practice will be described in this paper.

IDEOLOGY

The radical's commitment is to social change benefiting the economically disadvantaged. As a social worker, his goals involve the modification of institutions toward adequately serving the needs of the deprived and toward the creation of new need-meeting structures where such are necessary. At a community level, tactics are best defined in terms of processes to expand the influence of the poor over policy affecting them.

Despite our New Deals, Fair Deals, and Great Societies, the disadvantaged are becoming relatively more so. "While the in-

Note: Reprinted from *New Perspectives, 1*:83-88, 1967.

come share of the richest tenth of the general population has remained large and virtually constant over the past half century, the two lowest income-tenths have experienced a sharp decline . . ."[1] As Harrington has stated, America's social legislation has resulted in a situation of socialism for the economically able and free enterprise for the poor. Much of it, indeed, has affected the poor in clearly inimical fashion. Housing policy to 1950, for example, established the basis for much of today's residential segregation by assisting only those builders, buyers, and mortgage bankers who would conform to governmental regulations demanding "homogeneous" neighborhoods. Today's urban renewal policies result in the destruction of poor neighborhoods and the dispersion of residents to neighborhoods less stable, more expensive, and just as blighted.

Such are two examples of many. Our welfare state has little meaning and less legitimacy for millions of Americans, "having been built, not for the desperate, but for those who are already capable of helping themselves."[2] The poor, historically excluded from exerting influence proportionate to their numbers, have not been substantially aided by social legislation reflecting the interests of the organized.

On both a federal and community level, therefore, our democratic system of government reflects a *de facto* division of power between organized interests which singularly excludes the poor. In policy deliberations, the interests of the disenfranchised, the poor, are sacrificed. Since bureaucrats consider themselves entrusted in their public being to act as they see fit on public issues, the radical in social work does not rely on meaningful change to result from the natural process of governmental action. His primary efforts are toward expanding the public decision-making system to increase collaboration with that bottom two-tenths who bear the brunt of public action. As perhaps the only true generalist on the municipal scene, the community organization "radical" must direct his attention at humanizing institutions, at making the community more functional for its poor. His activity is most logically aimed toward neighborhood community development, the creation of neighborhood and action groups, and the enhancement of their influence upon the municipal system.

THE SOCIAL WORKER AS ADVOCATE

How does a social worker so intentioned act; what roles can he play? In the literature on administration two general role categories have often been posited. There is the "institutionalized personality," the bureaucrat whose first loyalty is to his organization, to his function as defined by his superiors. Secondly, there is the professional, the "cosmopolitan," one committed to general techniques and goals that stem from the heritage of his discipline rather than from the immediate needs of his organization. In actuality, of course, the roles often merge, generally toward the first rubric. The professional often chooses to work for an organization whose interests are congruent with his own. Or, as he rises in an organizational hierarchy, he progressively identifies with the organization, sees his interest furthered by its interest, sees slights to it as personal slights, and, more subtly, feels the need to justify the activities of that body in whose behalf so much of his lifetime and work has been expended.

It appears as though even the professional molds into the organization with time. In two thousand years, after all, how many ministers have chosen the Book over the church? Closer to home, how many social workers quit Alameda County's employ after the night raids? But such cowardice and parochial self-interest is apparently on the wane. There is talk of making Christianity work; it would appear our first task is to make social work work. For community organization at least, there is a sufficient commitment to radical change in the developing ideology to argue as a *standard* role in the practice *repertoire* one that emphasizes the proper representation of the interests of the economically disadvantaged.

Such a role, it is clear, involves a primary commitment not to an organization or to traditional social work "professional ethics," but to the poor. Such a social worker must take sides, become "a partisan in social conflict [whose] expertise is available exclusively to serve his clients' interests."[3] This is social work advocacy. Following the legal analogy, the advocate acts on behalf of a client against an adversary. Although conflict does not always become manifest, there is always an opponent. For the social worker as advocate, the client, individual or organization, is or represents the needy, and the need is one that can to some degree be met by the behavior of individuals or institutions. The adversary is usually the establishment, public and private.

The advocate plays essentially a disruptive role. His task is to remedy, to change, whereas institutions generally operate to minimize change not directed toward their own expansion. Organizational decision-makers "always have more at stake in preserving present social arrangements than they do in agitating particular decisions."[4] Such persons are "integratively" oriented, valuing consensus, and hostile to those with causes. The advocate *has* a cause, is impatient, willing to fight, and therefore in conflict with those who believe the path to social betterment lies in those "time-tested procedures" of rational discussion and gentlemanly compromise.

There are two general types of advocacy, generally corresponding to the nature of the clientele, the nature of change, and the nature of the social worker's background. What has often been described as the *social broker* role is most amenable to casework practice, serving individual clients to meet their specific needs. The community organization advocate works with groups and is primarily concerned with institutional change.

BROKER ADVOCACY

The advocate as broker functions on behalf of a client to remedy difficulties stemming from the actions of public bodies (as Public Welfare Departments) and private individuals and organizations (as slumlords, discriminatory employers). The client is an individual and complaints usually result from laxness or illegalities on the part of lower-level personnel in municipal departments. If the caseworker-advocate feels a complaint is legitimate and remediable, his task is to "directly intervene to bring the client and the community's institutions and services into a more congenial and beneficial juxtaposition."[5] Often a single complaint will involve the practices of many agencies. Purcell writes of the housing complaints of tenement dwellers in New York City that related to the functioning of six city agencies.[6]

It is unrealistic to expect a lower-class individual to be able to traverse through the bureaucratic maze, to say nothing of the bureaucratic hostility, awaiting one not satisfied with the system's operation. In the absence of an *ombudsman* function within the governmental structure, a variety of agencies and individuals have attempted to protect the rights of citizens confronted with the public behemoth. Some cities have established civilian review boards to deal with complaints against police malpractice. Many public agencies have built-in procedures for those wishing to appeal its decisions. Such measures generally are highly complex and structured and not very apt for the needs of those most likely to have complaints. Such procedures, furthermore, serve no function for those persons who do not know that such protections exist and that specific institutional practices may be, if not illegal, at least reversible.

The type of advocacy possible in such cases is obviously colored by the framework, the agency, within which one works. The Public Welfare caseworker, for example, operating within an essentially restrictive organization, is extremely vulnerable playing the role of advocate. In seeking to act in his client's best interest, the workers will consistently be at odds with an agency operating to keep people at lowest subsistence and highest humiliation. Arguing for "special needs" and increased allocations will place him in opposition to higher level personnel who are more concerned with holding down costs than meeting needs. The organization conspires against decency. A worker will be called down for showing his client his case record. A worker in New York City will be prohibited from going to court and speaking in behalf of a client against a landlord who has refused to keep his property up to code.

Although there will almost invariably be a tension between the advocate social worker and his agency, there are a variety of public and private bodies that provide settings more amenable to advocacy than do Public Welfare Departments. Human Rights Commissions often intervene in the municipal structure for individuals with valid complaints. Community Action Programs similarly act on behalf of the poor. In New York City, Mobilization For Youth workers, faced with myriad complaints against the city Public Welfare Department, time and time again had to "intervene between an agency of government and its client to secure an entitlement or right which [had] been obscured or denied."[7] A wide range of neighborhood groups, Welfare Rights Organizations, and tenant associations similarly occupy much of their time confronting the establishment in an effort to eke out justice for persons unfairly treated. Such bodies also often provide legal services when such is most appropriate to eliciting favorable institutional responses.

The caseworker as advocate does not usually have to confront institutions in their manifest authority. Especially in Public Welfare Departments where a great deal of discretion is embodied in the caseworker, relatively small pressures may be successful in changing a budget or suspending action that is viewed by the client as demeaning, harassing, or an invasion of privacy. Public Welfare Department caseworkers are often remarkably insensitive, and even the most humane worker, with sixty-plus cases, is unlikely to undertake the consistent argument and appeals necessary to provide clients with adequate allotments. So long as the caseworker is responsible only to his supervisors, whatever liberal intentions he may have will tend to be thwarted by the organization's desire to minimize expenses. Since the unprotected client rarely complains, the worker takes the path of least resistance, and niggardliness wins out over need. However, when counterpressures can be applied and bureaucratic ineptitude and parsimony challenged, the caseworker and supervisory personnel are more apt to see things as does the client. In both cases, personnel acts to limit conflict. The advocate's ability, therefore, to press an issue in and of itself can often result in beneficial action. Such counterpressures provide more liberal public welfare workers with protection when they seek to follow humane rather than organizational dictates. Furthermore, as Cloward and Elman state, by "serving notice upon the low level employee that he would be held responsible for his actions to his supervisor and on up the line [the New York City Public Welfare Department] was made responsive to a portion of its Lower East Side constituency."[8]

Such broker advocacy, however, can have only limited results *because* it focuses upon the line worker rather than on those who make the policy that results in hardship. The establishment is confronted on the basis of an individual's grievance and the remedial action sought is usually one that is obtained without changing general policy. Only minimal redress is received. Each victory, therefore, is unto itself, *sui generis,* and without carryover effect.

GROUP ADVOCACY

A second, more significant kind of advocacy is one emphasizing the creation and support of neighborhood and direct action groups representing the interests of the disadvantaged. Such advocacy is of especial interest for the community organizer, and can be meaningfully employed in a variety of agencies. The advocate, for example, can play a major role in the wide variety of agencies that have been created in recent years to work for intergroup harmony and the alleviation of poverty. In a number of Community Action Programs, for example, the radical as advocate is able to function in conjunction with both his ideals and the recognized organizational task. The "catalyst" stance emphasized by many projects can legitimize a variety of community development activities. Mobilization For Youth, for example, after three years of the broker advocacy described before, decided to assist in establishing "The Committee of Welfare Families," a neighborhood organization which grew progressively more independent of MFY as its own members acquired knowledge of welfare operations and skills and organizing for change. The Committee of Welfare Families actively challenged many welfare policies and carried their demands to the highest levels of Public Welfare Department administration.[9]

Office of Economic Opportunity personnel often engage themselves as advocates. OEO field representatives have often given advice and assistance to neighborhood and minority group organizations in their domain who are involved in struggles with the local establishment. The Community Action Program director in the Western Region has been outspoken in his emphasis on neighborhood organization, neighborhood planning, and a conflict orientation to change.

The advocate of this type can also play an important role *within* the system of municipal governmental bodies; and a variety of specific roles can be enumerated for those working on a community level for government bodies or in Community Action Programs. First of all, the advocate can act as a general spokesman for the disadvantaged community and their representatives in his day to day contacts with public officials and community influentials. The advocate represents such local groups in those councils to which they do not have access. The advocate will consistently demand from those operating within the blinders of their own organization's necessities the consideration of the needs of the disadvantaged. Secondly, as a result of his own access to the views, plans, and informational resources of the establishment, the advocate is well-equipped to provide local action groups with relevant knowldege. As Mike Miller has stated, the radical in public service can at least play the role of "spy." Thirdly, the advocate, on the basis of his training and expertise, can use such knowledge himself to offer advice concerning effective methods of action for local groups. Knowing of vulnerable institutional practices and the spots of maximum weakness in municipal plans and proposals, he often is able to suggest the most efficacious forms for direct action or other forms of pressure. Fourthly, the advocate as professional can offer a wide range of specialized assistance to local community organizations. He can help them "objectify" their views, present the considerations their adversaries consider paramount, fill in gaps in their information, and clarify distorted views or unfeasible plans or goals. Next, the advocate can attempt to create countervailing pressures to public or private activity not in the interest of the disadvantaged. He can help to create organizations in those instances where the need is great and action is possible. Sixthly, the advocate can do contingency planning so as to capitalize on crises. Violence and confrontation often create a mood in which advantageous social change can be effected. In the time of confusion and enthusiasm for change immediately following such crises, the advocate must be prepared with detailed proposals for change.

A range of professions other than that of social work can act as advocates in a variety of circumstances. Most obviously, lawyers can perform the role. In addition, city planners can be of assistance, especially to groups involved in disputes with urban renewal agencies. As a number of professional persons become increasingly interested in the connections between social dysfunctions and progressively more concerned with the needs of the disadvantaged, a form of coalitionism between politicians, lawyers, planners, mental health specialists, and social workers is developing within our communities. As Melvin Webber has stated, new groupings are "arising out of shared interests in social and intellectual problems, rather than out of occupational or disciplinary heritages."[10] City planners, to cite one example, are becoming less exclusively concerned with problems of physical planning, and are taking greater interest in social planning considerations. The expansion of delimited professional interests is certainly true in community organization where a more generalist approach to need-meeting is being applied as it is recognized that the social worker's clientele is affected by diverse actors and institutions.

CONCLUSION

The radical as a social work advocate must always remain somewhat of a free agent if he is not to become stifled in organizational complexity and agency needs. The trap is as major as it is subtle. We are all familiar with those who profess the most radical sentiments and yet, remarkably, never disturb the *status quo*. We all, indeed, like to think our politics somehow unique, special, or humanist, and yet, in practice, we all seem to behave quite alike. The radical can't be "quite alike"; he can't make-do; he can't justify complacency, indolence, and a good salary in terms of the supposed long-run virtues of cooperation, persuasion, etc.

The advocate must be a thorn. He must consistently articulate the alternative that public agents so often lose sight of.

The radical's tenure will generally be a short one. To insure that he will not become too far removed from the passion and urgency of the impoverished neighborhood and its spokesmen, and to prevent himself from becoming too tolerant and understanding of "organizational necessity," the social work advocate must at regular intervals work in radical ventures. The radical should always be ready to quit to dramatize injustice. The radical, obviously, will often be dismissed.

The advocate-radical must keep close to his ideological roots. Why are the radicals in the schools instead of the field? The task of the professional "change agent" would appear to be one of retaining his integrity, refusing to give into the sop system, resisting that individual "goal displacement" whereby one's own humanist ideals are replaced by the necessities of the establishment.

REFERENCES

1. Kolko, Gabriel: *Wealth and Power in America*. New York, Praeger, 1962, p. 15.
2. Harrington, Michael: *The Other America*. New York, Penguin, 1962, p. 158.
3. Grosser, Charles F.: Community organization programs serving the urban poor. *Social Work*, 10(No. 3):18, June, 1965.
4. Mogulof, Melvin B.: Emerging concepts of neighborhood planning: Significance for community-wide planning. Mimeographed, 1966, p. 7.
5. Mobilization for Youth: *A Proposal for the Prevention and Control of Delinquency by Expanding Opportunities*. New York, 1961, p. 215.
6. Purcell, Francis P. and Specht, Harry: The house on sixth street. *Social Work*, 10 (No. 4):72, Oct. 1965.
7. Cloward, Richard A. and Elman, Richard M.: Advocacy in the ghetto. *Trans-Action, IV (No. 4)*:28, 1966.
8. *Ibid.*, p. 29.
9. *Ibid.*, p. 34.
10. Webber, Melvin M.: The roles of intelligence systems in urban-systems planning. *J Am Inst Planners*, 31 (No. 4):290, Nov. 1965.

Chapter 38

FAMILY ADVOCACY:
FROM CASE TO CAUSE

ROBERT SUNLEY

T HE GAP BETWEEN THE INDIVIDUAL CASE of social injustice and broad-scale social action has been a continual source of frustration for the family worker and the family agency alike. The family worker struggles time after time to rectify wrongs suffered by clients. Sometimes he succeeds, often through some personal contact with a counterpart in the offending social institution, but he is only too aware of and further frustrated by the fact that ten or a hundred other people continue to suffer for lack of such influential intervention. His work on behalf of one client will bring about no change in the institution. The sheer immovability and unresponsiveness of the bureaucracy to his individual effort will tend to dull his enthusiasm and dedication as it does with many workers, who drift toward "adjustment" rather than attempt to change the organizations. The client may also be directly or subtly encouraged to come to terms with "reality"—the reality of formidable arrays of laws, rules, regulations, and practices.

For the agency, the gap has also posed a difficult problem. Though aware of the need for social action, most agencies—the board and administration—have had no agency-wide structure within which to operate. Isolated efforts by the board, such as passing resolutions or writing letters to legislators, hardly meet the need. There is little or no linkage between client, staff, board, and the needed action. At best, staff and board are linked by the traditional role of the caseworker in social action, as set out by Mary Richmond, Charlotte Towle, Gordon Hamilton, and most recently by Harry Specht, which may be summed up in Towle's brief description:

Note: Reprinted from *Social Casework,* 51:347-357, 1970. Copyright 1970, Family Service Association of America.

. . . the caseworker [would] be responsible for initiating or instigating social action by making known unmet needs and social ills as revealed in his practice. He would contribute his findings, through agency channels, to those writing social policy, conducting publicity campaigns, drafting legislation. . . .[1]

According to this point of view the family agency also has a limited function. Worker and agency together are only too likely to see themselves as small and rather inactive members of a large-scale process, limited to polite and long-range efforts at legislation, examples perhaps of that sense of powerlessness and of that disjunction between goals and structure fitting under the general catchword "anomie."[2]

Quite a few family agencies have recently made efforts to bridge this gap. Perhaps most notable was Project ENABLE, a national program which brought agencies into direct touch with the poor, those suffering daily from social injustices. This project, like other special programs, was not integral to the regular agency function; separately funded through the Office of Economic Opportunity, the programs for the most part ended with the termination of the special funding.[3] The regular agency programs remained as before, though the awareness of the need for something comparable was undoubtedly heightened. The prospect of large-scale ongoing funding for projects such as ENABLE appear quite dim for the near future; whatever agencies do must be done within the fairly narrow margins of regular budget allocations.

Family advocacy is a move toward bridging the gap, but within the regular agency functioning. It delineates a basic function of the caseworker and assures a continuing link with the action program. It recognizes the professional obligation (not option) of the worker for social action, for fighting through to the finish for clients' rights and needs.[4] The concept of family advocacy also embraces the vital principle of involving the client in the action, of helping the client to help himself in this area as well as in that of individual and family functioning.

As will be seen, family advocacy requires more than good intentions; in effect, it is a discipline in itself, as yet only partially developed. A body of knowledge, principles, and methods exists in part. Even interviewing, the specialty of the family worker, must take on an additional focus and objective. A new commitment by the agency is necessary to back up the family worker. It must be expressed in new structuring as well as in new distribution of staff time and emphasis.

Several of the important aspects of a family advocacy program—interviewing, case study, interventions and objectives, and agency structuring—are discussed here. Examples are given from one agency, the Family Service Association of Nassau County, which recently established a Department of Family Advocacy, headed by a full-time social worker, which embraces the work of the family workers, administration, and board.

INTERVIEWING FOR FAMILY ADVOCACY

By training and practice many family caseworkers focus on individual and family dysfunction or pathology. The material elicited from the client tends to bear upon this focus. Thus, when a child is referred as a slow learner, not achieving his potential, a family caseworker may accept this basic premise of the referral which is usually buttressed by evidence from the school. This evidence might include poor grades, I.Q. and other psychological tests, or examples of poor behavior. The caseworker does not usually make as careful a study of the school, the educational approach and philosophy, and the teacher as he does of the child and parents in his effort to determine the cause of the learning or behavior problem evidenced by the child.

Interviewing for advocacy introduces a range of new factors into the sessions with the client and "collateral" sources. Some of these perhaps sound obvious, but all reach much further than appears at first sight. Clients may not, for various reasons, give complete information, and the caseworker's skill is needed to develop a relationship of trust and confidence. In contacting public and private organizations on behalf of clients, workers have frequently been baffled in trying to find out precisely the relevant regulations, practices, requirements, or entitlements. The difficulties may be attributed to bureaucratic timidity or fearfulness, or as

Charles Grosser points out, some institutions are "overtly negative and hostile, often concealing or distorting information. . . ."[5] Reconciling conflicting stories of clients and professional colleagues in other organizations can be as difficult as reconciling those of husbands and wives in marital conflict.

Caseworkers themselves are often lax in facing or establishing facts, although their sympathies and actions may be in the right direction. For example, Daniel Thursz cites the example of a group of social workers who were called upon to document with cases the "man-in-the-house" rule; they "did not have one bit of supporting evidence."[6] Or, more serious yet, David Wineman and Adrienne James charged in a recent article that students are "systematically taught to abandon reality," describing the many abuses they encounter and the many "cop-outs" used by supervisors and administrators (and eventually by the students and caseworkers as well).[7]

DIFFICULTIES FACING THE WORKER

In addition to the problems centered around obtaining accurate information, the caseworker may well encounter his own difficulties stemming more directly from the "medical" model of pathology. For example, the assessment of pathology in a client may well affect the worker's perception and evaluation of an injustice the client is undergoing. Paranoid tendencies in the client may lead a worker to discount reality problems. The worker may see a sullen welfare recipient only as withdrawn, depressed, and distorting reality—the pathological view—instead of as a person who is suspicious out of experience and seeks to protect himself against further attack.

Also, value judgments enter in. For example, the client's mismanagement of money or time or role may offend the caseworker. In one situation, caseworkers from several agencies were in accord that a certain client was an unfit mother, leaving young children unattended on many occasions; yet her lawyer entered a suit against the department of welfare alleging that it had failed to make provision for sitters while she did necessary shopping and errands. Regardless of the merits of this situation, it is notable that caseworkers had not taken any advocacy position for their client, nor since then for clients in comparable difficulties. Perhaps as a result of interagency snafus and frustrating experiences in dealing with governmental bureaucracies, many caseworkers have tended to fall back onto the "adjustment" solution to environmental problems: the client adjusts, that is, if he or she possesses the "ego strengths" to do so. In fairness, the individual workers may well be aware of better solutions and approaches, but they have had within their job no channels or groups through which to exert pressure.

The caseworker may also be subject to other internal stresses. The nature of the issues involved may subtly "turn him off"; the fact that the client does not come into the situation with "clean hands" may keep him from seeing that legal or human rights have been violated; his own fear of authority may also induce him to hold back; or his identification with authority may predispose him to side with the world of rules and established practices, perhaps rationalized as a conviction that the authorities may make mistakes, but that they mean well. Yet another extreme may be that of the caseworker whose own rebellious feelings cause him to secretly provoke a client into arbitrary rebellion.

All these examples may be termed "countertransference" in a general way. Workers may have mastered such reactions in relation to individual and family relationship problems but be less able to recognize them in advocacy situations. The result may emerge not only in misjudgments or failure to elicit information, but more importantly in an inability to develop that outlook and commitment necessary for advocacy for the client.

A situation reported recently illustrates the possibilities and pitfalls. Three children in a family receiving public assistance were sent home the first day of school because of inadequate clothing. A recent New York state law eliminated all special grants, including clothing, for such families. In responding to the situation, the caseworker could see to it that the family received a donation of the necessary clothing, could help the mother with budgeting, or could try to help the mother with a presumed depression that kept her from managing her funds—possible solutions, but not advocacy. Or, the caseworker could ask such questions as: Are these and other children being denied their right to an education by the new welfare law? Is a mother being forced to put herself in risk of a charge of child neglect because of the new state law? The caseworker now has made the large first step in advocacy—a commitment to the client rather than to the existing system involved. The caseworker should then have recourse to a lawyer to determine whether there is a basis for a court case to test the constitutionality of the new law, or to a welfare rights group to determine if a public issue should be made of the situation. These alternatives, it should be noted, will involve the client acting on her own behalf.

Where does family counseling enter in? Its place is clear with clients who come for family problems and subsequently reveal social problems calling for advocacy, although the worker must as with any client be alert to the possibility that the actual injustice may also become a focal point in the client's defensive system to resist any internal change. On the other hand, clients who come essentially for redress of wrongs cannot be treated as if they are indirectly asking for personal counseling. Although this assumption has been made by many workers in the past, it may well run counter to the reality seen by the client. Low-income families (and others as well) tend to view such interviewing activity by the worker as prying into their personal lives, and from that may make a reasonable deduction that there is something behind the scenes they do not understand and do not trust. Also, the worker's eagerness to get to the family problems (as if this were the only justification for his job) may seriously disrupt the client's sense of priorities in his personal life, leaving the client overwhelmed and the worker helpless by premature exposure of all problems.

Case Study

Just as casework treatment is based on a study of background material, current situation, and related factors, a case for advocacy should rest upon a comparable study. More specifically, in advocacy the worker needs to familiarize himself not only with the specific client, problem, and situation but also with such factors as the institutions involved and the legal implications.

Broadly speaking, situations are presented to the caseworker either directly as situations for advocacy—the client comes seeking help for a problem in which rights are apparently being violated —or the client comes for some other difficulty but the caseworker elicits the advocacy need. As a first step, as already noted, the caseworker must be alert and committed to the client's position in relation to social institutions. Perhaps a good working method is to see every problem the client "has" as a possible problem that the social institution "has"; this is not to negate the client's possible internal problem but to ensure that we carefully examine in what ways this is a shared problem and whether solutions may not lie outside the client, either partly or wholly.

Many grievances relate to possible legal rights of the client. The caseworker has a responsibility to uncover such possibilities, to obtain necessary facts, and to consult a lawyer or legal service for the poor to ascertain whether a legal case exists. The caseworker is also responsible for helping the client understand that there may be possible publicity, delays, and other strains involved in pursuing a court case. He must inform him of possible alternative solutions. He must determine whether the client is assured of financial support and other needs during the trial period, if this enters into the situation. And he must help the client reach a decision, which may mean going into motivations, conflicts, and fears. Looking further ahead, the caseworker must plan to be available throughout and even after a case is settled, for it can happen that a client may win a court case but meet further delays and appeals. Thus, in the area of legal rights, caseworkers need not only some knowledge of law in those areas often involved in client problems, but also a working relationship with a legal service or lawyer who handles advocacy cases, to understand the practical workings of the legal system and to be able to obtain opinions quickly and informally.

For various reasons, however, legal recourse may not be sought even though rights have been violated. This may be the choice of the client or test cases may already be pending; nevertheless, other immediate action may be desired. In addition, in cases where legal rights have not been violated but other "human" rights are involved, resulting from instituational insensitivity to the needs of the poor and elderly, there may also be cause for further action. Interventions suitable in such cases will be described later.

Familiarity with pertinent law is but one of a number of areas of knowledge the caseworker needs. Credit practices, school policies and practices, family court, handling of alcoholics and drug addicts, probationary methods, psychiatric facilities, and systems theories are others. In short, the caseworker as advocate needs to develop knowledge and understanding of the institutions and systems with which clients are most often in contact. This refers not only to general knowledge but also to specific institutions in the community. While caseworkers perforce develop a working knowledge of local institutions, this is usually developed piecemeal and not fully shared and pooled with other staff to develop a full picture. The caseworker—not in isolation but with other staff—needs in effect an outline with which to study a given organization, just as he explicity or implicitly follows such an outline in developing his study of an individual or family, however imperfect such an outline may be in its ultimate explanations.

An institution or organization is first characterized by the fact that it has an entity (usually a legal base for its existence), its own structure, regulations, premises, staff; it is set off from other organizations by its clientele—it serves certain people for certain specified purposes only. There is a hierarchy of command and accountability. The worker should become familiar with these aspects of each important organizaton in the community. Beyond the formal structure, however, and perhaps more important, is the informal structure of the organization and its relationship to the community. The caseworker needs to ask the following questions: What is the orientation of the organization toward the people it serves? What is its tone and morale? How does one evaluate the discrepancy between clients' complaints and agency position? What efforts have been made to change policies, by whom and how, and with what results? What is the response of the organization to criticism or attack? Does it have vulnerabilities (adverse publicity, for example)? At what level, within or above the organization, is there discretionary power to make changes?

On a practical level the caseworker needs to know the following: procedural structure in relation to clients to whom grievances are first addressed and what further steps are specified, such as appeals or review boards; in what ways retaliation against the client may be resorted to, and what protection can be found for the client; and whether or not other clients of the agency encounter the same difficulty. He will also want to know if clients of other agencies have encountered similar difficulties and what if anything they have tried.

It becomes clear that an institution must be viewed more as an "adversary" in advocacy, rather than as a cooperating or allied agency (even though in other situations this may be true). "Adversary" does not perforce mean "enemy," but does require a different approach than the "consensus" approach to which caseworkers are accustomed.[8] Even from this brief description, it can be seen that the full ongoing assessment of an advocacy case may require case conferences or outside consultation—or both—just as in an evaluation of a family treatment case.

Interventions

In casework, the worker (and other staff at times) selects the methods and modes of treatment for each client, based on the initial case evaluation. In family advocacy, similar steps seem necessary, from the initial interviews, through the study and diagnostic thinking, to the selection of interventions; the necessary participation of the client or client group is, obviously, on a different level in this process.

Family agencies have traditionally used only a small number of the many kinds of interventions available for an advocacy program. The selection of which interventions to use in a given issue is a complex one, involving the nature of the problem, the objective, the nature of the adversary, the degree of militancy to which the agency will go, and the effectiveness of the method, generally and in relation to certain kinds of situations. All of these factors suggest the desirability of expert consultation for many agencies in an ongoing advocacy program. More than one method is usually included in an action program, with the result that the staff and the agency as a whole will become involved in various ways.

In advocacy programs it is important for the agency not to get caught in dilatory tactics so common in bureaucratic procedures; an overconcern for the niceties and politeness of "due process" may dishearten staff and cause suffering for the clients. Yet failure to study the situation carefully may result in a quick action being dismissed because a necessary step was omitted. For example, a case brought against a school system was dismissed after a period of months because the court ruled that the plaintiff had failed to exhaust other remedies first, namely, an appeal to the board of education. By this time, the school year was almost over, the complaint no longer had any validity, and the child had been subjected to adverse conditions.

The following methods of intervention hardly exhaust the possibilities or the many variations used by groups (mainly non-social work) but suggest the wide range and the many types suitable for a family advocacy program.

1. *Studies and surveys.* These often form the groundwork for further action, both for the advocacy program itself and for educational and publicity purposes. Whatever the sources of the material, staff and board must be prepared to answer penetrating or hostile questions, and material should in effect be subjected to such an approach before it is used. Otherwise embarrassing loopholes may be exposed and the effort weakened.

2. *Expert testimony.* Social workers may be called upon to testify as professionals or agency representatives, with or without the backing of studies and surveys. While this method may not have great effect upon legislators or public officials, the absence of the social work voice may be noted adversely.

3. *Case conferences with other agencies.* This has traditionally been one important way in which the agency tries to effect change; by presenting the conditions and results of certain practices and regulations in given cases, one hopes to induce the other agency to change. This method may be of value in early stages of

an advocacy effort, especially if it can involve higher officials of the other agency. It also elicits much about the potential adversary organization and may help to clarify just where the crux of the problem lies—at the level of staff practice, supervision, middle or top administration, board, or beyond the agency. Such conferences held with clients present can have other values as well and may be the first step in developing a client group determined to go further in action on its own behalf.

4. *Interagency committees.* Such commitees, which often have proven to be splendid time-wasters, can offer the advantages of case conferences mentioned above. They can also be developed into types of permanent bodies which can represent yet another method of action in a given locality. In large suburban areas, encompassing several small communities, various agencies may provide services within each small community but obviously cannot have a local base in each. An interagency committee can be developed involving local community agencies and the wider-based agencies to handle local issues. For example, Family Service Association of Nassau County along with another agency started such a committee in one community, originally around overlapping case concerns. Over a five-year period, the committee has developed into a kind of local welfare council, though without separate corporate existence. It takes up local issues and is called upon by other organizations to help in certain situations. This type of committee, for example, can be used by a local agency which may have complaints against the school system but hesitates to take action alone. It also provides a vehicle for the interagency sharing of grass-roots problems arising from specific cases, which councils embracing large areas and many agencies cannot do.

5. *Educational methods.* This refers to activities such as informational meetings, panels, exhibits, pamphlets, and press coverage, all aimed at educating segments of the population. These may include also public appeals on specific issues made through the press, radio, and television. Legislators and public officials may be somewhat influenced by these methods.

6. *Position taking.* The agency formally takes a position on an issue, making it known publicly through the press, as well as

to officials, legislators, and others directly. This goes beyond an educational effort in an attempt to put the weight of the agency onto a specific position. Generally, the agency's position will be newsworthy only if it is among the first to take the stand, or if board members represent an influence with important segment of the community. The taking of a formal position may be often of greatest value internally, that is, in conveying to staff and clientele that the agency is committed and moving.

7. *Administrative redress.* Governmental bodies usually provide for various steps to appeal decisions at the practice level. While such steps may appear to delay action, they may nonetheless be necessary preludes to further action (such as court suits) or desirable in that they will call the attention of higher officials within or without the agency to conditions. Also, where the imperfect working of a system has resulted in an injustice to one client, grievance procedures through an ombudsman often result in a correction for that one client. Taking such moves may be necessary although the advocacy program need not stop there in fighting a larger battle.

8. *Demonstration projects.* Even though focused directly on problems of the poor, demonstration projects are generally long-term methods of advocacy. They may be necessary in order to elicit the specific material needed for advocacy, and to help a group or community develop the awareness, leadership, and determination to embark upon a course of action. Further advocacy is usually needed to carry the message of the demonstration project into a larger scale service or institutional change affecting the total population involved in a problem.

9. *Direct contacts with officials and legislators.* The agency may approach them formally to make positions known, give relevant information, or protest actions carried out or contemplated. Informal meetings, individually or with groups of legislators, may be similarly used and may enable the legislator to reveal ignorance, ask questions, and listen to more specific material. The agency might attempt to set up some type of regular contact, which in time may result in greater impact as agency personnel and views become known.

10. *Coalition groups.* These can be described as ad hoc group-ings of organizations around a specific objective. The advantages lie not only in the combination of forces, but in the fact that agencies do not have to bear the burden and risk separately. The coalition concept also points to the involvement of disparate types of organizations and groups, which maintain autonomy while pur-suing a common goal. Each organization usually has a circle of adherents who in turn may be more willing to work in concert than alone. Drawbacks involve the danger of setting too general goals and methods, and a proliferation of meetings and com-mittees seeking to "clarify" and "cooperate."

11. *Client groups.* The wide-scale development of the poten-tial of client groups has occurred only recently, and has revealed that this is a major instrument of social change. By client groups is meant any local group or grouping of individuals sharing a problem; while they are not the traditional agency "clients," they are so termed in the sense that they are in some way helped through an agency service. This service may be limited to giving some impetus to the forming of the group, but may continue in the form of consultation to the group, supportive efforts in such ways as helping the group obtain information or gain access to certain people, or mounting collaborative efforts with other com-munity groups. At the outset the advocate may assist in helping the group role-play contemplated action, help solve problems with the group, or suggest ways of augmenting the group. Through community contacts the advocate may help in bringing several groups together to develop coalitions; he may also suggest various methods of action for the group's consideration. Some family agencies have already had valuable experience with such groups in Project ENABLE, which by its very name indicates the primary role of the advocate in relation to such groups.

There is already considerable literature on client groups that covers many aspects of this method of social change. There are, however, two dangers to which the caseworker-advocate should be alert from the start: one, being too verbal, directive, not remaining where the group is, or directly or indirectly using the group as a means to ends other than what the group develops; second, the failure to develop other sources of support toward the same general objectives and to help the group relate to other support in a meaningful but autonomous manner.

12. *Petitions.* While petitions appear to have little direct effect upon officials and legislators, they are valuable in calling attention to an issue. Getting petitions signed is also a valuable activity for a new group in that it mobilizes members around an action and gives them an opportunity to talk to people about the issue, develop their abilities in making public contacts, and formulate points and rebuttals. It may also provide a way of reaching other interested people who might join or support the group.

13. *Persistent demands.* This method in effect means bombardment of officials and legislators, going beyond the usual channels of appeal. Thus a welfare group protesting welfare cuts directed one effort against the local board of education, in an attempt to get the board to join in action to influence the state legislature. This method represents a kind of escalation of a campaign, and may be directed against figures inaccessible or unwilling to submit to personal contacts. While within lawful limits, it may be the precursor to "harassment" or other extralegal means.

14. *Demonstrations and protests.* These include marches, street dramas, vigils, picketing, sit-ins, and other public demonstrations. The family advocate should become familiar with these methods, although organizing and conducting them may lie beyond his competence and role. To what extent an agency as such will organize and participate in these methods will have to be determined within the agency. An agency will have to consider carefully, however, whether its other forms of action are not being conducted from too far behind the firing line, and whether commitment may not require some such firing line activity at times.

Selecting the Method of Intervention

The objectives of any plan of intervention are closely tied in with the methods selected and the nature of the issue and of the adversary organizations. An effort to challenge a state law usually will require a massive effort, on many levels and with various methods, whereas challenging a practice of a local organization may be accomplished through such means as meetings, pressures, client groups, and administrative redress. A demonstration project may represent a fresh and optimistic approach to a problem that has eluded solution for years; it cuts through a problem in a different way and represents a long-term investment toward an objective. For example, the very early childhood experimental programs now in progress in several places in the country, such as one being conducted by Family Service Association of Nassau County, represent a new approach to one goal of reformers and advocates—that of forcing the school systems to provide vast remedial and enrichment programs for the many low-income children who suffer cognitive deficiencies. The objective of these new programs is to foster early development in the child so that the need for later remedial efforts is minimized or even eliminated. The program conducted by Family Service Association of Nassau County has the additional objective of enhancing the role of mothers and fathers in low-income families, an objective pursued in the past through various other methods.

The family advocate and the agency must consider the order of priority of their objectives, leaving room for sharpening or shifting of focus as practice reveals more clearly the nature of the issues involved and points to new approaches, such as those mentioned in relation to demonstration projects. The family advocate should also be alert to the many seemingly minor petty harassments, indignities, and omissions he will suffer—these are often the only part of the Establishment iceberg that is visible to the poor. Ultimately they may become larger issues than the clear-cut injustices which are amenable to lawsuits or other definable actions. Behind the small indignities lie the encrusted attitudes and structures which are far more impervious to change than a given rule or regulation. As William Blake wrote in 1804, "He who would do good to another, must do it in Minute Particulars/General Good is the plea of the scoundrel hypocrite & flatterer."[9]

Agency Structure

The commitment of the agency to action on behalf of families is obviously the cornerstone of an advocacy program. But commitment can rather quickly be dissipated unless a workable structure for advocacy is established. The structure must be one which can and does involve the entire agency, including staff, board, and volunteers in an ongoing activity. Commitment must also be represented by a commitment of time; if advocacy is to be the second major function of a family agency, it must receive the time, attention, and thought that have gone into the counseling program. For example, does the staff time committed to advocacy equal that commited to recording interviews? The staff can tell by such allotments what the agency really means to emphasize. The board, with overall responsibility for the agency, will probably need to delegate to a committee the charge for advocacy. Such a committee, already existing in a number of agencies under such names as Public Issues or Social Concerns, should probably be separate from a committee focused on legislation per se, as the latter would be dealing primarily with bills introduced into legislative bodies. At times, of course, the two committees may be concerned with the same issue and even the same legislation.

The advocacy committee has several important functions. One is to become and keep informed on local problems and issues in order to make continuous assessments of priorities for action and give guidelines to staff involved in advocacy; staff in turn will inform the committee on the pressing concerns of the people. Also essential to advocacy is the potential for quick action. The committee consequently must establish methods by which the advocacy staff can move quickly and still be assured of its backing. This can be done only through an ongoing process in which the committee learns to set guidelines by considering the methods, successes, and failures of the staff and others involved in advocacy. A close and continuing contact between staff and committee is necessary.

The committee has a key responsibility in thinking through the implications of any course of action giving particular thought to follow-through so that client groups are not stirred up and then disappointed by an action that is abandoned. It must also consider the risks involved for the agency in taking action and in making alignments with various groups. Finally, the committee itself becomes involved in action. Members may attend public meetings and hearings or call upon officials and legislators. For example, the Public Issues Committee of the Family Service Association of Nassau County took up the transportation problem in the county as it affects the poor. The committee met with the County Planning Commission and with a representative of the bus companies, obtained much background material, and then, with staff, attended public hearings to present the agency position. Usually board members carry more weight in efforts to influence officials and legislators than do social workers; they may speak not only as residents of a community but may also be able to mobilize other local groups unaffiliated with the agency.

Agency staff also needs to be involved, so that advocacy is not an isolated, specialized function. While historically the caseworker has been seen as one who relays case material to administrators and board, it is evident that staff is for the most part not content with this role, which has no follow-through and which may only occasionally involve any given worker. On the other hand, not all caseworkers can be closely involved in every advocacy action, and there are aspects to advocacy which call for the development of expertise and knowledge to be exercised more centrally in an agency.

Different patterns for staff advocacy are possible, depending on agency size, funding, staff interests, and other considerations. The following are four examples:

1. An agency may have a full-time staff position of Family Advocate, or a Department of Advocacy headed by the Family Advocate. This position, as recently established at Family Service Association of Nassau County through a foundation grant, is initially projected to include two main functions: first, to work with staff, providing consultation on action on behalf of individual clients, or handling certain situations directly and compiling case material on problems for the Public Issues Committee. In addition, the Family Advocate will be working to involve the staff in further action, such as the formation of client groups concerned with specific problems, and participation in committees and hearings. It should be noted that clerical staff may also be involv-

ed in such actions; most clerical staff in social agencies have or develop a commitment to the purposes of social work, and should have opportunity to ally themselves in their capacity as agency personnel as well as private citizens.

The second major responsibility of the Family Advocate is to act as the staff person to the Public Issues Committee. He helps the members define priority problems through case material and background information and by bringing in officials and others who are involved in the problems; he works with them to set guidelines and steps for action, to think through implications, to review what has been done, and to evaluate methods. The Family Advocate may act as agency spokesman, and as liaison to officials and legislators; he may act as agency representative with coalition groups and community groups, and as consultant to client groups; or he may act as advisor to staff or board people who carry out these functions.

One example will illustrate how guidelines and priorities are established, and how the Family Advocate can take action accordingly. The Public Issues Committee defined several priority problem areas before adjourning for the summer; one involved what appeared to be the inequitable distribution and possible poor use of federal education funds siphoned through the state (Title I funds of the Elementary and Secondary Education Act provide added services for children of low-income families). The Committee had no specific cases with which to document this possible problem; it had been suggested by agency staff whose contacts with schools on behalf of clients gave them good reason to believe this was an area to explore further and possibly act upon. Shortly afterwards, the Family Advocate spoke with the superintendent of a school district which was rapidly becoming a ghetto and needed massive governmental funding to cope with educational needs. The superintendent, failing to obtain funds anywhere, was ready to explore this area.

The Family Advocate, acting as consultant and organizer, helped prepare factual material which documented the inequitable distribution of funds and helped assemble a group of other superintendents in similar situations. State education officials came to meetings, and one school district instituted a court suit to force redistribution. Throughout, the Advocate worked cooperatively with the Title I Director of the County Economic Opportunity Council. All this activity took place in line with the priorities set down by the Public Issues Committee, which had not anticipated that this particular problem would suddenly come alive —this rested upon the work of the Advocate and the decision of the executive director.

2. Variation on the establishment of a full-time Family Advocate might include creating a part-time position instead. Or, an "indigenous" worker might fill the position. This pattern might require the investment of more staff and consultation time but bring about other advantages such as better contact with local poverty groups.

3. A present staff member might be assigned in agencies where the budget does not permit expansion of staff at present. Or, a part-time assignment could be made, as an expedient only, since the conflict between the demands of a caseload and of the advocacy function would be frequent and onerous for the worker.

4. A staff committee might be formed, with a chairman bearing responsibility for the advocacy function, but delegating pieces of work to committee members. This method has the advantages of involving more staff directly, keeping the advocacy function related to the casework, and keeping the staff in direct contact with the board committee. Obviously it could present difficulties in carrying out actions, as well as in the kinds of demands upon the worker's attention and time mentioned above.

It may be possible in the context of the four patterns that have been described for the agency to obtain graduate social work students for the program. This would provide needed manpower. Students can, for example, do much of the background work which is time-consuming for the caseworker but essential to the advocacy function. Some schools of social work, in preparing "generic" workers, may find this a highly desirable type of placement, since it can provide the student with selected cases related to advocacy, client groups with which to work, again in connection with advocacy, and community organization and action experience.

In agencies where a separate position of Family Advocate cannot be established, staff members carrying the functions in one of the patterns suggested should have direct access to the responsible board committee and work with that committee. Otherwise the resulting delays in cross-communication and lack of clarity may impede any action. An agency may find it needs the advice of one or more specialists in the areas of agency structuring and functioning for advocacy, orientation to clientele, assisting client groups, and defining areas of action and strategies.

CONCLUSION

Family advocacy offers a way for agencies and staffs to bridge the gap between the many cases of individual grievances against social institutions and the broader-scale actions needed to bring about institutional change. The caseworker's intimate knowledge of individual families provides a grassroots basis for social action, and his concern for families becomes an integral and vital part of the advocacy process.

The defining of the function of family advocacy points to the need for special knowledge and skills, to support the caseworker's activity and to promote social change. A meaningful commitment by the agency is essential to carrying out the second major function of the family agency—improving the social environment of families.

REFERENCES

1. Towle, Charlotte: Social work: Cause and function. *Social Casework, 42:* 394, October 1961; see also Specht, Harry: Casework practice and social policy formulation. *Social Work, 13:*42-52, January 1968; and Hamilton, Gordon: The role of social casework in social policy. *Social Casework, 33:*315-24, October 1952.
2. Hartman, Ann: Anomie and social casework. *Social Casework, 50:*131-37, March 1969.
3. Manser, Ellen P.: *Project ENABLE: What Happened.* New York Family Service Association of America, 1968.

4. NASW Ad Hoc Committee on Advocacy: The social worker as advocate: Champion of social victims. *Social Work, 14*:16-22, April 1969.
5. Grosser, Charles F.: Community development programs serving the urban poor. *Social Work, 10*:18, July 1965.
6. Thursz, Daniel: Social action as a professional responsibility. *Social Work, 11*:17, July 1966.
7. Wineman, David and James, Adrienne: The advocacy challenge to schools of social work. *Social Work, 14*:26, April 1969.
8. Epstein, Irwin: Social workers and social action: Attitudes toward social action strategies. *Social Work, 13*:101-8, April 1968.
9. *Jerusalem,* Ch. 3, lines 60-61.

Chapter 39

THE SOCIAL AGENCY AS A
DISSEMINATOR OF INFORMATION

SHERMAN BARR

W HEN Mobilization For Youth began its operations there was
much evidence that settlement houses, hospitals, schools, and
other established social agencies on the Lower East Side were not
perceived, by low-income people or by the agencies themselves, as
sources of information relevant to the lives of the poor. If a resident wanted information about welfare, for example, he would
rely on the community grapevine; it would never occur to him to
go to an agency. Now, five years later, these agencies are clamoring
to get more information so that they can dispense it to the population they serve.

The limited success of these agencies in information dissemination was demonstrated by the adult survey of the neighborhood
carried out in 1961.[1]

Do you know any neighborhood organizations or local groups that
are trying to do something about problems in the area:

No:	don't know of any such organizations	681
Yes:	Lower East Side Neighborhoods Association	81
	Two Bridges Council; Good Neighbors	23
	Tenants' councils and block associations	48
	Settlement houses and community centers	140
	Churches	55
	Schools; PTA's; Board of Education	37
	Local political clubs	27
	Other organizations	61
	Know of some but can't name them	17
		———
		1,170

Note: Reprinted from Weissman, H. (Ed.) : *Individual and Group Services in the
Mobilization for Youth Experience.* New York, Association Press, 1969, pp.
54-61.

617

When you have a difficult personal or family problem who are you most likely to talk it over with:

Husband or wife	337
Brothers or sisters; brothers-in-law or sisters-in-law living in household	86
Children	86
Parents or parents-in-law; grandparents	69
Other relatives	53
Friends	98
Social worker; welfare worker; city state or private agency	37
Other professional (i.e. doctor, lawyer, counselor)	79
No one; myself; person having difficulty with	120
Don't know; vague irrelevant answer; no answer	19
	988

The problem of lack of information became apparent very early in the program. Large numbers of people came in for help with problems which can be solved rather easily by supplying information. One frequently heard such questions as, is it true that . . . where can I find . . . someone told me that . . . I heard. . . .

THE USE OF INFORMATION

The problem of disseminating information to the poor often devolves to their inability to use information that they have been given. For example, a client may be unable to use what he knows about a clinic or some other kind of service; he lacks the financial wherewithal to do so—perhaps carfare to get to the service or the very small fee connected to it. In time the information itself is regarded as irrelevant. The lack of child-care facilities also may prevent use of information or of a service. Telling a mother that the prenatal clinic at Beth Israel Hospital meets at 8:30 is rather useless unless arrangements have been made to care for her preschool children while she is at the clinic.

People often fail to use information because they do not understand it. Information is often given rather quickly, with the assumption that clients understand what is being said and can really follow through. For example, a client may be told, "Okay, go to

Welfare, you seem to be eligible; the center is at Fifth Street and bring this paper, that paper, that paper, this paper, the other paper, in order to do this, in order to do that." The client will simply nod his head and leave without admitting that he does not completely understand. Sometimes the information given is simply not accurate; after trial and error and frustration, people do not return to the source to get correct information, because they assume that the first negative experience is typical.

Still another factor preventing proper use of information is the transportation system; information has to be very precise, and maps or other directions given so that a person who does not understand English well can find his way. Frequently information is not given concerning geographical boundaries, how much time might be involved, or what telephone numbers to check. A physical orientation to an agency is sometimes necessary as part of the information picture. For instance, it is not helpful merely to tell a client to go to Bellevue Hospital. Bellevue is a complex of buildings which can be overwhelming to the ordinary citizen, let alone those who lack the necessary language skills. A client might go there, look at the place, and come back much too frightened to use it.

The information supplied by the local culture is very often in contradiction to what the social agency says. A worker may say, "Go to Welfare, they'll take care of you," but a friend in the community tells the client: "Welfare is a bunch of dogs, they won't treat you right, and they'll insult you; you shouldn't go there because no one will help you anyway." Or the community may offer him crippling misinformation, such as these remarks by the father of six children, who received Aid to Dependent Children funds:

> I never complain about anything to Welfare. The more you complain, the more angry they get. And the investigator gets $50 every time he closes a case, so he's going to cut you off if you complain too much. I shut up and just take it.

The same situation occurs often with medical facilities; the informal communication links take over and prevent adequate use of information. Good information-giving techniques have to anticipate such a situation and the client's problems, bring them out into the open, and help the client deal with them so that proper use can be made of information.

In terms of transmission of information, it is important not only to say just what the service is and what time to get there but also to warn the client of some of the problems he may meet—a snippy clerk, a cold official, an elevator operator who gives vague directions.

Information about social security or veteran's benefits is given in subway placards; other kinds of public benefits are advertised on television and in periodicals. This is not true in regard to most medical services, and certainly not to welfare services and education services. There appears to be an inclination to hold back information in the fear that extensive dissemination will result in a flood of applicants for the services, and thus will involve additional expenditures which the agency cannot afford.

Some people who have been on welfare for many years do not know what to do about eviction notices, utility bills, special clothing needs, and the like; it is obvious that information has not been shared. In case after case, the sharing of information by the Welfare Department would, indeed, result in a run on the services and tremendous expense. For example, although the manual states that the welfare recipient is supposed to have a minimum standard of furniture, clothing, and household equipment, this information is not given to him. As a matter of fact, if the client doesn't ask, the Welfare Department doesn't offer.

Regarding education, how many parents know what topics the teacher is supposed to cover over a period of time, or where they can go to protest a decision to put a child in a special class or in a 600 school for problem children? This sort of information is seldom shared with parents in other than crisis situations. By and large, the client gets to know what the agency wants him to know; beyond that he must rely on his own wits and on gossip within the community. Information obtained in this way is frequently inaccurate and may be damaging.

INFORMATION AND ACTION

The decision of an agency to give information and to provide the means for the clients to follow through on it implies that the agency has adopted a certain stance toward action. If it deliberately chooses to provide information about welfare which will increase the demands made on the welfare system and the amount of expenditure expected of it, that agency is not only providing more information to clients but is also taking the risk of creating problems in its relationship with the welfare system itself.

In its attitude toward providing information, an agency reflects its philosophy, its preferred clientele, and the kind of risks it is willing to take. If a clinic meets at an inconvenient hour, would it not be the responsibility of the agency providing the information to help clients organize to change the meeting time? In other words, where does the job of giving information develop into the job of counseling action? Or again, if the agency tells a client about a particular service and the service agency does not perform as expected, what responsibility does the worker or his agency have to do something about it? Clearly, good information requires a certain commitment, a certain stance on the part of the agency. A client seeking help in applying for public assistance said about a previous experience:

> Miss K., the social worker, gave us a letter to take to Welfare. If she had gone with us instead of just writing a letter, it would have been different. If you go alone, they treat you one way. But if you go with somebody from an organization, they treat you another way. She's very nice, Miss K., but I don't know what she's going to do for me. She looks at me, smiles and says, "Hm-um, Hm-um." Well, life just isn't that calm for us.

One well-known service agency has never given information concerning minimum standards or the right to appeal decisions of the Department of Welfare. Prior to the institution of Mobilization's services, only a handful of appeals had been made to the State Department of Social Welfare. Such fair hearings are now requested by the hundreds.

To obtain information for a client from the Board of Education, the social worker may have to use the legal service or some other weapon to force the information from the educational system. The reason people have not identified social-work agencies as places which hold information is not because of the agencies' unwillingness to transmit information, but because of their unwillingness to go to bat for the client in order to make sure the information is obtained and put to good use.

INFORMATION AND THE IMAGE OF THE SOCIAL AGENCY

The image of a social agency in the client's mind is crucial. For example, a publicity campaign was carried out by a neighborhood legal services unit in a large eastern city. The area was blanketed with notices announcing meetings, and lawyers were sent around to speak with local groups. The net result of all this effort was not any marked increase in the number of people using these services. Eventually it was discovered that the neighborhood legal service unit was not accepting any criminal cases. Since there was a great need for help in the criminal courts in this particular neighborhood, legal service had taken on a negative image—it simply wasn't viewed as a place where one could get help. As a result, the legal services which were provided were not fully utilized.

Mobilization has discovered that word of mouth is probably the best and most common means of transmitting information in a slum; mimeographed releases or sound trucks alone are not enough. Attendance at meetings of neighborhood organizations also helps to open up communication links. But what really paves the way to communication is long and persistent work to develop an image of an organization which the clients value and discuss with respect among themselves. Eighty-five percent of the new cases at MFY's neighborhood service centers are referred through word-of-mouth techniques, and the very successful welfare groups have developed primarily through word of mouth.

An interesting illustration of image as a factor in the dissemination of information occurred in the first local campaign around Operation Head Start. About ten summer workers and Vista volunteers were employed in a crash program to enlist youngsters in the program. Circulars were distributed, tables were set up on every street corner, sound trucks were used, workers approached people on the streets and on the stoops, they filled mailboxes and so on, but the response was very limited; many openings in the program were not filled. The following year registration was far better. Some of this improvement may be attributed to the use of better techniques throughout the city, but it is also true that Mobilization had improved its name and image in the area by making more services and information available. Since Mobilization was a source of information about Head Start, people were more receptive to such information.

Regarding the information provided by the neighborhood service centers, one of the psychiatric consultants observed that there was what he called a "place transference." Information or suggestions coming from neighborhood-service-center workers were especially valued because their source was the neighborhood service center. The image had been enhanced over the years, and thus information was shared and used much more broadly.

In the current cold war, jamming of radio frequencies is a much used tactic to prevent information from being used. MFY has sought to unjam the client's receivers by providing clear information and making sure that the information can be acted on, either by providing the needed ancillary services—e.g. day care—or by pressuring institutions to act, by insisting that institutions expand the information they transmit and cut down on conflicting messages and discordant techniques of dissemination, and by developing the image of MFY as a helping institution.

One of the major roles of voluntary social agencies is to act as watchdogs of the public agencies. Private agencies not only must give information to clients about the public agencies but also must make certain that public bodies are accountable to their clients. Private social agencies are admirably suited to do this since they depend on public bodies for neither funds nor legitimacy. They can both organize clients to seek their rights and arouse public opinion. They cannot really be effective in providing information unless they act as the champions and advocates of client needs. For it is not information alone that clients need but also the ability to use it.

REFERENCE

1. *Adult Survey Code Book.* New York, Mobilization For Youth, 1962, vol 1.

C. DELIVERY OF SERVICES

Chapter 40

"MENTAL HEALTH WITHOUT WALLS": COMMUNITY MENTAL HEALTH IN THE GHETTO

JACOB R. FISHMAN AND JOHN McCORMACK

GHETTO residents experience tremendous mental health problems that often appear resistant to treatment. Many psychiatrists and coworkers are baffled by the constellation of environmental problems and behavioral and emotional difficulties so acutely manifested by people attempting to survive in the ghetto. Elimination of the environmental problems has been attempted through several types of social action and community improvement programs, but ghettos still generate considerable unrest, thus increasing individual and group disturbance.

In the community mental health programs attempted, mental health workers often encounter problems that lie outside the range of problems they have been trained to treat.[7,8,13,14,15] In addition, application of relevant knowledge and techniques is greatly hindered by the constricted perspective afforded by the artificial walls of office, ward, and "center."

The model for community mental health centers evolved in recent years is essentially a modification of the usual institutional model of service and is built around a core of inpatient, clinic, and emergency services attached to some modified form of extended hospital care and a liaison staff based in an inpatient-outpatient complex. This model of "community" mental health service does not appear to work in the ghetto. Office and hospital walls, just like ghetto boundaries, have two sides. They keep people in; they keep people out; and they obstruct vision.

Note: Reprinted from the *Am J Psychiatry,* 26:1461-1467, 1970. Copyright 1970, the American Psychiatric Association.

Based on a paper read at the 123rd annual meeting of the American Psychiatric Association, Detroit, Mich., May 8-12, 1967.

Shut in by these walls, the practitioner has extreme difficulty in dealing with problems in the context of the ghetto environment in which the patient spends nearly all his time. Professionals working primarily in the artificial environment of office or ward cannot in a brief time sufficiently "influence" a person to initiate significant behavior modifications that will survive in the face of prevailing and complex ghetto life styles.

In our experience, program design and treatment methods, to be effective, must literally be based in the ghetto and in the realities and problems of the patient's living situation; they must include understanding of the psychological causes and consequences of these problems.[4] The goal must be a program "without walls."

During the course of several years' experience in developing comprehensive community mental health services in a ghetto area of Washington, D.C.* and in other cities, we identified a number of constantly appearing issues and developed innovations to meet the particular needs of ghetto residents. They extend beyond the traditional dimensions of diagnosis and treatment.

THE MAJOR ISSUES

Techniques

Conventional psychotherapeutic techniques frequently offer little assistance to the adult, adolescent, or child in the ghetto. Hard data on this subject are badly needed but several weeks in a hospital ward or fifty minutes a week in an office for a few months is obviously inadequate and frequently inappropriate.

Professionals, both Negro and white, usually live in the suburbs and have little experience with or understanding of ghetto life styles that differ from those of the middle class with whom they live, work, and socialize.[9] Consequently, their therapeutic focus is frequently irrelevant to the problems most pressing to ghetto residents—unemployment, lack of coping skills, family disintegration, and neighborhood pressures. Treatment goals often fail to provide motivation since they are generally not clearly

---

*Howard University D.C. Department of Health Center for Mental Health and Institute for Youth Studies.

defined or explained in terms of patients' problems and perspectives.

Traditional psychotherapy consists primarily of verbal exchange, relying on a combination of abstraction, insight, transference, and persuasion to produce behavioral change and resolution of problems. This process is appropriate to a middle-class population conditioned to delayed gratification, verbal exchange, and intellectual control over behavior. It does not appear to be effective in the ghetto context, since it differs so greatly from the activity-oriented patterns of living to which the ghetto resident is accustomed. Verbal interaction often fails to generate trust in people conditioned to distrust, disappointment, and the "snow job."

New, active forms of therapy are needed that are related to real-life problems. Activities must focus on modifying behavior as well as on the conditions that reinforce behavior: therapy must result in both internal (personal) and external (community) change. Therapeutic goals and methods must be organized and defined in terms of the social and behavioral skills people need to cope successfully with the problems they face. Concomitantly, social changes and opportunities must be developed that permit successful use of new skills and coping patterns.

Such an approach clearly involves the development of linkages with programs providing employment, education, training, legal aid, social services, and health care. In addition, we must try to bring about changes in community organization and structure that will facilitate improvement of mental health.

We must also recognize, help develop, and use in the therapeutic process those underlying group and individual strengths that are usually disregarded by the therapist but that have enabled people to survive in the face of enormous adversity. The ghetto dweller has grown up in a context of segregation, depreciation, and constriction and has had to learn to negotiate a system in which: (a) passive-aggressive dependency is encouraged if not required; (b) internal controls have few rewards; (c) impulsive, violent behavior is frequently the only outlet to gratification; and (d) distrust is justified by reality. Local values, traditions, and coping styles must be learned by the professional so he can help people use the positive strengths and potential of these resources to develop successful coping skills and competencies that lead to changed behavior. Failure to tap these resources is depreciating to the person, impairs the therapeutic relationship, and overlooks a potentially vital tool for help.

Location

Mental health facilities and resources are generally not located in the ghetto. Most residents are reluctant for economic, psychological, and social reasons to travel far for services. Facilities are generally not open evenings or weekends when people could fully use them. It is a great hardship for the employed poor to take time off and lose income.

Communication

When facilities are in the neighborhood, many residents are ill-informed about them, unaware of their need for service, or reluctant to use the facilities. As professionals, we often believe that if people do not come for help, they are either "resistant" or undesirous of receiving care. This premise is based on a middle-class model of motivation, in which patients conform to the expectations of private practitioners, rather than one in which services actively reach out to meet people's needs. Many problems like lack of finances, education, or information influence the seeking and acceptance of services.

Mental health programs seldom provide systematic outreach to the community by trained people who know the community and are accepted by local residents. Thus, a facility may be underused not through lack of need but through lack of necessary linkages to the community. Active outreach must be provided by easily accessible neighborhood workers who seek out people in need, provide a bridge to service, and actively arrange referral and follow-up.

Continuity

There must be adequate continuity of care provided by mental health and other human services, including education, employment, welfare, legal aid, and training. These are usually scattered in different parts of the city, disconnected geographically and functionally. No one location or unit provides for meeting the overall spectrum of related needs, and the system is too fragmented for the poor to negotiate successfully. In moving from one service to the next, the patient goes through a duplication of processing, evaluation, diagnosis, intake, and recommendations that delays service and wastes effort. He finds services hidden behind a maze of walls.

Participation

Most medical and social services in a poor community are based on a "charity model" in which people receive services without being permitted to participate in the identification of their needs or the goals of service. Policies regarding service are made by prominent citizens from other parts of the city and tend to emphasize professional training and knowledge in contrast to the recipients' needs for knowledge. This fosters and maintains dependency in patients and clients. The treatment process is presumably aimed at developing independence, competence, and autonomy in clients, yet the system of relationships undercuts achievement of these goals. To help overcome dependency and to develop coping skills, community residents can assist in defining needs, goals, programs, and services.

Community Development Efforts

Many social change and community improvement efforts have been mobilized in the ghetto with great rapidity in recent years. Some derive from federal antipoverty efforts to develop local leadership and self-help, others from civil rights and Black Power movements. Activities have ranged from sporadic demonstrations to more systematic development of neighborhood organization, political awareness, and community improvement. Even more rapid has been the increase in frustration and pressure enhanced by growing awareness of gaps between needs or expectations and reality. The result is an extremely explosive matrix, easily ignited by problems and incidents involving police, welfare, employment, and school conditions. Whether the goals and methods used in community development efforts are acceptable or workable, they represent important attempts on the part of people in need to develop positive identity and strength through organization and action to overcome a severely handicapped psychological and social state.[1,6,16]

The white liberal professional has many ambivalent feelings, based on stereotyped images of ghetto residents, about crime, delinquency, irresponsibility, and hostility just as he has about civil rights, antipoverty programs, Black Power, and school problems. But through the community mental health program, he can assist community attempts at problem-solving in constructive ways, helping to avoid destructive explosions and conflicts that increase social pathology. This vital support must be provided in the context of professional expertise rather than citizen advocacy.

Cost

The cost of extending mental health services to all who need them is prohibitive even in the most favorable community budget. It is even more costly when the inefficiency of existing methods is considered. Problems of total cost and cost effectiveness must be faced as programs expand and change in character.

For example, the rule of thumb currently in vogue suggests that ten percent of our national population needs some form of psychiatric help; the rate is higher in the ghetto. In the segment of Washington that we serve (roughly one-third of the city), there are approximately fifty thousand children under twelve, and it appears that at least 25 percent (or 12,500) of them need varying degrees of help. If a professional were to see five children a day five days a week, he could handle 1,250 visits a year, only one small segment of the total clinical need. If each child were seen only once a month for six visits, more than seventy full-time professionals would be needed. The overall cost would be more than $3 million a year. Since this represents just one segment of all needed services in the area, fiscal problems can be seen to be immense. And they must be viewed in the context of an increasing demand from other services for an expanded share of the strained public dollar.

Systematic determination of cost effectiveness thus becomes a major challenge. Systems of evaluation generally used in public agencies today rely most heavily on units of service provided, a doubtful basis on which to determine the effectiveness of techniques, goals, organization of delivery systems, and manpower utilization. Economic questions will have to be answered in the face of growing public demands for accountability and credibility.

TOWARD SOME ANSWERS

Community Involvement

We involved community residents and neighborhood groups in decision making processes regarding needs, program development, and operation. For example, an organized neighborhood group was invited to assume a major role in the development of a satellite neighborhood mental health center. The group made decisions with the staff through a joint committee in which the local representatives had the major voice. The committee interviewed the clinic director and staff, discussing standards and making choices regarding staff appointments. This group continues to involve and represent local residents in providing ongoing guidance, monitoring, and decision-making regarding policy, organization, and relevance of services.

Even though this process precludes any assumption of medical responsibilities by nonphysicians, it has not always been easy for professionals to accept. The group functions similarly to a board of directors elected by the people of the community, providing linkage between the patients and the staff. This brings the entire mental health process to the neighborhood and community level in a positive way and has the unique therapeutic effect of permitting people to achieve greater control over their own destinies.[4]

New Careers

Local residents were trained and employed to work as nonprofessionals in various parts of the mental health program. Supervised by professionals, they perform a variety of roles and functions in the delivery of preventive treatment and rehabilitative services. Career ladders are being developed for them within the structure of the program, providing them with support and opportunity for upward mobility. The new careers concept of community intervention has been discussed by one of us and others.[5, 10,11,12]

Community Outreach

Considerable emphasis is placed on community outreach services, including active case finding, early identification of needs, and bringing services to people. Outreach is provided primarily by nonprofessionals. Linkages are provided to other types of agencies by the mental health nonprofessional who provides for referrals, coordination, and follow-up while maintaining active contact with individuals and families.

Community Organization and Improvement

All staff take active parts in neighborhood groups involved in community improvement and social change. They provide education, consultation, guidance, and specialized knowledge on key issues, collaborating often with other service agencies. They assist the community in organizing itself, taking action, and developing a positive and constructive identity based on mutual selfhelp and social improvement. This involvement has contributed greatly to improved mental health within the community and has helped professionals to relate better to the client population.

Decentralization of Services

Unlike the usual arrangement, in which each particular kind of service is provided in one central location in a city, we have decentralized services to each local neighborhood and placed emphasis on outreach, follow-up, and continuity between care provided in the home, in the neighborhood, and in relevant community institutions such as schools, community centers, and places of employment.

This increases effectiveness and reaches the hard-core or otherwise unreachable individual and family who are frequently most in need of help. It also helps to overcome the underlying professional illusion of the need for four protective walls surrounding the clinic or hospital in which all "real" treatment must be provided.

Integration with Other Human Services

Close integration, geographically and functionally, with other human service agencies at the neighborhood level provides for major accessibility and allows true continuity of care for the typical multiproblem family and individual. It provides an opportunity for a flexible format that fits services to the needs of the individual rather than forcing the person to fit himself into nonfunctional and disconnected services.

To achieve this integration, we made our satellite neighborhood center an integral part of a local neighborhood center operated by a community group, Change, Inc. This center provides services such as employment, counseling, social welfare, health, legal aid, credit union, community organization, and youth services to a neighborhood of 40,000 people. Nonprofessionals, many of them initially trained in the new careers program, are employed in a variety of roles in the center.

Integration of the satellite mental health center into the structure of this neighborhood multipurpose center provides the advantages of decentralization and integration of a variety of services in one location. Psychiatric services have become a natural part of the overall services, and opportunity is provided for continuity of care, liaison, consultation, and provision of education to other services, neighborhood groups, and community organization workers. Centralized screening, intake, and coordinated referral all take place in the same location, removing walls between services.

Integration with other institutions and agencies also affords the opportunity for the various services to develop joint program goals and bring about planned change. By working closely with professionals in other fields, it is possible for us to encourage the inclusion of preventive and therapeutic principles of mental health in other services.

Consultation and Education

We extended the role of consultant, a familiar role of psychiatrists, to include consultation by other staff not only with respect to problem handling, early identification, and crisis intervention but also in relation to training, program structure, curriculum content, juvenile court operations, neighborhood organizations, churches, police, and other key groups. This maximizes preventive and therapeutic mental activity in the community.

For example, the consultant to the school seeks acceptance in a role in which he provides input with respect to mental health aspects of curriculum, techniques of teaching, and supervisory relationships as well as the handling of problem children. A task-oriented approach to the consultee has been found a most effective method of instilling sound mental health principles throughout the population.

These roles and activities are no less difficult than providing intensive psychotherapy. Learning to provide consultation and deal with the psychosocial realities of social institutions in the community, while maintaining necessary professional identity, involves the use of a system of information and experience not covered in professional education, yet urgently needed. Preparation for this role should be incorporated into standard training programs in all relevant fields.[4]

Treatment methods need to be tailored to the needs of disadvantaged multiproblem individuals and families and evaluated on the basis of success in meeting these needs. We have found that activities such as special education, vocational training, community organization, and rehabilitation, which have always been considered ancillary or supportive to "real psychiatry," must play a central role in our thinking and practice.

We developed therapeutic models based on meaningful task- and goal-directed activity. Directing and relating therapeutic activity to work, financial reward, social change, relevant education, and positive identity goals is effective and motivating for the ghetto population.

We built treatment goals and techniques into programs of

career training, skill development, and employment. Thus, goals and processes are more concrete, relevant, and meaningful to residents. The training program and the job, for example, replace verbal exchange as the major therapeutic vehicle for developing confidence and coping ability. Trainees provide support to each other in small-group training sessions, taking part in mutual problem solving and reality testing through techniques such as role-playing. Treatment and therapeutic discussion are provided in the context of real tasks rather than artificial situations.

Therapy has been provided quite successfully through the new careers program, which simultaneously provides training and employment, bridges the gap between professional and patient, and helps overcome manpower shortages in human service agencies. Success in a new careers program has an important therapeutic effect on the trainee, his family, and the community. Significant and lasting behavioral change has occurred in indigenous adolescents and adults trained for and placed in nonprofessional careers in mental health, child care, social service, education, rehabilitation, and other human services.[2,3,6]

The new careers program is group based and structured to motivate behavioral change by supplying ego and identity supports through meaningful work, group support, economic independence, and the acquisition of social and personal skills. The new self-concept and role developed through helping others appears to be an important aspect of individual growth. This program produces much more extensive and lasting change in ghetto residents than traditional forms of individual psychotherapy or usual work-training programs. New careers helps local residents help themselves and develop competency as they begin to assist in delivering the services in agencies upon which they were formerly dependent.

New careers has a positive effect on the human service agencies in which the nonprofessionals are employed, since the new careerists provide a link between the suburban professional and inner city population. Psychiatrists and other professionals are required to develop new roles as trainer, supervisor, or specialist, and a fundamental reorganization and reorientation of staff and service delivery patterns are often required. The result, however, in addition to improved relations between server and served, can also be increased cost effectiveness created by more economical staffing patterns and the assumption by new careerists of nonprofessional tasks formerly performed by professionals.

We also provided new careers training successfully to adolescents in high school whose training was combined with high school curriculums, remediation, and compensated on-the-job training. Such approaches to out-of-school and out-of-work problem youth have been more effective in producing lasting behavioral change than traditional psychotherapy, which has had little success with adolescents in general and lower socioeconomic class adolescents in particular.[5]

REFERENCES

1. Erikson, E.: *Youth, Change, and Challenge.* New York, Basic Books, 1966.
2. Fishman, J.R., Denham, W. and Shatz, E.: *New Careers for the Disadvantaged in Human Service.* Washington, D.C. Howard University Institute for Youth Studies, 1968, p. 250.
3. Fishman, J.R., Klein, W., MacLennan, B., Mitchell, L., Pearl, A. and Walker, W.: *Trianing for New Careers.* Washington, D.C., President's Committee on Juvenile Delinquency, 1965.   :
4. Fishman, J. R., Mitchell, L. and Blount, J.: *Model for a Community Mental Health Program for an Urban Ghetto Area.* Washington, D.C., D.C. Department of Health, Howard University College of Medicine, 1968, p. 180 (processed).
5. Fishman, J.R., Mitchell, L. and Wittenberg, C.: Baker's dozen: Training local problem youth as mental health aides. *Mental Health Training Reports, no. 2.* National Instiute of Mental Health, 1967, pp. 11-24.
6. Fishman, J.R. and Solomon, F.: Youth and social action. *J Social Issues, 20:*1-27, October 1964.
7. Grier, W. and Cobbs, P.: *Black Rage.* New York, Basic Books, 1968.
8. Group for the Advancement of Psychiatry: *The Dimensions of Community Psychiatry.* GAP Report no. 69. New York, GAP, 1968.
9. Kaplan, M.C. and Kurtz, R.M.: Psychiatric residents and lower class patients: Conflict in training. *Community Mental Health J, 4:*91-97, 1968.
10. Lynch, M., Gardner, E. and Felzer, S.B.: Role of indigenous personnel as clinical therapists. *Arch Gen Psychiat, 19:*528-534, 1968.

11. MacLennan, B.W., Klein, W., Pearl A. and Fishman, J.: Training for new careers. *Community Mental Health J, 2*:135-141, 1966.

12. Pearl, A. and Riessman, F.: *New Careers for the Poor.* New York, Free Press, 1965.

13. Peck, H.B., Kaplan, S. and Roman, M.: Prevention, treatment, and social action. *Am J Orthopsychiatry, 36*:57-69, 1966.

14. Riessman, F., Cohen, J. and Pearl, A.: *Mental Health for the Poor.* New York, Free Press, 1964.

15. Smith, M.B.: The revolution in mental health care—A bold new approach. *Trans-Action*:19-23, April 1968.

16. Solomon, F., Walker, W., O'Connor, B. and Fishman, J.R.: Civil rights activity and the reduction of crime among Negroes. *Arch Gen Psychiatry, 12*:227-236, 1965.

Chapter 41

THE NEIGHBORHOOD CENTER CONCEPT

MICHAEL S. MARCH

T HERE IS growing interest in the multipurpose neighborhood center as a means for improving the delivery of social services. Solution of social problems, especially in areas where poor people are concentrated, requires more effective services. This paper analyzes why public administrators and social scientists are seeking better ways of organizing health, educational, manpower, rehabilitation and other social services and outlines alternative models of center systems. The models presented in the charts are theoretical, and the reader is expected to judge the relevancy of each according to his own knowledge of the facts and the needs of his community.

The *neighborhood center* is defined in this paper as an organization for delivering a broad range of social services in a *co-ordinated* and highly *responsive* manner to individuals and families, and for serving the neighborhood at large. The principal focus is on the service delivery system as an instrument for preventing and treating disorders which undermine the satisfactory social and economic functioning of individuals, families, and communities. Co-location of various agencies and services in a single building or a "social services plaza" and integration of the services through central administration and core services are viewed as essential parts of the overall system concept. It is assumed throughout that *responsive* delivery of services requires effective community organization to achieve meaningful involvement of neighborhood residents, particularly the disadvantaged and the poor, in the development and the operation of the center system.

Note: Abridged and reprinted from the April, 1968 issue of *Public Welfare,* the journal of the American Public Welfare Association, pp. 97-111.

It is increasingly clear that there are a number of factors which suggest a major effort to find better ways for delivering and coordinating social services at the local level. Among these are the following:

1. The volume and number of programs providing services, facilities, and aid to communities has been stepped up significantly. Between fiscal years 1957 and 1969, Federal aid to state and local governments, exclusive of aid for highway construction, is estimated to increase more than fourfold, from about $4 billion to around $16 billion, of which $12 billion is in the health, labor, welfare and education categories. A recent study indicated that there were 162 major aid programs in effect early in 1966, and that they were provided under 399 different statutory authorizations.[1] The 1967 Office of Economic Opportunity catalog of Federal programs lists 459 separate programs which are available for aid to communities or to individuals.[2] Coordination has not kept pace with the accelerating fragmentation resulting from new programs. The volume of public services financed from state and local funds has also increased sharply in this period.

2. To deliver the services and benefits provided through these programs, new organizational units have been created by local, state, and Federal agencies. The compartmentalization and fragmentation of programs at the Federal level has often been replicated at the local level, often with corresponding lines leading through a state agency. Voluntary councils have been overshadowed and have been unable to control the programming of social service funds flowing into communities. The drive toward specialization and toward professional identity has often promoted compartmentalization. As compartmentalization grew and was extended vertically, horizontal integration of programs has tended to be neglected.

3. Initiation of the war on poverty in 1964 highlighted the importance of human resource development programs. It became increasingly clear that at the bottom of the social and economic heap, there were often individuals and families with multiple problems. They were the racial and ethnic minorities, the uneducated, the sick and untrained, the unemployed and the unemployable, and the socially and culturally alienated. The "postage stamp" programs could not cover their needs. Moreover, many existing programs were not responsive to their desires or needs.

4. The need for concerting and coordinating programs became more apparent and more widely understood. Urgency has been underlined by the rising problem of the Negroes, Puerto Ricans, and Mexicans in big-city ghettos, who have replaced European immigrants as

the most underprivileged. Effective assistance to the hard-core group requires concerted assistance from a number of programs over a substantial period of time under conditions where the disadvantaged and the poor are receptive and join in the effort to achieve their own uplift. One response to this challenge has been a recent surge by public agencies to decentralize their activities and create local offices, including neighborhood centers.

5. Many different types of centers are being tried including manpower centers, community action centers, human resource development centers, comprehensive health centers, maternal and child health centers, parent and child centers, welfare suboffices, employment offices, youth opportunity centers, rehabilitation centers, comprehensive mental health centers, and supplementary education centers—just to name a few. Experience with many of these projects has shown that increasingly they strive individually to become more comprehensive as they try to meet the complex needs of their clientele. There is growing need for effective coordination of the various centers or offices that are financed in a given community by different agencies. Advance community-wide planning of services and related facilities is necessary to overcome gaps, overlaps, and lack of coordination.

Public agencies have known for quite a number of years how to concert services actively to rehabilitate physically and mentally disabled or handicapped individuals. However, they have not yet solved the problem of concerting services for socially and economically disabled *families*. Even less is known about how to achieve the coordinated action necessary to rehabilitate a sick neighborhood or a sick community. Despite the admitted potential of neighborhood centers, and the hundreds or even thousands of various centers and local offices already in operation, it is hard to find examples where services are integrated and responsive. The effort to develop a better neighborhood service center represents an extension of the principle of rehabilitation to the provision of services to the socially and economically disadvantaged.

Succeeding sections outline various possible approaches to the solution of the problem of how to organize the delivery of services effectively. In considering all these models, it should be constantly borne in mind that the objective is not to operate or coordinate services for their own sake; the end purpose is to help solve the social or human resource problems of cities, suburban communities, or rural areas—and particularly the problems of families and individuals in such areas who are not capable of effective social and economic functioning. The purpose is to improve methods for prevention and treatment of socially and economically handicapping disorders and the rehabilitation of people who have them. And, while our most immediate concerns are the poor and disadvantaged, the methods should be applicable to all social services, and the services should be available to all residents who need them.

HOW ARE OUR SERVICES AND PROGRAMS ORGANIZED TODAY?

A simple sketch can perhaps indicate the organizational consequences in a local community of the present structure of Federal, state, and local programs. In Figure 41-1, the largest square represents the city and the circle stands for the neighborhood, which contains multiproblem Family A. The small rectangles depict major institutions, one of which is completely outside the urban area. The little triangles represent public and private service agencies. Let us assume that Family A is newly arrived in the ghetto, is destitute, and is composed of four persons:

- a father who is unemployed, addicted to drink, and untrained;
- a mother who is uneducated and sick, but energetic in attempting to hold the family together;
- a son, a school dropout, recently placed on probation for car theft;
- a little daughter, aged ten, three grades behind in school.

Figure 41-2 describes what happens when mother shoves father out the door one day and tells him not to come back until he gets a job. The Community Action Center is strong on organization but has few "hard" services; it refers him to the Employment Service. The Employment Service counselor smells alcohol on his breath and inquires enough to find that his real problem is not unemployment but health; he is referred to the nearby Health Center. The Health Center is a general health center which lacks capability in the mental health area. The father then is sent to

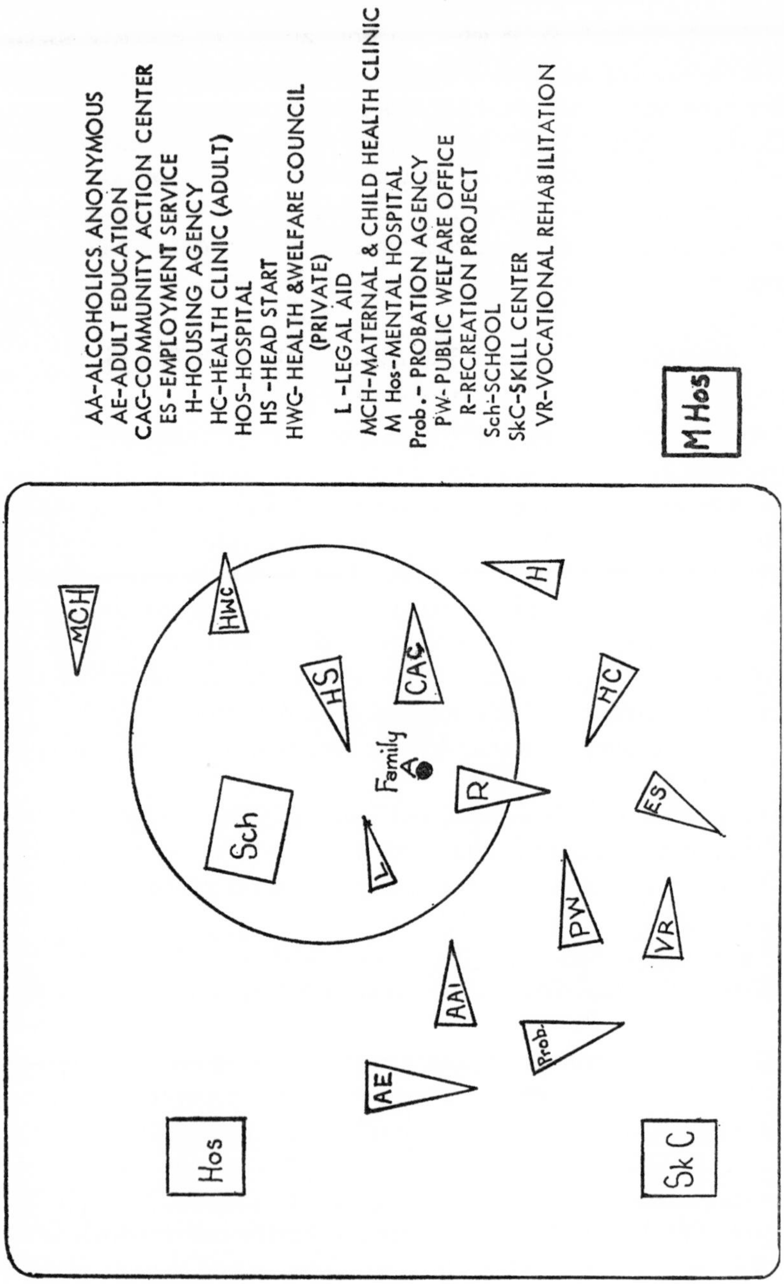
AA-ALCOHOLICS ANONYMOUS
AE-ADULT EDUCATION
CAC-COMMUNITY ACTION CENTER
ES-EMPLOYMENT SERVICE
H-HOUSING AGENCY
HC-HEALTH CLINIC (ADULT)
HOS-HOSPITAL
HS-HEAD START
HWC-HEALTH &WELFARE COUNCIL (PRIVATE)
L-LEGAL AID
MCH-MATERNAL & CHILD HEALTH CLINIC
M Hos-MENTAL HOSPITAL
Prob.-PROBATION AGENCY
PW-PUBLIC WELFARE OFFICE
R-RECREATION PROJECT
Sch-SCHOOL
SkC-SKILL CENTER
VR-VOCATIONAL REHABILITATION
M Hos
MCH
HWC
HS
CAC
H
HC
Sch
Family A
R
ES
L
PW
VR
AA
Prob.
AE
Hos
Sk C

Figure 41-1.

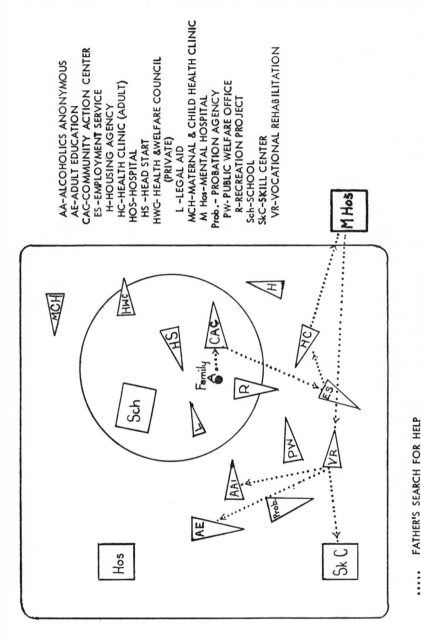

AA-ALCOHOLICS ANONYMOUS
AE-ADULT EDUCATION
CAC-COMMUNITY ACTION CENTER
ES-EMPLOYMENT SERVICE
H-HOUSING AGENCY
HC-HEALTH CLINIC (ADULT)
HOS-HOSPITAL
HS –HEAD START
HWG- HEALTH &WELFARE COUNCIL
(PRIVATE)
L –LEGAL AID
MCH-MATERNAL & CHILD HEALTH CLINIC
M Hos-MENTAL HOSPITAL
Prob.– PROBATION AGENCY
PW-PUBLIC WELFARE OFFICE
R-RECREATION PROJECT
Sch-SCHOOL
SkC-SKILL CENTER
VR-VOCATIONAL REHABILITATION

••••• FATHER'S SEARCH FOR HELP

Figure 41-2.

the Mental Hospital, which is the community's mental health resource. There it is ascertained that his problems are the sort that could be handled by Vocational Rehabilitation.

Vocational Rehabilitation develops a rehabilitation plan for him following medical consultation and counseling. He is scheduled for treatment at an out-patient alcoholic clinic, and encouraged to contact Alcoholics Anonymous. In the meantime tentative vocational plans are drawn up, including vocational training. Pending readiness and admittance to the school, he is referred to a rehabilitation workshop at a Skill Center for work-adjustment training and evaluation. Arrangements are then made for the provision of remedial reading and basic arithmetic training at Adult Education classes.

Figure 41-3 illustrates mother's search for help for herself and for her daughter. First they go to the Maternal and Child Health Clinic for health care for the daughter, then to the Public Welfare Department in search of welfare aid, only to be told that residence requirements prohibit any payments and that they must go to the privately funded Health and Welfare Council Office. Then mother goes to the Health Clinic, where a cursory examination indicates that she may need an operation and she is referred to the City Hospital.

Continuing her efforts to secure aid for her daughter, mother then visits the Head Start office and is told that the only possibility of help is to visit the psychologist at the Mental Hospital because her daughter has more fundamental troubles requiring thorough diagnosis.

Assume also that son visits the Recreation Project and there is urged to try to get back into School, but the School wants to be sure that he has a clear bill of health from the Probation Agency and sends him there for a visit. The probation officer encourages him to get work training and refers him to the Employment Service, which places him in a slot at the Skill Center.

Figure 41-4 illustrates the Odyssey of Family A in seeking to get help for their variegated problems. In the course of these visits, they probably spent a number of weeks; they were interviewed many times and filled out many forms or had many forms

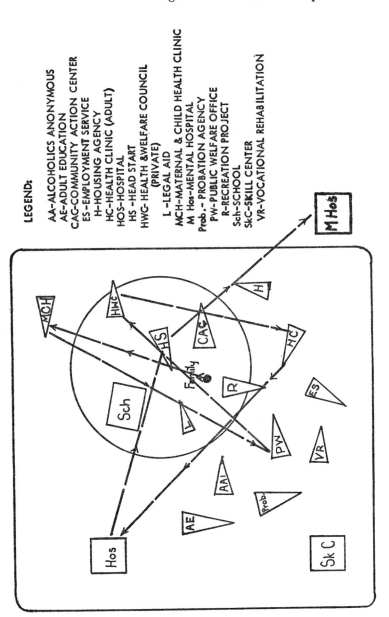

LEGEND:

AA-ALCOHOLICS ANONYMOUS
AE-ADULT EDUCATION
CAG-COMMUNITY ACTION CENTER
ES-EMPLOYMENT SERVICE
H-HOUSING AGENCY
HC-HEALTH CLINIC (ADULT)
HOS-HOSPITAL
HS -HEAD START
HWC- HEALTH &WELFARE COUNCIL
(PRIVATE)
L -LEGAL AID
MCH-MATERNAL & CHILD HEALTH CLINIC
M Hos-MENTAL HOSPITAL
Prob.- PROBATION AGENCY
PW-PUBLIC WELFARE OFFICE
R-RECREATION PROJECT
Sch-SCHOOL
SkC-SKILL CENTER
VR-VOCATIONAL REHABILITATION

— — — MOTHER'S SEARCH FOR HELP FOR SELF AND MENTALLY RETARDED DAUGHTER

Figure 41-3.

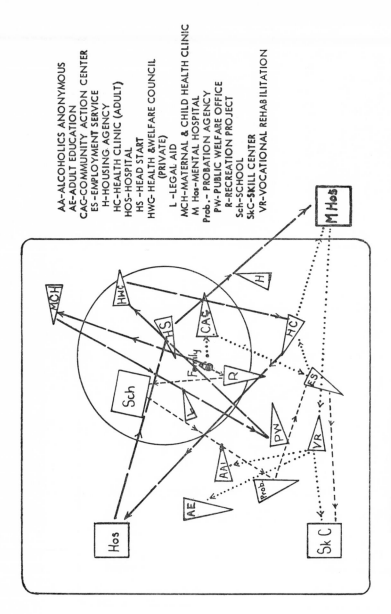

AA-ALCOHOLICS ANONYMOUS
AE-ADULT EDUCATION
CAG-COMMUNITY ACTION CENTER
ES-EMPLOYMENT SERVICE
H-HOUSING AGENCY
HC-HEALTH CLINIC (ADULT)
HOS-HOSPITAL
HS –HEAD START
HWG-HEALTH &WELFARE COUNCIL
        (PRIVATE)
L –LEGAL AID
MCH-MATERNAL & CHILD HEALTH CLINIC
M Hos-MENTAL HOSPITAL
Prob.– PROBATION AGENCY
PW-PUBLIC WELFARE OFFICE
R-RECREATION PROJECT
Sch-SCHOOL
SkC-SKILL CENTER
VR-VOCATIONAL REHABILITATION

········ FATHER'S SEARCH FOR HELP
— — — MOTHER'S SEARCH FOR HELP FOR SELF AND MENTALLY RETARDED DAUGHTER
------- SON

Figure 41-4.

filled out for them; and they had to meet differing eligibility requirements and in some cases were found ineligible. In some cases they got no service; in some cases they received piecemeal services; and in all cases it took them a number of stops even to partially solve their problems. Few poverty families would persist in fighting their way through such a web of red tape.

In summary, many valiant efforts are being made by numerous well-motivated and capable people in our local, state, and Federal agencies to provide needed social services to the poor and disadvantaged. Yet, as the preceding figures illustrate, present multiple, fragmented approaches to the funding and location of health, manpower, educational, training, and other social services have serious built-in handicaps:

- Services are not accessible; often they are not in the neighborhood, but are "downtown," requiring excessive travel.
- People are referred from agency to agency, subjected to repetitive interviews and differing eligibility standards. Frequently agencies are not attuned to the needs of people in the neighborhood, and the residents are alienated and distrustful of the agencies which give them the run-around. This fragmentation, complexity, and lack of coordination often mask large gaps and insufficiencies in services essential to assist the hard-core poor.
- Articulation of the programs is difficult because at least three different levels of government and private organizations are involved in their funding without any local master plan. The present fragmentation of grants-in-aid makes it hard for a community to apply practical cost-effectiveness (Planning-Programing-Budgeting) principles to the selection and administration of its social programs. Agencies take what they can get in the various grants available to them, often focussing more on grantsmanship than on the intrinsic benefit/cost returns. Very little cost-effectiveness analysis and evaluation are done.
- The family can hardly receive attention as a unit.
- The skills of capable professionals serving in the various community agencies are not fully or effectively used.

The reconstruction of service delivery systems in our communities is one of the major public administration problems confronting the country. It is unlikely that any single solution can be adequate or definitive. But preliminary experience and logic point toward the hypothesis that a quantum jump can be achieved in the effectiveness of delivery services to the poor through inaugurating an exemplary neighborhood center system which incorporates the best practices and theory on the coordination of service programs.

Various efforts now under way offer a starting point. The administration of rehabilitation services provides one well-tested, high-return example of effective service coordination. While many clients of rehabilitation are not hard-core cases, the task of rehabilitation is formidable. Yet studies show that the costs of rehabilitation are returned many times in increased earnings, and pay their way several times over in increased taxes.[3] The Concentrated Employment Programs are adopting some of these techniques. OEO Community Action Programs and neighborhood centers and the development of Model Cities projects, in which such centers may conceivably play a significant role, are useful attempts at service coordination on a broader scale in a context where participation of the poor and disadvantaged is encouraged. The following sections draw upon and attempt to order some of the emerging concepts.

RESIDENT INVOLVEMENT AND PARTICIPATION: AN ESSENTIAL INGREDIENT

The involvement of neighborhood residents in the planning, development, and operation of the Neighborhood Center System is an essential step toward its success. The antipoverty effort of the last several years has created a new and significant awareness of the extent to which the poor in ghettos and rural slums are alienated from the rest of society and of the necessity for involving them meaningfully in the planning and conduct of the service programs that are intended to help them. Such involvement can help assure that the services and programs provided conform to the desires and needs of residents and can add to the receptivity of the poor to the assistance which is being made available. The poor also become a major resource in accomplishing the Center's goals and in participating in their own self and community development.

Figures 41-5 and 41-6 represent schematically the contrast between an unorganized community where lassitude, hostility, and despair prevail and an effectively organized community where the residents are involved in a hopeful effort to create a community institution which will serve them and in which they can meaningfully participate. Figure 41-6 links a multipurpose neighborhood center and the community school, so that they can reinforce each other in assisting the neighborhood residents. With effective community organization, a neighborhood center complex of this sort can minister to the broader neighborhoodwide needs as well as to the specific needs of the individuals and of families.

Involvement of residents in the management of a neighborhood center offers an attractive potential for giving the disadvantaged an opportunity to share in the policy development and the general direction of the local center. A variety of arrangements for participation is possible. They range from utilization of neighborhood corporations which have a high degree of autonomy to centers which are administered by the city government but have local citizen advisory boards, either for the center or as part of the broader CAA involvement. The exact structuring of organizations for neighborhood participation by the disadvantaged is still in an early evolutionary stage. There is wide room for experimentation with alternative approaches. In the 14-city Pilot Program, Community Action Agencies have a role in each project, and seven cities have elected to develop neighborhood corporations to organize and operate the centers.

A particularly important facet of resident involvement can be the employment of so-called indigenous workers or subprofessionals in a neighborhood center. Employment of local residents can serve many purposes: provide a source of manpower; create significant job opportunities for the poor; increase the receptivity of neighborhood residents to the otherwise professional services

Figure 41-5.

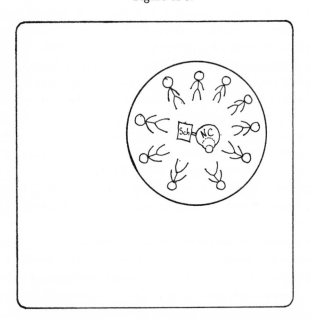

Sch-SCHOOL   **NC-NEIGHBORHOOD CENTER**

Figure 41-6.

provided by the center; and provide an opportunity for mutually supportive work by subprofessionals and trained professionals which can lead to new careers for the first and free the latter from tasks which drain their time, releasing them for more significant professional work.

With proper community organization the center will have the capability to reach into the community to the ill-informed, isolated and alienated, to bring them into the center, and to serve as an advocate to make sure they receive assistance. The organization also provides a forum where the needs of the entire neighborhood can be expressed to the community power structure and new patterns of meeting them more fully can be developed. Conflict can and does arise between established and new organizations, but this should be resolvable, especially if the needs of the poor are kept uppermost in mind by all.

A community organization does not mean, however, that effective professional techniques and services of professionals would be discarded, or that professionals lose their appropriate voice in the management of the center. The objective is to make sure that such professional services are addressed to the real needs of the poor and that the poor are given a voice in the planning and operation of services. It is a fair hypothesis that the disadvantaged will welcome services which are of genuine value to themselves, their families, and their neighborhoods.

THE SERVICE DELIVERY SYSTEM: WHAT SHAPE SHOULD IT TAKE?

The structuring of a new neighborhood organization for delivering services which will overcome the hit-or-miss characteristics of the present scattered and fragmented pattern prevailing will not be easy. No single solution can prevail, and there is great latitude for each neighborhood or community to develop its own improved pattern to better meet its particular requirements.

The direction of movement, however, is clear: It is toward *comprehensiveness* of services, toward *decentralization* of services into the ghetto, toward *concerting* of resources from different programs, toward *co-location* of service components, and toward

operational *integration* of services so that they can be geared together in a *continuum* ordered in proper sequence and effectively
administered without the present duplication and time-wasting
which goes on for clients and for employees.[4]

EMPHASIS ON DELIVERY SYSTEMS

The following sections sketch several kinds of possible models.
The emphasis is on the service delivery systems rather than on
brick and mortar aspects. Physical facilities are necessary, but
they should be tailored to the service system rather than determine the configuration of the relationship of services in a neighborhood.

Each model assumes that there is action taken to organize the
community adequately and to involve the residents meaningfully
in the undertaking.

Model I—The Advice and Referral Center

Figure 41-7 depicts the simplest and easiest model to establish.
The square in which this and the next three charts are set is just
the frame and does not symbolize the city as in the other charts in
this paper. The advice and referral center would have a very
small staff—possibly only one or two persons. They would inform
people about the available services, but the service agencies would
remain in their present scattered and/or downtown locations. In-

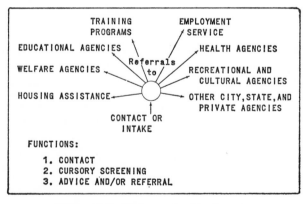

Figure 41-7. Advice and referral center.

take would largely be "walk-ins." Broadly trained "generalists," well-informed about the whole spectrum of public and private service agencies, would tell people authoritatively what services can be provided and where to go, and would do elementary screening. The staff could answer questions, hand out forms, and could even make appointments for clients. The approach is similar to that used in the Citizens' Advice Bureau in Great Britain.[5] Many OEO "store-front" centers perform these functions, at least partially.

This model would least disturb the operation of existing community agencies, and would be the easiest to sell; and it would also enhance them least. The burden of travel would still rest upon the clients, and many of the operational disadvantages inherent in the present system would remain.

The effectiveness of such centers would be increased if usable, indexed information were compiled on various Federal, state, and local benefits and services available to the people in the locality. A system of transportation could be coupled with the referrals, as well as outreach, advocacy, and follow-up. A network of these units could be established in a neighborhood to make their services more readily accessible, for example, at locations such as post offices.

Model II—The Diagnostic Center

The model presented in Figure 41-8 backstops the advice and referral unit with a professional, interdisciplinary counseling staff. The intake unit would handle the general run of cases as in the first model. For the hard-core cases—individual or ideally for entire problem families—the counseling staff would assume responsibility. For a multiproblem individual or family a team diagnosis might be made, a comprehensive service plan worked out, a schedule of appointments developed, and an assignment made for subsequent case management, including referral adequacy and periodic follow-up. Referral for specialized services would still be made to service agencies at the several locations, including downtown.

This model would require co-location of representatives of

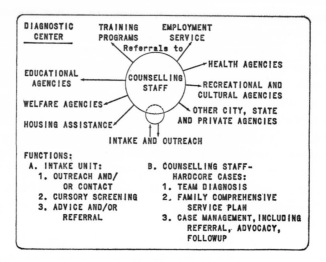

Figure 41-8.

service agencies under central administrative supervision, and development of strong ties to the service components to assure availability and continuing services pursuant to the service plan developed for a particular family or individual. It also offers an opportunity for unified intake, application, and eligibility procedures. Common case records would minimize competitive and duplicatory paper work and repetitive interviews. The outreach and many case management functions could be performed by neighborhood resident subprofessionals. A transportation unit could materially facilitate the effectiveness of the system.

The writer knows of no centers where these concepts have been fully implemented. However, some of the centers sponsored by the Chicago Committee on Urban Opportunity have made progress on the diagnostic front.[6] Community Research Associates in New York under an HEW supported project, have been continuing useful earlier work on a family-centered diagnostic and case management control system.[7]

Model III—The One-Stop, Multi Purpose
Neighborhood Service Center

The Neighborhood service delivery system in Figure 41-9 is the comprehensive model. The key service delivery components would be co-located at an appropriate place in the neighborhood. The objective would be to gather together and concert the service agencies of the neighborhood for human resource development so they can function as a single system in providing preventive, therapeutic, and rehabilitative services and assistance to restore the handicapped to social and economic self-sufficiency.

The heart of the system would be the units outlined in Model II—central intake and central diagnosis. Less complex cases could be referred to the specialized service agencies directly by intake.

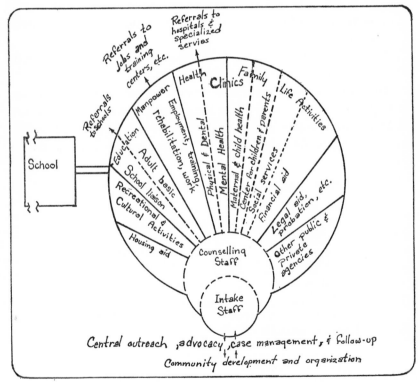

Figure 41-9. "One stop," multipurpose neighborhood center.

More complicated cases could be routed via central diagnosis for team review, development of a family service plan and a schedule, and for assignment to a regular case manager-advocate. The possibilities for standardized central records, simplified eligibility procedures, and one-stop interviews outlined in Model II could be used here.

Such a social service complex would:

- Be carefully administered so hours and operating procedures could be harmonized.
- Have a major community development and organization arm which would look to the neighborhood wide needs.
- Have "core service" units working with clients both in-center and out-center, performing the central outreach, advocacy, case-management and follow-up functions. Staff for such units would typically be subprofessionals who would work in close concert with the professionals on the central counseling staff.
- Co-locate the various specialized service agencies and ideally organize them along functional lines.

In addition to the in-center service components, as indicated in Figure 41-10, the center could sponsor extramural services such as Head Start activities, Manpower Development and Training Act projects, homemaker services, visiting health services, etc. In

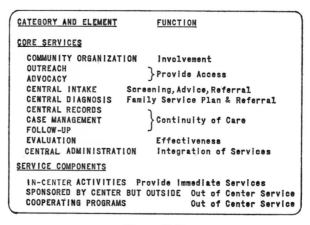

Figure 41-10.

addition it could develop close links with other cooperating programs sponsored by other agencies or arrange for provision of services which could not economically be decentralized to the neighborhood. Figure 41-9 indicates that even the most comprehensive center would have to make referrals for certain kinds of services, such as hospital care, specialized training, education, etc.

Agencies in a "one-stop" center could be located in separate buildings within walking distance of each other, just as little shops share common shopping centers, or they might be in one or several big buildings. Preliminary experience in California, noted below, suggests that a one-floor, relatively open building is conducive to cooperation among service agencies and free flow of clients.

It would be more economical to locate the center in close proximity to a school, and to arrange for the use of the school building during its off hours. Schools are typically used only part of the day and only part of the year, and many activities for adults as well as children and youths might overflow into the school building. The "community school" concept found in a few communities could be made a living reality in many more neighborhoods. The cooperative removal of artificial administrative walls between the school and other social service agencies can be a great forward step toward giving timely assistance to children and youth and striking effectively at the root causes of delinquency and poverty.

The concerting of services at a one-stop location would necessarily involve the relocation of many agencies and changes in their operating patterns. This would be found to stir up uncertainties, smoldering professional jealousies, and jurisdictional concerns which crop up in almost all human organizations faced with change. However, there would be attractive advantages:

- Increased *convenience* and *saving* of time and effort to the clients;
- Increased *access* to and *utilization* of services needed by the poor people;
- Benefits from the *mutual reinforcement* of services, coopera-

tively provided by the several specialized agencies to multiproblem families or individuals;
* Opportunity to provide *family-centered services* to help
  overcome the problems of all the family members;
* Enhanced opportunities to provide a greater *continuity* of
  scheduled services to the family;
* Increased *efficiency* of agencies through elimination of du-
  plicate interviews, repetitive paper work, and through the
  use of a central family file system which would follow the
  client from the intake and central counseling services to the
  specialized agencies and back again for follow-up;
* Possibilities for a more genuine *division of labor* among the
  several professional specialties and elimination of wasteful
  functions which result from the haphazard, even circular,
  routing of clients under the present system;
* Opportunities for extending *professional skills* by providing
  subprofessional aides and opportunities for *new careers* for
  for the less well-trained;
* An excellent source of data and focus for *interdisciplinary
  analysis* of the factors causing people to be poor, and *evaluation* of the cost/effectiveness of services, without resurvey-
  ing the poor until they begin to brood about being guinea
  pigs.

The advantages of the one-stop model are far from easy to
achieve. It is clear that a high degree of agreement and commitment among agencies which are diversely funded at the local,
state, and federal levels must be achieved. Resources would have
to be carefully balanced in such a center to avoid a queuing problem. There is risk that a large center or building might appear to
be too forbidding to the ghetto residents. The problem of central
administration would have to be resolved and the concept of
"core" or central services formulation developed in order to weld
the center into an operating entity rather than an agglomeration
of agencies.

There are, however, hopeful signs that this is practicable. Centers in Chicago, Detroit, New York City and other cities are
reaching in the direction of the one-stop model. The state of Cali-

fornia in the last two years has made large strides toward the development of working one-stop centers. One such center in East Los Angeles, located in a large open building providing space for about twenty service agencies, has been averaging two thousand new clients per month and two hundred and fifty to three hundred visitors per day, including repeats.[8]

Figure 41-11 traces the path of Family A as it visits a hypothetical one-stop center. The family goes *as a unit, is interviewed as a unit,* and receives most of its services *within the confines* of the center. A few specialized referrals to outside institutions will be necessary because economies of scale do not permit complete decentralization of some service units, such as hospitals or training centers. Compare this with the criss-cross paths in Figure 41-4 that the individual members of the family followed before the one-stop center was created.

Model IV—A Network or System of Centers

In a larger community area there would be possibilities for developing a balanced system of neighborhood centers. The one-stop center could stand at the hub. Outlying areas could be served by one or more diagnostic centers. Advice and referral stations could be established in between. The latter could refer to the larger centers as well as to cooperating agencies. Referrals, of course, could be made across neighborhood lines to a one-stop center. Thus, some areas which would not have such a facility would at least have the benefit of the smaller units. Figure 41-12 sketches this model.

Another alternative might be a nearby "one-stop" center, supported by a number of single service centers. The important point is that the decisions should be made on the basis of cost/ effectiveness and on what is good for serving the clients, rather than on the basis of happenstance, tradition, or bureaucratic prerogative.

SUMMARY

The shortcomings of the existing organizational patterns for social services are significant and clearly evident. The main targets

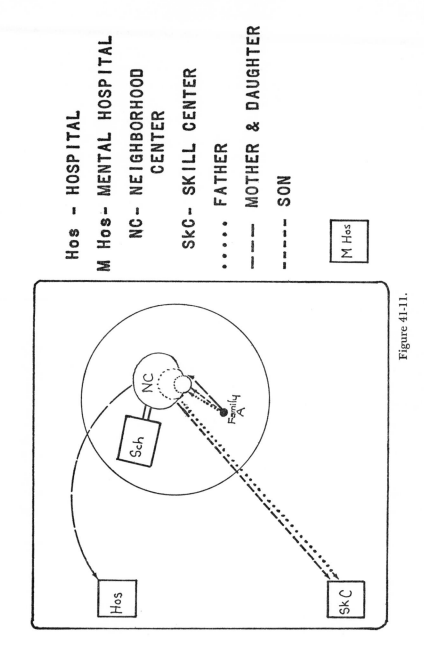

Hos – HOSPITAL

M Hos – MENTAL HOSPITAL

NC – NEIGHBORHOOD
        CENTER

SkC – SKILL CENTER

• • • • • FATHER

— — — MOTHER & DAUGHTER

– – – – SON

Figure 41-11.

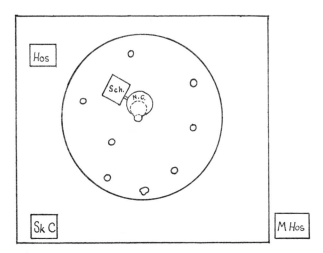

Figure 41-12.

are clear: achievement of improved community and neighborhood organization and participation, development of more effective and better articulated service delivery systems, broadening the objective of service beyond the individual to the family as a unit and the neighborhood, and aggressively directing services to the solution of real problems.

The specific principles or criteria for action might well include the following:

1. *decentralization* of services and programs to the neighborhood level;
2. Increased *responsiveness* of services to the needs and desires of the residents, especially the poor residents;
3. opening *access* to programs and services by *co-locating* some and building referral networks to others and by means such as outreach, advocacy, follow-up, etc.;
4. *coordination* of services into a *comprehensive* pattern in keeping with the best principles of social work and rehabilitation;
5. arranging a *continuum of services* in proper sequence for the individual or the family through development of a

service plan based on team analysis, scheduled appointments, implemented by follow-up;

6. *concerting* of resources by involving in the service system
both the old-established service agencies and the new OEO-
funded agencies, and by incorporating the *existing* resources as well as the possible *additional* increments;

7. *integration* of operations through core services which are
administered through central intake, diagnostic counseling,
case management, and records systems. This means surren-
der of some autonomy by component agencies and movement toward functional groupings.

8. direction of services and assistance *to strike at the root
causes* of social problems as they afflict individuals, families,
and the neighborhood.

The obstacles to development of a comprehensive and integrated services delivery system targeted at real causes of social
dysfunction are large. Success would require intergovernmental
cooperation among the local, state, and federal levels, and the involvement of the private organizations. The large number of
federal formula grants channeled through the states will have to
be involved and their restrictive provisions relaxed; two-way
cooperative relations between states and cities strengthened; and
neighborhood-centered programming emphasized by the cities.
The several federal agencies which fund services will have to
achieve new patterns for cooperative action to help the states and
cities assist effectively in the neighborhood efforts. Techniques
for working with poor people and involving them fully will have
to be improved. The different models of neighborhood service
centers and service systems will have to be carefully and scientifically tested and evaluated over a period of several years. A
reasonably full range of alternate models has not been systematically tested.

The importance of inventorying and drawing *existing* resources into this effort at the local level cannot be overemphasized.
Literally, billions of dollars are being spent for services in local
communities today. To create new service organizations with new
funds, without drawing the large base of established organizations

and resources into the effort will add to the complexity and duplication. An overall plan for a neighborhood service delivery system is necessary. To be truly effective as a coordinating mechanism, a neighborhood center system should have a real voice in determining for which services resources are to be allocated.

It would help to complete the array of services and to promote coordination, too, if a neighborhood service center had a pool of "free" or unearmarked funds for service purchase for its clients from other service agencies in the community. This is successfully done today as a matter of course by rehabilitation agencies. Service purchase gives a broader base for provision of coordinated services without the necessity for creating new service units or agencies.

The objectives of the neighborhood center approach to coordination of services are worthwhile because of the possibility that large quantitative and qualitative improvements can be made in the organization and delivery of social services. All our "people-serving" agencies can contribute through this means toward achievement of the goal of improving the overall effectiveness of social services at the local level, and in doing so they can increase their own effectiveness and public worth. There are many tools of program coordination, but the potentialities of the neighborhood center for reducing the present disorganization of social programs and providing social services more economically and effectively have not been tapped.

NOTES AND REFERENCES

1. Federal aid to state and local governments. *Special Analyses.* Budget of the United States, Fiscal Year 1968, pp. 145-150.
2. *Catalog of Federal Assistance Programs.* Washington, D.C., Office of Economic Opportunity, June 1, 1967.
3. An exploratory cost-benefits analysis of vocational rehabilitation. Department of Health, Education, and Welfare, Vocational Rehabilitation Administration, 1967.
4. A useful reference is a booklet *Community Action: The Neighborhood Center.* Office of Economic Opportunity, Washington, D.C., July 1966.
5. Kahn, Alfred J. *et al.: Neighborhood Information Centers: A Study and Some Proposals.* New York, Columbia University School of Social Work, 1966.

6. The writer is indebted to Dr. Deton J. Brooks, Jr., of the Chicago Committee on Urban Opportunity for many insights about neighborhood centers.
7. For an interesting statement of a rationale for a "therapeutic concept of preventive programming" in community planning for multi-problem families, see Buell, Bradley: Is prevention possible. Edward C. Lindeman Memorial Lecture, 86th Annual Forum of the National Conference on Social Welfare, published by Community Research Associates, N. Y., 1959, pp. 1-20.
8. The author expresses appreciation to Bertram S. Griggs of the California Department of Corrections and Dan Lopez, Manager of the East Los Angeles Center, for highly pertinent information about the organization and effectiveness of the California model, which in scope of resources moves in the direction suggested by Model III in this paper. California has six state-sponsored centers. The key role of the state in organizing and operating these centers contrasts with the local-initiative approach being used in the fourteen-city project.

PART IV:
ADDITIONAL RECOMMENDED READINGS

1. Brager, G.: Advocacy and political behavior. *Social Work, 13*:5-14, 1968.
2. Brager, G. and Purcell, F. (Eds.): *Community Action Against Poverty.* New Haven, College and University Press, 1967.
3. Cloward, R. and Elman, R.: Advocacy in the ghetto. *Trans-Action:* 27-35, 1966.
4. Fantl, B.: Integrating social and psychological theories in social work practice. *Smith College Studies in Social Work,* Memorial Issue, June, 1964.
5. Glueck, S. (Ed.): *Poverty and Mental Health.* Psychiatric Research Report 21. American Psychiatric Association, 1967.
6. Gould, R.: Dr. Strangeclass: Or how I stopped worrying about the theory and began treating the blue collar worker. *Am J Orthopsychiatry*:78-85, Jan. 1967.
7. Kramer, R. and Specht, H. (Eds.): *Readings in Community Organization Practice.* Englewood Cliffs, Prentice-Hall, 1969.
8. Mayer, J. and Timms, N.: *The Client Speaks: Working Class Impressions of Casework.* New York, Atherton, 1970.
9. Meyer, C.: Individualizing the multi-problem family. *Social Casework, 44*:267-272, 1963.
10. Meyer, C.: Casework below the poverty line. *Social Work Practice, 1965.* New York, Columbia University Press, 1966, pp. 229-242.
11. Miller, H.: Social work in the black ghetto: The new colonialism. *Social Work, 14 (3)*:65-77, 1969.
12. Purcell, F. and Specht, H.: The house on Sixth Street. *Social Work, 10 (4)*:69-76.
13. Richan, W. (Ed.): *Human Services and Social Work Responsibility.* New York, National Association of Social Workers, 1969.
14. Riessman, F. and Hallowitz, E.: The neighborhood service center: An innovation in preventive psychiatry. *Am J Psychiatry, 23*:1408-1413, 1967.
15. Riessman, F., Cohen, J. and Pearl A. (Eds.): *Mental Health of the Poor.* New York, Free Press, 1964.
16. Thurz, D.: The arsenal of social action strategies: Options for social workers. *Social Work, 16,* 27-34, 1971.

17. Thursz, D.: Social action as a professional responsibility. *Social Work,* *13*:12-21, 1968.
18. Weissman, H.: *The New Social Work.* New York, Association Press, 1969, 4 volumes.